ECONOMICS
PRINCIPLES AND POLICY
MACROECONOMICS
FOURTH EDITION

ECONOMICS
PRINCIPLES AND POLICY
MACROECONOMICS
FOURTH EDITION

WILLIAM J. BAUMOL

New York University
and
Princeton University

ALAN S. BLINDER

Princeton University

Harcourt Brace Jovanovich, Publishers

and its subsidiary, Academic Press

San Diego   New York   Chicago   Austin   Washington, D.C.
London   Sydney   Tokyo   Toronto

ISBN: 0-15-518853-4

Library of Congress Catalog Card Number: 87–81895

Printed in the United States of America

Note: This work is derived from *Economics: Principles and Policy*, Fourth Edition by William J. Baumol and Alan S. Blinder. Copyright © 1988, 1985, 1982, 1979 by Harcourt Brace Jovanovich, Inc.

ILLUSTRATION CREDITS

Page 12: © 1971, General Drafting Co.; Gousha-Chek Chart; p. 14: London School of Economics and Political Science; p. 47: National Portrait Gallery, London; p. 51: The Bettmann Archive, Inc.; p. 69: HBJ Photo; p. 84: Reproduced from the collections of the Library of Congress; p. 87: UPI/Bettmann Newsphotos; p. 101: From *The Wall Street Journal*—Permission, Cartoon Features Syndicate; p. 110: Camera Press-Photo Trends; p. 178: British Information Service; p. 240: UPI/Bettmann Newsphotos; p. 242: Drawing by Alex Mendoza; p. 252: By permission of Johnny Hart and Creators Syndicate, Inc.; p. 253: University Museum, University of Pennsylvania; p. 313: HBJ photo; p. 337: From *The Wall Street Journal*—Permission, Cartoon Features Syndicate; p. 340: HBJ photo; p. 387: Culver Pictures; p. 393: George H. Harrison from Grant Heilman; p. 397: Zephyr Pictures; p. 401: AP/Wide World; p. 402: Culver Pictures; p. 413: McDonald's Corporation; p. 452: © 1987 Peter Menzel/Stock, Boston; p. 454: Reuters/Bettmann Newsphotos; p. 467: Harvard University; p. 494: Du Pont Company; p. 520: Photothyne, Canadian National Film Board; p. 585: Krokodil/Sovfoto; p. 628: Douglas Aircraft Company; p. 647: © Bryce Flynn/Stock, Boston; p. 671: Courtesy of San Francisco Forty-Niners; p. 685: UPI/Bettmann Newsphotos; p. 693: Photo: © Houston Chronicle; p. 696: Courtesy of Union Electric Company; p. 700: Courtesy of AT&T Phone Service; p. 730: AP/Wide World; p. 736: UPI/Bettmann Newsphotos; p. 739: THE FAR SIDE, © 1985, Universal Press Syndicate, reprinted with permission. All rights reserved.; p. 754: Courtesy of John Palmisano, President, AER•X Division of RMT; p. 764: UPI/Bettmann Newsphotos; p. 795: © Bob Englehart. The Hartford Courant.; p. 807: UPI/Bettmann Newsphotos; p. 813: UPI/Bettmann Newsphotos; p. 826: Public Information Office, NY Urban Development Corp.; p. 842: UPI/Bettmann Newsphotos; p. 862: United Nations; p. 873: UPI/Bettmann Newsphotos; p. 888: UPI/Bettmann Newsphotos; p. 901: Sovfoto; p. 914: UPI/Bettmann Newsphotos; p. 915: UPI/Bettmann Newsphotos.

To my four children,
Ellen, Daniel,
and now Sabrina and Jim
W.J.B.

For Scott, now of age to read this book,
and William, who prefers Garfield
A.S.B.

Preface

For decades, the "principles of economics" book has been expected to codify the entire discipline of economics. In recent years, this has become at once more difficult and more imperative. The explosion of economic knowledge has made it impossible to put all of economics between two covers. But at the same time, more and more public policy issues either are basically economic in nature or involve important economic considerations. Intelligent citizens can no longer afford to be innocent of economics.

The preparation of this Fourth Edition continued to be guided by this dilemma. We have studiously avoided the encyclopedic approach and abandoned the fiction, so popular among textbook writers, that literally everything is of the utmost importance. Since students are sufficiently intelligent to see through this ruse in any event, we have tried to highlight those important ideas that are likely to be of lasting significance—principles that you will want to remember long after the course is over because they offer insights that are far from obvious, because they are of practical importance, and because they are widely misunderstood by intelligent laymen. A dozen of the most important of these ideas have been selected as **12 Ideas for Beyond the Final Exam** and are called to your attention when they occur through the use of the book's logo. ☑

All modern economics textbooks abound with "real world" examples, but we have tried to go beyond this, to elevate the examples to preeminence. For in our view, the policy issue or everyday economic problem ought to lead the student naturally to the economic principle, not the other way around. For this reason, many chapters start with a real policy issue or a practical problem that may seem puzzling or paradoxical to noneconomists, and then proceed to describe the economic analysis required to remove the mystery. In doing this, we have tried to utilize technical jargon and diagrams only where there is a clear need for them, never for their own sake.

Still, economics is a somewhat technical subject and, except for a few rather light chapters, this is a book for the desk, not for the bed. We have, however, made strenuous efforts to simplify the technical level of the discussion as much as we could without sacrificing content. Fortunately, almost every important idea in economics can be explained in plain English, and this, in general, is how we have tried to explain them. Yet, even while reducing the technical difficulty of the book, we have incorporated some elements of economic analysis that have traditionally been left out of introductory books but that are really too important to omit.

Foremost among these is our extensive treatment of prices and inflation in Parts 2 through 5. For years, textbooks devoted many chapters to unrealistic but simpler economic models in which prices never rose. Ours was the first introductory text to put inflation into the story from the very beginning, rather than as an afterthought—a practice we maintain and expand in the Fourth Edition.

Changes from the Third Edition

The most notable change in the Fourth Edition is the greater "internationalization" of the book, reflected especially in two new chapters and considerable reorganization of Part 4. *Economics: Principles and Policy* now places much more emphasis on the world economy and America's place in it. Recent events necessitate this reorientation. Students simply cannot understand the major economic controversies of the day—over large budget and trade deficits, dramatic swings in exchange rates, and international coordination of economic policy, for example—without a deeper understanding of international economics. Such issues are in the newspapers every day and promise to play a role in the 1988 presidential campaign and beyond.

International economics is the focus of Part 5 ("The United States in the World Economy"). Chapters 18 and 19 are extensively updated and revised, and Chapter 20 ("Macroeconomics in a World Economy") is entirely new. We think it is by far the most extensive treatment of open-economy macroeconomics to be found in any major principles textbook.

Although open-economy macroeconomics has long been standard fare in Europe and Canada, it has traditionally been considered too difficult for the principles course in the United States. However, we have concluded that the subject is far too important to omit and have therefore prepared an elementary treatment geared to the needs of the contemporary American student. Specifically, we avoid the traditional taxanomic approach by concentrating on the case that is most relevant to the contemporary United States: a large economy with a floating exchange rate and high (but not perfect) capital mobility.

The other new chapter is Chapter 7 on productivity ("Productivity, Progress, and Prosperity"), which represents a complete revision of Chapter 20 of the Third Edition. Not only does it come much earlier in the book, but it now has a much more international and historical flavor; it is intended to help students place our economy in a broader perspective. Finally, references to open-economy aspects of macroeconomics are sprinkled throughout Parts 3 and 4.

To make room for the new Chapter 20, we have consolidated materials that formerly took up six chapters into five (current Chapters 13–17). This required considerable reorganization, a little pruning, and some longer chapters. The ordering of certain topics differs from the Third Edition's but, in many ways, is more logical. For example, everything pertaining to the Keynesian–monetarist controversy now appears in a single chapter (Chapter 15), rather than being scattered over three chapters.

Most of the other macroeconomic chapters will look familiar to users of previous editions, although few paragraphs survived untouched. Some changes are worth noting, however. There is, of course, extensive revision and updating of the materials on Reaganomics and the events of the 1980s, especially in Chapters 5, 11, 12, and 16. Both Chapter 11's explanation of the aggregate supply curve and Chapter 13's explanation of deposit creation have been rewritten, based on helpful suggestions from readers. Chapter 14 has a new section explaining the relationship between bond prices and interest rates, and Chapter 17 has one on Martin Weitzman's "share economy" proposal.

Studying Principles of Economics

Whatever the nature of your course, we would like to offer one suggestion. Unlike some of the other courses you may be taking, principles of economics is cumulative—each week's lesson builds on what you have learned before. You will save yourself a lot of frustration (and also a lot of work) if you keep up on a week-to-week basis. To help you do this, there is a chapter summary, a list of important terms and concepts, and a selection of discussion questions to help you review at the end of each chapter. In addition to these aids, many students will find the *Study Guide*, designed specifically to accompany this text by Professor Craig Swan, helpful as a self-testing and diagnostic device. When you encounter difficulties in the *Study Guide*, you will know which sections of the text you need to review.

Note to the Instructor

In trying to improve the book from one edition to the next, we rely heavily on our own experiences as teachers. But our experience using the book is minuscule compared with that of the hundreds of instructors who use it nationwide. If you encounter problems, or have suggestions for improving the book, we urge you to let us know by writing to either one of us in care of Harcourt Brace Jovanovich, College Department, 1250 Sixth Avenue, San Diego, California 92101. Such letters are invaluable, and we are glad to receive them, even if they are critical.

What follows is a set of suggested course outlines.

OUTLINE FOR A ONE-SEMESTER COURSE IN MACROECONOMICS

Chapter Number	Title
1	What Is Economics?
2	The Use and Misuse of Graphs
3	Scarcity and Choice: *The* Economic Problem
4	Supply and Demand: An Initial Look
5	Macroeconomics and Microeconomics
6	Macroeconomic Maladies: Unemployment and Inflation
7	Productivity, Progress, and Prosperity
8	Income and Spending: The Powerful Consumer
9	Demand-Side Equilibrium: Unemployment or Inflation?
10	Changes on the Demand Side: Multiplier Analysis
11	Supply-Side Equilibrium: Unemployment *and* Inflation?
12	Fiscal Policy and Supply-Side Economics
13	Money and the Banking System
14	Monetary Policy and the National Economy
15	The Keynesian–Monetarist Debate
16	Budget Deficits and the National Debt: Fact and Fiction
17	The Trade-Off Between Inflation and Unemployment
18	International Trade and Comparative Advantage
19	The International Monetary System: Order or Disorder?
20	Macroeconomics in a World Economy
21	Growth in Developed and Developing Countries

OUTLINE FOR A ONE-QUARTER COURSE IN MACROECONOMICS

Chapter Number	Title
1	What Is Economics?
2	The Use and Misuse of Graphs
3	Scarcity and Choice: *The* Economic Problem
4	Supply and Demand: An Initial Look
5	Macroeconomics and Microeconomics
6	Macroeconomic Maladies: Unemployment and Inflation
8	Income and Spending: The Powerful Consumer
9	Demand-Side Equilibrium: Unemployment or Inflation?
10	Changes on the Demand Side: Multiplier Analysis
11	Supply-Side Equilibrium: Unemployment *and* Inflation?
12	Fiscal Policy and Supply-Side Economics
13	Money and the Banking System
14	Monetary Policy and the National Economy
15	The Keynesian–Monetarist Debate
16	Budget Deficits and the National Debt: Fact and Fiction
17	The Trade-Off Between Inflation and Unemployment

With Thanks

Finally, and with great pleasure, we turn to the customary acknowledgments of indebtedness. Ours have been accumulating now through four editions. In these days of specialization, not even a pair of authors can master every subject that an introductory text must cover. Our friends and colleagues Charles Berry, Rebecca Blank, William Branson, Lester Chandler, Gregory Chow, Avinash Dixit, Robert Eisner, Stephen Goldfeld, Claudia Goldin, Ronald Grieson, Daniel Hamermesh, Peter Kenen, Melvin Krauss, Arthur Lewis, Burton Malkiel, Edwin Mills, Janusz Ordover, Uwe Reinhardt, Harvey Rosen, Carl Shapiro, Hans Soderstrom, Laura Tyson, and Martin Weitzman have all given generously of their knowledge in particular areas over the course of four editions. We have learned much from them, and only wish we had learned more.

Many economists at other colleges and universities offered useful suggestions for improvements, many of which we have incorporated into the Fourth Edition. We wish to thank J. David Bowman of State University of New York—Oswego, Gerald Breger of University of South Carolina, Hsin Chang of University of Michigan, Carol Clark of Guilford College, Elizabeth Crowell of University of Michigan, Elizabeth Dickhaus of University of Missouri—Columbia, Patricia Euznet of University of Central Florida, Marianne Felton of Indiana University, Richard Fritz of University of Central Florida, Phillip Gilbert of Mira Costa College, Jonathan Goldstein of Bowdin College, Joseph Guerin of Saint Joseph's University, Thomas Hamer of Glassboro State College, James Hanson of Willamette University, Richard Harmstone of Pennsylvania State University, Benjamin Hitchner of Glassboro State College, John Isbister of University of California—Santa Cruz, Hassan Khademian of University of Missouri—St. Louis, Wolfgang Mayer of University of Cincinnati, John Mogab of Southwest Texas State University, David Ramsey of Illinois State University, Neil Reznik of Community College of Philadelphia, Steven Rock of Illinois Institute of Technology, Gary Sellers of University of Akron, Scott Sumner of Bentley College, Robert Thomas of Iowa State University, Roger Trenary of Kansas State University, Wayne Wangsness of Luther College, Walter Wessels of North Carolina State University, Travis Wilson of DeKalb Community College, and Anthony Zambelli of Cuyamaca College.

We also wish to thank the many economists who responded to our questionnaire; their responses were invaluable in planning this revision: Nick Adnett of California State University—Sacramento, Lori Alden of California State University—Sacramento, Polly Allen of University of Connecticut, Sandra Alvis of North Carolina State University, Kenneth Arakelian of University of Rhode Island, Robert Baade of Lake Forest College, Moshen Bahmani of University of Wisconsin, Barbara Bladwin of Diablo Valley College, Douglas Barnett of Biola University, Nancy Barry of Baldwin-Wallace College, Klaus Becker of Ohio University, Dwight M. Blood of Brigham Young University, Ronald Braeutigan of Northwestern University, Philip Bryson of University of Arizona, Judy Butler of Baylor University, David Butz of Northwestern University, Wendy A. Campione of Northern Arizona University, Thomas M. Carroll of Central Oregon Community College, Paula Cech of University of Arizona, Darrel Christy of University of Wisconsin, Carolyn Clark of Washington State University, Paul Coomes of University of Louisville, Granger Coudle of University of Colorado at Boulder, Dan Dabney of Southwest Texas State University, Rosalee Danielson of Illinois State University, Gary Dymski of University of Southern California, James Eaton of Bridgewater College, David Emery of St. Olaf College, Carol Engle of Auburn University—Montgomery, Homer Erekson of Miami University, Paul Farnham of Georgia State University, Ellen Foster of State University of New York—Albany, Jack Fulcher of University of Nebraska—Omaha, Albert Gray, Jr., of Baldwin-Wallace College, John Green of University of Northern Colorado, W. Clayton Hall of Illinois Institute of Technology, Thomas Hatcher of Fordham University, Charles Hegji of Auburn University—Montgomery, Bruce Herrick of Washington and Lee University, Harold H. Hiskey of Southern Utah State College, Paul Huszar of Colorado State University, Robert Jensen of Pacific Lutheran University, William Kammrath of Concordia College, Bruce Kanago of Miami University, Robert Walter Kerr of College of Lake County, Kusum Ketkar of Seton Hall University, Jong Seok Kim of Dartmouth College, Lori Kletzer of Williams College, L. Emil Kreider of Beloit College, Dale Kuntz of Bentley College, Thomas Leary of University of North Carolina—Greensboro, Michael Leonesio of University of Missouri, Dennis Leyden of University of North Carolina—Greensboro, John Wakeman-Linn of Williams College, R.F. Litro of Mattatuck Community College, John Lyons of Miami University, Bruce Mann of University of Puget Sound, Barbara Marcus of Davenport College of Business, Rebecca Marton of Nicholls State University, Lester McAllister of Beloit College, Peter McKay of Bakersfield College, Richard Megna of Kansas State University, Ruby Pandey of Southwest Texas State University, Theodore Paulos of Eastern Montana College, Rosemary Peavler of Morehead State University, Charles Revier of Colorado State University, Bruce Roberts of College of William and Mary, Robert Robertson of Indiana State University, Steve Russell of Arizona State University, Stephen Sacks of University of Connecticut, John Shaw of California State University—Fresno, John Shieh of California State Polytechnic University, William Sloan of North Carolina State University, John Ewing-Smith of Burlington County College, Steven Smith of Bakersfield College, Shane Stevens of Bridgewater College, Mary Stevenson of University of Massachusetts—Boston, Gabriel Talmain of State University of New York—Albany, Kenneth Taylor of Villanova University, Nita Thacker of State University of New York—Albany, Carolyn Tuttle of Lake Forest College, Terry Von Ende of Ohio University, Dale Warnke of College of Lake County, Chris Weber of University of North Carolina—Greensboro, Mark Weglarski of Macomb County Community College, Cathleen Whiting of Willamette University, John Wolfe of Michigan State University, William Wood of Bridgewater College, and William P. Yohe of Duke University.

We were, of course, most gratified by a number of spontaneous and kind letters from student readers. Since it is for such readers that the book is primarily intended, no other comments have meant as much to us.

The book you hold in your hand was not done by us alone. The fine people at Harcourt Brace Jovanovich, including Mimi Egan, Margie Rogers, Bruce Daniels, Lynn Edwards, Rebecca Lytle, and Diane Pella, worked hard and well to turn our manuscript into the book you see. We appreciate their efforts.

Our sanity and survival during the preparation of the Fourth Edition were assured by the intelligence, ability, and pleasantness of our secretaries, Phyllis Durepos and Karen Garner-Lipman, who did so many things and did them all so well. Sue Anne Batey Blackman, who seems to know our thoughts on the subject better than we do ourselves, besides catching a number of mistakes, brought up to date the chapter on the environment and the economics of natural resources. She and, more recently, Vacharee Devakula have both provided superb assistance.

And finally there are our wives, Hilda Baumol and Madeline Blinder. They have now participated in this project a dozen years, and with each successive revision they help in more and more ways. Their patience, good judgment, and love have made everything go more smoothly than we had any right to expect. This we appreciate deeply.

William J. Baumol
Alan S. Blinder

Contents

Preface   vii

PART 1   Getting Acquainted with Economics   1

1   WHAT IS ECONOMICS?   2

Ideas for Beyond the Final Exam*   2

Idea 1: The Trade-Off Between Inflation and Unemployment   3
Idea 2: The Illusion of High Interest Rates   3
Idea 3: The Consequences of Budget Deficits   4
Idea 4: Mutual Gains from Voluntary Exchange   4
Idea 5: The Surprising Principle of Comparative Advantage   4
Idea 6: The Overwhelming Importance of Productivity Growth in the Long Run   5
Idea 7: Attempts to Repeal the Laws of Supply and Demand: The Market Strikes Back   5
Idea 8: Externalities: A Shortcoming of the Market Cured by Market Methods   6
Idea 9: Rational Choice and True Economic Costs   6
Idea 10: The Importance of Marginal Analysis   7
Idea 11: The Cost Disease of the Service Sector   8
Idea 12: Increasing Output May Require Sacrificing Equality   8
Epilogue   9

Inside the Economist's Tool Kit   9

Economics as a Discipline   9

---

*Some of the Ideas for Beyond the Final Exam are in this textbook; others are in *Microeconomics: Principles and Policy* by Baumol and Blinder.

The Need for Abstraction 9
The Role of Economic Theory 13
What Is an Economic "Model"? 14
Reasons for Disagreements: Imperfect Information and
    Value Judgments 15
The Economist's Odd Vocabulary 16
Summary 17
Concepts for Review 17
Questions for Discussion 17

2   THE USE AND MISUSE OF GRAPHS 18

Graphs Used in Economic Analysis 18

Two-Variable Diagrams 18
The Definition and Measurement of Slope 20
Rays Through the Origin and 45° Lines 23
Squeezing Three Dimensions into Two: Contour Maps 24

Perils in the Interpretation of Graphs 25

Summary 32
Concepts for Review 33
Questions for Discussion 33

3   SCARCITY AND CHOICE: *THE
ECONOMIC PROBLEM* 34

Scarcity, Choice, and Opportunity Cost 35
Opportunity Cost and Money Cost 36
Production, Scarcity, and Resource Allocation 37
Scarcity and Choice for a Single Firm 37
The Principle of Increasing Costs 39
Scarcity and Choice for the Entire Society 39
Scarcity and Choice Elsewhere in the Economy 41
The Concept of Efficiency 43
The Three Coordination Tasks of Any Economy 44

Specialization, Division of Labor, and Exchange 44
Markets, Prices, and the Three Coordination Tasks 46
Radicalism, Conservatism, and the Market Mechanism 46
Summary 48
Concepts for Review 49
Questions for Discussion 49

4 SUPPLY AND DEMAND: AN INITIAL LOOK 50

Fighting the Invisible Hand 50
Demand and Quantity Demanded 52
Supply and Quantity Supplied 54
Equilibrium of Supply and Demand 56
Shifts of the Demand Curve 58
Shifts of the Supply Curve 61
Restraining the Market Mechanism: Price Ceilings 64
Restraining the Market Mechanism: Price Floors 66
A Can of Worms 67
Summary 69
Concepts for Review 70
Questions for Discussion 70

PART 2   The Realm of Macroeconomics 73

5 MACROECONOMICS AND MICROECONOMICS 74

Drawing a Line Between Macroeconomics and Microeconomics 74
Supply and Demand in Macroeconomics 76
Gross National Product 78
Limitations of the GNP: What GNP Is Not 80
The Economy on a Roller Coaster 81
The Great Depression of the 1930s 83
From World War II to 1973 85

The Great Stagflation, 1973–1980   86
The Reagan Years   86
The Problem of Macroeconomic Stabilization: A Sneak
   Preview   87
Summary   89
Concepts for Review   90
Questions for Discussion   90

6   MACROECONOMIC MALADIES:
UNEMPLOYMENT AND INFLATION   92

The Costs of Unemployment   93

Counting the Unemployed: the Official Statistics   94
Types of Unemployment   95
How Much Employment Is "Full Employment"?   96
Unemployment Insurance: The Invaluable Cushion   97
The Economic Costs of High Unemployment   97

The Costs of Inflation   100

Inflation: The Myth and the Reality   100
Inflation as a Redistributor of Income and Wealth   103
Real Versus Nominal Interest Rates   104
Inflation and the Tax System   105
Usury Laws, Interest Rate Ceilings, and Other
   Impediments   106
Other Costs of Inflation   108
Creeping Versus Galloping Inflation   109
The Costs of Creeping Versus Galloping Inflation   110
Creeping Inflation Does Not Necessarily Lead to
   Galloping Inflation   110
Summary   111
Concepts for Review   111
Questions for Discussion   112

Appendix: How Statisticians Measure Inflation   112

Index Numbers for Inflation   112
The Consumer Price Index   113

How to Use a Price Index to "Deflate" Monetary Figures 114
The GNP Deflator 114
Summary 115
Concepts for Review 115
Questions for Discussion 115

7 PRODUCTIVITY, PROGRESS, AND PROSPERITY 117

Life in the "Good Old Days" 117
The Magnitude of Productivity Growth 120
Significance of the Growth of Productivity 123
The Second Major Development: Convergence 123
Why International Equalization? 125
Are All Countries Participating in Equalization? 126
The Recent Productivity Slowdown in the United States 126
More Guarded Interpretations of the Slowdown 129
The Costs of Lagging Productivity 131
Productivity, Unemployment, and Deindustrialization 131
Concluding Comment 134
Summary 135
Concepts for Review 135
Questions for Discussion 135

PART 3 Aggregate Supply and Demand Analysis 137

8 INCOME AND SPENDING: THE POWERFUL CONSUMER 138

Aggregate Demand, National Product, and National
    Income 139
The Circular Flow of Spending, Production, and Income 140
Demand Management and the Powerful Consumer 142

Consumer Spending and Income: The Important
   Relationship   144
The Consumption Function and the Marginal
   Propensity to Consume   147
Movements Along Versus Shifts of the Consumption
   Function   149
Other Determinants of Consumer Spending   150
Why Tax Policy Failed in 1968 and 1975   152
The Predictability of Consumer Behavior   153
Summary   154
Concepts for Review   154
Questions for Discussion   155

**Appendix A: The Saving Function and the Marginal
Propensity to Save**   155
Summary   157
Concepts for Review   157
Questions for Discussion   157

Appendix B: National Income Accounting   157
Defining GNP: Exceptions to the Rules   158
GNP as the Sum of Final Goods and Services   158
GNP as the Sum of All Factor Payments   159
GNP as the Sum of Values Added   161
Alternative Measures of the Income of the Nation   162
Summary   163
Concepts for Review   164
Questions for Discussion   164

9   DEMAND-SIDE EQUILIBRIUM:
UNEMPLOYMENT OR INFLATION?   165

The Extreme Variability of Investment   166
A Simplified Circular Flow   167
The Meaning of Equilibrium GNP   168

Equilibrium on the Demand Side of the Economy   169
Constructing the Expenditure Schedule   170
The Mechanics of Income Determination   171
The Aggregate Demand Curve   173
Demand-Side Equilibrium and Full Employment   175
The Coordination of Saving and Investment   177
Summary   179
Concepts for Review   180
Questions for Discussion   180

Appendix A: The Saving and Investment Approach   181
Graphical Analysis   181
Induced Investment   181
Summary   182
Concepts for Review   182
Questions for Discussion   182

Appendix B: The Simple Algebra of Income Determination   182
Questions for Discussion   183

10 CHANGES ON THE DEMAND SIDE: MULTIPLIER ANALYSIS   184

The Magic of the Multiplier   184
Demystifying the Multiplier: How It Works   186
Algebraic Statement of the Multiplier   188
The Multiplier Effect of Consumer Spending   190
The Multiplier in Reverse   191
The Paradox of Thrift   192
The Multiplier and the Aggregate Demand Curve   193
Summary   194
Concepts for Review   194
Questions for Discussion   195

Appendix: The Simple Algebra of the Multiplier   195

11 SUPPLY-SIDE EQUILIBRIUM: UNEMPLOYMENT *AND* INFLATION?   197

The Supply-Side Matters   197
The Aggregate Supply Curve   198
Shifts of the Aggregate Supply Curve   200
The Shape of the Aggregate Supply Curve   202
Equilibrium of Aggregate Demand and Supply   202
Recessionary and Inflationary Gaps Revisited   204
Adjusting to an Inflationary Gap: Inflation   205
Demand Inflation and Stagflation   207
An Example from U.S. History: 1966 to 1970   207
Adjusting to a Recessionary Gap: Deflation or
　　Unemployment?   208
Does the Economy Have a Self-Correcting Mechanism?   210
Stagflation from Supply Shifts   212
Inflation and the Multiplier   213
A Role for Stabilization Policy   215
Summary   216
Concepts for Review   216
Questions for Discussion   216

PART 4　Fiscal and Monetary Policy   219

12 FISCAL POLICY AND SUPPLY-SIDE ECONOMICS   220

Government Purchases and Equilibrium Income   221
Income Taxes and the Consumption Schedule   224
Tax Policy and Equilibrium Income   225
Multipliers for Tax Policy   227
Government Transfer Payments   228
The Multiplier Revisited   229

Planning Expansive Fiscal Policy 230
Planning Restrictive Fiscal Policy 231
The Choice Between Spending Policy and Tax Policy 232
Some Harsh Realities 233
The Idea Behind Supply-Side Tax Cuts 234
Some Flies in the Ointment 237
Toward Assessment of Supply-Side Economics 241
Summary 243
Concepts for Review 243
Questions for Discussion 244

**Appendix: Algebraic Treatment of Fiscal Policy and
Aggregate Demand** 244
Questions for Discussion 246

13 MONEY AND THE BANKING SYSTEM 248

Policy Issue: Deregulating the Banks 248
Barter Versus Monetary Exchange 249
The Conceptual Definition of Money 251
What Serves as Money? 251
How the Quantity of Money Is Measured 253
How Banking Began 255
Principles of Bank Management: Profits Versus Safety 257
Bank Regulation 257
How Bankers Keep Books 258
The Limits to Money Creation by a Single Bank 259
Multiple Money Creation by a Series of Banks 261
The Process in Reverse: Multiple Contractions of the
    Money Supply 264
Why the Money Creation Formula is Oversimplified 265
The Need for Monetary Control 266
Summary 267
Concepts for Review 267
Questions for Discussion 268

14 MONETARY POLICY AND THE NATIONAL ECONOMY 269

The Federal Reserve System: Origins and Structure	269
The Independence of the Fed	271
Controlling the Money Supply: Open-Market Operations	272
Open-Market Operations, Bond Prices, and Interest Rates	273
Controlling the Money Supply: Reserve Requirements	274
Controlling the Money Supply: Lending to Banks	276
Proposals for Tightening Monetary Control	277
The Money Supply Mechanism	278
The Demand for Money	279
Equilibrium in the Money Market	280
Money and Income: The Important Difference	281
Interest Rates and Total Expenditure	282
Monetary Policy and Aggregate Demand in the Keynesian Model	283
Money and the Price Level in the Keynesian Model	285
From Models to Policy Debates	287
Summary	288
Concepts for Review	288
Questions for Discussion	289

15 THE KEYNESIAN–MONETARIST DEBATE 290

Velocity and the Quantity Theory of Money	290
The Determinants of Velocity	293
Monetarism: The Quantity Theory Modernized	294
Reconciling the Keynesian and Monetarist Views	296
Keynesians Versus Monetarists: Fiscal Versus Monetary Policy	298
Keynesians Versus Monetarists: Lags in Fiscal and Monetary Policy	298

Keynesians Versus Monetarists: Control of the Money
 Supply Versus Control of Interest Rates   300
Keynesians Versus Monetarists: The Aggregate Supply
 Curve   304
Keynesians Versus Monetarists: Should the Government
 Intervene?   306
Stabilization Policy: Discretionary Measures or Fixed
 Rules?   309
Techniques of Economic Forecasting   310
The Accuracy of Economic Forecasts   314
Other Dimensions of the Rules-Versus-Discretion
 Debate   314
Conclusion: What Should Be Done?   315
Summary   317
Concepts for Review   318
Questions for Discussion   318

16 BUDGET DEFICITS AND THE NATIONAL DEBT: FACTS AND FICTION   319

The Partisan Political Debate over the Budget Deficit   319
Should the Budget Be Balanced?   320
Deficits and Debt: Some Terminology   322
Some Facts About the National Debt   322
Interpreting the Budget Deficit   324
Bogus Arguments About the Burden of the Debt   330
Budget Deficits and Inflation   331
Deficits, Interest Rates, and Crowding Out   335
The True Burden of the National Debt   337
The Economic Effects of Budget Deficits: Causation
 Versus Correlation   338
Conclusion: The Partisan Debate over the Budget Deficit   341
Summary   342
Concepts for Review   343
Questions for Discussion   343

17 THE TRADE-OFF BETWEEN INFLATION AND UNEMPLOYMENT 344

Demand-Side Inflation Versus Supply-Side Inflation: A Review 344
Applying the Model to a Growing Economy 346
Demand-Side Inflation and the Phillips Curve 348
Supply-Side Inflation and the Collapse of the Phillips Curve 352
What the Phillips Curve Is Not 354
Fighting Inflation with Fiscal and Monetary Policy 356
What Should Be Done? 359
Inflationary Expectations and the Phillips Curve 360
The Theory of Rational Expectations 363
Fighting Recessions with Fiscal and Monetary Policy 365
Why Economists (and Politicians) Disagree 367
The Dilemma of Demand Management 368
Attempts to Improve the Trade-Off Directly 369
Incomes Policy 369
Tax-Based Incomes Policy 373
The Share Economy 373
Indexing 374
Summary 375
Concepts for Review 376
Questions for Discussion 377

PART 5   The United States in the World Economy 379

18 INTERNATIONAL TRADE AND COMPARATIVE ADVANTAGE 380

Why Trade? 381
Mutual Gains from Trade 382
International Versus Intranational Trade 383

Comparative Advantage: The Fundamental Principle of
  Specialization   384
The Arithmetic of Comparative Advantage   386
The Graphics of Comparative Advantage   388
Supply–Demand Equilibrium and Pricing in Foreign
  Trade   390
Comparative Advantage and Competition of "Cheap
  Foreign Labor"   392
Tariffs, Quotas, and Other Interferences with Trade   392
How Tariffs and Quotas Work   394
Tariffs Versus Quotas   396
Why Inhibit Trade?   397
Other Arguments for Protection   399
What Import Prices Benefit a Country?   402
Conclusion: A Last Look at the "Cheap Foreign Labor"
  Argument   403
Summary   404
Concepts for Review   405
Questions for Discussion   405

19 THE INTERNATIONAL MONETARY SYSTEM: ORDER OR DISORDER? 407

What Are Exchange Rates?   407
Exchange Rate Determination in a Free Market   409
The Purchasing-Power Parity Theory: The Long Run   411
Economic Activity and Exchange Rates: The Medium
  Run   413
Interest Rates and Exchange Rates: The Short Run   414
Market Determination of Exchange Rates: Summary   415
Fixed Exchange Rates and the Definition of the Balance
  of Payments   415
Defining the Balance of Payments in Practice   418
The U.S. Balance of Payments Accounts   418
A Bit of History: The Gold Standard   420

The Bretton Woods System and the International
   Monetary Fund   421
Adjustment Mechanisms Under the Bretton Woods
   System   422
Why Try to Fix Exchange Rates?   424
The Current Mixed System   425
Recent Developments in International Financial
   Markets   426
Summary   428
Concepts for Review   429
Questions for Discussion   429

20 MACROECONOMICS IN A WORLD ECONOMY   431

International Trade and National Incomes   432
The Multiplier in the Presence of Foreign Trade   435
Relative Prices, Exports, and Imports   438
The Effects of Changes in Exchange Rates   439
Lags in International Trade and the J Curve   440
Aggregate Supply in an Open Economy   442
The Macroeconomic Effects of Exchange Rates   443
Interest Rates and International Capital Flows   444
Fiscal Policy in an Open Economy   445
Monetary Policy in an Open Economy   447
International Aspects of Reaganomics   447
The Link Between the Budget Deficit and the Trade
   Deficit   449
On Curing the Trade Deficit   450
Conclusion: We Are Not Alone   453
Summary   455
Concepts for Review   455
Questions for Discussion   456

PART 6   Alternative Economic Systems   457

21 GROWTH IN DEVELOPED AND DEVELOPING COUNTRIES   458

Growth in General   458

How to Measure Growth: Total Output or Output per Capita?   458
On Growth in Population: Is Less Really More?   459
The Crowded Planet: Exponential Population Growth   461
Requirements for Increased Growth   463
Accumulating Capital by Sacrificing Consumption: The Case of Soviet Russia   463
The Payoff to Growth: Higher Consumption in the Future   464
Growth Without Sacrificing Consumption: Something for Nothing?   465
Is More Growth Really Better?   466

Problems of the Less Developed Countries   468

Living in the LDCs   468
Recent Trends   470
Impediments to Development in the LDCs   472
Help from Industrialized Economies   478
Loans and Grants by the United States and Others   479
Can LDCs Break Away from Poverty?   480
Summary   480
Concepts for Review   481
Questions for Discussion   481

Appendix   483

Glossary   G-1

Index   I-1

ECONOMICS
PRINCIPLES AND POLICY
MACROECONOMICS
FOURTH EDITION

PART 1

Getting Acquainted with Economics

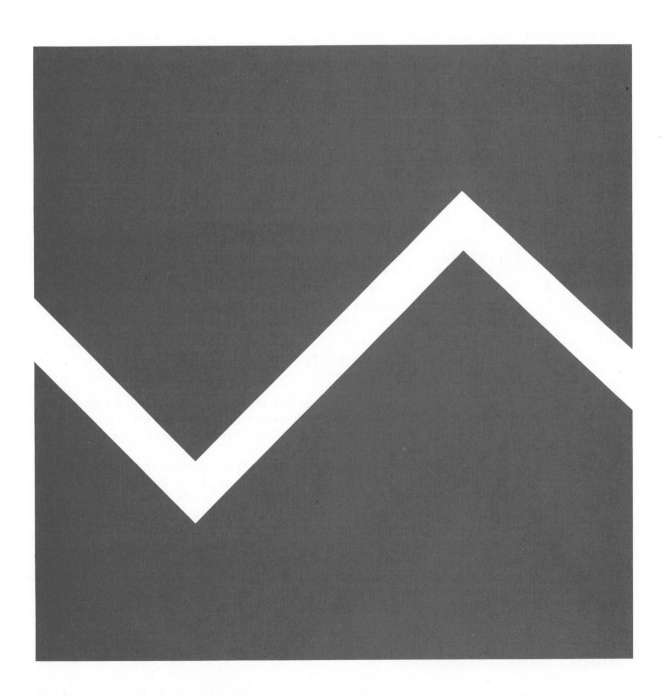

1

Why does public discussion of economic policy so often show the abysmal ignorance of the participants? Why do I so often want to cry at what public figures, the press, and television commentators say about economic affairs?

ROBERT M. SOLOW

What Is Economics?

Economics is a broad-ranging discipline, both in the questions it asks and the methods it uses to seek answers. Many definitions of economics have been proposed, but we prefer to avoid any attempt to define the discipline in a single sentence or paragraph. Instead, this chapter will introduce you to economics by letting the subject matter speak for itself.

The first part of the chapter is intended to give you some idea of the types of problems that can be approached through economic analysis and the kinds of solutions that economic principles suggest. Many of the world's most pressing problems are economic in nature. So a little knowledge of basic economics is essential to anyone who wants to understand the world in which we live.

The second part briefly introduces the methods of economic inquiry and the tools that economists use. These are tools you may find useful in your life as a citizen, consumer, and worker long after the course is over.

Ideas for Beyond the Final Exam*

As college professors, we realize it is inevitable that you will forget much of what you learn in this course — perhaps with a sense of relief — soon after the final exam. There is not much point bemoaning this fact; elephants may never forget, but people do.

Nevertheless, some economic ideas are so important that you will want to remember them well beyond the final exam. If you do not, you will have shortchanged your own education. To help you pick out a few of the most crucial concepts, we have selected 12 from among the many ideas contained in this book. Some offer critical and enduring insights into the workings of the economy. Others bear on important policy issues that often appear in the newspapers and that may have relevance to your own future decisions. Others point out common misunderstandings that occur among even the most thoughtful lay observers. As the opening quotation of this chapter suggests, many learned judges, politicians, business leaders, and university administrators who failed to

*Some of the Ideas are in this textbook; the others are in *Microeconomics: Principles and Policy.*

understand or misused these economic principles could have made far wiser decisions than they did.

Each of the **12 Ideas for Beyond the Final Exam** will be discussed in depth as it occurs in the course of the book, so you should not expect to understand them fully after reading this first chapter. Nonetheless, we think it useful to sketch them briefly here both to introduce you to economics and to provide a selective preview of what is to come.

We have organized our 12 Ideas into two groups, corresponding to the way economics is normally taught. The first six are likely to be encountered in courses that specialize in *macroeconomics* (the study of the national economy). The last six are likely to be covered in courses that specialize in *microeconomics* (the study of the price system). Some will appear in both types of courses.

The Trade-off Between Inflation and Unemployment   IDEA 1

At the start of the 1980s, U.S. policy makers declared all-out war on inflation. Some people, including some partisans of Reaganomics, claimed that this war could be waged without heavy casualties in the form of high unemployment. As things turned out, however, the battle against inflation proved to be costly. Inflation was reduced dramatically. But the national unemployment rate, which averaged 6.1 percent during the 1970s, averaged 8.1 percent during 1981–1986 and exceeded 9.5 percent in both 1982 and 1983.

Economists maintain that this conjunction of events was no coincidence. Owing to features of our economy that we will study in Parts 2 and 3, there is an agonizing *trade-off between inflation and unemployment,* meaning that most policies that bring down inflation also cause unemployment to rise.

Since this trade-off poses the fundamental dilemma of national economic policy, we will devote all of Chapter 17 to examining it in detail. And we shall also consider some suggestions for escaping from the trade-off, such as supply-side economics (Chapter 12) and wage-price controls (Chapter 17).

The Illusion of High Interest Rates   IDEA 2

Is it more costly to borrow money at 10 percent interest or at 14 percent interest? That would seem an easy question to answer, even without a course in economics. But, in fact, it is not. An example will show why.

In 1987, banks were lending money to home buyers at annual interest rates of 10 percent or less. Just seven years earlier, these rates had been 14 percent or more. Yet economists maintain that it was actually cheaper to borrow in 1980 than in 1987. Why? Because inflation in 1980 was running at about 12 percent per year while it was only about 4 percent in 1987.

But why is information on inflation relevant for deciding how costly it is to borrow? Consider the position of a person who borrows $100 for one year at a 14 percent rate of interest when the inflation rate is 10 percent. At the end of the year the borrower pays back his $100 plus $14 interest. But over that same year, because of inflation, his indebtedness declines by $10 *in terms of what that money will buy*. Thus, in terms of *purchasing power,* the borrower really pays only $4 in interest on his $100 loan, or 4 percent.

Now consider someone who borrows $100 at 10 percent interest when prices are rising only 4 percent a year. This borrower pays back the original $100 plus $10 in interest and sees the purchasing power of his debt decline by $4 due to inflation—for a net payment in purchasing-power terms of $6, or 6 percent. Thus, in the economically relevant sense, the 10 percent loan is actually more expensive than the 14 percent loan.

As we will learn in Chapter 6, the failure to understand this principle has caused troubles for our tax laws, for the financial system, and for the housing and public utility industries. And in Chapter 16 we will see that it has even led to misunderstanding of the size and nature of the government budget deficit.

IDEA 3 The Consequences of Budget Deficits

Large federal budget deficits have been much in the news in recent years. Congress has struggled continually to cut the deficit and has failed to comply with a deficit-reduction law (the Gramm-Rudman-Hollings Act of 1985) that it set for itself. President Reagan, while defending the policies that led to large deficits, has advocated a constitutional amendment to require a balanced budget.

The conflicting claims and counterclaims that have marked this debate are bound to confuse the layman. Some critics claim that deficits hold dire consequences — including higher interest rates, more inflation, a stagnant economy, and an irksome burden on future generations of Americans. Others deny these charges.

Who is right? Are deficits really malign or benign influences on our economy? The answers, economists insist, are so complicated that the only correct short answer is: It all depends. The precise factors on which the answers depend, and the reasons why, are sufficiently important that they merit an entire chapter of this book (Chapter 16). There we will learn that a budget deficit may be sound or unsound policy, depending on its size and on the reasons for its existence.

IDEA 4 Mutual Gains from Voluntary Exchange

One of the most fundamental ideas of economics is that in a voluntary exchange both parties must gain something, or at least expect to gain something. Otherwise why would they both agree to the exchange? This principle may seem self-evident, and it probably is. Yet it is amazing how often it is ignored in practice.

For example, it was widely believed for centuries that governments should interfere with international trade because one country's gain from a swap must be the other country's loss. (See Chapter 18.) Analogously, some people feel instinctively that if Mr. A profits handsomely from a deal with Mr. B, then Mr. B must have been exploited. Laws sometimes prohibit mutually beneficial exchanges between buyers and sellers — as when a loan transaction is banned because the interest rate is "too high" (Chapter 6), or when a willing worker cannot be hired because the wage rate is "too low" (Chapter 36), or when the resale of tickets to sporting events ("ticket scalping") is outlawed even though the buyer is happy to pay the high price (Chapter 4).

In every one of these cases, and many more, well-intentioned but misguided reasoning blocks the mutual gains that arise from voluntary exchange — and thereby interferes with one of the most basic functions of an economic system (see Chapter 3).

IDEA 5 The Surprising Principle of Comparative Advantage

The Japanese economy produces many products that Americans buy in huge quantities — including cars, TV sets, cameras, and electronic equipment. American manufacturers have complained about the competition and demanded protection against the flood of imports that, in their view, threatens American standards of living. Is this view justified?

Economists think not. But what if a combination of higher productivity and lower wages were to permit Japan to produce *everything* more cheaply than we could? Would it not then be true that Americans would have no work and that our nation would be impoverished?

A remarkable result, called the law of **comparative advantage,** shows that even in this extreme case the two nations should still trade and that each can gain as a result! We will explain this principle fully in Chapter 18, where we will also note some potentially valid arguments in favor of protecting particular domestic industries. But for now a simple parable will make the reason clear.

Suppose Sam grows up on a farm and is a whiz at plowing, but is also a successful country singer who earns $2000 a performance at hotels and nightclubs. Should Sam refuse some singing engagements to leave time for plowing? Of course not. Instead he should hire Alfie, a much less efficient farmer, to plow for him. Sam is the better farmer, but he earns so much more by specializing in singing that it pays him to leave the farming to Alfie. Alfie, though a poorer farmer than Sam, is an even worse singer. Thus Alfie earns a living by specializing in the job at which he at least has a *comparative* advantage (his farming is not quite as bad as his singing), and both Alfie and Sam gain. The same is true of two countries. Even if one of them is more efficient at everything, both countries can gain by producing the things they do best *comparatively*.

The Overwhelming Importance of Productivity Growth in the Long Run

IDEA 6

In Geneva a worker in a watch factory now turns out roughly one hundred times as many mechanical watches per year as his ancestor did three centuries earlier. The **productivity** of labor (output per worker hour) in cotton production has probably gone up more than a thousandfold in two hundred years. It is estimated that production per hour of labor in manufacturing in the United States has gone up about seven times in the past century. This means the average American can enjoy about seven times as much clothing, housewares, and luxury goods as were available to a typical inhabitant of the United States one hundred years before.

Economic issues such as inflation, unemployment, and monopoly are important to us all, and will receive great attention in this book. But in the long run nothing has as great an effect on our material well-being and the amounts society can afford to spend on hospitals, schools, and social amenities as the rate of growth of productivity. Chapter 7 points out that what appears to be a small increase in productivity growth can have a huge effect on a country's standard of living over a long period of time because productivity compounds like the interest on savings in a bank. Since 1870, for example, U. S. productivity is estimated to have grown only about 2 percent a year on the average. But that was enough to increase the volume of goods and services available to each person about twelve times—a truly incredible amount.

Attempts to Repeal the Laws of Supply and Demand: The Market Strikes Back

IDEA 7

When a commodity is in short supply, its price naturally tends to rise. Sometimes disgruntled consumers badger politicians into "solving" the problem by imposing a legal ceiling on the price. Similarly, when supplies are abundant—say, when fine weather produces extraordinarily abundant crops—prices tend to fall. This naturally dismays producers, who often succeed in getting legislation prohibiting low prices by imposing price floors. But such attempts to repeal the laws of supply and demand usually backfire and sometimes produce results virtually the opposite of those that were intended.

Where rent controls are adopted to protect tenants, housing grows scarce because the law makes it unprofitable to build and maintain apartments. When minimum wages are enacted to protect low-wage workers, low-wage jobs disappear. Price floors are placed under agricultural products and surpluses pile up. History provides spectacular examples of the way in which free markets strike back at attempts to interfere with the way they would otherwise work. In Chapter 4, we will see that price controls played a role in causing the oft-recounted hardships of Washington's army at Valley Forge. Two centuries earlier, when the armies of Spain surrounded Antwerp in 1584, hoping to starve the city into submission, profiteers kept Antwerp going by smuggling food and supplies through enemy lines. However, when the city fathers adopted price controls to end these "unconscionable" prices, supplies suddenly dried up and the city soon surrendered.

As we will see in Chapter 4 and elsewhere in this book, such consequences of interference with the price mechanism are no accident. They follow inevitably from the way free markets work.

IDEA 8

Externalities: A Shortcoming of the Market Cured by Market Methods

Markets are very efficient in producing the goods that consumers want in the quantities in which they are desired. They do so by offering large financial rewards to those who respond to what consumers want to buy and who produce these products economically. Similarly, the market mechanism minimizes waste and inefficiency by causing inefficient producers to lose money.

This works out well as long as an exchange between a seller and a buyer affects only those two parties. But often an economic transaction affects uninvolved third parties. Examples abound. A cigarette smoker blows smoke in your face. The utility which supplies electricity to your home also produces soot that discolors your curtains and pollutants that despoil the air and even affect your health. After a farmer sprays his crops with toxic pesticides, the poison may seep into the ground water and affect the health of neighboring communities.

Such social costs—called **externalities** because they affect parties *external* to the economic transaction that causes them—escape the control of the market mechanism, as we will learn in *Microeconomics* Chapter 13. There is no financial incentive that motivates polluters to minimize the damages they do. As a consequence, it pays firms to make their products as cheaply as possible, disregarding externalities that may damage the quality of life.

Yet, as we will learn in *Microeconomics* Chapters 13 and 18, there is a way for the government to use the market mechanism to control undesirable externalities. If the public utility and the farmer are charged for the harm they cause the public, just as they are charged when they use tangible resources such as coal and fertilizer, then they will have an incentive to reduce the amount of pollution they generate. Thus, in this case, economists believe that market methods are often the best way to cure one of the market's most important shortcomings.

IDEA 9

Rational Choice and True Economic Costs

Despite dramatic improvements in our standard of living since the industrial revolution, we have not come anywhere near a state of unlimited abundance, and so we must constantly make choices. If you purchase a new home, you may not be able to afford to eat at expensive restaurants as often as you used to. If a firm decides to retool its factories, it may have to postpone plans for new executive offices. If a government expands its defense program, it may be forced to reduce its outlays on roads or school buildings.

Economists say that the true costs of such decisions are not the number of dollars spent on the house, the new equipment, or the military establishment, but rather *the value of what must be given up in order to acquire the item* — the restaurant meals, the new executive offices, the improved roads and new schools. These are called **opportunity costs** because they represent the *opportunities* the individual, firm, or government must forego to make the desired expenditure. Economists maintain that opportunity costs must be considered in the decision-making process, if rational choices are to be made (see Chapter 3).

The cost of a college education provides a vivid example that is probably close to the hearts of all students reading this book. How much do you think it *costs* to go to college? Most likely you would answer this question by adding together your expenditures on tuition, room and board, books, and the like, and then deducting any scholarship funds you may receive. Economists would not. They would first want to know how much you could be earning if you were not attending college. This may sound like an irrelevant question; but because you give up these earnings by attending college, they must be added to your tuition bill as a cost of your education. Nor would economists accept the university's bill for room and board as a measure of your living costs. They would want to know by how much this exceeds what it would have cost you to live at home, and only this extra cost would be counted as an expense. On balance, a college education probably costs more than you think.

The Importance of Marginal Analysis   IDEA 10

Many pages in this book will be spent explaining, and extolling the virtues of, a type of decision-making process called **marginal analysis** (see especially *Microeconomics* Chapters 5–8), which can best be illustrated by an example.

Suppose that an airline is told by its accountants that the full cost of transporting one passenger from Los Angeles to New York is $180. Can the airline profit by offering a reduced rate of $100 to students who fly on a standby basis? The surprising answer is: probably yes. The reason is that most of the $180 cost per passenger must be paid whether the plane carries 20 passengers or 120 passengers. Marginal analysis points out that full costs — which include costs of maintenance, landing rights, ground crews, and so on — are irrelevant to an airline interested in making as much profit as possible. The only costs that are relevant in deciding whether to carry standby passengers for reduced rates are the *extra* costs of writing and processing additional tickets, the food and beverages these passengers consume, the additional fuel required, and so on. These costs are called **marginal costs,** and they are probably quite small in this instance. Any passenger who pays the airline more than its marginal cost will add something to the company's profit, so it probably is more profitable to let the students ride for the reduced fare than to fly the plane with empty seats.

There are many real cases in which decisionmakers, not understanding marginal analysis, have rejected advantageous possibilities like the reduced fare in our hypothetical example. These people were misled by calculating in terms of *average* rather than *marginal* cost figures — an error that can be quite costly.

IDEA 11   The Cost Disease of the Service Sector

There is a distressing phenomenon occurring throughout the industrialized world. Many community services have apparently been growing poorer — fewer postal deliveries, larger classes in public schools, less reliable garbage pickups — while the public is paying more and more for them. Indeed, the costs of providing public services have risen consistently faster than the rate of inflation. A natural response is to attribute the problem to political corruption and government inefficiency. But this is certainly not the whole story, because private services have also grown more costly.

As we shall see in *Microeconomics* Chapter 13, one of the major causes of the problem is economic. And it has nothing to do with corruption or inefficiency of public employees; rather, it has to do with the dazzling growth in efficiency of private manufacturing industries! Because technological improvements make workers more productive in manufacturing, wages rise. And they rise not only for the manufacturing workers but also for postal workers, teachers, and other public employees, because workers can leave industries with low-paying jobs and compete for jobs in high-paying industries. But in personal services technology is not easily changed. Since it still takes one person to drive a postal truck and one teacher to teach a class, the cost of these services is forced to rise. The same sort of cost disease affects other services like medical care, university teaching, restaurant cooking, retailing, and automobile repairs.

This is important to understand not because it excuses the financial record of our governments, but because an understanding of the problem suggests what we should expect the future to bring and, perhaps, indicates what policies should be advocated to correct it.

IDEA 12   Increasing Output May Require Sacrificing Equality

"Supply-side" economics was one of the cornerstones of President Reagan's economic policy. The basic idea behind supply-side tax cuts (which are discussed in detail in Chapter 12) is to spur productivity and efficiency by providing greater incentives for working, saving, and investing. Those were, for example, among the major goals of the large tax cuts of 1981.

Yet there is at least one problem with supply-side economics — a problem that has figured prominently in the debate over Reaganomics. In order to provide stronger incentives for success in the economic game, the gaps between the "winners" and the "losers" must necessarily be widened. For it is these gaps that, after all, provide the incentives to work harder, to save more, and to invest productively.

However, some observers feel that the unequal distribution of income in our society is unjust; that it is inequitable for the super rich to sail yachts and give expensive parties while poor people live in slums and eat inadequate diets. People who hold this view are disturbed by the fact that supply-side tax cuts are likely to make the distribution of income even more unequal than it already is.

This example illustrates a genuine and pervasive dilemma. There is often a *trade-off* between the *size* of a nation's output and the degree of *equality* with which that output is distributed. As illustrated by the example of supply-side tax cuts, programs that increase production often breed inequality. And, as we will see in *Microeconomics* Chapter 21, many policies designed to divide the proverbial economic pie more equally inadvertently cause the size of the pie to shrink.

Epilogue

These, then, are a dozen of the more fundamental concepts to be found in this book — ideas that we hope you will retain **Beyond the Final Exam.** Do not try to learn them perfectly right now, for you will hear much more about each as the book progresses. Instead, keep them in mind as you read — we will point them out to you as they occur by the use of the book's logo ☑ — and look back over this list at the end of the course. You may be amazed to see how natural, or even obvious, they will seem then.

Inside the Economist's Tool Kit

Now that you have some idea of the kinds of issues economists deal with, you should know something about the way they grapple with these problems.

Economics as a Discipline

Economics has something of a split personality. Clearly the most rigorous of the social sciences, it nevertheless looks decidedly more "social" than "scientific" when compared with physics. Economists strive to be humanists and scientists simultaneously. An economist is, by necessity, a jack of several trades. Economists borrow modes of investigation from numerous fields, adjusting each to fit the particular problems posed by economic events. Usefulness, not methodological purity, is the criterion for inclusion in the economist's tool kit.

Mathematical reasoning is used extensively in economics, but so is historical study. And neither looks quite the same as when practiced by a mathematician or a historian. Statistical inference, too, plays an important role in economic inquiry; but economists have had to modify standard statistical procedures to fit the kinds of data they deal with. In 1926, John Maynard Keynes, the great British economist, summed up the many faces of economic inquiry in a statement that still rings true today.

The master-economist . . . must understand symbols and speak in words. He must contemplate the particular in terms of the general, and touch abstract and concrete in the same flight of thought. He must study the present in the light of the past for the purposes of the future. No part of man's nature or his institutions must lie entirely outside his regard. He must be purposeful and disinterested in a simultaneous mood; as aloof and incorruptible as an artist, yet sometimes as near the earth as a politician.[1]

Economics is distinguished both by the types of *problems* it addresses and by the investigative *techniques* it employs to study them. An introductory course in economics cannot make you an economist, but it should help you approach social problems from a pragmatic and dispassionate point of view. Answers to all society's problems will not be found in this book. But you should learn how to pose questions in ways that will help produce answers that are both useful and illuminating.

The Need for Abstraction

Some students find economics unduly abstract and "unrealistic." The stylized world envisioned by economic theory seems only a distant cousin to the world

[1] See his *Essays in Biography* (New York: Norton, 1951), pages 140–141.

they see around them. There is an old joke about three people—a chemist, a physicist, and an economist—stranded on an isolated island with an ample supply of canned food but no implements to open the cans. In debating what to do, the chemist suggested lighting a fire under the cans, thus expanding their contents and causing the cans to burst. The physicist doubted that this would work. He advocated building a catapult with which they could smash the cans against some nearby boulders. Then they turned to the economist for his suggestion. After a moment's thought, he announced his solution: "Let's assume we have a can opener."

Economists *do* make unrealistic assumptions; you will encounter many of them in the pages that follow. But this propensity to abstract from reality results from the incredible complexity of the real world, not from any fondness economists have for sounding absurd.

Compare the chemist's simple task of explaining the interactions of compounds in a chemical reaction with the economist's complex task of explaining the interactions of people in an economy. Are molecules motivated by greed or altruism, by envy or ambition? Do they ever emulate other molecules? Do forecasts about them influence their behavior? People, of course, do all these things, and many, many more. It is therefore immeasurably more difficult to predict human behavior than it is to predict chemical reactions. If economists tried to keep track of every aspect of human behavior, they could surely never hope to understand the nature of the economy. Thus:

Abstraction from unimportant details is necessary to understand the functioning of anything as complex as the economy.

Abstraction means ignoring many details in order to focus on the most important factors in a problem.

To appreciate why the economist **abstracts** from details, put yourself in the following hypothetical situation. You have just arrived, for the first time in your life, in Los Angeles. You are now at the Los Angeles Convention Center. This is the point marked A in Figures 1–1 and 1–2, which are alternative maps of part of Los Angeles. You want to drive to the famous La Brea tar pits, marked B on each map. Which map would you find more useful? You will notice that Map 1 (Figure 1–1) has the full details of the Los Angeles road system. Consequently, it requires a major effort to read it. In contrast, Map 2 (Figure 1–2) omits many minor roads so that the freeways and major arteries stand out more clearly.

Most strangers to the city would prefer Map 2. With its guidance they are likely to find the tar pits in a reasonable amount of time, even though a slightly shorter route might have been found by careful calculation and planning using Map 1. Map 2 seems to *abstract* successfully from a lot of confusing details while retaining the essential aspects of the city's geography. Economic theories strive to do the same thing.

Map 3 (Figure 1–3), which shows little more than the major interstate routes that pass through the greater Los Angeles area, illustrates a danger of which all theorists must beware. Armed only with the information provided on this map, you might never find the La Brea tar pits. Instead of a useful idealization of the Los Angeles road network, the map makers have produced a map that is oversimplified for our purpose. Too much has been assumed away. Of course, this map was never intended to be used as a guide to the La Brea tar pits, which brings us to a very important point:

There is no such thing as one "right" degree of abstraction for all analytic purposes. The optimal degree of abstraction depends on the objective of the analysis. A model that is a gross oversimplification for one purpose may be needlessly complicated for another.

Economists are constantly treading the thin line between Map 2 and Map 3, between useful generalization about complex issues and gross distortions of the pertinent facts. How can they tell when they have abstracted from reality just enough? There is no objective answer to this question, which is why applied economics is as much art as science. One of the factors distinguishing good economics from bad economics is the degree to which analysts are able to find the factors that constitute the equivalent of Map 2 (rather than Maps 1 or 3) for the problem at hand. It is not always easy to do, as the following examples illustrate.

Example: The Distribution of Income

Suppose you are interested in learning why different people have different incomes, why some are fabulously rich while others are pathetically poor. People differ in many ways, too many to enumerate, much less to study. The economist ignores most of these details in order to focus on a few important facts. The color of a person's hair or eyes probably is not important to the problem at hand, but the color of his skin certainly is. Height and weight may not matter, but education probably does. Proceeding in this way, we pare Map 1 down to the manageable dimensions of Map 2. But there is a danger of going too far. To make it easy to analyze a problem, we can end up stripping away some of its most crucial features.

Example: The Determination of National Income

Suppose we want to know what factors determine the size of the output of the whole economy. Since the volume of goods and services turned out by the whole economy is affected by literally millions of decisions by investors,

Figure 1–1
MAP 1

Map 1 gives complete details of the road system of Los Angeles. If you are like most people, you will find it hard to read and not very useful for figuring out how to get from the Convention Center (point *A*) to the La Brea tar pits (point *B*). For this purpose, the map carries far too much detail, though for some other purposes (for example, locating some small street in Hollywood), it may be the best map available.
© MCMLXXV by North American Maps, P.O. Box 5850, San Francisco, CA 94101.

Figure 1–2

MAP 2

Map 2 shows a different perspective of Los Angeles. Minor roads are eliminated— we might say, *assumed away*—in order to present a clearer picture of where the major arteries and freeways go. As a result of this simplification, several ways of getting from the Convention Center (point *A*) to the La Brea tar pits (point *B*) stand out clearly. For example, we can take the Harbor Freeway north to Wilshire Boulevard, and then follow Wilshire west to the tar pits. While we might find a shorter route by poring over the details of Map 1, most of us will feel more comfortable with Map 2.

Figure 1–3

MAP 3

Map 3 strips away still more details of the Los Angeles road system. In fact, only major trunk roads and freeways remain. This map may be useful for passing through the city or getting around it, but it will not help the tourist who wants to see the sights of Los Angeles. For this purpose, too many details are missing.

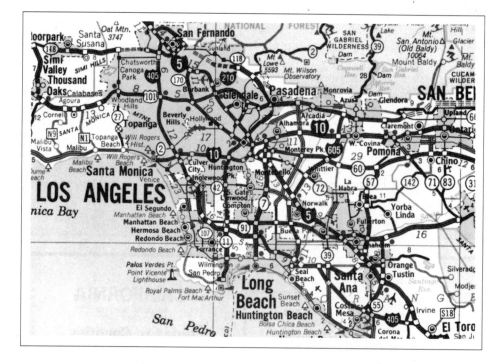

business managers, employees, government officials, and others, a complete enumeration of all the factors determining the nation's output clearly makes analysis unworkable (Map 1). Abstraction is necessary. We must prune the list to manageable size. Parts 3 and 4 of this book explain how economists do this;

that is, how they draw up a Map 2 of the nation's output. Several shortcuts to this process have been proposed, but in the opinion of their critics, they have proved on inspection to be like Map 3.

The Role of Economic Theory

A person "can stare stupidly at phenomena; but in the absence of imagination they will not connect themselves together in any rational way." These words of the renowned American philosopher-scientist C. S. Peirce succinctly express the crucial role of theory in scientific inquiry and help explain why economists are so enamored of it. To the economist or the natural scientist, the word *theory* does not mean what it does in common parlance. In scientific usage, a theory is *not* an untested assertion of alleged fact. The statement that saccharine causes cancer is not a theory, it is a *hypothesis*, which will either prove to be true or false after the right sorts of experiments have been completed.

Instead, a **theory** is a deliberate simplification (abstraction) of factual relationships that attempts to explain how those relationships work. In other words, it is an *explanation* of the mechanism behind observed phenomena. For example, astronomers' data describe the paths of the planets, and gravity forms the basis of theories that are intended to explain these data. Similarly, economists have data suggesting that government policies can affect the degree of a country's prosperity. Keynesian theory (which will be discussed in Parts 3 and 4) seeks to describe and explain these relationships.

A **theory** is a deliberate simplification of relationships whose purpose is to explain how those relationships work.

Economic theory has acquired an unsavory public image in recent years — partly because of inaccurate predictions by some economists, partly because doctrinal disputes have spilled over into the news media, and partly because some politicians have found it expedient to scoff at economists. This bad image is unfortunate because theorizing is not a luxury but a necessity. Economic theory provides a logical structure for organizing and analyzing economic data. It proceeds deductively from assumptions to conclusions — which can later be tested against data. Without theory, economists could only "stare stupidly" at the world. With theory, they can attempt to understand it.

People who have never studied economics often draw a false distinction between *theory* and *practical policy*. Politicians and business people, in particular, often reject abstract economic theory as something that is best ignored by "practical" policymakers. The irony of these statements is that:

It is precisely the concern for policy that makes economic theory so necessary and important.

If there were no possibility of changing the economy through public policy, economics might be a historical and descriptive discipline, asking, for example, what happened in the United States during the Great Depression of the 1930s or how is it that industrial pollution got to be so serious in the 1960s.

But deep concern about public policy forces economists to go beyond historical and descriptive questions. To analyze policy options, they are forced to deal with possibilities that have not actually occurred. For example, to learn how to prevent depressions, they must investigate whether the Great Depression could have been avoided by more astute government policies. Or to determine what environmental programs will be most effective, they must understand how and why a market economy produces pollution and what might happen if government placed taxes on industrial waste discharges and automobile emissions. As Peirce pointed out, not even a lifetime of ogling at real-world data will answer such questions.

Two variables are said to be **correlated** if they tend to go up or down together. But correlation need not imply causation.

An **economic model** is a simplified, small-scale version of some aspect of the economy. Economic models are often expressed in equations, by graphs, or in words.

Figure 1–4
THE PHILLIPS MACHINE
The late Professor A. W. Phillips, while teaching at the London School of Economics in the early 1950s, built this machine to illustrate Keynesian theory. This is the same theory that we will explain with words and diagrams later in the book; but Phillips's background as an engineer enabled him to depict the theory with the help of tubes, valves, and pumps. Because economists are not very good plumbers, few of them try to build models of this sort; most rely on paper and pencil instead. But the two sorts of models fulfill precisely the same role. They simplify reality in order to make it understandable

Indeed, the facts can sometimes be highly misleading. Statistics often indicate that two variables behave very similarly: Whenever one rises so does the other, and they also both go down simultaneously. But this **correlation** in the data does not prove that either of these variables *causes* the other. For example, in rainy weather, people tend to drive their cars more slowly, and there are also more traffic accidents. But this correlation does not mean that slow driving causes accidents. Rather, both phenomena can be attributed to a common underlying factor (more rain) which leads both to more accidents and to slower driving. Thus, just looking at the degree of correlation (the degree of similarity) between the behavior of two sets of statistics (like accidents and driving speeds) may not tell us much about cause and effect. We need to use theory as part of the analysis.

Because most economic issues hinge on some question of cause and effect, only a combination of theoretical reasoning and data analysis can hope to provide solutions. Simply observing correlations in data is not enough. We must understand how, if at all, different government policies will lead to a lower unemployment rate or how a tax on emissions will reduce pollution.

What Is an Economic "Model"?

An **economic model** is a representation of a theory or a part of a theory, often for the purpose of illuminating cause-and-effect relationships. The notion of a "model" is familiar enough to children, and economists (in common with other scientists) use the term in much the same way that children do.

A child's model automobile or airplane looks and operates much like the real thing, but it is much smaller and much simpler, and so it is easier to manipulate and understand. Engineers for General Motors and Boeing also build models of cars and planes. While their models are far bigger and much more elaborate than a child's toy, they use them for much the same purposes: to observe the workings of these vehicles "up close," to experiment with them in order to see how they might behave under different circumstances ("What happens if I do this?"). From these experiments, they make educated guesses as to how the real-life version will perform. Often these guesses prove uncannily accurate, as exemplified by the success of the Boeing 747. But sometimes they are wide of the mark: The chronic mechanical problems of General Motors' Corvair prompted Ralph Nader's acclaimed book *Unsafe at Any Speed*, which helped launch the consumer movement.

Economists use models for similar purposes and with similarly mixed results. A. W. Phillips, the famous engineer-turned-economist who discovered the "Phillips curve" (discussed in Chapter 17), was talented enough to construct a working model of the determination of national income in a simple economy, using colored water flowing through pipes. For years this contraption, depicted in Figure 1–4, graced the basement of the London School of Economics. However, most economists lack Phillips's manual dexterity, so economic models are generally built with paper and pencil rather than with hammer and nails.

Because many of the models used in this book are depicted in diagrams, we explain the construction and use of various types of graphs in the next chapter. But sometimes economic models are expressed only in words. The statement "Business people produce the level of output that maximizes their profits," is the basis for a behavioral model whose consequences are explored in some detail in Parts 6 through 9. Don't be put off by seemingly abstract models. Think of them as useful road maps, and remember how hard it would be to find your way around Los Angeles without one.

Reasons for Disagreements:
Imperfect Information and Value Judgments

"If all the earth's economists were laid end to end, they could not reach an agreement," or so the saying goes. And President Reagan once quipped that the special version of the game *Trivial Pursuit* for economists has 100 questions, but 3000 answers. If economics is a scientific discipline, why do economists quarrel so much? Politicians and reporters are fond of pointing out that economists can generally be found on both sides of every issue of public policy. Physicists, on the other hand, do not debate whether the earth revolves around the sun or vice versa.

The question reflects a misunderstanding of the nature of science. As a matter of fact, physicists formerly did argue over whether the earth revolves around the sun, often with rather grim results for themselves. (Economists, fortunately, are not often burned at the stake!) Nowadays, physicists argue about "black holes," the existence of certain subatomic particles, and other esoterica. These arguments often go unnoticed by the public because few of us understand what they are talking about. In contrast, everyone is eager to join economic debates over inflation, unemployment, pollution, and almost everything else. Because economics is a *social* science, its disputes are aired in public, and almost everyone is personally concerned with the subject matter. Anyone who has ever bought or sold anything, it seems, fancies himself an amateur economist.

Furthermore, the fact is that economists agree much more than is commonly supposed. Virtually all economists, regardless of their politics, agree that taxing polluters is one of the best ways to protect the environment (see *Microeconomics* Chapters 13 and 18), that rent controls can ruin a city (Chapter 4), and that free trade among nations is preferable to the erection of barriers through tariffs and quotas (see Chapter 18). The list could go on and on. It is probably true that the issues about which economists agree *far* exceed the subjects on which they disagree.

Finally, many disputes among economists are not scientific disputes at all. Economists, like everyone else, come in all political stripes: conservative, middle-of-the-road, liberal, radical. Each may have different values and hold a different view of what is best for society. So each may have a different opinion on what is the "right" solution to any problem of public policy. In addition, some of the pertinent facts might not be known.

While economists can contribute the best theoretical and factual knowledge there is on a particular issue, the final decision on policy questions often rests either on information that is not currently available or on tastes and ethical opinions about which people differ (the things we call "value judgments"), or on both.

Some examples will illustrate why pure scientific analysis often does not lead to a policy conclusion.

Taxing Industrial Wastes
As you will learn in *Microeconomics* Chapter 18, the proper tax to levy on industrial wastes depends on quantitative estimates of the harm done by the pollutant. For most waste products, these numbers are not yet known, although knowledge is accumulating rapidly. So a lack of complete information makes it difficult to formulate a concrete policy proposal.

Inflation and Unemployment

Government policies that succeed in shortening a recession are virtually certain to cause higher inflation for a while. Using tools that we will describe in Parts 2 through 5, many economists believe they can even measure how much more inflation the economy will suffer as the price of fighting a recession. Is it worth it? An economist cannot answer this any more than a nuclear physicist could have determined whether dropping the atomic bomb on Hiroshima was a good idea. The decision rests on value judgments about the moral trade-off between inflation and unemployment, judgments that can be made only by the citizenry through its elected officials.

These examples underscore something we said earlier in this chapter: Economics cannot provide all the *answers*, but it can teach you how to ask the right *questions*. By the time you finish studying this book, you should have a good understanding of when the right course of action turns on disputed facts, on value judgments, and on some combination of the two.

The Economist's Odd Vocabulary

George Bernard Shaw once remarked that America and England are two nations separated by a common language. Much the same might be said of economists and other people, for economists often assign peculiar meanings to familiar words. Here are two examples; you will find many others later on.

The **opportunity cost** of some decision is the value of the next best alternative which you have to give up because of that decision (for example, working instead of going to school).

1. *Cost.* We have already mentioned that when economists speak of "costs" they are normally referring to *opportunity costs*. Accountants, on the other hand, almost always measure costs as only the direct monetary expenses involved in any activity. Thus, in calculating the costs of the same activity, the accountant and the economist may arrive at two very different results, as the example of the costs of going to college illustrated. Accountants and economists are indeed divided by a common language.

2. *Money.* Most people work for money, or so they think. Again, the economist disagrees. He will insist that people work to earn *income*, which often happens to be paid — for reasons of convenience — in the form of *money*. What is the difference? To the economist *money* refers to the amount of cash and bank-account balances you own at any particular moment. Your holdings of money change frequently, often several times in a single day. But *income* refers to the rate at which you earn money over time. A worker would answer the question "What is your income?" by saying "$10,000 a year," or "$200 a week," or something like that. Income probably changes much less frequently than holdings of money, perhaps only once a year. The distinction between money and income is important, and it will occupy our attention in Part 4.

The economist, it would appear, is much like Humpty Dumpty in *Alice in Wonderland* who said imperiously, "When I use a word it means just what I choose it to mean — neither more nor less." Why such obstinacy? Because economists need a *scientific jargon*, just as other scientists do. Any dictionary will testify to the fact that most words in any language have a multiplicity of meanings. Scientists must be more precise than that. And, rather than conjure up entirely new words, as natural scientists frequently do, economists take ordinary words and give them slightly special meanings.

One wag once pointed out that Canada has a radical group called *separatists* whose members steadfastly refuse to speak English, and that America also has such a group—but calls them *economists*. Who, though, would prefer that we say "phlogiston" instead of "cost" or "nutches" instead of "money"?

Summary

1. To help you get the most out of your first course in economics, we have devised a list of *12 Important Ideas* that you will want to remember *Beyond the Final Exam*. Here we list them, very briefly, indicating where each idea occurs in the book.

   (1) Most government policies that reduce inflation are likely to intensify the unemployment problem, and vice versa. (Chapter 17)

   (2) Interest rates that appear very high may actually be very low if they are accompanied by rapid inflation. (Chapter 6)

   (3) Budget deficits may or may not be advisable, depending on the circumstances. (Chapter 16)

   (4) In a voluntary exchange, both parties must expect to benefit. (Chapters 3 and 18)

   (5) Two nations can gain from international trade, even if one is more efficient at making everything. (Chapter 18)

   (6) In the long run, productivity is almost the only thing that matters for a nation's material well-being. (Chapter 7)

   (7) Lawmakers who try to repeal the "law" of supply and demand are liable to open a Pandora's box of troubles they never expected. (Chapter 4)

   (8) Externalities cause the market mechanism to misfire, but this defect of the market can be remedied by market-oriented policies. (Chapters 29 and 34)

   (9) To make a rational decision, the opportunity cost of an action must be measured, because only this calculation will tell the decision-maker what he has given up. (Chapter 3)

   (10) Decisionmaking often requires the use of marginal analysis to isolate the costs and benefits of that particular decision. (Chapter 24)

   (11) The operation of free markets is likely to lead to rising prices for public and private services. (Chapter 29)

   (12) Most policies that equalize income will exact a cost by reducing the nation's output. (Chapter 37)

2. Economics is a discipline that uses a variety of approaches, some of them scientific and others humanistic, to address important social questions.

3. Because of the great complexity of human behavior, the economist is forced to abstract from many details, make generalizations that he knows are not quite true, and organize what knowledge he has according to some theoretical structure.

4. Correlation need not imply causation.

5. Economists use simplified models to understand the real world and predict its behavior, much as a child uses a model railroad to learn how trains work.

6. While these models, if skillfully constructed, can illuminate important economic problems, they rarely can answer the questions that policymakers are confronted with. For this purpose, value judgments are needed, and the economist is no better equipped to make them than is anyone else.

7. A course in economics seeks to teach the student how to formulate the right questions, questions that point to the value judgments or unknown pieces of data that must be obtained in order to make an intelligent decision. It does not try to provide all the answers.

Concepts for Review

Voluntary exchange	Marginal analysis	Correlation versus causation
Comparative advantage	Marginal costs	Model
Productivity	Abstraction and generalization	Opportunity cost
Externalities	Theory	

Questions for Discussion

1. Think about how you would construct a "model" of how your college is governed. Which officers and administrators would you include and exclude from your model if the objective were
   a. to explain how decisions on tuition payments are made?
   b. to explain the quality of the football team?
   Relate this to the map example in the chapter.

2. Relate the process of "abstraction" to the way you take notes in a lecture. Why do you not try to transcribe every word the lecturer utters? Why do you not just write down the title of the lecture and stop there? How do you decide, roughly speaking, on the correct amount of detail?

3. Explain why a government policymaker cannot afford to ignore economic theory.

2

The Use and Misuse of Graphs

Chapter 1 noted that economic models are frequently analyzed and explained with the help of graphs. This book is full of them. But that is not the only reason for you to study how they work. Most of you will deal with graphs in the future, perhaps frequently. They appear in newspapers. Doctors use graphs to keep track of patients' progress. Business firms use them to check their profit and sales performance. Persons concerned with social issues use them to examine trends in ethnic composition of cities and the relation of felonies to family income.

Graphs are invaluable because of the large quantity of data they can display and the way they facilitate interpretation and analysis of the data. They enable the eye to take in at a glance important statistical relationships that would be far less apparent from prose descriptions or long lists of numbers. But badly constructed graphs can confuse and mislead.

In this chapter we show, first, how to read a graph that depicts a relationship between two variables. Second, we define the term *slope* and describe how it is measured and interpreted. Third, we explain how the behavior of three variables can be shown on a two-dimensional graph. Fourth, we discuss how misinterpretation is avoided by adjusting economic graphs to take account of changes in the purchasing power of the dollar, in the population of the nation, and in other pertinent developments. And finally, we examine several other common ways in which graphs can be misleading if not drawn and interpreted with care.

Graphs Used in Economic Analysis*

Two-Variable Diagrams

Much of the economic analysis to be found in this and other books requires that we keep track of two **variables** simultaneously. For example, in studying the

A **variable** is an object, such as price, whose magnitude is measured by a number; it is used to analyze what happens to other things when the size of that number changes (varies).

*Students who have a nodding acquaintance with geometry and feel quite comfortable with graphs can safely skip the first sections of this chapter and proceed directly to the second part, which begins on page 25.

operation of markets, we will want to keep one eye on the price of a commodity and the other on the quantity that is bought and sold.

For this reason, economists frequently find it useful to display real or imaginary figures in a *two-dimensional graph*, which simultaneously represents the behavior of two economic variables. The numerical value of one variable is measured along the bottom of the graph (called the *horizontal axis*), starting from the **origin** (the point labeled "0"), and the numerical value of the other is measured up the side of the graph (called the *vertical axis*), also starting from the origin.

Figures 2–1(a) and 2–1(b) are typical graphs of economic analysis. They depict an (imaginary) *demand curve*, represented by the blue dots in Figure 2–1(a) and the heavy blue line in Figure 2–1(b). The graphs show the price of natural gas on their vertical axes and the quantity of gas people want to buy at each such price on the horizontal axes. The dots in Figure 2–1(a) are connected by the continuous blue curve labeled DD.

Economic diagrams are generally read as one reads latitudes and longitudes on a map. On the demand curve in Figure 2–1, the point marked *a* represents a hypothetical combination of price and quantity demanded in St. Louis. By drawing a horizontal line leftward from that point to the vertical axis, we learn that the average price for gas in St. Louis is $3 per thousand cubic feet. By dropping a line straight down to the horizontal axis, we find that 80 billion cubic feet are wanted by consumers at this price, just as the statistics in Table 2–1 show. The other points on the graph give similar information. For example, point *b* indicates that if natural gas in St. Louis cost only $2 per thousand cubic feet, quantity demanded would be higher—it would reach 120 billion cubic feet.

Notice that information about price and quantity is *all* we can learn from the diagram. The demand curve will not tell us about the kinds of people who

The lower left-hand corner of a graph where the two axes meet is called the **origin**. Both variables are equal to zero at the origin.

Figure 2–1
A DEMAND CURVE FOR NATURAL GAS IN ST. LOUIS
This demand curve shows the relationship between the price of natural gas and the quantity of it that will be demanded. For example, the point labeled *a* indicates that at a price of $3 per thousand cubic feet (point *P*), the quantity demanded will be 80 billion cubic feet (point *Q*).

Table 2–1
QUANTITIES OF NATURAL GAS DEMANDED AT VARIOUS PRICES

Price ($ per thousand cubic ft.)	$2	3	4	5	6
Quantity Demanded (billions of cubic feet)	120	80	56	38	20

live in St. Louis, the size of their homes, or the condition of their furnaces. It tells us about the price and the quantity demanded at that price; no more, no less. Specifically, it does tell us that when price declines there is an increase in the amount of gas consumers are willing and able to buy.

A diagram abstracts from many details, some of which may be quite interesting, in order to focus on the two variables of primary interest—in this case, the price of natural gas and the amount of gas that is demanded at each price. All the diagrams used in this book share this basic feature. They cannot tell the reader the "whole story" any more than a map's latitude and longitude figures for a particular city can make someone an authority on that city.

The Definition and Measurement of Slope

One of the most important features of the diagrams used by economists is the pace with which the line, or curve, being sketched runs uphill or downhill as we move to the right. The demand curve in Figure 2–1 clearly slopes downhill (the price falls) as we follow it to the right (that is, as more gas is demanded). In such instances we say that *the curve has a negative slope, or is negatively sloped, because one variable falls as the other one rises*.

The **slope of a straight line** is the ratio of the vertical change to the corresponding horizontal change as we move to the right along the line, or as it is often said, the ratio of the "rise" over the "run."

The four panels of Figure 2–2 show all the possible slopes for a straight-line relationship between two unnamed variables called Y (measured along the vertical axis) and X (measured along the horizontal axis). Figure 2–2(a) shows a negative slope, much like our demand curve. Figure 2–2(b) shows a positive slope, because variable Y rises (we go uphill) as variable X rises (as we move to the right). Figure 2–2(c) shows a *zero* slope, where the value of Y is the same irrespective of the value of X. Figure 2–2(d) shows an *infinite* slope, meaning that the value of X is the same irrespective of the value of Y.

Slope is a numerical concept, not just a qualitative one. The two panels of Figure 2–3 show two positively sloped straight lines with different slopes. The line in Figure 2–3(b) is clearly steeper. But by how much? The labels should help you compute the answer. In Figure 2–3(a) a horizontal movement, AB, of 10 units (13–3) corresponds to a vertical movement, BC, of 1 unit (9 − 8). So the slope is $BC/AB = \frac{1}{10}$. In Figure 2–3(b), the same horizontal movement of

Figure 2–2
DIFFERENT TYPES OF SLOPE OF A STRAIGHT-LINE GRAPH
In Figure 2–2(a), the curve goes downward as we read from left to right, so we say it has a negative slope. The slopes in the other figures can be interpreted similarly.

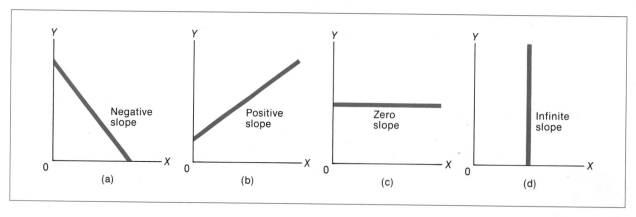

Negative slope (a)

Positive slope (b)

Zero slope (c)

Infinite slope (d)

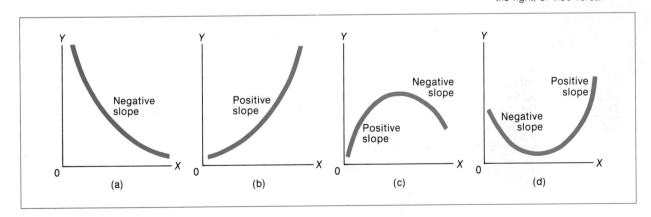

10 units corresponds to a vertical movement of 3 units (11 − 8). So the slope is $\frac{3}{10}$, which is larger.

By definition, the slope of any particular straight line is the same no matter where on that line we choose to measure it. That is why we can pick any horizontal distance, AB, and the corresponding slope triangle, ABC, to measure slope. But this is not true of lines that are curved.

Curved lines also have slopes, but the numerical value of the slope is different at every point.

The four panels of Figure 2–4 provide some examples of **slopes of curved lines.** The curve in Figure 2–4(a) has a negative slope everywhere, while the curve in Figure 2–4(b) has a positive slope everywhere. But these are not the only possibilities. In Figure 2–4(c) we encounter a curve that has a positive slope at first but a negative slope later on. Figure 2–4(d) shows the opposite case: a negative slope followed by a positive slope.

It is possible to measure the slope of a smooth curved line numerically *at any particular point*. This is done by drawing a *straight* line that *touches*, but does not *cut*, the curve at the point in question. Such a line is called a **tangent to the curve.**

Figure 2–3
HOW TO MEASURE SLOPE
Slope indicates how much the graph rises per unit move from left to right. Thus, in Figure 2–3(b), as we go from point A to point B, we go $13 − 3 = 10$ units to the right. But in that interval, the graph rises from the height of point B to the height of point C, that is, it rises 3 units. Consequently, the slope of the line is $BC/AB = 3/10$.

Figure 2–4
BEHAVIOR OF SLOPES IN CURVED GRAPHS
As Figures 2–4(c) and 2–4(d) indicate, where a graph is not a straight line it may have a slope that starts off as positive but that becomes negative farther to the right, or vice versa.

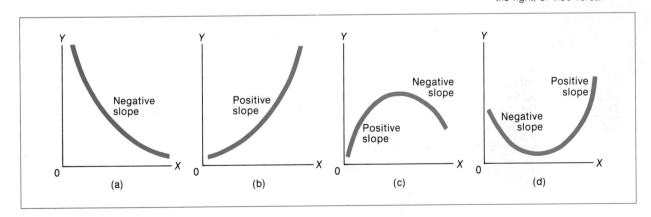

The slope of a curved line at a particular point is the slope of the straight line that is tangent to the curve at that point.

In Figure 2–5 we have constructed tangents to a curve at two points. Line tt is tangent at point C, and line TT is tangent at point F. We can measure the slope of the curve at these two points by applying the definition. The calculation for point C, then, is the following:

$$\text{Slope at point } C = \text{Slope of line } tt = \frac{\text{Distance } BC}{\text{Distance } AB}$$

$$= \frac{6-2}{10-0} = \frac{4}{10} = +0.4 .$$

A similar calculation yields the slope of the curve at point F, which, as we can see from Figure 2–5, must be smaller:

$$\text{Slope at Point } F = \text{Slope of line } TT = \frac{14-9}{50-0} = \frac{5}{50} = +0.1 .$$

EXERCISE

Show that the slope of the curve at point D is between $+0.1$ and $+0.4$.

What would happen if we tried to apply this graphical technique to the high point in Figure 2–4(c) or to the low point in Figure 2–4(d)? Take a ruler and try it. The tangents that you construct should be horizontal, meaning that they should have a slope of exactly zero. It is always true that where the slope of a smooth curve changes from positive to negative, or vice versa, there will be at least a single point with a zero slope.

Figure 2–5
HOW TO MEASURE SLOPE AT A POINT ON A CURVED GRAPH
To find the slope at point F, draw the line TT, which is tangent to the curve at point F; then measure the slope of the straight-line tangent TT as in Figure 2–3. The slope of the tangent is the same as the slope of the curve at point F.

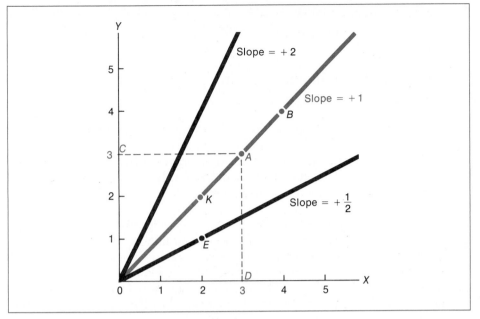

Figure 2–6
RAYS THROUGH THE
ORIGIN

Rays are straight lines drawn through the zero point on the graph (*the origin*). Three rays with different slopes are shown. The middle ray, the one with slope = +1, has two properties that make it particularly useful in economics: (1) it makes a 45° angle with either axis, and (2) any point on that ray (for example, point *A*) is exactly equal in distance from the horizontal and vertical axes (length *DA* = length *CA*). So if the items measured on the two axes are in equal units, then at any point on that ray, such as *A*, the number on the *X*-axis (the abscissa) will be the same as the number on the *Y*-axis (the ordinate).

Curves that have the shape of a hill, such as Figure 2–4(c), have a zero slope at their *highest* point. Curves that have the shape of a valley, such as Figure 2–4(d), have a zero slope at their *lowest* point.

Rays Through the Origin and 45° Lines

The point at which a straight line cuts the vertical (*Y*) axis is called the *Y-intercept*. For example, the *Y*-intercept of line *tt* in Figure 2–5 is 2, while the *Y*-intercept of line *TT* is 9. Lines whose *Y*-intercept is zero have so many special uses that they have been given a special name, a **ray through the origin,** or a **ray.**

Figure 2–6 contains three rays through the origin, and the slope of each is indicated in the diagram. The ray in the center—whose slope is 1—is particularly useful in many economic applications because it marks off points where *X* and *Y* are equal (as long as *X* and *Y* are measured in the same units). For example, at point *A* we have *X* = 3 and *Y* = 3, at point *B*, *X* = 4 and *Y* = 4, and a similar relation holds at any other point on that ray.

How do we know that this is always true for a ray whose slope is 1? If we start from the origin (where both *X* and *Y* are zero) and the slope of the ray is 1, we know from the definition of slope that:

$$\text{Slope} = \frac{\text{Vertical change}}{\text{Horizontal change}} = 1.$$

This implies that the vertical change and the horizontal change are always equal, so the two variables must always remain equal.

Rays through the origin with a slope of 1 are called **45° lines** because they form an angle of 45° with the horizontal axis. If a point representing some data

The point on the graph where both variables are zero is called **the origin.**

A straight line emanating from the origin, or zero point on a graph, is called a **ray through the origin** or, sometimes, just a **ray.**

A **45° line** is a ray through the origin with a slope of + 1. It marks off points where the variables measured on each axis have equal values.[1]

---

[1]The definition assumes that both variables are measured in the same units.

is above the 45° line, we know that the value of Y exceeds the value of X. Conversely, whenever we find a point below the 45° line, we know that X is larger than Y.

Squeezing Three Dimensions into Two: Contour Maps

Sometimes, because a problem involves more than two variables, two dimensions just are not enough, which is unfortunate since paper is only two dimensional. When we study the decision making process of a business firm, for example, we may want to keep track simultaneously of three variables: how much labor it employs, how much machinery it uses, and how much output it creates.

Luckily, there is a well-known device for collapsing three dimensions into two, namely a *contour map*. Figure 2–7 is a contour map of Mount Rainier, the highest peak in the state of Washington. On several of the irregularly shaped "rings" we find a number indicating the height above sea level at that particular spot on the mountain. Thus, unlike the more usual sort of map, which gives only latitudes and longitudes, this contour map exhibits three pieces of information about each point: latitude, longitude, and altitude.

Figure 2–8 looks more like the contour maps encountered in economics. It shows how some third variable, called Z (think of it as a firm's output, for example), varies as we change either variable X (think of it as a firm's employment) or variable Y (think of it as the use of a firm's machines). Just like the map of Mount Rainier, any point on the diagram conveys three pieces of data. At point A, we can read off the values of X and Y in the conventional way (X is 30 and Y is 40), and we can also note the value of Z by checking to see on which contour line point A falls. (It is on the Z = 20 contour.) So point A is able to tell us that 30 hours of labor and 40 hours of machine time produce 20 units of output.

While most of the analyses presented in this book will be based on the simpler two-variable diagrams, contour maps will find their applications, especially in the appendixes to Chapters 21 and 23.

Figure 2–7
A GEOGRAPHIC
CONTOUR MAP
All points on any particular contour line represent geographic locations that are at the same height above sea level.
SOURCE: U.S. Geological Survey.

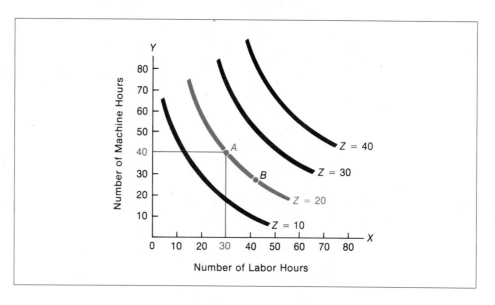

Figure 2–8
AN ECONOMIC
CONTOUR MAP
In this contour map, all points on a given contour line represent different combinations of labor and capital capable of producing a given output. For example, all points on the curve Z = 20 represent input combinations that can produce 20 units of output. Point A on that line means that the 20 units of output can be produced using 30 labor hours and 40 machine hours. Economists call such maps *production indifference maps*.

Perils in the Interpretation of Graphs

The preceding materials contain just about all you will need in order to understand the simple graphics used in economic models. We turn now to the second objective of this chapter: to show how statistical data are portrayed on graphs and some of the pitfalls to watch out for.

The Interpretation of Growth Trends

Probably the most common form of graph in empirical economics is a year-by-year (or perhaps a month-by-month) depiction of the behavior of some economic variable — the profits of a particular corporation, or its annual sales, or the number of persons unemployed in the U.S. economy, or some measure of consumer prices. For example, Figure 2–9 is this sort of **time series graph** showing year by year the total amount of money borrowed by U.S. corporations. It shows that the amount of money acquired increased almost constantly over the quarter century 1960–1986, although in the last few years it has declined. Time series graphs are a type of two-variable diagram in which time is always the variable measured along the horizontal axis.

A **time series graph** depicts how a variable changes over time.

Such graphs can be quite illuminating, offering an instant visual grasp of the course of the relevant events. *However, if misused, such graphs are very dangerous.* They can easily mislead persons who are not experienced in dealing with them.[2] Perhaps even more dangerous are the lies perpetrated accidentally and unintentionally by people who draw graphs without sufficient care and who may innocently mislead themselves as well as others.

A fine example of this latter occurrence is illustrated in Figure 2–10. Many people felt that there was a "cultural boom" underway in the period after World

---

[2]An interesting and informative book on the subject is called *How to Lie with Statistics*, by Darrell Huff and Irving Geis (New York: Norton, 1954).

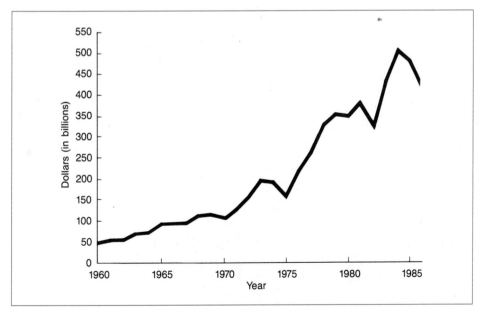

Figure 2–9
TIME SERIES GRAPH: FUNDS ACQUIRED BY U.S. CORPORATIONS, 1960–1986
This graph shows the amount of money acquired by U.S. non-farm corporations in each year from 1960 through 1986.
SOURCE: *Economic Report of the President*, Washington, D.C.: U.S. Government Printing Office, 1987, p. 348.

Figure 2–10
INDEX OF
EXPENDITURES ON
ADMISSIONS TO
ARTISTIC
PERFORMANCES
This graph, showing
expenditures on admissions
to artistic performances,
seems to indicate that since
about 1932 Americans have
become much more
interested in attending the
performing arts.
SOURCE: *Survey of Current
Business*, July issues, various
years; and *Economic Report of
the President*, Washington D.C.:
U.S. Government Printing Office,
various years.

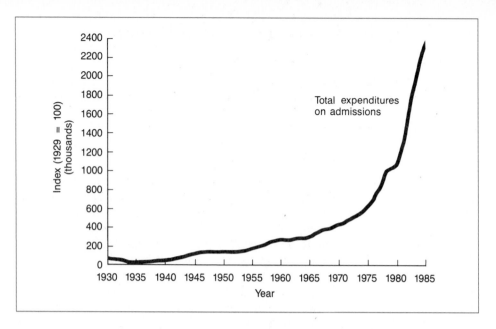

War II that led to an explosion in the demand for tickets to all sorts of artistic performances. This boom, it was thought, accounted for the rapidly rising prices of theater tickets. Figure 2–10 shows the time series graph that formed the basis for this allegation. The growth in spending for theater tickets certainly looks impressive; expenditures rose about 2300 percent from 1929 to 1985.

But there is less to this graph than meets the eye—much less. Most of the spectacular growth in spending on theater admissions was a reflection of three rather banal facts. First, there were many more Americans alive in 1982 than in 1929, so spending *per person* rose by much less than Figure 2–10 suggests. Second, the price of almost everything, not just theater tickets, was higher in 1985 than in 1929. In fact, average prices were more than five times their 1929 levels. Third, the average American was richer in 1985 than in 1929, and consequently was more inclined to spend money on everything—not just on cultural activities.

All three of these factors can be accounted for by expressing spending on theater admissions as a *fraction* of total consumer income. The results of this "correction" are shown in Figure 2–11. The explosive growth suggested by the uncorrected data really amounts to a decline in the share of income that the average American spent on theater tickets—from about 15 cents out of each $100 in 1929 to only 8 cents in 1985! How misleading it can be simply to "look at the facts." There is a general lesson to be learned from this example:

The facts, as portrayed in a time series graph, most assuredly do not "speak for themselves." Because almost everything grows in a growing economy, one must use judgment in interpreting growth trends. Depending on what kind of data are being analyzed, it may be essential to correct for population growth, for rising prices, for rising incomes, or for all three.[3]

Distorting Trends by Choice of the Time Period
In addition to possible misinterpretations of growth trends, users of statistical data must be on guard for distortions of trends caused by unskillfully or un-

[3]For a full discussion of how to use a "price index" to correct for rising prices, see the appendix to Chapter 6.

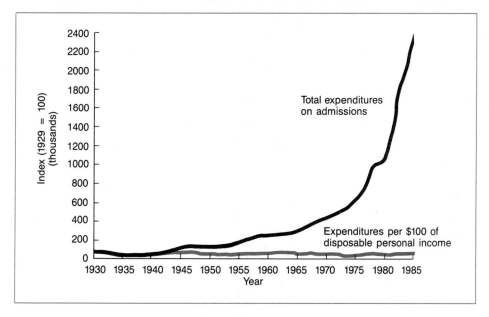

Figure 2–11
APPEARANCE AND
REALITY IN ARTS
EXPENDITURE
The curve in black shows
correctly that the number of
dollars spent on the arts by
Americans rose dramatically
after 1932. But because of
inflation, a dollar in 1985 was
worth much less than in
1929, and there were many
more Americans in the latter
year, who were also wealthier
on the average. After
correction for inflation,
population changes, and so
on, the black line is
transformed into the blue line,
showing that in 1985 an
average American actually
spent less of his purchasing
power on the arts than in
1929.
SOURCE: *Survey of Current
Business*, July issues, various
years; and *Economic Report of
the President*, Washington, D.C.:
U.S. Government Printing Office,
various years.

scrupulously chosen first and last periods for the graph. This is best explained by an example.

Figures 2–12 and 2–13 on the next page show the behavior of average stock market prices over the periods 1929–1932 and 1973–1975. They both display a clear downhill movement and would suggest to anyone who does not have other information that stocks are a terrible investment.

However, an unscrupulous seller of stocks could use the same set of stock market statistics to tell exactly the opposite story by carefully selecting another group of years. Figure 2–14 shows the behavior of average stock prices from 1940 through 1965. The persistence and size of the increase is quite dramatic. Stocks now look like a rather good investment.

An even longer and less biased period gives a less distorted picture (Figure 2–15). It indicates that investments in stocks are sometimes profitable and other times unprofitable.

The deliberate or inadvertent distortion resulting from an unfortunate or un-scrupulous choice of time period for a graph must constantly be watched for.

There are no rules that can give absolute protection from this difficulty, but several precautions can be helpful.

1. Make sure the first date shown on the graph is not an exceptionally high or low point. In comparison with 1929, a year of unusually high stock market prices, the years immediately following are bound to give the impression of a downward trend.

2. For the same reason, make sure the graph does not end in a year that is ex-traordinarily high or low (although this may be unavoidable if the graph simply ends with figures that are as up-to-date as possible).

3. Make sure that (in the absence of some special justification) the graph does not depict only a very brief period, which can easily be atypical.

Figure 2–12
STOCK PRICES,
1929–1932
This graph seems to show
that stock market prices
generally go down.

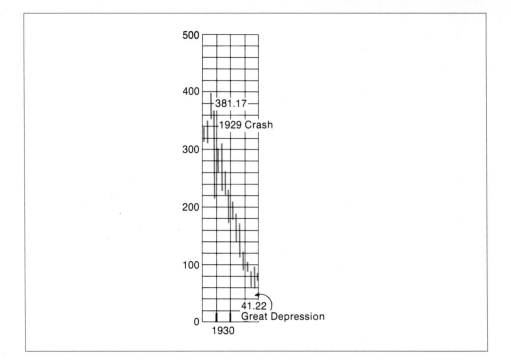

Figure 2–13
STOCK PRICES,
1973–1975
This figure also seems to
show that stock prices
generally fall.

Figure 2–14
STOCK PRICES,
1940–1965
This graph seems to indicate
that the value of stocks is on
a never-ending climb.

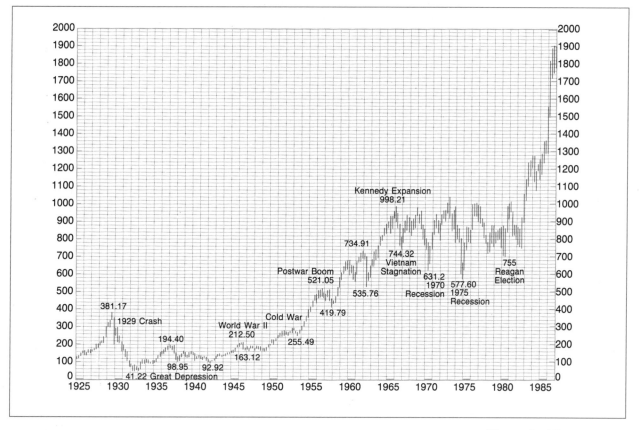

Dangers of Omitting the Origin

Frequently, the value of an economic variable described on a graph does not fall anywhere near zero during the period under consideration. For example, as Figure 2–16 shows, toward the end of 1983 the interest rate on three-month Treasury securities never rose as high as 9.5 percent and never fell as low as 8 percent. This means that a graph representing the behavior of interest rates in

Figure 2–15
THE FULL HISTORY OF STOCK PRICES, 1925–1987
Here we see that stock prices have lots of ups and downs, though they have risen quite a bit on the average.

Figure 2–16
A GRAPH SHOWING OMISSION OF THE ORIGIN
A hasty glance at this figure seems to show that, from the end of August to December 1983, the interest rate collapsed almost to zero, and then shot up again almost as fast.
SOURCE: *The New York Times*, December 6, 1983.

1983 would have a good deal of wasted space between the horizontal axis of the graph, where the interest rate is zero, and the level of the graph representing an 8 percent interest rate. In that area there are simply no data to plot. It is therefore tempting simply to eliminate this wasted space by beginning the graph at an 8 percent interest rate or higher. This was done by *The New York Times* at that time (Figure 2–16), where the lowest points shown in the figure involved an interest rate of 8.4 percent.

What is wrong with the drawing? The answer is that it vastly exaggerates the size of the drop and the rise in the interest rate that are depicted. It makes the drop in the interest rate that occurred in the middle of the period look like a complete crash in the interest rate's level. The more informative graph, which includes the origin as well as the "wasted space" in between is shown in Figure 2–17. Note how this alternative presentation puts matters into perspective. It shows that at the beginning of the period there was a fall in the interest rate, but that it was nowhere near as severe as the graph in *The New York Times* would have suggested to the unwary reader.

Omitting the origin in a graph is dangerous because it always exaggerates the magnitudes of the changes that have taken place.

Sometimes, it is true, the inclusion of the origin would waste so much space that it is undesirable to include it. In that case, a good practice is to put a very clear warning on the graph to remind the reader that this has been done. Figure 2–18 shows one way of doing so.

Unreliability of Steepness and Choice of Units
The last problem we will consider has consequences similar to the one we have just discussed. The problem is that we can never trust the impression we get from the steepness of an economic graph. A graph of stock market prices that

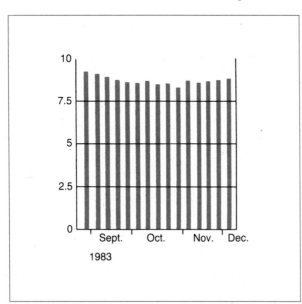

Figure 2–17
INTEREST RATE FIGURES INCLUDING POINT OF ORIGIN
Adding the point of zero interest rate to the previous graph shows that the fall and rise in the interest rate was in fact not so enormous as the earlier graph suggests.

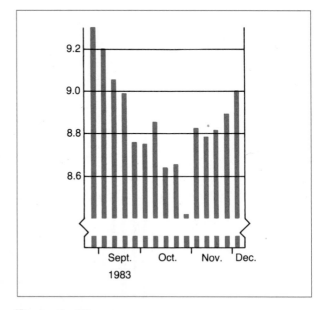

Figure 2–18
A BREAK IN A GRAPH
An alternative way of warning the reader that the zero point has been left out is to put a break in the graph, as illustrated here.

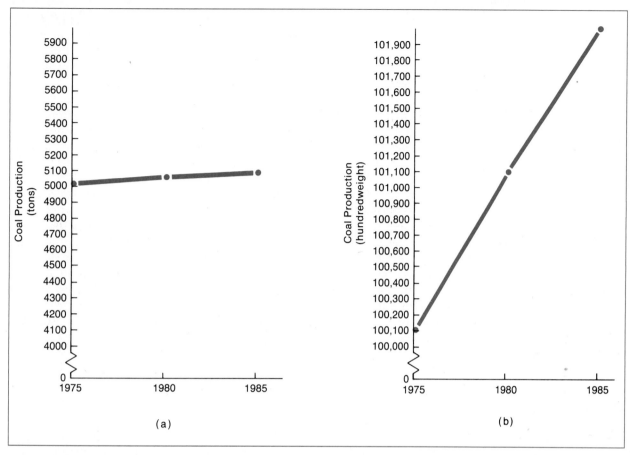

(a)

(b)

moves uphill sharply (has a large positive slope) appears to suggest that prices are rising rapidly, while another graph in which the rate of climb is much slower seems to imply that prices are going up sluggishly. Yet, depending on how one draws the graph, exactly the same statistics can produce a graph that is rising very quickly or very slowly.

The reason for this possibility is that in economics there are no fixed units of measurement. Coal production can be measured in hundredweight (hundreds of pounds) or in tons. Prices can be measured in cents or in dollars or in millions of dollars. Time can be measured in days or in months or in years. Any of these choices is perfectly legitimate, but it makes all the difference to the speed with which a graph using the resulting figures rises or falls.

An example will bring out the point. Suppose that we have the following (imaginary) figures on daily coal production from a mine, which we measure both in hundredweight and in tons (remembering that 1 ton = 20 hundredweight):

YEAR	PRODUCTION IN TONS	PRODUCTION IN HUNDRED WEIGHT
1975	5000	100,000
1980	5050	101,000
1985	5090	101,800

Look at Figures 2–19(a) and 2–19(b), one graph showing the figures in tons and the other showing the figures in hundredweight. The line looks quite flat in Figure 2–19(a), but quite steep in Figure 2–19(b).

Figure 2–19
SLOPE DEPENDS ON UNITS OF MEASUREMENT
(a) Coal production is measured in tons, and production seems to be rising very slowly.
(b) Production is measured in hundredweight (hundred-pound units) so the same facts now seem to say that production is rising spectacularly.

Unfortunately, we cannot solve the problem by agreeing always to stick to the same measurement units. Pounds may be the right unit for measuring demand for beef, but they will not do in measuring demand for cloth or for coal. A penny may be the right monetary unit for postage stamps, but it is not a very convenient unit for the cost of airplanes or automobiles.

A change in units of measurement stretches or compresses the axis on which the information is represented, which automatically changes the slope of a graph. Therefore, we must never place much faith in the apparent implications of the slope of an ordinary graph in economics.

Later, in Chapter 22 on demand analysis, we will encounter a useful approach economists have adopted to deal with this problem. Instead of calculating changes in "absolute" terms—like tons of coal—they use as their common unit the *percentage* increase. By using percentages rather than absolute figures the problem can be avoided. The reason is simple. If we look at our hypothetical figures on coal production again, we see that no matter whether we measure the increase in output from 1975 to 1980 in tons (from 5000 to 5050) or in hundredweight (from 100,000 to 101,000), the *percentage* increase has been the same. Fifty is 1 percent of 5000, and 1000 is 1 percent of 100,000. Since a change in units affects both the numbers *proportionately*, the result is a washout—it does not do anything to the percentage calculation.

Summary

1. Because graphs are used so often to portray economic models, it is important for students to acquire some understanding of their construction and use. Fortunately, the graphics used in economics are usually not very complex.
2. Most economic models are depicted in two-variable diagrams. We read data from these diagrams just as we read the latitude and longitude on a map: each point represents the values of two variables at the same time.
3. In some instances, three variables must be shown at once. In these cases, economists use contour maps, which, as the name suggests, show "latitude," "longitude," and "altitude" all at the same time.
4. Often, the most important property of a line or curve drawn on a diagram will be its slope, which is defined as the ratio of the "rise" over the "run," or the vertical change divided by the horizontal change. Curves that go uphill as we move to the right have positive slopes, while curves that go downhill have negative slopes.
5. By definition, a straight line has the same slope wherever we choose to measure it. The slope of a curved line changes, but the slope at any point on the curve can be calculated by measuring the slope of a straight line tangent to the curve at that point.
6. A time series graph is a particular type of two-variable diagram that is useful in depicting statistical data. Time is measured along the horizontal axis, and some variable of interest is measured along the vertical axis.
7. While time series graphs are invaluable in helping us condense a great deal of information in a single picture, they can be quite misleading if they are not drawn and interpreted with care. For example, growth trends can be exaggerated by inappropriate choice of units of measurement or by failure to correct for some obvious source of growth (such as rising population). Omitting the origin can make the ups and downs in a time series appear much more extreme than they actually are. Or, by a clever choice of the starting and ending points for the graphs, the same data can be made to tell very different stories. Readers of such graphs—and this includes anyone who ever reads a newspaper—must be on guard for problems like these or they may find themselves misled by "the facts."

Concepts for Review

Variable	Slope of a straight (or curved) line	Ray through the origin, or ray
Two-variable diagram	Negative, positive, zero, and infinite slope	45° line
Horizontal and vertical axes	Tangent to a curve	Contour map
Origin (of a graph)	Y-intercept	Time series graph

Questions for Discussion

1. Look for a graph in your local newspaper, on the financial page or elsewhere. What does the graph try to show? Is someone trying to convince you of something with this graph? Check to see if the graph is distorted in any of the ways mentioned in this chapter.

2. Portray the following hypothetical data on a two-variable diagram:

ENROLLMENT DATA: UNIVERSITY OF NOWHERE

ACADEMIC YEAR	TOTAL ENROLLMENT	ENROLLMENT IN ECONOMICS COURSES
1984–1985	3000	300
1985–1986	3100	325
1986–1987	3200	350
1987–1988	3300	375
1988–1989	3400	400

Measure the slope of the resulting line, and explain what this number means.

3. From Figure 2–5, calculate the slope of the curve at point D.

4. Sam believes that the number of dates he gets per week depends on the number of dabs of aftershave lotion he uses. He concludes from experience that the following figures are typical:

Number of dabs	0	1	2	3	4
Number of dates	1	3	4	5	6

Put these numbers into a graph like Figure 2–1a. Measure and interpret the slopes between adjacent dots.

5. In Figure 2–6, determine the values of X and Y at point K and at point E. What do you conclude?

6. In Figure 2–8, interpret the economic meaning of points A and B. What do the two points have in common? What is the difference in their economic interpretation?

7. Suppose that between 1987 and 1988 expenditures on dog food rose from $35 million to $70 million and that the price of dog food doubled. What do these facts imply about the popularity of dog food?

8. Suppose that between 1980 and 1988 U.S. population went up 10 percent and that the number of people attending professional wrestling matches rose from 3,000,000 to 3,100,000. What do these facts imply about the growth in popularity of professional wrestling?

3

Our necessities are few but
our wants are endless.

INSCRIPTION FOUND IN A
FORTUNE COOKIE

Scarcity and Choice:
The Economic Problem

This chapter examines a subject that many economists consider to be *the* fundamental issue of economics: the fact that since no resource is available in unlimited supply, people must consequently make decisions consistent with their limited means. A wild-eyed materialist may dream of a world in which everyone owns a yacht and five automobiles, but the earth almost certainly lacks the resources needed to make that dream come true. The scarcity of resources, both natural and man-made, makes it vital that we stretch our limited resources as far as possible.

The chapter introduces a way to analyze the limited choices available to any decision maker. The same sort of analysis, based on the concept of *opportunity cost*, will be shown to apply to the decisions of business firms, of governments, and of society as a whole. Many of the most basic ideas of economics—such as *efficiency, division of labor, exchange*, and the *role of markets* —are introduced here for the first time. These concepts are useful in an analysis of the unpleasant choices forced upon us by the scarcity of resources that constrains all economic decisions. This chapter also introduces a broad question that constitutes the central theme of this text: **What does the market do well and what does it do poorly?**

Application: The "Indispensable Necessity" Syndrome

It is natural but not rational for people to try to avoid facing up to the hard choices which scarcity makes necessary. This happened, for example, when governments at all levels were forced to tighten their belts sharply in the early 1980s. A series of recessions cut into tax revenues. At the same time, the Reagan administration reduced federal grants to state and local governments and looked for ways to trim federal civilian spending. (Actually, government spending rose despite these efforts, but not as much as it would have increased otherwise.)

Budget cuts forced politicians and administrators to make some hard decisions over which services to cut. As they struggled with these decisions, they learned to their dismay that their constituents often were unwilling to accept *any* reductions. Mayors who proposed closing a firehouse or a hospital were confronted by demonstrators decrying the proposed cutback as a "false economy" and describing the firehouse or hospital as "indispensable." Groups marched on Washington to oppose President Reagan's budget cuts. College administrators found that suggestions to eliminate poorly attended courses, cut library hours, or restrict access to the photocopy machine all too frequently were met with the cry that each of these was *absolutely* essential.

Yet, regrettable as it is to have to give up any of these good things, reduced budgets mean that *something* must go. If everyone reacts by declaring *everything* to be indispensable, the decision maker is in the dark and is likely to end up making cuts that are bad for everyone. When the budget must be reduced, it is critical to determine which cuts are likely to prove *least damaging* to the people affected.

It is nonsense to assign top priority to everything. No one can afford everything. An optimal decision is one that chooses the most desirable alternative *among the possibilities permitted by the quantities of scarce resources available*.

Scarcity, Choice, and Opportunity Cost

One of the basic themes of economics is that the **resources** of decision makers, no matter how large they may be, are always limited, and that as a result everyone has some hard decisions to make. The U.S. government has been agonizing over difficult budget decisions for years, though it spends more than a trillion dollars annually! Even Philip II, of Spanish Armada fame, ruler of one of the greatest empires in history, frequently had to cope with rebellion on the part of his troops, whom he was often unable to pay or to supply with even the most basic provisions.

But far more fundamental than the scarcity of funds is the scarcity of physical resources. The supply of fuel, for example, has never been limitless, and a sudden scarcity of fuel would force us to make some hard choices. We might have to keep our homes cooler in winter and warmer in summer, live closer to our jobs, or give up such fuel-using conveniences as dishwashers. While energy is the most widely discussed scarcity these days, the general principle of scarcity applies to all the earth's resources — iron, copper, uranium, and so on.

Even goods that can be produced are in limited supply because their production requires fuel, labor, and other scarce resources. Wheat and rice can be grown. But nations have nonetheless suffered famines because the land, labor, fertilizer, and water needed to grow these crops were unavailable. We can increase our output of cars, but the increased use of labor, steel, and fuel in auto production will mean that something else, perhaps the production of refrigerators, will have to be cut back. This all adds up to the following fundamental principle of economics, one we will encounter again and again in this text.

> **Resources** are the instruments provided by nature or by people that are used to create the goods and services humans want. Natural resources include minerals, the soil (usable for agriculture, building land, and so on) water, and air. Labor is another resource which is scarce partly because of time limitations (the day has only 24 hours). Factories and machines are resources made by man (or by woman). These three types of resources are often referred to as "land," "labor," and "capital." They are also called the **inputs used in production processes**.

Virtually all resources are *scarce*, meaning that humanity has less of them than we would like. So choices must be made among a *limited* set of possibilities, in full recognition of the inescapable fact that a decision to have more of one thing means we will have less of something else.

In fact, one popular definition of economics is that it is the study of how best to use limited means in the pursuit of unlimited ends. While this definition, like any short statement, cannot possibly cover the sweep of the entire discipline, it does convey the flavor of the type of problem that is the economist's stock in trade.

The Principle of Opportunity Cost

Economics examines the options available to households, business firms, governments, and entire societies given the limited resources at their command, and it studies the logic of how **rational decisions** can be made from among the competing alternatives. One overriding principle governs this logic—a principle we have already introduced in Chapter 1 as one of the **12 Ideas for Beyond the Final Exam.** With limited resources, a decision to have more of something is simultaneously a decision to have less of something else. Hence, the relevant *cost* of any decision is its **opportunity cost**—the value of the next best alternative that is given up. Rational decision making, be it in industry, government, or households, must be based on opportunity-cost calculations.

A **rational decision** is one that best serves the objective of the decision maker, whatever that objective may be. Such objectives may include a firm's desire to maximize its profits, a government's desire to maximize the welfare of its citizens, or another government's desire to maximize its military might. The term "rational" connotes neither approval nor disapproval of the objective itself.

The **opportunity cost** of any decision is the forgone value of the next best alternative that is not chosen.

To illustrate opportunity cost, we continue the example in which production of additional cars requires the production of fewer refrigerators. While the production of a car may cost $6000 per vehicle, or some other money amount, its real cost to society is the refrigerators it must forgo to get an additional car. If the labor, steel, and fuel needed to make a car are sufficient to make eight refrigerators, we say that the opportunity cost of a car is eight refrigerators. The principle of opportunity cost is of such general applicability that we devote most of this chapter to elaborating it.

Opportunity Cost and Money Cost

Since we live in a market economy where (almost) everything "has its price," students often wonder about the connection between the opportunity cost of an item and its market price. What we just said seems to divorce the two concepts. We stressed that the true cost of a car is not its market price but the value of the other things (like refrigerators) that could have been made instead. This *opportunity cost* is the true sacrifice the economy must incur to get a car.

But isn't the opportunity cost of a car related to its money cost? The answer is that the two are often closely tied because of the way a market economy sets the prices of the steel and electricity that go into the production of cars. Steel is valuable because it can be used to make other goods. If the items that steel can make are themselves valuable, the price of steel will be high. But if the goods that steel can make have little value, the price of steel will be low. Thus, if a car has a high opportunity cost, then a well-functioning price system will assign high prices to the resources that are needed to produce cars, and therefore a car will also command a high price. In sum:

If the market is functioning well, goods that have high opportunity costs will tend to have high money costs, and goods whose opportunity costs are low will tend to have low money costs.

Yet it would be a mistake to treat opportunity costs and explicit monetary costs as identical. For one thing, there are times when the market does not function well and hence does not assign prices that accurately reflect opportunity costs. Many such examples will be encountered in this book, especially in *Microeconomics* Chapters 13 and 18.

Moreover, some valuable items may not bear explicit price tags at all. We have already encountered one such example in Chapter 1, where we contrasted the opportunity cost of going to college with the explicit money cost. We learned that one important item typically omitted from the money-cost calculation is the value of the student's time; that is, the wages he or she could have earned by working instead of attending college. These forgone wages, which are given up by students in order to acquire an education, are part of the opportunity cost of a college education just as surely as are tuition payments.

Other common examples are goods and services that are given away, "free." You incur no explicit monetary cost to acquire such an item. But you may have to pay implicitly by waiting in line. If so, you incur an opportunity cost equal to the value of the next best use of your time.

Production, Scarcity, and Resource Allocation

Consumers do not obtain all the goods and services they would want to acquire if those goods and services were provided free; that is what we mean when we say that outputs are scarce. Scarcity forces consumers to make choices. If Jones buys a motorboat, she may be unable to replace her old coat. The scarcity of goods and services, in turn, is attributed to the scarcity of the land, labor, and capital used to produce **outputs.**

These resources are, after all, the means (instruments) of production, the **inputs** whose services cooperate in the production process, in the farm, and in the factory, to yield both the commodities that people consume, as well as produced means of production (machines, locomotives, and so on).

Scarcity of such input resources, then, means that the economy cannot produce all the bread, hats, cars and computers that consumers would want if they could be made available in limitless amounts. Somehow it must be decided whether or not to assign more fuel to the production of refrigerators, which will mean there is less fuel to use in the production of airplanes or washing machines.

The decision on how to **allocate resources** among the production of different commodities is made in different ways in different types of economies. In a centrally planned economy such as the U.S.S.R., many such decisions are made by government bureaus. In a free market economy such as the United States, Canada, or Great Britain, no one group or individual makes such resource allocation decisions explicitly. Rather, they are made automatically, often unobserved, by what are called "the forces of supply and demand." For example, if consumers want more beef than farmers now supply, that will make it profitable for ranchers to hire more labor to increase their beef herds, thus reallocating labor and other inputs away from other production activities and into increased production of beef.

Outputs are the goods and services that consumers want to acquire. **Inputs** or **means of production** are the natural resources, labor, and produced plant and equipment used to make the outputs.

The **allocation of resources** refers to the decision on how to divide up the economy's scarce input resources among the different outputs produced in the economy and among the different firms or other organizations that produce those outputs.

Scarcity and Choice for a Single Firm

The nature of opportunity cost is perhaps clearest in the case of a single business firm that produces two outputs from a fixed supply of inputs. Given the existing technology and the limited resources at its disposal, the more of one good the firm produces, the less of the other it will be able to produce. And unless management carries out an explicit comparison of the available choices, weighing the desirability of each against the others, it is unlikely that it will make rational production decisions.

Consider the example of a farmer whose available supplies of land, machinery, labor, and fertilizer are capable of producing the various combinations of soybeans and wheat listed in Table 3–1 on page 38. Obviously, the more land and other resources he devotes to production of soybeans, the less wheat he will be able to produce. Table 3–1 indicates, for example, that if he produces only soybeans, he can harvest 40,000 bushels. But, if soybean production

Table 3–1
PRODUCTION POSSIBILITIES OPEN TO A FARMER

BUSHELS OF SOYBEANS	BUSHELS OF WHEAT	LABEL IN FIGURE 3–1
40,000	0	A
30,000	38,000	B
20,000	52,000	C
10,000	60,000	D
0	65,000	E

is reduced to only 30,000 bushels, the farmer can also grow 38,000 bushels of wheat. Thus the opportunity cost of obtaining 38,000 bushels of wheat is 10,000 fewer bushels of soybeans. Or, put the other way around, the opportunity cost of 10,000 more bushels of soybeans is 38,000 bushels of wheat. The other numbers in Table 3–1 have similar interpretations.

Note that Figure 3–1 is a graphical representation of this same information. Point A corresponds to the first line of Table 3–1, point B to the second line, and so on. Curves like AE appear frequently in this book; they are called **production possibilities frontiers.** Any point *on or below* the production possibilities frontier is attainable. Points above the frontier cannot be achieved with the available resources and technology.

The production possibilities frontier always slopes downward to the right. Why? Because resources are limited. The farmer can *increase* his wheat production (move to the right in Figure 3–1) only by devoting more of his land and labor to growing wheat, meaning that he must simultaneously *reduce* his soybean production (move downward) because less of his land and labor remain available for growing soybeans.

Notice that in addition to having a negative slope, our production possibilities frontier AE has another characteristic — it is "bowed outward." Let us consider a bit carefully what this curvature means.

Suppose our farmer is initially producing only soybeans, so that he uses for this purpose even land that is much more suitable for wheat cultivation (point A). Now suppose he decides to switch some of his land from soybean production to wheat production. Which part of his land will he switch? Obviously, if he is sensible, he will use the part best suited to wheat growing. If he shifts to point B, soybean production falls from 40,000 bushels to 30,000 bushels as

A **production possibilities frontier** shows the different combinations of various goods that a producer can turn out, given the available resources and existing technology.

Figure 3–1
PRODUCTION POSSIBILITIES FRONTIER FOR PRODUCTION BY A SINGLE FIRM

With a given set of inputs, the firm can produce only those output combinations given by points in the shaded area. The production possibilities frontier, *AE*, is not a straight line but one that curves more and more as it nears the axes. That is, when the firm specializes in only one product, those inputs that are especially adapted to the production of the other good lose at least part of their productivity.

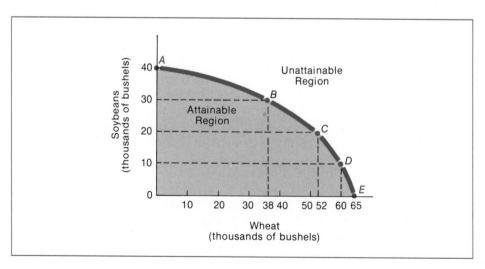

wheat production rises from zero to 38,000 bushels. A sacrifice of only 10,000 bushels of soybeans "buys" 38,000 bushels of wheat.

Imagine now that the farmer wants to produce still more wheat. Figure 3–1 tell us that the sacrifice of an additional 10,000 bushels of soybeans (from 30,000 down to 20,000) will yield only 14,000 more bushels of wheat (see point C). Why? The main reason is that inputs tend to be specialized. As we noted, at point A the farmer was using resources for soybean production that were much more suitable for growing wheat. Consequently, their productivity in soybeans was relatively low, and when they were switched to wheat production, the yield was very high. But this cannot continue forever. As more wheat is produced, the farmer must utilize land and machinery that are better suited to producing soybeans and less well-suited to producing wheat. This is why the first 10,000 bushels of soybeans forgone "buys" the farmer 38,000 bushels of wheat while the second 10,000 bushels of soybeans "buys" him only 14,000 bushels of wheat. Figure 3–1 and Table 3–1 show that these returns continue to decline as wheat production expands: the next 10,000-bushel reduction in soybean production yields only 8000 bushels of additional wheat, and so on.

We can now see that the *slope* of the production possibilities frontier represents graphically the concept of *opportunity cost*. Between points C and B, for example, the opportunity cost of acquiring 10,000 additional bushels of soybeans is 14,000 bushels of forgone wheat; and between points B and A, the opportunity cost of 10,000 bushels of soybeans is 38,000 bushels of forgone wheat. In general, as we move upward to the left along the production possibilities frontier (toward more soybeans and less wheat), the opportunity cost of soybeans in terms of wheat increases. Or, putting the same thing differently, as we move downward to the right, the opportunity cost of acquiring wheat by giving up soybeans increases.

The Principle of Increasing Costs

We have just described a very general phenomenon, which is applicable well beyond farming. The **principle of increasing costs** states that as the production of one good expands, the opportunity cost of producing another unit of this good generally increases.

This principle is not a universal fact; there can be exceptions to it. But it does seem to be a technological regularity that applies to a wide range of economic activities. As our example of the farmer suggests, the principle of increasing costs is based on the fact that resources tend to be specialized, at least in part, so that some of their productivity is lost when they are transferred from doing what they are relatively good at to what they are relatively bad at. In terms of diagrams like Figure 3–1, the principle simply asserts that the production possibilities frontier is bowed outward.

Perhaps the best way to understand this idea is to contrast it with a case in which there are no specialized resources. Figure 3–2 depicts a production possibilities frontier for producing black shoes and brown shoes. Because the labor and capital used to produce black shoes are just as good at producing brown shoes, the frontier is a straight line. If the firm cuts back its production of black shoes by 10,000 pairs, it always gets 10,000 additional pairs of brown shoes. No productivity is lost in the switch because resources are not specialized.

The **principle of increasing costs** states that as the production of a good expands, the opportunity cost of producing another unit generally increases.

Scarcity and Choice for the Entire Society

Like an individual firm, the entire economy is also constrained by its limited resources and technology. If society wants more aircraft and tanks, it will have to

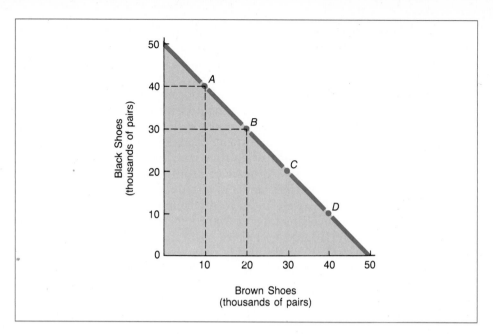

Figure 3–2

PRODUCTION POSSIBILITIES FRONTIER WITH NO SPECIALIZED RESOURCES

Resources that produce black shoes are just as good at producing brown shoes. So there is no loss of productivity when black shoe production is decreased in order to increase brown shoe production. For example, if the firm moves from point A to point B, black shoe output falls by 10,000 pairs and brown shoe output rises by 10,000 pairs. The same would be true if it moved from point B to point C, or from point C to point D. The production possibilities frontier is therefore a straight line.

give up some boats and automobiles. If it wants to build more factories and stores, it will have to build fewer homes and sports arenas. In general:

The position and shape of the production possibilities frontier that constrains the choices of the economy are determined by the economy's physical resources, its skills and technology, its willingness to work, and how much it has devoted in the past to the construction of factories, research, and innovation.

Since the debate over increasing our nation's military strength has been so much on the national agenda in recent years, let us illustrate the nature of society's choices by the example of choosing between military might (represented by missiles) and civilian consumption (represented by milk). Just like a single firm, the economy as a whole has a production possibilities frontier for missiles and milk determined by its technology and the available resources of land, labor, capital, and raw materials. This production possibilities frontier may look like curve BC in Figure 3–3.

If most workers are employed at dairy farms and supermarkets, the production of milk will be large but the output of missiles will be small. If resources are transferred from farms to factories, the mix of output can be shifted toward increased production of missiles at some sacrifice of milk (the move from D to E). However, something is likely to be lost in the transfer process—the hay that helped produce the dairy output will not help in missile production. As summarized in the principle of increasing costs, physical resources tend to be specialized, so the production possibilities frontier probably curves downward toward the axes.

We may even reach a point where the only resources left are items that are not very useful outside dairy farms and supermarkets. In that case, even a very large additional sacrifice of milk will enable the economy to produce very few more missiles. That is the meaning of the steep segment, FC, on the frontier. At point C there is very little more output of missiles than at F, even though at C milk production has been given up entirely.

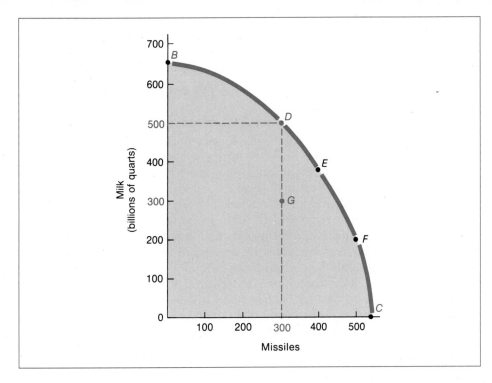

Figure 3–3
THE PRODUCTION POSSIBILITIES FRONTIER FOR THE ENTIRE ECONOMY
This production possibilities frontier is curved because resources are not perfectly transferable from milk production to missile production. The limits on available rescources place a ceiling, C, on the output of one product and a different ceiling, B, on the output of the other product.

The downward slope of society's production possibilities frontier implies that hard choices must be made. Our nation's military strength can be increased only by decreasing civilian consumption ("milk"), not by rhetoric nor by wishing it so. The curvature of the production possibilities frontier implies that, as defense spending increases, it becomes progressively more expensive to "buy" additional military strength ("missiles") by sacrificing civilian consumption.

Scarcity and Choice Elsewhere in the Economy

We have stressed that limited resources force hard choices upon business managers and society as a whole. But the same type of choices arise elsewhere—in households, in universities and other nonprofit organizations, and in the government.

The nature of opportunity cost is perhaps most obvious for a household that must decide how to divide its income among the goods and services that compete for the family's trade. If the Higgins family buys an expensive new car, it may be forced to cut back sharply on its other purchases. This does not make it unwise to buy the car. But it does make it unwise to buy the car until the full implications of the purchase for the family's overall budget are considered. If the Higgins family is to use its limited resources most effectively, it must explicitly acknowledge that the opportunity costs of the car are, say, a shorter vacation and making do with the old TV set.

Even a rich and powerful nation like the United States or Japan must cope with the limitations implied by scarce resources. The necessity for choice imposed on the governments of these nations by their limited budgets is similar in character to the problems faced by business firms and households. For the goods and services it buys from others, a government has to prepare a budget similar to that of a very large household. For the items it produces itself—education, police protection, libraries, and so on — it faces a production possibilities frontier much like that of a business firm. Even though the U.S. government will spend over $1100 billion in 1988, some of the most acrimonious debates between the Reagan administration and its critics have been over how to allocate the government's limited resources among competing programs.

Application: Economic Growth in the United States and Japan

Among the economic choices that any society must make, there is one extremely important choice that illustrates well the concept of opportunity cost. This choice is embodied in the question "How fast should the economy grow?"[1] At first, the question may seem ridiculous. Since **economic growth** means, roughly, that the average citizen has more and more goods and services, is it not self-evident that faster growth is always better?

Again, the fundamental problem of scarcity intervenes. Economies do not grow by magic. Scarce resources must be devoted to the process of growth. Cement and steel that could be used to make swimming pools and stadiums must be diverted to build more machinery and factories. Wood that could make furniture and skis must be used for hammers and ladders instead. Grain that could be eaten must be used as seed to plant additional acres. By deciding how large a quantity of resources to devote to future needs rather than to current consumption, society in effect *chooses* (within limits) how fast it will grow.

In diagrammatic terms, economic growth means that the economy's production possibilities frontier shifts outward over time — like the move from FF to GG in Figure 3–4(a). Why? Because such a shift means that the economy can produce more of both of the outputs shown in the graph. Thus, in the figure, after growth has occurred it is possible to produce the combination of products represented by points like N. Before growth had occurred point N was beyond the economy's means because it was outside the production possibilities frontier.

How does growth occur? That is, what shifts an economy's production frontier outward? There are many ways. For example, workers may acquire greater skill and learn to produce more output in an hour. Such increases in labor's productivity are discussed in Chapter 7. Perhaps even more important, the economy may construct more capital goods, temporarily giving up some consumption goods to provide the resources to build the factories and machines. Finally, inventions like the steam engine, AC electricity, and industrial robots can and do increase the economy's productive capacity, thereby shifting its production frontier outward.

Figure 3–4 illustrates the nature of the choice by depicting production possibilities frontiers for **consumption goods**, that are consumed today (like food and electricity) versus **capital goods** that provide for future consumption (like grocery stores and generating plants) for two different societies. Figure 3–4(a) depicts a society like the United States that devotes a relatively small quantity of resources to growth, preferring current consumption instead. It chooses a point like A on this year's production possibilities frontier, FF. At A, consumption is relatively high and production of capital is relatively low, so the production possibilities frontier shifts only to GG next year. Figure 3–4(b) depicts a society much more enamored of growth, like Japan. It selects a point like B on its production possibilities frontier, ff. At B, consumption is much lower and production of capital goods is much higher, so its production possibilities frontier moves all the way to gg by next year. Japan grows faster than the

Economic growth occurs when an economy is able to produce more goods and services for each consumer.

A consumption good is an item which is available for immediate use by households, and which satisfies wants of members of households without contributing directly to future production by the economy.

A capital good is an item that is used to produce other goods and services in the future, rather than being consumed today. Factories and machines are examples.

[1] Economic growth will be studied in detail in Chapter 21.

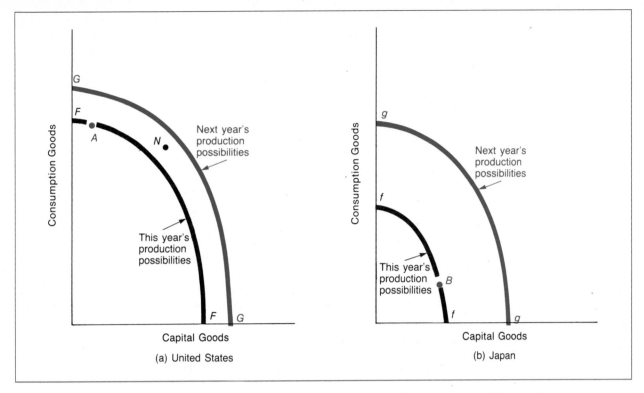

Figure 3–4
GROWTH IN TWO
ECONOMIES
Growth shifts the production
possibilities frontiers *FF* and
ff (black) outward to the
frontiers *GG* and *gg* (blue),
meaning that each economy
can produce more of both
goods than it could before. If
the shift in both economies
occurs in the same period of
time, then the Japanese
economy [part(b)] is growing
faster than the U.S. economy
[part (a)] because the
outward shift in (b) is much
greater than the one in (a).

U.S. But the more rapid growth has a price — an *opportunity cost*: The Japanese must give up some of the current consumption that Americans enjoy.

An economy grows by giving up some current consumption and producing capital goods for the future instead. The more capital it produces, the faster will its production possibilities frontier shift outward over time.

The Concept of Efficiency

So far in our discussion of scarcity and choice, we have assumed that either the single firm or the whole economy always operates on its production possibilities frontier rather than *below* it. In other words, we have tacitly assumed that, whatever it decides to do, the firm or economy does so *efficiently*. Economists define *efficiency* as the absence of waste. An efficient economy utilizes all of its available resources and produces the maximum amount of output that its technology permits.[2]

To see why any point on the economy's production possibilities frontier in Figure 3–3 represents an efficient decision, suppose for a moment that society has decided to produce 300 missiles. According to the production possibilities frontier, if 300 missiles are to be produced, then the maximum amount of milk that can be made is 500 billion quarts (point *D* in Figure 3–3). The economy is therefore operating efficiently if it actually produces 500 billion quarts rather than some smaller amount such as 300 billion quarts (as at point *G*). While point *D* is efficient, point *G* is not. This is so because the economy is capable of moving from *G* to *D*, thereby producing 200 billion more quarts of milk without giving up any missiles (or anything else). Clearly, failure to take advantage of the option of choosing point *D* rather than point *G* constitutes a wasted opportunity.

[2]A more formal definition of *efficiency* is offered in *Microeconomics* Chapter 10.

Note that the concept of efficiency does not tell us which point on the production possibilities frontier is *best*; it only tells us that no point that is *not* on the frontier can be best, because any such point represents wasted resources. For example, should society ever find itself at point G, the necessity of making hard choices would (temporarily) disappear. It would be possible to increase production of *both* missiles *and* milk by moving to a point such as E.

Why, then, would an economy ever find itself at a point below its production possibilities frontier? There are a number of ways in which resources are wasted in real life. The most important of them, unemployment, is an issue that will take up a substantial part of this book (especially in Parts 2 and 3). When many workers are unemployed, the economy finds itself at a point like G, below the frontier, because by putting the unemployed to work in both industries, the economy could produce more missiles *and* more milk. The economy would then move from point G to the right (more missiles) and upward (more milk) toward a point like E on the production possibilities frontier. Only when no resources are wasted by unemployment or misuse is the economy on the frontier.

Analogous problems occur on the farm. For example, if a farmer lets fertilizer fall off the rear end of his truck through sheer carelessness, he will end up at a point *inside* the production possibilities frontier. The farm will not be operating efficiently.

The Three Coordination Tasks of Any Economy

In deciding how to use its scarce resources, society must somehow make three sorts of decisions. First, as we have emphasized, it must figure out **how to utilize its resources efficiently;** that is, it must find a way to get *on* its production possibilities frontier. Second, it must decide **what combination of goods to produce** — how many missiles, how much milk, and so on; that is, it must select one specific point on the production possibilities frontier. Finally, it must decide **how much of each good to distribute to each person,** doing so in a sensible way that does not assign meat to vegetarians and wine to teetotalers.

Certainly, each of these decisions could be made in many ways. For example, a central planner could tell people how to produce, what to produce, and what to consume.[3] But they can also be made without central direction, through a system of prices and markets. Let us consider each task in turn.

Specialization, Division of Labor, and Exchange

Efficiency in production is one of the three basic tasks. Many features of society contribute to efficiency; others interfere with it. While different societies pursue the goal of economic efficiency in different ways, one source of efficiency is so fundamental that we must single it out for special attention: the tremendous gains in productivity that stem from **specialization** and the consequent **division of labor.**

Division of labor means breaking up a task into a number of smaller, more **specialized** tasks so that each worker can become more adept at his or her particular job.

Adam Smith, the founder of modern economics, first marveled at this mainspring of efficiency and productivity on a visit to a pin factory. In a famous passage near the beginning of his monumental book, *The Wealth of Nations* (1776), he described what he saw:

One man draws out the wire, another straightens it, a third cuts it, a fourth points it, a fifth grinds it at the top for receiving the head; to make the head requires two or three

[3]Central planning will be considered in some detail in *Microeconomics* Chapter 23.

distinct operations; to put it on is a peculiar business, to whiten the pins is another; it is even a trade by itself to put them into the paper. . . .[4]

Smith observed that by dividing the work to be done in this way, each worker became quite skilled in his particular specialty, and the productivity of the group of workers as a whole was enhanced enormously. As Smith related it:

I have seen a small manufactory of this kind where ten men only were employed. . . . Those ten persons . . . could make among them upwards of forty-eight thousand pins in a day. . . . But if they had all wrought separately and independently . . . they certainly could not each of them have made twenty, perhaps not one pin in a day. . . .[5]

In other words, through the miracle of division of labor and specialization, ten workers accomplished what would otherwise have required thousands. This was one of the secrets of the Industrial Revolution, which helped lift humanity out of the abject poverty that had for so long been its lot.

But specialization created a problem. With division of labor, people no longer produced only what they wanted to consume themselves. The workers in the pin factory had no use for the thousands of pins they produced each day; they wanted to trade them for things like food, clothing, and shelter. Specialization thus made it necessary to have some mechanism by which workers producing pins could **exchange** their wares with workers producing such things as cloth and potatoes.

Without a system of exchange, the productivity miracle achieved by the division of labor would have done society little good. With it, standards of living rose enormously. As we observed in Chapter 1:

Mutual Gains from Voluntary Exchange
Unless there is deception or misunderstanding of the facts, a *voluntary* exchange between two parties must make both parties better off. Even though no additional goods are produced by the act of trading, the welfare of society is increased because each individual acquires goods that are more suited to his needs and tastes. This simple but fundamental precept of economics is one of our **12 Ideas for Beyond the Final Exam.**

While goods can be traded for other goods, a system of exchange works better when everyone agrees to use some common item (such as pieces of paper) for buying and selling goods and services. Enter *money*. Then workers in pin factories, for example, can be paid in money rather than in pins, and they can use this money to purchase cloth and potatoes. Textile workers and farmers can do the same.

These two phenomena—specialization and exchange (assisted by money)—working in tandem led to a vast improvement in the well-being of mankind. But what forces induce workers to join together so that the fruits of the division of labor can be enjoyed? And what forces establish a smoothly functioning system of exchange so that each person can acquire what he or she wants to consume? One alternative is to have a central authority telling people what to do. But Adam Smith explained and extolled another way of organizing and coordinating economic activity—the use of markets and prices.

[4]Adam Smith, *The Wealth of Nations* (New York: Random House, Modern Library Edition, 1937), page 4.
[5]*Ibid.*, page 5.

Markets, Prices, and the Three Coordination Tasks

A **market system** is a form of organization of the economy in which decisions on resource allocation are left to the independent decisions of individual producers and consumers acting in their own best interests without central direction.

Smith noted that people are adept at pursuing their own self-interest, and that a **market system** is a fine way to harness this self-interest. As he put it, with pretty clear religious overtones, in doing what is best for themselves, people are "led by an invisible hand" to promote the economic well-being of society as a whole.

Since we live in a market economy, the outlines of the process by which the invisible hand works are familiar to all of us.[6] Firms are encouraged by the profit motive to use inputs efficiently. Valuable resources (like energy) command high prices, and so producers economize on their use. The price (market) system also guides firms' output decisions, and hence those of society. A rise in the price of wheat, for example, will persuade farmers to produce more wheat and fewer soybeans. Finally, a price system determines who gets what goods through a series of voluntary exchanges. Workers with valuable skills and owners of scarce resources will be able to sell what they have at attractive prices. With the incomes they earn, they can then purchase the goods and services they want most, within the limits of their budgets. Those with less to sell will have to live more frugally.

This, in broad terms, is how a market economy solves the three basic problems facing any society: how to produce any given combination of goods efficiently, how to select an appropriate combination of goods, and how to distribute these goods sensibly among the people. As we proceed through the following chapters, you will learn much more about these issues. You will see that they constitute the central theme that permeates not only this text, but the work of economists in general. As you progress through the book, keep in mind the following two questions: **What does the market do well, and what does it do poorly?** There are plenty of answers to both questions. As you will learn in coming chapters:

1. Society has many important goals. Some of them, such as producing goods and services with maximum efficiency (minimum waste), can in certain circumstances be achieved extraordinarily well by letting markets operate more or less freely.

2. Free markets will not, however, achieve all of society's goals. For example, as we will see in Part 3, they often have trouble keeping unemployment and inflation low. And there are even some goals—such as protection of the environment—for which the unfettered operation of markets may be positively harmful. Many observers also believe that markets do not necessarily lead to an equitable distribution of income.

3. But even in cases where the market does not perform at all well, there may be ways of harnessing the power of the market mechanism to remedy its own deficiencies, as you will learn particularly in Part 2 and *Microeconomics* Part 3.

Radicalism, Conservatism, and the Market Mechanism

Since economic debates often have political and ideological overtones, we think it important to close the chapter by stressing that the central theme that we have just outlined is neither a defense of nor an attack upon the capitalist

---

[6]This topic is studied in detail in *Microeconomics* Chapter 10.

Biographical Note: Adam Smith (1723–1790)

Adam Smith, who was to become the leading advocate of freedom of international trade, was born the son of a customs official in 1723 and ended his career in the well-paid post of collector of customs for Scotland. He received an excellent education at Glasgow College, where, for the first time, some lectures were being given in English rather than Latin. A fellowship to Oxford University followed, and for six years he studied there mostly by himself, since, at that time, teaching at Oxford was virtually nonexistent.

After completing his studies, Smith was appointed professor of logic at Glasgow College and, later, professor of moral philosophy, a field which then included economics as one of its branches. Fortunately, he was a popular lecturer because, in those days, a professor's pay in Glasgow depended on the number of students who chose to attend his lectures. At Glasgow, Smith was responsible for helping young James Watt find a job as an instrument maker. Watt later invented the steam engine, so in this and many other respects, Smith was present virtually at the birth of the Industrial Revolution, whose prophet he was destined to become.

After 13 years at Glasgow, Smith accepted a highly paid post as a tutor to a young Scottish nobleman with whom he spent several years in France, a customary way of educating nobles in the eighteenth century. Primarily because he was bored during these years in France, Smith began working on *The Wealth of Nations*. Several years after his return to England, in 1776, the book was published and rapidly achieved popularity.

The Wealth of Nations contains many brilliantly written passages. It was one of the first systematic treatises in economics, contributing to both theoretical and factual knowledge about the subject. Among the main points made in the book are the importance for a nation's prosperity of freedom of trade and the division of labor permitted by more widespread markets; the dangers of governmental protection of monopolies and imposition of tariffs; and the superiority of self-interest — the instrument of the "invisible hand" — over altruism as a means of improving the economy's service to the general public.

The British government was grateful for the ideas for new tax legislation Smith proposed, and to show its appreciation appointed him to the lucrative sinecure of collector of customs, which, together with the lifetime pension awarded him by his former pupil, left him very well-off financially, although he eventually gave away most of his money to charitable causes.

The intellectual world was small in the eighteenth century, and among the many people with whom Smith was acquainted were David Hume, Samuel Johnson, James Boswell, Benjamin Franklin, and Jean Jacques Rousseau. Smith got along well with everyone except Samuel Johnson, who was noted for his dislike of Scots. Smith was absent-minded and apparently timid with women, being visibly embarrassed by the public attention of the eminent ladies of Paris during his visits there. He never married, and he lived with his mother most of his life. When he died, the Edinburgh newspapers recalled only that when Smith was four years old he was kidnapped by gypsies. But thanks to his writings, he is remembered for a good deal more than that.

---

system. Nor is it a "conservative" position. One does not have to be a conservative to recognize that the market mechanism can be a helpful instrument for the pursuit of economic goals. A number of socialist countries, including Yugoslavia and Hungary, have openly and deliberately organized large parts of their economies along market lines, and the People's Republic of China is now rushing in that direction.

The point is not to confuse means and ends in deciding on how much to rely on market forces. Radicals and conservatives surely have different goals, and they may also differ in the means they advocate to pursue these goals. But means should be chosen on the basis of how effective they are in achieving the adopted goals, not on some ideological prejudgments.

For example, radicals may assign a much higher priority to pollution control than conservatives do. Consequently, radicals may favor strict controls even if such controls cut into business profits. Conservatives may prefer things the other way around. Nevertheless, each side may want to use the market mechanism to achieve its goals. Indeed, each side may conclude that, should it lose the political struggle and the other side's position be adopted, less damage will be done to its own goals if market methods are used.

Certainly, there are economic problems with which the market cannot deal. Indeed, we have just noted that the market is the *source* of a number of significant problems. But the evidence leads economists to believe that many economic problems are best handled by market techniques. The analysis in this book is intended to help you identify the strengths and weaknesses of the market mechanism. Forget the slogans you have heard—whether from the left or from the right—and make up your own mind after you have read this book.

Summary

1. Supplies of all resources are limited. Because resources are scarce, a rational decision is one that chooses the best alternative among the options that are possible with the available resources.

2. It is irrational to assign highest priority to everything. No one can afford everything, and so hard choices must be made.

3. With limited resources, if we decide to obtain more of one item, we must give up some of another item. What we give up is called the *opportunity cost* of what we get; this is the true cost of any decision. The concept of opportunity cost is one of the 12 Ideas for Beyond the Final Exam.

4. The allocation of resources refers to division of the economy's scarce inputs (fuel, minerals, machines, labor, and so on) among the economy's different outputs and the enterprises that produce them.

5. When the market is functioning effectively, firms are led to use resources efficiently and to produce the things that consumers want most. In such cases, opportunity costs and money costs (prices) correspond closely. When the market performs poorly, or when important items of cost do not get price tags, opportunity costs and money costs can be quite different.

6. A firm's production possibilities frontier shows the combinations of goods the firm can produce with a given quantity of resources, given the state of technology. The frontier usually is not a straight line, but is bowed outward because resources tend to be specialized.

7. The principle of increasing costs states that as the production of one good expands, the opportunity cost of producing another unit of this good generally increases.

8. The economy as a whole has a production possibilities frontier whose position is determined by its technology and by the available resources of land, labor, capital, and raw materials.

9. If a firm or an economy ends up at a point below its production possibilities frontier, it is using its resources inefficiently or wastefully. This is what happens, for example, when there is unemployment.

10. Economic growth means there is an outward shift in the economy's production possibilities frontier. The faster the growth, the faster this shift will occur. But growth requires a sacrifice of current consumption, and this is its opportunity cost.

11. Efficiency is defined by economists as the absence of waste. It is achieved primarily by gains in productivity brought about through specialization, division of labor, and a system of exchange.

12. If an exchange is voluntary, both parties must benefit even though no new goods are produced. This is another of the 12 Ideas for Beyond the Final Exam.

13. Every economic system must find a way to answer three basic questions: How can goods be produced most efficiently? How much of each good should be produced? How should goods be distributed?

14. The market system works very well in solving some of society's basic problems, but it fails to remedy others and may, indeed, create some of its own. Where and how it succeeds and fails constitute the theme of this book and characterize the work of economists in general.

Concepts for Review

Resources
Scarcity
Choice
Rational decision
Opportunity cost
Outputs
Inputs (means of production)

Production possibilities frontier
Allocation of resources
Principle of increasing costs
Consumption goods
Capital goods
Economic growth

Efficiency
Specialization
Division of labor
Exchange
Market system
Three coordination tasks

Questions for Discussion

1. Discuss the resource limitations that affect:
   a. the poorest person on earth.
   b. the richest person on earth.
   c. a firm in Switzerland.
   d. a government agency in China.
   e. the population of the world.
2. If you were president of your college, what would you change if your budget were cut by 5 percent? By 20 percent? By 50 percent?
3. If you were to drop out of college, what things would change in your life? What, then, is the opportunity cost of your education?
4. A person rents a house for which he pays the landlord $6000 a year and keeps money in a bank account that pays 7 percent interest a year. The house is offered for sale at $80,000. Is this a good deal for the potential buyer? Where does opportunity cost enter the picture?
5. Construct graphically the production possibilities frontier for Lower Slobovia given in the table. Does the principle of increasing cost hold in Lower Slobovia?
6. Consider two alternatives for Lower Slobovia in the year 1988. In case (a) its inhabitants eat 60 million

loaves of bread and build only 12,000 ovens. In case (b) the population eats only 15 million loaves but builds 36,000 ovens. Which case will lead to a more generous production possibilities frontier for Slobovia in 1989?

PRODUCTION POSSIBILITIES FOR LOWER SLOBOVIA, 1988

BREAD LOAVES (millions)	OVENS (thousands)
75	0
60	12
45	22
30	30
15	36
0	40

7. Mel's Sports Shop sells two brands of tennis balls. Brand X costs Mel $1.50 per can, and Brand Y costs Mel $2 per can. Draw Mel's production possibilities frontier if he has $60 to spend on tennis balls. Why is it not "bowed out"?

4

Supply and Demand: An Initial Look

If the issues of scarcity, choice, and coordination constitute the basic *problem* of economics, then the mechanism of supply and demand is its basic investigative tool. Whether your course concentrates on macroeconomics or microeconomics, you will find that the so-called law of supply and demand is the fundamental tool of economic analysis. Supply and demand analysis is used in this book to study issues seemingly as diverse as inflation and unemployment, the international value of the dollar, government regulation of business, and protection of the environment. So careful study of this chapter will pay rich dividends.

The chapter describes the rudiments of supply and demand analysis in steps. We begin with demand, then add supply, and finally put the two sides together. *Supply and demand curves* — graphs that relate price to quantity supplied and quantity demanded, respectively — are explained and used to show how prices and quantities are determined in a free market. Influences that shift either the demand curve or the supply curve are catalogued briefly. And the analysis is used to explain why airlines often run "sales," and why the home computer industry grew so fast.

One major theme of the chapter is that governments around the globe and throughout recorded history have attempted to tamper with the price mechanism. We will see that these bouts with Adam Smith's invisible hand often have produced undesired side effects that surprised and dismayed the authorities. And we will show that many of these unfortunate effects were no accidents, but were inherent consequences of interfering with the operation of free markets. The invisible hand fights back!

Finally, a word of caution. This chapter makes heavy use of graphs such as those described in Chapter 2. If you encounter difficulties with these graphs, we suggest you review pages 18–24 before proceeding.

Fighting the Invisible Hand

Adam Smith was a great admirer of the price system. He marveled at its intricacies and extolled its accomplishments — both as a producer of goods and a guarantor of individual freedom. Many people since Smith's time have shared his enthusiasm, but many others have not. His contemporaries in the American colonies, for example, were often unhappy with the prices produced by free markets and thought they could do better by legislative decree. (They could not, as the boxed insert on this page shows.) And there have been countless other instances in which the public's sense of justice was outraged by the prices charged on the open market, particularly when the sellers of the expensive items did not enjoy great popularity—landlords, moneylenders, and oil companies are good examples.

Attempts to control interest rates (which may be thought of as the price of borrowing money) go back hundreds of years before the birth of Christ, at least to the code of laws compiled under Hammurabi in Babylonia about 1800 B.C. Our historical legacy also includes a rather long list of price ceilings on foods and other products imposed in the reign of Diocletian, emperor of the declining Roman Empire. More recently, Americans have been offered the "protection" of a variety of price controls. Ceilings have been placed on some prices (such as

Price Controls at Valley Forge

George Washington, the history books tell us, was beset by many enemies during the winter of 1777–1778—including the British, their Hessian mercenaries, and the merciless winter weather. But he had another enemy that the history books ignore, an enemy who meant well but almost destroyed his army at Valley Forge. That enemy was the legislature of the Commonwealth of Pennsylvania, as the following excerpt explains.

In Pennsylvania, where the main force of Washington's army was quartered in 1777, . . . the legislature . . . decided to try a period of price control limited to those commodities needed for use by the army. The theory was that this policy would reduce the expense of supplying the army. . . . The result might have been anticipated by those with some knowledge of the trials and tribulations of other states. The prices of uncontrolled goods, mostly imported, rose to record heights. Most farmers kept back their produce, refusing to sell at what they regarded as an unfair price. Some who had large families to take care of even secretly sold their food to the British who paid in gold.

After the disastrous winter at Valley Forge when Washington's army nearly starved to death (thanks largely to these well-intentioned but misdirected laws), the ill-fated experiment in price controls was finally ended. The Continental Congress on June 4, 1778, adopted the following resolution:

"Whereas . . . it hath been found by experience that limitations upon the prices of commodities are not only ineffectual for the purposes proposed, but likewise productive of very evil consequences to the great detriment of the public service . . . resolved, that it be recommended to the several states to repeal or suspend all laws or resolutions within the said states respectively limiting, regulating or restraining the Price of any Article, Manufacture or Commodity."

SOURCE: Robert L. Schuettinger and Eamonn F. Butler, *Forty Centuries of Wage and Price Controls* (Washington, D.C.: Heritage Foundation, 1979), page 41. Reprinted by permission.

energy) to protect buyers, while floors have been placed under other prices (such as farm products) to protect sellers. Many if not most of these measures were adopted in response to popular opinion, and there is a great outcry whenever it is proposed that any one of them be weakened or eliminated.

Yet, somehow, everything such regulation touches seems to end up in even greater disarray than it was before. Despite rent controls, rents in New York City have considerably more than doubled in the last ten years. Despite laws against ticket "scalping," tickets for popular shows and sports events sell at tremendous premiums—$75 tickets to the 1987 Super Bowl, for example, reportedly were sold for prices as high as $1000. Taxis cost much more in New York City (where they are tightly regulated) than in Washington, D.C. (where they are not). And the list could go on.

Still, legislators continue to turn to controls whenever the economy does not work to their satisfaction, just as they did in 1777. The 1970s and 1980s have seen a return to rent controls in many American cities, a brief experiment with overall price controls by a Republican administration that had vowed never to turn to them, a web of controls over energy prices, and a revival of agricultural price supports.

Interferences with the "Law" of Supply and Demand
Public opinion frequently encourages legislative attempts to "repeal the law of supply and demand" by controlling prices. The consequences usually are quite unfortunate, exacting heavy costs from the general public and often aggravating the problem the legislation was intended to cure. This is another of the **12 Ideas for Beyond the Final Exam,** and it will occupy our attention throughout this chapter.

To understand what goes wrong when markets are tampered with, we must first learn how they operate when they are unfettered. This chapter takes a first step in that direction by studying the machinery of supply and demand. Then, at the end of the chapter, we return to the issue of price controls, illustrating the problems that can arise by case studies of rent controls in New York City and price supports for milk.

Every market has both buyers and sellers. We begin our analysis on the consumers' side of the market.

Demand and Quantity Demanded

Noneconomists are apt to think of consumer demands as fixed amounts. For example, when the production of a new type of machine tool is proposed, management asks "What is its market potential? How many will we be able to sell?" Similarly, government bureaus conduct studies to determine how many engineers will be "required" in succeeding years.

Economists respond that such questions are not well posed—that there is no *single* answer to such a question. Rather, they say, the "market potential" for machine tools or the number of engineers that will be "required" depends on a great number of things, *including the price that will be charged for each*.

The **quantity demanded** is the number of units consumers want to buy.

The **quantity demanded** of any product normally depends on its price. Quantity demanded also has a number of other determinants, including population size, consumer incomes, tastes, and the prices of other products.

Because of the central role of prices in a market economy, we begin our study of demand by focusing on the relationship between quantity demanded and price. Shortly, we will bring the other determinants of quantity demanded back into the picture.

Consider, as an example, the quantity of milk demanded. Almost everyone purchases at least some milk. However, if the price of milk is very high, its "market potential" may be very small. People will find ways to get along with less milk, perhaps by switching to tea or coffee. If the price declines, people will be encouraged to drink more milk. They may give their children larger portions or switch away from juices and sodas. Thus:

There is no *one* demand figure for milk, for machine tools, or for engineers. Rather, there is a different quantity demanded for each possible price.

The Demand Schedule

Table 4–1 displays this information for milk in what we call a **demand schedule**, which indicates how much consumers are willing and able to buy at different possible prices during a specified period of time. The table shows the quantity of milk that will be demanded in a year at each possible price ranging from $1 to 40¢ per quart. We see, for example, that at a relatively low price, like 50¢ per quart, customers wish to purchase 70 billion quarts per year. But if the price were to rise to, say, 90¢ per quart, quantity demanded would fall to 50 billion quarts.

Common sense tells us why this should be so.[1] First, as prices rise, some customers will reduce their consumption of milk. Second, higher prices will induce some customers to drop out of the market entirely—for example, by switching to soda or juice. On both counts, quantity demanded will decline as the price rises.

As the price of an item rises, the quantity demanded normally falls. As the price falls, the quantity demanded normally rises.

The Demand Curve

The information contained in Table 4–1 can be summarized in a graph, which we call a **demand curve**, displayed in Figure 4–1. Each point in the graph corresponds to a line in the table. For example, point B corresponds to the second line in the table, indicating that at a price of 90¢ per quart, 50 billion quarts

A **demand schedule** is a table showing how the quantity demanded of some product during a specified period of time changes as the price of that product changes, holding all other determinants of quantity demanded constant.

A **demand curve** is a graphical depiction of a demand schedule. It shows how the quantity demanded of some product during a specified period of time will change as the price of that product changes, holding all other determinants of quantity demanded constant.

[1]This common-sense answer is examined more fully in Chapter 21.

Table 4–1
DEMAND SCHEDULE FOR MILK

PRICE (dollars per quart)	QUANTITY DEMANDED (billions of quarts per year)	LABEL IN FIGURE 4–1
1.00	45	A
0.90	50	B
0.80	55	C
0.70	60	E
0.60	65	F
0.50	70	G
0.40	75	H

Figure 4–1
DEMAND CURVE
FOR MILK

This curve shows the relationship between price and quantity demanded. To sell 70 billion quarts per year, the price must be only 50¢ (point G). If, instead, price is 90¢, only 50 billion quarts will be demanded (point B). To sell more milk, the price must be reduced. That is what the negative slope of the demand curve means.

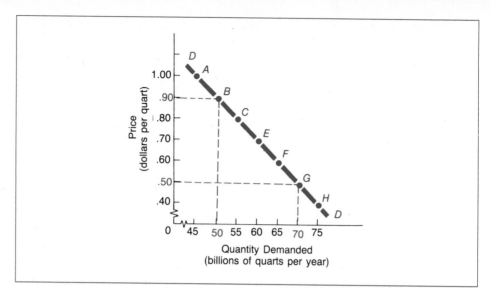

per year will be demanded. Since the quantity demanded declines as the price increases, the demand curve has a negative slope.[2]

Notice the last phrase in the definitions of the demand schedule and the demand curve: "holding all other determinants of quantity demanded constant." These "other things" include consumer incomes and preferences, the prices of soda and orange juice, and perhaps even advertising by the dairy association. We will examine the influences of these factors later in the chapter. First, however, let's look at the sellers' side of the market.

Supply and Quantity Supplied

Like quantity demanded, the quantity of milk that is supplied by dairy farmers is not a fixed number, but also depends on many things. Obviously, if there are more dairy farms, or larger ones, we expect more milk to be supplied. Or if bad weather deprives the cows of their feed, they may give less milk. As before, however, let's turn our attention first to the relationship between **quantity supplied** and one of its major determinants—the price of milk.

*The **quantity supplied** is the number of units sellers want to sell.*

Economists generally suppose that a higher price calls forth a greater quantity supplied. Why? Remember our analysis of the principle of increasing cost in Chapter 3 (page 39). According to that principle, as more of any farmer's (or the nation's) resources are devoted to milk production, the opportunity cost of obtaining another quart of milk increases. Farmers will therefore find it profitable to raise milk production only if they can sell the milk at a higher price— high enough to cover the higher costs incurred when milk production expands.

Looked at the other way around, we have just concluded that higher prices normally will be required to persuade farmers to raise milk production. This idea is quite general, and applies to the supply of most goods and services.[3] As long as suppliers want to make profits and the principle of increasing costs holds:

As the price of an item rises, the quantity supplied normally rises. As the price falls, the quantity supplied normally falls.

[2]If you need to review the concept of *slope*, refer back to Chapter 2, especially pages 20–23.
[3]This analysis is carried out in much greater detail in *Microeconomics* Chapters 7 and 8.

The Supply Schedule and the Supply Curve

The relationship between the price of milk and its quantity supplied is recorded in Table 4–2. Tables like this are called **supply schedules**; they show how much sellers are willing to provide (during a specified period) at alternative possible prices. This particular supply schedule shows that a low price like 50¢ per quart will induce suppliers to provide only 40 billion quarts, while a higher price like 80¢ will induce them to provide much more—70 billion quarts.

As you might have guessed, when information like this is plotted on a graph, it is called a **supply curve**. Figure 4–2 is the supply curve corresponding to the supply schedule in Table 4–2. It slopes upward because quantity supplied is higher when price is higher.

Notice again the same phrase in the definition: "holding all other determinants of quantity supplied constant." We will return to these "other determinants" a bit later in the discussion. But first we are ready to put demand and supply together.

A **supply schedule** is a table showing how the quantity supplied of some product during a specified period of time changes as the price of that product changes, holding all other determinants of quantity supplied constant.

A **supply curve** is a graphical depiction of a supply schedule. It shows how the quantity supplied of some product during a specified period of time will change as the price of that product changes, holding all other determinants of quantity supplied constant.

Table 4–2
SUPPLY SCHEDULE FOR MILK

PRICE (dollars per quart)	QUANTITY SUPPLIED (billions of quarts per year)	LABEL IN FIGURE 4–2
1.00	90	a
0.90	80	b
0.80	70	c
0.70	60	e
0.60	50	f
0.50	40	g
0.40	30	h

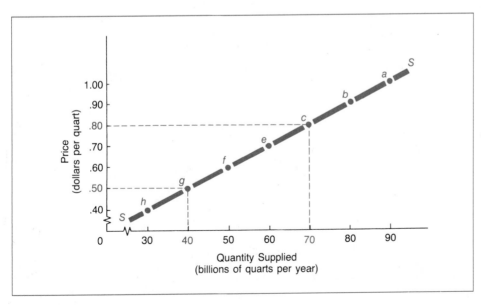

Figure 4–2
SUPPLY CURVE FOR MILK
This curve shows the relationship between the price of milk and the quantity supplied. To stimulate a greater quantity supplied, price must be increased. That is the meaning of the positive slope of the supply curve.

Equilibrium of Supply and Demand

To analyze how price is determined in a free market, we must compare the desires of consumers (demand) with the desires of producers (supply) and see whether the two plans are consistent. Table 4–3 and Figure 4–3 are designed to help us do this.

Table 4–3 brings together the demand schedule from Table 4–1 and the supply schedule from Table 4–2. Similarly, Figure 4–3 puts together the demand curve from Figure 4–1 and the supply curve from Figure 4–2 on a single graph. Such a graphic device is called a **supply–demand diagram**, and we will encounter many of them in this book. Notice that, for reasons already discussed, the demand curve has a negative slope and the supply curve has a positive slope. Most supply–demand diagrams are drawn with slopes like these.

There is only one point in Figure 4–3, point E, at which the supply curve and the demand curve intersect. At the price corresponding to point E, which is 70¢ per quart, the quantity supplied is equal to the quantity demanded. This means that, at a price of 70¢ per quart, consumers are willing to buy just what producers are willing to sell.

Table 4–3
DETERMINATION OF THE EQUILIBRIUM PRICE AND QUANTITY OF MILK

PRICE (dollars per quart)	QUANTITY DEMANDED	QUANTITY SUPPLIED	SURPLUS OR SHORTAGE?	PRICE WILL:
	(billions of quarts per year)			
1.00	45	90	Surplus	Fall
0.90	50	80	Surplus	Fall
0.80	55	70	Surplus	Fall
0.70	60	60	Neither	Remain the same
0.60	65	50	Shortage	Rise
0.50	70	40	Shortage	Rise
0.40	75	30	Shortage	Rise

Figure 4–3
SUPPLY–DEMAND EQUILIBRIUM

In a free market, price and quantity are determined by the intersection of the supply curve and the demand curve. In this example, the equilibrium price is 70¢ and the equilibrium quantity is 60 billion quarts of milk per year. Any other price is inconsistent with equilibrium. For example, at a price of 50¢, quantity demanded is 70 billion (point G), while quantity supplied is only 40 billion (point g), so that price will be driven up by the unsatisfied demand.

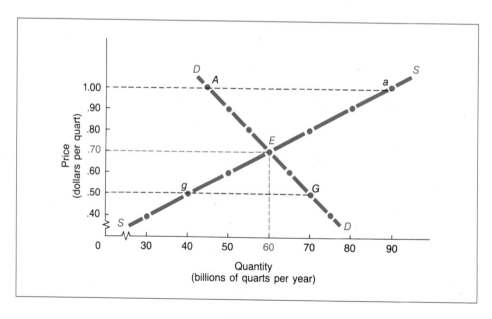

At a lower price, such as 50¢, only 40 billion quarts of milk will be supplied (point g) whereas 70 billion quarts will be demanded (point G). Thus, quantity demanded will exceed quantity supplied. There will be a **shortage** equal to 70 − 40 = 30 billion quarts. Alternatively, at a higher price, such as $1, quantity supplied will be 90 billion quarts (point a) while quantity demanded will be only 45 billion (point A). Quantity supplied will exceed quantity demanded, so there will be a **surplus** equal to 90 − 45 = 45 billion quarts.

Since 70¢ is the price at which quantity supplied and quantity demanded are equal, we say that 70¢ per quart is the **equilibrium price** in this market. Similarly, 60 billion quarts per year is the **equilibrium quantity** of milk.

The term "equilibrium" merits a little explanation, since it arises so frequently in economic analysis. An **equilibrium** is a situation in which there are no inherent forces that produce change; that is, a situation that does not contain the seeds of its own destruction. Think, for example, of a pendulum at rest at its center point. If no outside force (such as a person's hand) comes to push it, the pendulum will remain where it is; it is in *equilibrium*.

But, if someone gives the pendulum a shove, its equilibrium will be disturbed and it will start to move upward. When it reaches the top of its arc, the pendulum will, for an instant, be at rest again. But this is not an equilibrium position. A force known as gravity will pull the pendulum downward, and thereafter its motion from side to side will be governed by gravity and friction. Eventually, we know, the pendulum must return to the point at which it started, which is its only equilibrium position. At any other point inherent forces will cause the pendulum to move.

The concept of equilibrium in economics is similar and can be illustrated by our supply and demand example. Why is no price other than 70¢ an equilibrium price in Table 4–3 or Figure 4–3? What forces will change any other price?

Consider first a low price like 50¢, at which quantity demanded (70 billion) exceeds quantity supplied (40 billion). If the price were this low, there would be many frustrated customers unable to purchase the quantities they desire. They would compete with one another for the available milk. Some would offer more than the prevailing price and, as customers tried to outbid one another, the market price would be forced up. In other words, a price below the equilibrium price cannot persist in a free market because a shortage sets in motion powerful economic forces that push price upward.

Similar forces operate if the market price is *above* the equilibrium price. If, for example, the price should somehow get to be $1, Table 4–3 tells us that quantity supplied (90 billion) would far exceed quantity demanded (45 billion). Producers would be unable to sell their desired quantities of milk at the prevailing price, and some would find it in their interest to undercut their competitors by reducing price. This process of competitive price-cutting would continue as long as the surplus persisted, that is, as long as quantity supplied exceeded quantity demanded. Thus a price above the equilibrium price cannot persist indefinitely.

We are left with only one conclusion. The price 70¢ per quart and the quantity 60 billion quarts is the only price-quantity combination that does not sow the seeds of its own destruction. It is the only *equilibrium*. Any lower price must rise, and any higher price must fall. It is as if natural economic forces place a magnet at point E that attracts the market just like gravity attracts the pendulum.

A **shortage** is an excess of quantity demanded over quantity supplied. When there is a shortage, buyers cannot purchase the quantities they desire.

A **surplus** is an excess of quantity supplied over quantity demanded. When there is a surplus, sellers cannot sell the quantities they desire to supply.

An **equilibrium** is a situation in which there are no inherent forces that produce change. Changes away from an equilibrium position will occur only as a result of "outside events" that disturb the status quo.

The analogy to a pendulum is worth pursuing further. Most pendulums are more frequently in motion than at rest. However, unless they are repeatedly buffeted by outside forces (which, of course, is exactly what happens to pendulums used in clocks), pendulums gradually return to their resting points. The same is true of price and quantity in a free market. Markets are not always in equilibrium, but, if they are not interfered with, we have good reason to believe that they normally are *moving toward equilibrium*.

In principle, in a free market the forces of supply and demand are capable of selecting an equilibrium price and an equilibrium quantity toward which, in practice, we may expect actual price and actual quantity to gravitate.

The last interesting aspect of the analogy concerns the "outside forces" of which we have spoken. A pendulum that is being blown by the wind or pushed by a hand does not remain in equilibrium. Similarly, many outside forces can disturb a market equilibrium. A frost in Florida will disturb equilibrium in the market for oranges. A strike by miners will disturb equilibrium in the market for coal.

Many of these outside influences actually *change the equilibrium price and quantity* by shifting either the supply curve or the demand curve. If you look again at Figure 4–3, you can see clearly that any event that causes *either* the demand curve *or* the supply curve to shift will also cause the equilibrium price and quantity to change. Such events constitute the "other things" that we held constant in our definitions of supply and demand curves. We are now ready to analyze how these outside forces affect the equilibrium of supply and demand, beginning on the demand side.

Shifts of the Demand Curve

Returning to our example of milk, we noted earlier that the quantity of milk demanded is probably influenced by a variety of things other than the price of milk. Changes in population, consumer income, and the prices of alternative beverages such as soda and orange juice presumably cause changes in the quantity of milk demanded, even if the price of milk is unchanged.

Since the demand curve for milk depicts only the relationship between the quantity of milk demanded and the price of milk, holding all other factors constant, a change in any of these other factors produces a *shift of the entire demand curve*. That is:

A change in the price of a good produces a **movement along a fixed demand curve**. By contrast, a change in any other variable that influences quantity demanded produces a **shift of the demand curve**. If consumers want to buy *more* at any given price than they wanted previously, the demand curve shifts to the right (or outward). If they desire *less* at any given price, the demand curve shifts to the left (or inward).

To make this general principle more concrete and to show some of its many applications, let us consider some specific examples.

1. **Consumer incomes.** If average incomes increase, consumers may purchase more of many foods, including milk, even if the price of milk remains the same. That is, *increases in income normally shift demand curves outward to the right*, as depicted in Figure 4–4(a). In this example, the quantity demanded

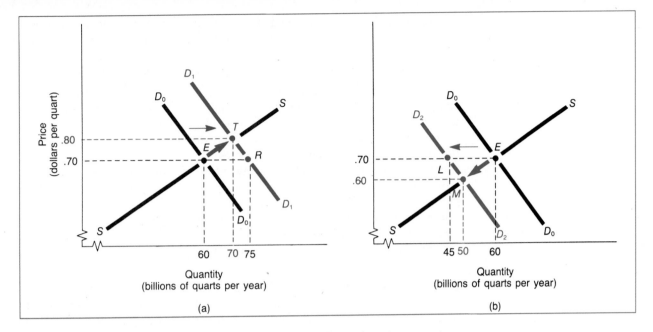

Quantity
(billions of quarts per year)

(a)

Quantity
(billions of quarts per year)

(b)

at the old equilibrium price of 70¢ increases from 60 billion quarts per year (point E on demand curve D_0D_0) to 75 billion (point R on demand curve D_1D_1). We know that 70¢ is no longer the equilibrium price, since at this price quantity demanded (75 billion) exceeds quantity supplied (60 billion). To restore equilibrium, price will have to rise. The diagram shows the new equilibrium at point T, where the price is 80¢ per quart and the quantity (demanded and supplied) is 70 billion quarts per year. This illustrates a general result.

Any factor that causes the demand curve to shift outward to the right, and does not affect the supply curve, will raise the equilibrium price and the equilibrium quantity.[4]

Everything works in reverse if consumer incomes fall. Figure 4–4(b) depicts a leftward (inward) shift of the demand curve that results from a decline in consumer incomes. For example, the quantity demanded at the previous equilibrium price (70¢) falls from 60 billion quarts (point E) to 45 billion (point L on demand curve D_2D_2). At the initial price, quantity supplied must begin to fall. The new equilibrium will eventually be established at point M, where the price is 60¢ and both quantity demanded and quantity supplied are 50 billion. In general:

Any factor that shifts the demand curve inward to the left, and does not affect the supply curve, will lower both the equilibrium price and the equilibrium quantity.

2. **Population.** Population growth should affect quantity demanded in more or less the same way as increases in average incomes. A larger population will presumably wish to consume more milk, even if the price of milk and

Figure 4–4
THE EFFECTS OF SHIFTS OF THE DEMAND CURVE
A shift of the demand curve will change the equilibrium price and quantity in a free market. In part (a), the demand curve shifts outward from D_0D_0 to D_1D_1. As a result, equilibrium moves from point E to point T; both price and quantity rise. In part (b), the demand curve shifts inward from D_0D_0 to D_2D_2, and equilibrium moves from point E to point M; both price and quantity fall.

[4]This statement, like many others in the text, assumes that the demand curve is downward-sloping and the supply curve is upward-sloping.

average incomes are unchanged, thus shifting the entire demand curve to the right as in Figure 4–4(a). The equilibrium price and quantity both rise. Similarly, a decrease in population should shift the demand curve for milk to the left, as in Figure 4–4(b), causing equilibrium price and quantity to fall.

3. **Consumer preferences.** If the dairy industry mounts a successful advertising campaign extolling the benefits of drinking milk, families may decide to raise their quantities demanded. This would shift the entire demand curve for milk to the right, as in Figure 4–4(a). Alternatively, a medical report on the dangers of high cholesterol may persuade consumers to drink less milk, thereby shifting the demand curve inward, as in Figure 4–4(b).

Again, these are general phenomena. *If consumer preferences shift in favor of a particular item, that item's demand curve will shift outward to the right, causing both equilibrium price and quantity to rise [Figure 4–4(a)]. Conversely, if consumer preferences shift against a particular item, that item's demand curve will shift inward to the left, causing equilibrium price and quantity to fall [Figure 4–4(b)].*

4. **Prices and availability of related goods.** Because soda, orange juice, and coffee are popular drinks that compete with milk, a change in the price of any of these beverages can be expected to shift the demand curve for milk. If any of these alternative drinks become cheaper, some consumers will switch away from milk. Thus the demand curve for milk will shift to the left, as in Figure 4–4(b). The introduction of an entirely new beverage — like coconut milk — can be expected to have a similar effect.

But other price changes shift the demand curve for milk in the opposite direction. For example, suppose that cookies, a commodity that goes well with milk, become less expensive. This may induce some consumers to drink more milk and thus shift the demand curve for milk to the right, as in Figure 4–4(a).

Common sense normally will tell us in which direction a price change for a related good will shift the demand curve for a good in question. *Increases in the prices of goods that are substitutes for the good in question (as soda is for milk) move the demand curve to the right, thus raising both the equilibrium price and quantity. Increases in the prices of goods that are normally used together with the good in question (such as cookies and milk) shift the demand curve to the left, thus lowering both the equilibrium price and quantity.* (See Discussion Question 11 at the end of the chapter.)

While the preceding list does not exhaust the possible influences on quantity demanded, enough has been said to indicate the principles involved. Let us therefore turn to a concrete example.

Application: Why Airlines Run Sales

Anyone who travels knows that airline companies reduce fares sharply to attract more customers at certain times of the year — particularly in winter (excluding the holiday period), when air traffic is light. Yet there is no reason to think that air transportation gets any cheaper in winter. Our supply and demand diagram makes it easy to understand why airlines run such "sales."

Given the number of planes in airlines' fleets, the supply of seats is relatively fixed, as indicated by the steep supply curve SS in Figure 4–5, and is more or less the same in summer and winter. During seasons when people want to travel less, the demand curve for seats shifts leftward from its normal

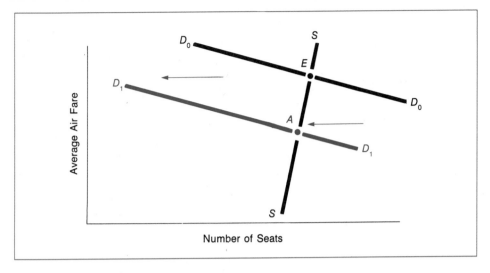

Figure 4–5
SEASONAL CHANGES IN
AIRLINE FARES
During seasons of slack
demand for air travel, the
demand curve shifts leftward
from $D_0 D_0$ to $D_1 D_1$. In
consequence, the market
equilibrium point shifts from E
to A, causing both price and
quantity to decline.

position, $D_0 D_0$, to a position such as $D_1 D_1$. Hence, equilibrium in the air-traffic market shifts from point E to point A. Thus both price and quantity decline at certain times of the year, not because of the generosity of the airlines, but because of the discipline of the market.

Shifts of the Supply Curve

Like quantity demanded, the quantity supplied on a market typically responds to a great number of influences other than price. The weather, the cost of feed, the number and size of dairy farms, and a variety of other factors all influence how much milk will be brought to market. Since the supply curve depicts only the relationship between the price of milk and the quantity of milk demanded, holding all other factors constant, a change in any of these other factors will cause the entire supply curve to shift. That is:

A change in the price of the good causes a **movement along a fixed supply curve**. But price is not the only influence on quantity supplied. And, if any of these other influences changes, the **entire supply curve shifts**.

Let us consider what some of these other factors are, and how they shift the supply curve.

1. *Size of the industry.* We begin with the most obvious factor. If more farmers enter the milk industry, the quantity supplied at any given price probably will increase. For example, if each farm provides 600,000 quarts of milk per year when the price is 70¢ per quart, then 100,000 farmers provide 60 billion quarts, and 130,000 farmers provide 78 billion. Thus, the more farms that are attracted to the industry, the greater will be the quantity of milk supplied at any given price, and hence the farther to the right will be the supply curve.

   Figure 4–6(a) illustrates the effect of an expansion of the industry from 100,000 farms to 130,000 farms—a rightward shift of the supply curve from $S_0 S_0$ to $S_1 S_1$. Notice that at the initial price of 70¢, the quantity supplied after the shift is 78 billion quarts (point I on supply curve $S_1 S_1$), which exceeds the quantity demanded of 60 billion (point E on supply curve $S_0 S_0$).

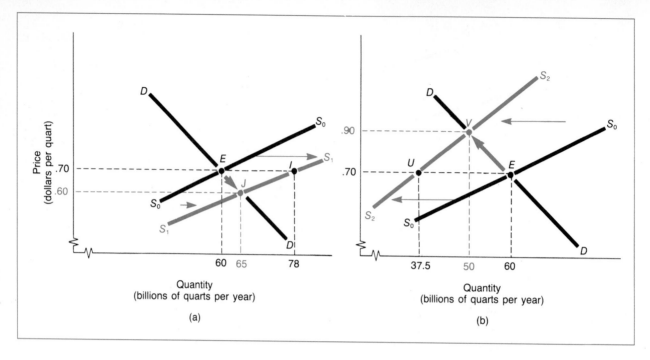

Figure 4–6

EFFECTS OF SHIFTS OF THE SUPPLY CURVE

A shift of the supply curve will change the equilibrium price and quantity in a market. In part (a), the supply curve shifts outward to the right, from $S_0 S_0$ to $S_1 S_1$. As a result, equilibrium moves from point E to point J; price falls as quantity increases. Part (b) illustrates the opposite case—an inward shift of the supply curve from $S_0 S_0$ to $S_2 S_2$. Equilibrium moves from point E to point V, which means that price rises as quantity falls.

We can see in the graph that the price of 70¢ is too high to be the equilibrium price; so the price must fall. The diagram shows the new equilibrium at point J, where the price is 60¢ per quart and the quantity is 65 billion quarts. The general point is that:

Any factor that shifts the supply curve outward to the right, and does not affect the demand curve, will lower the equilibrium price and raise the equilibrium quantity.

This must *always* be true if the industry's demand curve has a negative slope, because the greater quantity supplied can be sold only if price is decreased to induce customers to buy more.[5]

Figure 4–6(b) illustrates the opposite case: a contraction of the industry from 100,000 farms to 62,500 farms. The supply curve shifts inward to the left and equilibrium moves from point E to point V, where price is 90¢ and quantity is 50 billion quarts. In general:

Any factor that shifts the supply curve inward to the left, and does not affect the demand curve, will raise the equilibrium price and reduce the equilibrium quantity.

Even if no farmers enter or leave the industry, results like those depicted in Figure 4–6 can be produced by expansion or contraction of the existing farms. If farms get larger by adding more land, expanding the herds, and so on, the supply curve shifts to the right, as in Figure 4–6(a). If farms get smaller, the supply curve shifts to the left, as in Figure 4–6(b).

[5]Graphically, whenever a positively sloped curve shifts to the right, its intersection point with a negatively sloping curve must always move lower. Just try drawing it yourself.

2. **Technological progress.** Another influence that shifts supply curves is technological change. Suppose someone discovers that cows give more milk if Mozart is played during milking. Then, at any given price of milk, farmers will be able to provide a larger quantity of output; that is, the supply curve will shift outward to the right, as in Figure 4–6(a). This, again, illustrates a general influence that applies to most industries: *cost-reducing technological progress shifts the supply curve outward to the right*. Thus, as Figure 4–6(a) shows, the usual consequences of technological progress are lower prices and greater output.

3. **Prices of inputs.** Changes in input prices also shift supply curves. Suppose farm workers become unionized and win a raise. Farmers will have to pay higher wages and consequently will no longer be able to provide 60 billion quarts of milk profitably at a price of 70¢ per quart [point E in Figure 4–6(b)]. Perhaps they will provide only 37.5 billion (point U on supply curve $S_2 S_2$). This example illustrates that *increases in the prices of inputs that suppliers must buy will shift the supply curve inward to the left*.

4. **Prices of related outputs.** Dairy farms produce more than milk. If cheese prices rise sharply, farmers may decide to use some raw milk to make cheese, thereby reducing the quantity of milk supplied. On a supply–demand diagram, the supply curve would shift inward, as in Figure 4–6(b).

   Similar phenomena occur in other industries, and sometimes the effect goes in the opposite direction. For example, suppose the price of beef goes up, which increases the quantity of meat supplied. That, in turn, will cause a rise in the number of cowhides supplied at any given price of leather. Thus, a rise in the price of beef will lead to a rightward shift in the supply curve of leather. In general: *A change in the price of one good produced by a multiproduct industry may be expected to shift the supply curves of all the other goods produced by that industry.*

Application: A Computer in Every Home?

A dozen years ago, no one owned a home computer. Now there are millions, and enthusiasts look toward the day when computers will be as commonplace as television sets. What happened to bring the computer from the laboratory into the home? Did Americans suddenly develop a craving for computers?

Hardly. What actually happened is that scientists in the early 1970s invented the microchip—a major breakthrough that drastically reduced both the size of computers and, more important, the cost of manufacturing them. Within a few years, microcomputers were in commercial production. And microchip technology continued to improve throughout the 1970s and 1980s, leading to ever smaller, better, and cheaper computers. Today, for a few hundred dollars you can buy a desktop machine whose computing powers rival those of the giant computers of the early 1960s.

In terms of our supply and demand diagrams, the rapid technological progress in computer manufacturing shifted the supply curve dramatically to the right. As Figure 4–7 shows, a large outward shift of the supply curve should bring down the equilibrium price and increase the equilibrium quantity—which is just what happened in the computer industry. The figure calls attention to the fact that consumers naturally buy more computers as the price of computers falls (*a movement along* demand curve DD from E to A), even if the demand curve does not *shift*.

Figure 4–7
TECHNOLOGICAL CHANGE AND THE COMPUTER MARKET
The invention of the microchip, and subsequent improvements in microchip technology, caused the supply curve of microcomputers to shift outward to the right—moving from $S_0 S_0$ to $S_1 S_1$. Consequently, equilibrium shifted from point E to point A. The price of microcomputers fell from $10,000 to $3,000, and the quantity increased from 100,000 to 2 million per year. (The numbers in the diagram are roughly indicative of what happened in the U.S. market for microcomputers between 1978 and 1985, before correcting for the fact that the 1985 computer was vastly superior to the 1978 computer.)

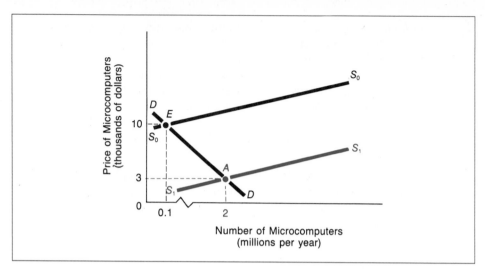

A **price ceiling** is a legal maximum on the price that may be charged for a commodity.

Restraining the Market Mechanism: Price Ceilings

As we have noted already, lawmakers and rulers have often been dissatisfied with the outcomes of the operation of the market system. From Rome to Pennsylvania and from biblical times to the space age, they have done battle with the invisible hand. Sometimes, rather than trying to make adjustments in the workings of the market, governments have sought to raise or to lower the prices of specific commodities by decree. In many of these cases, those in authority felt that the prices set by the market mechanism were, in some sense, immorally low or immorally high. Penalties were therefore imposed on anyone offering the commodities in question at prices lower or higher than those determined by the authorities.

But the market has proven itself a formidable foe that strongly resists attempts to circumvent its workings. In case after case where legal **price ceilings** are imposed, virtually the same set of consequences ensues:

1. A persistent shortage develops of the items whose prices are controlled. Queuing, direct rationing, or any of a variety of other devices, usually inefficient and unpleasant, have to be substituted for the distribution process provided by the price mechanism. *Example:* Price controls on gasoline led to long lines at service stations in 1979.

2. An illegal, or "black," market often arises to supply the commodity. There are usually some individuals who are willing to take the risks involved in meeting unsatisfied demands illegally, if legal means will not do the job. *Example:* Although most states ban the practice, ticket "scalping" occurs at most popular sporting events.

3. The prices charged on the black market are almost certainly higher than those that would prevail in a free market. After all, black marketeers expect compensation for the risk of being caught and punished. *Example:* Goods that are illegally smuggled into a country are normally quite expensive.

4. In each case, a substantial portion of the price falls into the hands of the black-market supplier instead of going to those who produce the good or who perform the service. *Example:* A constant complaint in the series of hearings that have marked the history of theater ticket price controls in New York City has been that the "ice" (the illegal excess charge) falls into

the hands of ticket scalpers rather than going to those who invested in, produced, or acted in the play.

These points and others are best illustrated by considering a concrete example of price ceilings.

A Case Study: Rent Controls in New York City

New York is the only major city in the United States that has had rent controls continuously since World War II. The objective of rent control is, of course, to protect the consumer from high rents. But most economists believe that rent control does not help the cities or their inhabitants and that, in the long run, it makes almost everyone worse off. Let's use supply–demand analysis to see what actually happens.

Figure 4–8 is a supply–demand diagram for rental units in New York. Curve *DD* is the demand curve and curve *SS* is the supply curve. Without controls, equilibrium would be at point *E*, where rents average $900 per month and 3 million units are occupied. Effective rent controls must set a ceiling price below the equilibrium price of $900, because otherwise the rent level would simply settle at the point determined by market forces. But with a low rent ceiling, such as, say, $500, the quantity of housing demanded will be 3.5 million (point *B*) while the quantity supplied will be only 2.5 million (point *C*).

The diagram shows a shortage of 1,000,000 apartments. This theoretical concept of a "shortage" shows up in New York City as an abnormally low vacancy rate—typically about half the national urban average.

As we expect, rent controls have spawned a lively black market in New York. The black market works to raise the effective price of rent-controlled apartments in many ways, including bribes, "key money" paid to move up on the waiting list, and requiring prospective tenants to purchase worthless furniture at inflated prices.

According to the diagram, rent controls reduce the quantity supplied from 3 million to 2.5 million apartments. What do we see in New York? First, some property owners, discouraged by the low rents, have converted apartment buildings into office space or other uses. Second, some apartments have not been maintained adequately. After all, rent controls create a shortage which makes even dilapidated apartments easy to rent. Third, some landlords have actually abandoned their buildings rather than pay rising tax and fuel bills. These abandoned buildings rapidly become eyesores and eventually pose threats to public health and safety.

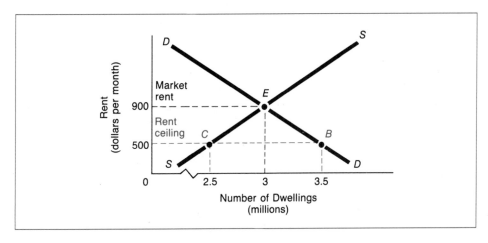

Figure 4–8
SUPPLY–DEMAND DIAGRAM FOR HOUSING
When market forces are permitted to set rents, the quantity of dwellings supplied will equal the quantity demanded. But when a rent ceiling forces rent below the market level, the number of dwellings supplied (point *C*) will be less than the number demanded (point *B*). Thus, rent ceilings induce housing shortages.

With all these problems, why do rent controls persist in New York City? And why are some other cities moving in the same direction? Part of the explanation is that many people simply do not understand the problems that rent controls cause. Another part is that landlords are unpopular politically. But a third, and important, part of the explanation is that not everyone is hurt by rent controls. Those who benefit from controls fight hard to preserve them. In New York, for example, many tenants pay rents that are only a fraction of what their apartments would fetch on the open market.

This last point illustrates another very general phenomenon:

Virtually every price ceiling or floor creates a class of people with a vested interest in preserving the regulations because they benefit from them. These people naturally use their political influence to protect their gains, which is one reason why it is so hard to eliminate price ceilings or floors.

Restraining the Market Mechanism: Price Floors

A **price floor** is a legal minimum on the price that may be charged for a commodity.

Interferences with the market mechanism are not always designed to keep prices low. Agricultural price supports and minimum wages are two notable examples in which the law keeps prices *above* free-market levels. **Price floors** are typically accompanied by a standard set of symptoms:

1. A surplus develops as some sellers cannot find buyers. *Example*: The minimum wage law helps create high unemployment among teen-agers.[6]

2. Where goods, rather than services, are involved, the surplus creates a problem of disposal. Something must be done about the excess of quantity supplied over quantity demanded. *Example:* The government has often been forced to purchase, and then store, large amounts of surplus agricultural commodities.

3. To get around the regulations, sellers may offer discounts in disguised — and often unwanted — forms. *Example:* When airline fares were regulated by the government, airlines offered more and better food and stylish uniforms for flight attendants instead of lowering fares. (Some still do; others offer "no frills" service with lower ticket prices.)

Once again, a specific example is useful.

A Case Study: Milk Price Supports

Perhaps you have seen television pictures of government workers giving away cheese to the needy. Perhaps you wondered where all that cheese came from. The answer is that the government's stockpiles of cheese are an indirect result of its efforts to set a floor under the price of milk. Explaining how this works provides a good illustration of the things that can happen when a price floor is imposed.

To help dairy farmers, the U.S. government sets a minimum support price for milk, just as it does for many agricultural products. In most times and places, this support price is well above the free-market level. So a surplus develops, as indicated in Figure 4–9. To maintain the price above the free-market level, the government must buy the surplus milk, which in recent years has

[6]This subject is dealt with more fully in *Microeconomics* Chapter 20.

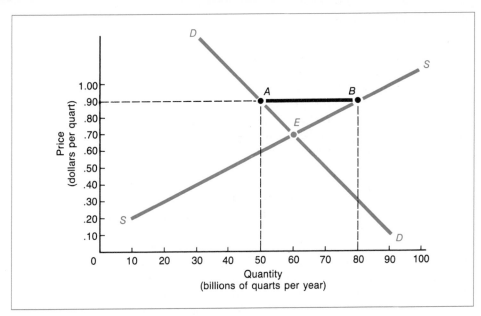

Figure 4-9
PRICE SUPPORTS
FOR MILK
In this diagram, which repeats the supply and demand curves from Figure 4-3, the support price for milk (90¢ per quart) is above the equilibrium price (70¢). Quantity supplied is 80 billion quarts per year (point B), while quantity demanded is only 50 billion (point A). To keep the price at 90¢, the government must buy 30 billion quarts of milk per year and store it as cheese.

amounted to 5–10% of all dairy products produced in the United States. But this creates a problem. Milk is so highly perishable that it must be turned into cheese or butter or dried milk before it can be stored. Buying and storing these products costs the U.S. government about $2–$3 billion per year. And every so often, the government accumulates so much cheese in its warehouses that its storage capacity is strained. It may then decide to give the surplus away. That is why the government gives cheese to the poor, instead of something else — such as milk.

A Can of Worms

Our two case studies — rent controls and milk price supports — illustrate some of the major side effects of price floors and ceilings, but barely hint at others. And there are yet more difficulties that we have not even mentioned, for the market mechanism is a tough bird that imposes suitable retribution on those who seek to circumvent it by legislative decree. Here is a partial list of other problems that may arise when prices are controlled.

Favoritism and Corruption
When price ceilings create a shortage, someone must decide who gets the limited quantity that is available. This can lead to political favoritism, to corruption in government, or even to discrimination along racial or religious lines.

Unenforceability
Attempts to control prices are almost certain to fail in industries with numerous suppliers, simply because the regulating agency must monitor the behavior of so many sellers. Some ways will be found to evade or to violate the law, and something akin to the free-market price will generally reemerge. But there is a difference: since the evasion mechanism, whatever its form, will have some operating costs, those costs must be borne by someone. Normally, that someone is the consumer.

Auxiliary Restrictions

Fears that a system of price controls will break down invariably lead to regulations designed to shore up the shaky edifice. Consumers may be told when and from whom they are permitted to buy. The powers of the police and the courts may be used to prevent the entry of new suppliers. Occasionally, an intricate system of market subdivision is imposed, giving each class of firms its protected category of operations in which others are not permitted to compete. Milk marketing orders are one good example. Laws banning conversion of rent-controlled apartments to condominiums are another.

Limitation of Volume of Transactions

To the extent that controls succeed in affecting prices, they can be expected to reduce the volume of transactions. Curiously, this is true whether the regulated price is above or below the free-market's equilibrium price. If it is set above the equilibrium price, quantity demanded will be below the equilibrium quantity. On the other hand, if the imposed price is set below the free-market level, quantity supplied will be cut down. Since sales volume cannot exceed either the quantity supplied or the quantity demanded, a reduction in the volume of transactions is likely to result.

Encouragement of Inefficiency

A price that is above the equilibrium level permits the survival of less-efficient firms whose high operating costs would doom them in an unrestricted market. This invitation to continued inefficiency becomes even more serious if entry of new suppliers is prevented as part of the program of enforcement of price regulations. (This is why deregulation of the airline industry has led to a painful "shake out" of the weaker companies in the 1980s.) Moreover, with the penalties for inefficiency severely restricted, the motivation for continued economy of operation by any firm is reduced.

Misallocation of Resources

Departures from free-market prices are likely to produce misuse of the economy's resources because the connection between production costs and prices is broken. For example, shippers use trucks or barges over routes where the resource cost of rail transportation is lower because artificial restrictions impose floors on railroad rates. In addition, just as more complex locks lead to more sophisticated burglary tools, more complex regulations lead to the use of yet more resources for their avoidance. New jobs are created for executives, lawyers, and economists. It may well be conjectured that at least some of the expensive services of these professionals could have been used more productively elsewhere.

Economists put it this way. Free markets are capable of dealing with the three basic coordination tasks outlined in Chapter 3: deciding *what* to produce, *how* to produce it, and *to whom* the goods should be distributed. Price controls throw a monkey wrench into the market mechanism. Though the market is surely not flawless, and government interferences often have praiseworthy goals, good intentions are not enough. Any government that sets out to repair what it sees as a defect in the market mechanism must take care lest it cause serious damage elsewhere. As a prominent economist once quipped, societies that are too willing to interfere with the operation of free markets soon find that the invisible hand is nowhere to be seen.

The Free Market and the Super Bowl

This excerpt from a newspaper article tells how the free market handled the shortage of tickets to the 1984 Super Bowl. The article uses the concept of opportunity cost from Chapter 3 without using the term. (Can you find where?)

Super Bowl XVIII provides a great illustration of how markets work. There are 72,000 seats in the Tampa stadium and roughly 40 million football fans. This creates a classic confrontation of supply and demand.

On the supply side of the market, quantity is absolutely limited.... Given Tampa's capacity, the supply-of-seats curve for Super Bowl XVIII is vertical.

Demand is another story. Tens of millions of fans would like to be there when the Los Angeles Raiders meet the Washington Redskins... and thus could be included in the market demand for seats....

The NFL does not permit the market to determine the ticket price, however. Instead, it rations tickets.... The market determines neither the initial price nor the initial distribution.

Holders, however, are permitted to resell their tickets, making for a lively market. Many are not willing to pay the full costs of attending the Super Bowl. For Raiders or Redskins home fans, full cost includes round-trip transportation (about $300), lodging ($200), the ticket ($60) and at least two days' time. The cash outlay is at least $600.

The economic cost of attendance is further increased by the implicit price of the ticket itself. The out-of-pocket cost is $60; however, the ticket can be sold for much more. This higher market value represents the ticket's implicit cost.

How high is that cost (price)? In Washington, a major ticket dealer says he bought more than 400 tickets at $350 apiece and resold them for $400 each. The Sunday edition of the *Washington Post* carried 109 ads each offering multiple tickets. The lowest offer was $350 a ticket, the highest $900. So it would appear that the equilibrium price in the aftermarket is about $500 a ticket. *

Are 72,000 fans really willing to pay more than $1,100 each to see the Super Bowl? Probably not. Most fans consider only the cash cost of their tickets, not the true economic cost. They don't realize how much they really are paying for their good fortune. If they acted like economists, the quantity of tickets supplied to the aftermarket would shift markedly to the right and the equilibrium price of a ticket would fall sharply (though not to $60).

SOURCE: Bradley R. Schiller, "Super Bowl Seats: Lucky Draw Costs a Fortune." *THE WALL STREET JOURNAL*, January 19, 1984.

*NOTE: For the 1987 Super Bowl in Los Angeles, ticket prices in the $750–$1000 range were common.

Summary

1. The quantity of a product that is demanded is not a fixed number. Rather, quantity demanded depends on such factors as the price of the product, consumer incomes, and the prices of other products.

2. The relationship between quantity demanded and price, holding all other things constant, can be displayed graphically on a demand curve.

3. For most products, the higher the price, the lower the quantity demanded. So the demand curve usually has a negative slope.

4. The quantity of a product that is supplied also depends on its price and many other influences. A supply curve is a graphical representation of the relationship between quantity supplied and price, holding all other influences constant.

5. For most products, the supply curve has a positive slope, meaning that higher prices call forth greater quantities supplied.

6. A market is said to be in equilibrium when quantity supplied is equal to quantity demanded. The equilibrium price and quantity are shown by the point on a graph where the supply and demand curves intersect. In a free market, price and quantity will tend to gravitate to this point.

7. A change in quantity demanded that is caused by a change in the price of the good is represented by a movement along a fixed demand curve. A change in quantity demanded that is caused by a change in any other determinant of quantity demanded is represented by a shift of the demand curve.

8. This same distinction applies to the supply curve:

Changes in price lead to movements along a fixed supply curve; changes in other determinants of quantity supplied lead to shifts of the whole supply curve.

9. Changes in consumer incomes, tastes, technology, prices of competing products, and many other influences cause shifts in either the demand curve or the supply curve and produce changes in price and quantity that can be determined from supply–demand diagrams.

10. An attempt by government regulations to force prices above or below their equilibrium levels is likely to lead to shortages or surpluses, black markets in which goods are sold at illegal prices, and to a variety of other problems. This is one of the **12 Ideas for Beyond the Final Exam.**

Concepts for Review

Quantity supplied	Supply curve	Equilibrium
Quantity demanded	Supply–demand diagram	Shifts in vs. movements along supply and
Demand schedule	Shortage	demand curves
Demand curve	Surplus	Price ceiling
Supply schedule	Equilibrium price and quantity	Price floor

Questions for Discussion

1. How often do you go to the movies? Would you go less often if a ticket cost twice as much? Distinguish between your demand curve for movie tickets and your "quantity demanded" at the current price.

2. What would you expect to be the shape of a demand curve
   a. for a medicine that means life or death for a patient?
   b. for the gasoline sold by Sam's gas station, which is surrounded by many other gas stations?

3. The following are the assumed supply and demand schedules for footballs:

DEMAND SCHEDULE		SUPPLY SCHEDULE	
	QUANTITY		QUANTITY
PRICE	DEMANDED	PRICE	SUPPLIED
$13	6,000	$13	71,000
11	13,000	11	63,000
9	29,000	9	29,000
7	50,000	7	11,000
5	61,000	5	0

   a. Plot the supply and demand curves and indicate the equilibrium price and quantity.
   b. What effect will an increase in the price of leather (a production input) have on the equilibrium price and quantity of footballs, assuming all other things remain constant? Explain

your answer with the help of a diagram.

   c. What effect will a decrease in the price of soccer balls (a substitute commodity) have on the equilibrium price and quantity of footballs, assuming again that all other things are held constant? Use a diagram in your answer.

4. Assume that the supply and demand schedules for economics textbooks at your college are the following:

PRICE	QUANTITY DEMANDED	QUANTITY SUPPLIED
$55	125	1400
45	250	900
35	500	500
25	1000	200
15	2000	0

   a. What is the equilibrium price and quantity of textbooks?
   b. In order to protect the profits of college bookstores, the state government sets a minimum textbook price of $45. How many economics textbooks will be sold now?
   c. Students protest and, as a result, the government abolishes the $45 price floor and imposes instead a $25 maximum price for textbooks. How many economics textbooks will be sold now?

d. While this price ceiling is in effect, computerization of publishing reduces the costs of producing textbooks. What effects will this have on the textbook market?

5. Show how the following demand curves are likely to shift in response to the indicated changes:
   a. The effect on the demand curve for boots when snowfall increases.
   b. The effect on the demand curve for tea when coffee prices rise.
   c. The effect on the demand curve for tea when sugar prices rise.

6. Discuss the likely effects of
   a. rent ceilings on the supply of apartments.
   x b. minimum wages on the demand for teen-age workers.
   Use supply–demand diagrams to show what may happen in each case.

7. Drinking water is costly to supply. Draw a supply–demand diagram showing how much water would be bought if water were supplied by a city government at zero charge. What do you conclude from these results about areas of the country in which water is in short supply?

8. On page 68 it is claimed that either price floors or price ceilings reduce the actual quantity exchanged in a market. Use a diagram, or diagrams, to support this conclusion, and explain the common sense behind it.

9. The same rightward shift of the demand curve may produce a very small or a very large increase in quantity, depending on the slope of the supply curve. Explain with diagrams.

10. In 1981, when regulations were holding the price of natural gas below its free-market level, Congressman Jack Kemp of New York said the following in an interview with *The New York Times*: "We need to decontrol natural gas, and get production of natural gas up to a higher level so we can bring down the price." [7] Evaluate the congressman's statement.

11. The two diagrams below show supply and demand curves for two substitute commodities: tapes and compact disks (CDs).
    a. On the left-hand diagram, show what happens when technological progress makes it cheaper to produce CDs.
    b. On the right-hand diagram, show what happens to the market for tapes.

12. (More difficult) Consider the market for milk discussed in this chapter (Tables 4–1 through 4–3 and Figures 4–1 through 4–3). Suppose the government decides to fight kidney stones by levying a tax of 30¢ per quart on sales of milk. Follow these steps to analyze the effects of the tax:
    a. Construct the new supply curve (to replace Table 4–2) that relates quantity supplied to the price consumers pay. (*Hint:* Before the tax, when consumers paid 70¢, farmers supplied 60 billion quarts. With a 30¢ tax, when consumers pay 70¢ farmers will receive only 40¢. Table 4–2 tells us they will provide only 30 billion quarts at this price. This is one point on the new supply curve. The rest of the curve can be constructed in the same way.)
    b. Graph the new supply curve constructed in part (a) on the supply–demand diagram depicted in Figure 4–3. What are the new equilibrium price and quantity?
    c. Does the tax succeed in its goal of reducing the consumption of milk?
    d. How much does the equilibrium price increase? Is the price rise greater than, equal to, or less than the 30¢ tax?
    e. Who actually pays the tax, consumers or producers? (This may be a good question to discuss in class.)

[7] *The New York Times*, December 23, 1981.

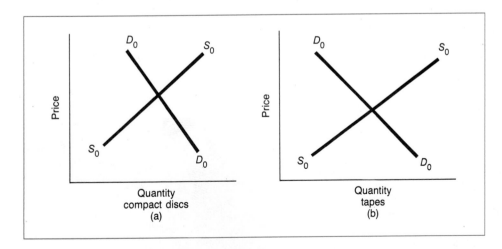

PART 2

The Realm of Macroeconomics

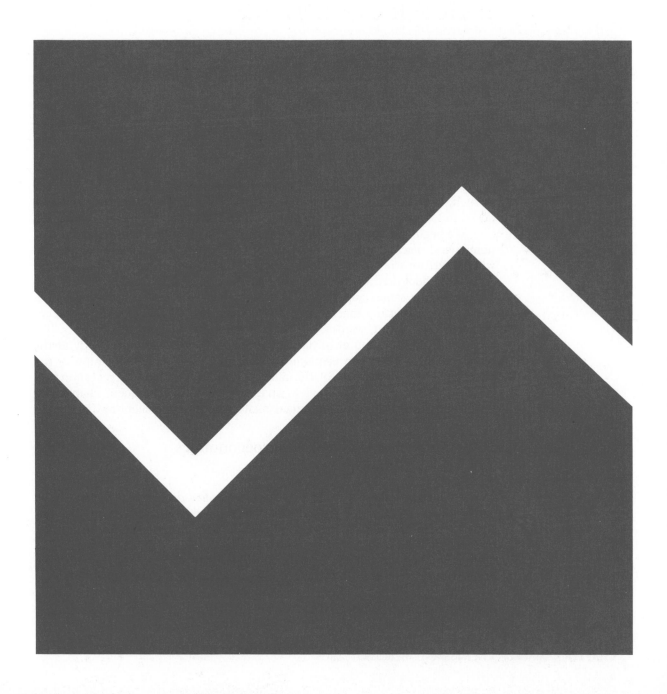

5

Where the telescope ends,
the microscope begins.
Which of the two has the
grander view?

VICTOR HUGO

Macroeconomics and Microeconomics

Economics traditionally has been divided into two fields: microeconomics and macroeconomics. These rather inelegant words are derived from the Greek—"micro" means something small and "macro" means something large. Although they were not specifically described as such, the basic notions and subject matter of **microeconomics** were introduced in Chapters 3 and 4. This chapter does the same for **macroeconomics**.

We begin the chapter by investigating the dividing line between microeconomics and macroeconomics: How do the two parts of the discipline differ and why? Next, we stress that while the *questions* studied by macroeconomists differ from those addressed by microeconomists, the underlying *tools* each group uses are almost the same. Supply and demand provide the basic organizing framework for constructing macroeconomic models, just as they do for microeconomic models. Third, we define some important macroeconomic concepts, like recession, inflation, and gross national product. Fourth, we look briefly at the broad sweep of American economic history to obtain some evaluation of the prevalence and seriousness of the macroeconomic problems of recession and inflation. And, finally, we preview what is to come in subsequent chapters by introducing the notion of government management of the economy.

Drawing a Line Between Macroeconomics and Microeconomics

In microeconomics *we study the behavior of individual decision-making units*. The dairy farmers of Chapter 4 are individual decision-making units; so are the consumers who purchase milk. How do they decide what courses of action are in their own best interests? How are these millions of decisions coordinated by the market mechanism, and with what consequences? Questions like these are the substance of microeconomics and are taken up in *Microeconomics* Parts 2 through 4.

Although Plato and Aristotle might wince at the abuse of their language, microeconomics applies to the decisions of some astonishingly large units.

Exxon and the American Telephone and Telegraph Company, for instance, have annual sales that exceed the total production of many nations. Yet someone who studies the pricing policies of AT&T is a microeconomist, whereas someone who studies inflation in Trinidad–Tobago is a macroeconomist. So the micro versus macro distinction in economics is certainly not based solely on size. What, then, is the basis for this time-honored distinction? Whereas microeconomics focuses on the decisions of individual units (no matter how large), *macroeconomics concentrates on the behavior of entire economies* (no matter how small). Rather than looking at the price and output decisions of a single company, macroeconomists study the overall price level, unemployment rate, and other things that we call *economic aggregates*.

Aggregation and Macroeconomics

What is an "economic aggregate"? Nothing but an *abstraction* that people find convenient in describing some salient feature of economic life. For example, while we observe the prices of butter, telephone calls, and movie tickets every day, we never observe "the price level." Yet many people (not only economists) find it both meaningful and natural to speak of "the cost of living"—so natural, in fact, that the Bureau of Labor Statistics' monthly attempts at measuring it are widely publicized by the news media.

Among the most important of these abstract notions is the concept of *national product,* which represents the total production of a nation's economy. The process by which real objects like hairpins, baseballs, cigarettes, and theater tickets get combined into an abstraction called national product is called **aggregation,** and it is one of the foundations of macroeconomics. We can illustrate it by a simple example.

Imagine a nation called Agraria, whose economy is far simpler than the U.S. economy: Business firms in Agraria produce nothing but foodstuffs to sell to consumers. Rather than deal separately with all the markets for pizzas, candy bars, hamburgers, and so on, macroeconomists group them all into a single abstract "market for output." Thus, when macroeconomists in Agraria announce that output in Agraria rose 10 percent this year, are they referring to more potatoes or hot dogs, more soybeans or green peppers? The answer is: They do not care. In the aggregate measures of macroeconomics, output is output, no matter what form it takes.

Amalgamating many markets into one means that distinctions among different products are ignored. Can we really believe that no one cares whether the national output of Agraria consists of $800,000 worth of pickles and $200,000 worth of ravioli rather than $500,000 each of lettuce and tomatoes? Surely this is too much to swallow! Macroeconomists clearly do not believe that no one cares; instead, they rest the case for aggregation on two foundations.

> **Aggregation** means combining many individual markets into one overall market.

1. While the *composition* of demand and supply in the various markets may be terribly interesting and important for *some* purposes (such as how income is distributed and what kinds of diets the citizens enjoy or endure), it may be of little consequence for the economy-wide issues of inflation and unemployment—the issues that concern macroeconomists.

2. During economic fluctuations, markets tend to move in unison. When demand in the economy rises, there is more demand for potatoes *and* tomatoes, more demand for artichokes *and* pickles, more demand for ravioli *and* hot dogs.

Though there are exceptions to these two principles, both seem serviceable enough as approximations. In fact, if they were not, there would be no discipline called macroeconomics, and this book would be only half as long as it is. (Lest this cause you a twinge of regret, bear in mind that many people feel that unemployment and inflation would be far more difficult to control without macroeconomics—which would be even more regrettable.)

The Line of Demarcation Revisited

These two principles—that markets normally move together and that the composition of demand and supply may be unimportant for some purposes—enable us to draw a different kind of dividing line between the territories of microeconomics and macroeconomics.

In macroeconomics, we typically assume that most details of resource allocation and income distribution are of secondary importance to the study of the overall rates of inflation and unemployment.

In microeconomics, we typically ignore inflation and unemployment and focus instead on how individual markets allocate resources and distribute income.

To use a well-worn metaphor, the macroeconomist analyzes the determination of the size of the economic "pie," paying scant attention to what is inside it or to how it gets divided among the dinner guests. A microeconomist, on the other hand, assumes that the pie is of the right size and shape, and frets over its ingredients and its division. If you have ever baked or eaten a pie, you will realize that either approach alone is a trifle myopic.

In some chapters of this book (especially in Parts 2–4), macroeconomic issues are discussed as if they could be divorced from questions of resource allocation and income distribution. In other chapters (especially those in *Microeconomics* Parts 2 through 5), microeconomic problems are investigated with scarcely a word about overall inflation and unemployment. Only in certain sections of the book (especially in Part 5 and *Microeconomics* Part 6) are the two modes of analysis brought to bear simultaneously on the same social problems. This is done solely for the sake of pedagogical clarity. In reality, the crucial interconnection between macroeconomics and microeconomics is with us all the time. There is, after all, only one economy.

Supply and Demand in Macroeconomics

Some students reading this book will be taking a course that concentrates on macroeconomics while others will be studying microeconomics. The discussion of supply and demand in Chapter 4 serves as an invaluable introduction to both fields because the basic apparatus of supply and demand is just as important in macroeconomics as it is in microeconomics.

Figure 5–1 shows two diagrams that should look familiar from Chapter 4. In Figure 5–1(a), there is a downward-sloping demand curve, labeled *DD*, and an upward-sloping supply curve, labeled *SS*. The axes labeled "Price" and "Quantity" do not specify what commodity they refer to because this is a multipurpose diagram. To start on familiar terrain, first imagine that this is a picture of the market for milk, so the price axis measures the price of milk while the quantity axis measures the quantity of milk demanded and supplied. As we know, if there are no interferences with the operation of a free market, equilibrium will be at point E with a price P_0 and a quantity of output Q_0.

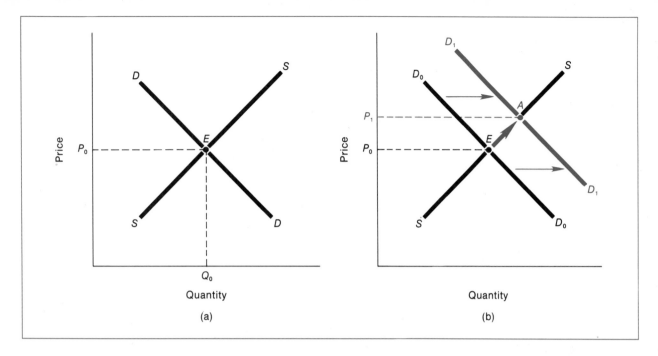

Figure 5–1
TWO INTERPRETATIONS OF A SHIFT IN THE DEMAND CURVE
Part (a) shows an equilibrium at point E, where demand curve DD intersects supply curve SS. Part (b) shows how this equilibrium moves from point E to point A if the demand curve moves outward. If this graph represents the market for milk, as it did in Chapter 4, then it shows an increase in the price of milk. But if the graph represents the aggregate market for "national product," then it shows inflation—a rise in the general price level.

Next, suppose something happens to shift the demand curve outward. For example, we learned in Chapter 4 that an increase in consumer incomes might have this effect. Figure 5–1(b) shows this shift as a rightward movement of the demand curve from $D_0 D_0$ to $D_1 D_1$. Equilibrium has shifted from E to A, so both price and output have risen.

Now let us reinterpret Figure 5–1 as representing an abstract market for "national product." This is one of those abstractions—an economic aggregate—that we described earlier. No one has ever seen, touched, smelled, or eaten a "unit of national product," but these are the kinds of abstractions upon which macroeconomic analysis is built. Consistent with this reinterpretation, think of the price measured on the vertical axis as being another abstraction— the overall price index, or "cost of living."[1] Then curve DD in Figure 5–1(a) is called an **aggregate demand curve**, and curve SS is called an **aggregate supply curve.** We will explain where these curves come from in Chapters 8–11.

With this reinterpretation, Figure 5–1(b) can depict the macroeconomic problem of **inflation.** We see from the figure that the outward shift of the aggregate demand curve, whatever its cause, pushes the price level up from P_0 to P_1. If aggregate demand keeps shifting out month after month, the economy will suffer from inflation, that is, a sustained increase in the general price level.

The other principal problems of macroeconomics, recession and unemployment, also can be illustrated on a supply-demand diagram, this time by shifting the demand curve in the opposite direction. Figure 5–2 repeats the supply and demand curves of Figure 5–1(a) and in addition depicts a leftward shift

The **aggregate demand curve** shows the quantity of national product that is demanded at each possible value of the price level.

The **aggregate supply curve** shows the quantity of national product that is supplied at each possible value of the price level.

Inflation refers to a sustained increase in the general price level.

[1]The appendix to Chapter 6 explains how such price indexes are calculated.

Figure 5–2

AN ECONOMY SLIPPING INTO A RECESSION
In this aggregate supply–demand diagram, there is an initial equilibrium at point E, where demand curve $D_0 D_0$ intersects supply curve SS. When the demand curve shifts inward from $D_0 D_0$ to $D_2 D_2$, equilibrium moves to point B, and output falls from Q_0 to Q_2.

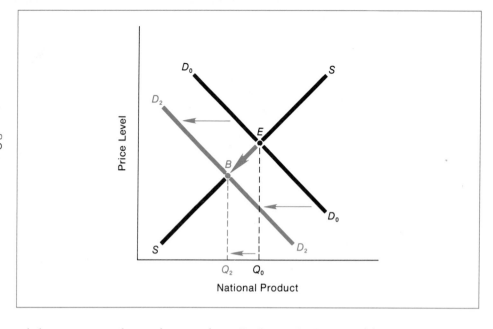

of the aggregate demand curve from $D_0 D_0$ to $D_2 D_2$. Equilibrium now moves from point E to point B so that national product (total output) declines from Q_0 to Q_2. This is what we normally mean by a **recession.**

Gross National Product

> **A recession** is a period of time during which the total output of the economy declines.

The economy's total output, we have just seen, is one of the major variables of concern to macroeconomists. While there are several ways to measure it, the most popular choice undoubtedly is the **gross national product**, a term you have probably encountered in the news media. The gross national product, or "GNP" for short, is the most comprehensive measure of the output of all the factories, offices, and shops in the U.S. economy. Specifically, it is the sum of the money values of all final goods and services produced within the year.

> **Gross national product (GNP)** is the sum of the money values of all final goods and services produced by the economy during a specified period of time, usually one year.

Several features of this definition need to be underscored.[2] First, you will notice that:

We add up the money values of things.

The GNP consists of a bewildering variety of goods and services: mousetraps and computers, bologna and caviar, ballet performances and rock concerts, tanks and textbooks. How are we to combine all of these into a single number? To an economist, the natural way to do this is first to convert every good and service into *money* terms. If we want to add 10 apples and 20 oranges, we first ask: How much *money* does each cost? If apples cost 20 cents and oranges cost 25 cents, then the apples count for $2 and the oranges for $5, so the sum is $7 worth of "output." The market *price* of each good or service is used as an indicator of its *value* to society simply because *someone* is willing to pay that much money for it.

This decision raises the question of what prices to use in valuing the different outputs. The official data offer two choices. First, we can value each good

---

[2]Certain exceptions to the definition are dealt with in Appendix B of Chapter 8, especially on page 158. Some instructors may prefer to take up that material here.

and service at the price at which it was actually sold during the year. If we do this, the resulting measure is called **nominal GNP,** or *money GNP,* or *GNP in current dollars*. This seems like a perfectly sensible choice. But as a measure of output, it has one serious drawback: nominal GNP rises when prices rise, even if there is no increase in actual production. For example, if hamburgers cost $1.50 this year but cost only $1.25 last year, then 100 hamburgers will contribute $150 to this year's nominal GNP but only $125 to last year's. But 100 hamburgers are still 100 hamburgers — output has not grown.

For this reason, government statisticians have devised an alternative measure that corrects for inflation by valuing all goods and services at some fixed set of prices. (Currently, the prices of 1982 are used.) For example, if the hamburgers were valued at $1.25 each in both years, $125 worth of hamburger output would be included in GNP in each year. When we treat every output in this way, we obtain the **real GNP** or *GNP in constant dollars*. The news media often refer to it as "GNP corrected for inflation." Throughout most of this book, and certainly when we are discussing the nation's output, it is the real GNP that we shall be concerned with. The distinction between nominal and real GNP leads us to a working definition of a *recession* as a period in which *real* GNP declines. For example, between 1981 and 1982, nominal GNP rose from $3053 billion to $3166 billion; but real GNP *fell* from $3249 billion to $3166 billion.

The next important aspect of the definition of GNP is that:

The GNP for a particular year includes only goods and services produced during that year. Sales of items produced in previous years are explicitly excluded.

For example, suppose you buy a perfectly beautiful 1974 Plymouth next week and are overjoyed by your purchase. The national income statistician will not share your glee because she already counted your car in the GNP in 1974 when it was first produced and sold; the car will never be counted again. The same holds true of houses. An old house (unlike an old car) often will sell for more than its original purchasers paid; yet the resale value of the house does not count in the GNP since it was already counted in the year it was built. For the same reason, exchanges of other existing assets are not included in the GNP.

Third, you will note the use of the phrase **final goods and services** in the definition. The adjective "final" is the key word here. For example, when a supermarket buys milk from a farmer, the transaction is not included in the GNP because the supermarket does not want the milk for itself. It buys milk only for resale to consumers. Only when the milk is sold to consumers is it considered a final product. When the supermarket buys it, economists consider it an **intermediate good.** The GNP does not include sales of intermediate goods or services.[3]

Finally, although the definition does not state this explicitly:

For the most part, only goods and services that pass through organized markets count in the GNP.

This, of course, excludes many economic activities. For example, illegal activities are not included in the GNP. Thus, gambling services in Chicago are not in the GNP, but gambling services in Atlantic City are. The definition reflects the statisticians' confession that they could not hope to measure the value of

Nominal GNP is calculated by valuing all outputs at current prices.

Real GNP is calculated by valuing all outputs at the prices that prevailed in some agreed-upon year (currently 1982). Therefore, real GNP is a far better measure of changes in national production.

Final goods and services are those that are purchased by their ultimate users.

An **intermediate good** is a good purchased for resale or for use in producing another good.

[3]Actually, there is another way to add up the GNP by counting a portion of each intermediate transaction. This is explained in Appendix B of Chapter 8, especially pages 161–62.

many of the economy's most important activities, such as housework, do-it-yourself repairs, and leisure time. While these are certainly economic activities that result in currently produced goods or services, they all lack that important measuring rod — a price.

This omission results in certain oddities. For example, suppose that each of two neighboring families hires the other to clean house, generously paying $1000 a week for the services. Each family can easily afford such generosity since it collects an identical salary from its neighbor. Nothing real changes, but GNP goes up by $104,000 a year.

Limitations of the GNP: What GNP Is Not

Having seen in some detail what the GNP *is*, it is worth pausing to expand upon what it *is not*. In particular:

Gross national product is not a measure of the nation's economic well-being.

The GNP is not intended to measure economic well-being, and does not do so for several reasons.

1. *Only market activity is included in GNP.* Work done by housewives and do-it-yourselfers certainly contributes to the nation's well-being, but it is not measured in the GNP because it has no price tag.

    One important implication of this exclusion arises when we try to compare the GNPs of developed and less-developed countries. Americans are always incredulous to learn that the per capita GNP of the poorest African countries is less than $250 a year. Surely, no one could survive in America on $5 a week. How can Africans do it? Part of the answer, of course, is that these people are incredibly poor. We shall study their plight in Chapter 38. But another part of the answer is that:

    International GNP comparisons are vastly misleading when the two countries differ greatly in the fraction of economic activity that each conducts in organized markets.

    This fraction is relatively large in the United States and relatively small in the less-developed countries, so when we compare their respective measured GNPs we are not comparing the same economic activities at all. Many things that get counted in the U.S. GNP are not counted in the GNPs of less-developed nations. So it is ludicrous to think that these people, poor as they are, survive on what to Americans would amount to $5 a week.

    A second implication is that GNP statistics take no account of the so-called "underground economy." This includes not just criminal activities, but a great deal of legitimate business activity that is conducted in cash (or by barter) to escape the tax collector. Naturally, we have no good data on the size of the underground economy; but some observers think it may amount to 10 percent or more of U.S. GNP. In some foreign countries, it is surely a much bigger share than this.

2. *GNP places no value on leisure.* As a country gets richer, one of the things that happens is that its citizens take more and more leisure time. The steady decrease in the length of the typical workweek in the United States is clear evidence for this. As a result, the gap is steadily widening between official

GNP and some truer measure of national well-being that would include the value of leisure time. For this reason, growth in GNP systematically *understates* the growth in national well-being. But there are also reasons why the GNP *overstates* how well-off we are. We consider these next.

3. *"Bads" as well as "goods" get counted in GNP.* Suppose there is a natural disaster—as when Mt. St. Helens erupted in the state of Washington in 1980. Surely the well-being of the nation was diminished by this catastrophe. Many homes, businesses, and resorts were destroyed; some people were killed; soot covered cities and towns miles from the blast. Yet the disaster probably caused GNP to rise. Consumers spent more to clean up and replace lost possessions. Businesses spent more to rebuild and repair damaged homes and stores. The government spent more for disaster relief and cleanup. Yet no one would think that the nation was better off for its higher GNP.

   Wars represent an extreme example. Mobilization for outright war always causes a country's GNP to rise rapidly. But men called into the army could be producing civilian output. Factories needed to produce armaments could instead be making cars, washing machines, and televisions. A country at war is surely worse off than a country at peace, but this fact will not be reflected in its GNP accounts.

4. *Ecological costs are not netted out of the GNP.* Many of the activities in a modern industrial economy that produce goods and services also have undesirable side effects on the environment. Automobiles provide enjoyment and a means of transportation, but they also despoil the atmosphere. Factories pollute rivers and lakes while manufacturing valuable commodities. Almost everything seems to produce garbage, which creates the problem of what to do with it. None of these ecological costs are deducted from the GNP in an effort to give us a truer measure of the *net* increase in economic welfare that our economy produces. Is this foolishness? Not if we remember the job that national income statisticians are trying to do: They are measuring the economic activity conducted through organized markets, not national welfare.

The Economy on a Roller Coaster

Having defined several of the basic concepts of macroeconomics, let us breathe some life into them by perusing the economic history of the United States. Figures 5–3 and 5–4 provide a capsule summary of this history since the Civil War. Figure 5–3 charts the behavior of the growth rate of real GNP over a period of almost 120 years. The fact that the growth rate has almost always been positive indicates that the main feature has been *economic growth*. In fact, the average annual growth rate over this period has been 3.4 percent. But the figure also shows that recessions—periods of falling real GNP—have been a persistent feature of America's economic performance. The ups and downs that are evident in Figure 5–3 are often referred to as *business cycles*.

The history of the inflation rate displayed in Figure 5–4 also shows more positive numbers than negative ones—more inflation than **deflation**. In total, the price level rose more than eleven-fold since 1869. But we also see some large gyrations in the inflation rate, including sharp bursts of inflation during and right after the two world wars and dramatic deflations in the 1870s, 1880s, 1921–1922, and 1929–1933.

The following exercise may be enlightening. Cover the portions of Figures 5–3 and 5–4 that deal with the period beginning in 1941, the portions to the right of the shaded area in each figure. The picture that emerges for the

Deflation refers to a sustained *decrease* in the general price level.

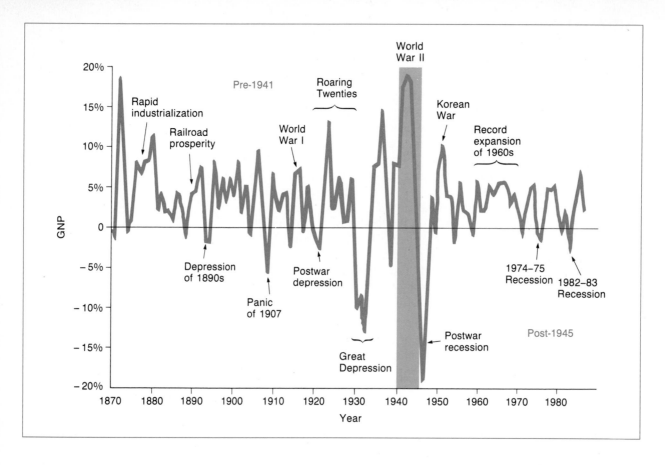

Figure 5–3

THE GROWTH RATE OF REAL GROSS NATIONAL PRODUCT OF THE UNITED STATES, 1870–1987

This time series chart displays the growth rate of real gross national product in the United States from 1870 to 1987. (Here real GNP is measured in 1982 prices.) The Great Depression (1929–1939) stands out vividly. The years during World War II are shaded. Does the growth rate look smoother to the right of this shaded area?

SOURCE: Constructed by authors from Commerce Department data for 1929–1987. Data for 1869–1928 were kindly provided by Professor Christina Romer.

1870–1940 period is of an economy on a roller coaster. In Figure 5–3, the ups and downs of the growth rate of real output are frequent and sometimes quite pronounced. In Figure 5–4 we see periods of both inflation and deflation with little or no tendency for one to be more common than the other. Indeed, prices at the eve of World War II were not much higher than they were at the close of the Civil War.

Now do the reverse. Cover the data prior to 1946 and look only at the postwar period. There is, indeed, a difference. Instances of negative real GNP growth are less common and business cycles are much less severe. While perfection has not been achieved, things do look much better. When we turn to inflation, however, things look rather worse. Gone are the periods of deflation and price stability that occurred before World War II. Prices now seem only to go up.

This quick inspection of the data suggests that something has happened. The U.S. economy behaved differently in 1946–1987 than it did in 1870–1940. Many economists attribute this shift in the economy's behavior to lessons the government has learned about managing the economy—lessons that we will be learning in Part 4. When you look at the pre-1941 data, you are looking at an unmanaged economy that went through booms and recessions for "natural" economic reasons. The government did little about either. When you examine the post-1945 data, on the other hand, you are looking at an economy that has been increasingly managed by government policy—sometimes successfully and sometimes unsuccessfully. While the recessions are less severe, a cost seems to have been exacted: the economy appears to be more inflation-prone than it was in the more distant past.

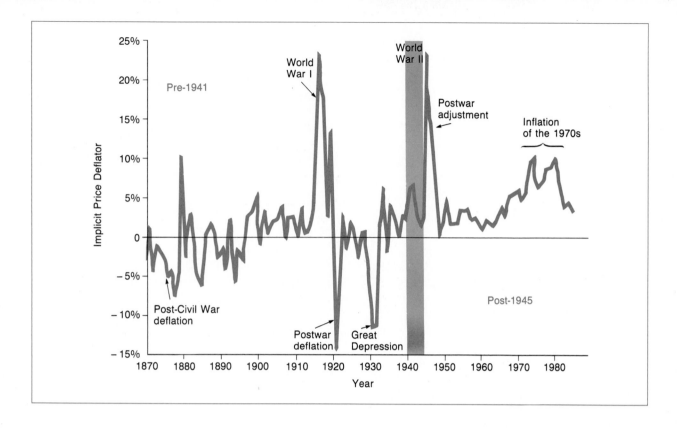

The Great Depression of the 1930s

As you look at these graphs, the Great Depression of the 1930s is bound to catch your eye. The decline in economic activity from 1929 to 1933 (see Figure 5–3) was the most severe in our nation's history, and the rapid deflation (see Figure 5–4) was most unusual. The Depression is but a dim memory now, but those who lived through it will never forget it.

While statistics usually conceal the true drama of economic events, this is not so of the Great Depression—they stand here as bitter testimony to its severity. From its 1929 high to its 1933 low, the production of goods and services dropped 30 percent and the price level fell 23 percent. Business investment almost ceased entirely, and stock market values slumped to less than one-sixth their 1929 level. The unemployment rate rose ominously from about 3 percent in 1929 to 25 percent in 1933—one person in four was jobless. From the data alone, one can virtually conjure up pictures of soup lines, beggars on street corners, closed factories, and homeless families. (See the boxed insert on the next page.)

Unlike many earlier and later recessions that plagued the U.S. economy, the Great Depression was a worldwide event. No country was spared its ravages. This traumatic episode literally changed the history of many nations. In Germany, it facilitated the ascendancy of the Nazi party. In the United States, it enabled Franklin Roosevelt's Democratic party to engineer one of the most dramatic political realignments in history and to push through a host of political and economic reforms.

The worldwide depression also caused a much-needed revolution in the thinking of economists. Up until the 1930s, the prevailing economic theory held that a capitalist economy, while it occasionally misbehaved, had a

Figure 5–4
THE INFLATION RATE IN THE UNITED STATES, 1870–1987
This time series chart portrays the behavior of the U.S. inflation rate from 1870 to 1987. (The specific price index used is called the GNP deflator, and it is defined as the ratio of nominal GNP divided by real GNP.) The difference between the 1870–1940 period and the 1946–1987 period is pronounced.
SOURCE: Constructed by authors from Commerce Department data for 1929–1987. Data for 1869–1928 were kindly provided by Professor Christina Romer.

Life in "Hooverville"

During the worst years of the Great Depression, unemployed workers often congregated in shanty-towns on the outskirts of many major cities. Conditions in these slums were deplorable. With a heavy dose of irony, these communities were known as "Hoovervilles," in honor of the president of the United States who preached rugged individualism. A contemporary observer described a Hooverville in New York City as follows:

A Hooverville in New York City.

It was a fairly popular "development" made up of a hundred or so dwellings, each the size of a dog house or chickencoop, often constructed with much ingenuity out of wooden boxes, metal cans, strips of cardboard or old tar paper. Here human beings lived on the margin of civilization by foraging for garbage, junk, and waste lumber. I found some splitting or sawing wood with dull tools to make fires; others were picking through heaps of rubbish they had gathered before their doorways or cooking over open fires or battered oilstoves. Still others spent their days improving their rent-free homes, making them sometimes fairly solid and weather-proof. . . . Most of them, according to the police, lived by begging or trading in junk; when all else failed they ate at the soup kitchens or public canteens. They were of all sorts, young and old, some of them rough-looking and suspicious of strangers. They lived in fear of being forcibly removed by the authorities, though the neighborhood people in many cases helped them and the police tolerated them for the time being.

SOURCE: Mathew Josephson, *Infidel in the Temple* (New York: Alfred A. Knopf, 1967), pages 82–83.

"natural" tendency to cure recessions or inflations by itself. The roller coaster bounced around but did not normally run off the tracks.

This optimistic view was not confined to academia. It characterized the views of most politicians (certainly including President Herbert Hoover) and business leaders as well. As the great American humorist Will Rogers remarked with characteristic sarcasm:

It's almost been worth this depression to find out how little our big men knew. Mayby [sic] this depression is just "normalcy" and we don't know it. It's made a dumb guy as smart as a smart one. . . . Depression used to be a state of mind, Now it's a state of coma, now it's permanent. Last year we said, "Things can't go on like this," and they didn't, they got worse.[4]

The stubbornness of the Great Depression shook almost everyone's faith in the ability of the economy to right itself. In Cambridge, England, this questioning attitude led John Maynard Keynes, one of the world's most respected economists, to write *The General Theory of Employment, Interest, and Money* (1936). Probably the most important book in economics of the twentieth century, it carried a rather revolutionary message. Keynes discarded the notion that the economy always gravitated toward high levels of employment, replacing it

[4]From *Sanity Is Where You Find It* by Will Rogers, edited by Donald Day; copyright © 1955 by Rogers Company; reprinted by permission of Houghton Mifflin Company; pages 120–21.

with the assertion that—if a pessimistic outlook led business firms and consumers to curtail their spending plans—the economy might be condemned to stagnation for years and years.

While this doleful prognosis sounded all too realistic at the time, Keynes closed his book on a hopeful note. For he showed how government actions might prod the economy out of its depressed state. The lessons he taught the world then are the lessons we shall be learning in Parts 3 and 4. They show how governments can manage their economies so that recessions will not turn into depressions and depressions will not last as long as the Great Depression. While Keynes was working on *The General Theory*, he wrote his friend George Bernard Shaw that, "I believe myself to be writing a book on economic theory which will largely revolutionize...the way the world thinks about economic problems." In many ways he was right, though parts of the Keynesian message remain controversial to this day.

From World War II to 1973

The Great Depression finally ended when the country mobilized for war in the early 1940s. With total spending at extraordinarily high levels during the war, mostly because of government expenditures, the economy boomed and the unemployment rate fell as low as 1.2 percent.

Wartime spending of this magnitude usually leads to inflation, but much of the potential inflation during World War II was contained by price controls. With prices held below the levels at which quantity supplied equaled quantity demanded, many goods had to be rationed, and shortages of consumer goods were common. All of this ended with a burst of inflation when controls were lifted after the war.

The period from the end of the war until the early 1960s resembled the earlier period of growth with recessions before 1929. The main difference was that the four recessions between 1948 and 1961 were noticeably shorter and less severe than their prewar counterparts. Moderate but persistent inflation also became a fact of life.

When the economy emerged from recession in 1961, it entered what proved to be the longest uninterrupted period of expansion in our nation's history. GNP grew smartly and unemployment declined steadily, while the price level, though continuing to rise, showed no tendency to accelerate. The noninflationary boom was credited widely to the success of what came to be called "The New Economics," a term the media created for the policy of economic management prescribed by Keynes in the 1930s. For a while it looked as if we could avoid both unemployment and inflation. But the optimistic verdicts were premature in both cases.

Inflation was the first problem to crop up, beginning in about 1966. Its major cause, as it had been so many times in the past, was high levels of wartime spending—this time for the Vietnam War. Unemployment came next, when the economic expansion ground to a halt in 1969. Despite a short and mild recession, inflation continued at rates that were considered high at the time—5 to 6 percent a year.

In the face of persistent inflation, and with the economy beginning to pick up steam once again, President Richard Nixon instituted his "New Economic Policy" in a dramatic radio and television address to the nation in August 1971. This sweeping change in policy included America's first experiment with wage and price controls during peacetime. The controls program, which will be discussed in Chapter 17, held the inflation rate in check for a while as economic expansion progressed. But inflation worsened dramatically in 1973, mainly because of an explosion in food prices caused by poor harvests around the world.

The Great Stagflation, 1973–1980

Then things began to get much worse, not only for the United States, but for all the oil-importing nations of the world. A 1973 war between Israel and the Arab nations led to a quadrupling of the price of oil by the Organization of Petroleum Exporting Countries (OPEC). At the same time, continued poor harvests in 1974 in many parts of the globe kept world food prices rising rapidly. Prices of other raw materials also skyrocketed. Naturally, higher costs of fuel and other materials soon were reflected in the prices of manufactured goods.

By unhappy coincidence, these events coincided with the lifting of wage and price controls. Just as had happened after World War II, the elimination of controls led to an acceleration of inflation as prices that had been held artificially below equilibrium levels were allowed to rise. For all these reasons, the inflation rate in the United States soared to above 12 percent during 1974.

Meanwhile, the U.S. economy was slipping into its longest and most severe recession since the 1930s. Real GNP fell by about $4\frac{1}{2}$ percent between late 1973 and early 1975, and the unemployment rate rose from less than 5 percent to nearly 9 percent. Thus, both the twin evils of macroeconomics—inflation and unemployment—were unusually virulent in 1974 and 1975. Indeed, a new term—**stagflation**—was coined to refer to the simultaneous occurrence of economic *stag*nation and rapid in*flation*.

Stagflation is inflation that occurs while the economy is growing slowly ("stagnating") or having a recession.

Thanks partly to government actions, but mostly to natural economic forces, the economic collapse ended in 1975, and a sustained recovery began. On the price front, three forces pushed inflation down rapidly. First, the explosion in food and fuel prices was not repeated. These prices settled down at *levels* far higher than in the early 1970s, but ceased being engines of *inflation*. Second, the adjustment to the end of price controls ended in late 1974, and price behavior returned to normalcy. Third, just as had happened in the past, the severity of the recession put a brake on inflation. The inflation rate tumbled from over 12 percent a year in 1974 to a range of 5 to 7 percent during 1976 and 1977.

But the price of oil began to misbehave again in 1979 when the revolution that deposed the shah of Iran sparked chaos in the world oil market. In a series of price increases, OPEC more than doubled the price of oil during 1979, and government allocation programs led to long lines of motorists at gasoline stations all over the country.

OPEC's actions brought stagflation back again. Inflation accelerated first—from a 9 percent rate in 1978 to over 13 percent in 1979 and then to an astonishing 16 percent during the first half of 1980. Output fell at an extraordinarily rapid rate, but the decline lasted for only about the first six months of 1980. Output began to recover during the second half of 1980.

The Reagan Years

As President Ronald Reagan assumed office in January 1981, the economy was showing signs of life but seemed stuck with a stubborn inflation rate near 10 percent. The new president promised to change things with a package of

The Promise of Reaganomics

President Reagan came to office with a plan to cure stagflation. Here are some excerpts from his first economic message to Congress:

> I believe these proposals will put the Nation on a fundamentally different course — a course leading to less inflation, more growth, and a brighter future for all. . . .
>
> The new policy is based on the premise that . . . government (should) provide a stable and unfettered environment in which private individuals can . . . make appropriate decisions. . . .
>
> As a result of the policies set forth here, our economy's productive capacity is expected to grow significantly faster than could be expected with a continuation of past policies. . . . Concurrently, the general rate of inflation is expected to decline steadily. . . .
>
> The economic assumptions contained in this message may seem optimistic to some observers. Indeed they do represent a dra-

matic departure from the trends of recent years — but so do the proposed policies.

SOURCE: *America's New Beginning: A Program for Economic Recovery*, White House economic paper, February 18, 1981, pages 1, 24, and 25.

policies he called "supply-side economics."[5] (See the boxed insert above.) And things did indeed change dramatically — though not always in the way President Reagan wanted.

Inflation fell remarkably from over 12 percent in 1980 to only about 4 percent in 1982, the lowest rate in a decade. But the economy did not perk up. Instead, it slumped into its worst recession since the Great Depression. By the time the 1981–1982 recession hit bottom, the unemployment rate was approaching 11 percent, the financial markets were in disarray, and the word "depression" had returned to the vocabulary of some economists.

Recovery from recession began in the winter of 1982–1983 and proceeded vigorously at first. With inflation still tame, proponents of what came to be called "Reaganomics" began to declare victory. But the pace of economic growth slowed markedly after mid-1984 and real GNP growth averaged just 2.8 percent over the ensuing three years. The unemployment rate fell rapidly in 1983, but only slowly thereafter. By mid-1987 it was still 6.1 percent.

The Problem of Macroeconomic Stabilization: A Sneak Preview

This brief look at the historical record shows that our economy has not generally produced a steady pattern of growth without inflation. Rather, it has been buffeted by periodic bouts of unemployment or inflation, and sometimes has

[5]Supply side economics is discussed further in Chapter 12.

been plagued by both. There was also a hint, in the discussion, that government policies may have had something to do with why macroeconomic performance during the years 1946 to 1973 was so vastly superior to what it had been prior to World War II. Let us now expand upon this hint a little bit.

We can provide a preliminary analysis of **stabilization policy,** the name given to government programs designed to prevent or shorten recessions and to counteract inflation, by using the basic tools of aggregate supply and aggregate demand analysis. To facilitate this, we have reproduced as Figures 5–5 and 5–6 two of the diagrams found earlier in this chapter [Figures 5–1(b) and 5–2], but we now give them slightly different interpretations.

Figure 5–5 gives a simplified view of government policy to fight unemployment. We suppose that, in the absence of government intervention, the economy would reach an equilibrium at point E, where demand curve $D_0 D_0$ crosses supply curve SS. Now if the output corresponding to point E is so low that many workers are unemployed, *the government can reduce unemployment if it can increase aggregate demand*. Chapter 12 will consider in detail how the government might try to do this. In the diagram, such an action would shift the demand curve to $D_1 D_1$, causing equilibrium to move to point A. In general:

Recessions and unemployment are often caused by insufficient aggregate demand. When this is so, government policies that successfully augment demand—such as increases in government spending—can be an effective way to increase output and reduce unemployment.

The opposite type of demand management is often called for when inflation is the main macroeconomic problem. Figure 5–6 illustrates this case. Here again, point E, the intersection of demand curve $D_0 D_0$ and supply curve SS, is the equilibrium that would be reached in the absence of government policy. But now we suppose that the price level corresponding to point E is considered "too high," meaning that the *change* in the price level from the previous period to this one would be too rapid if the economy moved to point E. A government program that reduces demand from $D_0 D_0$ to $D_2 D_2$ (for example, a reduction in government spending) can keep prices down and thereby reduce inflation. Thus:

Stabilization policy is the name given to government programs designed to prevent or shorten recessions and to counteract inflation (that is, to *stabilize* prices).

Figure 5–5
STABILIZATION POLICY TO FIGHT UNEMPLOYMENT
This diagram duplicates Figure 5–1(b), but here we assume that Point E — the intersection of demand curve $D_0 D_0$ and supply curve SS — corresponds to high unemployment. With the kind of policy tools that we will study in later chapters, the government can shift the aggregate demand curve outward to $D_1 D_1$. This would raise output and lower unemployment.

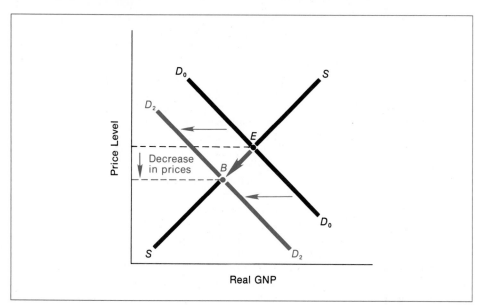

Figure 5–6
STABILIZATION POLICY
TO FIGHT INFLATION
This diagram duplicates
Figure 5–2, but here we
assume that point E — the
equilibrium the economy
would attain without
government
intervention — represents
high inflation (that is, the
price level corresponding to
point E is far above last
year's price level). By using
its policy instruments to shift
the aggregate demand curve
inward to $D_2 D_2$, the
government can keep this
year's price level lower than it
would otherwise have been;
in other words, the
government can reduce
inflation.

Inflation is frequently caused by aggregate demand racing ahead too fast. When this is the case, government policies that reduce aggregate demand can be effective anti-inflationary devices.

This, in brief, summarizes the intent of stabilization policy. When demand behavior is the source of economic instability, the government can limit both recessions and inflations by managing aggregate demand, pushing it ahead when it would otherwise lag, and restraining it when it would otherwise grow too quickly.

Sound simple? It's not. In reality, managing aggregate demand is a lot more complicated — both economically and politically — than shifting around lines on graphs with pencil and paper. We will spend much of Parts 3 and 4 examining the methods of demand management and learning why these methods do not always lead to the results that policymakers hope for.

In addition, the economy is sometimes plagued by both unemployment and inflation *at the same time*. In this case, the tools of demand management, even if wielded with great precision, are simply not up to the task. In Part 4 we will see why demand management is not enough and study some suggestions for dealing with unemployment and inflation at the same time.

Summary

1. Microeconomics studies the decisions of individuals and firms, how these decisions interact, and how they influence the allocation of society's resources and the distribution of income. Macroeconomics looks at the behavior of entire economies and studies the pressing social problems of inflation and unemployment.

2. While their respective subject matters differ greatly, the basic tools of microeconomics and macroeconomics are virtually identical. Both rely on the supply and demand analysis introduced in Chapter 4.

3. Macroeconomic models use abstract concepts like "the price level" and "national product" that are derived by amalgamating many different markets into one. This process is known as aggregation; it should not be taken literally but should be viewed as a useful approximation.

4. The best specific measure of the abstract concept "national product" is the gross national product (GNP), which is obtained by adding up the money values of all final goods and services produced in a given year. These outputs can be evaluated at current market prices (to get nominal GNP) or the prices of some previous year (to get real GNP). Neither intermediate goods nor transactions that take place outside organized markets are included in GNP.

5. The GNP is meant to be a measure of the *production* of the economy, not of the increase in its *well-being*. For example, the GNP places no value on housework and other do-it-yourself activities, nor on leisure time. On the other hand, even commodities that might be considered as "bads" rather than "goods" are counted in the GNP (for example, activities that harm the environment).

6. America's economic history is one of growth punctuated by periodic recessions; that is, periods in which real GNP declined. While the distant past included some periods of falling-prices (deflation), more recent history shows only rising prices (inflation).

7. The Great Depression of the 1930s was the worst in our country's history. It had profound effects both on our nation and on countries throughout the world and led also to a revolution in economic thinking, thanks to the work of John Maynard Keynes.

8. From World War II to the early 1970s, the American economy exhibited much steadier growth than it had in the past. Many observers attribute this to the implementation of the economic policies that Keynes suggested. At the same time, however, the price level seems only to rise, never to fall, in the modern economy. The economy seems to have become more "inflation prone."

9. During the 1970s and early 1980s the U.S. economy suffered through several serious recessions. At the same time, inflation was unusually virulent. This unhappy combination of economic stagnation with rapid inflation was nicknamed "stagflation."

10. One major cause of inflation is that aggregate demand may grow more quickly than aggregate supply. In such a case, a government policy that reduces aggregate demand may be able to check the inflation.

11. Similarly, recessions often occur because aggregate demand grows too slowly. In this case, a government policy that stimulates demand may be an effective way to fight the recession.

Concepts for Review

Microeconomics
Macroeconomics
National product
Aggregation
Aggregate demand and aggregate supply curves

Inflation
Deflation
Recession
Gross national product (GNP)
Nominal versus real GNP

Final goods and services
Intermediate goods
Stagflation
Stabilization policy

Questions for Discussion

1. Which of the following problems are likely to be studied by a microeconomist and which by a macroeconomist?
   a. The allocation of a university's limited budget.
   b. Why the Great Depression lasted so long.
   c. Why Japan's economy grows faster than the United States' economy, while Britain's grows slower.
   d. Why IBM sells more computers than Apple.

2. You probably use "aggregates" frequently in everyday discussions. Try to think of some examples. (Here is one: Have you ever said, "The student body at this college generally..."? What, precisely, did you mean?)

3. Use an aggregate supply and demand diagram to study what would happen to an economy in which the aggregate demand curve never moved while the aggregate supply curve shifted outward year after year.

4. Try asking a friend who has not studied economics in which year he or she thinks prices were higher: 1870 or 1900? 1920 or 1940? (In both cases, prices were higher in the earlier year.) Most people your age think that prices have always risen. Why do you think they have this opinion?

5. When were the two worst recessions of the past 60 years?

6. Which of the following transactions are included in the gross national product, and by how much does each raise GNP?
   a. Smith pays a carpenter $6000 to build a garage.
   b. Smith purchases $1000 worth of lumber and materials and builds himself a garage, which is worth $6000.

c. Smith goes to the woods, cuts down a tree, and uses the wood to build himself a garage that is worth $6000.

d. The Jones family sells its old house to the Reynolds family for $100,000. The Joneses then buy a newly constructed house from a builder for $150,000.

e. Your university purchases a used computer from another university, paying $400,000.

f. Your university purchases a new mainframe computer from IBM, paying $2 million.

g. You lose $200 in an Atlantic City casino.

h. You lose $200 in the stock market.

i. You sell a used economics textbook to your college bookstore for $15.

j. You buy a new economics textbook from your college bookstore for $20.

7. Give some reasons why the gross national product is not a suitable measure of the well-being of the nation. (Have you noticed newspaper accounts in which journalists seem to use GNP for this purpose?)

6

Macroeconomic Maladies: Unemployment and Inflation

When men are employed, they are best contented.

BENJAMIN FRANKLIN

Inflation is repudiation.

CALVIN COOLIDGE

Among the many trials faced by Odysseus, the hero of Homer's *Odyssey*, one of the most difficult was to steer his fragile boat through a narrow strait. On one side lay the rock of the monster Scylla, which threatened to break his craft into pieces, and on the other was the menacing whirlpool of Charybdis. The makers of national economic policy face a similarly difficult task in trying to chart a middle course between the Scylla of unemployment and the Charybdis of inflation. If they steer the economy far from the rocks of unemployment, they run the risk of being swept up in the swift currents of inflation. But if they maintain a safe distance from inflation, they may smash against the rocks of unemployment.

In Parts 3 and 4 we will explain how economic planners attempt to strike a balance between high employment and low inflation, why these goals cannot be attained with machinelike precision, and why improvement on one front generally spells deterioration on the other. A great deal of attention will be paid to the *causes* of inflation and unemployment.

But before getting involved in such weighty issues of theory and policy, we pause in this chapter to take a close look at the twin evils themselves: Why is it that a rise in unemployment is generally considered bad news? Why is inflation so loudly deplored? Can we measure the costs of unemployment and inflation? The answers to some of these questions may at first seem obvious, but we will see that there is more to them than meets the eye.

The chapter is divided into two parts. The first deals with unemployment. After a few words on the human costs of high unemployment, we explain how government statisticians measure unemployment and consider how the elusive concept of "full employment" can be defined. We turn next to our country's system of unemployment insurance, and we conclude by investigating—and quantifying—the economic losses associated with unemployment.

In the second part of the chapter, we turn to inflation. We begin by exploding some persistent myths about inflation, myths that help explain why inflation is so universally deplored. But the costs of inflation are not all mythical. The first real cost we consider is how and why inflation redistributes income and wealth from one group of people to another. Next, we learn how certain laws make inflation impose heavy economic costs that could be avoided if the laws were written differently. This leads us to one of our **12 Ideas for Beyond the Final Exam** mentioned in Chapter 1. We shall see that it is the failure to understand the effect of inflation on interest rates that explains the existence of some of these laws and accounts for other costs of inflation as well. Finally, we define and analyze the difference between creeping and galloping inflation and explode another myth about inflation: the myth that creeping inflation always leads to galloping inflation. An appendix explains how inflation is measured.

The Costs of Unemployment

The human costs of unemployment are probably sufficiently obvious. Years ago, loss of a job meant not only enforced idleness and a catastrophic drop in income, it often led to hunger, cold, ill health, and even death. This is the way one unemployed worker during the Great Depression described his family's plight in a mournful letter to the governor of Pennsylvania:

I have six little children to take care of. I have been out of work for over a year and a half. Am back almost thirteen months and the landlord says if I don't pay up before the 1 of 1932 out I must go, and where am I to go in the cold winter with my children? If you can help me please for God's sake and the children's sakes and like please do what you can and send me some help, will you, I cannot find any work. I am willing to take any kind of work if I could get it now. Thanksgiving dinner was black coffee and bread and was very glad to get it. My wife is in the hospital now. We have no shoes to were [sic]; no clothes hardly. Oh what will I do I sure will thank you. [1]

Nowadays, unemployment does not have such dire consequences for most families, although it still holds these terrors for some. Part of the sting has been taken out of temporary unemployment by our system of unemployment insurance (discussed below), and there are other social welfare programs to support the incomes of the poor (see *Microeconomics* Chapter 21). Yet most families still suffer a painful loss of income when their breadwinner becomes unemployed.

Even families that are well protected by unemployment compensation suffer when joblessness strikes. Ours is a work-oriented society. A man's "place" has always been in the office or factory or shop, and lately this has become increasingly true for women as well. A worker forced into idleness by a recession endures a psychological cost that is no less real for our inability to measure it. Martin Luther King put it graphically: "In our society, it is murder, psychologically, to deprive a man of a job... You are in substance saying to that man that he has no right to exist." [2] High unemployment has been linked to higher incidence of certain types of crimes, psychological disorders, divorces, suicides, and the like.

Nor are the costs only psychological. Accumulated work experience is a valuable asset. When forced into idleness, workers not only cease accumulating experience, but lengthy periods of unemployment may make them "rusty," and thus less productive when they are reemployed. Short periods of unemployment exact different kinds of costs. A record of steady employment is important in

---

[1] From *Brother, Can You Spare a Dime? The Great Depression 1929–1933*, by Milton Meltzer, page 103. Copyright © 1969 by Milton Meltzer. Reprinted by permission of Alfred A. Knopf, Inc.
[2] Quoted in Coretta Scott King (ed.), *The Words of Martin Luther King* (New York: Newmarket Press, 1983), page 45.

applying for a new job. And a worker who has frequently been laid off will lack this record of reliability.

It is important to realize that these costs, whether large or small in total, are distributed most unevenly across the population. At the bottom of the severe recession of 1981–1982, the **unemployment rate** among all workers approached 11 percent, a shockingly high figure. But over 16 percent of blue-collar workers were unemployed, as were 19 percent of nonwhite workers. For teen-agers the situation was worse still, with unemployment above 24 percent, and that of nonwhite teen-agers above 44 percent. Married men had the lowest rate—about 8 percent. Although all these rates were unusually high, the relations among them are typical:

In good times and bad, married men suffer the least unemployment and teen-agers suffer the most; nonwhites are unemployed much more often than whites; blue-collar workers have above-average rates of unemployment; and well-educated people have below-average unemployment rates.

Counting the Unemployed: The Official Statistics

The Bureau of Labor Statistics (BLS) is responsible for measuring unemployment. How do they do it? How accurate are their measurements?

The BLS's basic method for counting the unemployed is quite direct: it asks people. Specifically, a survey of over 50,000 households is conducted each month. The census-taker asks several questions about the employment status of each member of the household. On the basis of these answers, each person is categorized as being *employed, unemployed,* or *not in the labor force*.

The first category is simplest to define. It includes everybody currently working at a job, including part-time workers. Although some part-time workers work less than a full week because they choose to, others do so only because they cannot find a suitable full-time job. Nevertheless, these workers are not considered unemployed, though many would consider them "underemployed."

The second category is a bit trickier. For those not currently working, the BLS first determines whether they are temporarily laid off from a job to which they expect to return. If so, they are counted as unemployed. The remaining workers are asked whether they actively sought work during the previous week. If they did, they are also counted as unemployed. But if they did not, they are classified as *out of the labor force*; that is, since they failed to look for a job they are not considered unemployed.

This seems a reasonable way to draw the distinction—after all, we would not want to count all college students who work during the summer months as unemployed between September and May. Yet, there is a problem: Research has shown that many unemployed workers give up looking for jobs after a time. These so-called **discouraged workers** are victims of poor job prospects, just like the officially unemployed. Ironically, when they give up hope, the official unemployment statistics decline! Some critics have therefore argued that an estimate should be made of the number of discouraged workers and that these people should be added to the roles of the unemployed. In 1986 the BLS estimated that about 1 million workers fell into this category.

Involuntary part-time work, loss of overtime or shortened work hours, and discouraged workers are all examples of "hidden" or "disguised" unemployment. And those who are concerned about these phenomena argue that we should include them in the official unemployment rate because, if we do not, the magnitude of the problem will be *underestimated*.

The **unemployment rate** is the number of unemployed people, expressed as a percentage of the **labor force**.

The **labor force** is the number of people holding or seeking jobs.

A **discouraged worker** is an unemployed person who gives up looking for work and is therefore no longer counted as part of the labor force.

There is, however, an opposing school of thought that argues that the official unemployment rate really *overestimates* the unemployment problem. First, they argue, the unemployment rate of 1988 is not directly comparable to the unemployment rate of, say, 1958 because the composition of the labor force has changed dramatically over these years. Specifically, a larger fraction of all workers are young and female today than was the case 30 years ago. These groups have always had higher rates of unemployment than adult males. Therefore, even if adult men, adult women, and teen-agers each had the *same* unemployment rates in 1988 that they had in 1958, the unemployment rate for the entire population would have been higher in 1988 than in 1958.[3] Second, they argue, to count as unemployed, a person need only *say* that he is looking for work, even if he is not really interested in finding a job. No one knows to what extent the unemployment problem is overstated on account of this, but some think that it may be considerable.

Types of Unemployment

Providing jobs for those willing to work is one principal goal of macroeconomic policy. How are we to define this goal? One clearly *incorrect* answer would be "a zero measured unemployment rate." Ours is a dynamic and highly mobile economy. Households move from one state to another. Individuals quit jobs to look for better positions or to retool for more attractive occupations. These phenomena, and many more, produce some minimal amount of unemployment—people who literally are *between* jobs. Economists call this the level of **frictional unemployment**.

The critical distinguishing feature of frictional unemployment is that it is short-lived. A frictionally unemployed person has every reason to expect to find a new job soon. People tend to think of frictional unemployment as irreducible, but that is not the case. During World War II, for example, unemployment in this country fell below 2 percent—substantially below the frictional level.

Frictional unemployment is irreducible only in the sense that—under normal circumstances—it is socially undesirable to reduce it. Geographical and occupational mobility play important roles in our market economy—enabling people to search for better jobs. Similarly, waste is avoided by allowing inefficient firms, or firms producing items no longer in demand, to be replaced by new firms. Inhibition of either of these phenomena must hamper the workings of the market economy. But, if these adjustment mechanisms are allowed to operate, there will always be some temporarily unemployed workers looking for jobs just as there will always be some firms with unfilled positions looking for workers. This is the genesis of frictional unemployment.

A second type of unemployment is often difficult to distinguish from frictional unemployment, but it has very different implications. **Structural unemployment** arises when jobs are eliminated by changes in the structure of the economy, such as automation or permanent changes in demand. The crucial difference between frictional and structural unemployment is that, unlike a frictionally unemployed worker, a structurally unemployed worker cannot realistically be considered "between jobs." Instead, he may find his skills and experience unwanted in the changing economy in which he lives. He is thus faced with either a prolonged period of unemployment or the necessity of

Frictional unemployment is unemployment that is due to the normal workings of the labor market. It includes people who are temporarily between jobs because they are moving or changing occupations, or for similar reasons.

Structural unemployment refers to workers who have lost their jobs because they have been displaced by automation, because their skills are no longer in demand, or for similar reasons.

---

[3] If you do not understand why, consider the following analogy. Suppose your college class contains a mixture of "A" students and "C" students. If, between your freshman year and your senior year, more "C" students enter the class as transfers from other colleges, your class's overall grade point average will decline even if every student earns the same grades as a senior that he or she did as a freshman.

Cyclical unemployment is the portion of unemployment that is attributable to a decline in the economy's total production. Cyclical unemployment rises during recessions and falls as prosperity is restored.

making a major change in his occupation. For older workers, learning a new occupation may be nearly impossible.

The remaining type of unemployment, **cyclical unemployment,** will occupy our attention most in this book. Cyclical unemployment arises when the level of economic activity declines. Whenever the unemployment rate rises ominously or falls precipitously, the data are almost certainly reflecting changes in cyclical unemployment.

How Much Employment Is "Full Employment"?

Which of these types of unemployment is considered unavoidable — even under "full employment"? The **Employment Act of 1946,** the landmark piece of legislation in which the U.S. government first committed itself to maintain "conditions under which there will be afforded useful employment opportunities ... for those able, willing and seeking to work," was interpreted as a call to hold unemployment close to the frictional level. How much was that? During the prosperous years of the late 1940s and early 1950s, unemployment rates were consistently below 4 percent, dropping as low as 2.9 percent during the Korean War. This led President John F. Kennedy, in 1961, to select a 4 percent unemployment rate as an "interim target." The federal government was, for the first time, committed to a numerical goal.

Starting from a 6.7 percent rate in 1961, unemployment was eroded, more or less steadily, to 3.8 percent in 1966 — surpassing the interim target. Then the additional military spending for the Vietnam War pushed unemployment down still further. The unemployment rate reached 3.5 percent in 1969.

During the 1970s, the 4 percent goal posted by President Kennedy's New Frontier was rejected as being outmoded, although no new numerical target was put in its place. There were several reasons for this rejection of 4 percent.

First, some economists argued that the 4 percent target set during the Kennedy administration had to be adjusted upward for the early and middle 1970s because of the changed composition of the labor force that we have just mentioned. Second, they suggested, the increased generosity of unemployment compensation had reduced any individual's incentive to get himself off the unemployment rolls. Why work if unemployment benefits and other programs provide an income nearly as large as the salary one could earn on the job? This lack of work incentives made 4 percent unemployment much harder to achieve. Finally, these economists claimed, substantial increases in the federal minimum wage during the 1970s made it harder to employ teen-agers and other workers whose productivity was low. If, for example, their productivity was below the legal minimum wage, who would hire them?[4]

The last half of the 1970s saw considerable debate, both in government and in academia, over exactly how much measured unemployment corresponded to full employment. As is so often the case, actual events helped to settle the argument. Throughout 1978 and 1979, the measured unemployment rate hovered near 6 percent and the economy looked to be operating at approximately normal rates. Thus, by the early 1980s, many economists came to believe that **full employment** meant an unemployment rate close to 6 percent. But some felt it might be lower and others thought it was much higher — closer to the 7 percent rates that have prevailed from late 1984 into 1986. The definition of "full employment" remains controversial.

[4]For a full discussion of minimum wage laws, including their effect on unemployment, see *Microeconomics* Chapter 20.

Unemployment Insurance: The Invaluable Cushion

A surprising feature of the early 1980s was the equanimity with which the electorate tolerated high unemployment rates. One major reason for this was our system of **unemployment insurance.**

One of the most valuable pieces of legislation to emerge from the trauma of the Great Depression was the Social Security Act of 1935. Among other things, it established an unemployment insurance system which is now administered by each of the 50 states under federal guidelines. Thanks to this system, many—but, as we shall see, not all—American workers need never experience the complete loss of income that so many suffered during the 1930s.

While the precise amounts vary substantially, the average weekly benefit check to unemployed workers in 1986 was about $136. This amounted to about 45 percent of average earnings. Though a 55 percent drop in earnings still poses serious problems, the importance of this 45 percent income cushion can scarcely be exaggerated, especially since it may be supplemented by funds from other welfare programs. Families that are covered by unemployment insurance simply do not have to go hungry when they lose their jobs, and they are only rarely dispossessed from their homes.

Who is eligible to receive these benefits? Precise qualifications vary from state to state, but some stipulations apply quite generally. Only experienced workers qualify; so persons just joining the labor force (such as recent graduates of high schools and colleges) or reentering after a prolonged absence (such as women resuming work after years of child rearing) cannot collect benefits. Neither can those who have quit their jobs, except under unusual extenuating circumstances. You must be looking for work to qualify, and benefits end after a stipulated period of time. For all these reasons, only about one-third of the roughly 8.2 million persons who were unemployed during 1986 actually received benefits.

The importance of unemployment insurance to the unemployed is obvious. But there are also significant benefits to citizens who never become unemployed. During recession years many billions of dollars are paid out in unemployment benefits, and since recipients probably spend most of their benefits, unemployment insurance limits the severity of recessions by providing additional purchasing power when and where it is most needed.

The unemployment insurance system is one of several "cushions" that have been built into our economy since 1933 to prevent the possibility of another Great Depression. By giving money to those who become unemployed, the system helps prop up aggregate demand during recessions.

While the U.S. economy is now probably "depression proof," this should not be a cause for too much rejoicing, for the recessions of 1980 and 1981–1982 amply demonstrated that we are far from "recession proof."

The Economic Costs of High Unemployment

The fact that unemployment insurance and other social welfare programs replace a significant fraction of lost income has led some skeptics to claim that unemployment is no longer a serious problem. But the fact is that:

Unemployment insurance is just what the name says—an *insurance* program. And insurance can never prevent a catastrophe from occurring; it can only *spread the costs* of a catastrophe among many people instead of letting them all fall on the shoulders of those few unfortunate souls whom it affects directly.

Fire insurance is an example. If your family is covered by fire insurance and your house burns down, you will probably suffer only a small financial loss because the insurance company will pay most of the expenses. Where does it get the money? It cannot create it out of thin air. Rather, it must have collected the funds from the many other families who purchased insurance but did not suffer any fire damages. Thus, one family's loss of perhaps $80,000 is covered by the insurance payments of 400 families each paying $200 a year. In this way, the costs of the catastrophe are spread among hundreds of families, and in the process, made much more bearable.

But despite the insurance, the family whose house is destroyed by fire suffers anguish and inconvenience. No insurance policy can eliminate this. Furthermore, society loses a valuable resource—a house. It will take much wood, cement, nails, paint, and labor to replace the burnt-out home. *An insurance policy cannot insure society against losses of real resources.*

The case is precisely the same with insurance against unemployment. All workers and employers pay for the insurance policy by a tax that the government levies on wages and salaries. With the funds so collected, the government compensates the victims of unemployment. Thus, instead of letting the costs of unemployment fall entirely on the minority of workers who are out of work, the system of payroll taxes and unemployment benefits *spreads* the costs over the entire population. But it does not eliminate the basic economic cost.

When the economy does not generate enough jobs to employ all those who are willing to work, a valuable resource is lost. Potential goods and services that might have been enjoyed by consumers are lost forever. This is the real economic cost of high unemployment, and no insurance plan can eliminate it.

And these costs are by no means negligible. Table 6–1 summarizes the idleness of workers and machines, and the resulting loss of national output, for some of the years of lowest economic activity in recent decades. The second column lists the civilian unemployment rate, and thus measures unused labor resources. The third lists the percentage of industrial capacity that U.S. manufacturers were actually using, and thus indicates the extent of unused plant and equipment. And the fourth column is an estimate of how much more output (real GNP) could have been produced if these labor and capital resources had been fully employed.

Table 6–1
THE ECONOMIC COSTS OF HIGH UNEMPLOYMENT

YEAR	CIVILIAN UNEMPLOYMENT RATE (percent)	CAPACITY UTILIZATION RATE (percent)	PERCENTAGE OF REAL GNP LOST DUE TO IDLE RESOURCES
1958	6.8	75.0	4.2
1961	6.7	77.3	3.4
1975	8.5	72.3	5.3
1982	9.7	70.3	8.4
1983	9.6	74.0	7.6

SOURCES: Bureau of Labor Statistics; Federal Reserve System; and Robert J. Gordon, *Macroeconomics*, Fourth Edition (Boston: Little, Brown, 1987).

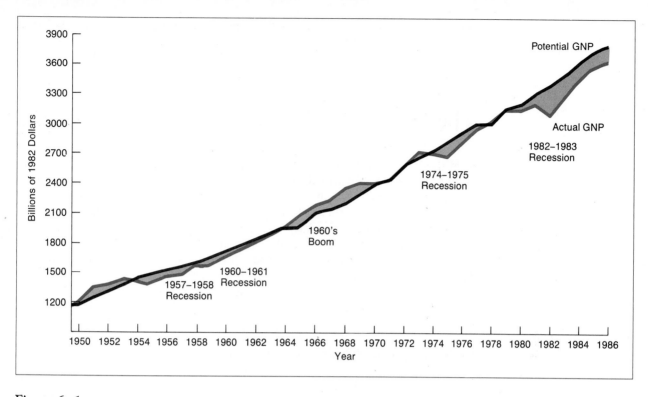

Figure 6–1

ACTUAL AND POTENTIAL GNP IN THE UNITED STATES, 1949–1986

This chart compares the growth of actual GNP (blue line) with that of potential GNP (black line). There have been two lengthy periods during which real GNP remained below its potential (1957–1963, and 1974 to the present), but only one lengthy period during which GNP remained above potential (1965–1970). The large shortfalls of GNP from potential in the 1980s stand out.

SOURCES: U.S. Department of Commerce and Robert J. Gordon, *Macroeconomics*, fourth edition (Boston: Little, Brown, 1987).

While these years are extreme examples, inability to utilize all of the nation's available resources has been a recurrent problem for our economy, especially in the 1980s. The blue line in Figure 6–1 shows the actual real GNP in the United States from 1949 to 1986, while the black line shows the real GNP we *could have* produced if "full employment" had been maintained. This last statement defines a concept called **potential GNP.** As our previous discussion of full employment pointed out, it *is* possible to push employment beyond its normal full employment level. This occurs whenever the unemployment rate dips below the "full employment unemployment rate"—a rate now thought to be 6 percent or so. Consequently, it *is* possible for actual GNP to exceed potential GNP. Figure 6–1 shows several instances where this happened. But it also shows, quite dramatically, that actual GNP has fallen short of potential GNP for most of the past dozen years—sometimes by huge amounts. In fact:

Potential gross national product is the real GNP the economy would produce if its labor and other resources were fully employed.

The cumulative gap between actual and potential GNP over the years 1974–1986 (all evaluated in 1982 prices) is an astounding $1577 billion. At 1988 levels of output, this loss in output as a result of unemployment would be almost five months' worth of production. And there is no way to redeem these losses. The labor wasted in 1985 cannot be utilized in 1989.

Those who argue that unemployment is nothing to worry about today because of unemployment insurance, or because unemployment is concentrated among certain kinds of workers (such as teen-agers), or because many unemployed workers become reemployed within a few weeks, should ponder

Figure 6–1. Is the loss of this much output really no cause for worry? Would these optimists react the same way if the government collected a fraction of the output of every factory in America and dumped it into the sea? Waste is waste no matter who ultimately pays the cost.

The Costs of Inflation

Both the human and economic costs of inflation are less obvious than the costs of unemployment. But this does not necessarily make them any less real, for if one thing is crystal clear about inflation, it is that people do not like it.

Public opinion polls consistently show that inflation ranks high on people's list of major national problems, generally even ahead of unemployment. Surveys also find that inflation, like unemployment, causes a deterioration in consumers' sense of well-being — it makes people unhappy. Finally, studies of voting behavior suggest that during congressional elections voters penalize the party that occupies the White House when inflation is high.

The fact is beyond dispute: People consider inflation to be something bad. Why?

Inflation: The Myth and the Reality

At first, the question may seem ridiculous. During times of inflation, people must keep paying higher prices for the same quantities of goods and services they had before. So more and more income is needed just to maintain the same standard of living. Is it not obvious that this erosion of **purchasing power** — that is, the decline in what money will buy — makes everyone worse off?

The **purchasing power** of a given sum of money is the volume of goods and services it will buy.

This would indeed be the case were it not for one very significant fact. The wages people earn are also prices — prices for labor services. During a period of inflation, wages also rise and, in fact, the average wage typically rises more or less in step with prices. Thus, contrary to popular myth, workers as a group are not usually victimized by inflation.

The **real wage rate** is the wage rate adjusted for inflation. It indicates the volume of goods and services that money wages will buy.

The purchasing power of wages — what is called the **real wage** — is not systematically eroded by inflation. Sometimes wages rise faster than prices, and sometimes prices rise faster than wages. The fact is that in the long run wages tend to outstrip prices as new capital equipment and innovation increase output per worker.

Figure 6–2 illustrates this simple fact. The blue line shows the annual rate of increase of consumer prices in the United States for each year since 1948, while the black line shows the annual rate of wage increase. The difference between the two indicates the rate of growth of *real* wages. Generally, wages rise faster than prices, reflecting the steady advance of technology and of labor productivity; so real wages rise. The years from 1974 to 1981 stand out as an unusual period in which real wages often did not rise. This single fact goes a long way toward explaining why people were so dissatisfied with economic performance when President Reagan took office.

The feature of Figure 6–2 that virtually jumps off the page is the way the two lines dance together. Wages normally rise rapidly when prices rise rapidly, and rise slowly when prices rise slowly. But you should not draw any hasty conclusions from this association. We cannot, for example, learn from this figure whether rising prices cause rising wages or whether rising wages cause rising

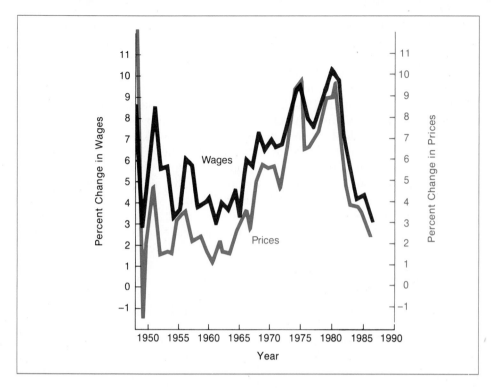

Figure 6–2
RATES OF CHANGE OF
WAGES AND PRICES IN
THE UNITED STATES,
1948–1986
This chart compares the rate
of price inflation (blue line)
with the rate of growth of
nominal wages (black line) in
the postwar period. The
patterns are clearly quite
similar, with wages and
prices normally accelerating
or decelerating together.
Notice that the traditional gap
between wage increases and
price increases did not
prevail in the middle and
late 1970s.
SOURCE: Bureau of Labor
Statistics.

prices. Remember the warnings given in Chapter 1 about trying to infer causation just by looking at data. But analyzing cause and effect is not our purpose right now. We merely want to explode the myth that inflation inevitably erodes real wages.

Why is this myth so widespread? Imagine a world without inflation in which wages are rising 2 percent a year because of the increasing productivity of labor. Now imagine that, all of a sudden, inflation sets in and prices start rising 4 percent a year but that nothing else changes. Figure 6–2 suggests that, with perhaps a small delay, wage increases will accelerate to 2 percent plus 4 percent, or 6 percent a year.

Will workers view this change with equanimity? Probably not. To each worker, the 6 percent wage increase will be seen as something he earned by the sweat of his brow. In his view, he *deserves* every penny of his 6 percent raise. And, in a sense, he is right because "the sweat of his brow" earned him a 2 percent increment in real wages that, when the inflation rate is 4 percent, can only be achieved by increasing his money wages by a total of 6 percent. An economist would divide the wage increase in the following way:

REASON FOR WAGE INCREASE	AMOUNT
Higher productivity	2%
Compensation for higher prices	4%
Total	6%

But the worker will probably keep score differently. Feeling that he earned the entire 6 percent by his own merits, he will view inflation as having "robbed" him of 4 percent of his just deserts. The higher the rate of inflation, the more of his raise the worker will feel has been stolen from him.

"Sure, you're raising my allowance. But am I actually gaining any purchasing power?"

Of course, nothing could be further from the truth. Basically, the economic system is rewarding the worker with *the same 2 percent real wage increment for higher productivity regardless of the rate of inflation*. The "evils of inflation" are often exaggerated because of a failure to understand this mechanism.

A second reason for misunderstanding the effects of inflation is that people are in the habit of thinking in terms of the number of dollars it takes to buy something rather than in terms of the *purchasing power* of these dollars. For example, if inflation doubles both prices and wages, workers will have to labor exactly the same amount of time as before to earn the price of a loaf of bread. But because they now pay $1 a loaf instead of 50 cents, they feel that the price of bread is scandalously high. In fact, nothing really has changed; but people cling to an outmoded idea of what bread *should* cost.

An item's **relative price** is its price in terms of some other item, rather than in terms of dollars.

A third misperception results from failure to distinguish between a *rise in the general price level* and a change in **relative prices,** that is, a rise in the price of one commodity relative to that of another. To see the distinction most clearly, imagine first a *pure inflation* in which *every* price rises by 10 percent during the year, so that relative prices do not change. Table 6–2 gives an example in which movie tickets go up from $4 to $4.40, candy bars from 50 cents to 55 cents, and automobiles from $8000 to $8800. After the inflation, just as before, it will still take 8 candy bars to buy a movie ticket, 2000 movie tickets to buy a car, and so on. A person who manufactures candy bars in order to purchase movie tickets is neither helped nor harmed by the inflation. Neither is a car dealer with a sweet tooth.

But real inflations are not like this. When there is 10 percent general inflation — meaning that the "average price" rises by 10 percent[5] — some prices may jump 20 percent or more while others actually fall. Suppose that, instead of the price increases shown in Table 6–2, prices rise as shown in Table 6–3. Movie prices go up by 25 percent, but candy prices do not change. Surely, candy manufacturers who love movies will be disgruntled because it now costs 10 candy bars instead of 8 to get into the theater. They will blame inflation for raising the price of movie tickets, even though their real problem stems from the *increase in the price of movies relative to candy*. (They would have been hurt as much if movie tickets had remained at $4 while the price of candy fell to 40 cents.)

[5]The way statisticians figure out "average" price increases is discussed in the appendix to this chapter.

Table 6–2

ITEM	LAST YEAR'S PRICE	THIS YEAR'S PRICE	PERCENT INCREASE
Candy bar	$0.50	$0.55	10
Movie ticket	4.00	4.40	10
Automobile	8000	8800	10

Table 6–3

ITEM	LAST YEAR'S PRICE	THIS YEAR'S PRICE	PERCENT INCREASE
Candy bar	$0.50	$0.50	0
Movie ticket	4.00	5.00	25
Automobile	8000	8400	5

Since car prices have risen by only 5 percent, theater owners in need of new cars will be delighted by the fact that an auto now costs only 1680 movie admissions (just as they would have cheered if car prices had fallen to $6720 while movie tickets remained at $4). However, they are unlikely to attribute their good fortune to inflation — as indeed they should not. What has actually happened.is that *cars became cheaper relative to movies*.

Because real-world inflation proceeds at *uneven* rates, relative prices are constantly changing. There are gainers and losers, just as some would gain and others lose if relative prices changed without any general inflation. Inflation, however, gets a bad name because losers often blame inflation for their misfortune while gainers rarely credit inflation for their good luck. Alas, nobody loves inflation.

These three kinds of misconceptions may go a long way toward explaining why respondents to public opinion polls consistently list inflation as a major national issue, why higher inflation rates depress consumers, and why voters express their ire at the polls when inflation is high.

Inflation does not systematically erode the purchasing power of wages. Nor does it lead to "unfair" prices. Nor is it usually to blame when some goods become more expensive relative to others.

But not all of the costs of inflation are mythical. Let us now turn to some of the real costs.

Inflation as a Redistributor of Income and Wealth

We have just seen that the *average* person is neither helped nor harmed by inflation. But almost no one is exactly average! Some persons gain from inflation and others lose. It is hard to say anything more systematic than this about the effects of inflation on particular prices and wages.

But inflation does have systematic effects on the distribution of income and wealth. Senior citizens trying to scrape by on pensions or other fixed incomes suffer badly from inflation. Since they earn no wages, it is little solace to them that wages are keeping pace with prices. Their pension incomes are not.[6]

This example actually illustrates a much more general problem. We can think of pensioners as people who "lend" money to an organization (the pension fund) when they are young in order to be "paid back" with interest when they are old. Because of the rise in the price level during the intervening years, the unfortunate pensioners get paid back in less valuable dollars than those they originally loaned. In general:

Those who lend money are usually victimized by rising inflation.

While lenders lose heavily, borrowers do quite well. For example, homeowners who borrowed money from banks in the form of mortgages back in the 1950s, when interest rates were 3 or 4 percent, gained enormously from the surprisingly virulent inflation of the late 1960s and 1970s. They paid back dollars

---

[6]This is not, however, true of recipients of social security. Social security benefits are financed out of tax revenues rather than directly through accumulated savings, and benefit levels are automatically increased to compensate recipients for changes in the price level. For further discussion of the social security system, see *Microeconomics* Chapter 17.

of much lower value than those that they borrowed. And the same is true of other borrowers.

Borrowers usually gain from rising inflation.

Since the redistribution caused by inflation generally benefits borrowers at the expense of lenders, and since both lenders and borrowers can be found at every income level, we must conclude that:

Inflation does not always steal from the rich to aid the poor, nor does it always do the reverse.

Why, then, is the redistribution caused by inflation so widely condemned? Because its victims are selected capriciously. Nobody legislates this redistribution. Nobody enters into it voluntarily. The gainers do not earn their spoils, and the losers do not deserve their fate. Moreover, there have been particular classes of people whom inflation has systematically robbed of purchasing power year after year — old-age pensioners, people who have saved money and "loaned" it to banks, and workers on long-term contracts or those whose wages and salaries do not adjust easily for some other reason. Even if people "on the average" suffer no damage from inflation, that offers little consolation to those who are hurt by it persistently and systematically. This is the fundamental indictment of inflation.

Inflation redistributes income in an arbitrary way that distorts society's distribution of income. The actual income distribution should reflect the interplay of the operation of free markets and the purposeful efforts of government to alter the distribution. Inflation interferes with and distorts this process.

Real Versus Nominal Interest Rates

But wait. Must inflation always rob lenders to bestow gifts upon borrowers? If both parties see inflation coming, won't lenders demand that borrowers pay a higher interest rate as compensation for the coming inflation? Indeed they will. For this reason, economists draw a sharp conceptual distinction between inflation that is *expected* and inflation that comes as a *surprise*.

What happens when inflation is fully expected by both parties? Suppose Diamond Jim wants to borrow $1000 from Scrooge, and both agree that, in the absence of inflation, which erodes the value of money, a fair rate of interest would be 3 percent on a one-year loan. This means that Diamond Jim would pay back $1030 at the end of the year for the privilege of having $1000 now.

If both expect prices to increase by 6 percent, Scrooge may reason as follows, "If Diamond Jim pays me back $1030 a year from today, that money will buy less than what $1000 buys today. Thus I'll really be *paying him* to borrow from me! I'm no philanthropist. Why don't I charge him 9 percent instead? Then he'll pay back $1090 at the end of the year. With prices 6 percent higher, this will buy roughly what $1030 is worth today. So I'll get the same 3 percent increase in purchasing power that we would have agreed on in the absence of inflation, and won't be any worse off. That's the least I'll accept."

Diamond Jim may follow a similar chain of logic. "With no inflation, I was willing to pay $1030 a year from now for the privilege of having $1000 today, and Scrooge was willing to lend it. He'd be crazy to do the same with a 6 percent inflation. He'll want to charge me more. How much should I pay? If I offer him $1090 a year from now, that will have roughly the same purchasing power as $1030 today, so I won't be any worse off. That's the most I'll pay."

This kind of thinking will lead Scrooge and Diamond Jim to write a contract with a 9 percent interest rate—3 percent as the increase in purchasing power that Diamond Jim pays to Scrooge and 6 percent as compensation for the expected inflation. Then, if the expected 6 percent inflation actually materializes, neither party will have been made better or worse off than was expected at the time the contract was signed.

This example illustrates a very general principle. The 3 percent increase in purchasing power that Diamond Jim agrees to hand over to Scrooge is called the **real rate of interest.** And the 9 percent contractual interest charge that Diamond Jim and Scrooge write into the loan agreement is called the **nominal rate of interest.** The nominal rate of interest is arrived at by adding the **expected rate of inflation** to the real rate of interest. Expected inflation is added to compensate the lender for the loss in purchasing power that he is expected to suffer as a result of inflation. Because of this:

Inflation that is accurately predicted need not redistribute income between borrowers and lenders. If the *expected* rate of inflation that is embodied in the nominal interest rate closely approximates the *actual* rate of inflation, no one gains and no one loses. However, to the extent that expectations prove incorrect, inflation will still redistribute income.[7]

It need hardly be pointed out that errors in predicting the rate of inflation are the norm, not the exception. Published forecasts bear witness to the fact that economists have great difficulty in predicting the rate of inflation. The task is no easier for businesses, consumers, and banks. This is one reason why inflation is so widely condemned as unfair and undesirable. It sets up a guessing game that no one likes.

Inflation and the Tax System

So inflation imposes costs on society because it is hard to predict. But there are other costs of inflation, perhaps even more serious, that arise from high inflation, even when inflation is predicted accurately. These costs stem from the fact that the laws and regulations that govern our financial system were designed for an inflation-free economy; and these laws may malfunction when inflation is high. The tax system is one important example.

Our tax law does not recognize the distinction between nominal and real interest rates. The law simply taxes nominal interest regardless of how much real interest it represents. As a result, strange things happen when there is high inflation. Our example of Scrooge's loan to Diamond Jim will illustrate the problem.

The top line of Table 6–4 shows how taxation affects the loan agreement when there is no inflation and the nominal and real interest rates are both 3 percent. Scrooge earns $30 in nominal interest income (column 3). Since there is no inflation, this also represents $30 in real interest income (column 5). If Scrooge pays one-third of his income in taxes, his tax bill rises by $10 (column 6), leaving him with $20 after tax (column 7). This $20 amounts to 2 percent of the $1000 originally loaned (column 8). Because his $10 tax payment is one-third of his $30 in real interest income, Scrooge's effective tax rate is $33\frac{1}{3}$ percent (column 9), just as Congress intended.

The **real rate of interest** is the percentage increase in purchasing power that the borrower pays to the lender for the privilege of borrowing. It indicates the increased ability to purchase goods and services that the lender earns.

The **nominal rate of interest** is the percentage by which the money the borrower pays back exceeds the money that he borrowed, making no adjustment for any fall in the purchasing power of this money that results from inflation.

[7]EXERCISE: Who gains and who loses if the inflation turns out to be only 4 percent instead of the 6 percent that Scrooge and Diamond Jim expected? What if the inflation rate is 8 percent?

Table 6–4
INFLATION AND THE TAXATION OF INTEREST INCOME

(1) INFLATION RATE (percent)	(2) NOMINAL INTEREST RATE (percent)	(3) INTEREST RATE (dollars)	(4) LOSS OF PURCHASING POWER DUE TO INFLATION (dollars)	(5) REAL INTEREST INCOME (dollars)	(6) TAXES PAID (dollars)	(7) REAL INCOME AFTER TAX (dollars)	(8) (as a percentage $1000 loan)	(9) EFFECTIVE RATE OF TAXATION (percent)
0	3	30	0	30	10	20	2%	33 1/3
6	9	90	60	30	30	0	0	100

Now let's consider the same transaction when the inflation rate is 6 percent and Scrooge and Diamond Jim settle on a 9 percent nominal interest rate. Scrooge collects $90 in interest (column 3). But, with 6 percent inflation, the purchasing power of the $1000 he lends declines by $60 (column 4). Thus his real interest income is again $30 (column 5). However, the tax collector taxes the $90 *nominal* interest income, not the $30 real interest income, so Scrooge must pay $30 (one-third of $90) in taxes (column 6). As we can see in column 7, his after-tax real income on the loan is zero since the tax collector takes all his real income. As column 9 shows, the effective tax rate on Scrooge's real interest income is thus 100 percent, far larger than the $33\frac{1}{3}$ percent rate intended by Congress.

So a tax system that works well at zero inflation misfires at 6 percent inflation because it taxes nominal, rather than real, interest. This little example illustrates a general, and very serious, problem:

Because it fails to recognize the distinction between nominal and real interest rates, our tax system levies high, and presumably unintended, tax rates on interest income when there is high inflation. And similar problems arise in the taxation of dividends, corporate profits, and other items.[8] Many economists feel that these high tax rates discourage saving, lending, and investing, and that high inflation therefore retards economic growth.

The Treasury Department's original tax reform package of 1984 proposed ways to correct most of these problems. But none of these proposals were included in the tax law that Congress passed in 1986. So the problems remain.

Usury Laws, Interest Rate Ceilings, and Other Impediments

A **usury law** sets down a maximum permissible interest rate for a particular type of loan. Loans at rates above the usury ceiling are illegal.

Another example of laws that malfunction under inflation is **usury laws,** which set *maximum* permissible interest rates on particular types of loans. Usury laws date back to biblical days and command rather widespread popular support. The problem is that they place ceilings on *nominal* interest rates, rather than on *real* interest rates and thus can have perverse effects in an inflationary environment.

In our previous example of Scrooge and Diamond Jim, suppose that a usury law sets a maximum rate of 8 percent on consumer loans. When he expects 6

[8]A particularly serious problem arises in the taxation of capital gains. (Capital gains are the difference between the price at which one sells an asset and the price at which one bought it.) In the United States, capital gains are taxed at their nominal values, without any adjustment for changes in their purchasing power resulting from inflation. An example will bring out the point. Between 1970 and 1980 the price level doubled, approximately. Consider some stock that was purchased for $5000 in 1970 and sold for $7500 in 1980. The investor would have lost purchasing power in the transaction because 7500 1980 dollars purchased less than 5000 1970 dollars. Yet, since the tax authorities do not correct for inflation, the investor will be forced to pay tax on the $2500 nominal capital gain as though there had been a profit rather than a loss.

percent inflation, Diamond Jim is willing to pay a 9 percent nominal interest rate and Scrooge is willing to lend at this rate. But the law intervenes. "Thou shalt not charge usurious interest." The deal cannot be completed, and both Diamond Jim and Scrooge go away disappointed.

The problem is that usury ceilings were set in periods of fairly steady prices, when there was no great difference between nominal and real interest rates. If, for example, the usury law had set the legal maximum at an 8 percent *real* rate of interest, it would not have prevented Scrooge from lending to Diamond Jim. As it is, however, a loan carrying a 3 percent real interest rate is perfectly legal at zero inflation but illegal at 6 percent inflation!

Usury laws set in nominal terms created so much havoc during the period of double-digit inflation in 1979–1980 that Congress took drastic action to eliminate them nationwide. Consequently, usury ceilings on interest rates are far less prevalent today than they were a decade ago.

Usury laws and problems with the tax system are just two examples of a general phenomenon:

Many of the laws that govern our financial system become extremely counter-productive in an inflationary environment, causing problems that were never intended by the legislators.

And it is important to note that *these are major costs of inflation that are not purely redistributive*. Society as a whole loses when mutually beneficial transactions are prohibited by law, when saving and investing are discouraged, when loans are not provided to those who need them, and when other useful acts are prevented by obsolete legislation.

Why do such laws stay on the books so long? One reason is a general lack of understanding of the difference between real and nominal interest rates. People seem not to understand that it is normally the *real* rate of interest that matters in an economic transaction because only that rate reveals how much borrowers pay (and lenders receive) *in terms of the goods and services which that money can buy*. They focus on the high nominal interest rates caused by inflation, even if these rates correspond to very low real interest rates. Here are some other examples that may help you appreciate how widespread and important this interest rate illusion is.

Interest Rate Regulations

Interest rate illusion is partly responsible for regulations that impose ceilings around 5 percent on interest paid on many bank accounts. Thus, *by government decree* small savers are condemned to earn *negative* real rates of interest during a period of rapid inflation.

Regulation of Public Utilities

During the early 1960s, when the rate of inflation averaged about $1\frac{1}{4}$ percent a year, interest rates on high-grade corporate bonds hovered just below $4\frac{1}{2}$ percent, yielding a real rate of interest of just over 3 percent. There were few public complaints suggesting that there was anything scandalous about such earning rates.

Yet during 1980 when the rate of inflation rose above 12 percent and corporate interest rates rose to perhaps 11 percent (a *negative* real rate of interest!), there was a public uproar. Regulated utilities, which asked the regulatory agencies to permit them a rate of return closer to 11 percent so that they could afford to borrow the money needed to serve expanding public demand, found that their requests were considered exorbitant by the commissons and by the general public. As a result, they failed to increase their capacities sufficiently.

Record Profit Rates

Amazingly, even business managers were subject to the same form of illusion. Often they were taken aback by the notion that their investors actually lost out (earned a negative *real* rate of return) when the company was earning a 10 percent profit. The managers noted that 10 percent was the company's highest earnings rate in recent history; but with inflation at 12 percent, it turned out that in real terms it was in fact the firm's lowest.

Thus, failure to understand that high *nominal* interest rates can signify low *real* interest rates has been known to impoverish savers during a period of inflation. It has made profits appear high when they were really low. It has sometimes made it impossible for electric companies and other public utilities to raise the capital they need to serve rising consumer demands, and power shortages and failures have been the predictable result.

The Illusion of High Interest Rates

The difference between real and nominal interest (and profit) rates, and the fact that the real rate matters more in terms of economic effects while the nominal rate is politically significant, are matters that are of the utmost importance and yet are understood by very few people, including many persons who make public policy decisions in these areas.

This concept is one of the **12 Ideas for Beyond the Final Exam,** and if you remember it ten years from now, you will truly have gotten a great deal out of studying economics.

Other Costs Of Inflation

Another cost of inflation is that rapidly changing prices make it risky to enter into long-term contracts. In an extremely severe inflation, the "long term" may be only a few days. But even moderate inflations can have remarkable effects on long-term loans. Suppose a corporation wants to borrow $1 million to finance the purchase of some new equipment and needs the loan for 20 years. If the inflation rate averages 4 percent over this period, the $1 million it repays at the end of 20 years will be worth $456,387 in today's purchasing power. If inflation averages 8 percent instead, it will be worth only $214,548. Lending or borrowing for this long a period is obviously a big gamble. With the stakes this high, the outcome may be that neither lenders nor borrowers want to get involved in long-term contracts. But without long-term loans, business investment becomes impossible. The economy stagnates.

Inflation also makes life difficult for the shopper. You probably have a group of stores that you habitually patronize because you know they generally carry the items you want to buy at (roughly) the prices you want to pay. This knowledge saves you a great deal of time and energy. But when prices are changing rapidly, your list quickly becomes obsolete. You return to your favorite clothing store to find that the price of jeans has risen drastically. Should you buy? Should you shop around at other stores? Will they have also raised their prices? Business firms have precisely the same problem with their suppliers. Rising prices force them to shop around more than they are accustomed to, which imposes costs on the firms and, more generally, reduces the efficiency of the whole economy.

Shopping costs may sound frivolous and unimportant, but they are not. Arthur Okun, who chaired the Council of Economic Advisers under President Johnson, suggested an ingenious mental exercise that illustrates the importance of shopping costs. Ask yourself the following question: How much would you have to be paid to promise never again to buy anything from any of the stores you have patronized in the past? When you ponder this for a while, you realize the great value of having normal places to shop. Inflation takes some of this value away.

Creeping Versus Galloping Inflation

The preceding litany of costs of inflation alerts us to one very important fact: *predictable inflation is far less burdensome than is unpredictable inflation*. When will an inflation be most predictable? When it proceeds year after year at more or less the same rate. Thus the *variability of the inflation rate* is a crucial factor. Inflation of 4 percent a year for three consecutive years will exact far lower social costs than inflation that is 2 percent in the first year, zero in the second, and 10 percent in the third. In general:

Steady inflation is much more predictable than variable inflation and therefore has much smaller social and economic costs.

But the *average level of the inflation rate* is also important. Partly because of the interest rate illusions mentioned above and partly because of the more rapid breakdown in normal customer relationships that we have just mentioned, a steady inflation of 6 percent a year is more damaging than a steady inflation of 4 percent a year.

Economists distinguish between **creeping inflations** and **galloping inflations** partly on their average level and partly on their variability. Under creeping inflation, prices rise for a long time at a moderate and fairly steady rate. Postwar Sweden provided a good example. During the 13-year period from 1954 to 1967, prices climbed a total of 64 percent (compared with only 24 percent in the United States), for an average annual inflation rate of 3.9 percent. And the pace of inflation was remarkably steady, rarely dropping below $2\frac{1}{2}$ percent or rising above 5 percent. Closer to home, though for a much shorter time, the U.S. inflation rate hovered near 4 percent during the years 1982–1985.

Galloping inflation refers to an inflation that proceeds at an exceptionally high rate, perhaps for only a relatively brief period. Germany after World War I suffered through one of the more severe inflations in history. Wholesale prices increased over 140 percent in 1921 and a colossal 4100 percent during 1922. At this point, what had been an impressive galloping inflation simply got out of control. Between December 1922 and November 1923, when a hard-nosed reform finally broke the inflationary spiral, wholesale prices in Germany increased by almost 100 million percent! But even this experience was dwarfed by the great Hungarian inflation of 1945–1946, the greatest inflation of them all. For a period of one year, the rate of inflation averaged about 20,000 percent *per month*. And in the final month, the price level skyrocketed 42 quadrillion percent!

While the distinction between creeping and galloping inflation is a quantitative one, we refrained from putting any specific numbers into the definitions. This is because different societies at different points in time hold very different conceptions of what rate constitutes creeping inflation and what rate

be able to differentiate

Creeping inflation refers to an inflation that proceeds for a long time at a moderate and fairly steady pace.

Galloping inflation refers to an inflation that proceeds at an exceptionally high rate, perhaps for only a relatively brief period. Galloping inflations are generally characterized by accelerating rates of inflation so that the rate of inflation is higher this month than it was last month.

These children in Germany during the hyperinflation of the 1920s are building a pyramid with cash, worth no more than the sand or sticks used by children elsewhere.

constitutes galloping inflation. For example, in the United States today, annual rates of inflation in the 2 to 5 percent range are generally considered to be "creeping," while rates in the 25 to 30 percent range would surely be construed as "galloping." In most Latin American countries, however, inflation consistently in the 25 to 30 percent range is viewed as "creeping." And in the United States of the 1950s, a 6 percent annual inflation might have been branded "galloping."

The Costs of Creeping Versus Galloping Inflation

If you review the costs of inflation that have been discussed in this chapter, you will see why the distinction beween creeping and galloping inflation is so fundamental. Many economists think we can live nicely, indeed can prosper, in an environment of creeping inflation. No one believes we can survive very well under galloping inflation.

Under creeping inflation, the rate at which prices rise is relatively easy to predict and to take into account in setting interest rates (as long as the law allows). Under galloping inflation, where prices are rising at ever-increasing rates, this is extremely difficult, and perhaps impossible, to accomplish. The potential redistributions become monumental, and as a result, lending and borrowing may cease entirely.

Any inflation makes it difficult to write long-term contracts. With creeping inflation, the "long term" may be 20 years, or 10 years, or 5. But with galloping inflation, the "long term" may be measured in weeks or even hours. Restaurant prices may change before you finish your dessert. Railroad fares may go up while you are in the middle of your journey. When it is impossible to enter into contracts of any duration longer than a few hours, economic activity becomes paralyzed. We conclude that:

The horrors of galloping inflation either are absent in creeping inflation or are present in such muted forms that they can scarcely be considered horrors.

Creeping Inflation Does Not Necessarily Lead to Galloping Inflation

We noted earlier that inflation is surrounded by a mythology that bears precious little relation to reality. It seems appropriate to conclude this chapter by disposing of one particularly persistent myth: that creeping inflation invariably leads to galloping inflation.

There is neither statistical evidence nor theoretical support for the myth that creeping inflation inevitably leads to galloping inflation. To be sure, creeping inflations sometimes accelerate. But at other times they slow down.

While creeping inflations have many causes, galloping inflations have occurred only when the government has printed incredible amounts of money, usually to finance wartime expenditures.

In the German inflation of 1923, the government finally found that its printing presses could not produce enough paper money to keep pace with the exploding prices. Not that it did not try. By the end of the inflation, the *daily* output of currency was over 400 quadrillion marks! The Hungarian authorities in 1945–1946 tried even harder. The average growth rate of the money supply was more than 12,000 percent *per month*. Needless to say, these are not the kind of inflation problems that are likely to face the United States in the foreseeable future.

But this should not be interpreted to imply there is nothing wrong with creeping inflation. Much of this chapter has been spent analyzing the very real costs of any inflation, no matter how slow. A case against even moderate inflation can indeed be built, but it does not help this case to shout foolish slogans like "Creeping inflation always leads to galloping inflation." Fortunately, it is simply not true.

Summary

1. Unemployment exacts heavy financial and psychological costs from those who are its victims, costs that are borne quite unevenly by different groups in the population.

2. Unemployment is measured by a government survey. Some critics claim that the survey methods understate the unemployment problem, while others contend that the methods overstate the problem.

3. Frictional unemployment arises when people are between jobs for normal reasons. Thus, most frictional unemployment is desirable.

4. Structural unemployment is due to shifts in the pattern of demand or to technological change that results in certain skills becoming obsolete.

5. Cyclical unemployment is the portion of unemployment that rises in recessions and falls when the economy booms.

6. The Employment Act of 1946 was widely interpreted as committing the government to limiting unemployment to the frictional variety. However, it set no numerical goals.

7. President Kennedy first enunciated the goal of 4 percent unemployment in 1961. But few economists think this is a realistic target for the 1980s. Many think that "full employment" now comes at an unemployment rate near 6 percent.

8. Unemployment insurance replaces nearly one-half the lost income of unemployed persons who are insured. But only about one-third of the unemployed collect benefits, and no insurance program can bring back the lost output that could have been produced had these people been working.

9. In recent decades, the U.S. economy often has produced less output than it could have were it operating at full employment. This shortfall has been particularly large since 1980.

10. People have many misconceptions about inflation. For example, many people believe that inflation systematically erodes real wages, are appalled by rising prices even when wages are rising just as fast, and blame inflation for any unfavorable changes in relative prices. All of these are myths.

11. Other costs of inflation are real, however. For example, inflation often redistributes income from lenders to borrowers.

12. This redistribution can be eliminated by adding the expected rate of inflation to the interest rate. But legal limitations sometimes prevent this, and expectations often prove to be inaccurate.

13. The real rate of interest is the nominal rate of interest minus the expected rate of inflation.

14. Since the real rate of interest indicates the command over real resources that the borrower surrenders to the lender, it is of primary economic importance.

15. Yet public attention often is riveted on nominal rates of interest, and this confusion can lead to costly policy mistakes when high inflation converts high nominal interest rates into very low real interest rates. This is one of the **12 Ideas for Beyond the Final Exam.**

16. Because nominal, not real, interest is taxed, our tax system levies heavy taxes on interest income when inflation is high.

17. Creeping inflation, which proceeds at moderate and fairly predictable rates year after year, carries far lower social costs than galloping inflation, which proceeds at high and variable rates.

18. The notion that creeping inflation inevitably leads to galloping inflation is a myth with no foundation in economic theory and no basis in historical fact.

Concepts for Review

Unemployment rate	Full employment	Real rate of interest
Labor force	Unemployment insurance	Nominal rate of interest
Discouraged workers	Potential GNP	Expected rate of inflation
Frictional unemployment	Purchasing power	Inflation and the tax system
Structural unemployment	Real wage	Usury laws
Cyclical unemployment	Relative prices	Creeping inflation
Employment Act of 1946	Redistribution by inflation	Galloping inflation

Questions for Discussion

1. Why is it not as terrible to become unemployed nowadays as it was during the Great Depression?

2. "Since unemployed workers receive unemployment benefits and other benefits that make up for most of their lost wages, unemployment is no longer a social problem." Comment.

3. Using what you learned about aggregate demand and aggregate supply in Chapter 5, try to explain why the U.S. economy has failed so frequently to produce up to its potential. (You will learn more about this question in later chapters, so don't worry if you find the question difficult now.)

4. Do you think that the Bureau of Labor Statistics overestimates or underestimates the number of people that are unemployed? Why?

5. Why is it so difficult to define "full employment"? What unemployment rate should the government be shooting for today?

6. Show why each of the following complaints is based on a misunderstanding about inflation:
   a. "Inflation must be stopped because it robs workers of their purchasing power."
   b. "Inflation is a terrible social disease. It leads to unconscionably high prices for basic necessities."
   c. "Inflation makes it impossible for working people to afford many of the things they were hoping to buy."
   d. "Inflation must be stopped today, for if we do not stop it, it will surely accelerate to ruinously high rates and lead to disaster."

7. What is the *real interest rate* paid on a loan bearing 16 percent nominal interest per year, if the rate of inflation is
   a. zero   d. 12 percent
   b. 2 percent   e. 18 percent
   c. 5 percent

8. Suppose you agree to lend money to your friend on the day you both enter college, at what you both expect to be a zero *real* rate of interest. Payment is to be made at graduation, with interest at a fixed *nominal* rate. If inflation proves to be *lower* during your four years in college than what you both had expected, who will gain and who will lose?

9. You have lived with inflation all your life. Think about the costs that inflation has imposed on you personally. How do these costs relate to the material in this chapter?

10. Add a third line to Table 6–4 showing what would happen if the inflation rate went to 12 percent and the real interest rate remained 3 percent.

Appendix
How Statisticians Measure Inflation

Index Numbers for Inflation

Inflation is generally measured by the change in some index of the general price level. For example, between 1973 and 1986, the Consumer Price Index (CPI), which stood at 100 in 1967, rose from 133.1 to 328.4, an increase of 147 percent. The meaning of the *change* is clear enough. But what is the meaning of the 133.1 figure for 1973 and the 328.4 figure for 1986?

These numbers are **index numbers,** each expresses the cost of a market basket of goods *relative to its cost in some "base" period*. Since the CPI uses 1967 as its base period, the CPI of 328.4 for 1986 means that it cost $328.40 to purchase the same basket of goods and services that cost $100 in 1967.

Now, the particular basket of consumer goods and services under scrutiny really did not cost $100 in 1967. When constructing index numbers, it is conventional to set the index at 100 in the base year. How is this conventional figure used in obtaining index numbers of other years? Very simply. Suppose the budget needed to buy the roughly 250 items included in the CPI was $500 per month in 1967 and $1642 per month in 1986. Then the index is defined by the following rule:

$$\frac{\text{CPI in 1986}}{\text{CPI in 1967}} =$$

$$\frac{\text{Cost of the 250-item market basket in 1986}}{\text{Cost of the 250-item market basket in 1967}}.$$

Since the CPI in 1967 is set at 100:

$$\frac{\text{CPI in 1986}}{100} = \frac{\$1642}{\$500} = 3.284$$

or

$$\text{CPI in 1986} = 328.4 \, .$$

Exactly the same sort of equation enables us to calculate the CPI in any other year. We have the rule:

CPI in given year =

$$\frac{\text{Cost of market basket in given year}}{\text{Cost of market basket in base year}} \times 100 \, .$$

Of course, not every combination of consumer goods that cost $500 in 1967 rose to $1642 by 1986. For example, a color TV set that cost $500 in 1967 might have sold for $450 in 1986, but a $500 hospital bill in 1967 might have ballooned to $3000. Since no two families buy precisely the same bundle of goods and services, no two families suffer precisely the same increase in their cost of living unless all prices rise at the same rate. Economists refer to this phenomenon as the **index number problem.**

When relative prices are changing, there is no such thing as a "perfect price index" that is correct for every consumer. Any statistical index will understate the increase in the cost of living for some families and overstate it for others. At best, the index can represent the situation of an "average" family.

The Consumer Price Index

The most closely watched price index is surely the **Consumer Price Index,** which is calculated and announced each month by the Bureau of Labor Statistics (BLS). When you read in the newspaper or see on television that the "cost of living rose by 0.4 percent last month," chances are the reporter is referring to the CPI.

The CPI is measured by pricing the items on a list representative of a typical urban household budget. To know what items to include and in what amounts, the BLS conducts an extensive survey of spending habits roughly once every decade (the last one was in 1982–1984). This means that the *same* bundle of goods and services is used as a standard for about 10 years, whether or not spending habits change.[9] Of course, spending habits do

[9]Economists call this a *base-period weight index,* because the relative importance it attaches to each price depends on how much money consumers actually chose to spend on it during the base period.

Table 6–5
RESULTS OF STUDENT EXPENDITURE SURVEY, 1983

ITEM	AVERAGE PRICE	AVERAGE QUANTITY PURCHASED PER MONTH	AVERAGE EXPENDITURE PER MONTH
Hamburger	$ 0.80	70	$ 56
Jeans	24.00	1	24
Movie ticket	5.00	4	20
		Total	$100

Table 6–6
PRICES IN 1988

ITEM	PRICE	PERCENTAGE INCREASE OVER 1973
Hamburger	$ 1.00	25
Jeans	24.00	0
Movie ticket	5.50	10

change; and this introduces a small error into the CPI's measurement of inflation.

A simple example will help us understand how the CPI is constructed. Imagine that college students purchase only three items — hamburgers, jeans, and movie tickets — and that we want to devise a cost-of-living index (call it SPI, for "student price index") for them. First we would conduct a survey of spending habits in the base year (suppose it is 1983). Table 6–5 represents the hypothetical results. You will note that the frugal students of that day spent only $100 per month: $56 on hamburgers, $24 on jeans, and $20 on movies.

Table 6–6 presents hypothetical prices of these same three items in 1988. Each price has risen by a different amount, ranging from zero for jeans up to 25 percent for hamburgers. By how much has the SPI risen? Pricing the 1983 student budget at 1988 prices, we find that what once cost $100 now costs $116, as the following calculation shows:

COST OF 1983 STUDENT BUDGET IN 1988 PRICES

70 hamburgers at $1	$70
1 pair of jeans at $24	24
4 movie tickets at $5.50	22
Total	$116

Thus the SPI, based on 1983 = 100, is

$$SPI = \frac{\text{Cost of budget in 1988}}{\text{Cost of budget in 1983}} \times 100$$

$$= \frac{\$116}{\$100} \times 100 = 116.$$

So the SPI in 1988 stands at 116, meaning that students' cost of living has increased 16 percent over the 5 years.

How to Use a Price Index to "Deflate" Monetary Figures

One of the most common uses of price indexes is in the comparison of monetary figures relating to two different points in time. The problem is that, if there has been inflation, the dollar is not a good measuring rod because it is worth less now than it was in the past.

Here is a simple example. Suppose that the average student spent $100 per month in 1983 and that this monthly spending figure had grown to $110 per month in 1988. If there was an outcry that students had become spendthrifts, how would you answer the charge?

The obvious answer is that a dollar in 1988 does not buy what it did in 1983. Specifically, our SPI shows us that it takes $1.16 in 1988 to purchase what $1 would purchase in 1983. To compare the spending habits of students in the two years, we must divide the 1988 spending figure by 1.16. Specifically, *real* spending per student in 1988 (where "real" is defined by 1983 dollars) is:

Real spending in 1988 =

$$\frac{\text{Nominal spending in 1988}}{\text{Price index of 1988}}.$$

Thus,

$$\text{Real spending in 1988} = \frac{\$110}{1.16} = \$94.83.$$

In sum, this calculation shows that, despite appearances to the contrary, the change in nominal spending from $100 to $110 actually represented a *decrease* in real spending.

This calculation procedure is called **deflating by a price index,** and it serves to translate noncomparable monetary figures into more directly comparable real figures.

Deflating is the process of finding the real value of some monetary magnitude by dividing by some appropriate price index.

A good practical illustration is the real wage, a concept we have discussed in this chapter. Average hourly earnings in the U.S. economy were $2.68 in 1967 and $8.76 in 1986. Since the CPI in 1986 was 328.4 (with 1967 as the base year), the real wage in 1986 (in 1967 dollars) was:

$$\text{Real wage in 1986} = \frac{\text{money wage in 1986}}{\text{price index of 1986}}$$

$$= \frac{\$8.76}{328.4} \times 100 = \$2.67$$

Thus, by this measure, the real wage was essentially the same in 1967 and 1986!

The GNP Deflator

In macroeconomics, one of the most important of the monetary magnitudes that we have to deflate is the nominal gross national product (GNP). The price index used to do this is called the **GNP deflator.** Our general principle for deflating a nominal magnitude tells us precisely how to go from nominal GNP to real GNP:

$$\text{Real GNP} = \frac{\text{Nominal GNP}}{\text{GNP deflator}} \times 100.$$

As with the CPI, the 100 simply serves to establish the base of the index as 100, rather than 1.00.

Economists often consider the GNP deflator to be a better measure of overall inflation in the economy than the Consumer Price Index. The main reason for this is that the two price indexes are based on different market baskets. As already mentioned, the CPI is based on the budget of a typical urban family. By contrast, the GNP deflator is constructed from a market basket that includes *every* item in the GNP—that is, every final good and service produced by the economy. Thus, in addition to prices of consumer goods the GNP deflator includes the prices of airplanes, lathes, and other goods purchased by business. It also includes government services. For this reason, the measures of inflation that these two indexes give are rarely the same. Usually their disagree-ments are minor. But sometimes they can be sub-stantial, as in 1979 when the CPI recorded a 13.3 percent inflation rate while the GNP deflator recorded only 8.9 percent.

Summary

1. Inflation is measured by the percentage increase in an index number of prices, which shows how the cost of some basket of goods has changed over a period of time.
2. Since relative prices are changing all the time, and since different families purchase different items, no price index can represent precisely the change in the cost of living for every family.
3. The Consumer Price Index (CPI) tries to measure the cost of living for an "average" urban household by pricing a "typical" market basket every month.
4. Price indexes like the CPI can be used to *deflate* monetary figures to make them more comparable. This amounts to dividing the monetary magnitude by the appropriate price index.
5. The GNP deflator is a better measure of economy-wide inflation than is the CPI because it includes the price of every good and service in the economy.

Concepts for Review

Index number
Index number problem

Consumer Price Index
Deflating by a price index

GNP deflator

Questions for Discussion

1. Just below you will find the amounts (in billions of dollars) that American consumers spent on various items in 1967 and in 1985. The Consumer Price Index in 1985 (on a base of 1967 = 100) was 322.2. Use this to deflate all the 1985 figures and to com-pare them with the 1967 figures. Which type of spending has grown most rapidly?

		ITEM	
YEAR	FOOD	GASOLINE AND OIL (billions of dollars)	HOUSING
1967	112.3	17.1	74.1
1985	469.3	91.9	403.3

2. Just below you will find nominal GNP and the GNP deflator for 1966, 1976, and 1986.
   a. Compute real GNP for each year.
   b. Compute the percentage change in nominal and real GNP from 1966 to 1976, and from 1976 to 1986.
   c. Compute the percentage change in the GNP deflator over these two periods.

	GNP STATISTICS		
	1966	1976	1986
Nominal GNP (billions of dollars)	772.0	1782.8	4235.0
GNP deflator	35.0	63.1	114.1

3. Fill in the blanks in the following table of GNP statistics.

YEAR	1984	1985	1986
Nominal GNP	3772.2		4235.0
Real GNP	3501.4	3607.5	
GNP deflator		111.2	114.1

4. Use the following data to compute the College Price Index for 1988, using the base 1972 = 100.

ITEM	PRICE IN 1972	QUANTITY PER MONTH IN 1972	PRICE IN 1988
Button-down shirts	$10	1	$22
Loafers	25	1	47
Sneakers	10	3	15
Textbooks	12	12	25
Jeans	12	3	36
Restaurant meals	5	11	12

5. Average hourly earnings in the U.S. economy dur-ing several past years were as follows:

1955	1965	1975	1985
$1.71	$2.76	$4.53	$8.57

Use the CPI numbers provided on the inside front cover of this book to calculate the real wage (in 1967 dollars) for each of these years. Which decade had the fastest growth of money wages? Which had the fastest growth of real wages?

6. The example in the appendix showed that the Student Price Index (SPI) rose by 16 percent from 1983 to 1988. You can understand the meaning of this better if you:

   a. Use Table 6–5 to compute the fraction of total spending accounted for by each of the three items in 1983. Call these the "expenditure weights."

   b. Compute the weighted average of the percentage increases of the three prices shown in Table 6–6, using the expenditure weights you have just computed.

   c. You should get 16 percent as your answer. This shows that "inflation," as measured by the SPI, is a weighted average of the percentage price increases of all the items that are included in the index.

7

Productivity, Progress, and Prosperity

Human history has never experienced anything like it. In the industrial countries, the quantity and quality of food, clothing, and comforts have reached levels that were never dreamed possible by earlier generations. The change has been so revolutionary that it is difficult to grasp its magnitude. This chapter helps us envision how great the accomplishment has been. It also suggests the source of the transformation: the fact that a person in the United States today can produce in an hour perhaps 20 times as much as was possible in 1800. Just two figures will suggest the magnitude of the achievement. In 1800 about 90 percent of America's labor force had to work on farms, and all that farm labor barely managed to produce enough food to provide adequate nutrition for the country. Today, in contrast, only about 3 percent of U.S. workers earn their living on farms. Yet those few farm workers provide an outpouring of surpluses which the U.S. government constantly struggles to contain.

Life in the "Good Old Days"

The United States, and the thirteen colonies before it, has always been a privileged land with relatively high levels of nutrition. In the eighteenth century, an average white, native-born male who reached the age of 10 could expect to live to somewhere between age 50 and 55. By contrast, an English *nobleman* at that time could expect to live only to something between age 39 and 46.

In the mid-nineteenth century, low incomes, local weather conditions, crop cycles, an almost complete lack of refrigeration, and limited transport of goods bound a large part of even the U.S. population to a minimal and nutritionally inferior variety of foods. Such uninspiring staples as potatoes, lard, cornmeal, and salt pork were the mainstays of diets, particularly outside the population centers. Most travelers' accounts of meals in nineteenth-century America mentioned the ubiquity of some kind of one-pot stew which constituted the main meal of the day for the family. According to one study, "There were, of course, a few people who knew what it was to . . . eat a meal that

The enormous wealth of Britain is attributable [primarily] to . . . the wonderful skill of her entrepreneurs . . . and the superiority of her workmen in rapid and masterly execution. . . . The English laborer . . . gives his work more care, attention and diligence, than the workmen of most other nations.

JEAN BAPTISTE SAY

Japan commercially, I regret to say, does not bear the best reputation for executing business. Inferior goods, irregularity and indifferent shipments have caused no end of worry . . . you are a very satisfied easy-going race . . . the habits of national heritage.

FROM A REPORT OF AN AUSTRALIAN EXPERT FOR THE JAPANESE GOVERNMENT, 1915 consisted of more than one course; but there were very, very few such people, and they were all very rich."[1]

Nevertheless, most Americans were right to feel that they lived in a land of unprecedented abundance, for that one-pot stew was quite sure to be there every day. For many centuries most Europeans had devoted nearly half their food budgets to breadstuffs; and, for most of them, the bread was of inferior quality. Often it took the form of gruel—what we would think of today as a cooked breakfast cereal—which was served in a single bowl with a single spoon, both of which were passed around the table to the entire family.

In bad years, even gruel was unavailable. Famine continued to threaten Europe until the beginning of the nineteenth century, and earlier it had constituted a normal fact of existence. One historian writes,

> . . . two consecutive bad harvests spelt disaster. . . . France, by any standards a privileged country, is reckoned to have experienced 10 general famines during the tenth century; 26 in the eleventh; 2 in the twelfth; 4 in the fourteenth; 7 in the fifteenth; 13 in the sixteenth; 11 in the seventeenth and 16 in the eighteenth.
>
> The same could be said of any country in Europe. In Germany, famine was a persistent visitor to the towns and the flatlands . . .
>
> . . . the countryside sometimes experienced far greater suffering. The peasants . . . had no solution in case of famine except to turn to the town where they crowded together, begging in the streets and often dying in public squares, as in Venice and Amiens in the sixteenth century.
>
> The towns soon had to protect themselves against these regular invasions. . . . Beggars from distant provinces appeared in the fields and streets of the town(s) . . . starving, clothed in rags and covered with fleas and vermin. [2]

Food shortages were not the only manifestation of unimaginably poor living conditions:

> [I]n Pescara on the Adriatic, a small town with about a thousand inhabitants, an inquiry in 1564 revealed that three-quarters of the families in the town . . . were virtually homeless, living in makeshift shelters. . . . In the very rich town of Genoa, the homeless poor sold themselves as galley slaves every winter. . . .
>
> The poor in the towns and countryside of [Europe] lived in a state of almost complete deprivation. Their furniture consisted of next to nothing, at least before the eighteenth century . . . only a few old clothes, a stool, a table, a bench, the planks of a bed, sacks filled with straw. Official reports for Burgundy between the sixteenth and the eighteenth centuries are full of "references to people [sleeping] on straw . . . with no bed or furniture" who were only separated "from the pigs by a screen." [3]

Even in the United States, living conditions in the nineteenth century were far from ideal. Most of the homes that travelers saw in rural America were tiny and crudely built, with no glass windows, no lighting except the fireplace,

[1] Ruth Schwartz Cowan, *More Work for Mother: The Ironies of Household Technology from the Open Hearth to the Microwave* (New York: Basic Books, 1983), Chapter 4.
[2] Fernand Braudel, *The Structures of Everyday Life: The Limits of the Possible*, vol. 1, *Civilization and Capitalism, 15th–18th Century* (New York: Harper and Row, 1979), pages 73–75 (footnotes omitted, Braudel's emphasis).
[3] *Ibid.*, pages 284–86.

no indoor plumbing, and scanty homemade furniture. Urban housing was not much better. In New York City in the 1860s, it was typical for six people to live in a ten-by-twelve room. In 1890 Jacob Riis wrote of the lower Manhattan tenements,

It is said that nowhere in the world are so many people crowded together on a square mile as here. In [one seven-story tenement building] there were 58 babies and 38 children that were over five years of age. . . . In Essex Street two small rooms in a six-story tenement were made to hold a "family" of father and mother, twelve children, and six boarders. . . .[4]

The worst evils of these overcrowded slums were insufficient light and air — narrow airshafts conveyed foul air and disease and served as inflammatory flues when fire broke out. There were no private water closets or washing facilities in these buildings, and cellars and courtyards were foul.

Like the common man, the rich have also gained much in terms of health and personal comfort in the course of two or three centuries. By the early 1900s, life expectancy at birth for a member of the British nobility had reached 65 years. But in the mid-sixteenth century, that figure was less than 40 years. More remarkable yet is the fact that longevity of the nobility in these centuries was no better than that of the population as a whole, despite the miserable living conditions of the bulk of the nation.

The dramatic improvement in the comforts enjoyed by the rich is illustrated by the development of home heating technology. The role of the draft in fireplace construction was not discovered until early in the eighteenth century. Until then, the huge fireplaces in the homes of the nobles, though beautiful, were extremely ineffective; they roasted nearby persons on one side and froze them on the other. Winter was a serious threat to rich and poor alike. "Cold weather . . . could be a public disaster, freezing rivers, halting mills [with little or no flour having been stored because preservation methods were largely unknown], bringing packs of dangerous wolves out into the countryside, multiplying epidemics."[5] Not even the highest nobility were spared. The Princess Palatine, the German sister-in-law of Louis XIV, reported that in February 1695 "in the Hall of Mirrors at Versailles at the King's table the wine and water froze in the glasses."[6]

Even the housing of relatively well-off nineteenth-century Americans (a very small proportion of the population) was still primitive by modern standards. Baths, for example, were rare even in the cities. No homes had electricity and few had gas. Fewer still had hot running water, and not even 2 percent had indoor toilets and cold running water. Boston, with a population of nearly 200,000 in 1860, had only 31,000 sinks, 4,000 baths, and 10,000 water closets — about half of which were extremely primitive affairs. Albany, with a population in 1860 of 62,000, had only 19 private baths and 160 water closets. Outdoor privies were the norm and baths, for the great majority, a luxury (and were still feared by many to be unhealthy).[7]

[4]Jacob Riis, *How the Other Half Lives* (New York: Hill and Wang, Inc., 1957), page 77. Originally published by Charles Scribner's Sons, New York, 1890.
[5]Braudel, page 299.
[6]*Ibid.* In 19th century rural America, it was not uncommon for ink to freeze in homes of people who were not wealthy.
[7]Edgar W. Martin, *The Standard of Living in 1860* (Chicago: University of Chicago Press, 1942).

Though living conditions were vastly improved from earlier centuries, by today's standards, life in the United States just 100 years ago was hard and primitive.

The Magnitude of Productivity Growth

Today, of course, things are vastly different. In 1980 only 2.2 percent of American housing units lacked complete plumbing—defined as hot and cold piped water, a flush toilet, and a bathtub or shower for the exclusive use of that housing unit. Only 4.5 percent were occupied by more than one person per room. Of the new, privately-owned, one-family houses built in 1981, fully 60 percent had three bedrooms, 46 percent had two bathrooms, and 65 percent had central air conditioning. And, 99.9 percent of all households had an electric vacuum cleaner, an electric toaster, a black and white television (89.8 percent had a color television), a radio, and an electric iron. Similarly, 99.8 percent were equipped with electric refrigerators, 92.8 percent had electric mixers, 77 percent had electric washing machines, 68 percent had electric frypans, 63.6 percent had electric can openers, and 64 percent had electric blankets![8]

This revolution in manner of living was made possible by an unprecedented rate of growth in human efficiency in producing output. Before reporting the facts, it is necessary to describe the two basic concepts, *labor productivity* and *output per capita*, usually employed to measure first, the productive efficiency of the working population, and second, the resulting average level of economic well-being.

Labor productivity refers to the amount of output a worker turns out in an hour (or a week or a year) of labor. It can be measured as total national output (GNP) in a given year divided by the total number of hours of work performed for pay in the country during that year. That is, labor productivity is defined as GNP per hour of labor.

Labor Productivity refers to the amount of output turned out by a *given* amount of labor. Obviously, an increase in productivity means that a human being has become a more effective instrument of production. This can be the result of harder work, better training, more or better equipment, innovative technology, or a variety of other causes.

The **standard of living,** on the other hand, is more naturally measured by **GNP per capita,** that is, by total output (GNP) divided by the number of persons among whom it will be distributed. The more output there is for each person, the better off in economic terms the average person must be.

The fantastic magnitude of the increases in both labor productivity and output per capita since, say, 1800 is best appreciated by contrasting it with the dismal average record of many previous centuries. In Europe, after a long decline, living standards had been increasing intermittently since the eleventh century—the century in which William the Conqueror acquired England. Yet, it is estimated that even by the time of the American Civil War neither labor productivity nor GNP per capita had yet reattained the levels that had been achieved in ancient Rome—about 16 centuries earlier! Thus, on the average, productivity and GNP per capita did not grow at all over 1600 years. Even for those wealthy enough to buy them, the number of important new consumer goods innovated in those 16 centuries was remarkably small. Firearms, glass windowpanes, eyeglasses, mechanical clocks, tobacco, and printed books constitute almost the entire list of major new consumer products invented between the fall of the Roman Empire and the beginning of the nineteenth century. Indeed, some significant amenities, notably elaborate bathing facilities and efficient home heating devices, had disappeared since the fall of Rome.

[8]U.S. Department of Commerce, Bureau of the Census, *Statistical Abstract of the United States, 1982–83* (Washington, D.C.: U.S. Government Printing Office, December 1982), pages 740, 754–55, 758.

In contrast, the period since, say, the 1830s has been characterized by an endless explosion of innovations. The railroad and the steamship revolutionized transportation. Steel-making technology changed drastically. The chemical industry was born and produced scores of new consumer products. The range of personal and household goods that we now take for granted—TV sets, dishwashers, cameras, automobiles, personal computers, and many, many others—appeared in an accelerating stream and became commonplace. This has reached a point where today our one unchanging expectation for the future is that it will be characterized by constant change.

Figure 7–1 shows, for five countries, the impressive growth of labor productivity over the past century. For example, it indicates that in this period Japanese productivity has risen about 2500 percent, French and German productivity levels each went up about 1500 percent, productivity in the United States increased about 1100 percent, and that even British productivity jumped by an astonishing 600 percent.

Figure 7–2 translates this productivity growth into the resulting rise in living standards—in national output per capita [**Gross Domestic Product (GDP)**].[9] In the countries shown, the number of hours worked per year has fallen significantly—by about 40 percent on the average. This is partly the result of a fall in work hours per day; typically from about 12 hours in 1870 down to some $7\frac{1}{2}$ hours per day in 1979. Also, the work week has declined from six days to five days. But most surprising is the almost total absence of any vacations for most of the population in 1870. The two- or four-week vacation is largely a twentieth-century invention—another luxury made possible by the rise in productivity. Largely because of this sharp fall in labor expended, output

[9]It should be noticed that the graphs measure outputs in terms of statistics on GDP (Gross Domestic Product) per capita. GDP, widely used by statisticians outside the United States, is a concept very similar to GNP. The former refers to all outputs produced within the geographic boundaries of a country, whether or not the producers were citizens of that country. GNP, in contrast, excludes all outputs produced by foreigners living or working in the country in question, and it includes outputs produced by citizens (nationals) of the country, even if they were working abroad.

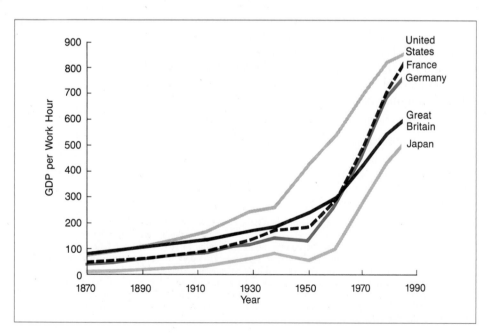

Figure 7–1
LABOR PRODUCTIVITY, 1870–1985
The productivity growth shown here for five industrial countries is typical of today's leading industrial economies. The explosive pattern of increase is unprecedented in previous history.
SOURCE: Angus Maddison, *Phases of Capitalist Development* (New York: Oxford University Press, 1982), page 8 and unpublished Maddison materials.

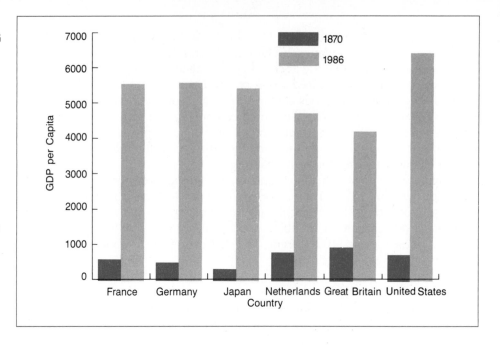

Figure 7–2
IMPROVEMENT IN LIVING STANDARDS, SIX COUNTRIES, 1870 VERSUS 1986
The graph shows how much higher GDP per capita is today than it was in 1870 in each of the six countries shown. The pattern is typical for free market industrialized countries. The numbers are in dollars adjusted to have roughly the same purchasing power in all countries and both dates listed.
Source: Angus Maddison, *Phases of Capitalist Development* (New York: Oxford University Press, 1982), page 8 and unpublished Maddison materials.

per person did not rise nearly as quickly as productivity. Yet the increases in output per person have also been spectacular. Over the 116-year period reported in the graph, output per person went up 1700 percent in Japan, 800 percent in Germany, 700 percent in the United States and France, and 300 percent in Great Britain.[10]

In other words, to take the U.S. case as an example, the average income of an American in 1870, measured in dollars of constant purchasing power, was only about one-eighth as large as it is today. To imagine what it is like to live with an income so small, one must go to *Egypt, Bolivia, or the Philippines*, whose per capita income today has been calculated to be on a par with that of an average American in 1870! Obviously, the rise in economic well-being of an average American, and of an average resident of the other countries in Figures 7–1 and 7–2, has been substantial. Indeed, it represents a rise to a standard of living a person in an earlier century can hardly have imagined.

Table 7–1 sums up the percentage increases since 1870 in **GDP per labor hour** and in **GDP per capita** for 16 leading industrialized countries. Obviously, the phenomenal growth in productivity and living standards extends to a considerable number of countries.

After some 1600 years of zero average growth in productivity and living standards, growth in both of these areas exploded in the world's industrial countries in the nineteenth and twentieth centuries, reaching levels previously unimaginable.

[10]It is important to notice that all of these numbers have been corrected to eliminate the effects of inflation in the manner already described in Chapter 2, pages 25–26, and in the appendix to Chapter 6. Thus, it is true, of course, that because of the subsequent inflation, a dollar in 1870 could purchase much more bread or many more shoes than it can today, so that a $12 weekly salary in 1870 is not as low, in purchasing power, as it may seem. But the statistics reported here have been corrected to eliminate this source of confusion, using the standard statistical method employed for the purpose. That is, since the statistics indicate that U.S. consumer prices have risen by about 6 times since 1870, a $12 1870 wage is counted as 6 × $12 = $72 in dollars of 1979 purchasing power (for more details on the method for correction for inflation see page 114 in the appendix to Chapter 6).

Table 7–1
Productivity and GDP Per Capita
Total Growth from 1870 to 1979* in 16 Industrialized Countries

	Real GDP per Work Hour	Real GDP Per Capita
Australia	398% growth	221% growth
Great Britain	585	310
Switzerland	830	471
Belgium	887	439
Netherlands	910	429
Canada	1,050	766
United States	1,080	693
Denmark	1,098	684
Italy	1,225	503
Austria	1,270	643
Germany	1,510	824
Norway	1,560	873
France	1,590	694
Finland	1,710	1,016
Sweden	2,060	1,083
Japan	2,480	1,661

Source: Angus Maddison, *Phases of Capitalist Development*. New York: Oxford University Press, 1982: pp. 8, 212.
*In 1970 U.S. dollars.

Significance of the Growth of Productivity

As we pointed out in our list of **12 Ideas for Beyond the Final Exam,** it is hardly an exaggeration to say that, in the long run, almost nothing counts for the determination of a nation's standard of living but its rate of productivity growth—for only rising productivity can raise standards of living in the long run.

Over long periods of time, small differences in rates of productivity growth compound like interest in a bank account, and they can make an enormous difference to a society's prosperity. Nothing contributes more to reduction of poverty, to increases in leisure, and to the country's ability to finance education, public health, environment, and the arts.

Since 1800, productivity in the United States has increased at an average annual rate slightly less than 2 percent. An apparently small change in this figure would have enormous consequences over a long period. Had productivity grown at an average rate of only 1 percent per year instead, an average American today would command about six times as large a quantity of goods and services as his forebears did in 1800. Actually, though it is hard to believe, real per capita income has risen about 20-fold in this period. And if productivity had grown over the entire interval at an annual rate of 3 percent, average living standards would be an incredible 137 times as high as they were in 1800.

Productivity growth can make an enormous difference in a nation's standing in the hierarchy of the world's economies. It has been remarked that the success of the United States in keeping its annual productivity growth about 1 percent ahead of Great Britain for about a century transformed America from a minor, developing country into a superpower and transformed the United Kingdom from the world's preeminent power into a second-rate economy. It is

Japan's 3-percent average annual productivity growth rate since 1870 that transformed it from one of the world's poorest countries into a nation with one of the highest GNP figures in the world.

The Second Major Development: Convergence

Not only have all the industrial countries grown in productivity and income per capita, but these countries have also become more similar to one another both in terms of labor productivity and GNP per capita. In other words, among the industrial countries, those which were furthest behind in 1870 have been catching up with those that were ahead. For example, considering the 16 countries represented in Table 7–1 (these are the only countries for which we have statistics that go back to 1870), the productivity level of the leading country (Australia) was about eight times as high as that of the least productive country (Japan) in 1870. By 1979 that ratio had declined to about two. That is, about three-quarters of the difference between the most productive and the least productive country were eliminated during the 109-year period.

Such a dramatic narrowing of productivity gaps among the industrial countries means that everyone else must be catching up with the leader, and that leader, ever since World War I, has been the United States. This is illustrated in Figure 7–3, which shows what happened to the *relative* living standards of several leading industrialized countries over the period 1950–1986, that is, GDP in each of those countries as a percentage of the U.S. level. It indicates that in 1950, per capita GDP for the average of the countries shown was almost 50 percent of that of the United States. By 1986 the average slightly exceeded 75 percent of the U.S. level. Figure 7–3 also shows that *each* of these countries has been moving closer to the United States (that is, closer to 100 percent of the U.S. level) in this 36-year period because for each country, the right-hand (1986) bar is equal to or taller than the left-hand (1950) bar. (The same is true

Figure 7–3

GDP PER CAPITA IN FIVE COUNTRIES AS PERCENT OF U.S. LEVEL, 1950 VERSUS 1986

The graph shows that four of the countries are approaching U.S. living standards (they have moved much closer to U.S. GDP per capita than they were in 1950). Only Great Britain has failed to come much closer, staying at about 2/3 of the U.S. GDP per capita.

SOURCE: Angus Maddison, *Phases of Capitalist Development* (New York: Oxford University Press, 1982), page 8 and unpublished Maddison materials.

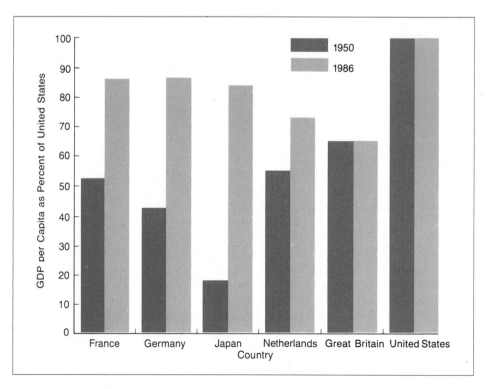

of each and every one of the other ten countries in Table 7–1). To interpret the graph, remember that if the bar representing some country were to reach precisely the top of the graph, it would mean that this country's standard of living is equal to that of the United States.

The data indicate that levels of labor productivity are converging among the leading industrialized countries.[11]

Has the same convergence process applied to countries other than the top industrial nations? Yes it has, at least for many of the medium-wealthy countries and even for the centrally planned economies. We have data on GDP per capita for seven centrally planned economies from 1950 to 1980. They show that GDP per capita of the richest of these countries in 1950 (Czechoslovakia) was more than 7 times as high as that of the poorest (China). By 1980 that distance between the richest (East Germany) and the poorest (still China) had declined to less than 5 to one.

The centrally planned economies have not only been catching up with one another, but they have also (slowly) been reducing the distance between themselves and the rest of the industrialized world. Thus, while GDP per capita in the average of these countries was slightly less than 25 percent of that of the United States in 1950, by 1980 it had reached 44 percent of that of the United States. Again, *every one* of the individual centrally planned economies for which we have data has benefitted from the catch-up.

The centrally planned economies seem to be growing closer to one another and to the United States in terms of income per capita.

Why International Equalization?

Why are all these countries growing more alike in productivity and average standards of living? No one has the entire answer, but a good part of the story is probably the speed-up of the international spread of new technology. Better communications permit innovative techniques to move from one country to another far more quickly than in the past. Better and more widespread education permits countries to learn technical details from one another and to train their labor forces rapidly to make use of them. At the beginning of the eighteenth century when the Newcomen steam engine (the predecessor of Watt's steam engine) was invented in England, it took half a century for the engine to spread to Western European countries and the American colonies. In contrast, the innovations in transistor and semiconductor technology since World War II have, on average, taken about two and one-half years to spread among countries.

All industrial countries benefit from the process of shared information; each learns from the innovations that occur in all the others. The British, the French, and the Germans benefit from American computer technology while the United States and others benefit from Japanese advances in robotics.

But there is one crucial asymmetry. Countries that are behind have a great deal to learn from countries that are ahead, but the leaders have less to learn

---

[11]The reader should be warned that this conclusion has been challenged, at least for the years before World War II, on the grounds that the sample of countries studied happens to include those that have been converging toward the United States because they are the success stories for which statistics are available. Thus, the critics point out, Argentina is omitted from the sample of countries, even though in 1870 many observers would have predicted a brilliant economic future for that country.

from those that have lagged behind. This is generally believed to be a prime explanation of the convergence in living standards. Meanwhile, the growing speed and efficiency of communications speeds up the entire process.

Lagging countries have more to learn from leaders than leaders can learn from laggards. This fact, and the growing speed with which innovations are spread, help explain why the world's economies are growing more equal.

Are All Countries Participating in Equalization?

So far we have seen that a considerable number of countries are growing increasingly similar to one another in terms of productivity and living standards. But we have yet to consider the world's poorest nations—usually referred to as "less developed countries," or LDCs. (See Chapter 38.) Have most of those countries also benefitted from the spread of innovation and closed the gap between themselves and the world's economic leaders? Unfortunately, among the LDCs, where equalization is most desperately needed, the picture is very mixed. Some economies, like Taiwan and South Korea, have achieved spectacular successes. But, as a group, the LDCs have grown less equal among themselves and have fallen further behind the United States. On average, GDP per capita grew about $3\frac{1}{2}$ percent per year in the industrialized countries in the period 1950–1980. But in the LDCs it rose only about $1\frac{1}{2}$ percent a year on average. A number of LDCs have fallen further behind the United States.

While the leading economies in the world are becoming more equal in terms of productivity and living standards, a number of the poorest countries are falling further behind and are holding back the average performance of the LDCs.

Why Some LDCs Are Falling Behind

In Chapter 21 we will discuss in detail the handicaps that have been blamed by specialist observers for the poor performance of many LDCs. Here we will only note briefly why the forces of equalization just described for the more developed countries do not work for a number of the LDCs.

Two influences are pertinent. First, the poor educational levels in the LDCs and the resulting scarcity of qualified engineers and technicians is a serious impediment to imitation and effective use of the complex technological advances of the industrialized countries. So they do not benefit by learning from others to nearly the extent the wealthier countries do. Second, the absence of products to which sophisticated production techniques can readily be applied makes it hard to participate in the growth gains from learning and imitation. A country that depends on products such as bananas, peanuts, and sugar for most of its income has little use for new robot designs or automated manufacturing processes, though it can and often does benefit from agricultural innovations, some of substantial importance. As a result, while the LDCs can and do learn to some degree from the technology of the industrialized economies, they suffer from serious handicaps in this process, handicaps from which the industrial countries are largely immune.

The Recent Productivity Slowdown in the United States

Since the mid-1960s there has been a sharp decline in the rate of growth of productivity in the United States. Some people fear that this threatens to turn America into a third-rate economy unable to compete with other nations. Others take a less alarmist view.

From the end of World War II until about 1965, productivity grew at an average rate of 3.2 percent per year, which is probably faster than it had ever grown before over so long a period. Then, between 1965 and 1972, productivity growth fell to something like 2.2 percent per year. From about 1972 to 1986, it fell to an annual rate of less than 1 percent.

It should be noted carefully that throughout most of this period the *level* of productivity continued to improve. In almost every year, it was higher than the last. But the *rate of improvement* slowed from a gallop to a walk, and finally to a crawl.

Why did U.S. productivity growth slow down? Many statisticians and economists have worked hard to determine why U.S. productivity growth has fallen so much since the mid-1960s. But because so many things have changed at once, no clear and easy answers have emerged. At least seven culprits have been identified.

Low Investment

Probably the most widely accepted cause of the slowdown is the lackluster performance of investment in plant and equipment, which is a prime determinant of labor productivity. The more a society invests, the more plant and equipment an average member of the labor force will have available to work with. More and better equipment will enable her to turn out more output per hour, so productivity will grow. Also, new machines usually incorporate the latest designs, and obsolete equipment tends to be kept longer when investment lags. Thus investment, and the savings that make investment possible, are crucial for productivity growth.

After World War II, business investment in the United States actually rose faster than GNP for a while. However, investment was not large enough to keep pace with the rapidly expanding labor force. Consequently, the amount of capital each worker had to work with fell after the 1960s. Because of differences in measurement procedures, there is some disagreement about the actual magnitude of this decline, but most analysts agree that lagging investment played a substantial role in the general decline in U.S. productivity growth. Most studies attribute from 20 to 40 percent of the slowdown in productivity growth to the shortfall in investment.

Slowdown in Research and Development

Another prime suspect in the slowing of U.S. productivity growth is business expenditure on applied research. Innovation is one of the main sources of productivity growth. New and more efficient productive procedures—from the steam engine to robotics—have multiplied the output a worker is capable of producing. However, innovation requires more than a new idea. It usually needs careful research to get out the "bugs" and to make the new procedures operational. This work is called **research and development (R and D),** and it is usually organized and financed by business firms. Because R and D is a critical step between the original invention and its final adoption by business enterprise, a big drop in R and D expenditures can do substantial damage to productivity growth.

The ratio of R and D outlays to GNP fell about 20 percent between the mid-1960s and the mid-1970s. There has been a decline in the number of scientists and engineers employed by U.S. industry. All in all, the statistical analysts generally attribute some 10 to 20 percent of the U.S. productivity slowdown to lagging R and D outlays.

Research and development (R and D) refers to the activity of business firms in which systematic efforts are undertaken to invent new or improved products or productive techniques and to make them ready to market or for use in production processes.

But what held back such outlays and generally impeded the pace of innovation? No one really knows. One hypothesis is that a decade of stagflation just made innovation and research less attractive to business. Another holds that rising real wages of scientists and engineers discouraged R and D activity by making it more expensive.

Government Regulations

Government regulation is also widely blamed for the slowdown. In the 1960s and 1970s, regulations for protection of the health and safety of workers and for defense of the environment were strengthened. These absorbed some of the investment outlays of business and increased the costs of production. Many business leaders believe that regulation has been a substantial impediment to productivity growth. But, while the statistics do not indicate that this development was completely blameless, they suggest that no more than 10 percent of the slowdown can be attributed to regulation.

Shift to the Service Industries

A **service industry** does not turn out any physical products. Telecommunications, medical care, teaching, police protection, and the work of lawyers are examples of service industries. Some, like telecommunications, use highly sophisticated equipment, and their productivity has grown rapidly. In many other services, such growth has been very slow.

Another possible culprit is the fact that during the period in question the share of the nation's labor force employed in **service industries** may have risen as much as 50 percent. Historically, growth of productivity in many (but by no means all) of the services has been far slower than in manufacturing. This is so in part because the quality of many services depends, or is believed to depend, directly on the amount of time the supplier devotes to the activity. The time devoted by a doctor to an average patient or the amount of faculty time per student are two prominent examples. Also, many services (such as diagnosis and treatment of a sick person) cannot be standardized and put on an assembly line. When workers leave manufacturing, with its relatively rapid productivity growth, and go into service industries where productivity growth is slower, overall productivity growth declines.

How serious is this phenomenon? Unfortunately, statistical estimates vary enormously. We really are not sure. In any event, the shift of the labor force toward the services cannot be considered an example of poor performance by our economy. Unlike lack of innovation, it is not something we must "cure."

Changes in the Makeup of the Labor Force

Discrimination has prevented many women and many members of minority groups from acquiring skills through on-the-job experience. To the extent that they have succeeded, therefore, efforts in recent decades to combat discrimination increased the flow of inexperienced workers into the labor force. The resulting impediment to productivity growth is probably temporary and, in any event, has partially been offset by rising educational attainment of the labor force as a whole.

Rising Energy Prices

The sharply rising price of energy was probably a major contributor to the slowdown in productivity growth. The 1970s was the period of the great petroleum shocks mentioned in Chapter 5. The sudden shortage of oil and the consequent leap in energy prices led to many economic changes. The building insulation business grew. The demand for large, gas-guzzling cars plunged. Much plant and equipment had to be changed to adapt to new patterns of consumer and business demands induced by rising energy prices and to substitute fuel-efficient equipment for items that had been installed when energy was cheap.

Because energy constitutes a small proportion of the nation's total expenditure on inputs, most statistical studies suggest that higher energy prices did not contribute much to the slowdown. A typical estimate is that they account for about 15 percent of the total decline in productivity growth.

Yet there are many, including the authors of this book, who suspect that energy may be responsible for more than that. The equipment which had to be replaced or modified to save on fuel probably used up a far from negligible portion of the country's investment. Moreover, as fuel prices rose, it sometimes became economical throughout the economy to employ more labor instead of using equipment that required expensive energy. So the ratio of labor to output rose, thus cutting directly into labor productivity. In addition, a sharp, sudden crisis and the resulting period of adjustment are never conducive to productivity growth. The fact that productivity growth plunged at just about the same time in most industrial countries suggests that the energy crisis was more important than the statistical studies show. The only explanations that apply to *all* countries are the energy problem and the influence of recession, to which we turn next.

Macroeconomic Conditions

Finally, some portion of the slowdown is probably attributable to the fact that the period since 1974 has not generally been characterized by healthy business conditions. Several recessions and an inflation of unprecedented severity and duration are not conditions that encourage business investment and innovation. There is no clear statistical evidence on the importance of this influence for the long-run behavior of productivity, but it is hard to believe that it was insignificant. Certainly a recession does cut productivity growth and the remaining question is how much of the U.S. economy's miserable productivity growth performance through 1986 was attributable to absence of buoyant prosperity.

The causes of the slowdown in U.S. productivity growth are far from certain. Lagging saving and investment, modest growth in R and D, increased government regulations, the shift to service industries, changes in the labor force, the energy crisis, and repeated recessions and protracted inflation probably all played a part.

More Guarded Interpretations of the Slowdown

Some analysts, however, question whether the U.S. productivity slowdown is as serious as it appears. They argue, first of all, that the U.S. is not alone in suffering a slowdown in productivity growth. The problem has affected virtually every industrial country. Figure 7–4 compares productivity growth rates during 1950–73 with those from 1973–84 for six industrial countries. We find that Great Britain's rate fell 25 percent, that of France declined 33 percent, West Germany's fell 50 percent, Holland's went down 57 percent, and Japan's fell 58 percent. Compared with these, the U.S.'s 60-percent decline does not seem so far out of line.

There is a second reason, based on the longer-run data, why some observers are less alarmed about the slowdown in U.S. productivity growth. Figure 7–5 shows a century of *growth rates* in U.S. labor productivity. The graph as a whole clearly exhibits neither a downward long-term trend nor a marked recent dip below the average growth rate of the preceding century. What we see is that the growth rate of productivity in the United States was virtually constant at

Figure 7–4

FALL IN PRODUCTIVITY GROWTH RATES, 1950–73 VERSUS 1973–84

This graph confirms that productivity growth has declined throughout the industrial world and not just in the United States. The decline is continuing in the 1980s.

SOURCE: Angus Maddison, *Phases of Capitalist Development* (New York: Oxford University Press, 1982), page 8 and unpublished Maddison materials.

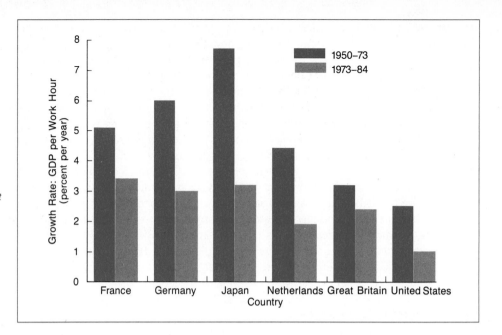

Figure 7–5

ANNUAL GROWTH RATES, U.S. PRODUCTIVITY, (1880–1985)

Aside from the sharp dip during the depression of the 1930s and the sharp rise after World War II, U.S. productivity has grown fairly steadily. However, during the 1980s it has fallen below its historical average of 2 percent improvement per year. No one knows how long the decline is likely to last.

SOURCE: Angus Maddison, *Phases of Capitalist Development* (New York: Oxford University Press, 1982), page 8 and unpublished Maddison materials.

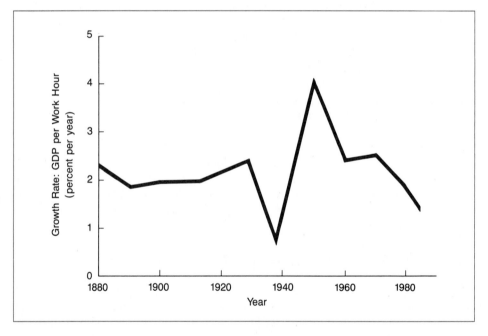

about 2 percent per year between about 1870 and 1930. Then, during the Great Depression of the 1930s, productivity growth plunged. With the advent of World War II and the postwar rebuilding of the devastated countries, U.S. productivity growth leaped upward. After this catch-up period, the growth rate fell back very close to its old historical level of 2 percent. On this view of the matter, then, the deceleration of the 1970s, rather than representing a drop below its historical norms, constitutes a return to that normalcy from a period of extraordinary growth which (in retrospect!) seems to have been predictably temporary. Much more disturbing is the fact that in the past few years productivity growth in the United States has fallen to perhaps half its historical average and has so far shown little sign of improvement. No one has any idea how long this problem, which has beset much of the industrial world, is likely to last.

What about the second disturbing fact about U.S. productivity growth—that it has recently been so much lower than that of other industrial countries? As a matter of fact that, too, is an old story. The growth rate of U.S. productivity has been just middling for the better part of a century. Between 1899 and 1913, the U.S. growth rate was already lower than that of Sweden, France, Germany, Italy, and Japan. Our growth rate was also below theirs (except for France) in 1924–1937. U.S. labor productivity grew rapidly relative to other nations only during both world wars, when many other countries were held back by the demands of their military activities.

There is a plausible explanation for the comparatively slow growth of U.S. productivity. It is the equalization of productivity in the world's industrial countries. If the forces making for equalization did in fact dominate the growth paths of those countries, it is necessarily true that productivity in the lagging countries *had* to grow more quickly than in the countries at the head of the line. Otherwise, they could never have grown more equal. The statistical evidence is consistent with the conjecture that the relative productivity growth rates of the various industrialized countries are largely explained by their distance behind the leader and the growth rates necessary for them to catch up. Viewed in this way, there need be little to be alarmed about in the relatively slow growth rate of U.S. productivity compared to that of other countries.

Viewed in long-term perspective, the recent slowdown in U.S. productivity growth and its lag behind other industrial countries seems somewhat less serious than it appears from an examination of the record of a briefer recent period.

The Costs of Lagging Productivity

Yet, despite what has just been said, there remain good reasons for concern about future productivity prospects. There certainly is no guarantee that productivity growth in the United States will continue at its old historical pace. To do so, the economy will require a continued flow of new and improving technology, new factories, new equipment, and the unslackening effort of engineers, scientists, technicians, management, and labor. None of this is easy or cheap, and none of it is guaranteed.

The costs of failure in this arena are very high. Above all, lagging productivity growth must slow or bring to an end the rising living standards and rising real wages which have so long been a prime accomplishment of the U.S. economy. If there is no rise in output per worker, then it will be impossible to keep increasing the quantity of goods and services provided to each consumer. Indeed, something of the sort has already happened. Since the beginning of the 1970s, the purchasing power of an average American worker's hourly wage has hardly increased at all.

Though we do not know whether long-run U.S. productivity growth has declined, for the past few years it has been well below its historical level. Failure to recoup threatens to hold back the growth in U.S. living standards.

Productivity, Unemployment, and Deindustrialization

Let us now use our long-term data to dispose of some popular myths about productivity growth and its consequences. Popular discussions of productivity growth often warn that rapid increases in labor productivity are not as beneficial as they are cracked up to be. We are told that each productivity increase reduces the demand for labor because it means that fewer work hours are needed to produce a given output. As a result, according to this view, productivity growth must create unemployment. Second, and perhaps somewhat inconsistently, it is argued that if an economy's productivity growth lags behind that of other countries, it will lose jobs to foreign workers, its industry will suffer, and its exports will fall. The resulting decline in industry has been given the catchy label "deindustrialization." However, the data do not support either of these conclusions, at least for the long run.

If the long-run unemployment spectre were a reality, we would expect that the 1100-percent increase in output per labor hour in the United States, its 600-percent increase in Great Britain, and its 1500-percent rise in Germany since 1870 would have had devastating effects on the demand for labor in these countries. After all, with productivity rising twelvefold during the last century, output per capita in the United States could have been kept about constant if employment were cut to one-twelfth its initial share of U.S. population. Even with a 50 percent fall in the number of hours an average person works per year, we might expect unemployment of perhaps five-sixths of the U.S. labor force by now.

Figure 7–6 shows that nothing of the sort has happened. The graph reports unemployment rates for Great Britain, the United States, and Germany in the periods 1874–1914 vs. 1952–1973. It is evident that over this long period there was no upsurge in unemployment, and the trend, if anything, has been somewhat downward. Before 1914, unemployment in the three countries averaged about 4 percent of the labor force, while in the 1952–1973 period it averaged a bit more than 3 percent. Even though there has been a rise in unemployment throughout the industrial world recently, much of it is attributable to short-term influences and reorientation of public policy away from government intervention to reduce unemployment. There is no evidence suggesting any *long-term* rise in unemployment.

How have we maintained unemployment in the face of rising productivity? The answer, of course, is that output per capita has hardly remained constant.

Figure 7–6
UNEMPLOYMENT RATES IN THE UNITED STATES, GREAT BRITAIN, AND GERMANY, 1874–1914 VERSUS 1952–1973
Over the long run, unemployment rates have not increased despite the enormous increase in productivity levels. Unemployment was much higher than is shown here during the 1930s. It has also gone up somewhat during the most recent decade.
SOURCE: R. C. O. Matthews, C. H. Feinstein, and J. C. Odling-Smee, *British Economic Growth 1856–1973* (Stanford: Stanford University Press, 1982), page 94.

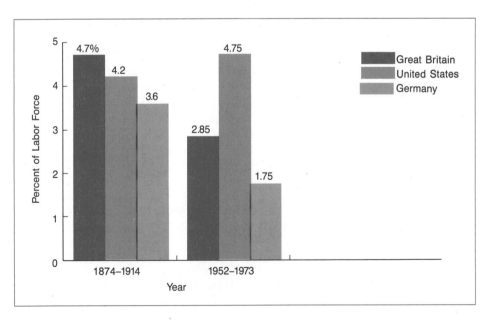

The demand for consumer goods and services, schools, hospitals, and factories has expanded explosively as productivity growth increased the purchasing power in the hands of the American public. That has sufficed to prevent any long-term increase in unemployment.

The same graph also undermines the (nearly) opposite apprehension. It shows that Great Britain, which has been the most noted laggard in productivity growth among industrialized countries, did not suffer from perpetually rising unemployment or unemployment problems more serious than those of other countries. Indeed, comparing the graph's bars for 1874–1914 with those of 1952–73, we see that Great Britain has made out relatively well on that score.

Neither rapid absolute productivity growth nor a slow relative productivity growth rate need subject a country to long-run and persistent increases in unemployment rates.

Before offering an explanation of this behavior of employment, we turn to the widely-held view that a persistent lag in a nation's productivity growth will place it at an increasing competitive disadvantage in international trade, and that it will thereby be excluded increasingly from its export markets, with devastating effects upon its industries.

Here again we use Great Britain, with its exceedingly poor productivity record, to examine these claims. It is true that the British *share* of exports declined from over 40 percent of world trade in 1870 to less than 10 percent a century later. But that is only because other countries' foreign sales rose even more rapidly than Britain's. The fact is that the total exports of Great Britain have risen spectacularly. Table 7–2 shows that between 1870 and 1979 the volume of British exports of goods and services increased about 930 percent; moreover, from 1855 to 1973, British exports of *goods* increased an astonishing 1200 percent.

Nor has Great Britain been forced to deindustrialize internally. In terms of the percent of the labor force employed in the industrial sector of its economy, Britain declined from first place in the sample of 16 countries in 1870 to fourth

Table 7–2
Exports: Total Percentage Growth, 1870–1979, in 15 Industrial Countries

Great Britain	930% growth
Germany	3,700
France	4,100
Switzerland	4,400
Austria	4,700
Sweden	5,100
Italy	6,200
Finland	6,200
Belgium	6,300
Denmark	6,800
Norway	7,700
Netherlands	8,000
United States	9,200
Canada	9,900
Japan	293,000

Source: Angus Maddison, *Phases of Capitalist Development*. New York: Oxford University Press, 1982: pp. 248–53.

place (behind Germany, Austria, and Switzerland) in 1979. But industry's share of employment in Great Britain was still 88 percent of that of Germany, the 1979 leader in terms of industrialization. And Great Britain continued to rank ahead of such countries as Sweden, France, the United States, Belgium, and Japan. If this is deindustrialization, it certainly is not very extreme.

The Real Cost of Lagging Productivity: Lagging Wages

From what has just been said, it may seem that it is not too bad to be a productivity laggard. After all, with no trend toward rising unemployment, with exports increasing, with the share of employment in manufacturing pretty well keeping up with other countries, what is so terrible about Great Britain's fate? Indeed, these observations may make one wonder how Britain was able to score these apparent successes despite its comparatively poor productivity performance.

The secret, which also shows the true price the British had to pay, is to be found in that country's lagging real wages. In the nineteenth century, British workers were the best paid in Europe. According to one estimate, which admittedly is not very reliable, in about 1860 an English worker's wages permitted the purchase of about $2\frac{1}{2}$ times the quantity of goods and services as a German worker's. Yet by 1980, the purchasing power of a German worker's wages was almost twice as great as that of a British worker. In other words, in a little more than a century the relative position of workers in the two countries had almost been reversed.

How are lagging British wages related to its productivity lag? The answer is straightforward. If Britain cannot compete on world markets by virtue of growing efficiency (productivity), it still can sell its products by providing cheap British labor. Of course, Britain does not volunteer to adopt low real wages; rather, market forces make it happen automatically, because inefficiently produced goods cannot be sold on the international marketplace unless those goods are produced by cheaper inputs. Hence, the invisible hand forces British wages to lag behind. Labor simply cannot extract higher wages from an economy that has little to give.

A country with lagging productivity is likely to be condemned to become an exporter of cheap labor. That is the only way it can keep its industry viable, maintain its exports, and preserve domestic jobs. This is the real danger that the United States faces if its productivity performance is unsatisfactory for any substantial period of time.

Concluding Comment

Productivity growth is indeed the stuff of which prosperity is made. The persistent record of U.S. productivity growth is the source of its high standard of living, which is extraordinary both in terms of previous history and in comparison with that of most nations in the world. In the long run, nothing is more important than productivity growth for the economic welfare of the country and for the world. In Chapter 21 we will examine some of the things that can help stimulate this vital ingredient of long-run well-being, which in two centuries transformed the focus of popular and political concerns in many industrial countries from the threat of starvation to the fear of overabundance of products.

Summary

1. Productivity growth over the past century has made a tremendous contribution to standards of living. Real U.S. per capita income is nearly 8 times as large as it was in 1870. Never in previous history have economic conditions improved so much.

2. For the first time in history, famine is no longer a constant threat in the world's industrialized countries. That is because productivity in agriculture has increased greatly. In 1800 about 90 percent of the U.S. labor force was needed to feed the nation poorly. Today, only about 3 percent of the labor force works on farms and yet produces great abundance.

3. Because of compounding, over longer periods a small increase in rate of productivity growth can make an enormous difference in the economic well-being of a nation. This is one of the **12 Ideas for Beyond the Final Exam.**

4. There is evidence suggesting that at least a small set of the world's leading economies are converging toward similar living standards and similar productivity levels.

5. All nations learn about new technological developments from one another. The international spread of inventions means that research in one country also benefits inhabitants in much of the rest of the world.

6. Since the 1960s, there has been a substantial slowdown in productivity growth in most industrial countries.

7. No one is quite sure of the reasons, but slowdown in saving and investment, the fuel crisis of the 1970s, and several recessions all probably played a significant role.

8. Lagging productivity holds back real wages and per capita incomes in a country. However, in the long run it will generally not cause unemployment or inability to export enough to pay for the nation's imports.

9. The growth rate of U.S. productivity has for many decades been slower than that of a number of other industrial countries. However, at least in part, that reflects the fact that the United States is still probably the world's productivity leader; so that while we have much to learn from others, they have even more to learn from us.

10. No one is sure whether or not the current slowdown in U.S. productivity and its lag behind that of other countries is a temporary matter. If it persists it can threaten relative U.S. living standards in the future.

11. The example of Great Britain shows that even if a country's productivity level and level of GDP per capita grow rapidly, it can appear to be depressed if it falls behind relatively, because other countries are growing even more rapidly.

Concepts for Review

Labor productivity	Gross Domestic Product (GDP)	Research and development (R and D)
Standard of living	GDP per labor hour	Service industry
GNP per capita	GDP per capita	

Questions for Discussion

1. Try to describe what family budgets were like 120 years ago when U.S. income per person (GDP per capita) was about one-eighth as high as it is today.

2. List some of the inventions that have increased agricultural output in the past century.

3. List some of the inventions that have increased manufacturing output in the last century.

4. List some of the new consumer products of the past century. Which of them became generally available only since World War II?

5. List some foreign inventions widely used in the United States.

6. List some American inventions widely used abroad.

7. If growing productivity has vastly reduced the amount of labor needed to produce a given output, why has it not caused massively growing unemployment?

8. If output per capita in a country doubles every 25 years, how much will it grow in a century?

9. Which do you think are more similar?
   a. Production methods in a U.S. and a German factory today.
   b. Production methods in the same U.S. factory today and the methods used there 25 years ago.

PART 3

Aggregate Supply and Demand Analysis

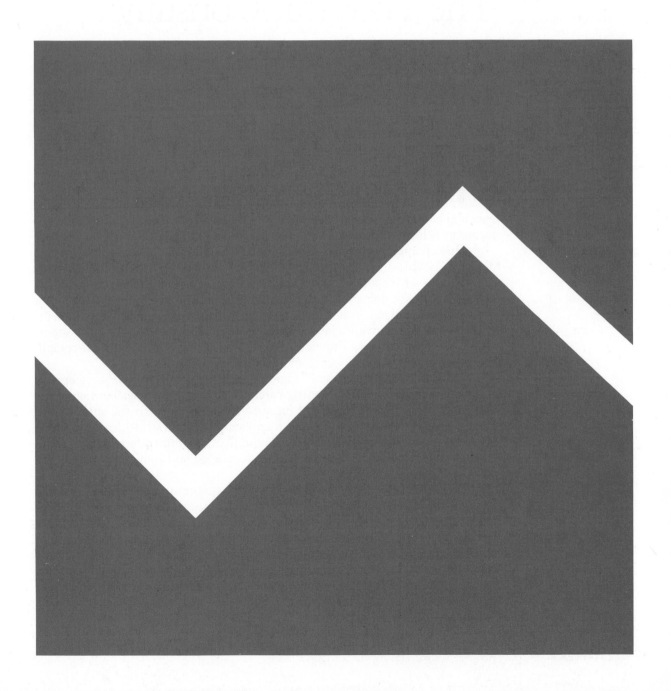

8

Income and Spending: The Powerful Consumer

Men are disposed, as a rule and on the average, to increase their consumption as their income increases, but not by as much as the increase in their income.

JOHN MAYNARD KEYNES

In Chapter 5 we saw how the strength of aggregate demand influences the performance of the economy. When aggregate demand is growing briskly, the economy is likely to be booming, though it may also be having trouble with inflation. When aggregate demand stagnates, a recession is likely to follow.

This chapter begins our detailed study of the *determination* of aggregate demand. In this and the next few chapters, we will learn why the *aggregate demand curve* of Chapter 5 has a negative slope and how the government can *manage* aggregate demand. Since consumer spending accounts for the lion's share of total demand, it is natural to begin with the consumer. The following chapters will bring investment spending, government spending, and the supply side of the economy into the picture. Still later chapters will add such complications as interest rates, money, and exports and imports.

We start the chapter with some definitions of alternative concepts of economic activity — distinguishing carefully among total *spending* (aggregate demand), total *output*, and total *income*. Next, we turn to the interactions among these three concepts, using a convenient pictorial device that shows how they are all interrelated. Then we note that government attempts to influence consumer spending have sometimes succeeded and sometimes failed, and we pose the question: Why?

The bulk of the chapter is devoted to this question. To answer it, we first describe the important relationship between consumer income and consumer spending, and we use this relationship to show how government policies have worked when they have been successful. Then we discuss some complications that arise from the fact that consumer income, though crucial, is not the only factor governing consumer spending. One of these complications holds the clue to why government policies have sometimes failed to influence consumer spending as expected.

Aggregate Demand, National Product, and National Income

We begin with some definitions. We have already introduced the concept of **gross national product** as the standard measure of the total output of the economy.[1]

For the most part, goods are produced in a market economy only if they can be sold. **Aggregate demand,** another concept encountered in Chapter 5, is the total amount that all consumers, business firms, government agencies, and foreigners wish to spend on all U.S. final goods and services. The downward-sloping aggregate demand curve of Chapter 5 suggested that aggregate demand is a *schedule,* not a fixed number. And several reasons why aggregate quantity demanded depends on the price level will emerge in coming chapters. But the level of aggregate demand also depends on a variety of other factors like consumer incomes, various government policies, and events in foreign countries. We can understand the nature of aggregate demand best if we break it up into its major components.

Consumer expenditure ("consumption" for short) is simply the total demand for all consumer goods and services. This is the focus of the current chapter, and we shall represent it by the letter C.

Investment spending, which we represent by the letter I, is the amount that firms spend on factories, machinery, and the like plus the amount that families spend on new houses. Notice that this is a very different usage of the word "investment" from that which is found in common parlance. Most people speak of "investing" in the stock market or in a bank account. This kind of "investment" merely swaps one form of financial asset (such as money) for another form (such as a share of stock). When economists speak of "investment," they mean instead the purchase of some *new physical* asset, like a drill press or an oil rig or a home. It is only this kind of investment that leads directly to additional demand for newly produced goods in the economy.

The third major component of aggregate demand is **government purchases** of goods and services; that is, things like paper, typewriters, airplanes, ships, and labor that are bought by all levels of government—federal, state, and local. We use the shorthand symbol G to denote this variable.

The final component of aggregate demand is **net exports,** which are simply defined as U.S. exports minus U.S. imports. The reasoning here is simple. Part of the demand for American goods and services originates beyond our borders—as when foreigners buy our wheat, our computers, or our banking services. So this must be added to domestic demand. Similarly, some items included in C and I are not American made—think, for example, of German beer, Japanese cars, and Korean textiles. So these must be subtracted, if we want to measure total spending on U.S. products. Making these two adjustments together amounts to including net exports, which we symbolize by $X - IM$ (exports minus imports), as part of aggregate demand.

Given all these abbreviations, we have the following shorthand definition of aggregate demand:

Aggregate demand is the sum $C + I + G + X - IM$.

The last concept we need is a measure of the total *income* of all the individuals in the economy. There are two versions of this: one for before-tax

[1] See Chapter 5, pages 78–80.

Aggregate demand is the total amount that all consumers, business firms, and government agencies are willing to spend on final goods and services.

Consumer expenditure, symbolized by the letter C, is the total amount spent by consumers on newly produced goods and services (excluding purchases of new homes, which are considered investment goods).

Investment spending, symbolized by the letter I, is the sum of the expenditures of business firms on new plant and equipment, plus the expenditures of households on new homes. Financial "investments" are not included, nor are resales of existing physical assets.

Government purchases, symbolized by the letter G, refers to all the goods (such as airplanes and paper clips) and services (such as school teaching and police protection) purchased by all levels of government. It does not include government **transfer payments,** such as social security and unemployment benefits.

Net exports, symbolized by $X - IM$, is the difference between U.S. exports and U.S. imports. It indicates the difference between what we sell to foreigners and what we buy from them.

National income is the sum of the incomes of all the individuals in the economy earned in the forms of wages, interest, rents, and profits. It excludes transfer payments and is calculated before any deductions are taken for income taxes.

Disposable income is the sum of the incomes of all the individuals in the economy after all taxes have been deducted and all transfer payments have been added.

incomes, called **national income,** and one for after-tax incomes, called **disposable income.**[2] The term "disposable income" is meant to be descriptive: it tells us how many dollars consumers actually have available to spend or to save. Because it plays such a prominent role in this chapter, we shall need an abbreviation for it as well; we call it **DI.**

The Circular Flow of Spending, Production, and Income

Enough definitions. How do these three concepts—national product, aggregate demand, and national income—interact in a market economy? We can answer this best with a rather elaborate diagram (Figure 8–1). For obvious reasons, Figure 8–1 is called a **circular flow diagram.** It depicts a large circular tube in which a fluid is circulating in a clockwise direction. There are several breaks in the tube where either some of the fluid leaks out or additional fluid is injected in.

Let us examine this system, beginning on the far left. At point 1 on the circle, we find consumers. Disposable income (*DI*) is flowing into them, and two things are flowing out: consumption (*C*), which stays in the circular flow, and saving (*S*), which "leaks out." This just says that consumers normally spend

[2]More detailed information on these and other concepts is provided in an appendix to this chapter.

Figure 8–1
THE CIRCULAR FLOW OF EXPENDITURE AND INCOME
The upper part of this circular flow diagram depicts the flow of expenditures on goods and services which comes from consumers (point 1), investors (point 2), government (point 3), and foreigners (point 4), and goes to the firms that produce the output (point 5). The lower part of the diagram indicates how the income paid out by firms (point 5) flows to consumers (point 1), after some is siphoned off by the government in the form of taxes and part of this is replaced by transfer payments (point 6).

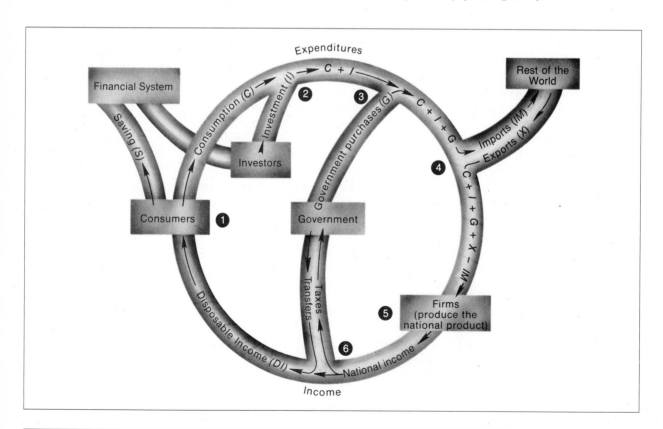

less than they earn and save the balance. The "leakage" to savings, of course, does not disappear, but flows into the financial system. We postpone consideration of what happens there until Chapter 13.

The upper loop of the circular flow represents expenditures, and as we move clockwise to point 2, we encounter the first "injection" into the flow: investment spending (I). The diagram shows this as coming from "investors"—a group that includes both business firms and consumers who buy new homes.[3] As the circular flow moves beyond point 2, it is bigger than it was before. Total spending has increased from C to $C + I$.

At point 3 there is yet another injection. The government adds its demand for goods and services (G) to those of consumers and investors ($C + I$). Now aggregate demand is up to $C + I + G$.

The final leakage and injection comes at point 4. Here we see export spending coming into the circular flow from abroad and import spending leaking out. The net effect of these two forces, net exports, may increase or decrease the circular flow. In either case, by the time we pass point 4 we have accumulated the full amount of aggregate demand, $C + I + G + X - IM$.

The circular flow diagram shows this aggregate demand for goods and services arriving at the business firms, which are located at point 5 at the southeast portion of the diagram. Responding to this demand, firms produce the national product. As the circular flow emerges from the firms, however, we have renamed it *national income*. Why? The reason is that, except for some complications explained in the appendix:

National income and national product must be equal.

Why is this the case? When a firm produces and sells $100 worth of output, it pays most of the proceeds to its workers, to people who have lent it money, and to the landlord who owns the property on which it is located. All of these payments are *income* to some individuals. But what about the rest? Suppose, for example, that the wages, interest, and rent that the firm pays add up to $90, while its output is $100. What happens to the remaining $10? The answer is that the owners of the firm receive it as *profits*. But these owners are also citizens of the country, so their incomes count in national income, too. Thus, when we add up all the wages, interest, rents, *and profits* in the economy to obtain the national income we must arrive at the value of the national output.

The lower loop of the circular flow diagram traces the flow of income by showing national income leaving the firms and heading for consumers. But there is a detour along the way. At point 6, the government does two things. First, it siphons off a portion of the national income in the form of taxes. Second, it adds back government **transfer payments,** like unemployment compensation and social security benefits, which are sums of money that certain individuals receive as outright *grants* from the government rather than as payments for services rendered to employers.

Transfer payments are sums of money that certain individuals receive as outright *grants* from the government rather than as payments for services rendered to employers.

When taxes are subtracted from GNP, and transfer payments are added, we obtain disposable income.[4]

$$DI = GNP - \text{Taxes} + \text{Transfer Payments}.$$

[3]You are reminded of the specific definition of investment on page 139.
[4]This definition omits a few minor details, which are explained in an appendix to this chapter.

Disposable income flows unimpeded to consumers at point 1, and the cycle repeats.

This diagram raises several complicated questions. Although we pose them here, we will not try to answer them at this early stage. The answers will be made clear in subsequent chapters.

1. Is the output that the firms produce at point 5 (the GNP) equal to aggregate demand? If so, what makes these two quantities equal? If not, what happens?
2. Is the flow of spending and income growing larger or smaller as we move clockwise around the circle, and why?

Chapter 9 provides the answers to questions 1 and 2.

3. Are the government's accounts in balance, so that what flows in at point 6 (taxes minus transfers) is equal to what flows out at point 3 (government purchases)? What happens if they are not?

This important question is first addressed in Chapter 12 and then recurs many times, especially in Chapter 16, which is devoted to discussing budget deficits.

4. Is our international trade balanced, so that exports equal imports? More generally, what factors determine net exports and what are the consequences of trade deficits or surpluses?

These questions, which have been much in the news of late, are postponed until Part 5, which is devoted to international economic issues.

But we cannot discuss any of these issues profitably until we first understand what goes on at point 1, where consumers make decisions, and point 2, where investors make decisions. We turn next, therefore, to the determinants of consumer spending.

Demand Management and the Powerful Consumer

As we suggested in Chapter 5, the government sometimes wants to shift the aggregate demand curve. There are a number of ways in which it can try to do so. One direct approach is to alter its own spending (G), becoming extravagant when private demand is weak and miserly when private demand is strong. But the government can also take a more indirect route by using taxes and other policy tools to influence *private* spending decisions.

A government desiring to change private spending can concentrate its energies on consumer spending (C), on investment spending (I), or on net exports ($X - IM$). At various times in our history, the U.S. government has endeavored to change each of these. Since consumer expenditures constitute nearly two-thirds of gross national product, C presents the most tempting target.

While there are many things it can do to alter consumer spending, the government's principal weapon is the personal income tax. Many of you already have encountered Form 1040, the unwelcome New Year's greeting that every taxpayer receives from the federal government each January. Many more of you probably have been on a payroll and seen a share of your wages deducted and sent to the Internal Revenue Service. It should be no mystery, then, how changes in personal taxes affect consumer spending. Any reduction in personal taxes leaves consumers with more disposable income to spend. Any increase in taxes leaves less.

The linkage from taxes to disposable income to consumer spending seems direct and unmistakable, and, in a certain sense, it is. But a look at the history of some major tax changes aimed at altering C is sobering. The varying degrees of success both of the measures themselves and of the predictions of their effects explain why economic research into the relationship between taxes and consumption continues.

Case 1: The 1964 Tax Reduction

The year 1964 was a good one for economists. For years they had been proclaiming that a cut in personal taxes would be an excellent way to stimulate a stagnating economy. But the plea fell on deaf ears until President John F. Kennedy was persuaded of the basic logic of the argument. Under his successor, Lyndon B. Johnson, Congress reduced personal taxes by about 18 percent. The legislation was designed to spur consumer spending, and it succeeded admirably. Consumers reacted just about as the textbooks of the day predicted, the economic situation improved rapidly and markedly, and economists smiled knowingly.

Case 2: The 1968 Tax Increase

The euphoria of 1964 proved to be short-lived. In 1968–1969 we learned—the hard way—that economists did not have all the answers. Because of the massive defense spending associated with the Vietnam War, the macroeconomic problem of 1966–1968 was precisely the opposite of that in 1964: too much demand rather than too little. It appeared logical, then, to prescribe the opposite medicine; and economists were quick to suggest a rise in personal income taxes to force consumers to spend less.

After a considerable delay, President Johnson recommended a temporary tax increase and Congress enacted a 10 percent rise in personal tax payments (calling it a "surcharge"). However, this attempt to cut aggregate demand by reducing C enjoyed only modest success. While consumer spending probably was below what it would have been in the absence of the surcharge, it was substantially above what the 1964 experience had led economists to predict.

Case 3: The 1975 Tax Reduction

The next major change in tax laws for stabilization purposes also met with partial success at best. In the spring of 1975, as the economy neared the bottom of a recession, President Gerald R. Ford and Congress agreed on a temporary tax cut to spur consumer spending: They returned to each taxpayer part of the taxes paid in 1974 and they reduced income tax rates for the balance of 1975. However, consumers confounded the wishes of the president and Congress by saving a good deal of their rebates rather than spending them.

Case 4: The 1981–1984 Tax Cuts

A series of reductions in personal income tax rates was a major campaign promise of Ronald Reagan, one which was promptly redeemed. Tax rates fell by about 23 percent between 1981 and 1984, and consumer spending increased by more or less the amounts that economists predicted.

What went wrong in 1968 and 1975 but did not go wrong in 1964 and 1981–1984? This chapter will attempt to provide some answers. We begin by exploring the important relationship between consumer income and consumer spending, more or less retracing the chain of logic that led government economists to the right conclusion in 1964. Once this is accomplished, we turn to some of the complications that made things go awry in 1968 and 1975.

Consumer Spending and Income: The Important Relationship

An economist interested in predicting how consumer spending will respond to a change in personal income tax payments must first ask how C is related to disposable income; for an increase in taxes is a decrease in after-tax income, and a reduction in taxes is an increase in after-tax income. This section, therefore, will examine what we know about the response of consumer spending to a change in disposable income.

Figure 8–2 depicts the historical paths of C and DI for the United States since 1929. The association is obviously rather close and certainly suggests that consumption will rise whenever disposable income does, and fall whenever income falls. The difference between the two lines is personal saving. Notice how little saving consumers did during the Great Depression of the 1930s, where the two lines are very close together, and how much they did during World War II, when many consumer goods were either unavailable or rationed so there was little on which to spend money.

Of course, knowing that consumer expenditures, C, will move in the same direction as disposable income, DI, is not enough for policy planners. They need to know *how much* one will go up when the other rises a given amount.

Figure 8–2

CONSUMER SPENDING AND DISPOSABLE INCOME IN THE UNITED STATES SINCE 1929
This time series chart shows the behavior of consumer spending and disposable income in the United States since 1929. Except for the World War II years, the correspondence between the two variables is remarkably close. The distance between the two lines represents consumer saving which was obviously quite small during the Great Depression of the 1930s and quite large during World War II.
SOURCE: U.S. Department of Commerce.

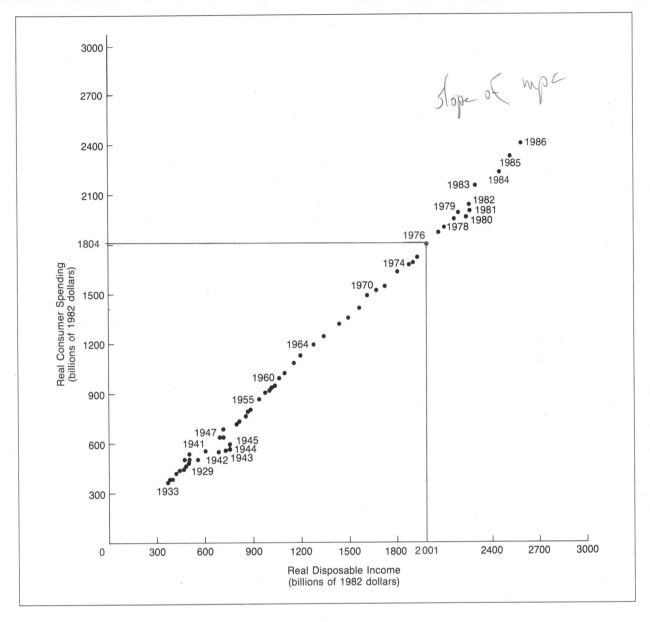

Figure 8–3

SCATTER DIAGRAM OF CONSUMER SPENDING AND DISPOSABLE INCOME IN THE
UNITED STATES, 1929–1986

This diagram shows the same data as depicted in Figure 8–2 but in a different manner. Each point
on the diagram represents the data for both consumer spending and disposable income during a
particular year. For example, the point labeled "1976" indicates that in that year consumer
spending was $1804 billion while disposable income was $2001 billion. Diagrams like this one are
called "scatter diagrams."

Figure 8–3 presents the same data that we saw in Figure 8–2 but in a way
designed to help answer the "how much" question.

  Economists call such pictures **scatter diagrams**, and they are very useful in
predicting how one economic variable (in this case, consumer spending) will
change in response to a change in another economic variable (in this case, disposable income). Each dot in the diagram represents the data on C and DI corresponding to a particular year. For example, the point labeled "1976" shows

A **scatter diagram** is a
graph showing the
relationship between two
variables (such as
consumption and
disposable income). Each
year is represented by a
point in the diagram.
The coordinates of each
year's point show the
value of the two variables
in that year.

that real consumer expenditures in 1976 were $1804 billion (which we read off the vertical axis), while real disposable incomes amounted to $2001 billion (which we read off the horizontal axis). Similarly, each year from 1929 to 1986 is represented by its own dot in Figure 8–3.

How can such a diagram assist the fiscal policy planner? Imagine that this is 1963 and you must decide whether to recommend to Congress a tax cut of $5 billion, $10 billion, or $15 billion. (It has already been decided that a cut smaller than $5 billion is not worth the legislative effort and that a cut of more than $15 billion is politically infeasible.) You have forecasts of what consumer expenditures are expected to be if taxes are not reduced. This, plus other forecasts of investment and government spending, has led you to conclude that aggregate demand in 1964 will be insufficient if taxes are not reduced.

To assist your imagination, another scatter diagram is given in Figure 8–4. This one removes the points for 1964 through 1986, which appear in Figure 8–3; after all, these were not known in 1963. Years prior to 1947 have also been removed because both the Great Depression and wartime rationing seriously disturbed the normal relationship between DI and C. With no more training in economics than you have right now, what would you do?

One rough-and-ready approach is to get a ruler, set it down on Figure 8–4, and sketch a straight line that comes as close as possible to hitting all the points. Try that now. You will not be able to hit each point exactly, but you will find that you can come remarkably close. The line you have just drawn summarizes, in a very rough way, the consumption-income relationship that is the focus of this chapter. We see at once that it confirms something we might have guessed—that a rise in income is associated with a rise in consumer spending. The slope of the line is certainly positive.

The slope of your line is very important.[5] That line has been drawn into Figure 8–5, and we note that its slope is:

$$\text{Slope} = \frac{\text{Vertical change}}{\text{Horizontal change}} = \frac{\$90 \text{ billion}}{\$100 \text{ billion}} = 0.90.$$

[5]To review the concept of *slope*, turn back to page 20.

Figure 8–4

SCATTER DIAGRAM OF CONSUMER SPENDING AND DISPOSABLE INCOME IN THE UNITED STATES, 1947–1963

This scatter diagram omits some of the data found in Figure 8–3 and indicates the information that policy planners might have used in deciding upon the size of the 1964 income tax cut.

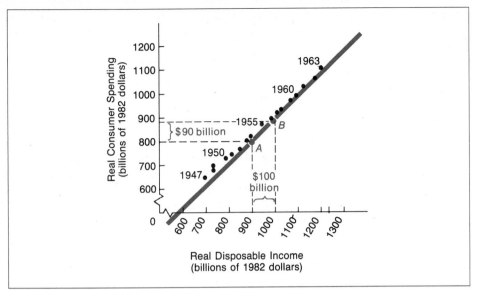

Figure 8–5
SCATTER DIAGRAM OF
CONSUMER SPENDING
AND DISPOSABLE
INCOME IN THE UNITED
STATES, 1947–1963
This diagram is the same as
Figure 8–4 except for the
addition of a straight line that
comes about as close as
possible to fitting all the data
points.

Since the horizontal change involved in the move from *A* to *B* represents a rise in disposable income of $100 billion (from $1000 billion to $1100 billion), and the corresponding vertical change represents the associated $90 billion rise in consumer spending (from $900 to $1000 billion), the slope of the line indicates how spending responds to changes in disposable income. In this case, we see that each additional $1 of income leads to 90 cents of additional spending.

In terms of the policy issue of 1964, this line can therefore help provide an answer to the question: How much more consumer spending will be induced by tax cuts of $5 billion, $10 billion, or $15 billion if the effects are similar to those observed in the past? First, we need to keep in mind that each dollar of tax cut increases disposable income by $1. Then we apply Figure 8–5's finding that each additional dollar of disposable income increases consumer spending by 90 cents, and we conclude that proposed tax cuts of $5 billion, $10 billion, or $15 billion would be expected to increase consumer spending by $4.5 billion, $9.0 billion, and $13.5 billion, respectively. Similar questions addressed by economists in 1964 led to a decision to cut taxes by about $9 billion.

Later in this and other chapters, we will encounter several reasons why this procedure, while basically valid, must be used with great caution.

The Consumption Function and the
Marginal Propensity to Consume

It has been said that economics is just systematized common sense. Let us, then, try to organize and generalize what has been a completely intuitive discussion thus far. One thing we have learned is that there is a close and apparently reliable relationship between consumer spending, *C*, and disposable income, *DI*. Economists call this relationship the **consumption function.**

A second fact we have picked up from these figures is that the slope of the consumption function is fairly constant. We infer this from the fact that the straight line in Figure 8–5 comes close to touching every point. If the slope of the consumption function had changed a lot, it would not be possible to do so well with a single straight line. Because of its importance in such applications as the tax-cut example, economists have given a special name to this slope — the

The **consumption function** is the relationship between total consumer expenditure and total disposable income in the economy, holding all other determinants of consumer spending constant.

The **marginal propensity to consume** (or **MPC** for short) is the ratio of the change in consumption to the change in disposable income that produces the change in consumption. On a graph, it appears as the slope of the consumption function.

marginal propensity to consume, or **MPC** for short. The MPC tells us how many more dollars consumers will spend if disposable income rises by $1 billion.

$$\text{MPC} = \frac{\text{Change in consumption}}{\begin{array}{c}\text{Change in disposable}\\ \text{income that produces}\\ \text{the change in}\\ \text{consumption}\end{array}}$$

The MPC is best illustrated by an example, and for this purpose we turn away from U.S. data for a moment and look at the consumption and income data of a hypothetical country called Macroland (see Table 8–1). The data for Macroland resemble those for the United States, except that in Macroland, C and *DI* figures happen to be nice round numbers, which facilitates computation.

Columns 1 and 2 of Table 8–1 show annual consumer expenditure and disposable income from 1983 to 1988. These two columns constitute Macroland's consumption function and are plotted in Figure 8–6. Column 3 in the table shows the marginal propensity to consume (MPC), which is the slope of the line in Figure 8–6; it is derived from the first two columns. We can see that between 1985 and 1986, *DI* rose by $500 billion (from $3000 to $3500) while C rose by $400 billion (from $2500 to $2900). Thus the MPC was:

$$\frac{\text{Change in consumption}}{\text{Change in disposable income}} = \frac{\$400}{\$500} = 0.80.$$

As you can easily verify, the MPC between any other pair of years in Macroland was also 0.80. This explains why the slope of the line in Figure 8–5 was so crucial in estimating the effect of a tax cut. This slope, which we found to be 0.90, is nothing but the MPC for the United States. And it is the MPC that tells us how much *additional* spending will be induced by each dollar *change* in disposable income. For each $1 of tax cut, economists expect consumption to rise by $1 times the marginal propensity to consume.

To estimate the *initial* effect of a tax cut on consumer spending, economists must first estimate the MPC and then multiply the amount of the tax cut by the estimated MPC. But since they never know the true MPC with certainty, this prediction is always subject to some margin of error.[6]

[6]The word "initial" in the first sentence is an important one. Later chapters explain why the effects discussed in this chapter are only the beginning of the story.

Table 8–1
CONSUMPTION AND INCOME IN MACROLAND

YEAR	(1) CONSUMPTION, C (billions of dollars)	(2) DISPOSABLE INCOME, *DI* (billions of dollars)	(3) MARGINAL PROPENSITY TO CONSUME, MPC
1983	1700	2000	
1984	2100	2500	0.8
1985	2500	3000	0.8
1986	2900	3500	0.8
1987	3300	4000	0.8
1988	3700	4500	0.8

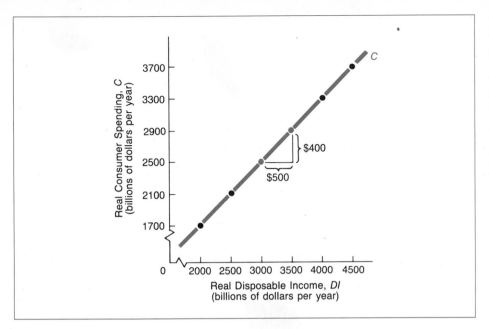

Figure 8–6
THE CONSUMPTION FUNCTION OF MACROLAND
This diagram is similar to Figure 8–5, except that it applies to a hypothetical (and blissfully simple!) economy called Macroland. As can be seen, a straight-line consumption function passes through every point exactly. The slope of this line is 0.8, which is the marginal propensity to consume in Macroland.

In 1963, for example, economists multiplied the anticipated $9 billion tax cut by the estimated MPC of 0.90 and concluded that consumer spending would rise initially by about $8 billion. Their estimate seems to have been remarkably accurate.

Movements Along Versus Shifts of the Consumption Function

Unfortunately, this sort of calculation does not always yield such precise results. Among the most important reasons for this is that the consumption function does not always stand still; sometimes it shifts.

You will recall from Chapter 4 the important distinction between a *movement along* a demand curve and a *shift* of the curve. A demand curve depicts the relationship between quantity demanded and only *one* of its many determinants—price. Thus, a change in price causes a *movement along the demand curve*, but a change in any other factor that influences quantity demanded causes a *shift of the entire demand curve*.

Because consumer spending is influenced by factors other than disposable income, a similar distinction is vital to understanding real-world consumption functions. Look back at the definition of the consumption function in the margin of page 147. A change in disposable income leads to a **movement along the consumption function** precisely because the consumption function depicts the relationship between C and *DI*. This is what we have been considering so far. But consumption also has other determinants, and a change in any of these "other determinants" will **shift the entire consumption function**—as indicated in Figure 8–7. These shifts account for many of the errors in forecasting consumption. To summarize:

Any change in disposable income moves us *along* a given consumption function. But a change in any of the other variables that influence consumption *shifts* the entire consumption schedule (see Figure 8–7).

Figure 8–7
SHIFTS OF THE
CONSUMPTION
FUNCTION

An increase in disposable income causes a movement along a fixed consumption function, such as the movement from point *A* to point *B* on consumption function C_0. But a change in any other determinant of consumer spending will cause the whole consumption function to shift upward (consumption function C_1) or downward (consumption function C_2).

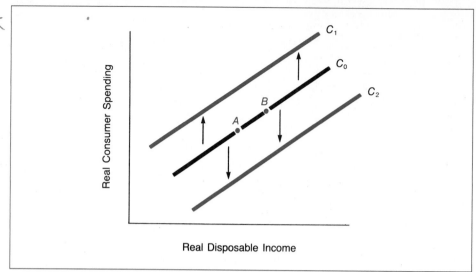

Let us now list some of these "other variables" that can shift the consumption function.

Other Determinants of Consumer Spending

Wealth

One factor affecting consumption is consumers' *wealth*, which is a source of demand in addition to income. Wealth and income are different things. A wealthy person may currently have little *income*. Similarly, a high-income individual who spends all he earns will not accumulate wealth. To appreciate the importance of the distinction, consider two consumers, both earning $35,000 this year. One of them has $100,000 in the bank, while the other has no assets at all. Who do you think will spend more this year? Presumably the one with the big bank account.

The general point is that current income is not the only source of funds that households have; they can also finance spending by withdrawals from their bank accounts or by cashing in other forms of wealth. A stock market boom may therefore raise the consumption function (see the shift from C_0 to C_1 in Figure 8–7), while a collapse of stock prices may lower it (see the shift from C_0 to C_2).

The Price Level

A good deal of consumer wealth is held in forms whose values are fixed in money terms. Money itself is the most obvious example of this, but government bonds, savings accounts, and corporate bonds are all assets with fixed face values in money terms. The purchasing power of any **money fixed asset** obviously declines whenever the price level rises, which means that the asset can buy less. For example, if the price level rises by 10 percent, a $1000 government bond will buy about 10 percent less than it could when prices were lower. Consequently:

A **money fixed asset** is an asset with a face value fixed in terms of dollars, such as money itself, government bonds, and corporate bonds.

Higher overall prices, by eroding the purchasing power of consumer wealth, decrease the demand for goods and services.

This is no trivial matter. It has been estimated that consumers in the United States hold money fixed assets worth over $3 *trillion,* so that each 1 percent rise in the price level reduces the purchasing power of consumer wealth by over $30 billion, a tidy sum. The process, of course, operates equally well in reverse. A decline in the price level increases the purchasing power of money fixed assets. So:

Lower overall prices, by enhancing the purchasing power of consumer wealth, increase the demand for goods and services.

For these reasons a change in the price level will shift the entire consumption function. Specifically,

A higher price level leads to lower real wealth and therefore to less spending *at any given level of real income.* Thus, a higher price level leads to a lower consumption function (such as C_2 in Figure 8–7). Conversely, a lower price level leads to a higher consumption function (such as C_1 in Figure 8–7).

Since students are often confused on this point, it is worth repeating that the depressing effect of the price level on consumer spending works through real *wealth,* not through real *income.* The consumption function is a relationship between *real* consumer *income* and *real* consumer *spending.* Thus any decline in *real income,* regardless of its cause, moves the economy *leftward along a fixed consumption function;* it does not shift the consumption function.[7] By contrast, any decline in *real wealth* will *shift the whole consumption function downward,* meaning that there is less spending at any given level of real income.

The Inflation Rate

Prices may be high and rising slowly, or they may be low but rising rapidly. Therefore, the depressing effect of a high *price level* on real consumer spending must be distinguished from any effect on spending of the *rate of inflation* (that is, the rate at which prices are rising).

Any effect of the inflation rate on consumer spending appears to be small; we are not even sure whether inflation stimulates or depresses spending. In the past, economists believed that high rates of inflation caused consumers to spend more to "beat" the inflation. That is, people were thought to purchase goods ahead of their needs in order to avoid the higher prices that loomed on the horizon. But behavior during the period of "double-digit" inflation in 1974 belied this contention: consumer spending was actually unusually *low* during this episode of high inflation, perhaps because of the uncertainty engendered by inflation. However, the opposite happened when inflation returned to double-digit levels in 1979–1980; this time, consumers started spending like mad.

Because there is no strong evidence that the rate of inflation shifts the consumption function systematically in one direction or the other, we shall assume that the position of the consumption function is influenced by the *price level,* but not by the *inflation rate.*

Expectations of Future Incomes

It will hardly be considered earth shattering to suggest that consumers' expectations about future income may affect how they spend today. This final determinant of consumer spending turns out to hold the key to answering the question

[7]This is true even if a rise in the price level lies behind the decline in real income. However, wages and prices normally move together, so there is no reason to expect real wages to fall when the price level rises.

we posed earlier. Why did the tax policy that succeeded so well in 1964 and the early 1980s fail to alter consumer spending as much in 1968 and 1975?

Why Tax Policy Failed in 1968 and 1975

To understand how expectations of future incomes affect current consumer expenditures, consider the abbreviated life histories of three consumers given in Table 8–2. The reason for giving our three imaginary individuals such odd names will be apparent shortly.

The consumer named "No Change" earned $100 in each of the four years considered in the table. The consumer named "Temporary Rise" earned $100 in three of the four years, but had a good year in 1975. The consumer named "Permanent Rise" enjoyed a permanent rise in income in 1975 and was clearly the richest.

Now let us use our common sense to figure out how much each of these consumers might have spent in 1975. "Temporary Rise" and "Permanent Rise" had the same income that year. Do you think they spent the same amount? Not if they had some ability to foresee their future income, because "Permanent Rise" was richer in the long run.

Now compare "No Change" and "Temporary Rise." Temporary Rise had 20 percent higher income in 1975 ($120 versus $100) but only 5 percent more over the entire four-year period ($420 versus $400). Do you think her spending was closer to 20 percent above No Change's or closer to 5 percent above it? Most people guess the latter.

The point of this example is that it is reasonable for consumers to decide on their *current* consumption spending by looking at their *long-run* income prospects. This should not be a shocking idea to most college students. How many of you are spending only what you earn this year? Probably not very many. And this is not because you are all foolish spendthrifts. On the contrary, you are rational planners. Knowing that your college education gives you a reasonable expectation of future income prospects much greater than those you now have, you are no doubt spending with that in mind.

Now let us see what all this has to do with the failure of the 1975 income tax rebate. For this purpose, imagine that the three rows in Table 8–2 now represent the entire economy under three different government policies. Recall that 1975 was the year of the rebate. The first row ("No Change") shows the unchanged path of disposable income if no tax cut was enacted. The second ("Temporary Rise") shows an increase in disposable income attributable to a tax cut *for one year only*. The bottom row ("Permanent Rise") shows a policy that increases DI in *every future year* by cutting taxes permanently in 1975. Which

Table 8–2
INCOMES OF THREE CONSUMERS

CONSUMER	INCOMES IN EACH YEAR				TOTAL INCOME
	1974	1975	1976	1977	
No Change	100	100	100	100	400
Temporary Rise	100	120	100	100	420
Permanent Rise	100	120	120	120	460

of the two lower rows do you imagine would have generated more consumer spending in 1975? The bottom row ("Permanent Rise"), of course. What we have concluded, then, is this:

Permanent cuts in income taxes cause greater increases in consumer spending than do temporary cuts of equal magnitude.

The application of this analysis to the case of the 1975 tax cut is immediate. The rebates were clearly one-time increases in income like that experienced by "Temporary Rise" in Table 8–2; no future income was affected. Hence, it is not surprising that statistical studies show that the 1975 tax cut had little effect on consumer spending.

Much the same situation prevailed in 1968, when Congress enacted a temporary 10 percent increase in income taxes to help finance the Vietnam War. Consumers considered the resulting decrease in their disposable income as only a *temporary* loss and did not curtail their spending as much as government officials had hoped. The general lesson is:

A permanent increase in income taxes provides a greater deterrent to consumer spending than does a temporary increase of equal magnitude.

We have, then, what appears to be a general principle, backed up both by historical evidence and common sense. Permanent changes in income taxes have a more significant impact on consumer spending than do temporary changes. Though it may now seem obvious, this is not a lesson you would have learned from the introductory textbooks of 1968. It is one that we learned the hard way, through bitter experience.

The Predictability of Consumer Behavior

We have now learned enough to see why the economist's problem in predicting how consumers will react to an increase or decrease in taxes is not nearly as simple as suggested earlier in this chapter.

The principal problem seems to be anticipating how taxpayers will view any changes in the income tax law. If the government *says* that a tax cut is permanent, will consumers *believe* it and increase their spending accordingly? Perhaps not, if the government has a history of raising taxes after promising to keep them low. Similarly, when (as in 1968) the government explicitly announces that a tax increase is temporary, will consumers always believe this? Or might they greet such an announcement with a hefty dose of skepticism? This is quite possible if there is a long history of "temporary" tax increases that stayed on the books indefinitely.

Thus the effectiveness of any *future* tax policy move may well depend on the government's *past* track record. A government that repeatedly uses a succession of so-called "permanent" tax cuts and tax increases for short-run stabilization purposes may find consumers beginning to ignore the tax changes entirely. The story of the boy who cried wolf is not yet required reading for fiscal policy planners, but it probably should be recommended.

Nor is this the only problem. Economists may fail to take adequate account of large and rapid accumulations of wealth (as happened immediately after World War II, when consumption forecasts were notoriously low) or of sizable losses of wealth (such as the drastic decline in the stock market in 1973–1975, when consumption forecasts were too high). Poor forecasts of future prices may lead consumption forecasts astray. And there are further hazards that we have not even mentioned here. Economic predictions are inexact, and predictions of consumption illustrate this well.

There is much more that can be said about the determinants of consumption, but it is best to leave the rest to more advanced courses. For we are now ready to apply our knowledge of the consumption function to the construction of the first model of the whole economy. While it is true that income determines consumption, the consumption function in turn helps to determine the level of income. If that sounds like circular reasoning, read the next chapter!

Summary

1. Aggregate demand is the total amount of goods and services that consumers, businesses, government units, and foreigners are willing to purchase. It can be expressed as the sum $C + I + G + X - IM$, where C is consumer spending, I is investment spending, G is government purchases, X is exports, and IM is imports.

2. Economists reserve the term "investment" to refer to purchases of newly produced factories, machinery, and houses.

3. National product is the total output of final goods and services of the economy. It is most commonly measured by the gross national product.

4. National income is the sum of the *before-tax* wages, interest, rents, and profits earned by all individuals in the economy. By necessity, it must be equal to national product.

5. Disposable income is the sum of the incomes of all individuals in the economy *after taxes and transfers,* and is the chief determinant of consumer expenditure.

6. All of these concepts, and others, can be depicted in a circular flow diagram that shows expenditures on all four sources flowing into business firms and national income flowing out.

7. The government often has tried to manipulate aggregate demand by influencing private consumption decisions, usually through the personal income tax. Although this policy seemed to work well in 1964 and 1981, it did not work well in 1968 and 1975.

8. The close relationship between consumer spending, C, and disposable income, DI, is called the consumption function. Its slope, which is used to predict the change in consumption that will be caused by a change in income taxes, is called the marginal propensity to consume (MPC).

9. Changes in disposable income move us along a given consumption function. Changes in any of the other variables that affect C shift the entire consumption function. Among the most important of these other variables are total consumer wealth, the price level, and expected future incomes.

10. Because consumers hold so many money fixed assets, they lose out when prices rise, which leads them to reduce their spending.

11. Future income prospects help explain why tax policy did not affect consumption as much as was hoped in 1968 and 1975. This is because the 1968 tax increase and the 1975 tax cut were both temporary, and therefore left future incomes unaffected. By contrast, the 1964 and 1981–1984 tax cuts were permanent, and affected future as well as current incomes. It is no surprise, then, that the 1964 and 1981 actions had stronger effects on spending than did the 1968 or 1975 actions.

Concepts for Review

Aggregate demand
Consumer expenditure (C)
Investment spending (I)
Government purchases (G)
Net exports ($X - IM$)
$C + I + G + X - IM$

National income
Disposable income (DI)
Circular flow diagram
Transfer payments
Scatter diagram
Consumption function

Marginal propensity to consume (MPC)
Movements along versus shifts of the consumption function
Money fixed assets
Temporary versus permanent tax changes

Questions for Discussion

1. What are the four components of aggregate demand? Which of these is the largest? Which is the smallest?
2. What is the difference between "investment" as the term is used by most people and "investment" as defined by an economist? Which of the following acts constitute "investment" according to the economist's definition?
   a. General Motors constructs a new assembly line.
   b. You buy 100 shares of General Motors stock.
   c. A small steel company goes bankrupt, and Bethlehem Steel purchases its factory and equipment.
   d. Your family buys a newly constructed home from a developer.
   e. Your family buys an older home from another family. (*Hint:* Are any *new* products demanded by this action?)
3. What would the circular flow diagram (Figure 8–1, page 140) look like in an economy with no government and no foreign trade? Draw one for yourself.
4. The marginal propensity to consume (MPC) for the nation as a whole is roughly 0.90. Explain in words what this means. What is your personal MPC?
5. Look at the scatter diagram in Figure 8–3 (page 145). What does it tell you about what was going on in this country in the years 1942–1945?
6. What is a "consumption function," and why is it a useful device for government economists planning a tax cut?
7. On a piece of graph paper, construct the consumption function for Simpleland from the data given below and determine the MPC.

YEAR	CONSUMER SPENDING	DISPOSABLE INCOME
1984	900	1000
1985	1350	1500
1986	1800	2000
1987	2250	2500
1988	2700	3000

8. In which direction will the consumption function for Simpleland shift if the price level rises? Show this on your graph.
9. Explain why permanent tax cuts are likely to lead to bigger increases in consumer spending than are temporary tax cuts.
10. (More difficult) Between 1984 and 1985, real disposable income (in 1982 dollars) rose from $2470 billion to $2542 billion. Use the data on real consumption expenditures given on the inside front cover of this book to compare the change in C to the change in DI. Explain why dividing the two does not give a good estimate of the marginal propensity to consume.

Appendix A
The Saving Function and the Marginal Propensity to Save

There is an alternative way of looking at the relationships we have discussed in this chapter. Disposable income that is not spent must be saved. Therefore, we can examine the effect of income on *saving* as well as its effect on consumer *spending*.

To see how saving appears on the consumption function diagram, we have repeated the consumption function of Macroland (see Figure 8–6) in Figure 8–8 and added a 45° line. You will recall that a 45° line marks those points where the distances along the horizontal and vertical axes are equal. (If you wish to review, see page 23.) Since the consumption schedule is below the 45° line, the figure shows that consumer spending is less than income, so some is being *saved*.

To find the amount of saving at each level of income, we need only read the vertical distance from the consumption function up to the 45° line. For example, when income is $4000 billion, saving is the distance AB, or $700 billion.

There is also a more direct way to find saving. Table 8–3 repeats the consumption and disposable income data for Macroland from Table 8–1 (page 148). Then, in column 3, we compute the difference between disposable income and consumption, which gives us **aggregate saving.**

Aggregate saving is the difference between disposable income and consumer expenditure. In symbols, $S = DI - C$.

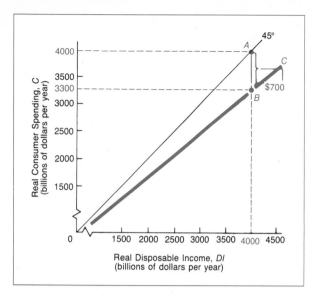

Figure 8–8

THE CONSUMPTION FUNCTION OF MACROLAND
The consumption function of Macroland, which we
encountered in Figure 8–6 (page xxx), is repeated here, and a
45° line is added for convenience. Since consumption and
saving must always add up to disposable income, the vertical
distance between the two lines represents saving. For
example, points A and B indicate that when disposable
income is $4000 billion, saving is $700 billion.

This subtraction is exactly what we showed graphically in Figure 8–8. Columns 2 and 3 of Table
8–3 constitute what economists call the **saving
function.**

The **saving function** is the relationship between
total consumer saving and total disposable income
in the economy, holding other determinants of
saving constant.

The data of Table 8–3 are portrayed in
Figure 8–9, which could equally well have been

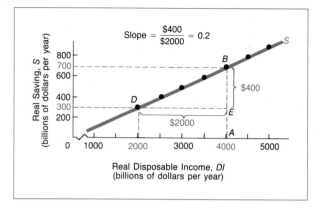

Figure 8–9

THE SAVING FUNCTION OF MACROLAND
The saving function of Macroland, depicted here, can
be constructed either from the data in Table 8–3 or from
Figure 8–8. This is because when we plot saving against
disposable income (as we do here), we are also plotting the
difference between consumption and disposable income
(the vertical distance between line C and the 45° line in
Figure 8–8) against disposable income.

constructed as the difference between the 45° line
and the C line in Figure 8–8. (Because saving is
so much less than consumption, we have stretched
the scale of the vertical axis considerably.) Points
A and B correspond to the same points in
Figure 8–8. When the consumption function is a
straight line, and thus has a constant slope, the
same will be true of the saving function. In
Figure 8–9, we show this slope as the ratio of distance EB to distance DE or $400/$2000 = 0.2.
Economists call this slope the **marginal propensity
to save.**

The **marginal propensity to save** (or **MPS**) is the
slope of the saving function. It tells us how much
more consumers will save if disposable income
rises by $1 billion.

Table 8–3

SAVING IN MACROLAND

YEAR	(1) CONSUMPTION, C (billions of dollars)	(2) DISPOSABLE INCOME, DI (billions of dollars)	(3) SAVINGS, S (billions of dollars)	(4) MARGINAL PROPENSITY TO SAVE, MPS
1983	1700	2000	300	
1984	2100	2500	400	0.2
1985	2500	3000	500	0.2
1986	2900	3500	600	0.2
1987	3300	4000	700	0.2
1988	3700	4500	800	0.2

You may have noticed that the MPS is 0.2 while the MPC for Macroland is 0.8. They add up to 1, and not by accident. Since the portion of each additional dollar of disposable income that is not spent must be saved, the MPC and the MPS always add up to 1. It is a simple fact of accounting.

The MPC and the MPS always add up to 1, meaning that an additional dollar of income must be divided between consumption and saving. In symbols:

$$MPC + MPS = 1.$$

This enables us to compute either one of them from the other.

Summary

1. Instead of studying the consumption function, it is possible to study the same data by looking at the saving function, which is defined as the relationship between disposable income and consumer saving.
2. Since consumer saving is merely the difference between disposable income and consumer expenditure, everything we have learned about the consumption function applies to the saving function.
3. The amount of additional saving caused by a $1 increase in disposable income is called the marginal propensity to save, or MPS.
4. Since each additional $1 of disposable income is either spent or saved, the MPC and the MPS must always add up to 1. Thus, knowledge of one implies knowledge of the other.

Concepts for Review

Aggregate saving
Saving function
Marginal propensity to save

Questions for Discussion

1. Look at the circular flow diagram in Figure 8–1 (page 140). Where does the saving function enter the picture?
2. If the MPC in the U.S. economy is about 0.90, how large is the MPS?
3. Take the data from Simpleland in Question 7 on page 140 and use them to construct a saving function for Simpleland on a piece of graph paper.
4. (More difficult) If taxes are cut *temporarily* and consumer spending does not increase much, what must happen to consumer saving? Ask your instructor what happened to consumer saving immediately after the 1975 tax cuts.

Appendix B
National Income Accounting

The type of macroeconomic analysis presented in this book dates from the publication of John Maynard Keynes's *The General Theory of Employment, Interest, and Money* in 1936. But at that time there was really no way to test Keynes's theories because the necessary data did not exist. It took some years for the theoretical notions used by Keynes to find concrete expression in real-world data. The system of measurement devised for this purpose is called **national income accounting.**

The development of this system of accounts ranks as a great achievement in applied economics, perhaps as important in its own right as Keynes's theoretical work. For without it the practical value of Keynesian analysis would be severely limited. Many men and women spent long hours wrestling with the numerous difficult conceptual questions that arose in translating the theory into numbers, but they had one acknowledged leader: Professor Simon Kuznets of Harvard University, who, in 1971, was awarded the Nobel Prize in economics for his contributions to economic measurement techniques. Along the way some more-or-less arbitrary decisions and conventions had to be made. You may not agree with all of them, but the accounting framework that was devised is eminently serviceable, though, inevitably, it has some limitations that must be understood.

Defining GNP: Exceptions to the Rules

We first encountered the concept of **gross national product (GNP)** in Chapter 5.

Gross national product (GNP) is the sum of the money values of all final goods and services produced during a specified period of time, usually one year.

However, the definition of GNP has certain exceptions we have not yet noted.

First, the treatment of government output involves a minor departure from the principle of using market prices. Outputs of private industries are sold on markets, so their prices are observed. But "outputs" of government offices are not sold; indeed, it is sometimes even difficult to define what those outputs are. Lacking prices for outputs, national income accountants fall back on the only prices they have: prices for the inputs from which the outputs are produced. Thus:

Government outputs are valued at the cost of the inputs needed to produce them.

This means, for example, that if a clerk at the Department of Motor Vehicles earns $8 an hour and spends one-half hour torturing you with explanations of why you cannot get a driver's license, that particular government "service" is considered as being worth $4, and will increase GNP by that amount.

Second, some goods that are not actually sold on markets during the year are nonetheless counted in that year's GNP. These are the goods that are produced during the year but not sold; that is, goods that firms stockpile as *inventories*. Goods that are added to inventories count in GNP even though they do not pass through markets.

National income statisticians treat inventories as if they were "bought" by the firms that produced them, even though this "purchase" never takes place.

Finally, the treatment of investment goods runs slightly counter to the rule that only final goods are to be counted. In a broad sense, factories, generators, machine tools, and the like might be considered as intermediate goods. After all, their owners want them only for use in producing other goods, not for any innate value that they possess. But this would present a real problem, for factories and machines normally are never sold to consumers. So when would we count them in GNP? National income statisticians avoid this problem by defining investment goods as final products demanded by the firms that buy them.

Now that we have a more complete definition of what the GNP is, let us turn to the problem of actually measuring it. National income accountants have devised three ways to perform this task, and we consider each in turn.

GNP as the Sum of Final Goods and Services

The first way to measure GNP seems to be the most natural, since it follows so directly from the circular flow diagram in this chapter. It also turns out to be the most useful definition for macroeconomic analysis. We simply add up the final demands of all consumers, business firms, government, and foreigners. Using the symbols C, I, G, and X − IM just as we did in the text, we have:

$$GNP = C + I + G + X - IM.$$

The I that appears in the actual U.S. national accounts is called **gross private domestic investment.** The word "gross" will be explained presently. "Private" indicates that government investment is considered part of G, and "domestic" just means that machinery sold by American firms to foreign companies is included in exports rather than in I. Gross private domestic investment in the United States has three components: business investment in plant and equipment, residential construction (home building), [8] and inventory

[8]Thus purchases of new homes are considered part of I rather than part of C.

investment. We repeat again that *only* these three things are **investment** in national income accounting terminology.

As defined in the national income accounts, **investment** includes only newly produced capital goods, such as machinery, factories, and new homes. It does not include exchanges of existing assets.

In common parlance, all sorts of activities that are not part of the GNP are often called "investment." People are said to "invest" in the stock market when they purchase shares. Or wealthy individuals "invest" in works of art. But since transactions like these merely exchange one type of asset (money) for another (stock or art works), they are not included in the GNP.

The symbol G, for government purchases, represents the *volume of current goods and services purchased by all levels of government*. Thus, anything the government pays to its employees is counted in G, as are its purchases of paper, pencils, airplanes, bombs, typewriters, and so forth.

Few citizens realize that *most of what the federal government spends its money on is not for purchases of goods and services*. Instead, it is on **transfer payments** — literally, giving away money — either to individuals or to other levels of government.

The importance of the conceptual distinction lies in the fact that G represents the part of the national product that government uses up for its own purposes — to pay for armies, bureaucrats, paper, and ink — whereas transfer payments merely represent shuffling of purchasing power from one group of citizens to another group. Except for the administrators needed to run the programs, real economic resources are not used up in this process.

In adding up the nation's total output as the sum of $C + I + G + X - IM$, we are summing the shares of GNP that are used up by consumers, investors, government, and foreigners, respectively. Since transfer payments merely give someone the capability to spend on C, it is logical to exclude them from our definition of G, including in C only the portion of these transfer payments that is spent. If we included them in G, the same spending would get counted twice: once in G and then again in C.

The final component of GNP is net exports, which are simply exports of goods and services minus imports of goods and services. Notice that both goods *and services* count, though the news media devote most attention to the monthly data on trade in goods ("merchandise trade").

Table 8–4 shows GNP for 1986, in both nominal and real terms, computed as the sum of $C + I + G + X - IM$. The most stunning numbers in the table are the large negative figures for net exports. We will have much to say about America's huge trade deficit in Part 5.

GNP as the Sum of All Factor Payments

There is another way to count up the GNP — *by adding up all the incomes in the economy*. Let's see how this method handles some typical transactions. Suppose General Electric builds a generator and sells it to General Motors for $1 million. The first method of calculating GNP simply counts the $1 million as part of *I*. The second method asks: What incomes resulted from the production of this generator? The answer might be something like this:

Wages of G.E. employees	$400,000
Interest to bondholders	$50,000
Rentals of buildings	$50,000
Profits of G.E. stockholders	$100,000

The total is $600,000. The remaining $400,000 is accounted for by inputs that G.E. purchased from

Table 8–4

GROSS NATIONAL PRODUCT IN 1986
AS THE SUM OF FINAL DEMANDS

ITEM	AMOUNT (billions of current dollars)	AMOUNT (billions of 1982 dollars)
Personal consumption expenditures (C)	2799.8	2450.5
Gross private domestic investment (I)	671.0	654.0
Government purchases of goods and services (G)	869.7	754.5
Net exports (X − IM)	−105.5	−145.8
Exports (X)	376.2	377.4
Imports (IM)	481.7	523.2
Gross national product (Y)	4235.0	3713.3

SOURCE: U.S. Department of Commerce. Totals do not add up precisely due to rounding.

other companies: steel, circuitry, tubing, rubber, and so on.

But if we traced this $400,000 back further, we would find that it is accounted for by the wages, interest, and rentals paid by these other companies, *plus* their profits, *plus* their purchases from other firms. In fact, for *every* firm in the economy, there is an accounting identity that says:

$$\text{Revenues from sales} = \begin{cases} \text{Wages paid } + \\ \text{Interest paid } + \\ \text{Rentals paid } + \\ \text{Profits earned } + \\ \text{Purchases from} \\ \quad \text{other firms.} \end{cases}$$

Why must this always be true? Because profits are the balancing item; they are what is *left over* after the firm has made all its other payments. In fact, this accounting identity is really just the definition of profits: sales revenue less all costs of production.

Now apply this accounting identity to *all the firms in the economy*. Total purchases from other firms are precisely what we call *intermediate goods*. What, then, do we get if we subtract these intermediate transactions from both sides of the equation?

$$\left.\begin{array}{c} \text{Revenues from sales} \\ \text{minus} \\ \text{Purchases from} \\ \text{other firms} \end{array}\right\} = \begin{cases} \text{Wages paid } + \\ \text{Interest paid } + \\ \text{Rentals paid } + \\ \text{Profits earned.} \end{cases}$$

On the right-hand side, we have the sum of all factor incomes: payments to labor, land, and capital. On the left-hand side, we have total sales minus sales of intermediate goods. This means that we have only sales of *final* goods, which is precisely our definition of GNP. Thus, the accounting identity for the entire economy can be rewritten as:

$$\text{GNP} = \text{Wages} + \text{Interest} + \text{Rents} + \text{Profits},$$

and this gives national income accountants another way to measure the GNP.

Table 8–5 shows 1986's GNP measured by the sum of all incomes. Once again, a few details have been omitted in our discussion. The sum of wages, interest, rents, and profits actually adds up

SOURCE: U.S. Department of Commerce. Totals do not add up precisely due to rounding.

Table 8–5

GROSS NATIONAL PRODUCT IN 1986 AS THE SUM OF INCOMES

ITEM	AMOUNT (billions of dollars)	
Compensation of employees (wages)	2504.9	
plus		
Net interest	326.1	
plus		
Rental income	16.7	
plus		
Profits	574.2	
Corporate profits		284.4
Proprietors' income		289.8
equals		
National income	3422.0	
plus		
Indirect business taxes and miscellaneous items	356.4	
equals		
Net national product	3778.4	
plus		
Depreciation	456.6	
equals		
Gross national product	4235.0	

to only $3422 billion (whereas GNP is $4235 billion). We call this sum the **national income** because it is the sum of all factor payments. But the actual selling prices of goods include another category of income that we have ignored so far: sales taxes, excise taxes, and the like. National income statisticians call these *indirect business taxes*, and when we add these to national income we obtain the **net national product (NNP).**

Now we are almost at the GNP. The only difference between GNP and NNP is **depreciation** of the nation's capital stock.

Depreciation is the value of the portion of the nation's capital equipment that is used up within the year. It tells us how much output is needed just to keep the economy's capital stock intact.

The difference between "gross" and "net" simply refers to whether depreciation is included or excluded. We add depreciation to NNP to get GNP. Thus, GNP is a measure of all final output, taking no account of the capital used up in the process (and therefore in need of replacement).

NNP deducts the required replacements to arrive at a *net* production figure.

From a conceptual point of view, most economists feel that NNP is a more meaningful indicator of the economy's output than GNP. After all, the depreciation component of GNP represents the output that is needed just to repair and replace worn out factories and machines; it is not available for anybody to consume.[9] So NNP seems to be a better measure of well-being than GNP. But, alas, GNP is much easier to measure because depreciation is a particularly tricky item. What fraction of his tractor did Farmer Jones "use up" last year? How much did the Empire State Building depreciate during 1987? If you ask yourself these difficult questions, you will understand why most economists feel that GNP is measured more accurately than is NNP. For this reason, most economic models are based on GNP.

In Table 8–5 you can hardly help noticing the preponderant share of employee compensation in total national income—about 73 percent. Labor is by far the most important factor of production. The return on land is truly minute—under 1 percent; and interest accounts for under 10 percent. Profits account for the remaining 17 percent, though the size of corporate profits (less than 9 percent of GNP) is much less than the public thinks. If, by some magic stroke, we could eliminate all corporate profits without upsetting the performance of the economy, the average worker would get a raise of about 11 percent!

GNP as the Sum of Values Added

It may strike you as strange that national income accountants include only *final* goods and services in GNP. Aren't *intermediate* goods part of the nation's product? They are, of course. The problem is that, if all intermediate goods were included in GNP, we would wind up double and triple counting things and therefore get an exaggerated impression of the amount of economic activity that is actually going on.

To explain why, and to show how national income accountants cope with this difficulty, we must introduce a new concept, called **value added.**

The **value added** by a firm is its revenue from selling a product minus the amount paid for goods and services purchased from other firms.

The intuitive sense of the concept is clear: If a firm buys some inputs from other firms, does something to them, and sells the resulting product for a price higher than it paid for the inputs, we say that the firm has "added value" to the product. If we sum up the values added in this way by all the firms in the economy, we must get the total value of all final products. Thus:

GNP can be measured as the sum of the values added by all firms.

To verify that this is so, look back at the last accounting identity on page 160. The left-hand side of this equation, sales revenue minus purchases from other firms, is precisely the firm's value added. Thus:

$$\text{Value added} = \frac{\text{Wages + Interest +}}{\text{Rents + Profits.}}$$

Since the second method we gave for measuring GNP is to add up wages, interest, rents, and profits, we see that the value-added approach must also yield the same answer.

The value-added concept is useful in avoiding double counting. Often it is hard to distinguish intermediate goods from final goods. Paint bought by a painter, for example, is an intermediate good. But paint bought by a do-it-yourselfer is a final good. What happens, then, if the professional painter has some paint left over and uses it to refurbish his own garage? The intermediate good becomes a final good. You can see that the line between intermediate goods and final goods is a fuzzy one in practice.

If we measure GNP by the sum of values added, however, it is not necessary to make such subtle distinctions. In this method, *every* purchase of a new good or service counts, but we do not count the entire selling price, only the portion that represents value added.

To illustrate this idea, consider the data in Table 8–6 and how they would affect GNP as the sum of final products. Our example begins when a farmer who grows soybeans sells them to a mill for $3 a bushel. This transaction does *not* count in the GNP, because the miller does not purchase the soybeans for his own use. The miller then

---

[9]If it is used for consumption, the capital stock will decline, and the nation will wind up poorer than before.

Table 8–6
AN ILLUSTRATION OF FINAL
AND INTERMEDIATE GOODS

ITEM	SELLER	BUYER	PRICE
Bushel of soybeans	Farmer	Miller	$ 3
Bag of soy meal	Miller	Factory	4
Gallon of soy sauce	Factory	Restaurant	8
Gallon of soy sauce used as seasoning	Restaurant	Consumers	10
		Total:	$25
	Addendum: Contribution to GNP:		**$10**

grinds up the soybeans and sells the resulting bag of soy meal to a factory that produces soy sauce. The miller receives $4, but GNP still has not increased because the ground beans are also an intermediate product. Next, the factory turns the beans into soy sauce, which it sells to your favorite Chinese restaurant for $8. Still no effect on GNP. But then the big moment arrives: The restaurant sells the sauce to you and other customers as a part of your meals, and you eat it. At this point, the $10 worth of soy sauce becomes a final product and is included in the GNP. Notice that if we had also counted the three intermediate transactions (farmer to miller, miller to factory, factory to restaurant), we would have come up with $25 — two and one-half times too much.

Why is it too much? The reason is straightforward. Neither the miller nor the factory owner nor the restauranteur value the product we have been considering *for its own sake*. Only the customers who eat the final product (the soy sauce) have had an increase in their material well-being. So only this last transaction counts in the GNP. However, as we shall now see, value-added calculations enable us to come up with the right answer ($10) by counting only *part* of each transaction. The basic idea is to count at each step only the contribution to the value of the ultimate final

product that is made at that step, excluding the values of items produced at earlier steps.

Ignoring the minor items (such as fertilizer) that the farmer purchases from others, the entire $3 selling price of the bushel of soybeans is new output produced by the farmer; that is, the whole $3 is value added. The miller then grinds the beans and sells them for $4. He has added $4 − $3 = $1 to the value of the beans. When the factory turns this soy meal into soy sauce and sells it for $8, it has added $8 − $4 = $4 more in value. And finally, when the restaurant sells it to hungry customers for $10, a further $2 of value is added.

Table 8–7 shows this chain of creation of value added by appending another column to Table 8–6. We see that the total value added by all four firms is $10, exactly the same as the restaurant's selling price. This is as it must be, for only the restaurant sells the soybeans as a final product.

Alternative Measures of the Income of the Nation

Economists use the term *national income* in two different ways. The most common usage is as a general term indicating the size of the income of the nation as a whole, without being specific about exactly how this income is to be measured. This is the sense in which the term "national income" is used in this book. The second, and much more precise, use of the term refers to a particular concept in national income accounting which we encountered in Table 8–5 on page 160: the sum of wages, interest, rents, and profits.

Aside from this formal definition of national income, what other accounting concept might be used to measure the total income of the nation? The first and most obvious candidate is the GNP

Table 8–7
AN ILLUSTRATION OF VALUE ADDED

ITEM	SELLER	BUYER	PRICE	VALUE ADDED
Bushel of soybeans	Farmer	Miller	$ 3	$ 3
Bag of soy meal	Miller	Factory	4	1
Gallon of soy sauce	Factory	Restaurant	8	4
Gallon of soy sauce used as seasoning	Restaurant	Consumers	10	2
		Totals:	$25	$10
	Addendum: Contribution to GNP			
	Final products...		$10	
	Sum of values added......................................		$10	

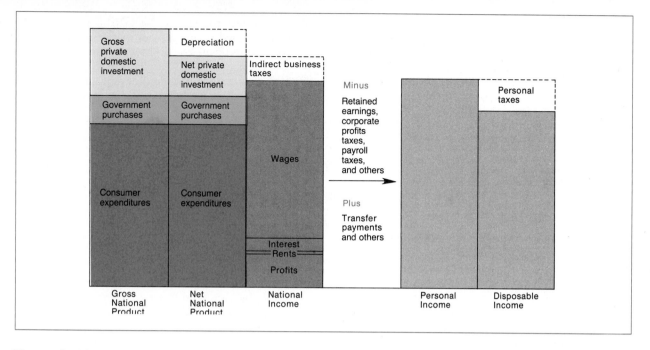

Figure 8–10
ALTERNATIVE MEASURES OF THE INCOME OF THE NATION
This bar chart indicates the relationships among the five alternative measures of the total income of the nation, starting with the largest and most comprehensive measure (GNP) and ranging down to the measure that most closely approximates the spendable income of consumers (disposable income).

itself. GNP, however, is intended to be a measure of *production*, and so has several drawbacks as a measure of *income*. First, it includes some output that represents income to no one—output that simply replaces worn-out machinery and buildings (depreciation). When we deduct this depreciation, we obtain the net national product (NNP), as shown in Figure 8–10. Second, because of sales taxes and related items (indirect business taxes), part of the price paid for each good and service does not represent the income of any individual. When we deduct these indirect business taxes from NNP, we arrive again at the formal definition of national income (refer to Figure 8–10).

There are, however, two other measures of income. **Personal income** is meant to be a better measure of the income that actually accrues to individuals. It is obtained from national income by *subtracting* corporate profits taxes, retained earnings, and payroll taxes (because these items are never received by individuals), and then *adding in* transfer payments (because these sources of income are not part of the wages, interest, rents, or profits that constitute the national income). As Figure 8–10 suggests, this adding and subtracting normally results in a number that is rather close to national income. Finally, if we subtract personal income taxes from personal income, we obtain **disposable income.**

Among all the concepts of the nation's income depicted in Figure 8–10, only two are used frequently in the construction of models of the economy: gross national product (GNP) and disposable income (*DI*). Since the models presented in this book ignore depreciation and indirect business taxes, GNP is basically identical to national income (see Figure 8–10). Similarly, if we ignore retained earnings, GNP and *DI* differ only by the amounts of taxes and transfers (again, see Figure 8–10).

Summary

1. Gross national product (GNP) is the sum of the money values of all final goods and services produced during a year and sold on organized markets.

There are, however, certain exceptions to this definition.

2. One way to measure the GNP is to add up the final

demands of consumers, investors, government, and foreigners: $GNP = C + I + G + X - IM$.

3. A second way to measure the GNP is to start with all the factor payments—wages, interest, rents, and profits—that constitute the national income, and then add indirect business taxes and depreciation.

4. A third way to measure the GNP is to sum up the values added by every firm in the economy (and then once again add indirect business taxes and depreciation).

5. Except for possible bookkeeping and statistical errors, all three methods must give the same answer.

Concepts for Review

National income accounting	Transfer payments	Depreciation
Gross National Product (GNP)	Net exports	Value added
Gross private domestic investment	National Income	Personal Income
Government purchases	Net National Product (NNP)	Disposable Income (*DI*)

Questions for Discussion

1. Which of the following transactions are included in the gross national product, and by how much does each raise GNP?
   a. You buy a new car, paying $8000.
   b. You buy a used car, paying $3000.
   c. IBM builds a $50 million factory to make computers.
   d. An unemployed worker receives a government check for $400 in unemployment compensation.
   e. General Motors builds 2000 Cadillacs at a cost of $14,000 each. Unable to sell them, it holds them as inventories.
   f. Mr. Black and Mr. Blue, each out for a Sunday drive, have a collision in which their cars are destroyed. Black and Blue each hire a lawyer to sue the other, paying the lawyers $1000 each for services rendered. The judge throws the case out of court.
   g. You sell a $400 painting to your roommate.

2. Explain the difference between final goods and intermediate goods. Why is it sometimes difficult to apply this distinction in practice? In this regard, why is the concept of value added useful?

3. Explain the difference between government spending and government purchases of goods and services (G). Which is larger?

4. Explain why national income and gross national product would be exactly equal if there were no depreciation and no indirect business taxes.

5. The following is a complete description of all economic activity in Trivialand for 1987. Draw up versions of Tables 8–4 and 8–5 for Trivialand showing GNP computed in two different ways.
   a. There are thousands of farmers but only two big business firms in Trivialand: Specific Motors (an auto company) and Super Duper (a chain of food markets). There is no government and no depreciation.
   b. Specific Motors produced 1000 small cars, which they sold at $6000 each, and 100 trucks, which they sold at $8000 each. Consumers bought 800 of the cars, and the remaining 200 cars were exported to the United States. Super Duper bought all the trucks.
   c. Sales at Super Duper markets amounted to $14 million, all of it sold to consumers.
   d. All the farmers in Trivialand are self-employed and sell all their wares to Super Duper.
   e. The costs incurred by all the businesses were as follows:

	SPECIFIC MOTORS	SUPER DUPER	FARMERS
Wages	$3,800,000	$4,500,000	$ 0
Interest	100,000	200,000	700,000
Rent	200,000	1,000,000	2,000,000
Purchases of food	0	7,000,000	0

6. (More difficult) Now complicate Trivialand in the following ways and answer the same questions. In addition, calculate national income, personal income, and disposable income.
   a. The government bought 50 cars, leaving only 150 cars for export. In addition, the government spent $800,000 on wages for soldiers and made $1,200,000 in transfer payments.
   b. Depreciation for the year amounted to $600,000 for Specific Motors and $200,000 for Super Duper. (The farmers had no depreciation.)
   c. The government levied sales taxes amounting to $500,000 on Specific Motors and $200,000 on Super Duper (none on farmers). In addition, the government levied a 10 percent income tax on all wages, interest, and rental income.
   d. In addition to the food and cars mentioned in Question 5, consumers in Trivialand imported 500 computers from the United States at $2,000 each.

9

Demand-Side Equilibrium: Unemployment or Inflation?

Investment . . . is a flighty bird, which needs to be controlled.

J. R. HICKS

As we learned in Chapter 5, the interaction of aggregate demand and aggregate supply determines whether the economy will stagnate or prosper, whether our resources of labor and capital will be fully employed or unemployed. This is the first of a series of chapters devoted to studying this important process.

A simplified model of aggregate demand is constructed in Chapters 9 and 10, and the supply side is added in Chapter 11. This first model of the economy teaches us much about the causes of unemployment and inflation, but it is too simple to deal with policy issues, because the government and the financial system are largely ignored. Chapters 12–14 remedy these omissions, thereby making it possible to study how government policies affect unemployment and inflation. By the end of Chapter 14 we will have a model that is capable of dealing with a wide variety of policy issues; and we will make extensive use of that model in Chapters 15–17. Then, in Chapters 18–20, we will consider some of the complications that arise from international economic relations.

In Chapter 8 we examined the largest component of aggregate demand, consumer expenditure (C). Here we turn our attention first to the most volatile component, investment (I), and discuss its determinants and the reasons why investment spending is so variable and so difficult to predict.[1] Then, rather than waiting for a full discussion of the other components of aggregate demand, we construct an abbreviated model of the determination of national income based only on the C and I components. We use this model to provide a preliminary description of how the state of aggregate demand influences the level of the gross national product, and to consider a question of great importance to policymakers: Can the economy be expected to achieve full employment of its resources if the government does not intervene?

---

[1]We repeat the warning given in the previous chapter about the meaning of the word *investment*. It *includes* spending by businesses and individuals on *newly produced* factories, machinery, and houses. But it *excludes* sales of used industrial plants, equipment, and homes, and it *also excludes* purely financial transactions, such as the purchase of stocks and bonds.

The Extreme Variability of Investment

The first thing to be said about investment spending is that it is extraordinarily variable.

Unlike consumer spending, which follows movements in disposable income with great (though not perfect) reliability, investment spending swings from high to low levels with annoying rapidity. During recessions, for example, the decline in investment generally constitutes by far the greatest part of the total drop in real GNP, despite the fact that investment is only a small portion of GNP—about 17 percent in the postwar United States. What accounts for these movements of investment demand?

Business Confidence and Expectations About the Future

While many factors influence business people's desires to invest, Keynes himself laid great stress on the *state of business confidence*, which in turn depends on *expectations about the future*.

While tricky to measure, it does seem obvious that businesses will build more factories and purchase more new machines when their expectations are optimistic. Conversely, their investment plans will be very cautious if the economic outlook appears bleak. Keynes pointed out that psychological perceptions like these are subject to abrupt shifts, so that fluctuations in investment can be a major cause of instability in aggregate demand. Hence, Hicks's analogy to a "flighty bird."

Unfortunately, neither economists nor, for that matter, psychologists have any very good ideas about how to *measure*—much less how to *control*—business confidence. Therefore, economists usually focus on several more objective determinants of investment—determinants that are easy to quantify and, perhaps even more important, are more easily influenced by government policy.

The Rate of Interest

The interest rate is the determinant of investment that is most extensively studied by economists, and it will play a pivotal role in later chapters. A good deal of business investment is financed by borrowing, and the interest rate indicates how much firms must pay for that privilege. Some investment projects that look profitable at an interest rate of 7 percent will look disastrous if the firm has to pay 12 percent.

The amount that businesses will want to invest depends on the real interest rate they have to pay on their borrowings. The lower the real rate of interest, the more investment spending there will be.

In Chapter 14 we will study in some detail how the government can influence the rate of interest. Since interest rates affect investment, policymakers have a handle on aggregate demand—a handle they do not hesitate to use. The point is that, unlike business confidence, interest rates are visible and manipulable. Therefore, even if investment responds much more dramatically to changes in confidence than to changes in interest rates, interest rates are nonetheless a more important instrument of government policy.

The State of Demand and Capacity Utilization

There will be a strong incentive to invest when firms find that demand is pressing against their capacity. Under these circumstances, firms are likely to feel that new factories and machinery can be employed profitably. By contrast, if there is a great deal of spare capacity (unused machinery, empty factories, and so on), business managers will not find investment attractive even at low interest rates.

The Growth of Demand

Since it takes a substantial amount of time to order machinery or to build a factory, investment plans are made with an eye on the future. Even when pressures on current capacity are not particularly severe, a firm experiencing rapid growth in sales may start investing now so that it will have adequate capacity when it is needed in the future. In addition, briskly growing sales are likely to make business people more optimistic. Conversely, slow growth of output will discourage investment. We can summarize these last two points by saying that:

High levels of sales in relation to available capacity and rapid economic growth create an atmosphere favorable to investment. On the other hand, low levels of sales and slow growth are likely to discourage investment.

Government stabilization policy thus has another handle on investment spending, for by stimulating aggregate demand it can induce business firms to invest more, though the precise amount may be hard to predict.

Tax Provisions

The government has still another important way to influence investment spending—by altering various provisions of the tax law. Most obviously, there is a tax on corporate profits and the government may reduce the statutory tax rate as a way to spur investment—as it did in 1986. That same tax bill, however, reduced the incentives for many companies to invest by ending the *investment tax credit*, a special subsidy for certain types of investment spending. Finally, the tax law sets maximum **depreciation allowances** which govern how firms may deduct the costs of investment from their taxable income. In 1981, when the Reagan administration wanted to encourage investment spending, it made these allowances more generous as a way to enhance the profitability of investment. To summarize:

Depreciation allowances are tax deductions that businesses may claim when they spend money on investment goods.

The tax law gives the government several ways to influence business spending on investment goods. But influence is far from control. Investment remains a "flighty bird."

A Simplified Circular Flow

Let us now put consumption and investment together and see how they interact, using as our organizing framework the circular flow diagram introduced in the last chapter. For this purpose, we simplify the circular flow somewhat by leaving out the government and the foreign sector.

There are two reasons for doing this. The first is pedagogical: The workings of the model will be clearer if we strip away some complications. But there is an equally important reason. One of the crucial questions surrounding government attempts to stabilize the economy is whether the economy would *automatically* gravitate toward full employment if the government simply left it alone. John Maynard Keynes, contradicting the teachings of generations of economists before him, claimed that it would not. But Keynes' views remain controversial to this day. We can study this issue best by imagining an economy that has no government, so that all the aggregate demand comes from the private sector. This is just what we do in this chapter.

Look now at Figure 9–1, which is the same as Figure 8–1 of the last chapter except that the government and foreign sectors have been omitted. The first thing you may notice is that, with the government out of the picture, there is no longer any leakage out of the national income for taxes (nor are there transfer payments); so there is no important difference between national income and disposable income. Second, there are no government or net export components of total spending; instead, spending is represented by the sum $C + I$.

The Meaning of Equilibrium GNP

We can use Figure 9–1 to begin the construction of a simple model of the determination of national income. A first step is to understand what we mean by "equilibrium income."

As was explained in the last chapter, national *product* and national *income* must, of necessity, be equal. But the same cannot automatically be said of total *spending*. Look again at Figure 9–1 and imagine that, for some reason, the total expenditures $(C + I)$ that are being made at point 3 are greater than the output that is being produced by the business firms at point 4.

Two things may happen in such a situation. Since consumers and firms together are buying (in the forms of C and I) more than firms are producing, business firms are being forced to take goods out of their warehouses to meet customer demands. Thus, inventory stocks must be falling. These inventory reductions are a signal to retailers of a need to increase their orders, and to manufacturers of a need to step up their production. Consequently, production is likely to rise. At some later date, if there is evidence that the high level of

Figure 9–1
A SIMPLIFIED
CIRCULAR FLOW
Here we show a simplified version of the circular flow of income and expenditures that we introduced in Chapter 8. The simplification amounts to shutting off the pipes leading into and out of the government. Thus, this circular flow represents an economy with no government and no foreign trade. Notice that aggregate demand now has only two components (consumer spending and investment spending) and that the entire national income flows to consumers without taxation.

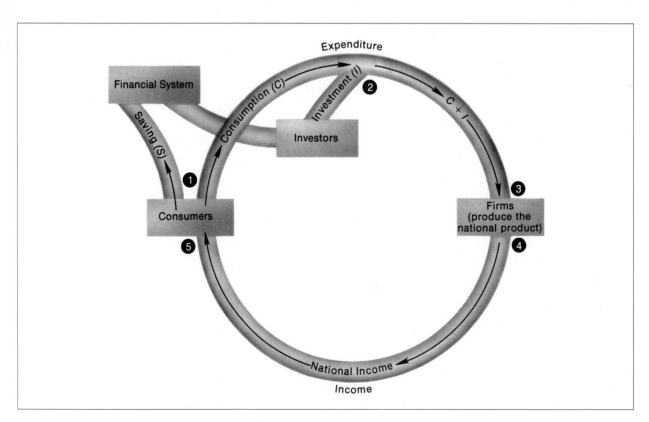

aggregate demand is not just a temporary aberration, either manufacturers or retailers (or both) may also respond to the buoyant sales performances by raising their prices. Economists therefore say that neither output nor the price level is in **equilibrium** when aggregate demand exceeds the current rate of production.

It is clear from the definition of equilibrium that the economy cannot be in equilibrium when aggregate demand exceeds production, for the falling inventories demonstrate to firms that their production and pricing decisions were not quite appropriate.[2] Thus, since we normally use GNP to measure output:

Equilibrium refers to a situation in which consumers and firms have no incentive to change their behavior. They are content to continue with things as they are.

The equilibrium level of GNP cannot be one at which total spending exceeds output because firms will notice that inventory stocks are being depleted. They may first decide to increase production sufficiently to meet the higher demand. Later they may decide to raise prices as well.

Now imagine the other case, in which the flow of spending reaching firms falls short of current production. Some output cannot be sold and winds up as additions to inventories. The inventory pile-up acts as a signal to firms that at least one of their decisions was wrong. Once again, they will probably react first by cutting back on production, causing the GNP to fall. If the imbalance persists, they may also lower prices in order to stimulate sales. But they certainly will not be happy with things as they are. Thus:

The equilibrium level of GNP cannot be one at which total spending is less than output, because firms will not allow inventories to continue to pile up. They may decide to decrease production, or they may decide to cut prices in order to stimulate demand. Normally, firms are reluctant to cut prices until they are certain that the low level of demand is not a temporary phenomenon. So they rely more heavily on reductions in output.

Equilibrium on the Demand Side of the Economy

You may have noticed that we have now determined, through a process of elimination, the level of national income and product that is consistent with peoples' desires to spend. We have reasoned that whenever GNP is below total spending $(C + I)$, the GNP will rise; and that whenever GNP is above $C + I$, the GNP will fall. Equilibrium can only occur, then, when there is just enough spending to absorb the current level of production. Under such circumstances, producers conclude that their price and output decisions are correct, and they have no incentive to change them. We conclude that:

The **equilibrium level of GNP on the demand side** is the one at which total spending equals production. In such a situation, firms find their inventories remaining at desired levels; so there is no incentive to change output or prices.

The simple circular flow diagram, then, has helped us to understand the concept of equilibrium of GNP on the demand side. It has also shown us how the economy is driven toward this equilibrium. It leaves unanswered, however, three important questions:

1. How large is the equilibrium level of GNP?
2. Will the economy suffer from unemployment, inflation, or both?

[2]All the models in this book assume, strictly for simplicity, that firms never want to change their inventories. Deliberate changes in inventories are treated in more advanced courses.

EQUILIBRIUM ON THE DEMAND SIDE OF THE ECONOMY   169

3. Is the equilibrium level of GNP on the demand side also consistent with firms' desires to produce? That is, is it also an equilibrium on the *supply* side?

The first two questions will occupy our attention in this chapter; the third question is reserved to Chapter 11.

Constructing the Expenditure Schedule

Our first objective is to determine precisely the equilibrium level of GNP and to see what factors it depends upon. To make the analysis more concrete, we turn to a numerical example. Specifically, we examine the relationship between aggregate demand and GNP in Macroland, the hypothetical economy that was introduced in the last chapter.

Columns 1 and 2 of Table 9–1 repeat the consumption function of Macroland that we first encountered in Table 8–1. They show how consumer spending, C, depends on national income, which we now begin to symbolize by the letter Y. However, one thing has changed here. The consumption function in Chapter 8 related C to *disposable* income (DI), whereas the consumption function in Table 9–1 relates C to *national* income (Y). This change is legitimate because, in this chapter, we have eliminated the government from the picture. With no taxes and no transfer payments, there is no difference between DI and Y.

Column 3 provides the other component of aggregate demand, I, through the simplifying assumption that investment spending is $700 billion in Macroland, regardless of the level of GNP. By adding together the second and third columns, we calculate C + I, or total expenditure, which is displayed in column 4. Columns 1 and 4, shaded in blue, show how total expenditure depends on income in Macroland. We call this the **expenditure schedule**.

Figure 9–2 shows the construction of the expenditure schedule graphically. The line labeled C is the consumption function of Macroland and simply duplicates Figure 8–6 of the last chapter, except that GNP, not DI, appears on the horizontal axis. It plots on a graph the numbers given in columns 1 and 2 of Table 9–1. The line labeled I displays our assumption that investment is fixed

An **expenditure schedule** shows the relationship between national income (GNP) and total spending.

Table 9–1
TOTAL EXPENDITURE IN MACROLAND (billions of dollars)

(1) GNP INCOME (Y)	(2) CONSUMPTION (C)	(3) INVESTMENT (I)	(4) TOTAL EXPENDITURE (C + I)
2000	1700	700	2400
2500	2100	700	2800
3000	2500	700	3200
3500	2900	700	3600
4000	3300	700	4000
4500	3700	700	4400
5000	4100	700	4800
5500	4500	700	5200
6000	4900	700	5600

This table illustrates the derivation of the expenditure schedule, which is shaded in blue. It is derived from the consumption schedule, columns 1 and 2, and from the investment schedule, columns 1 and 3, by simple addition. This is because total spending is the sum C + I.

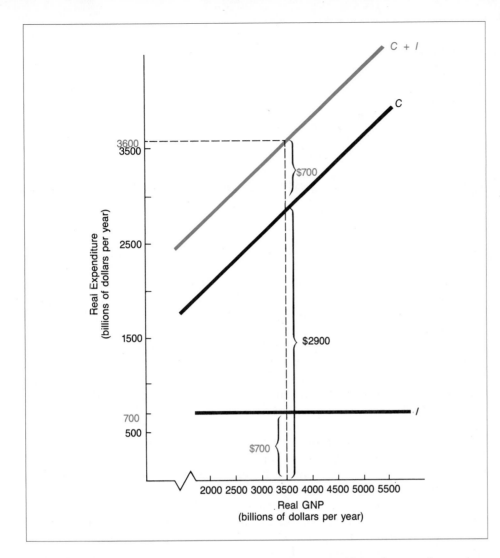

Figure 9–2
CONSTRUCTION
OF THE EXPENDITURE
SCHEDULE
This figure shows in a
diagram what Table 9–1
showed numerically—the
construction of a total
expenditure schedule from its
components. Line C is the
consumption function that we
first encountered in
Figure 8–6 except that GNP,
not disposable income, is
measured along the
horizontal axis. Line I is the
investment schedule
(assumed always to be $700
billion in this example). Line
C + I is the expenditure
schedule and is obtained by
adding investment to the
consumption function. For
example, when GNP is
$3500, C is $2900 and I is
$700, for a total of $3600.

at $700 billion, regardless of the level of GNP. By adding the two lines verti-
cally—that is, by summing consumption and investment at each level of
GNP—we derive the total expenditure schedule that was shown in columns 1
and 4 of Table 9–1. In the diagram, it is the blue line labeled C + I.

In our simple example investment is a fixed number, so the C and C + I
lines are parallel; that is, the distance between them is always the same. This
distance is $700 billion—the volume of investment assumed. If investment
were not always $700 billion, the two lines would either move closer together
(at income levels at which investment was below $700 billion) or grow farther
apart (at income levels at which investment was above $700 billion). For exam-
ple, our list of determinants of investment spending suggested that I might be
larger at higher levels of GNP. Because of this added investment—which is
called **induced investment**—the resulting C + I schedule would have a steeper
slope than the C schedule.

Induced investment is
the part of investment
spending which rises
when GNP rises and falls
when GNP falls.

The Mechanics of Income Determination

We are now ready to determine demand-side equilibrium in Macroland. Look
first at Table 9–2, which presents the logic of our circular flow argument in

Table 9–2
THE DETERMINATION OF EQUILIBRIUM OUTPUT

(1) OUTPUT (Y) (billions of dollars)	(2) TOTAL SPENDING (C + I) (billions of dollars)	(3) BALANCE OF SPENDING AND OUTPUT	(4) INVENTORIES ARE:	(5) PRODUCERS WILL RESPOND BY:
2000	2400	Spending exceeds output	Falling	Producing more
2500	2800	Spending exceeds output	Falling	Producing more
3000	3200	Spending exceeds output	Falling	Producing more
3500	3600	Spending exceeds output	Falling	Producing more
4000	4000	Spending = output	Constant	Not changing production
4500	4400	Output exceeds spending	Rising	Producing less
5000	4800	Output exceeds spending	Rising	Producing less
5500	5200	Output exceeds spending	Rising	Producing less
6000	5600	Output exceeds spending	Rising	Producing less

tabular form. The first two columns of this table reproduce the expenditure schedule that was constructed in Table 9–1. The other columns explain the process by which equilibrium is approached. Let us see why a GNP of $4000 billion must be the equilibrium level.

Consider first any output level below $4000 billion. For example, at output level Y = $3500 billion, total expenditure is $3600 billion (column 2), which is $100 billion more than production. With spending greater than output (column 3), inventories will be falling (column 4). As the table suggests, this will be a signal to producers to raise their output (column 5). Clearly, then, no output level below Y = $4000 billion can be an equilibrium. Output is too low.

A similar line of reasoning can eliminate any output level above $4000 billion. Consider, for example, Y = $4500 billion. The table shows that total spending would be $4400 billion if national income were $4500 billion. So $100 billion of the GNP would go unsold. This would raise producers' inventory stocks and signal them that their rate of production is too high.

Just as we concluded from our circular flow diagram, equilibrium will be achieved only when total spending (C + I) is equal to GNP (Y). In symbols, our condition for equilibrium GNP is:

$$C + I = Y.$$

The table shows that this occurs only at a GNP of $4000 billion. This, then, must be the equilibrium level of GNP.

Figure 9–3 shows this same conclusion graphically, by adding a 45° line to Figure 9–2. Why a 45° line? Recall from Chapter 2 that a 45° line marks all points on a graph at which the value of the variable measured on the horizontal axis is equal to the value of the variable measured on the vertical axis. In this convenient graph of the expenditure schedule, gross national product (Y) is measured on the horizontal axis and total expenditure (C + I) is measured on the vertical axis. So the 45° line shows all the points at which output and spending are equal; that is, where Y = C + I. The 45° line therefore displays all the points at which the economy *can possibly* be at equilibrium, for if C + I is not equal to Y, firms will not be content with current output levels.

Now we must compare these potential equilibrium points with the actual combinations of spending and output that the economy can attain, given the behavior of consumers and investors. That behavior, as we have seen, is described by the C + I line in Figure 9–3, which shows how total expenditure

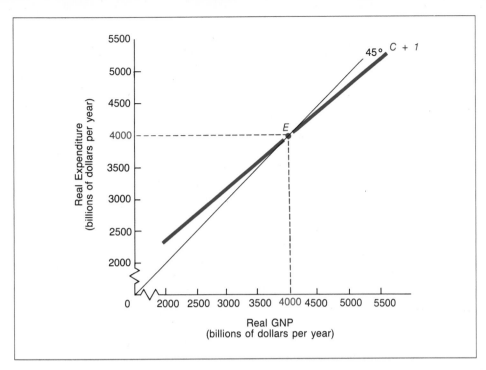

Figure 9–3

INCOME-EXPENDITURE DIAGRAM

This figure adds a 45° line—which marks off points where expenditure and output are equal—to Figure 9–2. Since the condition for equilibrium GNP is that expenditure and output must be equal, this line can be used to determine the equilibrium level of GNP. In this example, equilibrium is at point *E*, where GNP is $4000 billion—precisely as we found in Table 9–2.

varies as income changes. Thus, the economy will *always* be on the C + I line because only points on the C + I line are consistent with the spending plans of consumers and investors. Similarly, *if* the economy is in equilibrium, it *must* be on the 45° line. As Figure 9–3 shows, these two requirements together imply that the only viable equilibrium is at point E, where the C + I line intersects the 45° line. Only this point is consistent both with equilibrium and with the actual desires to consume and invest.

Notice that to the left of the equilibrium point, E, the C + I line lies above the 45° line. This means that total spending exceeds total output, as we have already noted in words and with numbers. Hence inventories will be falling and firms will conclude that they should increase production. The opposite is true to the right of equilibrium point E. Here spending falls short of output, inventories are rising, and firms will cut back production.

Diagrams like this one will recur so frequently in this and the next several chapters that it will be convenient to have a name for them. Let us therefore call them **income-expenditure diagrams** since they show how expenditures vary with income. Sometimes we shall also refer to them simply as **45° line diagrams.**

The Aggregate Demand Curve

Chapter 5 sketched a framework for macroeconomic analysis by introducing aggregate demand and aggregate supply curves which relate aggregate quantities demanded and supplied to the price level. Yet the price level has not even been mentioned so far in our discussion of equilibrium. It is now time to remedy this omission, for only by explicit analysis of the determination of the price level will we be able to deal with important issues relating to inflation.

Fortunately, no further mechanical apparatus is required. The price level can be brought into our income-expenditure analysis by recalling something we learned in the last chapter: At any given level of real income, higher prices lead to lower real consumer spending. The reason, you will recall, is that consumers

An **income-expenditure diagram,** also called a **45° line diagram,** plots total real expenditure (on the vertical axis) against real income (on the horizontal axis). The 45° line marks off points where income and expenditure are equal.

own many assets whose values are fixed in money terms, and which therefore lose purchasing power when prices rise.[3] With real wealth lower, consumers spend less and therefore total spending in the economy falls.

In terms of our 45° line diagram, then, a rise in the price level will lower the consumption function depicted in Figure 9–2 and, hence, will lower the total expenditure schedule as well. Conversely, a fall in the price level will raise both the C and C + I schedules in the diagram. The two parts of Figure 9–4 illustrate both these sorts of shifts.

What, then, do changes in the price level do to the equilibrium level of real GNP on the demand side? Common sense says that, with lower spending, equilibrium GNP should fall. And Figure 9–4 shows that this conclusion is correct. Part (a) shows that a rise in the price level, by shifting the expenditure schedule downward from $C_0 + I$ to $C_1 + I$ leads to a reduction in the equilibrium quantity of real GNP demanded from Y_0 to Y_1. Part (b) shows that a fall in the price level, by shifting the expenditure schedule upward from $C_0 + I$ to $C_2 + I$ leads to a rise in the equilibrium quantity of real GNP demanded from Y_0 to Y_2. In summary:

A rise in the price level leads to a lower equilibrium level of real aggregate quantity demanded. This relationship between the price level and the equilibrium quantity of real GNP demanded is depicted in Figure 9–5 and is precisely what we called the **aggregate demand curve** in earlier chapters. It comes directly from the 45° line diagrams in Figure 9–4. Thus, points E_0, E_1, and E_2 in Figure 9–5 correspond precisely to the points bearing the same labels in Figure 9–4.

Thus we have now learned the first reason why the aggregate demand curve relating the price level to real GNP demanded slopes downward. (More

[3]Two warnings issued in Chapter 8 (pages 150–51) are worth repeating: First, the effect referred to here comes from changes in the *price level*, not from changes in the *inflation rate*. Second, a higher price level does not reduce spending by reducing real income. Quite to the contrary, real income is held constant when we compare consumer expenditures at different price levels.

Figure 9–4
THE EFFECT OF THE PRICE LEVEL ON EQUILIBRIUM AGGREGATE QUANTITY DEMANDED
Because a change in the price level causes the expenditure schedule to shift, it changes the equilibrium quantity of real GNP demanded. Part (a) shows what happens when the price level rises, causing the expenditure schedule to shift downward from $C_0 + I$ to $C_1 + I$. Equilibrium quantity demanded falls from Y_0 to Y_1. Part (b) shows what happens when the price level falls, causing the expenditure schedule to shift upward from $C_0 + I$ to $C_2 + I$. Equilibrium quantity demanded rises from Y_0 to Y_2.

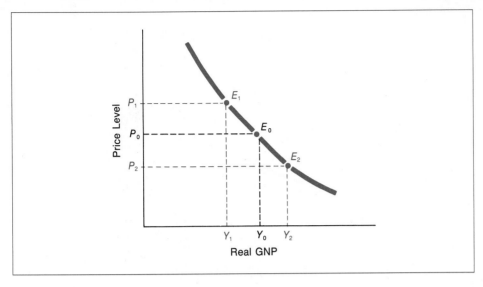

Figure 9–5
THE AGGREGATE
DEMAND CURVE
The graphical analysis in
Figure 9–4 showed that
higher prices lead to lower
aggregate quantity
demanded. This relationship
is called the aggregate
demand curve and is shown
in this figure.

reasons will come later in the book, after we have studied money and interest rates.) We have also been warned that:

An income-expenditure diagram like Figure 9–3 can be drawn up only for a *specific* price level. At different price levels, the $C + I$ schedule will be different and, hence, the equilibrium quantity of GNP demanded will be different.

As we shall now see, this finding is critical to understanding the genesis of unemployment and inflation.

Demand-Side Equilibrium and Full Employment

We now turn to the second major question of this chapter: Will the economy achieve an equilibrium at full employment without inflation, or will there be unemployment, inflation, or both?

In the income-expenditure diagrams used so far, the equilibrium level of GNP demanded has been shown as the intersection of the expenditure schedule and the 45° line, regardless of whatever level of GNP might correspond to full employment. However, as we will see now, when equilibrium GNP falls above full employment, the economy probably will be plagued by inflation. And when equilibrium falls below full employment, there will be unemployment and recession.

This remarkable fact was one of the principal messages of Keynes's *General Theory of Employment, Interest, and Money*. Writing during the Great Depression, it was natural for him to stress the case in which equilibrium falls short of full employment so that there are unemployed resources. Figure 9–6 illustrates this possibility. A vertical line has been erected at the full-employment level of GNP (called "potential GNP"), which is assumed to be $5000 billion in the example. We see that the $C + I$ curve cuts the 45° line at point E, which corresponds to a GNP ($Y = \$4000$ billion) below potential GNP. In this case, the $C + I$ curve is too low to lead to full employment. Such a situation might arise because either consumers or investors are unwilling to spend at normal rates, or because the price level is "too high," thereby depressing the $C + I$ curve. Unemployment must occur because not enough output will be demanded to keep the entire labor force busy.

Figure 9–6

A RECESSIONARY GAP
Sometimes equilibrium GNP
may fall below potential GNP,
so that some workers are
unemployed. This diagram
illustrates such a case. The
horizontal distance *EB*
between equilibrium GNP
and potential GNP is called
the recessionary gap.

The **recessionary gap** is
the amount by which the
equilibrium level of real
GNP falls short of
potential GNP.

The distance between the equilibrium level of output demanded and the full-employment level of output (that is, potential GNP) is called the **recessionary gap**—and is shown by the horizontal distance from *E* to *B*.

It is clear from Figure 9–6 that full employment can be reached only by raising the total spending schedule to eliminate the recessionary gap. Specifically, the *C* + *I* schedule must move upward until it cuts the 45° line at point *F*. Can this happen without government intervention? We know that a sufficiently large drop in the price level could do the job. But is that a realistic prospect? We shall return to this question after we have brought the supply side into the picture. But first let us consider the other case, in which equilibrium GNP exceeds full employment.

Figure 9–7 illustrates this possibility. The expenditure schedule intersects the 45° line at point *E*, where GNP is $6000 billion. But this exceeds the full employment level, Y = $5000 billion. A case like this can arise when consumer or investment spending is unusually buoyant or when a "low" price level pushes the *C* + *I* curve upward.

The **inflationary gap**
is the amount by which
equilibrium real GNP
exceeds the full-
employment level
of GNP.

To reach an equilibrium at full employment, the price level would have to rise enough to drive the *C* + *I* schedule *down* until it passed through point *F*. The horizontal distance *BE*—which indicates the amount by which the quantity of GNP demanded exceeds potential GNP—is called the **inflationary gap**. If there is an inflationary gap, a higher price level or some other means of reducing total expenditure is necessary to reach an equilibrium at full employment.

In sum, only if the price level and the spending plans of consumers and investors are "just right" will the *C* + *I* curve intersect the 45° line precisely at full employment, so that neither a recessionary gap nor an inflationary gap occurs. Are there reasons to expect this outcome? Does the economy have a self-correcting mechanism that automatically eliminates recessionary or inflationary gaps and propels it toward full employment? And how is it that inflation and unemployment sometimes occur together? These are questions we are not ready to address because we have not brought *aggregate supply* into the picture.

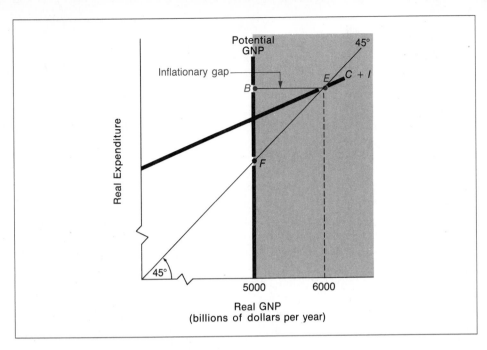

Figure 9–7

AN INFLATIONARY GAP
Sometimes equilibrium GNP
may lie above potential GNP,
meaning that there are more
jobs than required for full
employment. This diagram
illustrates such a case. The
horizontal distance *BE*
between potential GNP and
equilibrium GNP is called the
inflationary gap. It is
gradually eliminated by rising
prices, which pull the *C + I*
schedule down until it passes
through point *F*.

And, as we learned in Chapter 5, the price level is determined by the interaction of *both* aggregate demand *and* aggregate supply. However, it is not too early to get an idea about why things can go wrong, why the economy can find itself far away from full employment.

The Coordination of Saving and Investment

To understand what goes wrong with the economy in a recession, it is useful to pose the following question: How can the full-employment level of GNP fail to be an equilibrium?

To find an answer, look back at the simplified circular flow diagram (Figure 9–1 on page 168). Suppose that firms produce the full-employment level of GNP, and this becomes the national income that emerges at point 4 in the diagram. This full-employment level of income then flows to consumers at point 5, who save some of it and spend the rest. The saving, you will note, "leaks out" of the circular flow at point 1. So, once we pass this point, consumption is less than full-employment GNP. But then, at point 2, an additional source of spending enters: investment. Recalling that the condition for equilibrium is that the sum *C + I* equals the GNP, we have the following conclusion:

The economy will reach an equilibrium at full employment only if the amount that consumers wish to save out of full-employment incomes is precisely equal to the amount that investors want to invest. If these two magnitudes happen to be unequal, then full employment will not be an equilibrium for the economy.

Specifically, we can see from the circular flow diagram that if saving exceeds investment at full employment, then the total demand arriving at the firms (point 3) will fall short of total output because the added investment spending is not enough to replace the leakage to saving. With demand inadequate to support production at full employment, we know that the GNP must fall below potential. There will be a recessionary gap. Conversely, if investment

John Maynard Keynes was something of a child prodigy. After an outstanding scholastic career at Eton and Cambridge, Keynes took the civil service examination. His second-place score was not good enough to land him the position he wanted (in the Treasury), so in 1907 he found himself in the India Office. Some years later, reflecting on the fact that his lowest score on the exam was in the economics section, he suggested with characteristic immodesty that, "The examiners presumably knew less than I did." He was probably right.

During World War I, Keynes was called to the Treasury to assist in planning various financial aspects of the war. There his "unique combinations of the guts of a burglar and the intellect of a first-class economist" quickly established him as a dominant figure. At the war's end, he represented the British Treasury at the peace conference in Versailles. The conference was a turning point in Keynes's life, though it was one of his few failures. He sought unsuccessfully to persuade the Allies to take a less punitive attitude toward the vanquished Germans, and then left the conference in protest in June 1919 to work on his *Economic Consequences of the Peace*, which created a furor when it was published. In it Keynes argued that the Germans could never meet the harsh economic terms of the treaty and that its viciousness posed the threat of continued instability and perhaps another war in Europe.

No longer welcome in government, Keynes returned to Cambridge and to his circle of literary and artistic friends in London's Bloomsbury district—a group that included Virginia Woolf, Lytton Strachey, and E. M. Forster. In 1925 he married the beautiful ballerina Lydia Lopokova, who gave up her stage career for him (though she later acted in a theater that Keynes himself established).

Between the wars, Keynes devoted himself to making money, to economic theory, and to political economy. He managed to make both himself and King's College rich by speculating in international currencies and commodities—allegedly by studying the newspapers while still in bed each morning! As a scholar, he wrote the *Tract on Monetary Reform* (1923), a stunning denunciation of the gold standard, which was published two years before Churchill once again tied the pound to gold. In 1936, he published his masterpiece, *The General Theory of Employment, Interest, and Money*, on which modern macroeconomics is based.

A heart attack in 1937 reduced Keynes's activities somewhat, but he returned to the Treasury during World War II and conducted several delicate financial negotiations with the Americans. Then as the capstone to a truly remarkable career, he represented the United Kingdom—and by all accounts dominated the proceedings—at the conference in Bretton Woods, New Hampshire, in 1944 that established an international financial system that served the Western world for 27 years. (See Chapter 19.)

He died of a heart attack at his home on Easter Sunday of 1946 as Lord Keynes, Baron of Tilton, a man who had achieved almost everything that he sought, and who had only one regret: He wished he had drunk more champagne.

---

exceeds saving when the economy is at full employment, then total demand $(C + I)$ will exceed potential GNP and production will rise above the full-employment level. There will be an inflationary gap.

Now this discussion does nothing but restate what we already know in different words.[4] But these words hold the key to understanding why the economy can find itself stuck below full employment (or above it, for that matter), for *the people who do the investing are not the same people who do the saving*. In a modern capitalist economy, investing is done by one group of individuals (corporate

---

[4]In symbols, our previous equilibrium condition was $C + I = Y$. If we note that Y is also the sum of consumption plus saving, $Y = C + S$, it follows that $C + I = C + S$, or $I = S$, is a restatement of the equilibrium condition. The saving = investment approach is described in an appendix to this chapter.

executives and home buyers) while saving is done by another group.[5] It is easy to imagine that their plans may not be well coordinated. If they are not, we have just seen how either unemployment or inflation can arise.

Notice that these problems would never arise if the acts of saving and investing were not separated. Imagine a primitive economy of farmers, each of whom invests only in his own farm. There is no borrowing or lending, and no financial system. In this world, any farmer wanting to buy a new plow or tractor (that is, wanting to invest) would have to refrain from consuming part of his income (that is, would have to *save*). Therefore, the amount that all farmers together planned to save out of full-employment income would of necessity be equal to the amount of planned investment. Total spending and production would always have to be equal at full employment.

Almost the same holds true in a centrally planned economy like that of Soviet Russia. There, the state decides how much will be invested and has a great deal of leverage over how much saving people do. If the planners do their calculations correctly, they can force saving to be equal to investment at full employment. Consequently, business fluctuations are not a major problem in the Soviet Union. (They have plenty of others!)

Keynes observed that modern market economies differ from either primitive societies or centrally planned societies in this fundamental way, and that this flaw in the market mechanism is what leaves them vulnerable to recessions. However, one should not conclude that in order to avoid unemployment and recession the U.S. economy should revert to either a primitive form of capitalism or to rigid central planning. These "remedies" are far worse than the disease. Fortunately, there are policies the government can follow in an advanced capitalist economy to ease the pain of unemployment and recession—policies that we shall be studying in the following chapters.

[5]In a modern economy, it is not only households that save. Businesses save also, in the form of retained earnings. Nonetheless, households are the ultimate source of the saving needed to finance investment.

Summary

1. Investment is the most volatile component of aggregate demand, largely because it is tied so closely to the state of business confidence and to expectations about the future performance of the economy.

2. Government policy cannot influence business confidence in any reliable way, so policies designed to alter investment spending are aimed at more objective, though possibly less important, determinants of investment. Among these are interest rates, the overall state of aggregate demand, and tax incentives.

3. The equilibrium level of national income on the demand side is the level at which total spending just equals production (GNP). In this chapter we ignore government and foreign demand, so total spending is the sum of consumption plus investment. Thus, in symbols, the condition for equilibrium is $Y = C + I$.

4. Income levels below equilibrium are bound to rise because, when spending exceeds output, firms will see their inventory stocks being depleted and will react by stepping up production.

5. Income levels above equilibrium are bound to fall because, when total spending is insufficient to absorb total output, inventories will pile up and firms will react by curtailing production.

6. The determination of the equilibrium level of GNP on the demand side can be portrayed on a convenient "income-expenditure diagram" as the point at which the expenditure schedule—defined as the sum of the consumption and investment schedules—crosses the 45° line. The 45° line is significant because it marks off points at which spending and output are equal (that is, at which $C + I = Y$), and this is the basic condition for equilibrium.

7. An income-expenditure diagram can only be drawn up for a specific price level, however. Thus the equilibrium GNP so determined depends on the price level.

8. Because higher prices reduce the purchasing power of consumers' wealth and hence reduce their spending, equilibrium real GNP demanded is lower when prices are higher. This downward-sloping relationship is known as the aggregate demand curve.

9. Equilibrium GNP can be above or below potential GNP, which is defined as the GNP that would be produced if the labor force were fully employed.
10. If equilibrium GNP exceeds potential GNP, the difference is called an inflationary gap. If equilibrium GNP falls short of potential GNP, the resulting difference is called a recessionary gap.
11. Such gaps can occur because the saving that consumers want to do at full-employment income levels may differ from the investing that investors want to do. This problem is not likely to arise in a planned economy or in a primitive economy.

Concepts for Review

Depreciation allowances	Income-expenditure	Recessionary gap
Equilibrium level of GNP	(or 45° line) diagram	Inflationary gap
Expenditure schedule	Aggregate demand curve	Coordination of saving and investment
Induced investment	Full-employment level of GNP	
$C + I = Y$	(or potential GNP)	

Questions for Discussion

1. Why would someone interested in stabilization policy want to study a model of an economy in which there is no government?
2. When President Reagan took office, there was a feeling that the rate of business investment in the United States was too low. Does this chapter give you any ideas about what is meant by the phrase "too low"? What factors do you think accounted for the low level of investment spending? (You may want to discuss this last issue with your instructor.)
3. Why is not any arbitrary level of GNP an equilibrium for the economy? (Do not give a mechanical answer to this question, but explain the economic mechanism involved.)
4. From the following data, construct an expenditure schedule on a piece of graph paper. Then use the income-expenditure (45° line) diagram to determine the equilibrium level of GNP.

INCOME	CONSUMPTION	INVESTMENT
1100	990	120
1150	1035	120
1200	1080	120
1250	1125	120
1300	1170	120

5. From the following data, construct an expenditure schedule on a piece of graph paper. Then use the income-expenditure (45° line) diagram to determine the equilibrium level of GNP. Compare your answer with your answer to Question 4.

INCOME	CONSUMPTION	INVESTMENT
1100	1020	90
1150	1050	105
1200	1080	120
1250	1110	135
1300	1140	150

6. Suppose investment spending were always $250, government spending were always $150, and consumer spending depended on the price level in the following way:

PRICE LEVEL	CONSUMER SPENDING
80	740
90	720
100	700
110	680
120	660

On a piece of graph paper, use these data to construct an aggregate demand curve. Why do you think this example supposes that consumption declines as the price level rises?
7. Does the economy this year seem to have an inflationary gap or a recessionary gap? (If you do not know the answer from reading the newspaper, ask your instructor.)
8. Why are there no recessions in the Soviet Union?
9. (More difficult)* Consider an economy in which the consumption function takes the following simple algebraic form:

$$C = 100 + 0.8Y$$

and in which investment (I) is always 700. Find the equilibrium level of GNP from the requirement that $C + I = Y$. Compare your answer to Table 9–2 and Figure 9–3.

*The answer to this question is provided in Appendix B.

Appendix A
The Saving and Investment Approach

As we mentioned in the chapter, there is another way of looking at the determination of the equilibrium level of GNP on the demand side. Instead of studying the condition that total expenditure ($C + I$) is equal to production (Y), we can study the condition that saving (S) is equal to investment (I). This is what we will do in this appendix.

It must be emphasized at the outset that this is not a *new* approach. It is merely another way of looking at precisely the same phenomenon. The reason is that income (Y) must be either spent on consumer goods (C) or saved (S). Since $Y = C + S$ *always*, and since $Y = C + I$ when Y is at its equilibrium value, we can describe equilibrium by the condition that $C + S = C + I$, or simply:

$$S = I.$$

Graphical Analysis

This way of looking at equilibrium has a different graphical representation: It does not use the 45° line diagram, but it contains precisely the same information. Recall that in an appendix to Chapter 8 we constructed the saving schedule, which we repeat here as Figure 9–8. Since the equilibrium condition now under scrutiny is $S = I$, we can complete the story by using the investment schedule shown in Figure 9–2 (page 171).

To find the point at which saving and investment are equal, we need only put both curves on the same diagram, which we have done in Figure 9–9. Point E shows the equilibrium level of GNP, which is at an income level of $4000 billion. As must be the case, this is the same answer we obtained with the 45° line diagram.

You will notice that at income levels below $4000 billion, investment exceeds saving, just as $C + I$ exceeded output in the 45° line diagram. Similarly, at income levels above $4000 billion, S exceeds I. (In the 45° line diagram, Y exceeded $C + I$ in this range.) This must be the case since the two graphs are alternative depictions of the same phenomena. The economic analyses behind them are precisely the same.

Induced Investment

In the chapter we mentioned the possibility of *induced investment*, that is, of an investment schedule that rises as GNP rises, but we did not examine this possibility in our graphs. (However, this case did arise in Discussion Question 5.) The reason is that what matters in the 45° line diagram is the slope of the *combined* $C + I$ schedule, not

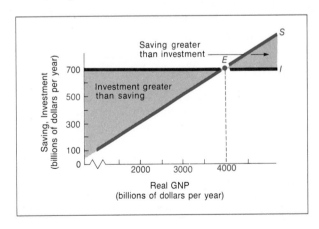

Figure 9–9
DETERMINATION OF EQUILIBRIUM GNP BY SAVING = INVESTMENT
This diagram depicts the equilibrium of the economy at point E, where the saving and investment schedules intersect. The equilibrium is at a real GNP of $4000 billion, which, as must be the case, is the same conclusion that we reached with the aid of the 45° line diagram (Figure 9–3 on page 173).

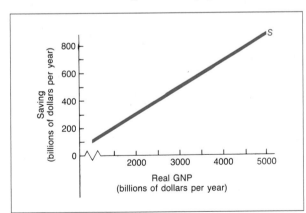

Figure 9–8
THE SAVING SCHEDULE
This diagram shows the relationship between saving and income in Macroland and duplicates Figure 8–9 (page 156).

the *individual* slopes of the C and I schedules. So an upward-sloping investment schedule makes little difference to the analysis.

When using the saving and investment approach, however, the slope of the investment schedule becomes more apparent, if not more important. So Figure 9–10 illustrates the case of induced investment. In this diagram, the investment schedule is upward sloping. Equilibrium, however, is still at point E—where the S and I schedules cross. Thus, allowance for induced investment does not change our analysis in any significant way.[6]

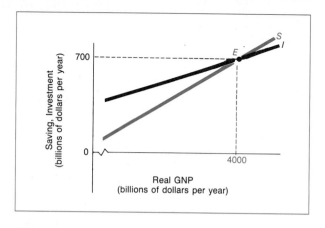

Figure 9–10
INCOME DETERMINATION WITH INDUCED INVESTMENT
When investment rises with GNP ("induced investment"), the investment schedule acquires a positive slope. Apart from this, the determination of equilibrium output is precisely as it was before. Point E, where the S and I schedules cross, is the equilibrium.

[6]Some students may wonder what happens if the slope of the investment schedule exceeds that of the saving schedule. This is a difficult question that is best reserved for more advanced courses. Suffice it to say here that the simple model of income determination constructed in this chapter will not work in such a case.

Summary

1. The condition for equilibrium GNP—which we gave in the chapter as the equation of total spending with output (C + I = Y)—can be restated as the requirement that saving and investment be equal (S = I). This does not change anything, but simply says the same thing in different words.
2. These different words lead to a different graphical presentation, in which we look for equilibrium at the point where the saving schedule crosses the investment schedule.
3. Induced investment—that is, investment that rises as the GNP rises—leads to an upward-sloping investment schedule, but requires no other change in the analysis.

Concepts for Review

S = I   Investment schedule
Saving schedule   Induced investment

Questions for Discussion

1. From the data in Discussion Question 4 at the end of the chapter, construct the saving schedule and the investment schedule on a piece of graph paper. (In doing so, remember that any income that is not consumed must have been saved.) Use these constructions to find the equilibrium level of GNP.
2. Do the same thing with the data in Discussion Question 5.

Appendix B
The Simple Algebra of Income Determination

The model of demand-side equilibrium that the chapter presented graphically and in tabular form can also be handled with some simple algebra.

Written as an equation, the consumption function in our example is:

$$C = 100 + 0.8Y.$$

This is simply the equation of a straight line with intercept 100 and slope 0.8. Investment in the example was assumed to be 700, regardless of the level of income. So the sum C + I is:

$$C + I = 100 + 0.8Y + 700 = 800 + 0.8Y,$$

which describes the $C + I$ curve in Figure 9–3. Since the equilibrium quantity of GNP demanded is defined by:

$$Y = C + I,$$

we can solve for the equilibrium value of Y by substituting $800 + 0.8Y$ for $C + I$, to get:

$$Y = C + I = 800 + 0.8Y.$$

To solve this equation for Y, first subtract $0.8Y$ from both sides to get:

$$0.2Y = 800.$$

Then divide both sides by 0.2 to obtain the answer:

$$Y = 4000.$$

This, of course, is precisely the solution we found by graphical and tabular methods in the chapter.

The method of solution is easily generalized to deal with any set of numbers in our equations. Suppose the consumption function is:

$$C = a + bY.$$

(In the example, $a = 100$ and $b = 0.8$.) Then the equilibrium condition that $Y = C + I$ implies:

$$Y = a + bY + I.$$

Subtracting bY from both sides leads to:

$$(1 - b)Y = a + I,$$

and dividing through by $1 - b$ gives:

$$Y = \frac{a + I}{1 - b}.$$

This formula, which is certainly not to be memorized, is valid for any numerical values of a, b, and I (so long as b is between zero and one.)

Questions for Discussion

1. Find the equilibrium level of GNP demanded in an economy in which investment is always $300 and the consumption function is described by the following algebraic equation:

$$C = 150 + 0.8Y.$$

2. Do the same for an economy in which investment is fixed at $250 and the consumption function is:

$$C = 250 + 0.5Y.$$

3. In each of the above cases, how much saving is there in equilibrium? (*Hint:* Income not consumed must be saved.) Is saving equal to investment?

4. Imagine an economy in which consumer expenditure is represented by the following equation:

$$C = 50 + .75Y.$$

Imagine also that investors want to spend 500 at every level of income: $I = 500$.

a. What is the equilibrium level of income?
b. If the full employment level of income is 2000, is there a recessionary or inflationary gap? If so, how much?
c. What will happen to the equilibrium level of income if investors become pessimistic about the country's future and reduce their investment to 400?
d. Is there a recessionary or inflationary gap now? How much?

5. Ivyland has the following consumption function:

$$C = 100 + .75Y.$$

Firms in Ivyland always invest $200.
a. Find the equilibrium level of GNP.
b. How much is saved? Is saving equal to investment?
c. Suppose consumers are given an inducement to save, so that the consumption function falls to $C = 50 + .75Y$, but at the same time firms boost investment spending to $240. Answer (a) and (b) under these new circumstances.

10

A definite ratio, to be called the *Multiplier*, can be established between income and investment.

JOHN MAYNARD KEYNES

Changes on the Demand Side: Multiplier Analysis

In the last chapter we derived the economy's *aggregate demand curve*, which shows how the equilibrium quantity of real GNP demanded depends on the price level—holding all other factors constant. But often these "other factors" do not remain constant and, as a consequence, the entire aggregate demand curve shifts. This chapter is the first of several that are devoted to enumerating these "other factors" and explaining how and why they make the aggregate demand curve shift.

The central concept of this short chapter is the *multiplier*—the idea that an increase in spending will bring about an *even larger* increase in equilibrium GNP. We approach this idea from three different perspectives, each of which provides different and significant insights into the multiplier process. First, the multiplier is illustrated graphically using the income-expenditure diagram from Chapter 9. Next, we reach the same conclusion through the use of a numerical example, and finally, we offer an algebraic statement. Each of these is an expression of the remarkable multiplier result.

Near the end of the chapter, we use multiplier analysis to explain why a drive to increase national saving might not succeed.

The Magic of the Multiplier

Because it is subject to such abrupt swings, investment spending is often the cause of business fluctuations in the United States and elsewhere. Let us, therefore, ask what would happen to equilibrium income in our fictitious country, Macroland, if firms there suddenly decided to spend more on investment goods. As we shall see, such a decision would have a *multiplied* effect on GNP in Macroland. The same would be true in the U.S. economy.

The **multiplier** is the ratio of the change in equilibrium GNP (Y) divided by the original change in spending that causes the change in GNP.

For simplicity, we begin by assuming that the price level is fixed—an assumption we maintain *only* for this short chapter. Refer first to Table 10–1, which looks very much like Table 9–1 (page 170). The only difference is that we assume here that, for some reason, firms in Macroland now want to invest $200 billion more than they previously did—for a total of $900 billion. The **multiplier** principle says that Macroland's GNP will rise by more than the $200

Table 10–1
TOTAL EXPENDITURE AFTER THE RISE IN INVESTMENT SPENDING
(billions of dollars)

(1) INCOME (Y)	(2) CONSUMPTION (C)	(3) INVESTMENT (I)	(4) TOTAL EXPENDITURE (C + I)
2000	1700	900	2600
2500	2100	900	3000
3000	2500	900	3400
3500	2900	900	3800
4000	3300	900	4200
4500	3700	900	4600
5000	4100	900	5000
5500	4500	900	5400
6000	4900	900	5800

This table shows the construction of a total expenditure schedule for Macroland after investment has risen to $900 billion. As indicated by the shaded numbers, only income level Y = $5000 billion is an equilibrium on the demand side of the economy because only at this level is total spending (C + I) equal to production (Y).

billion increase in investment. Specifically, the multiplier is defined as the ratio of the change in equilibrium GNP (Y) divided by the original change in spending that causes the change in GNP. In shorthand, when we deal with the multiplier for investment (I), the formula is:

$$\text{Multiplier} = \frac{\text{Change in Y}}{\text{Change in I}}.$$

Let us verify that the multiplier is indeed greater than 1. Table 10–1 shows how to derive a new expenditure schedule by adding up C and I at each level of Y, just as we did in Chapter 9. If you compare the last column of Table 10–1 to that of Table 9–1, you will see that the new expenditure schedule lies uniformly above the oid one by $200 billion. Figure 10–1 illustrates this diagrammatically. The schedule marked $C + I_0$ is derived from the last column of Table 9–1, while the higher schedule marked $C + I_1$ is derived from the last column of Table 10–1. The two $C + I$ lines are parallel and $200 billion apart.

So far no act of magic has occurred — things look just as you might expect. But one more step will bring the multiplier rabbit out of the hat. Let us see what the upward shift of the $C + I$ line does to equilibrium income. In Figure 10–1, equilibrium moves outward from point E_0 to point E_1, that is, from $4000 billion to $5000 billion. The difference is an increase in national income of $1000 billion. All this from a $200 billion stimulus to investment? That is the magic of the multiplier.

Because the change in I is $200 billion and the change in equilibrium Y is $1000 billion, by applying our definition, the multiplier is:

$$\text{Multiplier} = \frac{\text{Change in Y}}{\text{Change in I}} = \frac{\$1000}{\$200} = 5.$$

This tells us that, in our example, every additional dollar of investment demand will add $5 to the equilibrium GNP!

This does indeed seem mysterious. Can something be created from nothing? Let us, therefore, check to be sure that the graph has not deceived us. The first and last columns of Table 10–1 show in numbers what Figure 10–1 shows

Figure 10–1

ILLUSTRATION OF
THE MULTIPLIER

This figure depicts the
multiplier effect of a rise in
investment spending of $200
billion. The expenditure
schedule shifts upward from
$C + I_0$ to $C + I_1$, thus moving
equilibrium from point E_0 to
point E_1. The rise in income
is $1000 billion, so the
multiplier is $1000/$200 = 5.

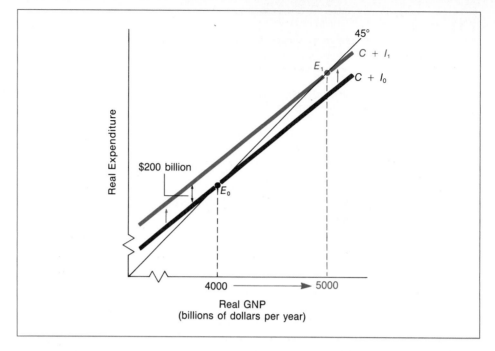

in a picture. Notice that, at any income level below $5000, spending ($C + I$) exceeds output ($Y$). As we know, this cannot be an equilibrium situation because inventories would be disappearing. On the other hand, at any income level above $5000 inventories would be piling up, since $C + I$ is less than Y.

Only at $Y = $5000 billion are spending and production in balance, as Table 10–1 shows. This is $1000 billion higher than the $4000 billion equilibrium GNP obtained in the discussion of Table 9–1, where investment was only $700 billion. Thus a $200 billion rise in investment leads to a $1000 billion rise in equilibrium GNP. The multiplier really is 5.

Demystifying the Multiplier: How It Works

The multiplier result seems peculiar at first, but it loses its mystery once we remember the circular flow of income and expenditure and the simple fact that one person's spending is another person's income. To illustrate the logic of the multiplier, and see why it is exactly 5 in our model economy, let us look more closely at what actually happens if businesses decide to spend an additional $1 million on investment goods. If GNP is to rise by $5 million, and $Y = C + I$, then consumer spending must rise by $4 million. Let's see how.

Suppose that Generous Motors—a major corporation in Macroland—decides to spend $1 million to retool a factory to manufacture pollution-free, electronically powered automobiles. Its $1 million expenditure goes to construction workers and owners of construction companies as wages and profits. That is, it becomes their *income*.

But the owners and workers of the construction firms will not simply keep their $1 million in the bank. They will spend some of it. If they are "typical" consumers, their spending will be $1 million times the marginal propensity to consume (MPC). In our example, the MPC is 0.8. So let us assume that they spend $800,000 and save the rest. *This $800,000 expenditure is a net addition to the nation's demand for goods and services exactly as GM's original $1 million expenditure was.* So, at this stage, the $1 million investment has already pushed GNP up some $1.8 million.

But the process by no means stops here. Shopkeepers receive the $800,000 spent by construction workers, and these shopkeepers in turn also spend 80 percent of their new income. This accounts for $640,000 (80 percent of $800,000) in additional consumer spending in the "third round." Next follows a fourth round in which the recipients of the $640,000, in their turn, spend 80 percent of this amount, or $512,000, and so on. At each stage in the spending chain, people spend 80 percent of the additional income they receive, and the process continues. Consumption grows in each round.

Where does it all end? Does it all end? The answer is that it does, indeed, eventually end—with GNP a total of $5 million higher than it was before Generous Motors spent the original $1 million. The multiplier, as stated, is 5.

Table 10–2 displays the basis for this conclusion. In the table, "round 1" represents GM's initial investment, which creates $1 million in income for construction workers; "round 2" represents the construction workers' spending which creates $800,000 in income for shopkeepers. The rest of the table proceeds accordingly. Each entry in column 2 is 80 percent of the previous entry, and column 3 tabulates the running sum of column 2.

We see that after 10 rounds of spending, the initial $1 million investment has mushroomed to nearly $4.5 million, and the sum is still growing. After 20 rounds, the total increase in GNP is over $4.9 million—near its eventual value of $5 million. While it takes quite a few rounds of spending before the multiplier chain is near 5, we see from the table that it approaches 4 rather quickly. If each income recipient in the chain waits, say, two months before spending his new income, the multiplier will reach 4 in only about 14 months.

Table 10–2
THE MULTIPLIER SPENDING CHAIN

(1) ROUND NUMBER	(2) SPENDING IN THIS ROUND	(3) CUMULATIVE TOTAL
1	$1,000,000	$1,000,000
2	800,000	1,800,000
3	640,000	2,440,000
4	512,000	2,952,000
5	409,600	3,361,600
6	327,680	3,689,280
7	262,144	3,951,424
8	209,715	4,161,139
9	167,772	4,328,911
10	134,218	4,463,129
⋮	⋮	⋮
20	14,412	4,942,354
⋮	⋮	⋮
50	18	4,999,929
⋮	⋮	⋮
"Infinity"	0	5,000,000

This table shows how the multiplier unfolds through time. Round 1 is GM's initial spending, which leads to $1 million in additional income to construction workers. Round 2 shows the construction workers spending 80 percent of this amount, since the marginal propensity to consume is 0.8. The other rounds proceed accordingly, with spending in each successive round equal to 80 percent of that in the previous round. Technically, the full multiplier of 5 is reached only after an "infinite" number of rounds. But, as can be seen, we are close to the full amount after 20 rounds.

Figure 10–2
HOW THE
MULTIPLIER BUILDS
This diagram portrays the
numbers from Table 10–2
and shows how the multiplier
builds through time. Notice
how the effect grows quickly
at first and how the full effect
is almost reached after 20
rounds.

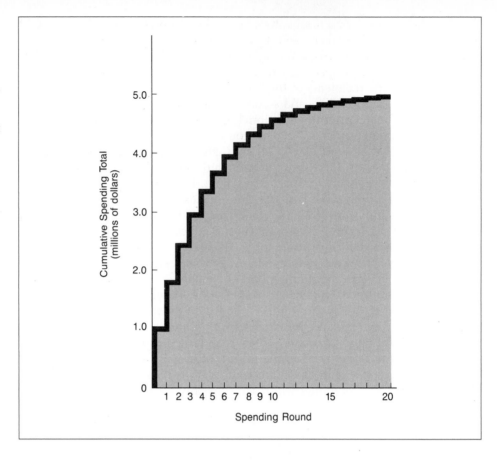

Figure 10–2 provides a graphical presentation of the numbers in the last column of Table 10–2. Notice how the multiplier builds up rapidly at first and then tapers off to approach its ultimate value (5 in this example) gradually.

Algebraic Statement of the Multiplier

Figure 10–2 and Table 10–2 probably make a persuasive case for the fact that the multiplier eventually reaches 5. But for the remaining skeptics we offer a simple algebraic proof.[1] Most of you learned about an "infinite geometric progression" in high school. This is simply an infinite series of numbers, each one of which is a fixed fraction of the previous one. This fraction is called the "common ratio." A geometric progression beginning with 1 and having a common ratio equal to 0.8 would look like this:

$$1 + 0.8 + (0.8)^2 + (0.8)^3 + \ldots .$$

More generally, a geometric progression beginning with 1 and having a common ratio R would be:

$$1 + R + R^2 + R^3 \ldots$$

[1]Students who blanch at the sight of algebra should not be put off. Anyone who can balance a checkbook (even many who cannot!) will be able to follow the argument.

A simple formula enables us to sum such a progression as long as R is less than 1.[2] The formula is:[3]

$$\text{Sum of infinite geometric progression} = \frac{1}{1 - R}.$$

Now we can recognize that the multiplier chain in Table 10–2 is just an infinite geometric progression with 0.8 as its common ratio. That is, each \$1 spent by GM leads to a $(0.8) \times \$1$ expenditure by construction workers, which in turn leads to a $(0.8) \times (0.8 \times \$1) = (0.8)^2 \times \$1$ expenditure by the shop-keepers, and so on. Thus, for each initial dollar of investment spending, the progression is:

$$1 + 0.8 + (08)^2 + (0.8)^3 + (0.8)^4 + \dots.$$

Applying the formula for the sum of such a series, we find that:

$$\text{Multiplier} = \frac{1}{1 - 0.8} = \frac{1}{0.2} = 5.$$

Notice how this result can be generalized. If we did not have a specific numerical value for the marginal propensity to consume, but simply called it "MPC," the geometric progression in Table 10–2 would have been:

$$1 + \text{MPC} + (\text{MPC})^2 + (\text{MPC})^3 + \dots,$$

which has the MPC as its common ratio. Applying the same formula for summing a geometric progression to this more general case gives us the following general result:

✳ OVERSIMPLIFIED FORMULA FOR THE MULTIPLIER

$$\text{Multiplier} = \frac{1}{1 - \text{MPC}}.$$

We call this formula "oversimplified" because it ignores many factors that are important in the real world. One of them is *inflation*, a complication to which we will turn in the next chapter. A second is *income taxation*, a point we will elaborate in Chapter 12. A third factor arises from the *financial system* and, after we discuss money and banking in Chapters 13 and 14, we will explain it in

---

[2] If R exceeds 1, nobody can possibly sum it — not even with the aid of a modern computer!
[3] The proof is simple. Let the symbol S stand for the (unknown) sum of the series:

$$S = 1 + R + R^2 + R^3 + \dots.$$

Then, multiplying by R,

$$RS = R + R^2 + R^2 + R^3 + \dots.$$

By subtracting RS from S, we obtain:

$$S - RS = 1$$

or

$$S = \frac{1}{1 - R}.$$

Chapter 15. A final factor relates to *international trade*, and will wait until Chapter 20. As it turns out, each of these factors *reduces* the size of the multiplier.

We can begin to appreciate just how unrealistic the "oversimplified" formula is by considering some real numbers for the U.S. economy. The marginal propensity to consume (MPC) has been estimated many times and is about 0.9. From our oversimplified formula, then, it would seem that the multiplier should be:

$$\text{Multiplier} = \frac{1}{1 - 0.9} = \frac{1}{0.1} = 10.$$

In fact, the actual multiplier for the U.S. economy is believed to be less than 2. This is quite a discrepancy! But it does not mean that anything we have said about the multiplier so far is incorrect. Our story is simply incomplete. As we progress through the following chapters, you will learn why the multiplier is below 2 even though the MPC is close to 0.9. For now we simply point out that:

While the multiplier is larger than 1 in the real world, it cannot be calculated with any degree of accuracy from the oversimplified formula. The actual multiplier is *lower* than the formula suggests.

The Multiplier Effect of Consumer Spending

Business firms that invest are not the only ones that can work the magic of the multiplier; so can consumers. Let us see how the multiplier works when the process is initiated by an upsurge in consumer spending.

First, we need to distinguish between two types of change in consumer spending. When C rises because income rises — that is, when consumers move outward *along a fixed consumption function* — we call the increase in C an **induced increase in consumption.** However, if instead C rises because the entire consumption function *shifts* up, we call this an **autonomous increase in consumption.** The name indicates that consumption changes independently of income, and Chapter 8's discussion pointed out that a number of events, such as a change in the price level or in the value of the stock market, can initiate such a shift.

Let us suppose that, for some reason, consumer spending rises autonomously by $200 billion. In this case, our table of aggregate demand would have to be revised to look like Table 10–3. Comparing this to Table 10–1 on page 185, we note that each entry in column 2 is $200 billion *higher* than the corresponding entry in Table 10–1 (because consumption is higher), and each entry in column 3 is $200 billion *lower* (because investment is lower).

The equilibrium level of income is clearly Y = $5000 billion once again. Indeed the entire expenditure schedule is the same as it was in Table 10–1. The initial rise of $200 billion in spending leads to an ultimate rise of $1000 billion in GNP, just as occurred in the case of higher investment spending. In fact, Figure 10–1 applies to this case without any changes. The multiplier for autonomous changes in consumer spending, then, is also 5 ($1000/$200).

An **induced increase in consumption** is an increase in consumer spending that stems from an increase in consumer incomes. It is represented on a graph as a movement along a fixed consumption function.

An **autonomous increase in consumption** is an increase in consumer spending without any increase in incomes. It is represented on a graph as a shift of the entire consumption function.

Table 10–3

TOTAL EXPENDITURE AFTER CONSUMERS DECIDE TO SPEND $200 BILLION MORE
(billions of dollars)

(1) INCOME (Y)	(2) CONSUMPTION (C)	(3) INVESTMENT (I)	(4) TOTAL EXPENDITURE (C + I)
2000	1900	700	2600
2500	2300	700	3000
3000	2700	700	3400
3500	3100	700	3800
4000	3500	700	4200
4500	3900	700	4600
5000	4300	700	5000
5500	4700	700	5400
6000	5100	700	5800

This table shows the construction of the total expenditure schedule for Macroland following an autonomous increase of $200 billion in consumption rather than in investment. Notice that columns 2 and 3 differ from the corresponding columns in Table 10–1, but column 4 is the same in both tables. Thus the expenditure schedule in the 45° line diagram is the same as in the earlier example.

The reason is straightforward. It does not matter who injects an additional dollar of spending into the economy, whether it is business investors or consumers. Wherever it comes from, 80 percent of it will be respent if the MPC is 0.8, and the recipients of this second round will in turn spend 80 percent of their additional income, and so on and on. And that is what constitutes the multiplier process.

The Multiplier in Reverse

A good way to check your understanding of the multiplier process is to run it in reverse: What happens if, for example, consumers autonomously decide to spend less? For example, suppose a wave of thriftiness comes over the people of Macroland so that, no matter what their total income, they now want to spend $200 billion *less* than they did previously.

A decision to spend $200 billion less out of any given level of income is, by definition, a *downward* shift of the total expenditure schedule by $200 billion. This is shown in Figure 10–3, where the $C + I$ schedule falls from $C_0 + I$ to $C_1 + I$. The horizontal distance between these two parallel lines is the $200 billion drop in spending.

There are two ways of calculating the multiplier. First, our oversimplified multiplier formula tells us that the multiplier is

$$\frac{1}{1 - \text{MPC}} = \frac{1}{1 - 0.8} = \frac{1}{0.2} = 5.$$

So a $200 billion drop in spending will lead to a multiplier effect of $1000 billion. Alternatively, we can read this conclusion from Figure 10–3. Here the economy's equilibrium point moves down the 45° line from point E_0 to E_1; income drops from $4000 billion to $3000 billion—a decline of $1000 billion.

Figure 10–3
THE MULTIPLIER IN REVERSE
This diagram shows the multiplier effect of an autonomous decline in consumer spending of $200 billion. The decline appears as a downward shift of $200 billion in the expenditure schedule, which falls from $C_0 + I$ to $C_1 + I$. Equilibrium, which is always at the intersection of the expenditure schedule and the 45° line, moves from point E_0 to point E_1, and income falls from $4000 billion to $3000 billion.

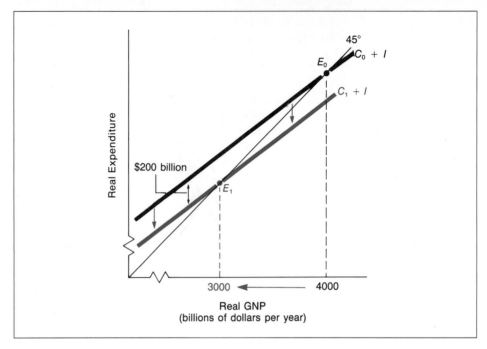

Now compare the analysis of a decline in spending that is summarized in Figure 10–3 with our previous analysis of an increase in spending, as shown in Figure 10–1 on page 186. You will see that everything is simply turned in the opposite direction. The multiplier works in both directions.

 ## The Paradox of Thrift

This last example of multiplier analysis teaches us an important lesson: It shows that an increase in the desire to save will lead to a cumulative fall in GNP. And, *because saving depends on income,* the resulting decline in national income will pull saving down.

Let us be a bit more specific about this. Before the upsurge in saving, consumers were spending $3300 billion out of a total national income of $4000 billion, as we can see in Table 9–1 on page 170. Hence $700 billion was being saved. In Figure 10–3, income falls to $3000 billion. Since investment is still $700 billion, and C + I must add up to Y, we know that consumption at point E must be $2300. So total saving is still $700 (= $3000 − $2300) billion. The effort to save more has been totally frustrated by the decline in GNP.[4]

The **paradox of thrift** is the fact that an effort by a nation to save more may simply reduce national income and fail to raise total saving.

This remarkable result is called the **paradox of thrift,** because it shows that, while saving may pave the road to riches for an individual, if the nation as a whole decides to save more, the result may be a recession and poverty for all. The paradox of thrift is important because it is contrary to most people's thinking, and it means that greater saving may be a mixed blessing if it is not accompanied by equally greater investment.

[4]It is even possible to devise examples in which total saving goes *down* when people attempt to save more. Just suppose there is *induced investment;* that is, suppose that investment spending rises with GNP. Then, when GNP falls, so does *I*. Since *S = I* in equilibrium, savings must decline.

The Multiplier and the Aggregate Demand Curve

At this point we must recall something that was mentioned at the start of the chapter: Income-expenditure diagrams such as Figure 10–1 or 10–3 can be drawn up only for a given price level. A different price level leads to a different total expenditure curve. This means that our oversimplified multiplier formula measures *the increase in real GNP demanded that would occur if the price level were fixed*. That is, it measures the *horizontal shift* of the economy's aggregate demand curve.

Figure 10–4 illustrates this conclusion by supposing that the price level that underlies Figure 10–1 is $P = 100$. The top panel simply repeats Figure 10–1 and shows how an increase in investment spending from $700 to $900 billion leads to an increase in GNP from $4000 to $5000 billion.

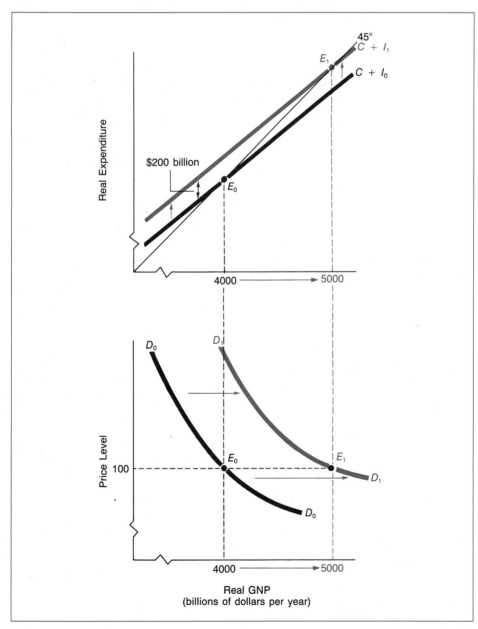

Figure 10–4
TWO VIEWS OF THE MULTIPLIER
The top panel repeats Figure 10–1. The bottom panel shows two aggregate demand curves. Curve D_0D_0, which applies when investment is $700 billion, shows that equilibrium GNP on the demand side comes at $Y = \$4000$ billion when $P = 100$ (point E_0). Curve D_1D_1, which applies when investment is $900 billion, shows that equilibrium GNP on the demand side comes at $Y = \$5000$ billion when $P = 100$ (point E_1). The horizontal distance between points E_0 and E_1 in the bottom panel indicates the oversimplified multiplier effect.

The bottom panel shows two downward-sloping aggregate demand curves. The first, labeled D_0D_0, depicts the situation when investment is $700 billion. Point E_0 on this curve indicates that, at the given price level ($P = 100$), the equilibrium quantity of GNP demanded is $4000 billion. It corresponds exactly to point E_0 in the top panel. The second aggregate demand curve, D_1D_1, depicts the situation after investment has risen to $900 billion. Point E_1 on this curve indicates that the equilibrium quantity of GNP demanded when $P = 100$ has risen to $5000 billion, which corresponds exactly to point E_1 in the top panel.

As Figure 10–4 shows, the horizontal distance between the two aggregate demand curves is exactly equal to the increase in real GNP shown in the income-expenditure diagram — in this case, $1000 billion. Thus:

An autonomous increase in spending leads to a horizontal shift of the aggregate demand curve by an amount given by the oversimplified multiplier formula.

Thus everything we have said about the multiplier applies to shifts of the economy's aggregate demand curve. If businesses decide to increase their investment spending, or if the consumption function shifts up, the aggregate demand curve moves horizontally to the right — as indicated in Figure 10–4. If either investment decreases or the consumption function shifts down, the aggregate demand curve moves horizontally to the left. In subsequent chapters we will learn, not surprisingly, that the same applies to changes in either of the other two components of total spending: government purchases and net exports.

Thus the economy's aggregate demand curve cannot be expected to stand still. Autonomous changes in spending by consumers, investors, government units, or foreigners all cause the aggregate demand curve to move around. But to understand the consequences of shifts of aggregate demand, we must bring the aggregate supply curve into the picture. That is the task of the next chapter.

Summary

1. Any autonomous increase in expenditure has a multiplier effect on GNP; that is, it increases GNP by more than the original increase in spending.
2. The reason for this multiplier effect is that one person's additional expenditure constitutes a new source of income for another person, and this additional income leads to still more spending, and so on.
3. The multiplier also works in reverse: an autonomous decrease in any component of aggregate demand leads to a multiplied decrease in national income.
4. A simple formula for the multiplier says that its numerical value is $1/(1 - \text{MPC})$. This formula, which is too simple to give accurate results, measures the horizontal shift of the aggregate demand curve.
5. If the nation as a whole decides to save more, that is, to consume less, the resulting decline in national income may serve to make everyone poorer. This possibility that thriftiness, while a virtue for the individual, may be disastrous for an entire nation, is called the paradox of thrift.

Concepts for Review

The multiplier

Induced increase in consumption

Autonomous increase in consumption

Paradox of thrift

Questions for Discussion

1. Try to remember where you last spent a dollar. Explain how this dollar will lead to a multiplier chain of increased income and spending. (Who received the dollar? What will he or she do with it?)
2. Use both numerical and graphical methods to find the multiplier effect of the following shift in the consumption function in an economy in which investment is always $110.

INCOME	CONSUMPTION BEFORE SHIFT	CONSUMPTION AFTER SHIFT
$510	$430	$470
540	450	490
570	470	510
600	490	530
630	510	550
660	530	570
690	550	590
720	570	610

(*Hint:* What is the marginal propensity to consume?)

3. Turn back to Discussion Question 4 in Chapter 9 (page 180). Suppose investment spending rises to $130, and the price level is fixed. By how much will the equilibrium GNP increase? Derive the answer both numerically and graphically.
4. Explain the paradox of thrift. Why do you think it is called a paradox?
5. (More difficult) Suppose the consumption function is as given in Discussion Question 9 of Chapter 9 (page 180)

$$C = 100 + 0.8Y$$

and investment (I) rises to 900. Use the equilibrium condition $Y = C + I$ to find the equilibrium level of GNP. (In working out the answer, assume the price level is fixed.) Compare your answer to Table 10–1 and Figure 10–1. Now compare your answer to the answer to Discussion Question 9 of Chapter 9. What do you learn about the multiplier?

Appendix
The Simple Algebra of the Multiplier

In Appendix B to Chapter 9, we worked out a general expression for the equilibrium level of GNP when the price level is fixed, investment is some fixed number, I, and the consumption function is:

$$C = a + bY.$$

The answer obtained there (which can be found on page 183) was:

$$Y = \frac{a + I}{1 - b}.$$

From this formula, it is easy to derive the oversimplified multiplier formula algebraically and to show that it applies equally well to a change in investment or to a change in autonomous consumer spending. To do this, suppose that *either I*

or *a* increases by 1 unit. In either case, the sum $C + I$ would rise from:

$$C + I = a + bY + I,$$

to:

$$C + I = a + bY + I + 1.$$

Using the equilibrium condition that Y must be equal to $C + I$, we can solve for Y just as we did in Appendix B of Chapter 9:

$$Y = C + I$$

so that:

$$Y = a + bY + I + 1$$

and therefore:

$$(1 - b)Y = a + I + 1,$$

or:

$$Y = \frac{a + I + 1}{1 - b}.$$

By comparing this with our previous expression for Y, we see that a 1 unit change in *either a or I* changes equilibrium GNP by:

$$\text{change in } Y = \frac{a + I + 1}{1 - b} - \frac{a + I}{1 - b}$$

$$\text{change in } Y = \frac{a + I + 1 - (a + I)}{1 - b}$$

or:

$$\text{change in } Y = \frac{1}{1 - b}.$$

Recalling that b is the marginal propensity to consume, we see that this is precisely the over-simplified multiplier formula.

11

Supply-Side Equilibrium: Unemployment *and* Inflation?

We might as well reasonably dispute whether it is the upper or the under blade of a pair of scissors that cuts a piece of paper, as whether value is governed by [demand] or [supply].

ALFRED MARSHALL

In Chapter 9 we learned that the level of prices, in conjunction with the economy's consumption and investment schedules, governs whether the economy will experience a recessionary or an inflationary gap. If the $C + I$ schedule is "too low," a *recessionary gap* will arise, while a $C + I$ schedule that is "too high" leads to an *inflationary gap*. Which sort of gap actually occurs is of some importance because, as we shall confirm in this chapter, a recessionary gap normally spells unemployment while an inflationary gap means inflation.

The tools provided in Chapter 9, however, are not sufficient to determine which sort of gap will arise because, as we know, the position of the $C + I$ schedule depends on the price level. And the price level is determined by *both aggregate demand and aggregate supply*. Thus, the task of the present chapter is to bring the supply side of the economy into the picture.

We begin by explaining how the *aggregate supply* curve is derived from business costs. Next we consider the interaction of aggregate supply and aggregate demand, and the joint determination of output and the price level. With this apparatus in hand, we return to the phenomena of recessionary and inflationary gaps and study how the economy adjusts to each type. Doing this puts us in a position to deal with the crucial question raised in earlier chapters: Does the economy have an efficient self-correcting mechanism? As we shall see, the economy is better at curing inflationary gaps than recessionary gaps. Finally, we use aggregate supply–aggregate demand analysis to explain the vexing problem of *stagflation* — the simultaneous occurrence of high unemployment *and* high inflation — that has plagued the economy so often since the mid-1970s. The chapter ends by explaining how inflation affects the multiplier.

The Supply Side Matters

The Reagan administration took office in January 1981 espousing a new doctrine called "supply-side economics" — an allegedly new theory designed to supplant the Keynesian theory we have studied in the last two chapters. Supply-side economics was controversial from the start, and it remains so to this day. Supporters credit it with spurring economic growth and conquering inflation. Detractors blame it for many of our current problems, especially the huge federal budget and foreign trade deficits.

Actually, however, supply-side economics was not a new theory at all. Rather, it was a collection of activist policies aimed at the supply side of the economy—plus a claim that these policies were just what the U.S. economy needed after the inflationary 1970s. The policies naturally provoked considerable debate; and we will review that debate in the next chapter. But one supply-side proposition never was controversial: that what happens on the supply side of the economy matters a great deal for inflation, unemployment, and economic growth. It is therefore time for us to consider the origins of the aggregate supply curve and the factors that can make it shift.

The Aggregate Supply Curve

In earlier chapters we noted that aggregate demand is a schedule, not a fixed number. The quantity of real GNP that will be demanded depends on the price level, as summarized in the economy's *aggregate demand* curve.

Analogously, the concept of *aggregate supply* does not refer to a fixed number but, rather, to a schedule (to a supply curve). The volume of goods and services that will be provided by profit-seeking enterprises depends on the prices they obtain for their outputs, on wages and other production costs, on the state of technology, and on other things. The relationship between the price level and the quantity of real GNP supplied, *holding all other determinants of quantity supplied constant*, is called the economy's **aggregate supply curve.**

The **aggregate supply curve** shows, for each possible price level, the quantity of goods and services that all the nation's businesses are willing to produce, holding all other determinants of aggregate quantity supplied constant.

A typical aggregate supply curve is drawn in Figure 11–1. It slopes upward, meaning that as prices rise more output is produced, *other things held constant*. It is not difficult to understand why this is so. Producers in the U.S. economy are motivated mainly by profit. Since the profit made by producing a unit of output is simply the difference between the price at which it is sold and the unit cost of production,

$$\text{profit per unit} = \text{price} - \text{cost per unit},$$

Figure 11–1
AN AGGREGATE SUPPLY CURVE
This graph shows a typical aggregate supply curve. It has a positive slope (that is, it rises as we move to the right), meaning that the quantity of output supplied rises as the price level rises.

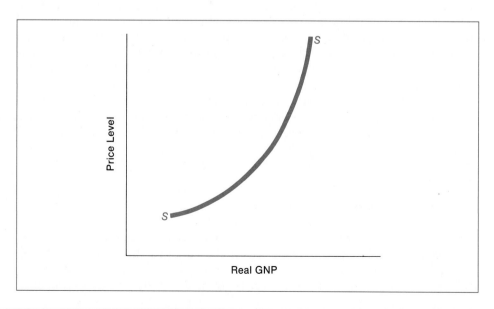

it is clear that the response of production to a rising price level (henceforth, P) depends on the response of costs.[1]

One critical fact affecting this response is that labor and other inputs used by firms normally are available at *relatively fixed prices* for some period of time — though certainly not forever. There are many reasons for this. Some workers and firms enter into long-term labor contracts that set money wages up to three years in advance. Even where there are no explicit contracts, employees typically have their wages increased only about once per year. During the interim period, money wages are fixed. Much the same is true of other factors of production. Many firms get deliveries of raw materials under long-term contracts according to which suppliers have agreed to provide the materials at prearranged prices. None of these contracts lasts forever, of course, but many of them last long enough to matter.

Why is it significant that firms often purchase inputs like labor and raw materials at prices that stay fixed for considerable periods? Because firms decide how much to produce by comparing selling prices with costs of production; and production costs obviously depend on input prices. If the selling prices of the firm's products rise while wages and other factor costs are relatively fixed, production becomes more profitable, and so firms are persuaded to increase output.

A simple example will illustrate the idea. Suppose a firm uses one hour of labor time to manufacture a gadget that sells for $9. If workers earn $8 per hour, and the firm has no other production costs, its profit per unit is:

$$\text{profit per unit} = \text{price} - \text{cost per unit}$$
$$= \$9 \quad - \$8$$
$$= \$1.$$

Now what happens if the price of a gadget rises to $10, but wage rates remain constant? The firm's profit per unit becomes:

$$\text{profit per unit} = \text{price} - \text{cost per unit}$$
$$= \$10 \quad - \$8$$
$$= \$2.$$

With production more profitable, it is likely that the firm will supply more gadgets.

The same process operates in reverse. Suppose selling prices fall while input costs are relatively fixed. Since this squeezes their profit margins, firms may react by cutting back on production. For example, if the price of a gadget fell from $9 to $8.50, profit per unit would fall from $1 to 50 cents, and firms would probably produce less.

The behavior we have just described is summarized by the upward slope of the aggregate supply curve: Production rises when the price level (P) rises, and falls when P falls. In other words:

The aggregate supply curve slopes upward because firms normally can purchase labor and other inputs at fixed costs for some period of time. Thus, higher selling prices make production more attractive.

---

[1]For a full discussion of business output decisions and how they respond to costs, see *Microeconomics* Chapter 8.

The phrase "for some period of time" alerts us to the possibility that the aggregate supply curve may not stand still for long. If wages or prices of other inputs change, as they surely will during inflationary times, then the aggregate supply curve will shift.

Shifts of the Aggregate Supply Curve

We have concluded so far that, for any given levels of wages and other input prices, there will be an upward-sloping aggregate supply curve relating the price level to aggregate quantity supplied. But what factors determine the *position* of this curve? What things can make it shift?

The Money Wage Rate

Our previous discussion suggests that the most obvious determinant of the position of the aggregate supply curve is the money wage rate. Wages are the major element of cost for most firms, typically accounting for something like 70 percent of all expenses. Higher wages spell higher costs, thereby lowering profits at any given prices.

Let us return to our example and consider what would happen to a gadget producer if the money wage rose to $8.75 per hour while the price of a gadget remained $9. Profit per unit would decline from:

$$\$9 - \$8 \quad = \$1$$

to:

$$\$9 - \$8.75 = \$0.25.$$

With profits squeezed, the firm would probably cut back on production.

This is the typical reaction of firms in our economy to a rise in wages. Therefore, a wage increase leads to a decrease in aggregate quantity supplied at current prices. Graphically, the aggregate supply curve shifts to the left (or inward), as shown in Figure 11–2. In this diagram, when wages are low, firms

Figure 11–2

A SHIFT OF THE AGGREGATE SUPPLY CURVE

This diagram shows what happens to the economy's aggregate supply curve when money wages rise. Higher wages shift the supply curve inward from $S_0 S_0$ to $S_1 S_1$, leading, for example, to an output level of $3500 billion (point *B*), rather than $4000 (point *A*), when the price level is 100. The aggregate supply curve will shift inward in the same manner if the price of any other input (such as energy) increases.

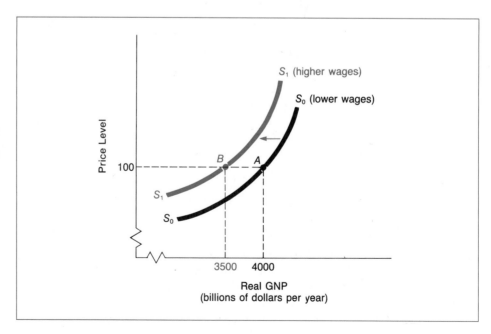

are willing to supply $4000 billion in goods and services at a price level of 100 (point A). After wages increase, however, these same firms are willing to supply only $3500 billion at this price level (point B). By similar reasoning, the aggregate supply curve will shift to the right (or outward) if wages fall. Thus:

A rise in the money wage rate causes the aggregate supply curve to shift *inward*, meaning that the quantity supplied at any price level declines. A fall in the money wage rate causes the aggregate supply curve to shift outward, meaning that the quantity supplied at any price level increases.

Prices of Other Inputs

In this regard, there is nothing special about wages. An increase in the price of *any* input that firms buy will shift the aggregate supply curve in the same way. That is:

The aggregate supply curve is shifted inward by an increase in the price of any input to the production process, and it is shifted outward by a decrease.

While there are many inputs other than labor, the one that has attracted the most attention in recent years is energy. We shall have much to say about energy in this book, including further discussion in this chapter and in Chapter 34. But for present purposes the important thing to realize is that increases in the price of energy, such as those that took place in the 1970s and early 1980s, push the aggregate supply curve inward more or less as shown in Figure 11–2. By the same token, a rise in the price of *any* input we import from abroad would have the effect shown in the figure.

Technology and Productivity

Another factor that determines the position of the aggregate supply curve is the state of technology. Suppose, for example, that a technological breakthrough increases the **productivity** of labor. If wages do not change, such an improvement in productivity will *decrease* business costs and thus improve profitability and encourage more production.

Productivity is the amount of output produced by a unit of input.

Once again, our gadget company will help us understand how this works. Suppose the price of a gadget stays at $9 and the hourly wage rate stays at $8, but gadget workers become much more productive. Specifically, suppose the labor input required to manufacture a gadget falls from one hour (which costs $8) to three-quarters of an hour (which costs $6). Then profit per unit rises from $9 − $8 = $1 to $9 − $6 = $3. The lure of higher profits should induce gadget manufacturers to increase production. In brief, we have concluded that:

Improvements in productivity shift the aggregate supply curve outward.

Figure 11–2 can be viewed as applying to a *decline* in productivity. As we noted earlier in Chapter 7, slow growth of productivity has been a problem for the United States of late, and it remains a source of great concern. Many people feel that the productivity slowdown contributed to the stagflation of the 1970s.

Available Supplies of Labor and Capital

The last determinant of the position of the aggregate supply curve is obvious, but we list it anyway both for the sake of completeness and for its importance in the debate over supply-side economics. The bigger the economy — as measured by its available supplies of labor and capital—the more it is capable of producing. So:

As the labor force grows, and as the capital stock is increased by investment, the aggregate supply curve shifts outward (to the right), meaning that more output can be produced at any given price level.

These, then, are the major "other things" that we hold constant when drawing up an aggregate supply curve: wage rates, prices of other inputs (like energy), technology, labor force, and capital stock. While a change in the price level moves the economy *along a given supply curve*, a change in any of these other determinants of aggregate quantity supplied *shifts the entire supply schedule*.

The Shape of the Aggregate Supply Curve

One other feature of the aggregate supply curve depicted in Figure 11–1 merits comment. We have drawn our supply curve with a characteristic curvature: It is relatively flat at low levels of output and gets steeper at high levels of output (as we move to the right). There is a reason for this.

When economic activity is weak, product demand slack, and capacity utilization low, firms are likely to respond to an upsurge in demand by bringing their unused capital and labor resources back into production. They will find, therefore, that unit costs of production do not rise much as output expands. As a result, they will find it neither necessary nor advisable to raise prices much. Rapidly rising output with relatively unchanged prices means an aggregate supply curve that is relatively flat.

By contrast, if the economy is booming, demand is buoyant, and production is straining capacity, firms will be able to increase output only by hiring more workers, acquiring more capital, or putting workers on overtime. Whatever they do, unit costs of production rise. Price increases will thus be encouraged by cost developments and, incidentally, will not be resisted forcefully on the demand side. In this case, the aggregate supply curve is steep. Thus:

The slope of the aggregate supply curve, which tells us the price increase that is associated with a unit increase in quantity supplied, generally rises as the degree of resource utilization rises.

Equilibrium of Aggregate Demand and Supply

In Chapter 9 we learned that the level of prices is a crucial determinant of whether equilibrium GNP is below full employment (a "recessionary gap"), precisely at full employment, or above full employment (an "inflationary gap"). We are now in a position to analyze which type of gap, if any, will actually occur in any particular case by combining the analysis of aggregate supply just completed with the analysis of aggregate demand from the last two chapters to determine *simultaneously* the equilibrium level of real GNP (Y) and the equilibrium price level (P).

Figure 11–3 displays the mechanics. The aggregate demand curve DD and the aggregate supply curve SS intersect at point E, where real GNP is $4000 billion and the price level is 100. As can be seen in the graph, at any higher price level, such as 120, aggregate quantity supplied would exceed aggregate quantity demanded. There would be a glut on the market as firms found themselves unable to sell all their output. As inventories piled up, firms would compete

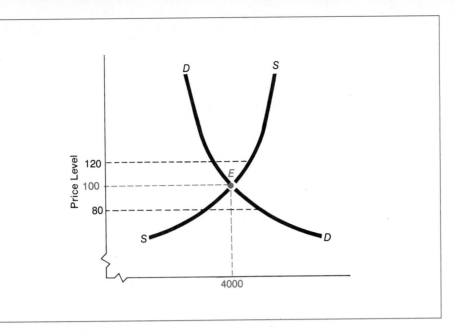

Figure 11–3
EQUILIBRIUM OF REAL
GNP AND THE PRICE
LEVEL
This diagram shows how the
equilibrium levels of real GNP
and the price level are
simultaneously determined by
the intersection of the
aggregate demand curve
(*DD*) and the aggregate
supply curve (*SS*). In this
example, equilibrium occurs
at point *E*, with a real GNP of
$4000 billion and a price
level of 100.

more vigorously for the available customers, thereby forcing prices down. The
price level would fall, as would production.

At any price level lower than 100, such as 80, quantity demanded would
exceed quantity supplied. There would be a shortage of goods on the market.
With inventories disappearing and customers knocking on their doors, firms
would be encouraged to raise prices. The price level would rise, and so would
output.

Only when the price level is 100 are the quantities of real GNP demanded
and supplied equal. Hence, only the combination $P = 100$, $Y = \$4000$ is an
equilibrium.

Table 11–1 illustrates the same conclusion in another way, using a tabular
analysis similar to that of Chapter 9 (refer back to Table 9–2, page 172).
Columns 1 and 2 constitute an aggregate demand schedule corresponding to the
aggregate demand curve *DD* in Figure 11–3. Columns 1 and 3 constitute an

Table 11–1
THE DETERMINATION OF THE EQUILIBRIUM PRICE LEVEL

(1)	(2)	(3)	(4)	(5)
	AGGREGATE QUANTITY DEMANDED	AGGREGATE QUANTITY SUPPLIED	BALANCE OF	
PRICE LEVEL	(billions of dollars)	(billions of dollars)	SUPPLY AND DEMAND	PRICES WILL:
75	4400	3600	Quantity demanded exceeds quantity supplied	Rise
80	4300	3700	Quantity demanded exceeds quantity supplied	Rise
100	4000	4000	Quantity demanded equals quantity supplied	Remain the same
120	3800	4200	Quantity supplied exceeds quantity demanded	Fall
150	3600	4400	Quantity supplied exceeds quantity demanded	Fall

aggregate supply schedule with the general shape discussed in this chapter. It corresponds exactly to aggregate supply curve SS in the figure.

It is clear from the table that equilibrium occurs only at $P = 100$ and $Y = \$4000$. At any other price level, aggregate quantities supplied and demanded would be unequal, with consequent upward or downward pressure on prices. For example, at a price level of 80, customers demand $4300 billion worth of goods and services, but firms wish to provide only $3700 billion. The price level is too low and will be forced upward. Conversely, at a price level of, say, 120, quantity supplied ($4200 billion) exceeds quantity demanded ($3800 billion), implying that the price level must fall.

Recessionary and Inflationary Gaps Revisited

how do they solve themselves

Let us now reconsider a question we posed, but could not answer, in Chapter 9: Will equilibrium occur at, below, or beyond full employment?

We could not give a complete answer to this question in Chapter 9 because we had no way to determine the equilibrium price level, and therefore no way to tell which type of gap, if any, would arise. The aggregate supply and demand analysis summarized in Figure 11–3 gives us the information we need to determine the price level. But we find that our answer is nonetheless the same as it was in Chapter 9: Anything can happen.

The reason is that nothing in Figure 11–3 tells us where full employment is; it could be above the $4000 billion equilibrium level or below it. Depending on the locations of the aggregate demand and aggregate supply curves, then, we can reach equilibrium above full employment (an inflationary gap), at full employment, or below full employment (a recessionary gap).

All three possibilities are illustrated in Figure 11–4. The three upper panels are familiar from Chapter 9. As we move from left to right, the $C + I$ schedule rises from $C + I_0$ to $C + I_1$ to $C + I_2$, leading respectively to a recessionary gap, an equilibrium at full employment, and an inflationary gap. In fact, the upper left-hand diagram is a repeat of Figure 9–6 (page 176), and the upper right-hand diagram repeats Figure 9–7 (page 177). We stressed in Chapter 9 that any one of the three cases is possible, depending on the price level and on the consumption and investment schedules.

In the three lower panels, the equilibrium price level is determined at point E by the intersection of the aggregate supply curve (SS) and the aggregate demand curve (DD). But the same three possibilities emerge nonetheless.

In the lower left-hand panel, aggregate demand is too small to provide jobs for the entire labor force, so there is a recessionary gap equal to distance EB, or $1000 billion. This corresponds precisely to the situation depicted on the income-expenditure diagram immediately above it.

In the lower right-hand panel, aggregate demand is so high that the economy reaches an equilibrium well beyond full employment. There is an inflationary gap equal to BE, or $1000 billion, just as in the diagram immediately above it.

In the lower middle panel, the aggregate demand curve D_1D_1 is at just the right level to produce an equilibrium at full employment. There is neither an inflationary nor a recessionary gap, as in the diagram just above it.

It may seem, therefore, that we have done nothing but restate our previous conclusions. But, in fact, we have done much more. Because now that we have studied the determination of the equilibrium price level, we are able to examine how the economy adjusts to either a recessionary gap or an inflationary gap.

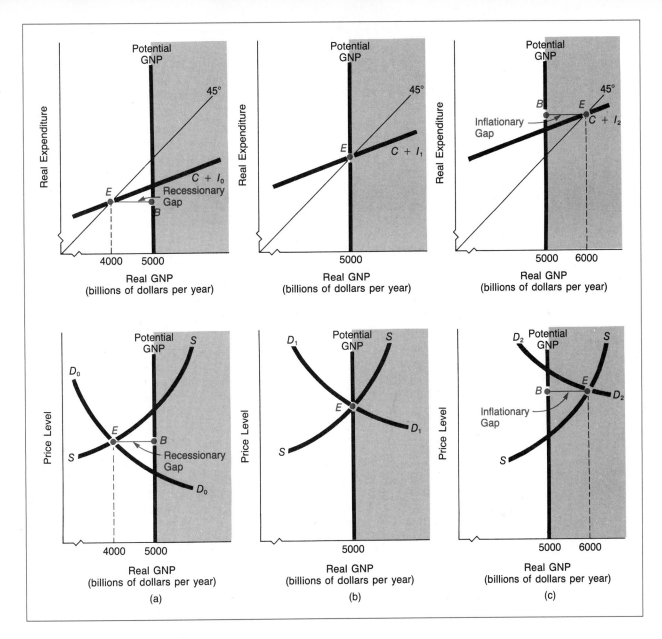

Figure 11–4

RECESSIONARY AND INFLATIONARY GAPS REVISITED

This diagram shows three possible types of equilibrium on two different diagrams. In the top row, income-expenditure diagrams from Chapter 9 are used to depict a recessionary gap, an equilibrium at full employment, and an inflationary gap. In the bottom row, these same three situations are shown on aggregate supply and demand diagrams. In each case, the aggregate supply curve is the same (SS), equilibrium occurs at point E, and full employment GNP is $5000 billion. In part (a), the aggregate demand curve $D_0 D_0$ is relatively low, so that equilibrium falls below full employment. There is a recessionary gap measured by the distance EB, or $1000 billion. In part (b), the aggregate demand curve $D_1 D_1$ is higher, and equilibrium occurs precisely at full employment. There is no gap of either kind. In part (c), the aggregate demand curve $D_2 D_2$ is so high that equilibrium occurs beyond full employment. There is an inflationary gap measured by the distance BE, or $1000 billion.

Adjusting to an Inflationary Gap: Inflation

We have already suggested that an inflationary gap sets the stage for inflation. As we shall see now, the economy, if left to its own devices, produces an inflation that eventually eliminates an inflationary gap. In other words, the gap self-destructs, although the process may be slow and painful. Let us see how this works.

Suppose equilibrium GNP is above potential, as in the lower right-hand panel of Figure 11–4. Jobs are plentiful and labor is in great demand. Although some workers are unemployed, this minimal unemployment is less than the frictional levels — that is, less than the number we usually expect to be jobless because they are moving, changing occupations, and so on. Many firms, on the other hand, are having trouble finding workers. They may even be having trouble hanging on to their current employees, as other firms try to lure them away with higher wages.

Such a situation is bound to lead to rising money wages, and rising wages add to business costs, thus shifting the aggregate supply curve inward. (Remember, the aggregate supply curve is drawn for a *given* money wage.) But as the aggregate supply curve shifts inward — eventually moving from $S_0 S_0$ to $S_1 S_1$ in Figure 11–5, for example — the size of the inflationary gap steadily declines. Thus, inflation erodes the inflationary gap, eventually leading the economy to an equilibrium at full employment (point F in Figure 11–5).

There is a straightforward way of looking at the economics that underlies the self-correcting process. The trouble arises because consumers and investors are demanding more output than the economy is capable of producing at normal operating rates. To paraphrase an old cliché, there is too much demand chasing too little supply. Naturally, prices will be rising in such an environment. And rising prices will eat away at the purchasing power of consumers' wealth, forcing them to cut back on consumption, as explained in Chapter 8. Eventually, consumers' appetites for goods will be scaled down to the economy's capacity to provide those goods; and at this point, the self-correcting process stops. That, in essence, is the unhappy process by which the economy cures itself of the problem of excessive aggregate demand.

One caveat should be entered. The conclusion that an inflationary gap sows the seeds of its own destruction holds *only in the absence of further forces propelling the aggregate demand curve outward*. But in Chapter 10 we have already encountered several forces that might shift the aggregate demand curve outward. As you can see by manipulating the aggregate demand-aggregate supply

Figure 11–5
THE ELIMINATION OF AN INFLATIONARY GAP
When the aggregate supply curve is $S_0 S_0$ and the aggregate demand curve is *DD*, the economy will initially reach equilibrium (point E) with an inflationary gap. The resulting inflation of wages will push the supply curve inward until it has shifted to the position indicated by curve $S_1 S_1$. Here, with equilibrium at point F, the economy is at normal full employment. But, during the adjustment period from E to F, there will have been inflation.

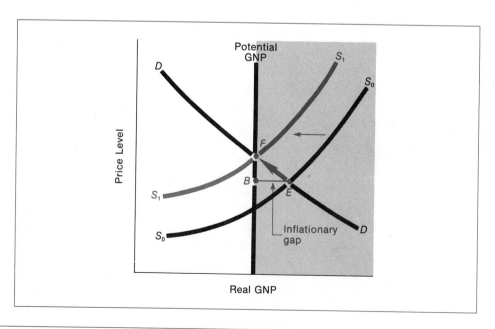

diagram, if aggregate demand is shifting out at the same time that aggregate supply is shifting in, there will certainly be inflation, but the inflationary gap may not shrink. (Try this as an exercise, to make sure you understand how to use the apparatus.) So not all inflations come to a natural end.

Demand Inflation and Stagflation

Simple as it is, this adjustment model teaches us a number of important lessons about inflation in the real world. First of all, Figure 11–5 reminds us that the real culprit in this particular inflation is the excessive level of aggregate demand. The aggregate demand curve is initially so high that it intersects the aggregate supply curve at an output level higher than full employment. The resulting intense demand for workers pushes wages higher; and higher wages spell higher prices. While excessive demand is not the only possible cause of inflation in the real world, it certainly is the cause in our example.

However, business managers and journalists are likely to blame inflation on rising wages. In a superficial sense, of course, they are right, because higher wages do indeed lead firms to raise their prices. But in a deeper sense they are wrong. Both rising wages and rising prices are only symptoms of an underlying malady: too much aggregate demand. Blaming labor for inflation in such a case is a bit like blaming high doctor bills for making you ill.

Second, we see that output falls while prices rise as the economy adjusts from point E to point F in Figure 11–5. This process thus provides our first (but not our last!) explanation of the phenomenon of **stagflation.** We see that:

A period of stagflation is part of the normal aftermath of a period of excessive aggregate demand.

Stagflation is inflation that occurs while the economy is growing slowly or having a recession.

It is easy enough to understand why stagflation occurs in this case. When aggregate demand is excessive, the economy will temporarily produce beyond its normal capacity. Labor markets tighten and wages rise. Machinery and raw materials may also become scarce and so start rising in price. Faced by higher costs, the natural reaction of business firms is to produce less and to charge a higher price. That is stagflation.

It may be useful to review what we have learned about inflationary gaps thus far.

If aggregate demand is exceptionally high, the economy may reach an equilibrium above full employment (an inflationary gap). When this occurs, the tight situation in the labor market soon forces wages to rise. Since wages are business costs, prices rise and there is inflation. With cuts in consumer purchasing power, the inflationary gap begins to close. As the inflationary gap is closing, output falls while prices continue to rise, so the economy experiences stagflation until the inflationary gap is eliminated. At this point, a long-run equilibrium is established with a higher price level and with GNP equal to potential GNP.

An Example from U.S. History: 1966 to 1970

The stagflation that follows a period of excessive aggregate demand is, you will note, a rather benign form of the dreaded disease. After all, while output is falling, it nonetheless remains above potential GNP; and unemployment is low. The U.S. economy has not experienced anything like this for many years. In fact, you have to go back to the late 1960s to find a "textbook" example of an inflationary gap that extinguished itself in this way.

During 1966–1968, the U.S. economy was booming, unemployment was below 4 percent, and jobs were plentiful. There was an inflationary gap, like that shown in the lower right-hand panel of Figure 11–4. Our analysis suggests that wages should have been accelerating, and indeed they were. The gray bars in Figure 11–6 illustrate this acceleration. The blue bars show that, with one minor exception, the rate of inflation followed the rate of increase of wages — rising from about 2 percent a year to over 5 percent. This is, again, in line with what our model predicts.

The upsurge in inflation naturally ate away at the inflationary gap, as shown in Figure 11–5, and the gap was gone by the end of 1970. Yet inflation continued unabated through a mild recession in 1969–1970. The U.S. economy was in the stagflation phase. Despite outcries of "excessive" wage demands that "caused" inflation, it is clear that the ultimate cause of the acceleration in both wages and prices was the excessive aggregate demand of the Vietnam War episode. The economy behaved just as our simple model suggests.

Adjusting to a Recessionary Gap: Deflation or Unemployment?

Let us now consider what can happen when the economy finds itself in equilibrium *below* full employment — that is, when there is a *recessionary* gap. This might be caused, for example, by inadequate consumer spending or by anemic investment spending.

Figure 11–7 illustrates such a case and gives an impression of the economic situation we faced at the bottom of the 1981–1982 recession. According to one estimate, real GNP was about $265 billion below potential GNP. And the unemployment rate stood at 10.7 percent.

You might expect that we could just run our previous analysis in reverse: High unemployment leads to falling wages; falling wages reduce business costs and shift the aggregate supply curve outward, so firms cut prices (see Figure 11–7); falling wages and prices eliminate the recessionary gap by propping up

Figure 11–6
GROWTH RATES OF WAGES AND PRICES IN THE UNITED STATES, 1965–1970
These data illustrate what happened when an inflationary gap arose in the United States during 1966–1968. Notice the acceleration of both wages and prices. By 1970, the gap was eliminated, and wage increases leveled off. There was a minor recession in 1969–1970, but inflation continued.
SOURCE: *Economic Report of the President*, 1987.

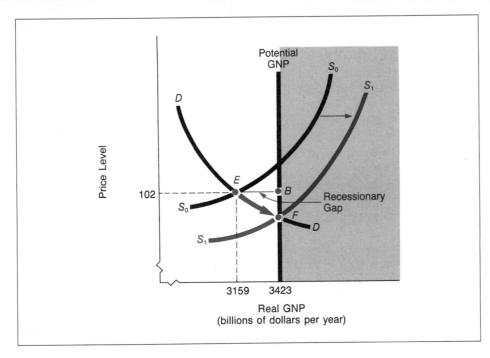

Figure 11–7

THE ELIMINATION OF A RECESSIONARY GAP? At point *E* there is a recessionary gap because the aggregate demand curve *DD* crosses the aggregate supply curve $S_0 S_0$ below the level of potential GNP. If wages fall, the aggregate supply curve gradually shifts outward until it reaches the position indicated by supply curve $S_1 S_1$. Here the economy has attained a full-employment equilibrium at point *F*. But if wages refuse to fall, the economy gets stuck with a recessionary gap and a long period of unemployment.

consumer spending; and full employment is restored. The economy moves smoothly from point *E* to point *F* in Figure 11–7. Very simple. And very misleading in our modern economy!

Why is it misleading? Our brief review of the historical record in Chapter 5 showed that, while the economy may have operated like this long ago, it certainly does not work this way now. The history of the United States shows many examples of falling wages and prices before World War II but none since then. Not even the severe recession of 1981–1982, during which unemployment climbed above 10 percent, was able to force average prices and wages down—though it certainly slowed their rate of increase.

Exactly why wages and prices are rigid in the downward direction in our modern economy has been a subject of intense and continuing controversy among economists for years.

Some economists emphasize institutional features like minimum wage laws, union contracts, and a variety of government regulations that place legal floors under particular wages and prices. Because most of these institutions are of relatively recent vintage, this theory successfully explains why wages and prices are more rigid now than they were before World War II. However, most of the U.S. economy is not subject to legal restraints on wage and price cutting. So it seems doubtful that legal restrictions can provide a complete explanation.

Other observers subscribe to the theory that workers have a profound psychological resistance to accepting a wage reduction. This theory certainly has the ring of truth. Think how you would react if your boss announced that she was cutting your hourly wage rate. You might quit, or you might devote less care and attention to your job. Genuine wage reductions are rare enough to be newsworthy. For example, Chrysler workers accepted hefty pay cuts in the early 1980s, but only when it appeared that the company was in grave danger of going bankrupt. In 1983, the Greyhound bus company grabbed the headlines by insisting that its drivers accept a large wage reduction; the drivers refused, and a nasty strike followed. In more recent years, money wages have been cut by several airline companies as the industry suffered through a painful shakeout.

While no one doubts that wage cuts are bad for morale, the psychological theory has one major drawback. It fails to explain why the psychological resistance to wage cuts apparently started only after World War II. Until a satisfactory answer to this question is provided, many economists will remain skeptical.

A third explanation is based on a fact we emphasized in Chapter 5—that business cycles were less severe in the postwar period than they were in the prewar period. Because workers and firms came to believe that recessions would not turn into depressions, the argument goes, they may have decided to wait out the bad times rather than accept wage or price reductions that they would later regret.

There are other theories as well, none of which commands anything like universal assent. But, regardless of the cause, we might as well accept the fact that, in our modern economy, prices and wages will rise when demand is strong but generally will not fall when demand is weak.

The implications of this rigidity are quite serious, for a recessionary gap cannot cure itself without some deflation. And if wages and prices will not fall, *the economy gets stuck at a point like E in Figure 11–7, that is, at an equilibrium below full employment.* Keynes was the first economist to point out that wage rigidity could lead to a long-lasting equilibrium below full employment and to distinguish it from the full-employment equilibrium that we have just been considering.

When aggregate demand is low, the economy may get stuck in an *unemployment equilibrium*. There is a recessionary gap, but wages and prices refuse to fall; so the gap persists. The economy endures a prolonged period of production below potential GNP.

Does the Economy Have a Self-Correcting Mechanism?

Now a situation like this would, presumably, not last forever. As the recession lengthened, and perhaps deepened, more and more workers would be unable to obtain jobs at the prevailing high wages. Eventually their resistance to wage cuts, whatever the cause, would be worn down by their need to be employed.

Firms, too, would become increasingly willing to cut prices as the period of weak demand lasted longer and longer and managers became convinced that the slump was not merely a temporary aberration. Prices and wages did, in fact, fall during the Great Depression of the 1930s. And they might fall again if a sufficiently drastic depression were allowed to occur. They certainly slowed markedly in the weak markets of the early 1980s.

Nowadays, political leaders of both parties believe it is folly to wait for falling wages and prices to eliminate a recessionary gap. But while they agree that *some* government action is both necessary and appropriate under recessionary conditions, there is still vocal—and highly partisan!—debate over how much and what kind of intervention is warranted.

One reason for this disagreement is that the **self-correcting mechanism** does operate—if only weakly—to cure recessionary gaps. Recent history provides a vivid illustration.

Disinflation and Recovery in the 1980s: A Case Study

The recession of 1981–1982 opened up the largest recessionary gap since the Great Depression. By the end of 1982, when the slump hit bottom, real GNP was estimated to be some $265 billion (in 1982 dollars) below potential. (See

Figure 11–7.) Our theory suggests that such a large gap should push inflation down strongly, and it did. While wages and prices did not actually decline, their rates of increase tumbled from 9–10 percent in 1981 to about 4 percent by 1983. (See Figure 11–8.)

But what about the self-correcting mechanism? Did falling inflation eat away at the recessionary gap? Yes, but slowly and painfully. Recovery from recession began in the winter of 1982–1983 and proceeded rapidly at first: the civilian unemployment rate tumbled from its peak of 10.7 percent to only 7.2 percent within about two years. But then it stalled out, and unemployment hovered near 7 percent of the labor force for some time. Some observers at the time claimed that 7 percent was now the "full employment" unemployment rate. If so, the self-correcting mechanism worked just as our simple model says—although millions of unemployed workers and thousands of bankrupted businesses suffered along the way. However, most economists believe that full employment today corresponds to an unemployment rate closer to 5.5 or 6 percent. In that case, the self-correcting mechanism still had some way to go. And, indeed, unemployment started falling again in late 1986 and early 1987.

Our overall conclusion about the economy's ability to right itself, then, seems to run something like this:

The economy does indeed have a self-correcting mechanism that tends to eliminate either unemployment or inflation. However, this mechanism is much more efficient at curing inflationary gaps through inflation than at curing recessionary gaps through deflation. In addition, its beneficial effects on inflation are sometimes swamped by strong inflationary forces (such as rapid increases in aggregate demand). Thus the self-correcting mechanism cannot always be relied upon.

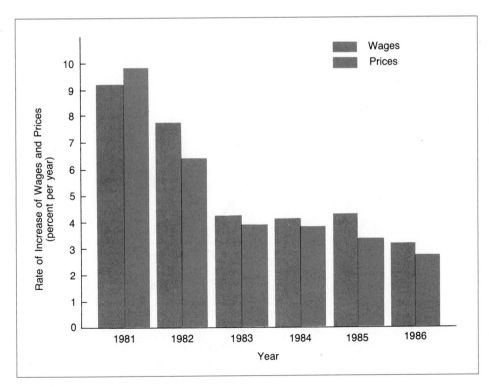

Figure 11–8
GROWTH RATES OF WAGES AND PRICES IN THE UNITED STATES, 1981–1986
These data illustrate what happened when the U.S. economy developed a large recessionary gap in 1981–1982. Notice that wage and price inflation slowed down dramatically in 1981–1983, but then stabilized.
SOURCE: *Economic Report of the President, 1987.*

Stagflation from Supply Shifts

We have so far encountered one type of stagflation in this chapter—the stagflation that often follows in the aftermath of an inflationary boom. However, that is not what happened in the more serious stagflationary episodes of 1973–1975 and 1979–1981. What was going on during those years that caused so much more unemployment and inflation than was expected? What were the causes of this new, more virulent type of stagflation? Several things, but the principal villain was the rising price of energy.

In 1973 the Organization of Petroleum Exporting Countries (OPEC) reached a collusive agreement to limit production that succeeded in quadrupling the price of crude oil in only a few months. American consumers soon found the prices of gasoline and home heating fuels increasing sharply. American businesses found that one of the important inputs to the production process—energy—rose drastically in price, thus increasing the cost of doing business. In 1979, the world oil market went into a panic again following the ouster of the Shah of Iran. Oil prices escalated as buyers scrambled to secure supplies and build inventories. Seizing the opportunity, OPEC this time doubled the price of oil.

Higher energy prices, we observed earlier, make the economy's aggregate supply curve shift inward in the manner shown in Figure 11–2 (page 200). If the aggregate supply curve shifts inward, as it surely did in 1973–1974 and again in 1979–1980, production will be reduced. And in order to reduce demand to the available supply, prices will have to rise. The result is the worst of both worlds: falling production and rising prices.

This conclusion is shown in Figure 11–9, which superimposes an aggregate demand curve, DD, on the two aggregate supply curves of Figure 11–2. The economy's equilibrium shifts upward to the left, from point E to point A. Thus, output falls while prices rise. In brief:

Stagflation is the typical result of adverse supply shifts.

Figure 11–9
STAGFLATION FROM A
SHIFT IN AGGREGATE
SUPPLY
This diagram illustrates how stagflation arises if the aggregate supply curve shifts inward to the left (from $S_0 S_0$ to $S_1 S_1$). If the aggregate demand curve does not change, equilibrium moves from point E to point A. Output falls as prices rise, which is what we mean by stagflation. The diagram indicates roughly what happened in the U.S. during 1973–1975, when higher energy prices caused stagflation.

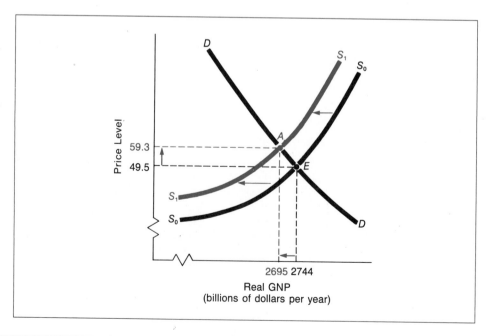

The numbers used in Figure 11–9 are roughly indicative of what happened in the United States between 1973 (represented by supply curve $S_0 S_0$ and point E) and 1975 (represented by supply curve $S_1 S_1$ and point A). Real GNP, in 1982 prices, fell by about $50 billion, while the price level rose almost 20 percent.

The story of the early 1980s is more complicated because so many other things were going on at the same time—especially the sharp changes in national economic policy ushered in by President Reagan. But, in broad outline, the 1979–1982 economy followed the script that had been written in 1973–1975 (see Figure 11–9). The inflation rate rose to an astonishing 13.3 percent in 1979 and to a sizzling 16 percent in the first half of 1980. Americans were almost panic-stricken over these unprecedented inflation rates, which exceeded even the worst months of 1974. Recession followed inflation. The economy began to weaken slightly in 1979, slipped into a small recession in early 1980, and experienced a huge recession in 1981–1982.

The general lesson to be learned from the experience of the 1970s and early 1980s is as important as it is clear:

The typical results of an adverse supply shock are a fall in output and an acceleration in inflation. This is one reason why the world economy was plagued by stagflation in the mid-1970s and early 1980s. And it can happen again if another series of supply-reducing events takes place.

Of course, supply shifts can work in the other direction as well. The world oil market softened in 1982–1983, OPEC weakened, and oil prices declined. At the same time, bountiful harvests around the world depressed agricultural prices. The aggregate supply curve was shifting outward, which helped the U.S. and other countries to reduce inflation rapidly. Then in early 1986 OPEC collapsed and oil prices plummeted. For a few months, the Consumer Price Index actually fell; and the inflation rate for 1986 as a whole was only 1.1 percent.

Favorable supply shocks tend to push output up and reduce inflation.

Inflation and the Multiplier

When we introduced the concept of the multiplier in Chapter 10, we said that there were several reasons why its actual value is smaller than suggested by the oversimplified multiplier formula. We are now in a position to understand one of these reasons: Inflation reduces the size [impact] of the multiplier.

The basic idea is simple. In Chapter 10, we described a multiplier process in which one person's spending became another person's income, which led to further spending by the second person, and so on. But this story is confined to the demand side of the economy. Let us therefore consider what is likely to happen on the supply side as the multiplier process unfolds. Will the additional demand be taken care of by firms without raising prices?

If the aggregate supply curve is upward sloping, the answer is no; more goods will only be provided at higher prices. Thus, as the multiplier chain progresses, pulling income and employment up, prices will also be rising. And this, as we know from Chapter 8, will dampen consumer spending because rising prices reduce the purchasing power of consumers' wealth. So the multiplier chain will not proceed as far as it would have in the absence of inflation.

How much inflation results from the rise in demand? How much of the multiplier chain is cut off by inflation? The answers depend on the slope of the economy's aggregate supply curve.

For a concrete example of the analysis, let us return to the $200 billion increase in investment spending used in Chapter 10. As we learned there (see especially page 185), $200 billion in additional investment spending eventually leads—through the multiplier process—to *a horizontal shift of $1000 billion in the aggregate demand curve*. But to know the actual quantity that will ultimately be produced, and the actual price level, we must bring the aggregate supply curve into the picture.

Figure 11–10 does this. Here we show the $1000 billion horizontal shift of the aggregate demand curve, from $D_0 D_0$ to $D_1 D_1$, that is derived from the oversimplified multiplier formula (which ignores rising prices). The aggregate supply curve, SS, then tells us how this expansion of demand is apportioned between higher output and higher prices. We see that as the economy's equilibrium moves from point E_0 to point E_1, real GNP does not rise by $1000 billion. Instead, prices rise, which, as we know, tends to cancel out part of the rise in quantity demanded. So output increases only from $4000 billion to $4800 billion—an increase of $800 billion. Thus, in our example, inflation reduces the multiplier from $1000/$200 = 5 to $800/$200 = 4. In general:

As long as the aggregate supply curve is upward sloping, any increase in aggregate demand will push up the price level. This will, in turn, drain off some of the higher real demand by eroding the purchasing power of consumer wealth. Thus, inflation reduces the value of the multiplier below that suggested by the oversimplified formula.

Notice also that the price level in this example has been pushed up (from 100 to 120, or 20 percent) by the rise in investment demand. This, too, is a general result:

As long as the aggregate supply curve is upward sloping, any outward shift of the aggregate demand curve will cause some rise in prices in the economy.

Figure 11–10
INFLATION AND THE MULTIPLIER
This figure illustrates the complete analysis of the multiplier, including the effect of inflation. The simple multiplier of Chapter 10, which ignored changes in the price level, appears here as a *horizontal* shift of $1000 billion in the aggregate demand curve, meaning that the multiplier would be $1000/200 = 5 if prices did not rise. However, when aggregate demand shifts from $D_0 D_0$ to $D_1 D_1$, prices rise. In the diagram, the price level increases from 100 to 120 or by 20 percent. Consequently, equilibrium real income increases from $4000 billion to only $4800—for a rise of $800 billion, or a multiplier of $800/$200 = 4.

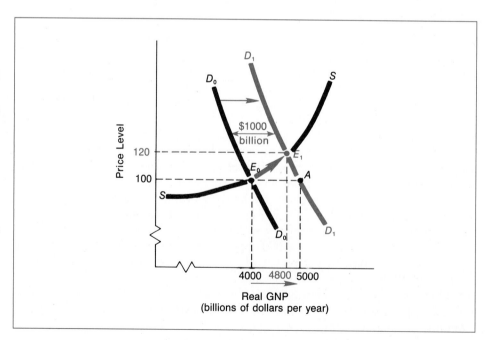

The economic behavior behind these results certainly cannot be considered surprising. Firms faced with large increases in quantity demanded at their original prices respond to these changed circumstances in two natural ways: They raise production (so GNP rises), and they raise prices (so the price level rises). But this rise in the price level reduces the purchasing power of the bank accounts and bonds held by consumers, and they too react in the natural way: They cut down on their spending. Such a reaction amounts to a movement *along* aggregate demand curve $D_1 D_1$ in Figure 11–10 from point A to point E_1.

Higher prices thus play their usual dual role in a market economy: They encourage suppliers to produce more and, at the same time, encourage demanders to consume less. In this way, equilibrium is reestablished at higher levels of output and higher prices through the process of inflation.

Figure 11–10 also shows us exactly where the oversimplified multiplier formula goes wrong. By ignoring the effects of the higher price level, the oversimplified formula supposes the economy moves horizontally from point E_0 to point A. As the diagram clearly shows, output does not actually rise this much. Output *would* rise this much only if the aggregate supply curve were horizontal. (Verify this for yourself by penciling in an imaginary horizontal aggregate supply curve through points E_0 and A in Figure 11–10.) That is, the oversimplified multiplier formula tacitly assumes that the aggregate supply curve is horizontal. Normally, this is an unrealistic assumption, and that is one reason why the oversimplified formula exaggerates the size of the multiplier.

As a summary, it may be useful to put together what we have learned about multiplier analysis in Chapters 10 and 11.

STEPS IN CALCULATING THE MULTIPLIER

1. Shift the expenditure schedule in the 45° line diagram vertically by the amount of the autonomous shift in spending (as, for example, in Figure 10–1 on page 186).

2. Use the 45° line diagram, or the oversimplified multiplier formula, to calculate the multiplier effect on GNP that *would* occur *if* the price level did not change (again, see Figure 10–1).

3. Now move from the 45° line diagram to an aggregate supply and demand diagram like Figure 11–10 to see how the price level will react. Enter the multiplier effect calculated in step 2 as a horizontal shift of the aggregate demand curve in the supply-demand diagram.

4. The supply-demand diagram will now show the actual effect on real output as well as the resulting inflation or deflation.[2]

A Role for Stabilization Policy

Chapter 9 emphasized the volatility of investment spending, and Chapter 10 noted that changes in investment have multiplier effects on aggregate demand. This chapter took the next step by showing how shifts in the aggregate demand curve cause fluctuations in both real GNP growth and inflation—fluctuations which are widely decried as undesirable. It also suggested that the economy's self-correcting mechanism works rather slowly, thereby leaving room for government stabilization policy to improve the workings of the free market. Can the government really do this? If so, how? These are the questions for Part 4.

---

[2]The change in the price level reacts back on the 45° diagram. See Discussion Question 11 at the end of the chapter.

Summary

1. The economy's aggregate supply curve relates the quantity of goods and services that will be supplied to the price level. It normally slopes upward to the right because the costs of labor and other inputs are relatively fixed in the short run, meaning that higher selling prices make input costs relatively "cheaper" and therefore encourage greater production.
2. The position of the aggregate supply curve can be shifted by changes in money wage rates, prices of other inputs, technology, or quantities of labor and capital available for employment.
3. The aggregate supply curve normally gets steeper as output increases. This means that, as output and capacity utilization rise, any given increase in aggregate demand leads to more inflation and less growth of real output.
4. The equilibrium price level and the equilibrium level of real GNP are jointly determined by the intersection of the economy's aggregate supply and aggregate demand schedules. This intersection may come at full employment, below full employment (a recessionary gap), or above full employment (an inflationary gap).
5. If there is an inflationary gap, the economy has a mechanism that erodes the gap through a process of inflation. Specifically, unusually strong job prospects push wages up, which shifts the aggregate supply curve to the left and reduces the inflationary gap.
6. One consequence of this self-correcting mechanism is that, if a surge in aggregate demand opens up an inflationary gap, part of the economy's natural adjustment to this event will be a period of stagflation; that is, a period in which prices are rising while output is falling.
7. The economy also has a self-correcting mechanism that erodes a recessionary gap. However, this mechanism works much more slowly and less reliably than the inflationary-gap mechanism because it relies on falling wages to shift the aggregate supply curve outward, and wages do not fall easily.
8. An inward shift of the aggregate supply curve will cause output to fall while prices rise; that is, it will cause stagflation. Among the events that have caused such a shift are the abrupt increases in the price of foreign oil.
9. Adverse supply shifts like this apparently plagued our economy in 1973–1974 and again in 1979–1980, leading to stagflation both times.
10. Among the reasons why the oversimplified multiplier formula is wrong is the fact that it ignores any inflation that may be caused by an increase in aggregate demand. Such inflation decreases the multiplier by reducing consumer spending, because consumers as a group suffer a loss of purchasing power when prices rise.

Concepts for Review

Aggregate supply curve	Inflationary gap	Recessionary gap
Productivity	Self-correcting mechanism	Inflation and the multiplier
Equilibrium of real GNP and the price level	Stagflation	

Questions for Discussion

1. In an economy with the following aggregate demand and aggregate supply schedules, find the equilibrium levels of real output and the price level. Graph your solution. If full employment comes at $1600 billion, is there an inflationary or a recessionary gap?

AGGREGATE QUANTITY DEMANDED (in billions)	PRICE LEVEL	AGGREGATE QUANTITY SUPPLIED (in billions)
2000	75	1400
1950	80	1450
1800	90	1600
1700	110	1700
1600	140	1800

2. Suppose a worker receives a wage of $10 per hour. Compute the real wage (money wage deflated by the price index) corresponding to each of the following possible price levels: 85, 95, 100, 110, 120. What do you notice about the relationship between the real wage and the price level? Relate this to the slope of the aggregate supply curve.
3. In 1986, capacity utilization averaged 80 percent. In 1982, it averaged 72 percent. In which year do you think the economy found itself on a steeper portion of its aggregate supply curve? Explain why.
4. Explain why a decrease in the price of foreign oil shifts the aggregate supply curve outward to the right. What are the consequences of such a shift?
5. Comment on the following statement: "Inflationary and recessionary gaps are nothing to worry about because the economy has a built-in

mechanism that cures either type of gap automatically."

6. Give *two* different explanations of how the economy can suffer from stagflation.

7. Why do you think wages tend to be rigid in the downward direction?

8. Add the following aggregate supply and demand schedules to the data in Question 3 of Chapter 10 (page 195) to see how inflation affects the multiplier.

(1) PRICE LEVEL	(2) AGGREGATE DEMAND (when investment is $120)	(3) AGGREGATE DEMAND (when investment is $130)	(4) AGGREGATE SUPPLY
90	$1210	$1310	$1110
95	1205	1305	1155
100	1200	1300	1200
105	1195	1295	1245
110	1190	1290	1290
115	1185	1285	1335

Draw these schedules on a piece of graph paper. Then:

a. Notice that the difference between columns 2 and 3 (the aggregate demand schedule at two different levels of investment) is always $100. Discuss how this relates to your answer in the previous chapter.

b. Find the equilibrium GNP and the equilibrium price level both before and after the increase in investment. What is the value of the multiplier?

9. Explain in words why rising prices reduce the multiplier effect of an autonomous increase in aggregate demand.

10. Use an aggregate supply and demand diagram to show that multiplier effects are smaller when the aggregate supply curve is steeper. Which case gives rise to more inflation — the steep aggregate supply curve or the flat one? What happens to the multiplier if the aggregate supply curve is vertical?

11. (More difficult) Assume that investment spending rises. Draw a set of graphs illustrating the Steps in Calculating the Multiplier listed on page 215. Your aggregate supply and demand diagram from steps 3 and 4 will show a change in the price level. How would this change in the price level react back on the 45° line diagram you used in step 1? In view of this, use the 45° line diagram to show that inflation reduces the multiplier.

PART 4

Fiscal and Monetary Policy

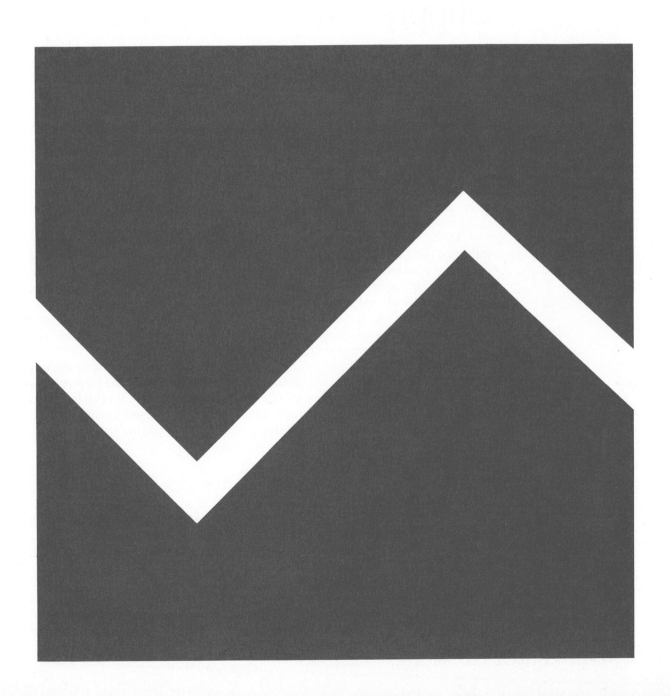

12

Next, let us turn to the problems of our fiscal policy. Here the myths are legion and the truth hard to find.

JOHN F. KENNEDY

Fiscal Policy and Supply-Side Economics

In Part 3, we constructed and analyzed a model of an economy with no government. We concluded that such an economy has only weak tendencies to move toward high employment with low inflation. Furthermore, we hinted that well-designed government policies might improve the economy's performance. It is now time to pick up that hint—and to get acquainted with some of the difficulties the government must overcome if it is to conduct a successful stabilization policy.

Traditionally, the government has used its taxing and spending powers to influence the demand side of the economy. So this chapter begins there, in the domain of conventional *fiscal policy*. Specifically, we expand the basic model to allow, first, for government purchases of goods and services as a component of aggregate demand, and second, for taxes that make disposable income less than national income. As we shall see, neither of these complications requires any fundamental change in the way we analyze the determination of GNP and the price level, although taxes do reduce the multiplier.

When President Reagan assumed office in 1981, he rejected the customary emphasis on aggregate demand management and argued that the government could and should use tax policy to influence aggregate *supply*. So the last parts of the chapter examine "supply-side economics"—the controversial analysis that was used to explain the president's program and to predict its effects.

Tax Reform and Fiscal Policy

In January 1987 a sweeping revision of the U.S. income tax code went into effect. The tax reform act that President Reagan signed into law in October 1986 was the culmination of an epic two-year legislative struggle during which legislators and the administration locked horns over numerous provisions. But, as the tax reform debate progressed, one ground rule was observed by all the participants: The bill was to be "revenue neutral," meaning that total tax collections were to neither rise nor fall.

Why was revenue neutrality so important? Because the president and members of Congress wanted to separate heated debates over the *structure* of taxation—which is what tax reform was all about—from equally heated debates over the government's **fiscal policy,** that is, the overall balance of spending and taxation. Many senators and representatives felt that taxes should be raised to reduce the budget deficit. The president agreed that the deficit was too large, but insisted that raising taxes was not the way to reduce it. Had the total volume of taxation been at issue, the White House and Congress probably never would have reached agreement on a tax bill.

But why all this fuss about fiscal policy? How do our political leaders decide how much spending or taxation is the right amount? Perhaps more to the point, how can you as a voter decide whether your elected representatives have made sound decisions? These are the questions for this chapter.

Government Purchases and Equilibrium Income

Before attempting to answer such difficult questions, we must integrate the government into our model of the determination of national income and the price level. We do this in stages, starting first with **government purchases of goods and services (G),** and then adding taxes. Thus, in bringing the government back into the circular flow of income and expenditure (see Figure 12–1), we ignore for the moment the flows of tax revenues and transfer payments at point 5. How would the equilibrium level of GNP be determined in an economy in which the state bought goods but did not levy taxes or make transfers?

The circular flow diagram shows us the answer, just as it did in an economy with no government (Chapter 9). If the size of the circular flow of income and expenditure is to be maintained, then the total amount of new goods and services that firms produce at point 4 (Y) must be equal to the sum of the demands of consumers at point 1 (C), investors at point 2 (I), and government

The government's **fiscal policy** is its plan for spending and taxation. It is designed to steer aggregate demand in some desired direction.

Figure 12–1
THE CIRCULAR FLOW OF
EXPENDITURE AND
INCOME WITH NO
FOREIGN TRADE

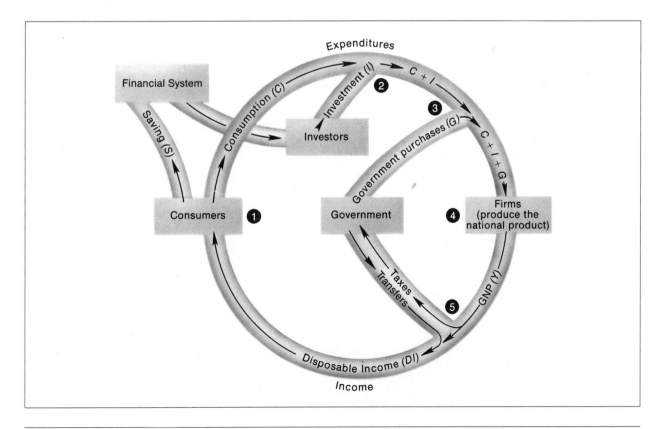

at point 3 (G). We thus obtain the following restatement of the condition for equilibrium on the demand side of the economy:[1]

For any given price level, equilibrium GNP on the demand side of the economy occurs when the sum of consumption demand, investment demand, and government demand for goods and services just equals output. In symbols:

$$(GNP) \quad Y = C + I + G.$$

The reasoning behind this equilibrium condition is precisely the same as it was in Chapter 9. At income levels below equilibrium, the sum $C + I + G$ would exceed Y; and so inventories would be disappearing, signaling firms that they should raise their production. Conversely, at income levels above equilibrium, $C + I + G$ would be less than Y, so that unwanted inventories would be accumulating and firms would have incentives to cut back production.

Table 12–1, which may usefully be compared to Table 9–1 in Chapter 9 (page 170), illustrates this process. The first three columns give the same consumption and investment schedules that we worked with there. The fourth column reflects the assumption that government purchases are $800 billion irrespective of the level of GNP. Summing these three components gives us our new total expenditure schedule in columns 1 and 5.

What, then, is the equilibrium level of GNP? As the table indicates, only a GNP of $8000 billion can be an equilibrium, for only at this level is total spending in balance with production.

Figure 12–2 shows the same conclusion graphically. The line labeled C is the same consumption function we used in previous chapters. The line labeled $C + I$ adds the fixed $700 billion in investment to this; again, this amount is taken from previous chapters. Finally, the line labeled $C + I + G$ adds an additional $800 billion in government spending to the $C + I$ line, which gives us our new total expenditure schedule.

[1] We are still leaving exports and imports out of the picture. They are the subject of Part 5.

Table 12–1
DERIVATION OF A TOTAL EXPENDITURE SCHEDULE WITH GOVERNMENT PURCHASES

(1) NATIONAL INCOME (Y) (billions)	(2) CONSUMPTION (C) (billions)	(3) INVESTMENT (I) (billions)	(4) GOVERNMENT PURCHASES (G) (billions)	(5) TOTAL EXPENDITURE (C + I + G) (billions)
$4000	$3300	$700	$800	$4800
4500	3700	700	800	5200
5000	4100	700	800	5600
5500	4500	700	800	6000
6000	4900	700	800	6400
6500	5300	700	800	6800
7000	5700	700	800	7200
7500	6100	700	800	7600
8000	6500	700	800	8000
8500	6900	700	800	8400

This table adds government purchases of $800 billion to our model economy. Notice that the equilibrium level of GNP grows to $8000 billion, for this is the level at which output is equal to total spending (the sum of $C + I + G$).

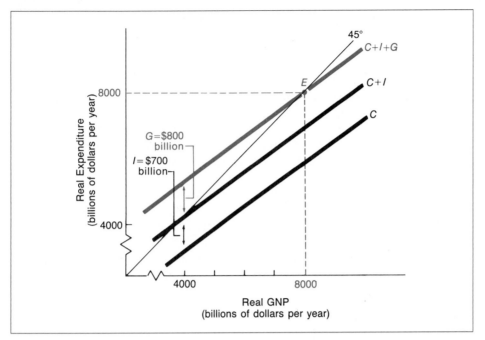

Figure 12–2
INCOME
DETERMINATION WITH
GOVERNMENT
SPENDING
This diagram adds
government purchases of
goods and services (G) to
the income expenditure
diagrams that we have been
using. The C + I + G curve
is the total expenditure
schedule for an economy
with no foreign trade, and the
point where it crosses the 45°
line (point E) marks the
equilibrium level of GNP. The
C + I + G line is parallel to
the C + I line because of the
assumption that whatever the
level of GNP, government
spending remains at $800
billion.

Just as in previous chapters, the equilibrium of the economy is at point *E*, where the total expenditure schedule crosses the 45° line. This is because the 45° line includes all the points at which *C* + *I* + *G* add up to *Y*. The diagram shows that equilibrium is at a GNP of $8000 billion, which consists of $6500 billion in consumption, $700 billion in investment, and $800 billion in government purchases. This agrees precisely with Table 12–1, as it must. If all this seems familiar from previous chapters, it should; for the analysis is precisely the same.[2]

In Chapter 10 we stated that when government spending was introduced, the multiplier for *G* would be the same as the multiplier for autonomous changes in *C* and *I*. We can now demonstrate this conclusion.

If you turn back to page 173, you will see that the equilibrium reached there was at a level of output *Y* = $4000 billion. Now, in an economy that is identical with the one in Chapter 9 except for the $800 billion in government spending, we see that the equilibrium is at *Y* = $8000 billion. Thus an $800 billion increment in *G* (from zero to $800 billion) has pushed up GNP by $4000 billion. In this example, then, the multiplier for government spending is $4000/$800 = 5, which, you will recall, was also the value of the multiplier for autonomous increases in investment or consumption.

The two multipliers are identical because the logic behind them is identical. In Chapter 10 we studied an example of a multiplier spending chain set in motion when Generous Motors spent $1 million to build a factory. This process could equally well have been kicked off by the federal government buying $1 million worth of new cars from GM. Thereafter, each recipient of additional income would spend 80 percent of it (the assumed marginal propensity to consume), until $5 million in new income had eventually been created.

And the qualification that we placed on the oversimplified multiplier formula in Chapter 11 also applies here. Government spending normally leads to some inflation, which pulls down consumer spending and thus reduces the value of the multiplier below our illustrative figure of 5.

[2]An algebraic version of this and other topics discussed here can be found in the appendix to this chapter.

Income Taxes and the Consumption Schedule

You can see, then, that it takes little effort to bring government purchases into our model of income determination. Let us turn our attention next to taxes and, in particular, to the personal income tax.

For present purposes, the most important aspect of taxes is that they create a discrepancy between gross national product (GNP) and disposable income (*DI*), as can be seen in the circular flow diagram (Figure 12–1). Tax revenues flow out of the circular flow and into the hands of the government. (The effects of transfer payments, which enter the circular flow at point 5, will be considered presently.)

We learned in Chapter 8 that there is a close and reliable relationship between consumer spending and *disposable* income. Therefore, if we want to construct a relationship between consumer spending and GNP, we first have to allow for the fact that taxes are deducted from GNP before *DI* is arrived at. The importance of this piece of accounting is that when taxes are increased, disposable income falls — and hence so does consumption — *even if GNP is unchanged*. As a result:

An increase in personal income taxes shifts the consumption schedule in our 45° line diagram downward. Similarly, a reduction in taxes shifts the consumption schedule upward.

The specific manner in which the consumption schedule shifts depends on the nature of the tax change. One way to reduce taxes is to increase the per person exemption, as was done in the 1986 tax reform act. The increase in disposable income from this provision is the *same* regardless of the level of GNP; hence the increase in consumer spending is the same. In a word, the C schedule shifts upward in a parallel manner, as shown in Figure 12–3(a).

But often tax policy is designed to make the change in disposable income depend on the level of income, normally being larger at high income levels than at low ones. This is true, for example, when Congress reduces the bracket

Figure 12–3
HOW TAX POLICY SHIFTS THE CONSUMPTION SCHEDULE
Because consumption depends on disposable income, not GNP, any change in taxes will shift the consumption schedule relating consumption to GNP. Part (a) shows how the curve shifts for changes in taxes of fixed amounts. Part (b) shows how the C curve shifts if the tax cut (or tax increase) is larger at high incomes than at low incomes.

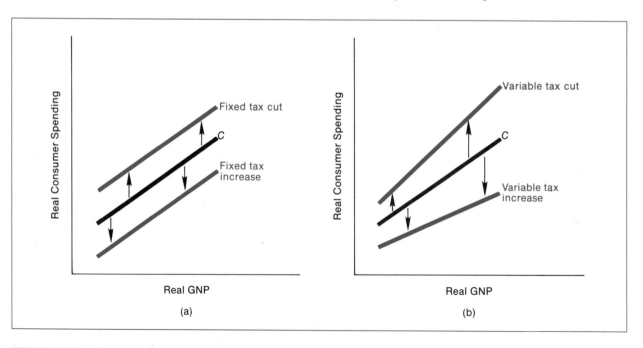

rates in the personal income tax code, which it also did in the 1986 tax act.[3] Since this sort of tax policy raises disposable income more when GNP is higher, the downward shift in the C schedule is sharper at high income levels than at low ones. Figure 12–3(b) illustrates how this type of tax policy shifts the consumption schedule.

Tax Policy and Equilibrium Income

We are now in a position to put taxes into our model of income determination. To do so, we must first adjust the consumption schedule we have been using to allow for an income tax.

Table 12–2 does this on the assumption that taxes are 25 percent of GNP. Column 1 shows alternative values of GNP ranging from $2.5 trillion to $5.5 trillion, and column 2 indicates that taxes are always one-quarter of this amount. Column 3 subtracts column 2 from column 1 to arrive at disposable income (DI). Column 4 then shows the amount of consumer spending corresponding to each level of DI. Note that columns 3 and 4 just repeat the consumption function that we studied in Chapter 8. But the consumption schedule that we need for our 45° line diagram relates C to Y, not to DI — that is, it relates spending to total consumer income, not to income net of taxes — and that schedule is therefore found in columns 1 and 4.

To derive the new expenditure schedule for an economy with taxes, we need only replace the old consumption schedule with this new one — that is, we must replace column 2 of Table 12–1 with column 4 of Table 12–2. This is done numerically in Table 12–3, and the results are shown diagrammatically in Figure 12–4. In particular, the expenditure schedule contained in columns 1 and 5 of Table 12–3 is shown as the C + I + G line in Figure 12–4. Naturally, the inclusion of taxes has lowered the expenditure schedule.

Since the 45° line is given in the diagram, we can immediately locate the equilibrium level of GNP at point E. Here, gross national product is

[3]You may be wondering how a tax law could raise the personal exemption, lower bracket rates, and yet remain revenue neutral. The answer is that the 1986 tax act closed many loopholes and raised taxes on corporations.

Table 12–2
DERIVATION OF A CONSUMPTION SCHEDULE WITH INCOME TAXATION

(1) GROSS NATIONAL PRODUCT (billions)	(2) TAXES (billions)	(3) DISPOSABLE INCOME (GNP minus taxes) (billions)	(4) CONSUMPTION (billions)
$2500	$ 625	$1875	$1600
3000	750	2250	1900
3500	875	2625	2200
4000	1000	3000	2500
4500	1125	3375	2800
5000	1250	3750	3100
5500	1375	4125	3400

Because taxes (column 2) must be subtracted from gross national product (column 1) to get disposable income (column 3), this table shows how an income tax lowers the consumption schedule (column 4) in a concrete example. (Compare column 4 with the consumption schedule in Table 12–1 to see that the C schedule has indeed fallen.)

Table 12–3
TOTAL EXPENDITURE SCHEDULE WITH TAXES AND GOVERNMENT PURCHASES

(1) NATIONAL INCOME (Y) (billions)	(2) CONSUMPTION (C) (billions)	(3) INVESTMENT (I) (billions)	(4) GOVERNMENT PURCHASES (G) (billions)	(5) TOTAL EXPENDITURE (C + I + G) (billions)
$2500	$1600	$700	$800	$3100
3000	1900	700	800	3400
3500	2200	700	800	3700
4000	2500	700	800	4000
4500	2800	700	800	4300
5000	3100	700	800	4600
5500	3400	700	800	4900

This table replaces the previous consumption schedule with a new one that adjusts for the income tax (as shown in Table 12–2) and shows that the equilibrium level of income is $4000 billion.

Figure 12–4
INCOME DETERMINATION WITH GOVERNMENT SPENDING AND TAXATION

This diagram adds a 25 percent income tax to the model economy portrayed in Figure 12–2. Because of this, the C schedule is shifted down (and hence the C + I and C + I + G schedules are also shifted down). Equilibrium is at point E, where the C + I + G schedule crosses the 45° line. Thus equilibrium GNP is $4000 billion, the same as it was in the economy with no government. This however, is certainly not a general result; government actions can either raise or lower GNP.

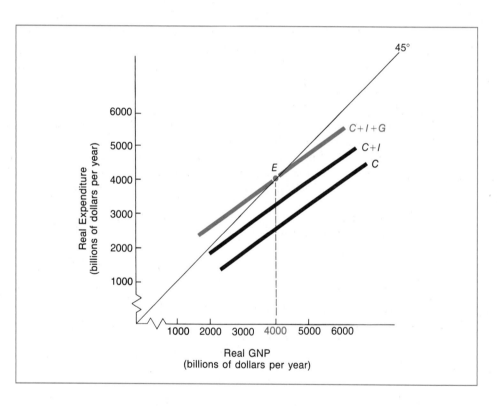

$4000 billion, consumption is $2500 billion, investment is $700 billion, and government purchases are $800 billion. As we know, full employment may occur above or below Y = $4000 billion. If below, there is an inflationary gap. Prices probably will start to rise, pulling the expenditure schedule down and reducing equilibrium GNP. If above, there is a recessionary gap, and history suggests that prices will fall only slowly. In the interim, there will be a period of high unemployment.

In short, once we adjust the expenditure schedule to include the effects of taxes, the determination of national income proceeds exactly as before. The effects of government spending and taxation, therefore, are fairly straightforward and can be summarized as follows:

Government purchases of goods and services *add* to total spending directly through the G component of $C + I + G$. Taxes indirectly reduce total spending by lowering disposable income and thus reduce the C component of $C + I + G$. On balance, then, the government's actions may raise or lower the equilibrium level of GNP, depending on how much spending and taxing it does.

Notice one interesting feature of our example. With government purchases of $800 billion and taxes equal to 25 percent of GNP, the economy's equilibrium is at $Y = \$4000$ billion (see Figure 12–4 or Table 12–3), the same as it was with $G = 0$ and no taxes. But tax receipts are $1000 billion when GNP is $4000 billion. This means that $1000 billion in taxes must have decreased GNP by the same amount as $800 billion in spending increased it. Apparently:

The multiplier for changes in taxes is smaller than the multiplier for changes in government purchases.

Let us see why.

Multipliers for Tax Policy

Because they work indirectly via consumption, multipliers for tax changes must be worked out in two steps.

Step 1. Before turning to the 45° line diagram, we must figure out what any proposed change in the tax law is likely to do to the consumption schedule.

Step 2. We can then enter this effect as a shift of the $C + I + G$ schedule in the 45° line diagram and work out the multiplier.

A reduction in income taxes provides a convenient example of this two-step analysis, because we have already done step 1 in an earlier chapter. Specifically, in Chapter 8 we studied how consumer spending would respond to a cut in income taxes. We concluded that if the tax reduction were viewed as permanent, consumers would increase their spending by an amount equal to the tax cut times the marginal propensity to consume. (If you need review, turn back to pages 144–48.)

This is the shift that must be entered in the 45° line diagram to complete step 2, and Figure 12–5 displays such a shift. The tax cut raises the expenditure schedule from $C_0 + I + G$ to $C_1 + I + G$ by raising its C component. The diagram then shows the multiplier effect on GNP, which rises from Y_0 to Y_1.

In our numerical example, income tax receipts rise from zero to $1000 billion. So step 1 instructs us to multiply the $1000 billion in added income taxes by the marginal propensity to consume (MPC), which is 0.8, to get $800 billion as the estimated vertical shift of the consumption schedule at $Y = \$4000$ billion. Notice that this is precisely equal to the $800 billion increase in government purchases. So, in this example, the *downward* shift of the C schedule exactly offsets the *upward* shift of the G schedule when $Y = \$4000$, leading to no net change in the $C + I + G$ schedule. That is why the equilibrium level of GNP did not change when we introduced the government.

Figure 12–5

THE MULTIPLIER FOR A REDUCTION IN INCOME TAXES

In this example, the $C + I + G$ schedule is shifted upward from $C_0 + I + G$ to $C_1 + I + G$, by a tax cut. Equilibrium GNP therefore increases from Y_0 to Y_1.

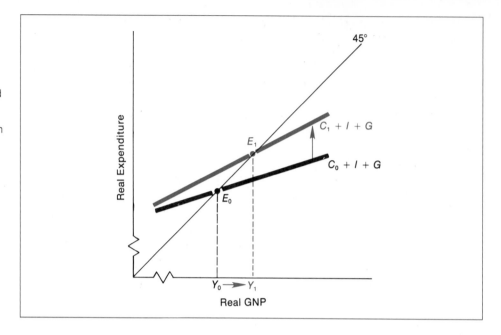

Thus we see the reason why the multiplier for income taxes is lower than the multiplier for government purchases: while G is a direct component of $C + I + G$, taxes are not. Taxes work indirectly, first by changing disposable income and then by changing C. That is why we had to multiply the $1000 billion change in taxes by 0.8 to get the $800 billion shift of the C schedule. Economically, some of the change in disposable income affects *saving* rather than *spending*; so a one-dollar tax cut does not pack as much punch as a dollar of G. The fact that the multipliers for G and taxes differ in this way has an interesting implication:

If government purchases and taxes rise by equal amounts, the equilibrium level of GNP on the demand side will rise. If G and taxes fall by equal amounts, the equilibrium level of GNP on the demand side will fall.

Thus fiscal policies that keep the deficit the same do not keep aggregate demand the same — a lesson that politicians frequently forget.

Government Transfer Payments

called reverse taxation

Finally, we should mention the last major tool of fiscal policy: **government transfer payments.** How are transfers treated in our models of income determinations — like purchases of goods and services (G) or like taxes?

The answer follows readily from the circular flow diagram on page 221 or the accounting identity back on page 140. The important thing to understand about transfer payments is that they intervene between gross national product (Y) and disposable income (DI) in precisely the *opposite* way from income taxes. Specifically, starting with the wages, interest, rents, and profits that constitute the national income, we *subtract* income taxes to calculate disposable income. We do so because these taxes represent the portion of incomes that are *earned* but never *received* by consumers. But then we must *add* transfer payments because they represent sources of income that are *received* though they were not *earned* in the process of production. Thus, *transfer payments are basically negative taxes*; giving a consumer $1 in the form of a transfer payment is equivalent to reducing her taxes by $1.

So, in terms of the 45° line diagram, increases in transfer payments can be treated simply as decreases in taxes. And we see that Figure 12–5, which we devised to illustrate a tax cut, can also be used to illustrate a rise in unemployment benefits, or in social security benefits, or in any other such transfer payment. Similarly, the analysis of a decrease in transfer payments would proceed exactly like the analysis of an increase in taxes.

The Multiplier Revisited

We have now acquired most of the tools we need to understand how fiscal policy decisions are made. But, before senators or congressmen vote on the budget, they should have an idea of the magnitude of the multiplier. Our figure of 5 is too high, and we can now understand how the income tax works to lower its value. But before getting involved in the mechanics, let us understand the basic reason.

As we learned in Chapter 10, the multiplier works through a chain of spending and respending, as one person's expenditure becomes another's income. But, through taxation, some of the additional income leaks out of the circular flow at each stage. Specifically, if the income tax rate is 25 percent, when Generous Motors spends $1 million on salaries, workers actually receive only $750,000 in *after-tax* (or disposable) income. If workers spend 80 percent of this amount (based on an MPC of 0.8), spending in the next round will be only $600,000. Notice that this is only 60 *percent* of the original expenditure, not 80 *percent* as in our earlier example. Thus the multiplier chain for each original dollar of spending shrinks from:

$$1 + 0.8 + (0.8)^2 + (0.8)^3 + \ldots = \frac{1}{1 - 0.8} = \frac{1}{0.2} = 5$$

to:

$$1 + 0.6 + (0.6)^2 + (0.6)^3 + \ldots = \frac{1}{1 - 0.6} = \frac{1}{0.4} = 2\frac{1}{2}.$$

This is clearly a very large reduction in the multiplier. We thus have a second reason why our oversimplified multiplier formula of Chapter 10 gives an exaggerated impression of the size of the multiplier:

REASONS WHY THE OVERSIMPLIFIED MULTIPLIER FORMULA
IS WRONG

1. It ignores price-level changes, which serve to reduce the size of the multiplier.

2. It ignores income taxes, which serve to reduce the size of the multiplier.

Of the two reasons, the second is much the more important in practice. In later chapters, we shall encounter still more reasons.

This conclusion about the multiplier is shown graphically in Figure 12–6, where we have drawn our $C + I + G$ schedules with a slope of 0.6 to reflect an MPC of 0.8 and a tax rate of 25 percent rather than the 0.8 slope that we used previously. The figure depicts the effect of an increase in government purchases

Figure 12–6

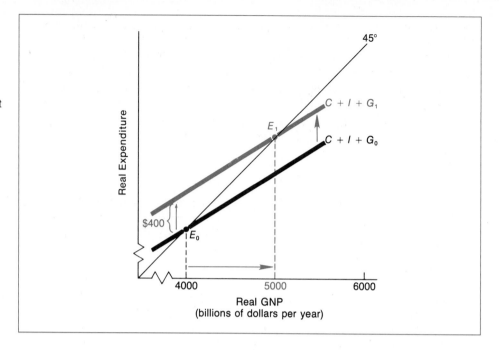

of goods and services of $400 billion, which shifts the $C + I + G$ schedule from $C + I + G_0$ to $C + I + G_1$. Equilibrium moves from point E_0 to point E_1—a growth in GNP from $Y = $4000 billion to $Y = $5000 billion. Thus, if we ignore for the moment any increases in the price level (which would reduce the multiplier shown in Figure 12–6), a $400 billion increment in government spending leads to a $1000 billion increment in GNP. So when taxes are included in our model, the multiplier is only $1000/$400 = $2\frac{1}{2}$, just as we concluded before.

Planning Expansive Fiscal Policy

Now, at last, you are ready to pretend that you are a member of Congress deciding how to respond to the president's proposed budget. Suppose that the economy would have a GNP of $4000 billion if last year's budget were simply repeated. Suppose further that your goal is to achieve a fully employed labor force and that staff economists tell you that your goal can be achieved with a GNP of approximately $5000 billion. Finally, just to keep the calculations manageable, suppose the price level is fixed. (We will drop this unrealistic assumption in just a few pages.) What budget should you vote for?

This question is far from hypothetical. When President Ronald Reagan took office in January 1981, the unemployment rate was 7.4 percent, and the gap between actual and potential GNP (in current prices) was estimated to be about $40 billion. He immediately scrapped President Carter's proposed budget and urged Congress to enact an entirely different fiscal policy, one which led to the largest peacetime budget deficits in American history. The ensuing debate over the budget has continued to this day.

Returning to our hypothetical example, what options are available if we want to raise GNP by $1000 billion? This chapter has taught us that Congress can raise government purchases, reduce taxes, or increase transfer payments by enough to close the recessionary gap between actual and potential GNP.

Figure 12–7 illustrates the problem, and its cure through higher government spending, on our 45° line diagram. Figure 12–7(a) shows the equilibrium

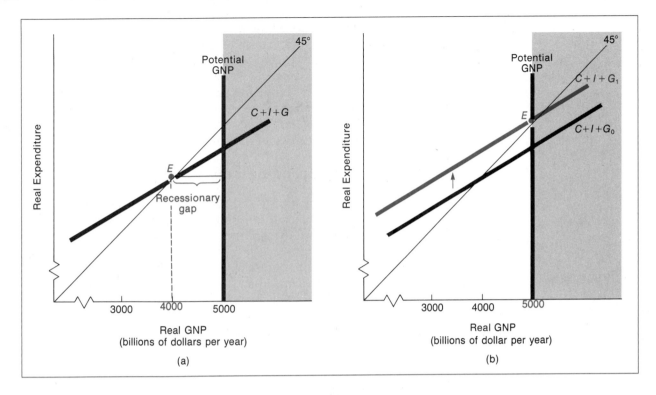

of the economy if no changes are made in the budget. Except for the full-employment line at $Y = \$5000$ and the corresponding recessionary gap, it looks just like Figure 12–4. With an expenditure multiplier of $2\frac{1}{2}$, you can figure out that an additional $400 billion of government spending will be needed to push the GNP up $1000 billion and eliminate this gap ($1000 \div 2\frac{1}{2} = \$400$).

So you might vote to raise G from $G_0 = \$800$ billion to $G_1 = \$1200$ billion, hoping to move the $C + I + G$ curve in Figure 12–7(a) out to the position indicated in Figure 12–7(b), thereby achieving full employment. Of course, you might prefer to achieve this fiscal stimulus by lowering income taxes rather than by increasing expenditures, as President Reagan did in 1981. Or you might prefer to rely on more generous transfer payments. The point is that there are a variety of budgets capable of pushing the economy up to full employment by increasing GNP by $1000 billion. Figure 12–7 applies equally well to any of them.

Planning Restrictive Fiscal Policy

The preceding example assumed that the basic problem of fiscal policy is to overcome a deficiency of aggregate demand, as was the case at the start of the Reagan administration. Often this is so. But at other times the problem is that demand is excessive relative to the economy's capacity to produce. In this case, fiscal policy should assume a restrictive stance in order to reduce inflation.

It does not take much imagination to run our previous analysis in reverse. If, under a continuation of current budget policies, there would be an inflationary gap, contractionary fiscal policy tools can eliminate it. Either by cutting spending programs out of the budget, or by raising taxes, or by some combination of these policies, the government can pull the $C + I + G$ schedule down to a noninflationary position and achieve an equilibrium at full employment.

Figure 12–7
FISCAL POLICY TO ELIMINATE A RECESSIONARY GAP
This diagram shows, with more precision than can actually be achieved in practice, how fiscal policy can eliminate a recessionary gap. Part (a) shows the gap: Equilibrium GNP ($4000 billion) falls short of potential GNP ($5000 billion). Part (b) shows how fiscal policy—by moving the $C + I + G$ curve up just enough—can wipe out this gap and restore full employment. With a multiplier of $2\frac{1}{2}$, a rise in G of $400 billion or a cut in taxes large enough to shift C up by $400 billion would do the trick.

Notice the difference between this way of eliminating an inflationary gap and the natural self-correcting mechanism of the economy that we discussed in Chapter 11. There we observed that, if the economy were left to its own devices, a cumulative but self-limiting process of inflation eventually would eliminate the inflationary gap and return the economy to full employment. Here we see that it is not necessary to put the economy through the inflationary wringer. Instead, a restrictive fiscal policy can limit aggregate demand to the level that the economy can produce at full employment.

The Choice Between Spending Policy and Tax Policy

In principle, fiscal policy can nudge the economy in the desired direction equally well by changing government spending or by changing taxes. For example, if the government wants to expand the economy, it can raise G or lower taxes. Either policy shifts the total expenditure schedule upward, as depicted in Figure 12–7, thereby raising the equilibrium GNP on the demand side.

In terms of our aggregate demand and supply diagram, either policy shifts the aggregate demand curve outward, from $D_0 D_0$ to $D_1 D_1$ in Figure 12–8. As a result, the economy's equilibrium moves from point E to point A. Both real GNP and the price level rise. As this diagram points out, any combination of higher spending and lower taxes that produces the same aggregate demand curve leads to the same increases in real GNP and prices.

How, then, do we decide whether it is better to raise spending or to cut taxes? The answer depends mainly on how large a public sector we want, and this is a contentious issue.

One point of view, expressed most eloquently in the writings of John Kenneth Galbraith, is that there is something amiss when a country as wealthy as the United States has such an impoverished public sector. In Galbraith's view, America's most pressing needs are not for more designer jeans, sports cars, and VCRs, but rather for better schools, more efficient public transportation systems, and cleaner and safer city streets. Those who agree with him believe that we should *increase* G when the economy needs stimulus, and pay for these improved public services by *increasing taxes* when the economy needs to be reined in.

Figure 12–8
EXPANSIONARY FISCAL POLICY
Any of a variety of expansionary fiscal policies will push the aggregate demand curve outward to the right as depicted by the shift from $D_0 D_0$ to $D_1 D_1$ in this aggregate supply and demand diagram. The economy's equilibrium moves upward to the right along aggregate supply curve SS, from point E to point A. Comparing A with E, we note that output is higher but prices are also higher. The expansionary policy has caused some inflation.

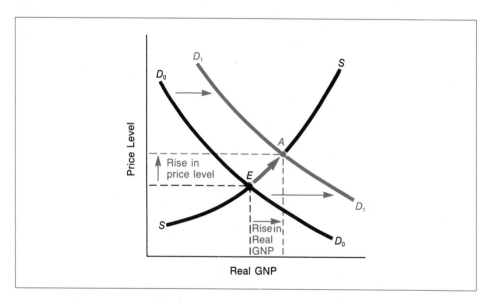

An opposing opinion, advocated most forcefully by President Ronald Reagan, gained the ascendancy in the 1980s. In this view, the government sector is already too large; we are foolish to rely on government to do things that private individuals and businesses could do better on their own; and the growth of government interferes too much in our everyday lives, and in so doing circumscribes our freedom. Those who hold this view argue for *tax cuts* when macroeconomic considerations call for expansionary fiscal policy, and for *reductions in public spending* when restrictive policy is required. That is precisely what President Reagan tried to do.

Too often the use of fiscal policy for economic stabilization is erroneously associated with a large and growing public sector—that is, with "big government." This need not be the case. Individuals favoring a smaller public sector can advocate an active fiscal policy just as well as those who favor a larger public sector. Advocates of big government budgets should seek to expand demand (when appropriate) through higher government spending and contract demand (when appropriate) through tax increases. By contrast, advocates of small public budgets should seek to expand demand by cutting taxes and reduce demand by cutting expenditures.

Some Harsh Realities

The mechanics outlined so far in this chapter make the fiscal policy planner's job look rather simple. The elementary diagrams suggest, rather misleadingly, that the authorities can drive GNP to any level they please simply by manipulating spending and tax programs. It seems as though they should be able to hit the full-employment bull's eye every time.

But, in fact, a better analogy is to shooting through dense fog at an erratically moving target with an inaccurate gun. The target is moving because, in the real world, the investment schedule (and, to a lesser extent, the consumption schedule) is constantly shifting on account of changes in expectations, new technological breakthroughs, changes in consumers' tastes, and the like. This means that the policies decided upon today, which are to take effect at some future date, may no longer be appropriate by the time that future date rolls around. Policy must be based, to some extent, on *forecasting*, and no one has yet discovered a foolproof method of economic forecasting.[4] Since our forecasting ability is so modest, and because fiscal policy decisions sometimes take a long time to be carried out, the government may occasionally find itself fighting the last inflation just when the new recession gets under way.

A second misleading feature of our diagrams is that multipliers are not known with as much precision as our examples suggest. Thus while the "best guess" may be that a $20 billion cut in government purchases will reduce GNP by $40 billion, the actual outcome may be as little as $24 billion or as much as $56 billion. It is therefore impossible to "fine tune" every wobble out of the economy's growth path through fiscal policy; economic science is simply not that precise. The point is even more cogent with respect to tax policy, for here we get involved in trying to guess whether consumers will view tax changes as permanent or temporary.

A third complication is that our target—full-employment GNP—may be only dimly visible, as if through a fog. Especially when the economy's last experience with full employment is far in the past, economists may have difficulty

---

[4]Some problems and techniques of economic forecasting are considered in Chapter 15.

estimating the GNP level that represents full employment. In fact, as mentioned in Chapter 6, there is much controversy right now over how much unemployment constitutes "full employment."

Finally, in trying to decide whether to push the unemployment rate lower, legislators would like to know what the inflationary costs are likely to be. As Figure 12–8 reminds us, any expansionary fiscal policy that closes a recessionary gap by increasing aggregate demand also pushes prices higher, that is, causes more inflation. This undesired side effect may make the government hesitant to use fiscal policy to end a recession.

Is there a way out of this dilemma? Can we stimulate the economy by fiscal policy without worsening inflation? During the late 1970s and 1980s, a small but influential minority of economists, journalists, and politicians argued that we could. They called their approach "supply-side economics."

The Idea Behind Supply-Side Tax Cuts

The central idea of supply-side economics is that certain types of tax cuts can be expected to increase aggregate supply. What kinds of measures are these? The basic principle is simple to state but not so simple to carry out in practice.

If taxes can be cut in a way that increases people's incentives to work, *and if people actually respond to these incentives,* then the tax system can be used to increase the total amount of labor that is available for employment. Similarly, if the tax system is changed in ways that encourage households to save more and businesses to invest more, *and if people respond to these changes in the way policymakers hope,* then the total amount of capital that is available for use will begin to rise. Both sorts of tax policies, then, if successful, will increase aggregate supply.

Figure 12–9 illustrates this conclusion on an aggregate supply and demand diagram. If policy measures can shift the economy's aggregate supply to position $S_1 S_1$, then prices will be lower and output higher than if the aggregate supply curve were $S_0 S_0$. Policymakers will have succeeded in reducing inflation and raising real output (lowering unemployment) at the same time. The trade-off between inflation and unemployment will have been defeated. This is the goal of supply-side economics.

Figure 12–9

THE IDEA BEHIND SUPPLY-SIDE TAX CUTS
The basic idea of supply-side cuts is that if they achieve their desired objective they will cause the economy's aggregate supply curve to shift outward to the right. For example the aggregate supply curve might be $S_1 S_1$ under a program of supply-side tax cuts, whereas it would only be $S_0 S_0$ without such tax cuts. In this case, if aggregate demand is the same in either case, the tax cuts would lead to the equilibrium point B instead of the equilibrium point A. Comparing B with A, we see that the program leads to lower prices and higher output.

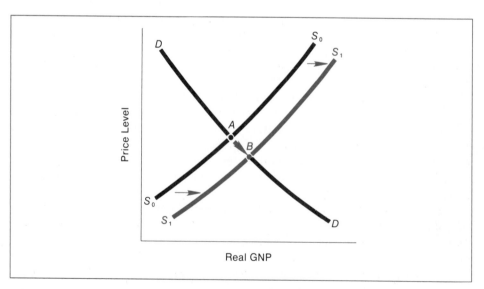

What sorts of policies do supply siders advocate? There is a long list, but most supply-side tax cuts are aimed at stimulating capital formation. For example:

1. **Accelerated Depreciation.** As mentioned in Chapter 9, a company investing in a machine or factory is not permitted to take the entire cost of that asset as a tax write-off in the year it is purchased. Instead, it must spread the cost over the lifetime of the asset in a series of **depreciation allowances** — annual tax deductions that in total add up to the value of the asset. Naturally, firms prefer to take their depreciation allowances sooner rather than later, because higher depreciation allowances in the early years of an investment mean lower immediate tax burdens.

    Many supply siders argue that an effective way to provide greater incentives for investment is to speed up ("accelerate") depreciation allowances. There are many ways to do this, and the details are best left to courses on accounting. However, one straightforward way is simple enough to explain right here. If Congress reduces the "lifetime" of a machine for tax purposes from, say, seven years to five years, then firms will get the tax savings from depreciation faster. That is precisely what President Reagan and Congress did in 1981.

2. **Reducing the Corporation Income Tax.** Another type of tax cut that supply siders often favor is reducing the statutory rates of taxation on corporate income. By letting companies retain more of their pre-tax income, it is argued, government will provide both greater investment incentives (by raising the profitability of investments) and more investable funds (by letting companies keep more of their earnings). This step was taken as part of the 1986 tax reform.[5]

3. **Reducing Taxes on Capital Gains.** Many investments, particularly financial investments such as stocks and bonds, often lead to **capital gains and losses.** For example, if Mr. Cabot purchases 100 shares of IBM stock in 1960 for $10,000 and sells them in 1988 for $100,000, the law says he has reaped a $90,000 *capital gain*, and must pay tax accordingly. Supply siders argue that lower taxes on capital gains provide greater incentives for individuals and firms to invest more, and, partly for these reasons, Congress reduced taxes on capital gains in 1979 and again in 1981. However, capital gains taxes were raised as part of the 1986 tax reform.

    Not all supply-side tax cuts are aimed at spurring investment. If there is to be more investment, someone must be providing the saving to finance it. Thus, supply siders typically favor:

> A **capital gain** is an increase in the market value of a piece of property, such as a common stock or a parcel of land, that occurs during the period between when it is bought and when it is sold. A **capital loss** is a decrease in that property's value.

4. **Reducing Taxes on Income from Savings.** One extreme form of this proposal would simply exempt from taxation all income from interest and dividends. Since income must be either consumed or saved, this would, in effect, change our present personal income tax into a tax on consumer spending. While this has not been adopted, the income tax changes introduced in 1981 did contain several significant steps in this direction — including, most notably, permitting almost all wage-earners to shelter limited amounts of saving from taxation in Individual Retirement Accounts (IRAs). Supply siders promoted and applauded these changes. Nonetheless, the use of IRAs was restricted by the 1986 tax bill.

---

[5]However, in return, Congress eliminated the investment tax credit, an investment subsidy mentioned in Chapter 9.

Supply siders recognize that capital is not the only factor of production. Aggregate supply can be expanded by increasing the supply of labor services as well. For this reason, they generally advocate:

5. ***Lowering Personal Income Tax Rates.*** Such cuts, they argue, will encourage people to work harder and for longer hours, and will induce them to spend more time at productive activities and less time worrying about how to avoid taxes. In fact, sharp cuts in personal taxes have been the cornerstone of President Reagan's economic strategy. At the urging of the president, Congress passed a massive three-stage reduction in personal income taxes under which tax rates were reduced by 5 percent in 1981, an additional 10 percent in 1982, and a final 10 percent in 1983. Five years later, bracket rates were slashed again in the Tax Reform Act of 1986. Now, except in unusual circumstances, no American is in a tax bracket above 33 percent, and most taxpayers are in the 15 percent bracket. Such low tax rates, supply siders argue, should bolster incentives to work, to save, and to invest.

Finally, aggregate supply depends on the state of technology. So supply siders are interested in using the tax system to encourage technological progress by such measures as:

6. ***Tax Credits for Research and Development.*** Under a law enacted in 1981, companies that spend money on research and development (R & D) are entitled to reductions in their tax bills. The hope is obvious: Tax incentives should increase spending on R & D, and more R & D should lead to improvements in technology.

Let us suppose, for the moment, that a successful supply-side tax cut is enacted to help close a recessionary gap. Since *both* aggregate demand *and* aggregate supply increase simultaneously, the economy may be able to avoid the painful inflationary consequences of an expansionary fiscal policy that were shown in Figure 12–8.

Figure 12–10 illustrates this conclusion. The two aggregate demand curves and the initial aggregate supply curve $S_0 S_0$ are carried over directly from Figure 12–8. But we have introduced an additional supply curve, $S_1 S_1$, to

Figure 12–10
A SUCCESSFUL SUPPLY-SIDE TAX REDUCTION

A tax cut specifically aimed at the supply side, if successful, will shift *both* aggregate demand *and* aggregate supply to the right. In this diagram, equilibrium is initially at point *E*, where demand curve $D_0 D_0$ intersects supply curve $S_0 S_0$. After the supply-side tax cut, the aggregate demand curve is $D_1 D_1$ and the aggregate supply curve is $S_1 S_1$, so equilibrium is at point *C*. As compared with the results of a tax cut that works only on the demand side (point *A*), the supply-side tax cut raises output more and prices less

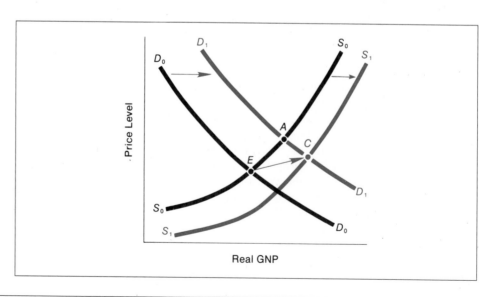

reflect the successful supply-side tax cut depicted in Figure 12–9. The equilibrium of the economy moves from E to C, whereas with a conventional demand-side tax cut it would have moved from E to A. As compared with point A, output is higher and prices are lower at point C.

A good deal, you say! Indeed it is. The supply-side argument is extremely attractive. It certainly appealed to candidate Ronald Reagan in 1980 and, as a consequence, it has had a profound influence on our nation's economic policy. But will it work in practice? Can we actually do what is depicted in Figure 12–10? Let us consider some difficulties.

Some Flies in the Ointment

Supply-side economics was, and remains, controversial. Supporters have touted it as a painless remedy for all our economic ills. Detractors have derided it as wishful thinking and branded it "voodoo economics."

Although supply-side economics has its critics, the critics rarely question the goals of the program or the basic idea that the tax system can be used to improve incentives. They argue, instead, that supply siders exaggerate the beneficial effects of supply-side tax cuts and ignore some undesirable side effects. Here is a list of the main objections to supply-side tax cuts that have fueled the great national debate since the late 1970s, a debate that is by no means over.

1. *Small Magnitude of Supply-Side Effects.* The first objection is that supply siders are simply too optimistic: We really do not know how to do what Figure 12–9 shows. It is easy to design tax cuts that, for example, make working more *attractive* financially, that is, which raise take-home pay. All you have to do is cut tax rates. Doing this, however, does not guarantee that people will actually work more. Instead, they may find themselves able to afford the goods and services they want with fewer hours of labor, and react by working *less*. Similarly, if tax cuts raise the return on savings, people may find their savings goals easier to achieve, and react by saving less.

   Most of the statistical evidence suggests that it is unrealistic to expect tax reductions to lead to substantial increases in either labor supply or household savings. Consequently, most economists expected President Reagan's tax cuts to lead to only modest increases in labor supply and saving— far less than avid supply siders predicted. As Charles Schultze, chief economic adviser to President Carter, quipped: "There's nothing wrong with supply-side economics that division by ten couldn't cure."

2. *Demand-Side Effects.* The second objection is that supply siders underestimate the effects of tax cuts on aggregate demand. If you cut personal taxes, individuals *may possibly* work more, but they *will certainly* spend more. If you reduce business taxes and thereby encourage expansion of industrial capacity, business firms will demand more investment goods.

   Two responses to this criticism have been made. Some of the more extreme proponents of supply-side economics have sought to deny the obvious, that is, to deny that supply-side tax cuts will stimulate aggregate demand. For example, according to supply-side advocate George Gilder: "The supply-sider denies that a tax cut can have any immediate effect on total disposable income or real aggregate demand."

   This wishful thinking was, fortunately, not President Reagan's response—at least in principle. His plan was to link the tax cuts to reductions in government spending that would cancel out the demand-side effects. Let us review the reasoning briefly. We learned in earlier chapters that tax cuts raise aggregate demand while reductions in government spending reduce it. Thus, whatever demand stimulus is caused by the tax cuts, there is some expenditure reduction big enough to cancel its demand-side effects. By combining these two programs into a fiscal package, it may be possible to obtain the situation depicted in Figure 12–9: a rise in aggregate supply with no accompanying rise in aggregate demand.

The problem with this strategy is that if *large* tax cuts are made, then *large* spending cuts must accompany them. Many observers in the early 1980s worried that the expenditure cuts proposed by President Reagan, while substantial, were much smaller than the tax cuts. In fact, we learned later that the president's own budget director, David Stockman, was among the skeptics. (See the boxed insert on page 240.) We also learned that the skeptics were right: The Reagan program actually cut taxes far more than it cut spending.

If we put these two objections together, we are led to Figure 12–11. Here we depict a small outward shift in the aggregate supply curve (which reflects the first objection) and a large outward shift of the aggregate demand curve (which reflects the second). The result is that the economy's equilibrium moves from point A (the intersection of $S_0 S_0$ and $D_0 D_0$) to point E (the intersection of $S_1 S_1$ and $D_1 D_1$). Prices rise as output expands. The outcome differs only a little from the straight "demand-side" fiscal stimulus depicted in Figure 12–8 (page 232).

3. ***Problems in Timing.*** The most promising types of supply-side tax cuts seek to encourage greater business investment by, for example, making depreciation allowances more generous. But investment does not create new industrial capacity overnight. It takes time to plan new investment projects, arrange the financing, get delivery on machinery, build factories, and then actually put these things into operation. The crucial point is that the *expenditures* on investment goods come before the *expansion of capacity*. Thus, even a supply-side optimist, if he is realistic, should recognize that supply-side tax cuts have their primary effects on aggregate demand in the short run. Effects on aggregate supply come later.

Figure 12–11
A MORE PESSIMISTIC VIEW OF SUPPLY-SIDE TAX CUTS
If the effect of supply-side tax initatives on the aggregate supply curve is actually much smaller than suggested by Figure 12–9, the anti-inflationary impact will be correspondingly smaller. As you can see in this diagram, it is possible that a large shift in the aggregate demand curve could overwhelm the favorable effects of the tax cuts on the price level.

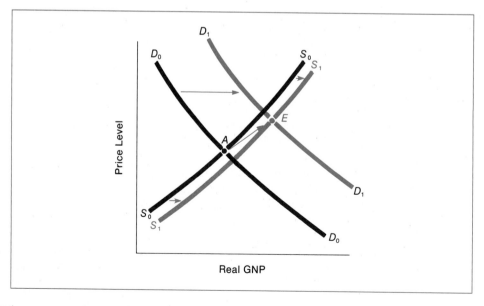

4. **_Limited Effect on Inflation._** Supply-side policies were offered as a cure for inflation. Unfortunately, even a very successful supply-side program can be expected to make only a small dent in the inflation rate. The reason is a matter of simple arithmetic.

Inflation depends on the _difference_ between the rates at which the _aggregate demand_ and _aggregate supply_ curves are shifting outward over time. Aggregate supply is, as a matter of definition, the product of the amount of labor available times the amount of output produced by each hour of labors—the **productivity** of labor. There is little that can be done to affect the long-run growth rate of labor supply, which depends fundamentally on population growth. Thus, if supply-side policies are to increase the growth rate of aggregate supply, they must focus on productivity.

But we learned in Chapter 7 that the historical growth rate of productivity in the United States is only about 2 percent per year. A 50 percent improvement in productivity growth would constitute a remarkable achievement. No serious economist thinks we really know how to achieve such a feat. But even a supply-side miracle of this magnitude would add only 1 percentage point to the growth rate of aggregate supply and therefore would lower the inflation rate by only about 1 percentage point—a very small effect.

5. **_Effect on the Distribution of Income._** The preceding objections all pertain to the likely effects of supply-side policies on aggregate supply and demand. But there is a very different problem that bears mention: Most supply-side initiatives would increase income inequality. Why? Because, while raising the incomes of the wealthiest members of our society may not be their primary aim, most supply-side cuts cannot help but concentrate benefits on the rich simply because it is the rich who earn most of the capital gains, interest, and dividends, and who own most of the corporations.

Indeed, this tilt toward the rich is almost an inescapable corollary of supply-side logic. The basic aim of supply-side economics is to increase the incentive for working and investing, that is, to increase the gap between the rewards of those who succeed in the economic game (by working hard, investing well, and so on) and those who fail. It can hardly be surprising, therefore, that supply-side policies tend to increase economic inequality.

6. **_Losses of Tax Revenue._** You can hardly help noticing that most of the policies suggested by supply siders involve reductions in one tax or another. Thus, unless some other tax is raised or spending is cut, supply-side tax cuts are bound to raise the government budget deficit. Critics of President Reagan's program, for example, argued that such large tax cuts would leave monstrous budget deficits for years to come.

Once again, extreme supply siders answered this objection by denying the obvious. Lower tax rates, they argued, need not lead to lower tax revenues if the tax base grows quickly enough. For example, suppose the GNP starts at $4000 billion when the tax rate is 25 percent; so the government collects $1000 billion in tax revenues. Then, if the tax rate is cut to 20 percent, but GNP grows to $5000 billion as a result, tax receipts will remain at $1000 billion. Reasoning like this led extreme supply siders like Professor Arthur Laffer to predict that the Reagan tax cuts would actually lead to more tax revenue and smaller budget deficits![6]

---

[6]The famous Laffer Curve is a graph showing how tax revenues first rise, but then fall, as the tax rate rises from zero, to 10 percent, then 20 percent, and so on up to 100 percent. Therefore, if tax rates are high enough, the reasoning goes, we can actually raise more revenue by cutting rates.

Reaganomics and the Budget: An Insider's View

President Reagan's original economic package was advertised as an equal reduction in taxes and spending. The incoming administration actually promised to balance the budget by fiscal year 1984[*]—a promise greeted with disbelief by those outside the administration. Later we learned that the most knowledgeable insider, Budget Director David Stockman, was the biggest skeptic of all. He told his story in his controversial book, *The Triumph of Politics: Why the Reagan Revolution Failed* (New York: Harper & Row, 1986), from which the following quotations are taken.

Even before he took over the Office of Management and Budget (OMB) in January 1981, Stockman realized that supply-side tax cuts would open a huge budget gap that could be closed only by gigantic budget cuts. Though worried that "I was the only one who had done even a minimal degree of . . . homework on the fundamental fiscal math," he welcomed the opportunity. "We would have the . . . politicians pinned to the wall. They would have to dismantle . . . bloated, wasteful, and unjust spending enterprises—or risk national ruin." Only in retrospect did he realize that, "Designing a comprehensive plan to bring about a sweeping change in national economic governance in forty days is a preposterous, wantonly reckless notion."

Energized by an ideological commitment to smaller government, Stockman prepared thick books of proposed budget cuts "chock-a-block with details and apparent precision (to) give the impression that the economic program was being launched with . . . admirable preparation. In fact, . . . critical loose ends were left unresolved everywhere." Then, in early February, bad news came: The OMB's computer models said the tax cuts would leave a 1984 deficit of $130 billion even with an optimistic forecast and all the proposed cuts. After that, Stockman "became a veri-

table incubator of shortcuts, schemes, and devices to overcome the truth."

Time was short, however, for the president was to present his program to Congress on February 18th. "As we went into the final ten days, the President of the United States was not even given the slightest warning that his economic policy revolution was bursting at the seams . . . the final week of White House deliberations on the economic plan gave new meaning to the concept of chaos." The document issued on February 18th claimed that the tax cuts would reduce revenues in fiscal year 1982 by $54 billion, most of which would be paid for by $41 billion in budget cuts. It projected budget balance by 1984 even though Stockman's internal calculations were showing a deficit of $130 billion or more. "The original budget plan I had devised . . . had been fatally flawed . . . the massive tax cut . . . never stood a chance of being paid for by a commensurate shrinkage of the welfare state."

Negotiations with Congress widened the budget gap as spending cuts were trimmed and tax cuts fattened. Stockman's budgeteers tried to square the circle with accounting gimmicks, but by November 1981 "it had become overwhelmingly clear that the . . . original political and economic assumptions were wrong by a country mile. . . . Now even the most outlandishly optimistic forecast . . . gave us triple-digit deficits . . . as far as the eye could see." We still have them.

[*]The fiscal year of the U.S. government runs from October 1st to September 30th. Thus fiscal year 1984 began on October 1, 1983.

To the vast majority of economists, this claim was implausible on its face. In the preceding example, if the GNP starts at $4000 billion, a cut in the tax rate from 25 percent to 20 percent lowers tax revenues initially by $200 billion (from $1000 billion to $800 billion). For this to cause a $1000 billion increase in the GNP (from $4000 billion to $5000 billion), the tax multiplier would have to be $1000/$200 = 5. This is about three times as large as the actual multiplier is believed to be. Turning from hypothetical examples to reality, federal tax revenues did not rise, but rather fell sharply after the 1982–1983 tax cuts—just as the critics had predicted. And the large budget deficits that ensued have been a major economic issue ever since.[7]

Toward Assessment of Supply-Side Economics

On balance, most economists have reached the following conclusions about supply-side tax initiatives:

1. The likely effectiveness of supply-side tax cuts depends very much on what kinds of taxes are cut. Tax reductions aimed at stimulating business investment are likely to pack more punch than tax reductions aimed at getting people to work longer hours or to save more.

2. Such tax cuts probably will increase aggregate supply, but the increase in aggregate supply will come much more slowly than the increase in aggregate demand. Thus supply-side policies should not be thought of as a substitute for short-run stabilization policy, but rather as a way to promote (slightly) faster economic growth in the long run.

3. Demand-side effects of supply-side tax cuts are likely to be much larger than supply-side effects, especially in the short run.

4. Supply-side policies can be expected to make, at most, only a small dent in the inflation rate.

5. Supply-side tax cuts are likely to benefit the rich more than the poor.

6. Supply-side tax cuts are almost certain to lead to bigger, not smaller, budget deficits.

But this list does not close the books on the issue. It does not even tell us whether supply-side tax cuts are a good idea or a bad one. Some people will look over this list and decide that they favor supply-side tax cuts; indeed, many economists and most of the Congress supported President Reagan's program in 1981. Others, perusing the same facts, will reach the opposite conclusion. We cannot say that either group is "wrong" because, like almost every economic policy, supply-side economics has its pros and cons.

Why, then, did so many economists and politicians react so negatively to supply-side economics in the early 1980s? The main reason seems to be that the claims made by the most ardent supply siders were clearly excessive. Naturally, these claims were proven wrong. But showing that wild claims are wild does not dispose of the kernel of truth in supply-side economics: Reductions in marginal tax rates do improve economic incentives. Any specific supply-side tax cut must be judged on its individual merits.

How did things work out after the Reagan tax cuts of 1981? Although supply siders had predicted an exuberant boom, the U.S. economy in 1981–1982 suffered through its worst recession since the Great Depression. But, when recovery finally came, the economy grew rapidly in 1983 and into 1984—

[7]Chapter 16 is devoted to the causes and consequences of budget deficits.

Are Marginal Tax Rates of Marginal Importance?

When Congress passed President Reagan's program of supply-side tax cuts in 1981, not everyone was convinced that they would have the dramatic effects that the president predicted. Here's how two humorists greeted the president's policy.

The Reagan administration has launched a radical economic experiment based on top officials' Promethean understanding of the psyches of American workers. The new economic team has divined that only one question burns in the mind of the modern American worker: What is my marginal tax rate?

Let us look in on a typical American family as they make crucial economic decisions. The digital alarm woke John Galt Workingstiff at 7:14 A.M., confronting him with the first of many rational choices of the day. Could he increase his family's economic well-being more by resting, thus boosting his productivity later in the day, or by rising early to check the economic indicators?

Kemp, 10, and Roth, 8, were at their Radio Shack microcomputer consoles. "We're going short in rutabagas today, Dad," said the eldest, his shoe-button eyes alight with glee. Workingstiff was stern. "You know the rules," he said. "If you can't net enough income today to offset my property tax, you have to recoup it by going to school."

Workingstiff glanced at the digital clock. 8:36. His shift at the Wonder Widget factory was set to start at 9. But what did it matter if he was a little late? Venal union officials would protect his featherbedding habits. And his union dues were fully deductible.

Anyway, why shouldn't he stay home and miss a half day's work? The worst that could happen was that he would lose his job. Unemployment benefits, after all, were tax free.

Suddenly, burbles of excitement echoed from Kemp and Roth. "Daddy!" they cried. "In a dramatic late-night session, Congress passed a major tax-cut bill! It's retroactive! President Reagan is to sign it this morning!"

But Workingstiff was apathetic. "I don't care about a general tax bill," he grumbled. "What does it do to my marginal tax rate?"

"That's cut 10 percent in the first year!" said Kemp.

"And there's more to come. And it's predictable!" chimed in Roth.

The effect was galvanic. Workingstiff reached for his coat, calculator and lunch pail. As he swung behind the wheel, he felt bullish on America. "Don't wait dinner for me," he shouted, "I think I'll work the second shift."

He backed down the drive and into Elm Street. Around him spread the productive pageant of his beloved Anytown, U.S.A., bustling with economic vigor and unleashed productive energy. Before him, in the direction of the Wonder Widget factory, loomed high vistas of achievement: zooming productivity, tranquil labor management relations, victory over the Japanese and Germans. As his father had before him in 1941, he turned toward those mountains, and his face was bright with hope.

SOURCE: Excerpted with permission from Garrett Epps and Walter Shapiro, "You're the Marginal Tax Rate of My Eye," *The Washington Post*, March 1, 1981.

confounding many pessimistic forecasters. Since then, however, the expansion has been sluggish. There has been little if any evidence to date that supply-side incentives have increased saving, investment, or labor supply to any noticeable degree. But inflation did fall rapidly in the early 1980s and has remained low. Finally, income inequality did grow larger and, as already mentioned, the budget deficit grew ominously.

In a nutshell, then, the specific supply-side tax cuts enacted in 1981 appear to have had some beneficial effects and some harmful ones—as was to be expected. Was the program a good idea, on balance? America is still making that judgment.

Summary

1. The government's fiscal policy is its plan for managing aggregate demand through its spending and taxing programs. It is made jointly by the president and Congress.

2. Government purchases of goods and services (G) are a direct component of total spending. Therefore, they have the same multiplier as do autonomous changes in consumption or investment.

3. When income taxes are introduced, there is a difference between GNP and disposable income. Since consumer spending (C) depends on disposable income, any change in taxes will shift the consumption schedule on a 45° line diagram.

4. Shifts in the consumption function caused by tax policy are subject to the same multiplier as autonomous shifts in the consumption schedule. However, the income tax reduces the size of this common multiplier just as it reduces the size of the multiplier for G or for I.

5. Government transfer payments are treated like negative taxes, not like government purchases of goods and services, because they influence total spending only indirectly through their effect on consumption.

6. The net effect of the government on aggregate demand—and hence on equilibrium output and prices—depends on whether the expansionary effects of its spending are greater or smaller than the contractionary effects of its taxes.

7. The multiplier for changes in taxes is smaller than the multiplier for changes in government purchases.

8. If the multipliers were known precisely, it would be possible to plan any of a variety of fiscal policies to eliminate either a recessionary or an inflationary gap. Recessionary gaps can be cured by raising G, cutting taxes, or increasing transfers. Inflationary gaps can be cured by cutting G, raising taxes, or reducing transfers.

9. Active stabilization policy can be carried out either by means that tend to expand the size of government (by raising either G or taxes when appropriate) or by means that hold back the size of government (by reducing either G or taxes when appropriate).

10. Expansionary fiscal policy can cure recessions, but it normally exacts a cost in terms of higher inflation. This dilemma has led to a great deal of interest in "supply-side" tax cuts designed to stimulate aggregate supply.

11. Supply-side tax cuts aim to push the economy's aggregate supply curve outward to the right. If successful, they can expand the economy and reduce inflation at the same times—a highly desirable outcome.

12. But critics point out five problems of supply-side tax cuts: They also stimulate aggregate demand; the beneficial effects on aggregate supply may be small; the demand-side effects occur before the supply-side effects; they make the income distribution more unequal; and large tax cuts lead to large budget deficits.

13. Supply-side policies can be expected to make only a small contribution to the long-term battle against inflation.

Concepts for Review

Fiscal policy	Government transfer payments	Depreciation allowances
Goverment purchases of goods and services (G)	Effect of income taxes on the multiplier	Capital gains and losses
	Supply-side tax cuts	Productivity

Questions for Discussion

1. Where in its annual budget cycle is the federal government right now? (Bring yourself up to date by reading the financial page of your local newspaper.)

2. Consider an economy in which tax collections are always $200 and in which the three components of aggregate demand are as follows:

GNP	TAXES	DI	C	I	G
$480	$200	$280	$210	$100	$200
540	200	340	255	100	200
600	200	400	300	100	200
660	200	460	345	100	200
720	200	520	390	100	200

Find the equilibrium of this economy graphically. What is the marginal propensity to consume? What is the multiplier? What would happen to equilibrium GNP if government purchases were raised by $15 and the price level were unchanged?

3. Now consider a related economy in which investment is also $100, government purchases are also $200, and the price level is also fixed. But taxes now vary with income, and as a result the consumption schedule looks like the following:

GNP	TAXES	DI	C
$480	$160	$320	$240
540	180	360	270
600	200	400	300
660	220	440	330
720	240	480	360

Find the equilibrium graphically. What is the marginal propensity to consume? What is the tax rate? Use your diagram to show the effect of an increase of $30 in government purchases. What is the multiplier? Compare this answer to your answer to Question 2 above. What do you conclude?

4. Explain why G has the same multiplier as autonomous shifts in C or I, while taxes have a different multiplier.

5. Return to the hypothetical economy in Question 2 and suppose that both taxes and government purchases are increased by $60. Find the new equilibrium under the assumption that consumer spending continues to be exactly three-quarters of disposable income (as it is in Question 2).

6. If the government today decides that aggregate demand is excessive and is causing inflation, what options are open to it? What if it decides that aggregate demand is too weak instead?

7. Discuss the difference between a government purchase of a good or service and a government transfer payment.

8. Suppose that you are in charge of the fiscal policy of the economy in Question 2. There is an inflationary gap with income at $600, and you want to reduce income to $540. What specific actions can you take to achieve this goal?

9. Now put yourself in charge of the economy in Question 3, and suppose that full employment comes at a GNP of $720. How can you push income up to that level?

10. Which of the proposed supply-side tax cuts appeals to you most? Draw up a list of arguments for and against enacting such a cut right now.

11. (More difficult) Consider an economy with a horizontal aggregate supply curve. Investment is fixed at $700, government purchases are $800, the consumption function is:

$$C = 100 + 0.8 \, DI,$$

and taxes are one-quarter of GNP—making disposable income (DI) equal to three quarters of GNP. Find the equilibrium level of GNP. How would this equilibrium change if taxes were abolished? Compare your answer with the examples in this chapter.

Appendix
Algebraic Treatment of Fiscal Policy and Aggregate Demand

In this appendix we explain the simple algebra behind the fiscal policy multipliers discussed in the chapter. In so doing, we deal only with a simplified case in which prices do not change. While it is possible to work out the corresponding algebra for the more realistic aggregate demand–aggregate supply analysis with variable prices, the analysis is rather complicated and is best left to more advanced courses.

We start with the example used in the chapter (especially on pages 222–23 and 225–28). The government spends $800 billion on goods and services ($G = 800$) and levies an income tax equal to 25 percent of GNP. So if the symbol T denotes tax receipts:

$$T = .25\,Y.$$

Since the consumption function we have been working with is

$$C = 100 + 0.8\,DI,$$

where DI is disposable income, and since disposable income and GNP are related by the accounting identity

$$DI = Y - T,$$

it follows that the C schedule used in the 45° line diagram is described by the algebraic equation:

$$
\begin{aligned}
C &= 100 + 0.8(Y - T) \\
&= 100 + 0.8(Y - .25Y) \\
&= 100 + 0.8(.75Y) \\
&= 100 + 0.6\,Y.
\end{aligned}
$$

We can now apply the equilibrium condition for an economy with a government, which is:

$$Y = C + I + G.$$

Since investment in this example is $I = 700$, substituting for C, I, and G into this equation gives:

$$
\begin{aligned}
Y &= 100 + 0.6\,Y + 700 + 800 \\
0.4Y &= 1600 \\
Y &= 4000.
\end{aligned}
$$

This is all there is to finding equilibrium GNP in an economy with a government.

To find the multiplier for government spending, increase G by 1 and resolve the problem:

$$
\begin{aligned}
Y &= C + I + G \\
Y &= 100 + 0.6Y + 700 + 801 \\
0.4Y &= 1601 \\
Y &= 4002.5
\end{aligned}
$$

So the multiplier is $4002.5 - 4000 = 2.5$, as stated in the text.

To find the multiplier for an increase in fixed taxes, change the tax schedule to:

$$T = .25Y + 1.$$

Disposable income is then

$$DI = Y - T = Y - (.25Y + 1) = .75Y - 1,$$

so the consumption function is

$$
\begin{aligned}
C &= 100 + 0.8DI \\
&= 100 + 0.8(.75Y - 1) \\
&= 99.2 + 0.6Y.
\end{aligned}
$$

Solving for equilibrium GNP as usual gives:

$$
\begin{aligned}
Y &= C + I + G \\
Y &= 99.2 + 0.6Y + 700 + 800 \\
0.4Y &= 1599.2 \\
Y &= 3998.
\end{aligned}
$$

So a \$1 increase in fixed taxes lowers Y by \$2. The tax multiplier is -2.

Now let us proceed to a more general solution, using symbols rather than specific numbers. The equations of the model are as follows:

$$(1) \quad Y = C + I + G$$

is the equilibrium condition, as usual;

$$(2) \quad C = a + bDI$$

is the same consumption function we have used in the appendixes of Chapters 9 and 10;

$$(3) \quad DI = Y - T$$

is the accounting identity relating disposable income to GNP;

$$(4) \quad T = T_0 + tY$$

is the tax function, where T_0 represents fixed taxes (which were zero in our numerical example) and t represents the tax rate (which was 0.25 in the example). Finally, I and G are just fixed numbers.

We begin the solution by substituting (3) and (4) into (2) to derive the consumption schedule relating C to Y:

$$C = a + b\, DI$$

$$C = a + b(Y - T)$$

$$C = a + b(Y - T_0 - tY)$$

$$(5) \quad C = a - b\, T_0 + b(1 - t)Y.$$

You will notice that a change in fixed taxes (T_0) shifts the *intercept* of the C schedule while a change in the tax rate (t) changes its *slope*, as explained in the text (pages 224–25).

Next substitute (5) into (1) to find equilibrium GNP:

$$Y = C + I + G$$

$$Y = a - b\, T_0 + b(1 - t)Y + I + G$$

$$[1 - b(1 - t)]Y = a - b\, T_0 + I + G$$

or

$$(6) \quad Y = \frac{a - bT_0 + I + G}{1 - b(1 - t)}.$$

Equation (6) shows us that G has the same multiplier as *I* or *a*, and that this multiplier is:

$$\text{Multiplier} = \frac{1}{1 - b(1 - t)}.$$

To see that this is in fact the multiplier, raise G or I or a by 1 unit. In each case, equation (6) would be changed to read:

$$Y = \frac{a - b\, T_0 + I + G + 1}{1 - b(1 - t)}.$$

Subtracting equation (6) from this expression gives the change in Y stemming from a one-unit change in G or I or a:

$$\text{Change in Y} = \frac{1}{1 - b(1 - t)}.$$

We noted in Chapter 10 (page 190) that if there were no income tax ($t = 0$), a realistic value for b (the marginal propensity to consume) would yield a multiplier of 10, which is much bigger than the true multiplier. Now that we have added taxes to the model, our multiplier formula produces much more realistic numbers. Reasonable values for the parameters for the U.S. economy are $b = \frac{9}{10}$ and $t = \frac{1}{3}$. The multiplier formula then gives:

$$\text{Multiplier} = \frac{1}{1 - \frac{9}{10}\left(1 - \frac{1}{3}\right)} = \frac{1}{1 - \frac{9}{10} \times \frac{2}{3}}$$

$$= \frac{1}{1 - \frac{6}{10}} = \frac{1}{\frac{4}{10}} = 2.5,$$

which is not far from its actual estimated value, nearly 2.

Finally, we can see from equation (6) that the multiplier for a change in fixed taxes (T_0) is:

$$\text{Tax multiplier} = \frac{-b}{1 - b(1 - t)}.$$

For the example considered in the text and earlier in this appendix, $b = 0.8$ and $t = 0.25$, so the formula gives:

$$\frac{-.8}{1 - .8(1 - .25)} = \frac{-.8}{1 - .8(.75)}$$

$$= \frac{-.8}{1 - .6} = \frac{-.8}{.4} = -2.$$

According to these figures, each $1 *increase* in T_0 *reduces* Y by $2.

Questions for Discussion

1. In an economy described by the following set of equations:

$$C = 10 + .9DI$$

$$I = 200$$

$$G = 360$$

$$T = 100 + (1/3)Y,$$

find the equilibrium level of GNP. Then find the multipliers for government purchases and for fixed taxes. If it is desired to lower GNP by 100, what are some policies that would do the trick?

2. This is a variant of the previous problem that approaches things the way a fiscal policy planner might. In an economy whose consumption function and tax function are as given in Question 1, and with investment fixed at 200, find the value of G that would make GNP equal to 1400.

3. You are given the following information about an economy.

$$C = 20 + .8(Y - T)$$

$$I = 100$$

$$G = 520$$

$$T = .25Y$$

a. Find equilibrium GNP and the budget deficit.
b. Suppose the government, unhappy with the budget deficit, decides to cut government spending by precisely the amount of the deficit in (a). What actually happens to the budget deficit and why?

4. (More difficult) In the economy considered in Question 3, suppose the government, seeing that it has not wiped out the deficit, keeps cutting G until it succeeds in balancing the budget. What levels of GNP will then prevail?

13

Money and the Banking System

The circular flow diagrams that were used in earlier chapters to explain equilibrium GNP (see, for example, Figure 12–1 on page 221) had a "financial system" in their upper left-hand corners. Savings flowed into this system and investment flowed out. Something obviously goes on inside the financial system to channel the saving into investment, and it is time we learned just what this something is.

There is another, equally important, reason for studying the financial system. *Fiscal policy* is not the only lever the government has on the economy's aggregate demand curve: It also exercises significant control over aggregate demand by manipulating *monetary policy*. If we are to understand monetary policy (the subject of Chapters 14 and 15), we must first acquire some understanding of the financial system.

The present chapter has three major objectives. It first seeks to explain the nature of money: what it is, what purposes it serves, and how it is measured. Once this is done, we turn our attention to the banking system, explaining its historical origins, the nature of banking as a business, and why this industry is so heavily regulated. Finally, we learn how banks create money—a subject that is of great importance because it is simply impossible to understand monetary policy without knowing how money is created.

At the end of the chapter, we will see why government authorities must exercise control over the supply of money in a modern economy, and this leads naturally into the discussion in Chapter 14 of *central banking*, that is, the techniques used to implement monetary policy. Then, we will integrate what we will by then have learned about money and monetary policy into our model of income determination.

Policy Issue: Deregulating the Banks

The United States is in the process of deregulating its banking system. Almost all legal limitations on interest rates have been abolished, and the government is allowing banks to engage in an ever-widening spectrum of financial activities. As a result, banks are rapidly becoming supermarkets of finance where, in addition to normal banking services like keeping an account and taking out loans, you can buy or sell stocks and bonds, purchase life insurance, have your electric bill paid, and many other things.

Bank deregulation has sparked controversy. Most observers applaud deregulation and believe it will make our economy more efficient. But some fear that deregulation will change our financial system in unpredictable ways, perhaps making it more fragile and harder to control. To make an informed judgment on deregulation, we must first ask a basic question: Why were banks so heavily regulated in the first place?

Banking is certainly not heavily monopolized. While there are financial giants such as Citibank (New York) and Bank of America (California), the industry is populated by literally thousands of small banks located in cities and towns throughout the country. There are more than 14,000 commercial banks and over 5000 savings institutions nationwide. So why did government regulations formerly tell banks, to some degree, how much they could accept in deposits, how much interest they could pay on these deposits, what types of investments they could make, and so on?

A first reason is that the major "output" of the banking industry—the nation's supply of money—is an important determinant of aggregate demand, as we will see in Chapter 14. Bank managers presumably do what is best for their stockholders. That, at any rate, is their job. But as we shall see, what is best for bank stockholders may not be best for the whole economy. For this reason, the government does not allow bankers to determine the level of the nation's money supply by profit considerations alone.

A second reason for the extensive regulation of banks is concern for the safety of depositors. In a free-enterprise system, new businesses are born and die every day; and no one save those people immediately involved takes much notice of these goings-on. When a firm goes bankrupt, stockholders lose money and employees may lose their jobs. (The latter may not even happen if new management takes over the assets of the bankrupt firm.) But, except for the case of very large firms, that is about it.

But banking is different. If banks were treated like other firms, depositors would lose money whenever one went bankrupt. That is bad enough by itself, but the real danger comes in the case of a **run on a bank.** When depositors get jittery about the security of their money, they may all rush in at once to cash in their accounts. For reasons we will learn in this chapter, most banks could not survive a "run" like this and would be forced into insolvency. Worse yet, this disease is highly contagious. If Mrs. Smith hears that her neighbor has just lost her life savings because the Main Street National Bank went broke, she is quite likely to rush to her own bank to make a hefty withdrawal. In fact, that is precisely what happened in 1985 when savings banks in Ohio and Maryland got into trouble.

A **run on a bank** occurs when many depositors withdraw cash from their accounts all at once.

Without modern forms of bank regulation, therefore, one bank failure might lead to another; and indeed, bank failures were common throughout most of American history (see Figure 13–1 on page 250). But despite the upsurge in bank failures in recent years, the failure of a major bank nowadays is still rare enough to be newsworthy. The reason is that government has taken steps to ensure that such an infectious disease, if it occurs, will not spread. It has done this in several ways that will be mentioned in this chapter.

Barter Versus Monetary Exchange

Money is so much a part of our day-to-day existence that we are likely to take it for granted, failing to appreciate all that it accomplishes. But it is important to

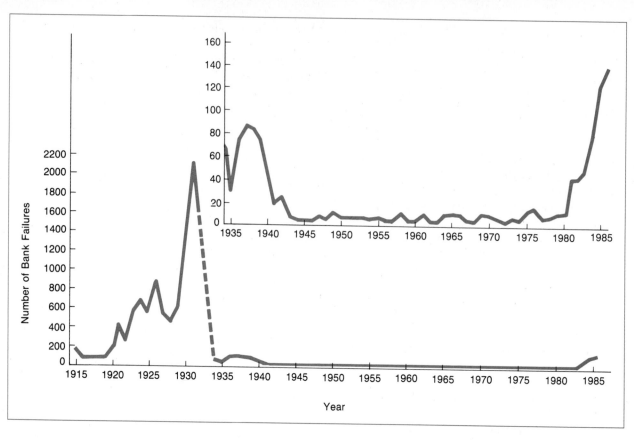

Figure 13–1
BANK FAILURES IN THE
UNITED STATES,
1915–1986
This chart shows the number
of commercial banks that
failed each year from 1915
through 1986. Notice the
sharp drop in the number of
failures from 1932 to 1934
and the steep rise in recent
years. Failures clearly are
much less common in the
postwar period than they
were in earlier years.
SOURCE: Federal Deposit
Insurance Corporation.

Barter is a system of
exchange in which
people directly trade one
good for another, without
using money as an
intermediate step.

realize that money is very much a social contrivance. Like the wheel, it had to
be invented. The most obvious way to trade commodities is not by using
money, but by **barter**—a system in which people exchange one good directly
for another. And the best way to appreciate what monetary exchange accomplishes is to imagine a world without it.

Under a system of direct barter, if Farmer Jones grows corn and has a craving for peanuts, he has to find a peanut farmer, say, Farmer Smith, with a taste
for corn. If he finds such a person (this was called the *double coincidence of wants*
by the classical economists), they make the trade. If this sounds easy, try to
imagine how busy Farmer Jones would be if he had to repeat the sequence for
every commodity he consumed in a week. For the most part, the desired double
coincidences of wants are more likely to turn out to be double wants of coincidence, where Jones gets no peanuts and Smith gets no corn. Worse yet, with so
much time spent looking for trading partners, Jones would have far less time to
grow corn. Thus:

Money greases the wheels of exchange, and thus makes the whole economy
more productive.

Under a monetary system, Farmer Jones gives up his corn for money. He
does so not because he wants the money per se, but because of what that money
can buy. Money makes his shopping tasks much easier, for it allows him simply
to locate a peanut farmer who wants money. And what peanut farmer does not?
For these reasons, monetary exchange replaced barter at a very early stage of
human civilization, and only extreme circumstances, like massive wars and runaway inflations, have been able to bring barter (temporarily) back.

The Conceptual Definition of Money

Monetary exchange is the alternative to barter. In a system of monetary exchange, people trade **money** for goods when they purchase something and trade goods for money when they sell something; but they do not trade goods directly for other goods. This defines money's principal role as the **medium of exchange.** But once it has become accepted as the medium of exchange, whatever object is serving as money is bound to take on other functions as well. For one, it will inevitably become the **unit of account,** that is, the standard unit for quoting prices. Thus, if inhabitants of an idyllic tropical island used coconuts as money, they would be foolish to quote prices in terms of sea shells.

Money may also come to be used as a **store of value.** If Farmer Jones temporarily produces and sells corn of more value than he wants to consume, he may find it convenient to store the difference in the form of money until he wants to use it. This is because he knows that money can be "sold" easily for goods and services at a later date, whereas land, gold, and other stores of value might not be. Of course, if money pays no interest and inflation is substantial, he may decide to forgo the convenience of money and store his wealth in some other form rather than see its purchasing power rapidly eroded. So this role of money is far from inevitable.

Since money may not always serve as a store of value, and since there are many stores of value other than money, it is best not to include the store-of-value function as part of our conceptual definition of money. Instead, we simply label as "money" whatever serves as the medium of exchange.

> **Money** is the standard object used in exchanging goods and services. In short, money is the **medium of exchange.**

> The **unit of account** is the standard unit for quoting prices.

> A **store of value** is an item used to store wealth from one point in time to another.

What Serves as Money?

Anthropologists and historians will testify that a bewildering variety of things have served as money in different times and places. Cattle, stones, candy bars, cigarettes, woodpecker scalps, porpoise teeth, and giraffe tails are a few of the more colorful examples.

In primitive or less organized societies, the commodities that served as money generally had value in themselves. If not used as money, cattle could be slaughtered for food, cigarettes could be smoked, and so on. But such **commodity money** generally runs into several severe difficulties. To be useful as a medium of exchange the commodity must be divisible. This makes cattle a poor choice. It must also be of uniform, or at least readily identifiable, quality so that inferior substitutes are easy to recognize. This may be why woodpecker scalps never achieved great popularity. The medium of exchange must also be storable and durable, which presents a serious problem for candy-bar money. Finally, because commodity money needs to be carried and stored, it is helpful if the item is compact, that is, has high value per unit of volume and weight. (See the boxed insert on page 253).

> A **commodity money** is an object in use as a medium of exchange, but which also has a substantial value in alternative (nonmonetary) uses.

All of these traits make it sensible that gold and silver have circulated as money since the first coins were struck about 2500 years ago. As they have high value in nonmonetary uses, a lot of purchasing power can be carried without too much weight. Pieces of gold are also storable, divisible (with a little trouble), and of identifiable quality (with a little more trouble).

The same characteristics suggest that paper would make an ideal money. Since we can print any number on it that we please, we can make paper money as divisible as we like and also make it possible to carry a large value in a lightweight and compact form. Paper is easy to store and, with a little cleverness, we can make counterfeiting hard (though never impossible). The Chinese originated paper money in the eleventh century and Marco Polo brought word of this invention to Europe.

Paper cannot, however, serve as a commodity money because its value per square inch in alternative uses is so small. A paper currency that is repudiated by its issuer can, perhaps, be used as wallpaper or to wrap fish, but these uses will surely represent only a small fraction of the paper's value as money.[1] Contrary to the popular expression, such a currency literally *is* worth the paper it is printed on, which is to say that it is not worth much. Thus paper money is always **fiat money.**

Fiat money is money that is decreed as such by the government. It is of little value as a commodity, but it maintains its value as a medium of exchange because people have faith that the issuer will stand behind the pieces of printed paper and limit their production.

Money in the contemporary United States is almost entirely fiat money. Look at a dollar bill. Next to George Washington's picture it states: "This note is legal tender for all debts public and private." Nowhere on the certificate is there a promise, stated or implied, that the U.S. government will exchange it for anything else. A dollar bill is convertible into 4 quarters, 10 dimes, 20 nickels, or any other similar combination, but not into gold, chocolate, or any other commodity.

Why do people hold these pieces of paper? Only because they know that others are willing to accept them for things of intrinsic value—food, rent, shoes, and so on. If this confidence ever evaporated, these dollar bills would cease serving as a medium of exchange and, given that they make ugly wallpaper, would become virtually worthless.

But don't panic. This is not likely to occur. Our current monetary system has evolved over hundreds of years during which *commodity* money was first replaced by *full-bodied paper money* — paper certificates that were backed by gold or silver of equal value held in the issuer's vaults. Then the full-bodied paper money was replaced by certificates that were only partially backed by gold and silver. Finally, we arrived at our present system, in which paper money has no "backing" whatsoever. Like a hesitant swimmer who first dips her toes, then her legs, then her whole body into a cold swimming pool, we have "tested the water" at each step of the way—and found it to our liking. It is unlikely that we will ever take a step back in the other direction.

[1]The first paper money issued by the federal government, the Continental dollar, was essentially repudiated. (Actually, the new government of the United States redeemed the Continentals for 1 cent on the dollar in the 1790s.) This gave rise to the derisive expression, "It's not worth a Continental."

Dealing by Wheeling on Yap

Primitive forms of money still exist in some remote places, as this extract from a newspaper article shows.

Stone wheel money from Yap.

YAP, Micronesia—On this tiny South Pacific Island...the currency is as solid as a rock. In fact, it is rock. Limestone to be precise.

For nearly 2,000 years the Yapese have used large stone wheels to pay for major purchases, such as land, canoes and permission to marry. Yap is a U.S. trust territory, and the dollar is used in grocery stores and gas stations. But reliance on stone money...continues.

Buying property with stones is "much easier than buying it with U.S. dollars," says John Chodad, who recently purchased a building lot with a 30-inch stone wheel. "We don't know the value of the U.S. dollar."

Stone wheels don't make good pocket money, so for small transactions, Yapese use other forms of currency, such as beer. . . .

Besides stone wheels and beer, the Yapese sometimes spend *gaw*, consisting of necklaces of stone beads strung together around a whale's tooth. They also can buy things with *yar*, a currency made from large sea shells. But these are small change.

The people of Yap have been using stone money ever since a Yapese warrior named Anagumang first brought the huge stones over from limestone caverns on neighboring Palau, some 1,500 to 2,000 years ago. Inspired by the moon, he fashioned the stone into large circles. The rest is history. . . .

By custom, the stones are worthless when broken. You never hear people on Yap musing about wanting a piece of the rock. . .

SOURCE: Adapted from Art Pine, "Hard Assets, or Why a Loan in Yap is Hard to Roll Over," *The Wall Street Journal*, March 29, 1984, page 1.

How the Quantity of Money Is Measured

Since the amount of money in circulation is of profound importance for the determination of national product and the price level, it is important for the government to know how much money there is, that is, to devise some *measure* of the money supply.

Our conceptual definition of money describes it as the medium of exchange. But this raises questions about just what items should be included and what items excluded when we count up the money supply. Some items are easy. All of our coins, the small change of our economic system, clearly should count as money. So should paper money, which accounts for a far greater volume of transactions. But we cannot stop here if we want to include the main vehicle for making payments in our society, for the lion's share of our nation's payments are made neither in metal nor in paper money, but by check.

Checking deposits are actually no more than bookkeeping entries in bank ledgers. Many people think of checks simply as a convenient way to give coins or dollar bills to someone else. But that is not so. In fact, the volume of money held in the form of checking deposits far exceeds the volume of currency. For example, when you pay the grocer $50 by check, dollar bills rarely change hands. Instead, that check normally travels back to your bank, where $50 is deducted from the bookkeeping entry that records your account and added to the bookkeeping entry for your grocer's account. (If you and the grocer hold accounts at different banks, more books get involved; but still no coins or bills are likely to be moved.)

Since so many transactions are made by check, it seems imperative that checking deposits be included in any specific definition of the money supply. Unfortunately, this is not an easy task nowadays because of the bewildering variety of checkable accounts that are available to depositors. Traditional checking accounts in commercial banks are the most familiar; they offer unlimited check writing privileges, often free of charge, but pay no interest.

In the past decade, however, many other financial institutions have gotten into the act. For example, both banks and savings institutions offer *NOW* (negotiable order of withdrawal) accounts that pay a low, fixed rate of interest (about $5\frac{1}{2}$ percent) in return for certain service charges. These institutions also offer so-called *Super NOW* accounts, which pay market-determined interest rates that are higher than the rates paid by NOW accounts.

One popular definition of the money supply stops here and includes coins, paper money, travelers' checks, and *only* these three types of checking accounts. In the official U.S. statistics, this narrowly defined concept of money is called **M1.** The left-hand side of Figure 13–2 shows the composition of M1 as of August 1987.

But there are other types of accounts that allow withdrawals by check and which therefore are candidates for inclusion in the money supply. Most prominently, *money market deposit accounts* allow only a few checks per month but pay market-determined interest rates. Consumers have found these accounts extremely attractive vehicles for short-term investment, and balances in them now exceed all the checkable deposits included in M1.

[2]This includes travelers' checks and both NOW (negotiable order of withdrawal) and Super NOW accounts.

The narrowly defined money supply, usually abbreviated **M1,** is the sum of all coins and paper money in circulation, plus certain checkable deposit balances at banks and savings institutions.[2]

Figure 13–2
DEFINITIONS OF THE MONEY SUPPLY
(September 1987)
SOURCE: Federal Reserve.

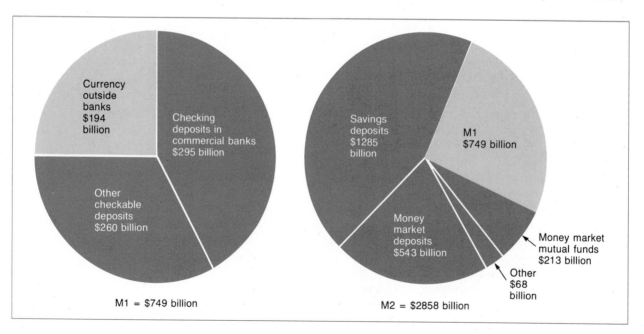

M1 = $749 billion

M2 = $2858 billion

In addition, many mutual fund organizations and brokerage houses offer *money market mutual funds*. These funds sell shares and use the proceeds to purchase a variety of short-term securities. But the important point, for our purposes, is that owners of shares in money market mutual funds can withdraw their funds simply by writing a check. So depositors can use their holdings of fund shares just like checking accounts—and they do.

Finally, although you cannot write a check on a *savings account*, many economists feel that modern banking procedures have blurred the distinction between checking balances and savings balances. For example, many banks offer convenient electronic transfers of funds from one account to another, either by telephone or by pushing a button on an automated teller. Consequently, savings balances can serve the same purposes as checking balances. For this reason, savings accounts are included—along with money market deposit accounts, money market mutual fund shares, and a few other small items—in the broader definition of the money supply known as **M2**.

The composition of M2 as of August 1987 is shown on the right-hand side of Figure 13–2. You can see that savings accounts predominate, dwarfing everything that is included in M1. Figure 13–2 illustrates two points that are worth remembering. First, our money supply comes not only from banks, but also from savings institutions, brokerage houses, and mutual fund organizations. Second, however, banks still play a predominant role.

Some economists do not want to stop counting at M2; they prefer still broader definitions of money (M3, and so on) which include more types of bank deposits and other closely related assets. The problem with this approach is that there is no obvious place to stop, no clear line of demarcation between those assets that *are* money and those that are merely *close substitutes* for money—so called **near moneys**.

If we define an asset's **liquidity** as the ease with which it can be converted into cash, there is a range of assets of varying degrees of liquidity. Everything in M1 is completely "liquid"; the money market fund shares and passbook savings accounts included in M2 are a bit less so; and so on, until we encounter such things as short-term government bonds, which, while still quite liquid, would not normally be included in the money supply. Any number of different "Ms" can be defined—and have been—by drawing the line in different places.

And there are still more complexities. For example, credit cards clearly serve as a medium of exchange. So should they be included in the money supply? Yes, you say. But how would we do this? How much money does your credit card represent? If you think about questions like this for a while, you will realize that there are no easy answers—which is one reason why research on the definition of money continues.

But we do not want to get bogged down in complex definitional issues in a first course in economics. So we will simply adhere to the convention that *"money" consists only of coins, paper money, and checkable deposits.*

Now that we have defined money and seen how it can be measured, we turn our attention to the principal creators of money—the banks.

The broadly defined money supply, usually abbreviated **M2**, is the sum of all coins and paper money in circulation, plus all types of checking account balances, plus most forms of savings account balances, plus shares in money market mutual funds, and a few other minor items.

Near moneys are liquid assets that are close substitutes for money.

An asset's **liquidity** refers to the ease with which it can be converted into cash.

How Banking Began

When Adam and Eve left the Garden of Eden, they did not encounter a branch of Citibank. Banking had to be invented, and some time passed before it came to be practiced as it is today. With a little imagination, we can see how the first banks must have begun.

When money was made of gold it was most inconvenient for consumers and merchants to carry it around and weigh and assay it for purity every time a transaction was made. So it is not surprising that the practice developed of leaving one's gold in the care of a goldsmith, who had safe storage facilities, and carrying in its place a receipt from the goldsmith stating that John Doe did indeed own five ounces of gold of a certain purity. When people began trading goods and services for the goldsmiths' receipts, rather than for the gold itself, the receipts became an early form of paper money.

At this stage, paper money was fully backed by gold. But gradually the goldsmiths began to notice that the amount of gold they were actually required to pay out in a day was but a small fraction of the total gold they had stored in their warehouses. Then one day some enterprising goldsmith hit upon a momentous idea that must have made him fabulously wealthy.

His thinking probably ran something like this. "I have 2000 ounces of gold stored away in my vault, for which I collect storage fees from my customers. If I get much more, I'll need an expensive new vault. But in the last year, I was never called upon to pay out more than 100 ounces on a single day. What harm could it do if I lent out, say, half the gold I now have? I'll still have more than enough to pay off any depositors that come in for a withdrawal, so no one will ever know the difference. And I could earn 30 additional ounces of gold each year in interest on the loans I make (at 3 percent interest on 1000 ounces). With this profit, I could lower my service charges to depositors and so attract still more deposits. I think I'll do it."

With this resolution, the modern system of **fractional reserve banking** was born. This system has three important features—features that are crucially important to this chapter.

Fractional reserve banking is a system under which bankers keep as reserves only a fraction of the funds they hold on deposit.

1. **Bank profitability.** By getting deposits at zero interest and lending some of them out at positive interest rates, goldsmiths made a profit. The history of banking as a profit-making industry was begun and has continued to this date. *Banks, like other enterprises, are in business to earn profits.*

2. **Bank discretion over the money supply.** When goldsmiths decided that they could get along by keeping only a fraction of their total deposits on reserve in their vaults and lending out the balance, they acquired the ability to *create money*. As long as they kept 100 percent reserves, each gold certificate represented exactly one ounce of gold. So whether people decided to carry their gold or leave it with their goldsmith did not affect the money supply, which was set by the volume of gold.

   With the advent of fractional reserve banking, however, new paper certificates were added whenever goldsmiths lent out some of the gold they held on deposit. The loans, in effect, created new money. In this way, the total amount of money came to depend on the amount of gold that each goldsmith felt compelled to maintain as reserves in his vault. For any given volume of gold on deposit, the lower the reserves the goldsmiths kept, the more loans they could make, and therefore the more money there would be. While we no longer use gold to back our money, this principle remains true today. *Bankers' business decisions influence the supply of money.*

3. **Exposure to runs.** A goldsmith who kept 100 percent reserves never had to worry about a run on his vault. Even if all his depositors showed up at the door at once, he always had enough gold to return their deposits. But as soon as the first goldsmith decided to get by with only fractional reserves, the possibility of a run on the vault became a real concern. If that first

goldsmith who lent out half his gold had found 51 percent of his customers at his door one unlucky day, he would have had a lot of explaining to do. Similar problems have worried bankers for centuries. *The danger of a run on the bank has induced bankers to keep prudent reserves and to lend out money carefully.*

Principles of Bank Management: Profits Versus Safety

Bankers have a reputation, probably deserved, for conservatism in politics, dress, and business affairs. From what has been said so far, the economic rationale for this conservatism should be clear. Checking deposits are pure fiat money. Years ago, these deposits were "backed" by nothing more than the bank's promise to convert them into currency on demand. If people lost trust in a bank, the bank was doomed.

Thus, it has always been imperative for bankers to acquire a reputation for prudence. This they did (and continue to do) in two principal ways. First, they had to maintain a sufficiently generous level of reserves to minimize their vulnerability to runs. Second, they had to be somewhat cautious in making loans and investments, since any large losses on their loans would undermine the confidence of depositors.

It is important to realize that banking under a system of fractional reserves is an inherently risky business that is rendered relatively safe only by cautious and prudent management. America's continuing history of bank failures bears sober testimony to the fact that many bankers have been neither cautious nor prudent. Why? Because this is not a recipe for high profits. Bank profits are maximized by keeping reserves as low as possible, by making at least some risky investments, and by giving loans to borrowers of questionable credit standing (because these borrowers will pay the highest interest rates). The art of bank management is to strike the appropriate balance between the lure of profits and the need for safety. When a banker errs by being too stodgy, his bank will earn inadequate profits. When he errs by taking unwarranted risks, his bank may not survive at all. Many banks have perished in this latter way in recent years.

Bank Regulation

The public authorities, however, apparently have decided that the balance struck by profit-minded bankers often would not be at the place where society would like it struck. So government has thrown up a web of regulations designed to insure the safety of depositors and to control the supply of money.

The principal innovation guaranteeing the safety of bank deposits is **deposit insurance.** Today most bank deposits are insured against loss by the **Federal Deposit Insurance Corporation (FDIC)** or by the **Federal Savings and Loan Insurance Corporation (FSLIC)**—two agencies of the United States government. If your bank belongs to the FDIC or the FSLIC (and most do), your checking account is insured for up to $100,000 regardless of what happens to the bank. Thus, while bank failures may spell disaster for the bank's stockholders, they do not give many depositors cause for concern. Deposit insurance eliminates the motive for customers to rush to their bank just because they hear some bad news about the bank's finances. Many observers give this innovation much of the credit for the pronounced decline in bank failures since 1933, the year in which the FDIC was established. (Refer back to Figure 13–1 on page 250.) But the recent rash of bank failures has put a strain on the deposit insurance system.

Deposit insurance is a system that guarantees that depositors will not lose money even if their bank goes bankrupt.

In addition to insuring depositors against loss, the government takes steps to see that banks do not get into financial trouble. For one thing, various regulatory authorities conduct periodic *bank examinations and audits* in order to keep tabs on the financial condition and business practices of the banks under their purview. For another, laws and regulations *limit the kinds and quantities of assets in which banks may invest.* For example, most banks are prohibited from purchasing common stock. Both these forms of regulation are clearly aimed at maintaining bank safety.

A final type of regulation also has some bearing on safety but is motivated primarily by the government's desire to control the money supply. We have seen that the amount of money any bank will issue depends on the amount of reserves it elects to keep. For this reason, most banks are subject by law to minimum **required reserves.** While banks may (and sometimes do) keep reserves in excess of these legal minimums, they may not keep less. It is this regulation that places an upper limit on the money supply. The rest of this chapter is concerned with the details of this mechanism.

How Bankers Keep Books

Before we can fully understand the mechanics of modern banking and the process by which money is "created," we must acquire at least a nodding acquaintance with the way in which bankers keep their books. The first thing to know is how to distinguish assets from liabilities.

An **asset** of a bank is something of value that the bank *owns*. This "thing" may be a physical object, such as the bank building, a computer, or a vault, or it may be just a piece of paper, such as an IOU of a customer to whom the bank has made a loan. A **liability** of a bank is something of value that the bank *owes*. Most bank liabilities take the form of bookkeeping entries. For example, if you have a checking account in the Main Street Bank, your bank balance is a liability of the bank. (It is, of course, an asset to you.)

There is an easy test to see whether some piece of paper or bookkeeping entry is a bank's asset or liability. Ask yourself whether, if this paper were converted into cash, the bank would receive the cash (if so, it is an asset) or pay it out (if so, it is a liability). This test makes it clear that loans to customers are bank assets (when loans are repaid, the bank collects), while customers' deposits are bank liabilities (when deposits are cashed in, the bank must pay). Of course, things are just the opposite to the bank's customers: the loans are liabilities and the deposits are assets.

When accountants draw up a complete list of all the bank's assets and liabilities, the resulting document is called the bank's **balance sheet.** Typically, the value of all the bank's assets exceeds the value of all its liabilities. (On the rare occasions when this is not the case, the bank is in serious trouble.) In what sense, then, do balance sheets "balance"?

They balance because accountants have invented the concept of **net worth** to balance the books. Specifically, they have defined the net worth of a bank to be the difference between the value of all its assets and the value of all its liabilities. Thus, by definition, when accountants add net worth to liabilities, the sum they get must be the same as the value of the bank's assets. In short:

$$\text{Assets} = \text{Liabilities} + \text{Net Worth}.$$

Table 13–1 illustrates this with the balance sheet of a fictitious bank, Bank-a-mythica, whose finances are extremely simple. On December 31, 1987,

Required reserves are the minimum amount of reserves (in cash or the equivalent) required by law. Normally, required reserves are proportional to the volume of deposits.

An **asset** of an individual or business firm is an item of value that the individual or firm owns.

A **liability** of an individual or business firm is an item of value that the individual or firm owes. Many liabilities are known as "debts."

A **balance sheet** is an accounting statement listing the values of all the assets on the left-hand side and the values of all the liabilities and **net worth** on the right-hand side.

Net worth is the value of all assets minus the value of all liabilities.

Table 13-1

BALANCE SHEET OF BANK-A-MYTHICA, DECEMBER 31, 1987

ASSETS		LIABILITIES AND NET WORTH	
Assets		**Liabilities**	
Reserves	$1,000,000	Checking deposits	$5,000,000
Loans outstanding	4,500,000		
Total	$5,500,000		
Addendum: Bank Reserves		**Net Worth**	
Actual reserves	$1,000,000	Stockholders' equity	500,000
Required reserves	1,000,000		
Excess reserves	0		
		Total	$5,500,000

it had only two kinds of assets (listed on the left-hand side of the balance sheet) — $1 million in cash, which it held as reserves, and $4,500,000 in outstanding loans to its customers, that is, in customers' IOUs. And it had only one type of liability (listed on the right-hand side) — $5 million in checking deposits. The difference between total assets ($5.5 million) and total liabilities ($5 million) was the bank's net worth ($500,000), shown on the right-hand side of the balance sheet.

The Limits to Money Creation by a Single Bank

Let us now turn to the process of deposit creation. Many bankers will deny that they have any ability to "create" money. (The phrase itself has a suspiciously hocus-pocus sound to it.) But they are not quite right. For although any individual bank's ability to create money is severely limited in a system with many banks, the banking system as a whole can achieve much more than the sum of its parts. Through the modern alchemy of **deposit creation,** it can turn one dollar into many dollars. But to understand this important process, we had better proceed in steps, beginning with the case of a single bank, our hypothetical Bank-a-mythica.

According to the balance sheet in Table 13–1, Bank-a-mythica is holding cash reserves that are equal to 20 percent of its deposits ($1 million in cash is equal to 20 percent of the $5 million in deposits). Let us assume that this is the minimum reserve ratio prescribed by law and that the bank strives to keep its reserves down to the legal minimum; that is, it strives to keeps its **excess reserves** down to zero.

Now let us suppose that on January 2, 1988, an eccentric widower comes into Bank-a-mythica and deposits $100,000 in cash in his checking account. The bank now has acquired $100,000 more in cash reserves, and $100,000 more in checking deposits. But since deposits are up by $100,000, *required* reserves are up only by 20 percent of this amount, or $20,000, leaving $80,000 in *excess* reserves. Table 13–2 illustrates the effects of this transaction on Bank-a-mythica's balance sheet. It is tables such as this, which show *changes* in balance sheets rather than the balance sheets themselves, that will help us follow the money-creation process.[3]

Excess reserves are any reserves held in excess of the legal minimum.

---

[3]Notice that in all such tables, which are frequently called "T accounts," the two sides of the ledger must balance. This is because changes in assets and changes in liabilities must be equal if the balance sheet is to balance both before and after the transaction.

Table 13–2

CHANGES IN BANK-A-MYTHICA'S BALANCE SHEET, JANUARY 2, 1988

ASSETS		LIABILITIES	
Reserves	+ $100,000	Checking deposits	+ $100,000

Addendum: Changes in Reserves

Actual reserves	+ $100,000
Required reserves	+ 20,000
Excess reserves	+ $ 80,000

Bank-a-mythica receives a $100,000 cash deposit. It now holds excess reserves of $80,000, since required reserves rise by only $20,000 (20 percent of $100,000).

If Bank-a-mythica does not want to hold excess reserves, it will be unhappy with the situation illustrated in Table 13–2, for it is holding $80,000 in excess reserves on which it earns no interest. So as soon as possible it will lend out the extra $80,000 — let us say to Hard-Pressed Construction Company. This loan leads to the balance sheet changes shown in Table 13–3: Bank-a-mythica's loans rise by $80,000 while its holdings of cash reserves fall by $80,000.

By combining Tables 13–2 and 13–3, we arrive at Table 13–4, which summarizes all the bank's transactions for the week. Reserves are up $20,000, loans are up $80,000, and now that the bank has had a chance to adjust to the inflow of deposits, it no longer holds excess reserves.

Looking at Table 13–4 and keeping in mind our specific definition of money, it appears at first that the chairman of Bank-a-mythica is right when he claims not to have engaged in the nefarious practice of "money creation." All that happened was that, in exchange for the $100,000 in cash it received, the bank issued the widower a checking balance of $100,000. This does not change M1; it merely converts one form of money into another.

But wait. What happened to the $100,000 in cash that the eccentric man brought to the bank? The table shows that $20,000 was retained by Bank-a-mythica in its vault. Since this currency is no longer in circulation, it no longer counts in the official money supply. (Notice that Figure 13–2 included only "currency outside banks.") But the other $80,000, which the bank lent out, is still in circulation. It is held by Hard-Pressed Construction, which probably will redeposit it in some other bank. But even before this happens, the original

Table 13–3

CHANGES IN BANK-A-MYTHICA'S BALANCE SHEET, JANUARY 3–6, 1988

ASSETS		LIABILITIES
Loans outstanding	+ $80,000	No change
Reserves	− 80,000	

Addendum: Changes In Reserves

Actual reserves	− $80,000
Required reserves	No change
Excess reserves	− $80,000

Bank-a-mythica gets rid of its excess reserves by making a loan of $80,000 to Hard-Pressed Construction Company.

Table 13–4

CHANGES IN BANK-A-MYTHICA'S BALANCE SHEET, JANUARY 2–6, 1988

ASSETS		LIABILITIES	
Reserves	+ $20,000	Checking deposits	+ $100,000
Loans outstanding	+ 80,000		
Addendum: Changes in Reserves			
Actual reserves	+ $20,000		
Required reserves	+ $20,000		
Excess reserves	No change		

When it receives $100,000 in cash deposits, Bank-a-mythica keeps only the required $20,000 in reserves and lends out the remaining $80,000 to Hard-Pressed Construction Company. Its excess reserves return to zero.

$100,000 in cash has supported a rise in the money supply: there is now $100,000 in checking deposits and $80,000 in cash in circulation, making a total of $180,000. The money-creation process has begun.

Multiple Money Creation by a Series of Banks

Let us now trace the $80,000 in cash and see how the process of money creation gathers momentum. Suppose that Hard-Pressed Construction Company, which banks across town at the First National Bank, deposits the $80,000 into its bank account. First National's reserves increase by $80,000. But because deposits are up by $80,000, *required* reserves rise by only 20 percent of this amount or $16,000. If the management of First National Bank behaves like that of Bank-a-mythica, the $64,000 of excess reserves will be lent out.

Table 13–5 shows the effects of these events on First National Bank's balance sheet. (The preliminary steps corresponding to Tables 13–2 and 13–3 are not shown separately.) At this stage in the chain, the original $100,000 in cash has led to $180,000 in deposits — $100,000 at Bank-a-mythica and $80,000 at First National Banks — and $64,000 in cash, which is still in circulation (in the hands of the recipient of First National's loans — Al's Auto Shop). Thus, from the original $100,000, a total of $244,000 has been added to the money supply ($180,000 in checking deposits plus $64,000 in cash).

But, to coin a phrase, the bucks do not stop here. Al's Auto Shop will presumably deposit the proceeds from its loan into its own account at Second

Table 13–5

CHANGES IN FIRST NATIONAL BANK'S BALANCE SHEET

ASSETS		LIABILITIES	
Reserves	+ $16,000	Checking deposits	+ $80,000
Loans outstanding	+ 64,000		
Addendum: Changes In Reserves			
Actual reserves	+ $16,000		
Required reserves	+ 16,000		
Excess reserves	No change		

Hard-Pressed deposits its $80,000 in First National Bank, which sets aside the required $16,000 in reserves (20 percent of $80,000) and lends $64,000 to Al's Auto Shop.

Table 13-6
CHANGES IN SECOND NATIONAL BANK'S BALANCE SHEET

ASSETS		LIABILITIES	
Reserves	+ $12,800	Checking deposits	+ $64,000
Loans outstanding	+ 51,200		
Addendum: Changes In Reserves			
Actual reserves	+ $12,800		
Required reserves	+ 12,800		
Excess reserves	No change		

When Al deposits his $64,000 in Second National Bank, that bank retains $12,800 as required reserves (20 percent of $64,000) and lends out the remaining $51,200.

National Bank, leading eventually to the balance sheet adjustments shown in Table 13–6 when Second National makes an additional loan rather than hold on to excess reserves. You can see how the money-creation process continues.

Table 13–7 is a convenient tabular summary of the balance-sheet changes of the first five banks in the chain (from Bank-a-mythica through the Fourth National Bank) on the assumptions that each bank holds exactly the 20 percent required reserves (no excess reserves), and that each loan recipient redeposits the proceeds in the next bank. But the chain does not end there. For the Main Street Movie Theatre, which received the $32,768 loan from the Fourth National Bank, then deposits these funds into the Fifth National Bank. Fifth National has to keep only 20 percent of this deposit, or $6,553.60, on reserve and will lend out the balance. And so the chain continues.

Where does it all end? The last two lines of Table 13–7 show what eventually happens to all other banks and to the entire banking system. The initial deposit of $100,000 in cash ultimately leads to a total of $500,000 in new deposits (column 1) and a total of $400,000 in new loans (column 4). The money supply (column 5) rises by $400,000 because the initial transaction at Bank-a-mythica merely exchanges one form of money (currency in circulation) for another (checking deposits) and hence has no net effect on the money supply. But all the other transactions in the chain increase the money supply by the amount of new deposits.

Table 13-7
THE PROCESS OF MULTIPLE MONEY CREATION

BANK	(1) DEPOSIT RECEIVED	(2) REQUIRED RESERVES	(3) EXCESS RESERVES	=	(4) NEW LOANS	(5) ADDITION TO MONEY SUPPLY
Bank-a-mythica	+ $100,000	+ $20,000	+ $80,000		+ $80,000	0
First National Bank	+ 80,000	+ 16,000	+ 64,000		+ 64,000	+ $80,000
Second National Bank	+ 64,000	+ 12,800	+ 51,200		+ 51,200	+ 64,000
Third National Bank	+ 51,200	+ 10,240	+ 40,960		+ 40,960	+ 51,200
Fourth National Bank	+ 40,960	+ 8,192	+ 32,768		+ 32,768	+ 40,960
All other banks	+ 163,840	+ 32,768	—		+ 131,072	+ 163,840
TOTALS	+ $500,000	+ $100,000	0		+ $400,000	+ $400,000

So there really is some hocus-pocus. Somehow, an initial deposit of $100,000 leads to $500,000 in new bank deposits—a multiple expansion of $5 for every original dollar—and a net increase of $400,000 in the money supply. We had better understand why this is so. But first let us verify that the calculations in Table 13–7 are correct.

If you look carefully at the table, you will see that each column of numbers forms a *geometric progression*; specifically, each entry is equal to exactly 80 percent of the entry that preceded it. Recall that in our discussion of the multiplier in Chapter 10 we learned how to sum an infinite geometric progression, which is just what each of these chains eventually will be. In particular, if the common ratio is R, the sum of an infinite geometric progression is

$$1 + R + R^2 + R^3 + \ldots = \frac{1}{1 - R}.$$

By applying this formula to the chain of checking deposits in column 1 of Table 13–7, we get:

$$\$100,000 + \$80,000 + \$64,000 + \$51,200 + \ldots$$
$$= \$100,000 \times (1 + 0.8 + 0.64 + 0.512 + \ldots)$$
$$= \$100,000 \times (1 + 0.8 + 0.8^2 + 0.8^3 + \ldots)$$
$$= \$100,000 \times \frac{1}{1 - 0.8} = \frac{\$100,000}{0.2} = \$500,000.$$

Proceeding similarly, we can verify that both columns 4 and 5 sum to $400,000 and that column 2 sums to $100,000. (Check these as exercises.)

So the numbers in Table 13–7 seem to be correct. Let us, therefore, think through the logic behind them. The chain of deposit creation can end only when there are no more excess reserves to be loaned out; that is, when the entire $100,000 in cash is tied up in *required* reserves. That explains the last entry in column 2. But, with a reserve ratio of 20 percent, excess reserves disappear only when checking deposits expand by $500,000—which is the last entry in column 1. Finally, since balance sheets must balance, the sum of all newly-created assets (reserves plus loans) must equal the sum of all newly-created liabilities ($500,000 in deposits). That leaves $400,000 for new loans—which is the last entry in column 4.

More generally, if the reserve ratio is some number R (rather than the $\frac{1}{5}$ in our example) each dollar of deposits requires only a fraction R of a dollar in reserves. Hence, deposits must expand by $1/R$ for each dollar of new reserves that are injected into the system. This suggests the general formula for multiple money creation when the required reserve ratio is some number R:

OVERSIMPLIFIED MONEY MULTIPLIER FORMULA

If the required reserve ratio is some fraction, R, an injection of $1 of excess reserves into the banking system can lead to the creation of $1/R$ in new money. That is, the so-called "money multiplier" is given by:

Change in deposits = $(1/R)$ × Change in excess reserves.

Notice that this formula correctly describes what happens in our example. The initial deposit of $100,000 in cash at Bank-a-mythica creates $80,000 in *excess* reserves (the top entry in column 3 of Table 13–7). Applying a multiplier of $1/R = 1/0.2 = 5$ to this $80,000, we conclude that the money supply will rise by $400,000—which is just what happens.

The Process in Reverse: Multiple Contractions of the Money Supply

Let us now briefly consider how this deposit-creation mechanism operates in reverse—as a system of deposit *destruction*. In particular, suppose that our eccentric widower came back to Bank-a-mythica to withdraw $100,000 from his checking account and return it to his mattress, where it rightfully belongs. Bank-a-mythica's *required* reserves would fall by $20,000 as a result of this transaction (20 percent of $100,000), but its *actual* reserves would fall by $100,000. The bank would be $80,000 short, as indicated in Table 13–8(a).

How does it react to this discrepancy? As some of its outstanding loans are routinely paid off, the bank will cease granting new ones until it has accumulated the necessary $80,000 in required reserves. The data for Bank-a-mythica's contraction are shown in Table 13–8(b), assuming that borrowers pay off their loans in cash.[4]

But where did the borrowers get this money? Probably by making withdrawals from other banks. In this case, let us assume it all came from First National Bank, which loses an $80,000 deposit and $80,000 in reserves. It finds itself short some $64,000 in reserves [see Table 13–9(a)] and therefore must reduce its loan commitments by $64,000 [see Table 13–9(b)]. This, of course, causes some other bank to suffer a loss of reserves and deposits of $64,000, and the whole process repeats just as it did in the case of deposit expansion.

After the entire banking system had become involved, the picture would be just as shown in Table 13–7, except that all the *plus* signs would be *minus* signs. Deposits would shrink by $500,000, loans will fall by $400,000, bank reserves would be reduced by $100,000, and the money supply would fall by

[4]In reality, they would probably pay with checks drawn on other banks. Bank-a-mythica would then cash these checks to acquire the reserves.

Table 13–8
CHANGES IN THE BALANCE SHEET OF BANK-A-MYTHICA

(a) ASSETS		(a) LIABILITIES		(b) ASSETS		(b) LIABILITIES
Reserves	− $100,000	Checking deposits	− $100,000	Reserves	+ $80,000	
				Loans outstanding	− 80,000	
Addendum: Changes In Reserves				**Addendum: Changes In Reserves**		
Actual reserves	− $100,000			Actual reserves	+ $80,000	
Required reserves	− 20,000			Required reserves	No change	
Excess reserves	− $ 80,000			Excess reserves	+ $80,000	

When Bank-a-mythica loses a $100,000 deposit, it must reduce its loans by $80,000 to replenish its reserves.

Table 13–9
CHANGES IN THE BALANCE SHEET OF FIRST NATIONAL BANK

(a) ASSETS		LIABILITIES		(b) ASSETS		LIABILITIES
Reserves	− $80,000	Checking deposits	− $80,000	Reserves	+ $64,000	
				Loans outstanding	− 64,000	
Addendum: Changes In Reserves				**Addendum: Changes In Reserves**		
Actual reserves	− $80,000			Actual reserves	+ $64,000	
Required reserves	− 16,000			Required reserves	No change	
Excess reserves	− $ 64,000			Excess reserves	+ $64,000	

First National Bank's loss of an $80,000 deposit forces it to cut back its loans by $64,000.

$400,000. As suggested by our money multiplier formula with $R = 0.2$, the decline in the money supply is $1/0.2 = 5$ times as large as the decline in excess reserves.

During the height of the radical student movement of the late 1960s, a circular appeared in Cambridge, Massachusetts, urging citizens to withdraw all funds from their checking accounts on a prescribed date, hold them in cash for one week, and then redeposit them. This act, the circular argued, would surely wreak havoc upon the capitalist system. Obviously, some of these radicals were well-schooled in modern money mechanics, for the argument was basically correct. The tremendous multiple contraction of the banking system and consequent multiple expansion that a successful campaign of this sort could have caused might have seriously disrupted the local financial system. But history records that the appeal met with little success. Checking-account withdrawals are not the stuff of which revolutions are made.

Why the Money Creation Formula is Oversimplified

So far, our discussion of the process of money creation has made it all seem rather mechanical. If all proceeds according to formula, each $1 in new excess reserves will lead to a $1/R$ increase in the money supply. But in reality things are not this simple. Just as we did in the case of the expenditure multiplier, we must stress that the oversimplified formula for money creation is accurate only under very particular circumstances. These circumstances require that:

1. Every recipient of a bank loan must redeposit the proceeds of that loan into another bank rather than hold it in cash.
2. Every bank must hold reserves no larger than the legal minimum.

Let us see what happens to the chain of deposit creation when either of these assumptions is violated.

Suppose first that the business firms and individuals who receive bank loans decide not to redeposit all of the proceeds into their bank accounts. For example, Hard-Pressed Construction Company and all the other borrowers might decide to hold half of their loan proceeds in cash and deposit only the remaining half. Then First National Bank would receive only a $40,000 deposit and could, therefore, make only a $32,000 loan. Second National Bank would then receive only $16,000 (half of $32,000), and so on. The whole chain of money creation would be reduced drastically. Thus:

If individuals and business firms decide to hold more cash, the multiple expansion of the money supply will be curtailed because fewer dollars of cash will be available to be used as reserves to support new checking deposits. Consequently, the money supply will be smaller.

The basic idea here is simple. Each $1 of cash held by a bank can support several dollars (specifically, $1/R$) of money. But $1 of cash held by an individual is exactly one dollar of money; it supports no bank deposits. Hence, any time cash leaves the banking system, the money supply will decline. And any time cash enters the banking system, the money supply will rise.

Next, suppose that Bank-a-mythica's management becomes more conservative, or that the outlook for loan repayments worsens because of a recession. The bank might then decide to keep more reserves than the legal requirement (say, 30 percent) and lend out less than the $80,000 assumed in Table 13–4 (say, $70,000). If this happens, then First National Bank will receive a smaller injection of cash reserves than that shown in Table 13–5. And if First National's management is as jittery as Bank-a-mythica's, it too will hold more in reserves and lend out less. Thus:

If banks wish to keep excess reserves, the multiple expansion of the money supply will be restricted. A given amount of cash will support a smaller supply of money than would be the case if banks held no excess reserves.

The Need for Monetary Control

If we pursue this point a bit further, we will see why government regulation of the money supply is so important for economic stability. We have just suggested that banks will wish to keep excess reserves when they do not foresee profitable and secure opportunities to make loans. This is likely to happen during the downswing and around the bottom of a business contraction. If it occurs, the propensity of banks to hold excess reserves will turn the money creation process into one of money destruction. Thus:

During a recession, profit-oriented banks would be prone to reduce the money supply by increasing their excess reserves — if the monetary authorities did not intervene. As we will learn in subsequent chapters, the money supply is an important influence on aggregate demand, so such a contraction of the money supply would exacerbate the severity of the recession.

On the other hand, banks will want to squeeze the maximum possible money supply out of any given amount of cash reserves by keeping their reserves at the bare minimum when the demand for bank loans is buoyant, profits are high, and many investments suddenly start to look profitable. This reduced incentive to hold excess reserves in prosperous times means that:

During an economic boom, the behavior of profit-oriented banks is likely to make the money supply expand, adding undesirable momentum to the booming economy and paving the way for a burst of inflation. The authorities must intervene to prevent this.

Regulation of the money supply, then, is necessary because bankers, in the pursuit of profit, might otherwise provide the economy with a wildly gyrating money supply that dances to the tune of the business cycle. Precisely how the authorities can keep the money supply under control is the subject of the next chapter.

Summary

1. It is more efficient to exchange goods and services by using money as a medium of exchange than by bartering them directly.

2. In addition to being the medium of exchange, whatever serves as money is likely to become the standard unit of account and a popular store of value.

3. Throughout history, all sorts of things have served as money. Commodity money gave way to fullbodied paper money (certificates backed 100 percent by some commodity, like gold), which in turn gave way to partially backed paper money. Nowadays our paper money has no commodity backing whatsoever; that is, it is pure fiat money.

4. The most widely used definition of the U.S. money supply is M1, which includes coins, paper money, and several types of checking deposits. However, many economists prefer the M2 definition, which adds to M1 most savings deposits and several other types of checkable accounts, some of which are not held in banks.

5. Under our modern system of fractional reserve banking, banks keep cash reserves equal to only a fraction of their total deposit liabilities. This is the key to their profitability, since their remaining funds can be loaned out at interest. But it also leaves them potentially vulnerable to runs.

6. Because of this vulnerability, bank managers are generally conservative in their investment strategy, and they also keep a prudent level of reserves. Even so, the government keeps a watchful eye over banking practices.

7. Before 1933, bank failures were common; but they are rare today. Many observers attribute this development to deposit insurance. Nonetheless, recent years have witnessed an upsurge of bank failures.

8. Because it holds only fractional reserves, even a single bank can create money. But its ability to do so is severely limited because the funds it lends out probably will be deposited in another bank.

9. As a whole, the banking system can create several dollars of money for each dollar of excess reserves it receives. Under certain assumptions, the ratio of new money to new excess reserves will be $1/R$, where R is the required reserve ratio.

10. The same process works in reverse, as a system of money destruction, when cash is withdrawn from the banking system.

11. Because banks and individuals may want to hold more cash when the economy is shaky, the money supply would probably contract under such circumstances if the monetary authorities did not intervene. Similarly, the money supply would probably expand rapidly in boom times if it were unregulated.

Concepts for Review

Run on a bank
Barter
Unit of account
Money
Medium of exchange
Store of value
Commodity money
Fiat money

M1 versus M2
Near moneys
Liquidity
Fractional reserve banking
Deposit insurance
Federal Deposit Insurance Corporation (FDIC)
Federal Savings and Loan Insurance Corporation (FSLIC)

Required reserves
Asset
Liability
Balance sheet
Net worth
Deposit creation
Excess reserves

Questions for Discussion

1. If ours were a barter economy, how would you pay your tuition bill? What if your college did not want the goods or services you offered in payment?

2. How is "money" defined, both conceptually and in practice? Does the U.S. money supply consist of commodity money, full-bodied paper money, or fiat money?

3. What is fractional reserve banking, and why is it the key to bank profits? (Hint: What opportunities to make profits would banks have if reserve

requirements were 100 percent?) Why does fractional reserve banking give bankers discretion over how large the money supply will be? Why does it make banks potentially vulnerable to runs?

4. Do you hold a checking account in a bank? If so, what will happen to your account if the bank goes bankrupt?

5. Suppose that no banks keep excess reserves and no individuals or firms hold on to cash. If someone suddenly discovers $4 million in buried treasure, explain what will happen to the money supply if the required reserve ratio is one-sixth (16.67 percent).

6. How would your answer to Question 5 differ if the reserve ratio were 25 percent? If the reserve ratio were 100 percent?

7. Each year during Christmas shopping season, consumers and stores wish to increase their holdings of cash. Explain how this could lead to a multiple contraction of the money supply. (As a matter of fact, the authorities prevent this contraction from occurring by methods explained in the next chapter.)

8. Excess reserves make a bank less vulnerable to runs. Why, then, don't bankers like to hold excess reserves? What circumstances might persuade them that it would be advisable to hold excess reserves?

9. Use tables such as Tables 13-2 and 13-3 to illustrate what happens to bank balance sheets when each of the following transactions occurs:
   a. You withdraw $100 from your checking account to purchase textbooks at the university book store.
   b. Paul steals $150 in cash from Peter and deposits it into his checking account.
   c. Mary Q. Contrary withdraws $600 in cash from her account at Hometown Bank, carries it to the city, and deposits it into her account at Big City Bank.

10. For each of the transactions listed in Question 9, what will be the ultimate effect on the money supply if the required reserve ratio is 10 percent? (Assume that the oversimplified money multiplier formula applies.)

14

Monetary Policy and the National Economy

This chapter adds our analysis of money and the banking system from Chapter 13 to the model of income determination and the price level that we have been developing since Chapter 8. By the end of the chapter, we will have in hand a complete model of the macroeconomy. We will then use this model to see how *monetary policy* affects aggregate demand and hence influences unemployment and inflation.

We begin by learning about the operations of America's *central bank*, the *Federal Reserve System*. The "Fed," as it is often called, is a very special kind of bank. Its customers are banks rather than individuals, and it performs some of the same services for them as your bank performs for you. Though it turns out to be an effective profit maker, its actions are not guided by the profit motive. Instead, the Fed tries to manage the money supply in what it perceives to be the national interest. Just how the Fed does its job, and why its performance has fallen short of perfection, are the first subjects of this chapter.

Next we integrate money into the Keynesian $C + I + G$ model. The mechanisms through which monetary policy affects aggregate demand are spelled out and analyzed in detail, and we learn an additional reason why the aggregate demand curve slopes downward. This sets the stage for the rest of Part 4, where we use the model to investigate a variety of important policy issues.

The Federal Reserve System: Origins and Structure

When the **Federal Reserve System** was established in 1914, the United States joined the company of most of the other advanced industrial nations. Up until then, the United States, distrustful of centralization of economic power, was almost the only important nation without a **central bank.** Britain's central bank, the Bank of England, for example, dates from 1694.

The impetus for the establishment of a central bank in the United States came not from the power of economic logic but from some painful experiences with economic reality. Four severe banking panics between 1873 and 1907 convinced legislators and bankers alike that a central bank that would regulate

A **central bank** is a bank for banks. America's central bank is the **Federal Reserve System.**

credit conditions was not a luxury but a necessity. After the 1907 crisis, the National Monetary Commission was established to find out just what was wrong with America's banking system. Its report in early 1912 led directly to the establishment of the Federal Reserve System.

Although the basic idea of central banking came from Europe, some changes were made when it was imported, making the Federal Reserve System a uniquely American institution. Owing to the vastness of our country, the extraordinarily large number of commercial banks, and our tradition of dual state–federal regulations, it was decided that the United States should have not one central bank but 12. The boundaries of the 12 Federal Reserve districts and the location of each of the 12 district banks are shown in Figure 14–1.

Technically, each of the Federal Reserve banks is a corporation; its stockholders are the banks that belong to it. But your bank, if it is a member of the System, does not enjoy the privileges normally accorded to stockholders: It receives only a token share of the Federal Reserve's immense profits (the bulk is donated to the U.S. Treasury), and it has no say in the decisions of the corporation. The private banks are more like customers of the Fed than like owners.

Who, then, controls the Fed? Most of the power resides in the seven-member Board of Governors of the Federal Reserve System, headquartered in Washington, and especially in its chairman, who is now Alan Greenspan, an economist. Members of the board are appointed by the president of the United States, with the advice and consent of the Senate, for 14-year terms. The president also designates one of the members to serve a four-year term as chairman of the board, and thus to be the most powerful central banker in the world; for the United States differs from many other countries in that the Federal Reserve Board, once appointed by the president, is *independent* of the rest of the government. So long as it stays within the statutory authority delineated by Congress, it alone has responsibility for determining the nation's monetary policy. The power of appointment, however, gives the president considerable long-run influence over Federal Reserve policy.

Figure 14–1

THE TWELVE FEDERAL RESERVE DISTRICTS

This map shows the boundaries of the 12 Federal Reserve districts and the locations of the 12 Federal Reserve banks. In which Federal Reserve district do you live?

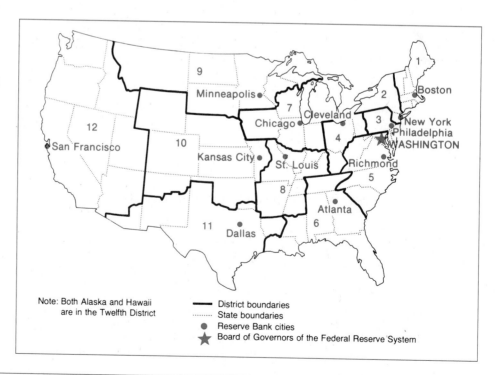

Note: Both Alaska and Hawaii are in the Twelfth District

—— District boundaries
········ State boundaries
● Reserve Bank cities
★ Board of Governors of the Federal Reserve System

Closely allied with the Board of Governors is the powerful **Federal Open Market Committee (FOMC),** which meets periodically in Washington. For reasons to be explained shortly, the decisions of the FOMC largely determine the size of the U.S. money supply. This 12-member committee consists of the seven governors of the Federal Reserve System and the presidents of five of the district banks.

The Independence of the Fed

The institutional independence of the Federal Reserve System is looked upon as a source of pride by some and as an antidemocratic embarrassment by others. The proponents of Federal Reserve independence argue that it enables monetary policy decisions to be made on objective, technical criteria and keeps monetary control out of the "political thicket." Without this independence, it is argued, there would be a tendency for politicians to force the Fed to expand the money supply too rapidly, thereby contributing to chronic inflation and undermining faith in America's financial system.

Opponents of this view counter that there is something profoundly undemocratic about having a group of unelected bankers and economists make decisions that affect the well-being of 240 million Americans. Monetary policy, they argue, ought to be formulated by the elected representatives of the people, just like fiscal policy. Those who argue for executive or congressional control over the Fed can point to historical instances in which monetary and fiscal policy have been at loggerheads—with the Fed undoing or even overwhelming the effects of fiscal policy decisions.

There is plenty of middle ground between the two extremes. One less drastic proposal would simply shift the term of the chairman of the Federal Reserve Board to make it coincide with that of the president. As things stand today, a newly elected president must retain the chairman that his predecessor appointed whether or not he agrees with his policies.

Another suggested reform would require the Fed to announce its ultimate targets for unemployment and inflation and explain how it expects its monetary policy actions to promote these goals. An extreme version of this proposal would require that the Fed adhere to the goals of the administration or of Congress. But a softer version simply would require that the Fed announce its own goals and subject them to public scrutiny. A small step in this direction was taken in 1975 when the Fed, in response to congressional wishes, began announcing "ranges of tolerance" for growth rates of the money supply (by several definitions!). That is, the chairman of the Federal Reserve Board now periodically tells Congress *in advance* what the maximum and minimum permissible growth rates for the money stock are in the coming months.

How people view these and other reform proposals that revolve around the issue of the Fed's independence depends on how they perceive the office. Are governors of the Federal Reserve System akin to judges and therefore, at least in principle, best thought of as nonpartisan and independent technocrats? The 14-year term of office certainly suggests an analogy to the judiciary, but the board's role is most assuredly one that involves policy making, not just "impartial" interpretation of the law. Or are the governors more like members of the Cabinet, that is, policy-making officials who should properly serve only at the pleasure of the president? Since neither analogy fits precisely, the issue is a vexing one.

Controlling the Money Supply: Open-Market Operations

Open-market operations refer to the Fed's purchase or sale of government securities through transactions in the open market.

Partly for historical reasons, the Fed normally relies on what are called **open-market operations** to manipulate the money supply. Open-market operations have the effect of giving the banks more reserves or taking reserves away from them, thereby triggering a multiple expansion or contraction of the money supply as in Chapter 13.

How does this work? Suppose the Federal Open Market Committee decides that the money supply is too low. It can issue instructions that the money supply be expanded through operations in the open market. Specifically, this means that the Federal Reserve System *purchases* U.S. government securities (generally short-term securities called "Treasury bills") from any individual or bank that wishes to sell, thus putting more reserves in the hands of the banks.[1]

An example will illustrate the mechanics of open-market operations. Suppose the order is to purchase $100 million worth of securities and that commercial banks are the sellers. *The Fed makes payment by giving the banks $100 million in new reserves.* So, if they held only the required amount of reserves initially, the banks now have $100 million in excess reserves, as shown in Table 14–1.

Where does the Fed get the money that it gives to the banks in return for the securities? It could pay in cash, but normally does not. Instead, it manufactures the funds out of thin air or, more literally, by punching the keyboard of a computer terminal. Specifically, the Fed pays the banks for the securities by adding the appropriate sums to the accounts that the banks maintain at the Fed. Balances held in these accounts constitute bank reserves, just like cash in bank vaults.

While this process of creating bookkeeping entries at the Federal Reserve is commonly referred to as "printing money," the Fed does not literally run the

---

[1]In fact, the Fed almost always deals with one of a small group of dealers who "make a market" in government securities. However, this detail has no effect on the basic principles. The dealers are simply intermediaries, intervening between the ultimate buyer (the Fed) and the ultimate seller.

Table 14–1

EFFECTS OF AN OPEN-MARKET PURCHASE OF SECURITIES ON THE BALANCE SHEETS OF BANKS AND THE FED

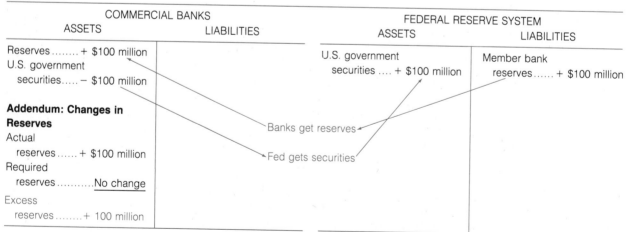

When the Fed buys $100 million worth of securities from the banks, it adds this amount to the bookkeeping entries that represent the banks' accounts at the Fed (called "member bank reserves"). Since deposits have not increased at all, required reserves are unchanged by this transaction. But actual reserves are increased by $100 million, so there are $100 million in excess reserves. This will trigger a multiple expansion of the banking system.

printing presses. Instead, it simply exchanges its IOUs for an existing asset (a government security). But unlike your IOUs, the Fed's IOUs constitute legal bank reserves, and thus are the equivalent of cash in their ability to support a multiple expansion of the money supply. The banks, not the Fed, actually increase the money supply; but the Fed's actions give the banks the wherewithal to do it.

Once the excess reserves are created, multiple expansion of the banking system proceeds in the usual way. It is not hard for the Fed to estimate the ultimate increase in the money supply that will result from its actions. As we saw in the last chapter, each dollar of excess reserves can support $1/R$ dollars of checking deposits if R is the required reserve ratio. In our example, $R = 0.20$; so $100 million in new reserves can support $100/0.2 = $500 million in new money.

But *estimating* the ultimate monetary expansion is a far cry from *knowing it* with certainty. As we know from Chapter 13, the simple money multiplier formula is predicated on the assumptions that people will want to hold no more cash, and that banks will want to hold no more excess reserves, as the monetary expansion proceeds. In practice, these assumptions are unlikely to be literally true. So, if the Fed is to predict the eventual effect of its action on the money supply correctly, it must estimate both the amount that firms and individuals will want to add to their currency holdings and the amount that banks will want to add to their excess reserves. Neither of these can be estimated with great precision. In summary:

When the Federal Reserve System wants to increase the money supply, it purchases U.S. government securities in the open market. It pays for these securities by creating new bank reserves, and these additional reserves lead to a multiple expansion of the money supply.

However, because of fluctuations in people's desires to hold cash and banks' desires to hold excess reserves, the Fed cannot predict the consequences of these actions with perfect accuracy. Thus, over short periods, control over the money supply must of necessity be imperfect.

The procedures followed when the FOMC wants to *contract* the money supply are just the opposite of those we have just explained. In brief, it orders a *sale* of government securities in the open market. This takes reserves *away* from banks, since banks pay for the securities by drawing down their deposits at the Fed. A multiple *contraction* of the banking system ensues. The principles are exactly the same as when the process operates in reverse—and so are the uncertainties.

Open-Market Operations, Bond Prices, and Interest Rates

By offering more government bonds for sale on the open market, the Federal Reserve will normally depress the price of bonds. This is illustrated by Figure 14–2, which shows a rightward shift of the (vertical) supply curve of bonds—from $S_0 S_0$ to $S_1 S_1$—with an unchanged demand curve, DD. The price of bonds falls from P_0 to P_1 as equilibrium in the bond market shifts from point A to point B.

Falling bond prices translate into rising interest rates. You cannot have one without the other. Why is that? Most bonds pay a fixed number of dollars of interest per year. For concreteness, consider a bond that pays $90 each year. If the bond sells for $1000, bondholders earn a 9 percent return on their

Figure 14–2
OPEN-MARKET SALES
AND BOND PRICES

If the Fed offers bonds for sale in the open market, the supply curve of bonds shifts rightward from S_0S_0 to S_1S_1. In consequence, equilibrium in the bond market shifts from point A to point B. The price of bonds declines from P_0 to P_1. By the same reasoning, an open-market purchase drives bond prices up.

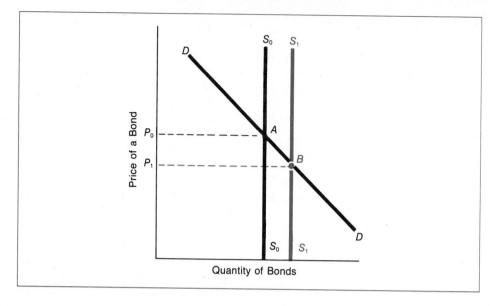

investment since $90 is 9 percent of $1000. We say that *the interest rate on the bond is 9 percent*. Now suppose the price of the bond falls to $900. The annual interest payment is still $90, so bondholders now earn 10 percent on their money ($90 is 10 percent of $900). *The effective interest rate on the bond has risen to 10 percent*. This relationship between bond prices and interest rates is completely general:

When bond prices fall, interest rates rise. When bond prices rise, interest rates fall.

In fact, the relationship amounts to nothing more than two ways of saying the same thing. Higher interest rates *mean* lower bond prices; lower interest rates *mean* higher bond prices.

We thus see that the Fed, through its open-market operations, exercises direct influence over interest rates. Specifically:

An open-market purchase of bonds by the Fed not only raises the money supply but also drives up bond prices and pushes interest rates down. Conversely, an open-market sale of bonds, which reduces the money supply, lowers bond prices and raises interest rates.

Controlling the Money Supply: Reserve Requirements

The Fed also has another way to control the money supply: by varying the minimum required reserve ratio. To see how this works, consider the balance sheet of a hypothetical bank shown in Table 14–2. If the minimum required reserve ratio is 20 percent, and the bank wishes to hold only the legal minimum in reserves, Middle American Bank is in equilibrium on October 25, 1988. Its $1 million in checking deposits mean that its required reserves amount to $200,000, which just matches its actual reserves. Excess reserves are zero.

Now suppose that the Federal Reserve Board decides that the money supply needs to be increased. One action it can take is to lower the required reserve ratio. As an exaggerated example, suppose it reduces reserve requirements to 15 percent of deposits.

Table 14–2

BALANCE SHEET OF MIDDLE AMERICAN BANK, October 25, 1988

ASSETS		LIABILITIES AND NET WORTH	
Reserves	$ 200,000	Checking deposits	$1,000,000
Loans outstanding	1,000,000	Net worth	200,000
Total assets	$1,200,000	Total liabilities plus net worth	$1,200,000

If the required reserve ratio is 20 percent, Middle American Bank holds exactly its required reserved on October 25, 1988—no more and no less. However, if the reserve ratio falls to 15 percent, its required reserves will fall to only $150,000 (15 percent of $1 million), and it will have $50,000 in excess reserves.

Middle American Bank's balance sheet is unaffected by this action, but the bank's managers are sure to react to it. For now required reserves are only $150,000 (15 percent of $1 million), so the bank is holding $50,000 in excess reserves—funds that are earning no interest for the bank. The effect is the same as if a new depositor had brought in cash: The bank now has more money to lend. Once it lends out this $50,000, its balance sheet will be as shown in Table 14–3; it now holds $50,000 less in reserves and $50,000 more in loans.

Although no new deposits are created by this transaction, we know from the previous chapter that the wheels of a multiple expansion of the banking system have been set in motion. For the recipient of the loan will deposit the proceeds in his own bank, giving that bank excess reserves and, therefore, the ability to grant more loans, and so on.

Once again, while the Fed's control over banks' excess reserves may be quite precise, its control over the money supply is a good deal looser. It can and will rely on its past experience to *estimate* the ultimate effect of any change in reserve requirements on the money supply. In normal times, these estimates are quite accurate (that, presumably, is the definition of "normal times"). But at other times banks may surprise the Fed by holding larger or smaller excess reserves than anticipated, or businesses and consumers may surprise it by holding more or less currency. In such cases, the Fed will not get the money supply it was shooting for and will have to readjust its policies.

It does not take much imagination to see what the Fed must do to reserve requirements when it wants to engineer a *contraction* of the money supply. If banks are not holding excess reserves, an increase in the required reserve ratio will force them to contract their loans and deposits until their reserve deficiencies are corrected. Of course, if banks do have sufficient excess reserves, they can flout the Fed's wishes. But the Fed normally will be trying to rein in the money supply when the economy is booming, and these are precisely the times when banks will not want to hold more idle reserves than they have to.

Table 14–3

BALANCE SHEET OF MIDDLE AMERICAN BANK, October 26, 1988

ASSETS		LIABILITIES AND NET WORTH	
Reserves	$ 150,000	Checking deposits	$1,000,000
Loans outstanding	1,050,000	Net worth	200,000
Total assets	$1,200,000	Total liabilities plus net worth	$1,200,000

If Middle American Bank does not wish to hold excess reserves, its balance sheet will look like this after it loans out the extra $50,000 in excess reserves. At this point, it once again has no excess reserves.

In fact, the Fed has not relied much on the reserve ratio as a weapon of monetary control. Current legislation provides for a basic reserve ratio of 12 percent against checking deposits, which is not expected to change frequently.

Controlling the Money Supply: Lending to Banks

When the Federal Reserve System was first established, its founders did not intend it to pursue an active monetary policy to stabilize the economy. Indeed, the basic ideas of stabilization policy were foreign at the time, dating only from Keynes's *General Theory of Employment, Interest, and Money* in 1936. Instead, the Fed's founders viewed it as a means of preventing the supplies of money and credit from drying up during economic contractions, as had happened so often in the pre-1914 period.

One of the principal ways in which the Fed was to provide such insurance against financial panics was to act as a "lender of last resort." That is, when risky business prospects made commercial banks hesitant to extend new loans, or when banks were in trouble, the Fed would step in by lending money to the banks, thus inducing the banks to lend more money to their customers.

Loans from the Federal Reserve banks to individual commercial banks have existed from the first days of the System. When the Fed extends borrowing privileges to a bank in need of reserves, that bank receives a credit in its deposit account at the Fed (see Table 14–4). This addition to bank reserves may lead to an expansion of the money supply; or it may eliminate a reserve deficiency and thereby prevent a multiple contraction of the banking system. In either case, the Fed makes monetary conditions more expansive by making borrowing easier.

The **discount rate** is the interest rate the Fed charges on loans it makes to banks.

Federal Reserve officials can influence the volume of member bank borrowing by setting the *rate of interest charged on these loans*. For historical reasons, this is called the **discount rate** in the United States. In most foreign countries, it is known as the "bank rate." If the Fed wants to give banks more reserves, it can reduce the interest rate that it charges, thereby tempting banks to borrow more. Alternatively, it can soak up reserves by raising its rate and persuading the banks to reduce their borrowings.

Table 14–4
BALANCE SHEET CHANGES FOR BORROWING FROM THE FED

COMMERCIAL BANKS		FEDERAL RESERVE SYSTEM	
ASSETS	LIABILITIES	ASSETS	LIABILITIES
Reserves .... + $5 million	Loan from Fed.... + $5 million	Loans to banks .. + $5 million	Bank reserves .... + $5 million
Addendum: Changes in Reserves			
Actual reserves... + $5 million			
Required reserves .... No change			
Excess reserves .... + $5 million			

Bank borrows $5 million and the proceeds are credited to its reserve account

When the Fed lends $5 million to a bank, it simply adds this amount to the bookkeeping entry that represents that bank's account at the Fed. Once again, actual reserves increase while required reserves do not change (because commercial bank deposits do not change). Hence this loan would be expected to initiate a multiple expansion of the banking system.

While this type of *active* manipulation of the discount rate is practiced widely in foreign countries, where the bank rate is often the centerpiece of monetary policy, it is much less common in the United States, where the Fed usually relies on open market operations in conducting its monetary policy. More often the Fed adjusts the discount rate *passively* to keep it in line with market interest rates. Nonetheless, changes in the discount rate have important psychological effects on financial markets, where they are widely interpreted as signals of the Fed's attitude toward interest rates.

As in the case of changes in reserve requirements and open market operations, the Fed cannot know for sure how banks will react to changes in the discount rate. Sometimes they may respond vigorously to a cut in the rate, borrowing a great deal from the Fed and lending a correspondingly large amount to their customers. At other times they may essentially ignore the Fed's actions. The link between the lending rate and the money supply is a loose one.

Often, though, the Fed tries to tighten this link by using a more direct way of controlling the volume of bank borrowing—**moral suasion.** This phrase refers to some not-so-subtle methods that the Fed has for letting banks know when it thinks they are borrowing too much. Since banks are anxious to maintain the good will of the Fed, they often respond to warnings that they they have overused their borrowing privileges—especially when such warnings are accompanied by a veiled threat that these privileges might be suspended if the offending bank does not mend its ways. As the Fed often reminds the banks, borrowing is "a privilege, not a right."

Moral suasion refers to informal requests and warnings designed to persuade banks to limit their borrowings from the Fed.

Proposals for Tightening Monetary Control

The fact that each of the Federal Reserve's principal instruments of monetary control is somewhat imperfect has led to a number of suggestions designed to improve the System's ability to regulate the supply of money.

Because banks' discretion over the amount of reserves they hold (subject only to the legal minimums) makes the link between changes in Federal Reserve policy and changes in the money supply rather slippery, some economists would like to see a return to a system of 100 percent reserve requirements. Under such a rule, no bank could add to or subtract from its excess reserves because there would never be any excess reserves. Each dollar of bank reserves would support exactly one dollar of deposits, no more and no less; so there would be no such thing as a multiple expansion or contraction of the banking system. The Fed can now control bank reserves with great precision; and under a system of 100 percent reserve requirements, its control over the money supply would be equally precise.

While such a change in banking regulations undoubtedly would make the Fed's job easier, it would also change the face of banking in dramatic and possibly unpredictable ways. It will be recalled from Chapter 13 that banking as we know it today evolved from that first goldsmith's momentous discovery that he could get along with only fractional reserves. This discovery has been the mainspring of bank profits ever since. Abolition of fractional reserve banking should therefore be viewed as a major overhaul of the financial system. This does not necessarily mean that it is a bad idea, only that it should be approached with some caution.

Some observers have suggested that lending to banks, far from aiding the Fed's monetary control, actually undermines it, and therefore the Fed should stop lending except in emergency cases. Their reasoning is as follows: When the Fed tries to force a contraction of the banking system, some banks may resist this desire by borrowing the reserves they need. Similarly, some banks may relinquish reserves to pay back loans just when the Fed wants the money supply to expand.

No doubt this occasionally happens. But there are also times when Federal Reserve lending is a valuable supplement to open market policy. Since it is by no means clear that monetary control would be tighter if lending were abolished, the Fed is understandably reluctant to give up one of its major traditional weapons.

The Money Supply Mechanism

This completes our discussion of the Fed's methods of controlling the money supply and the limitations of these methods. One point, however, merits further emphasis. We have noted several times that the Fed's control of the money supply is imperfect because banks can and do vary their holdings of excess reserves. Since reserves earn no interest, banks will hold substantial *excess* reserves only when they feel that funds cannot be put to profitable uses. This may happen if shaky business conditions make loans to customers look unusually risky or if interest rates are very low. Conversely, banks will work hard to hold reserves to the legal minimum when loans to customers look safe and when interest rates are high. Thus:

As interest rates rise, banks normally find it more profitable to expand their volume of loans and deposits, thus increasing the supply of money. However, the Fed can shift the relationship between the money supply and interest rates by employing any of its principal weapons of monetary control: open market operations, changes in reserve requirements, or changes in lending policy to banks.

These ideas are depicted graphically in Figure 14–3. Figure 14–3(a) shows a typical money supply schedule labeled MS, illustrating the fact that bank behavior makes the money stock rise as interest rates rise.[2] Notice that the sensitivity of the money supply to interest rates is rather weak in the diagram—a

Figure 14–3
THE SUPPLY SCHEDULE FOR MONEY
Part (a) shows a typical supply schedule for money. It is rising as we move toward the right, meaning that banks will supply more money when interest rates are higher. Part (b) illustrates what happens to the money supply schedule when the Fed purchases securities in the open market, or lowers required reserves, or provides banks with more loans. The supply schedule shifts outward. Part (c) depicts the effect of using these same policy instruments in the opposite (contractionary) direction. The supply schedule shifts inward.

[2]There are many interest rates in the economy. However, they all tend to move up and down together. Hence, for present purposes, we can speak of "the" rate of interest.

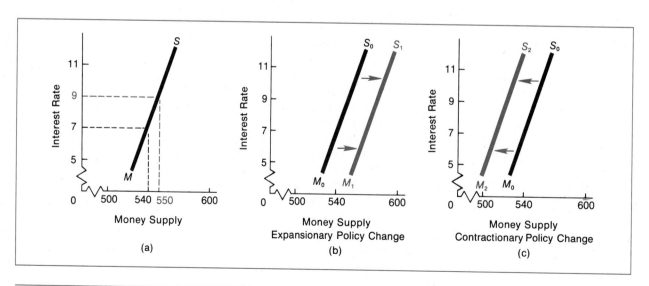

large rise in the rate of interest (from 7 percent to 9 percent) induces only a small increase in the supply of money (from $540 billion to $550 billion). The drawing is deliberately constructed that way because that is what the statistical evidence shows.

The curve in Figure 14–3(a) shows the money supply schedule corresponding to some specific monetary policy. Figure 14–3(b) portrays how the money supply schedule responds to an *expansionary change in monetary policy*, such as an open market purchase of government bonds, a reduction in reserve requirements, or a drop in the Fed's lending rate. The money supply schedule shifts outward from $M_0 S_0$ to $M_1 S_1$, as indicated by the arrows. After banks have adjusted to the change, there is more money at any given interest rate.

Figure 14–3(c) shows what happens in the reverse case — *contractionary monetary policy*, such as an open market sale of securities, an increase in reserve requirements, or a rise in the lending rate. The money supply shifts inward from $M_0 S_0$ to $M_2 S_2$.

As we have stressed, the diagrams make things look rather more precise than they actually are. Since the Fed's control over the money supply schedule is imperfect in the short run, the actual MS schedule is obscured by a bit of fog. In what follows, we portray all the graphs as clean straight lines only for pedagogical simplicity. The Fed wishes things were so simple in the real world!

The Demand for Money

Just as we must know something about both the supply of and the demand for wheat before we can predict how much will be sold and at what price, it is necessary to know something about the **demand for money** if we are to understand the amount of money actually in existence and the prevailing interest rate.

The definition of money given in Chapter 13 suggests the most important reason why people hold money balances: the medium of exchange is needed to carry out purchases and sales of goods and services. More dollars are needed to conduct the nation's business if more purchases and sales are made or if each transaction takes place at a higher price. Since the real gross national product (GNP) is normally considered to be the best measure of the total volume of goods and services traded in the economy, it seems safe to assume that the demand for money will rise as real GNP rises. And, indeed, an impressive amount of statistical evidence supports this supposition. In addition, both common sense and mountains of evidence point to the conclusion that a higher price level leads to a higher demand for money simply because more dollars are needed to conduct the same transactions.

But real output and the price level are not the only factors affecting the demand for money; interest rates matter, too. At first, that may seem surprising because most forms of money pay either no interest or an interest rate which is fixed by law. Why, then, are interest rates relevant? They are relevant because money is only one of a variety of forms in which individuals can hold their wealth. Holders of money *give up* the opportunity to hold one of these other assets, such as government bonds, in order to gain the convenience of money. In so doing, they *give up* the interest that they could have earned on one of these alternative assets.

This is another example of the concept of **opportunity cost.**[3] On the surface, it seems virtually costless to hold money. But, *compared with the next best alternative*, this action is not costless at all. For example, if the best alternative

---

[3]If you need to review this concept, see Chapter 3.

to holding $100 in cash is to put those funds into a government bond that pays 8 percent interest, then the opportunity cost of holding that money is $8 per year (8 percent of $100).

How, then, should the rate of interest influence the quantity of money that people demand? It is natural to assume that when interest rates are high people will make strenuous efforts to economize on their holdings of money balances, efforts that would not be worthwhile at lower interest rates. In a word, rational behavior of consumers and business firms should make the demand to hold money *decline* as the interest rate *rises*. And, once again, careful analysis of the data shows this to be true. To summarize:

People and business firms hold money primarily to finance their transactions. Therefore, the quantity of money demanded increases as real output rises or as prices rise. However, the quantity of money demanded decreases as the rate of interest rises because the rate of interest is the opportunity cost of holding money balances.

It is possible to portray the demand for money by a graphical device, as shown in the three panels of Figure 14–4. In panel (a) we show a downward-sloping demand schedule for money (the curve labeled MD)—the quantity of money demanded decreases as the rate of interest rises. But since the quantity of money demanded also depends on real output and the price level, we must hold both real output and the price level constant in drawing up such a curve. Changes in either of these variables will shift the MD curve in the manner indicated in the other two panels because at higher levels of real GNP and higher prices, demand for money is greater; and at lower levels of real GNP and lower prices, demand for money is smaller.

Equilibrium in the Money Market

As is usual in supply and demand analysis, it is useful to put both sides of the market together on a single graph. Figure 14–5 combines the money supply schedule of Figure 14–3(a) (labeled MS) with the money demand schedule of Figure 14–4(a) (labeled MD). Point E is the equilibrium of the money market. The diagram thus shows that *given* real output and the price level (which locates the MD curve) and *given* the Federal Reserve's monetary policy (which locates the MS curve), the money market is in equilibrium at an interest rate of

Figure 14–4
THE DEMAND SCHEDULE FOR MONEY
The downward-sloping line *MD* in part (a) is a typical demand curve for money. It slopes down because money is a less-attractive asset when interest rates on alternative assets are higher. However, such a curve can be drawn up only for particular levels of output and prices. A rise in either real output or the price level will shift the money-demand curve outward, as shown in part (b). Conversely, a fall in either real output or the price level will shift the curve inward, as in part (c).

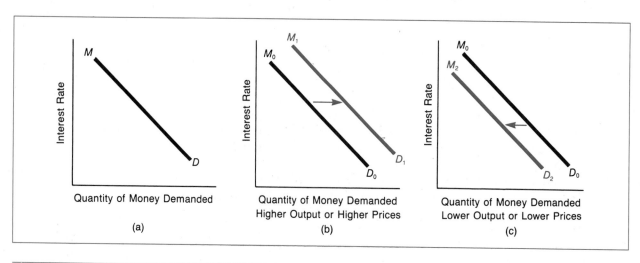

(a) — M, D — Interest Rate / Quantity of Money Demanded

(b) — M_0, M_1, D_0, D_1 — Interest Rate / Quantity of Money Demanded / Higher Output or Higher Prices

(c) — M_0, M_2, D_2, D_0 — Interest Rate / Quantity of Money Demanded / Lower Output or Lower Prices

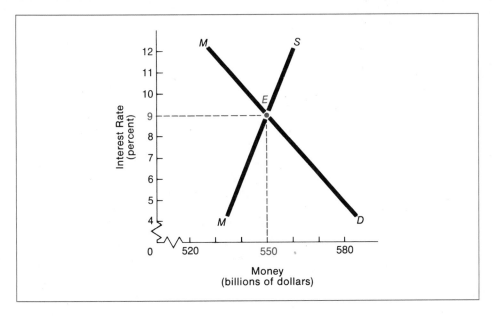

Figure 14–5
EQUILIBRIUM IN THE
MONEY MARKET
Equilibrium in the market for
money is determined by the
intersection of demand curve
MD and supply curve *MS*. At
point *E*, the interest rate is 9
percent, and the money
supply is $550 billion. At no
other interest rate would the
demand for and the supply of
money be in balance.

9 percent and a money stock of $550 billion. At any interest rate above 9 percent, the quantity of money supplied would exceed the quantity demanded and the interest rate—which is the price for renting money—would therefore decline. At any interest rate below 9 percent, more money would be demanded than supplied, and so the interest rate would rise. This is familiar ground.

Since the Fed can shift the MS curve, it can alter this equilibrium through its **monetary policy.** Expansionary monetary policy actions include purchasing government securities in the open market, reducing reserve requirements, and encouraging banks to borrow. Any of these actions will provide additional excess reserves to the banking system, thus encouraging banks to increase their loans and deposits. As money becomes more plentiful, interest rates drop.

Our supply-demand analysis of the money market shows this in Figure 14–6(a). By shifting the money supply schedule outward from $M_0 S_0$ to $M_1 S_1$, the Fed moves the market equilibrium from point *E* to point *A*—thus forcing the interest rate down.

Contractionary monetary policy actions, such as selling securities in the open market, raising reserve requirements, and discouraging borrowing, have the opposite effect. They push interest rates up, as Figure 14–6(b) shows. Thus:

Monetary policy refers to actions that the Federal Reserve System takes in order to change the equilibrium of the money market; that is, to alter the money supply, move interest rates, or both.

Monetary policies that expand the money supply normally lower interest rates. Monetary policies that reduce the money supply normally raise interest rates.

Money and Income: The Important Difference

We are now ready to see precisely how the Federal Reserve's monetary policy decisions affect unemployment, inflation, and the overall state of the economy. But first a review of some important vocabulary. As pointed out in Chapter 1, the words "money" and "income" are used almost interchangeably in common parlance. This is a pitfall we must learn to avoid.

Money is a snapshot concept. It is the answer to questions like: "How much money do you have right now?" or "How much money did you have at 3:32 P.M. on Friday, November 5th?" To answer questions like these, you would add up the cash you are (or were) carrying and whatever checking balances you

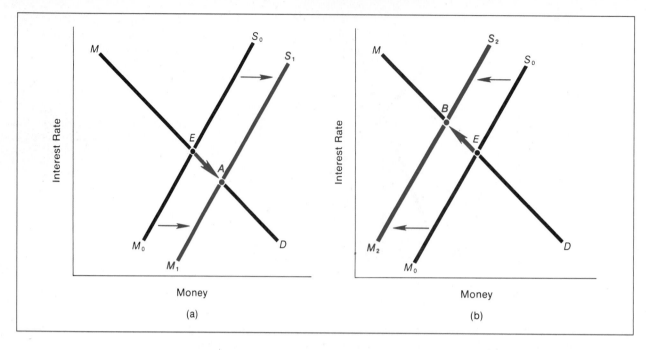

(a)

(b)

Figure 14–6
THE EFFECTS OF MONETARY POLICY ON THE MONEY MARKET
The two parts of this figure show the effects of monetary policy on the money supply (M) and the rate of interest (r). In part (a), expansionary monetary policies shift the supply schedule from M_0S_0 to M_1S_1, and push the equilibrium from point E to point A; M rises while r falls. In part (b), contractionary policies pull the supply schedule in from M_0S_0 to M_2S_2 causing equilibrium to move up from point E to point B; M falls as r rises.

have (or had), and answer something like: "I have $126.33," or "On Friday, November 5th, at 3:32 P.M., I had $31.43."

Income, by contrast, is more like a motion picture; it comes to you only over a period of time. If you are asked "What is your income?" you must respond by saying "$150 *per week,*" or "$600 *per month,*" or "$7200 *per year,*" or something like that. Notice that there is a unit of time attached to each of these responses. If you just say "My income is $452," without indicating whether it is per week or per month or per year, no one will understand what you mean.

That the two concepts are very different is easy to see. A typical American family has an *income* of about $30,000 per year, but its holdings of *money* at any point in time (using the M1 definition) are under $2000. Similarly, at the national level, nominal GNP in 1987 was around xxx billion, while the money stock (M1) in the middle of the year was only about $4500 billion.

While money and income are very different, they are certainly related. The rest of this chapter is precisely about that relationship. Specifically, we will look at how the stock of *money* in existence at any moment of time influences the rate at which people will be earning *income,* that is, how money affects the GNP.

Interest Rates and Total Expenditure

To begin, we go back to the analysis of Chapters 8–12, where we learned that aggregate demand is the sum of consumption spending (C), investment spending (I), and government purchases of goods and services (G).[4] We know that *fiscal policy* controls G directly and exerts influence over both C and I through the tax laws. We now want to find out how *monetary policy* affects C + I + G.

Most economists agree that, of the three components of aggregate demand, investment (I) is the most sensitive to monetary policy. *Business investment* in new factories and machinery is sensitive to interest rates for reasons that have

[4]We continue to ignore exports and imports until Part 5.

been explained in earlier chapters.[5] Since the rate of interest that must be paid on borrowings is one element of the cost of making an investment, business executives will find investment prospects less attractive as interest rates rise. Therefore, they will spend less. For similar reasons, *investment in housing* by individuals may also be deterred by high interest rates. Since the interest cost of a home mortgage is the major component of the total cost of owning a home, fewer families will want to buy a new home when interest rates are high than when interest rates are low. We conclude that:

Higher interest rates lead to lower investment spending. But investment (I) is a component of total spending (C + I + G). Therefore, when interest rates rise, total spending falls. In terms of the 45° line diagram of previous chapters, a higher interest rate leads to a lower C + I + G schedule. Conversely, a lower interest rate leads to a higher C + I + G schedule. (See Figure 14–7.)

Monetary Policy and Aggregate Demand in the Keynesian Model

The effect of interest rates on spending provides the mechanism by which monetary policy affects aggregate demand in the Keynesian model. We know from our analysis of the money market that monetary policy can have a profound effect on the rate of interest. Let us, therefore, outline the effects of monetary policy, starting first on the demand side of the economy.

Suppose the Federal Reserve, seeing the economy stuck with unemployment and a recessionary gap, raises the money supply. It would normally do this by purchasing government securities in the open market, but the specific weapon that the Fed uses is not terribly important for present purposes. What matters is that the money supply (M) expands.

With the demand schedule for money (temporarily) fixed, such an increase in the supply of money has the effect that an increase in supply always has in a

[5]See, for example, Chapter 9, page 166.

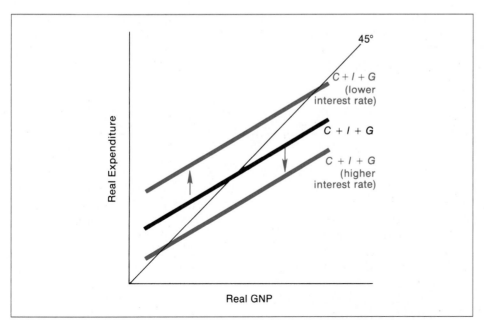

Figure 14–7
THE EFFECT OF INTEREST RATES ON AGGREGATE DEMAND
Because interest rates are an important determinant of investment spending, *I*, the C + I + G schedule shifts whenever the rate of interest changes. Specifically, as shown here, lower interest rates shift the curve upward and higher interest rates shift it downward.

Figure 14–8

THE EFFECT OF
EXPANSIONARY
MONETARY POLICY ON
THE MONEY SUPPLY
AND RATE OF INTEREST
An expansionary monetary
policy pushes the money
supply schedule outward
from M_0S_0 to M_1S_1, causing
equilibrium in the money
market to shift from point E_0
to point E_1. The money
supply rises from \$550 billion
to \$590 billion, while the
interest rate falls from 9
percent to 7 percent.

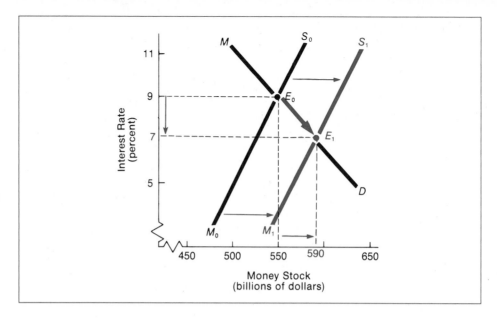

free market — it lowers the price. (See Figure 14–8.) In this case, the price of renting money is the rate of interest, r; so r falls.

Next, for reasons we have just outlined, investment spending (I) rises in response to the lower interest rates. But, as we learned in Chapter 10, such an autonomous rise in investment kicks off a multiplier chain of increases in output and employment. Thus, finally, we have completed the links from the money supply to the level of aggregate demand. In brief, monetary policy works as follows:

A higher money supply leads to lower interest rates, and these lower interest rates encourage investment, which has multiplier effects on aggregate demand.

The process operates equally well in reverse. By contracting the money supply, the Fed can force interest rates up, causing investment spending to fall and pulling down aggregate demand via the multiplier mechanism.

This, in outline form, is how monetary policy operates in the Keynesian model. Since the chain of causation is fairly long, the following schematic diagram may help clarify it.

In this causal chain, link 1 indicates that the actions of the Federal Reserve affect money and interest rates. Link 2 stands for the effect of interest rates on investment. Link 3 simply notes that investment is one component of total spending. And link 4 is the multiplier, relating an autonomous change in investment to the ultimate change in aggregate demand.

Let us next review what we know about each of these links and fill in some illustrative numbers. In the process, we will see what economists must study if they are to estimate the effects of monetary policy.

Link 1 is the subject of this chapter and of Figure 14–8. Given the initial level of real GNP and prices, the demand schedule for money is shown by curve

MD. The Fed's expansionary action shifts the supply schedule out from M_0S_0 to M_1S_1, resulting in an increase in the money stock from \$550 billion to \$590 billion in this example, and a decline in the interest rate from 9 percent to 7 percent. Thus the first thing an economist must know is how sensitive interest rates are to changes in the supply of money.

Link 2 translates the drop in the interest rate into an increase in investment spending (I), which we take to be \$100 billion in this example. To estimate this effect in practice, economists must study the sensitivity of investment to interest rates.

Link 3 instructs us to enter this \$100 billion rise in I as an autonomous shift in the $C + I + G$ schedule of a 45° line diagram. Figure 14–9 carries out this step. The expenditure schedule rises from $C + I_0 + G$ to $C + I_1 + G$.

Finally, link 4 applies multiplier analysis to this vertical shift in the expenditure schedule in order to predict the eventual increase in real GNP demanded. In our examples, we have been using a multiplier of 2.5, so multiplying \$100 billion by 2.5 gives the final effect on aggregate demand—a rise of \$250 billion. This is shown in Figure 14–9 as a shift in equilibrium from E_0 (where GNP is \$4000 billion) to E_1 (where GNP is \$4250 billion). Of course, the size of the multiplier itself must also be estimated. To summarize:

The effect of monetary policy on aggregate demand depends on the sensitivity of interest rates to the money supply, on the responsiveness of investment spending to the rate of interest, and on the size of the multiplier.

Money and the Price Level in The Keynesian Model

One need only recall the inflation of the 1970s to realize that we have forgotten something. What happens to the price level? To answer this, we must simply remember once again that prices and output are determined jointly by aggregate demand *and* aggregate supply. The analysis of monetary policy that we have completed so far has shown us how an increase in the money supply shifts the aggregate demand curve, that is, increases the *aggregate quantity demanded at any*

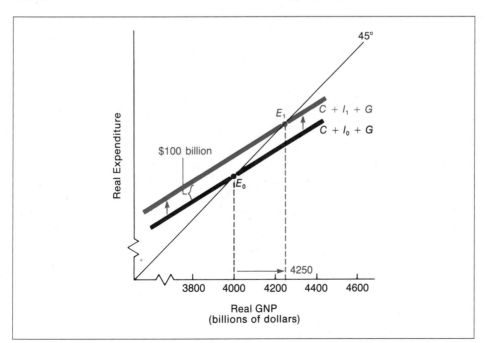

Figure 14–9
THE EFFECT OF EXPANSIONARY MONETARY POLICY ON AGGREGATE DEMAND
Expansionary monetary policies, which lower the rate of interest, will cause the $C + I + G$ schedule to shift upward from $C + I_0 + G$ to $C + I_1 + G$, as shown here. In this example, since the multiplier is 2.5, a \$100 billion rise in investment leads, via the multiplier process, to a \$250 billion rise in GNP.

given price level. But to learn what happens to the price level and to real output, we must consider *aggregate supply* as well.

Specifically, in considering shifts in aggregate demand caused by *fiscal* policy in Chapter 12, we noted that an upsurge in total spending normally induces firms to increase output somewhat *and* to raise prices somewhat. This is just what an aggregate supply curve shows. Whether prices or real output exhibit the greater response depends mainly on the degree of capacity utilization. An economy operating near full employment has but a limited ability to increase production; it therefore responds to greater demand mainly by raising prices. On the other hand, an economy with a substantial amount of unemployed labor and unused capital can produce a great deal more output without raising prices.

Now this analysis of output and price responses applies equally well to monetary policy or, for that matter, to anything else that raises aggregate demand. We conclude, then, that:

Expansionary monetary policy causes some inflation under normal circumstances. But how much inflation it causes depends on the state of the economy. If the money supply is expanded when unemployment is high and there is much unused industrial capacity, then the result may be little or no inflation. If, however, increases in the money supply occur when the economy is fully employed, then the main result is likely to be inflation.

The effect of a rise in the money supply on the price level is depicted graphically on an aggregate supply and demand diagram in Figure 14–10. The curved shape of aggregate supply curve *SS* reflects the assumptions that output rises with little inflation when the economy is depressed, while prices rise with little gain in output when the economy is near full employment.

In the example we have been using, the Fed's actions raise the money supply by $40 billion, and this increases aggregate demand (through the multiplier) by $250 billion. We enter this in Figure 14–10 as a horizontal shift of $250 billion in the aggregate demand curve, from D_0D_0 to D_1D_1. The diagram shows that this expansionary monetary policy raises the economy's equilibrium from

Figure 14–10
THE INFLATIONARY
EFFECTS OF
EXPANSIONARY
MONETARY POLICY
Raising the money supply
normally causes inflation.
When expansionary monetary
policy causes the aggregate
demand curve to shift
outward from D_0D_0 to D_1D_1,
the economy's equilibrium
shifts from point E to point B.
Real output expands (in this
case by $200 billion), but
prices also rise (in this case
by 3 percent).

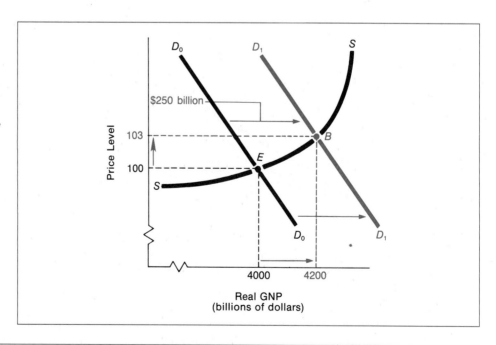

point E to point B — the price level therefore rises from 100 to 103, or 3 percent. The diagram also shows that real GNP rises by only $200 billion, which is less than the $250 billion stimulus to aggregate demand. The reason, as we know from earlier chapters, is that rising prices stifle demand.

By taking account of the effect of an increase in the money supply on the price level, we have completed our story about the role of monetary policy in the Keynesian model. We can thus expand our schematic diagram of monetary policy as follows:

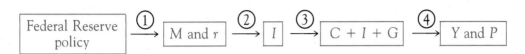

The last link now recognizes that *both* output *and* prices normally are affected by changes in the money supply.

Application: Why the Aggregate Demand Curve Slopes Downward

This analysis of the effect of money on the price level puts us in a better position to understand why higher prices reduce aggregate quantity demanded; that is, why the aggregate demand curve slopes downward. In earlier chapters, we explained this phenomenon by observing that rising prices reduce the purchasing power of certain assets held by consumers, especially money and government bonds, and that this in turn retards consumption spending. There is nothing wrong with this analysis. But higher prices have a much more important effect on aggregate demand through a channel that we are now in a position to understand.

Money is demanded primarily to conduct transactions and, as we have noted in this chapter, a rise in the *average money cost* of each transaction — as a result of a rise in the price level — will increase the quantity of money demanded. This means that when expansionary policy of any kind pushes the price level up, more money will be demanded at any given interest rate.

But, if the supply of money is *not* increased, an increase in the quantity of money demanded at any given interest rate must force the cost of borrowing money — the rate of interest — to rise. As we know, increases in interest rates reduce investment and, hence, reduce aggregate demand. This, then, is the main reason why the economy's aggregate demand curve has a negative slope, meaning that aggregate quantity demanded is lower when prices are higher. In sum:

At higher price levels, the quantity of money demanded is greater. Given a fixed supply schedule, therefore, a higher price level must lead to a higher interest rate. Since high interest rates discourage investment, aggregate quantity demanded is lower when the price level is higher. That is, the aggregate demand curve slopes downward to the right.

From Models to Policy Debates

You will no doubt be relieved to hear that we have now developed just about all the technical apparatus we need to analyze stabilization policy. To be sure, you will encounter many graphs in the next few chapters. But most of them are repeats of diagrams with which you are already familiar. Our attention now turns from *building* models to *using* models to understand important policy issues. The next three chapters take up a trio of important and controversial policy debates that surface regularly in the newspapers: the Keynesian–monetarist debate over stabilization policy (Chapter 15), the Reagan-era debate over the government budget deficit (Chapter 16), and the controversy over the tradeoff between inflation and unemployment (Chapter 17).

Summary

1. A central bank is a bank for banks.

2. The Federal Reserve System is America's central bank. There are 12 Federal Reserve banks, but most of the power is held by the Board of Governors in Washington and by the Federal Open Market Committee.

3. The Federal Reserve is independent of the rest of the government. There is controversy over whether this independence is a good idea, and a number of reforms have been suggested in recent years that would make the Fed more accountable to the president or to Congress.

4. The Fed has three major weapons for control of the money supply: open-market operations, reserve requirements, and its lending policy to the banks.

5. By lowering or raising reserve requirements, the Fed makes it possible for each dollar of reserves to support more or fewer dollars of deposits. Thus, lowering or raising the reserve ratio is one way to increase or decrease the money supply.

6. But the Fed does not do this very often. More typically, it raises the money supply by purchasing government securities in the open market. The Fed's payments to the banks for such purchases provide banks with new reserves and, hence, lead to a larger money supply. Conversely, open market sales of securities take reserves from the banks and lead to a smaller money supply.

7. When the Fed buys bonds, bond prices rise and interest rates fall. When the Fed sells bonds, bond prices fall and interest rates rise.

8. The Fed can also increase the money supply by allowing banks to borrow more reserves, perhaps by reducing the interest rate it charges on such loans. Alternatively, by discouraging borrowing, it can make the money supply contract.

9. None of these weapons, however, gives the Fed perfect control over the money supply in the short run, because it cannot predict perfectly how far the process of deposit creation or destruction will go.

10. The money supply schedule shows that more money is supplied at higher interest rates because, as interest rates rise, banks find it more profitable to expand their loans and deposits. This schedule can be shifted by Federal Reserve policy.

11. The money demand schedule shows that less money is demanded at higher interest rates because interest is the opportunity cost of holding money. This schedule shifts when output or the price level changes.

12. The equilibrium money stock (M) and the equilibrium rate of interest (r) are determined by the intersection of the money supply and money demand schedules.

13. Federal Reserve policy can shift this equilibrium. Expansionary policies cause M to rise and r to fall. Contractionary policies reduce M and increase r.

14. Investment spending (I), including business investment and investment in new homes, is sensitive to interest rates (r). Specifically, I is lower when r is higher.

15. This fact explains how monetary policy works in the Keynesian model. Raising the money supply (M) leads to lower r; the lower interest rates stimulate more investment spending; and this investment stimulus, via the multiplier, then raises aggregate demand.

16. However, prices are likely to rise as output rises. The amount of inflation caused by increasing the money supply depends on the levels of unemployment and of capacity utilization. There will be much inflation when the economy is near full employment, but little inflation when there is a great deal of slack.

17. The main reason why the aggregate demand curve slopes downward is that higher prices increase the demand to hold money in order to finance transactions. Given the money supply, this pushes interest rates up; and this, in turn, discourages investment.

Concepts for Review

Central bank
Federal Reserve System
Federal Open Market Committee (FOMC)
Independence of the Fed
Reserve requirements
Open-market operations

Bond prices and interest rates
Contraction and expansion of the money supply
Federal Reserve lending to banks
Moral suasion
Supply of money

Demand for money
Opportunity cost
Equilibrium in the money market
Monetary policy
Why the aggregate demand curve slopes downward

Questions for Discussion

1. Why does a modern industrial economy need a central bank?

2. Do you think it is a good idea to have an independent central bank? Explain your reasons.

3. Suppose there is $60 billion of cash in existence, and that half of it is held in bank vaults as *required* reserves (that is, banks hold no *excess* reserves). How large will the money supply be if the required reserve ratio is $16\frac{2}{3}$ percent? 20 percent? 25 percent?

4. Show the balance sheet changes that would take place if the Federal Reserve Bank of San Francisco purchased an office building from the Bank of America for a price of $100 million. Compare this to the effect of an open-market purchase of securities shown in Table 14–1. What do you conclude?

5. Suppose that the Fed purchases $8 million worth of government bonds from David Rockefeller, who banks at the Chase Manhattan Bank of New York. Show the effects on the balance sheets of the Fed, the Chase Manhattan Bank, and David Rockefeller. (*Hint:* What will Rockefeller do with the $8 million check he receives from the Fed?) Does it make any difference if the Fed buys bonds from a bank or from an individual?

6. Why would the Fed's control over the money supply be tighter under a system of 100 percent reserves?

7. Explain why the quantity of money supplied normally is higher and the quantity of money demanded normally is lower at higher interest rates.

8. What steps can the Fed take if it wants to drive the interest rate down? Illustrate on a diagram.

9. Explain why both business investments and purchases of new homes are expected to decline when interest rates rise.

10. Explain what a $40 billion increase in the money supply will do to real GNP under the following assumptions:
    a. Each $20 billion increase in the money supply reduces the rate of interest by 1 percentage point.
    b. Each 1 percentage point decline in interest rates stimulates $30 billion of new investment spending.
    c. The expenditure multiplier is 2.5.
    d. There is so much unemployment that prices do not rise noticeably when demand increases.

11. Explain how your answer to Question 10 would differ if each of the assumptions were changed. Specifically, what sorts of changes in the assumptions would make monetary policy very weak?

12. Use graphs like Figures 14–5 and 14–7 to explain why the aggregate demand curve has a negative slope.

13. (More difficult) Consider an economy in which government purchases and taxes are both zero, the consumption function is:

$$C = 100 + 0.8\,Y,$$

and investment spending (I) depends on the rate of interest (r) in the following way:

$$I = 500 - 800\,r.$$

Find the equilibrium GNP if the Fed makes the rate of interest (a) 5 percent ($r = 0.05$), (b) 10 percent, (c) zero.

15

The Keynesian–Monetarist Debate

The love of money is the root of all evil.

THE NEW TESTAMENT

Lack of money is the root of all evil.

GEORGE BERNARD SHAW

Up to now our discussion of stabilization policy has been almost entirely objective and technical. In seeking to understand how the national economy works and how government policies affect it, we have mostly ignored the intense economic and political controversies that surround the actual conduct of stabilization policy. Chapters 15 through 17 are about precisely these issues. The present chapter derives its name from the fact that the protagonists in several of these debates are groups of economists that the news media have dubbed *Keynesians* and *monetarists*.

We begin the chapter by explaining the monetarist view of how money affects the economy. Although the monetarist and Keynesian theories seem to be two contradictory views of how monetary and fiscal policy work, we will see that the conflict is more apparent than real. In fact, the disagreement is akin to hearing a Briton say, "Yes," and a Frenchman say, "Oui." The uninitiated hear two different languages, but knowledgeable listeners understand that they mean the same thing.

However, while one major objective of this chapter is to show that the differences between the two theories are greatly exaggerated, there *are* significant differences between the two schools of thought — not outright contradictions but differences in emphasis. These differences occupy the rest of the chapter. We shall see that monetarists and Keynesians disagree over the nature of aggregate supply, over the relative importance of monetary and fiscal policy, over whether the Federal Reserve should try to control the money stock or interest rates, and, indeed, over whether the government should try to conduct any stabilization policy at all. Since economists' abilities to forecast the future is critical to the success or failure of stabilization efforts, considerable time is spent in this chapter on the techniques and accuracy of economic forecasting.

Velocity and the Quantity Theory of Money

We saw in the last chapter how money influences real output and the price level in the Keynesian model. But there is another way to look at these matters, using a model that is much older than the Keynesian model and yet is at the heart of modern critiques of Keynesian economics. This model is known as the

quantity theory of money, and it is easy to understand once we have introduced one new concept — *velocity*.

We learned in Chapter 13 that because barter is so cumbersome, virtually all economic transactions in advanced economies are conducted by the use of money. This means that if there are, say, $4500 billion worth of transactions in the economy during a particular year, and there is an average money stock of $900 billion during that year, then each dollar of money must get used an average of five times during the year (since 5 × $900 billion = $4500 billion).

The number 5 in this example is called the **velocity of circulation,** or just **velocity** for short, because it indicates the speed at which money circulates. For example, a particular dollar bill might be used to buy a haircut in January; the barber might use it to buy a sweater in March; the storekeeper might then use it to pay for gasoline in May; the gas station owner could pay it out to the painter who paints his house in October; and the painter might spend it on a Christmas present in December. This would mean that the dollar was used five times during the year. If it were used only four times during the year, its velocity would be only 4, and so on. Similarly, a $20 bill circulating with a velocity of 8 would be the monetary instrument used to finance $160 worth of transactions in that year.

No one has data on all the transactions in the economy. To make velocity an operational concept, we must settle on a precise definition of transactions that we can actually measure. The most popular choice is gross national product in current dollars (nominal GNP), even though it ignores many transactions which use money — such as sales of existing assets. If we accept nominal GNP as a measure of the money value of transactions, we are lead to a concrete definition of velocity as the ratio of nominal GNP to the number of dollars in the money stock. Since nominal GNP is the product of real GNP times the price level, we can write this definition in symbols as:

$$\text{Velocity} = \frac{\text{Value of transactions}}{\text{Money Stock}} = \frac{\text{Nominal GNP}}{M} = \frac{P \times Y}{M}.$$

By multiplying both sides of the equation by M, we arrive at an identity called the **equation of exchange** that relates the money supply and nominal GNP:

$$\text{Money supply} \times \text{Velocity} = \text{Nominal GNP}.$$

Alternatively, stated in symbols, we have:

$$M \times V = P \times Y.$$

Here we have quite an obvious link between the stock of money, M, and the nominal value of the nation's output. But it is only a matter of arithmetic, not of economics. For example, it does not imply that the Fed can raise nominal GNP by increasing M. Why not? Because V might simultaneously fall by enough to prevent M × V from rising. That is, if there were more dollar bills in circulation than before, but each bill changed hands more slowly, total spending would not necessarily rise. Thus:

The *quantity theory of money* transforms the equation of exchange from an accounting identity into an economic model by assuming that changes in velocity are so minor that velocity can be taken to be virtually constant.

Velocity indicates the number of times per year that an "average dollar" is spent on goods and services. It is the ratio of nominal GNP to the number of dollars in the money stock. That is:

$$\text{Velocity} = \frac{\text{Nominal GNP}}{\text{Money stock}}$$

The **equation of exchange** states that the money value of GNP transactions must be equal to the product of the average stock of money times velocity. That is:

$$M \times V = P \times Y.$$

You can see that if V never changed, the equation of exchange would be a marvelously simple model of the determination of nominal GNP—far simpler than the Keynesian model. To see this, we need only to turn the equation of exchange around to read,

$$P \times Y = V \times M.$$

This equation says, for example, that if the Federal Reserve wants to increase nominal GNP by 12.7 percent, it need only raise the money supply by 12.7 percent. In such a simple world, economists could use the equation of exchange to *predict* nominal GNP simply by predicting the quantity of money. And policymakers could *control* nominal GNP simply by controlling the money supply.

In the real world things are not so simple because velocity is not a fixed number. But this does not necessarily destroy the usefulness of the quantity theory. We explained in Chapter 1 why all economic models make assumptions that are at least mildly unrealistic—without such assumptions they would not be models at all, just tedious descriptions of reality. The question is really whether the assumption of constant velocity is a useful abstraction from annoying detail or a gross distortion of facts.

Figure 15–1 sheds some light on this question by showing the behavior of velocity since 1929. You will undoubtedly notice a downward trend in the graph from 1929 until 1946, an upward trend until 1981, and a downward movement in recent years. Clearly, *velocity is not constant over long periods of time*. Closer examination of monthly or quarterly data reveals some rather substantial fluctuations of velocity about its trend. Such fluctuations have led most economists to the conclusion that *velocity is not constant in the short run either*. Nor have predictions of nominal GNP based on the product of V times M fared very well. It seems, then, that the strict quantity theory of money is not an adequate model of aggregate demand.

Figure 15–1
VELOCITY OF
CIRCULATION,
1929–1986
During a period of American history of nearly 60 years, velocity fell from 3.5 in 1930 to about 2 in 1946, and then rose to almost 7 in 1981 before falling again. Clearly, velocity is not constant over long periods of time.
NOTE: This graph uses the M1 definition of money.

SOURCE: Constructed by the authors; data from Bureau of Economic Analysis and Federal Reserve Board.

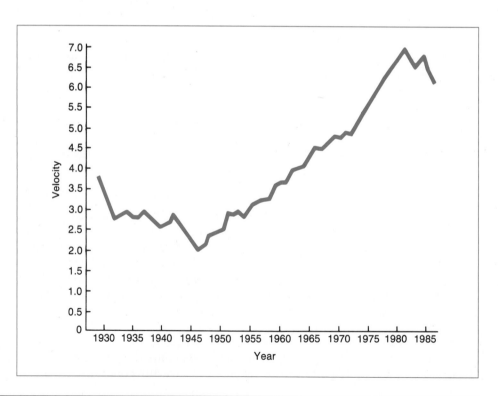

The Determinants of Velocity

Since it is abundantly clear that velocity is a variable, not a constant, we can use the equation of exchange as a model of GNP determination only by examining the determinants of velocity. What factors decide whether V will be 4 or 5 or 6; that is, whether a dollar will be used to buy goods and services four or five or six times a year?

Perhaps the principal factor is the *frequency with which paychecks are received*. This can best be explained through a numerical example. Consider a worker who earns $24,000 a year, paid to her in 12 monthly paychecks of $2000 each. Suppose that she spends the whole $2000 over the course of each month and maintains a minimum balance in the checking account of $500. Each payday her bank balance will shoot up to $2500 and then be gradually whittled down as she makes withdrawals to purchase goods and services. Finally, on the day before her next paycheck arrives, her checking balance will be just $500. Over the course of a typical month, then, her average checking account balance will be $1500 (halfway between $2500 and $500).

Now suppose her employer switches to a twice-a-month payroll. Her paychecks come twice as often, but are reduced to $1000 each. There is no reason for her rate of spending to change, but her *cash balances* will change. For now her checking balance will rise only to $1500 on payday (the $500 minimum balance plus the $1000 paycheck), and it will still be drawn down gradually to $500. Her average cash balance will therefore decline to $1000 (halfway between $1500 and $500). Why is this so? Because, with the next paycheck coming sooner than before, it is not necessary to keep as much cash in the bank in order to carry out a given quantity of transactions.

But what does this have to do with velocity? Notice that when she was on a monthly payroll, this worker's personal velocity was:

$$V = \frac{\text{Annual income}}{\text{Average cash balance}} = \frac{\$24,000}{\$1500} = 16.$$

When she switched to a semimonthly payroll, velocity rose to:

$$V = \frac{\text{Annual income}}{\text{Average cash balance}} = \frac{\$24,000}{\$1000} = 24.$$

The general lesson to be learned is that:

More frequent wage payments mean that people can conduct their transactions with lower average cash balances. Since they will want to hold less cash, money will circulate faster. In other words, velocity will rise.

A second factor influencing velocity is the *efficiency of the payments mechanism*, including how quickly checks clear banks, the use of credit cards, and other methods of transferring funds. It is easy to see how this works.

The example in the previous paragraph assumed that our worker holds her entire paycheck in the form of money until she uses it to make a purchase. But, given that many forms of money pay little or no interest, this method may not be the most rational behavior. If it is possible to convert interest-bearing assets into money on short notice and at low cost, a rational individual might use her paycheck to purchase such assets and then use credit cards for most purchases, making periodic transfers to her checking account as necessary. For the same amount of total transactions, then, she would require lower money balances. This means that money would circulate faster: Velocity would rise.

The incentive to limit cash holdings depends on the ease and speed with which it is possible to exchange money for other assets. This is what we mean by the "efficiency of the payments mechanism." As computerization has speeded up the bookkeeping procedures of banks, as financial innovations have made it possible to transfer funds rapidly between checking accounts and other assets, and as credit cards have come to be used instead of cash, the need to hold money balances has declined. By definition, then, velocity has risen.

Fortunately such basic changes in the payments mechanism usually take place only gradually, and thus often are easy to predict. But this is not always so. For example, a host of financial innovations in the 1970s and 1980s — some of which were mentioned in Chapter 13's discussion of the definitions of money — have given analysts fits in predicting velocity.

A third determinant of velocity is the *rate of interest*. The basic motive for economizing on money holdings is that most money (at least M1) pays little or no interest, while many alternative stores of value pay higher rates. The higher these alternative rates of interest, the greater the incentive to economize on holding money. Therefore, as interest rates rise, people want to hold less money. So the existing stock of money circulates faster, and velocity rises.

It is this factor that most directly undercuts the usefulness of the quantity theory of money as a guide for monetary policy. For in the last chapter we learned that expansionary monetary policy, which increases M, normally also decreases the interest rate. But if interest rates fall, other things being equal, velocity (V) will also fall. Thus, *when the Fed raises the money supply (M), the product* M × V *may go up by a smaller percentage than does* M *itself*.

One component of the interest rate is worth singling out for special attention: *the expected rate of inflation*. We explained in Chapter 6 why an "inflation premium" equal to the expected inflation rate often gets built into market interest rates.[1] Thus, in many instances, high inflation is the principal cause of high nominal interest rates. High rates of inflation, which erode the purchasing power of money, therefore lead both individuals and businesses to hold as little money as they can get by on — actions that increase velocity. To summarize this discussion of the determinants of velocity:

Velocity is not a strict constant but depends on such things as the frequency of payments, the efficiency of the financial system, the rate of interest, and the rate of inflation. Only by studying these determinants of velocity can we hope to predict the level of nominal GNP from knowledge of the money supply.

Monetarism: The Quantity Theory Modernized

The foregoing does not mean, however, that the equation of exchange cannot be a useful framework within which to organize macroeconomic analysis. Under the right circumstances, it can be. And during the past 30 years or so a group of economists called *monetarists* has convincingly demonstrated that this is so.

Monetarists recognize that velocity is not a constant. But they stress that it is fairly *predictable* — certainly in the long run and probably also in the short

[1] If you need review, turn back to pages 104–105.

run. This leads them to the conclusion that the best way to study economic activity is to start with the *equation of exchange:* $M \times V = P \times Y$. From here, careful study of the determinants of M (which we provided in the previous two chapters) and of V (which we just completed) can be used to *predict* the behavior of nominal GNP. Similarly, given an understanding of movements in V, control over the money supply gives the Fed *control* over nominal GNP.

These are the central tenets of **monetarism**. When something happens in the economy, monetarists ask two questions:

Monetarism is a mode of analysis that uses the equation of exchange to organize and analyze macroeconomic data.

1. What does this event do to the stock of money?

2. What does this event do to velocity?

From the answers, they assert that they can predict the path of nominal GNP.

By comparing the monetarist approach with the Keynesian approach that we described in the previous chapter, we can put both doctrines into perspective and understand the limitations of each. As we mentioned earlier, they differ more in style than in substance. Keynesians divide economic knowledge into three neat compartments—marked "*C*," "*I*," and "*G*"—and unite them all with the equilibrium condition that $C + I + G = Y$. In Keynesian analysis, money affects the economy by first affecting interest rates.

Monetarists, on the other hand, organize their knowledge into two alternative boxes—labeled "*M*" and "*V*"—and then use a simple identity that says $M \times V = P \times Y$ to bring this knowledge to bear in predicting aggregate demand. In the monetarist model, the role of money in the national economy is not necessarily limited to working through interest rates.

The bit of arithmetic that multiplies M and V to get $P \times Y$ is neither more nor less profound than the one that adds up C and I and G to get Y. And certainly both identities are correct. The only substantive difference is that the monetarist equation leads to a prediction of *nominal* GNP, that is, the demand for goods and services measured in money terms, while the Keynesian equation leads to a prediction of *real* GNP, that is, the demand for goods and services measured in dollars of constant purchasing power.

Why, then, do we not simply mesh the two theories—using the monetarist approach to study nominal GNP and the Keynesian approach to study real GNP? It seems that by doing so we could use the separate analyses of real and nominal GNP to obtain a prediction of the future behavior of the price level, which, of course, is the source of any difference in behavior between real and nominal GNP.

The reason that this appealing procedure will not work helps point out the major limitation of each theory. *Taken by itself, either theory is incomplete*. Each gives us a picture of the *demand* side of the economy without saying anything about the *supply* side. To try to predict both the price level and real output solely from these demand-oriented models would be like trying to predict the price of peanuts by studying only the behavior of consumers and ignoring that of farmers. It just will not work. In terms of our earlier aggregate supply and demand analysis:

Both the monetarist and Keynesian analyses are ways of studying the *aggregate demand curve*. In neither case is it possible to learn anything about both output and the price level without also studying the *aggregate supply curve*.

Economists thus are forced to choose between two alternative ways of predicting aggregate demand. Those who choose the monetarist route will use velocity and the money supply to study the demand for *nominal* GNP, and then turn to the supply side to estimate how any predicted change in nominal income gets apportioned between changes in production and changes in prices. The schematic diagram on page 284, with its emphasis on interest rates, plays little role in the monetarist analysis of the transmission mechanism for monetary policy.

On the other hand, an economist working with the Keynesian $C + I + G$ approach will start by using the schematic diagram on page 284 to predict how monetary policy affects the demand for *real* GNP. Then he will turn to the aggregate supply curve to estimate the inflationary consequences of this real demand.

Which approach works better? There is no generally correct answer for all economies in all periods of time. Therefore, it is not surprising that some economists prefer one approach while others favor the alternative. However, velocity has behaved in an erratic, and to some extent inexplicable, manner in the U.S. during the 1980s—which has led many economists to abandon monetarism.

Reconciling the Keynesian and Monetarist Views

We have already come a long way toward reconciling the Keynesian and monetarist views of how the economy operates. Keynesian analysis lends itself naturally to the study of fiscal policy, since G is a part of $C + I + G$. But we learned in the previous chapter that Keynesian economics also provides a powerful and important role for monetary policy: An increase in the money supply reduces interest rates, which, in turn, stimulates the demand for investment.

Monetarist analysis provides an obvious and direct route by which monetary policy influences both output and prices. But can the monetarist approach also handle fiscal policy? It can, because fiscal policy has an important effect on the rate of interest. And it is not hard to understand how this effect operates.

Let's see what happens to real output and the price level following, say, a rise in government purchases of goods and services. We learned in Chapter 12 that both real GNP (Y) and the price level (P) rise. But Chapter 14's analysis of the demand for money taught us that rising Y and P push the demand curve for money outward to the right. With no change in the supply curve for money, the rate of interest must rise. So expansionary fiscal policy raises interest rates.

If the government uses its spending and taxing weapons in the opposite direction, the same process works in reverse. Falling output and (possibly) falling prices shift the demand curve for money inward to the left. With a fixed supply curve for money, equilibrium in the money market leads to a lower interest rate. Thus:

Monetary policy is not the only type of policy that affects interest rates. Fiscal policy also affects interest rates. Specifically, increases in government spending or tax cuts normally push interest rates up, whereas restrictive fiscal policies normally pull interest rates down.

The fact that fiscal policy affects interest rates gives it a role in the monetarist model despite the fact that the equation of exchange, $M \times V = P \times Y$, does not include either government spending or taxation among its variables. Any fiscal policy that a Keynesian would call expansionary—higher spending, lower taxes, and so on—pushes up the rate of interest. And rising interest rates push up velocity because people want to hold less money when the interest they can earn on alternative assets increases. So it is through the V term in $M \times V$ that fiscal policy does its work in the monetarist framework. The equation of exchange, $M \times V = P \times Y$, then implies that nominal GNP must rise when, say, government spending increases—even if M is fixed. The given supply of money can finance more transactions when velocity is higher.

Conversely, restrictive fiscal policies like tax increases and expenditure cuts reduce the quantity of money demanded and lower interest rates. The consequent drop in velocity reduces income through the equation of exchange, because the money supply circulates more slowly.

The translation, then, seems to be complete. The Keynesian story about how fiscal policy works can be phrased in the monetarist dialect. And the monetarist tale about monetary policy can be told with a Keynesian accent. Furthermore, both modes of analysis help only to explain the mysteries of aggregate *demand* and must be supplemented by an analysis of aggregate *supply* to be complete. We must conclude, then, that:

The differences between Keynesians and monetarists have been grossly exaggerated by the news media. Indeed, when it comes to matters of basic economic theory, there are hardly any differences at all.

But this does not mean that Keynesians and monetarists must agree on everything any more than the fact that English prose can be translated into French implies that the English and the French always see eye to eye. There are important differences of emphasis and policy that we will take up in the remainder of this chapter.

Application: The Multiplier Formula Once Again

But first the fact that expansionary fiscal policy pushes up interest rates has another important consequence that we should mention. Recall that higher interest rates deter private investment spending. This means that when the government raises the G component of $C + I + G$, one of the side effects of its action will be to reduce the I component (by raising interest rates). Consequently, the sum $C + I + G$ will not rise as much as simple multiplier analysis might suggest. The fact that a surge in government demand (G) discourages some private demand (I) provides another reason why the oversimplified multiplier formula, $1/(1 - MPC)$, exaggerates the size of the multiplier:

Because any rise in G (or, for that matter, any autonomous rise in C or I) pushes interest rates higher, and hence deters some investment spending, the increase in the sum $C + I + G$ is smaller than what the oversimplified multiplier formula predicts.

Combining this observation with our previous analysis of the multiplier, we now have the following list of:

REASONS WHY THE OVERSIMPLIFIED MULTIPLIER FORMULA IS WRONG

1. It ignores price-level changes, which reduce the size of the multiplier.
2. It ignores the income tax, which reduces the size of the multiplier.
3. It ignores the rising interest rates that accompany any autonomous increase in spending, which also reduce the size of the multiplier.

Keynesians Versus Monetarists: Fiscal Versus Monetary Policy

Although the Keynesian and monetarist approaches can be thought of as two languages, it is well known that language can influence attitudes in many subtle ways. And it must be admitted that Keynesians and monetarists have not lacked things to argue about.

For years they conducted a spirited, and well publicized, debate over whether the government should rely mainly on fiscal policy or monetary policy to manage aggregate demand. While one would guess from reading the newspapers that this is the most important issue in the Keynesian–monetarist debate today, it is in fact the *least* important. It is unimportant because, as we have seen, each approach allows a role for each type of policy.

Nonetheless, the Keynesian language biases things subtly toward thinking that fiscal policy is central simply because fiscal actions influence aggregate demand so directly. G is, after all, a part of $C + I + G$. Monetarists, on the other hand, see a more indirect channel that works through interest rates and velocity, and they wonder if something might not go wrong along the way.

The roles are reversed in the analysis of monetary policy. To monetarists, the effect of the money supply on aggregate demand is simple — it follows directly from velocity through the equation of exchange: $M \times V = P \times Y$. While monetary policy also affects aggregate demand in the Keynesian model, the mechanisms are rather complex, and there is obviously room for a slip-up. Monetary expansion might not affect the interest rate much, or a fall in the interest rate might not induce much additional investment. Thus, some Keynesians have had their doubts when monetarists attributed great powers to monetary policy.

During the 1960s and early 1970s the choice between fiscal and monetary policy dominated the debate between the more partisan Keynesians and monetarists. Extreme monetarists claimed that fiscal policy was futile, while extreme Keynesians argued that monetary policy was useless. But during the 1970s, accumulating evidence made each extreme view seem less and less tenable. More and more monetarists had to admit that fiscal policy did affect output and prices, and more and more Keynesians had to concede the same to monetary policy. By 1976, two economists surveying the debate could write that "the shift has been so great that we wonder whether anything more than machismo and habit propels the controversy today." Nonetheless, echoes of this battle are occasionally heard today.

While Keynesians and monetarists agree that both fiscal and monetary policy have significant effects on aggregate demand, Keynesians tend to look more toward fiscal policy while monetarists tend to rely more on monetary policy.

This, however, is not a major difference.

Keynesians Versus Monetarists: Lags in Fiscal and Monetary Policy

More important than the issue of which type of policy is more *powerful* is the question of which type of medicine — fiscal or monetary — cures the patient more *quickly*. In our discussions of fiscal and monetary policy so far, we have ignored such subtle questions of timing and proceeded as if the authorities instantly noticed the need for stabilization policy, decided upon a course of action, and administered the appropriate medicine. In reality, each of these steps takes time.

First, delays in data collection and processing mean that the latest macroeconomic data pertain to the economy as it was a few months ago. Second, one of the prices of democracy is that the government often takes a distressingly long time to decide what should be done, to muster the necessary political support, and to put its decisions into effect. Finally, our $5 trillion economy is a bit like a sleeping elephant—it reacts rather sluggishly to moderate fiscal and monetary prods. As it turns out, these **lags in stabilization policy**, as they are called, play a pivotal role in the choice between fiscal and monetary policy. It is not hard to see why.

The main policy tool for manipulating consumer spending (C) is the personal income tax, and Chapter 8 documented why the fiscal policy planner can feel fairly secure that each $1 of tax reduction will lead to about 90 to 95 cents of additional spending *eventually*. But not all of this will happen at once.

First, consumers must learn about the tax change. Then more time may elapse before many consumers are convinced that the change is permanent. Finally, there is the simple force of habit: Households need time to adjust their spending habits when circumstances change. For all these reasons, consumers may increase their spending by only 30 to 50 cents for each $1 of additional income within the first few months after a tax cut. Only gradually, over a period of perhaps several years, will they raise their spending until they are finally consuming 90 to 95 cents of each additional dollar of income.

Lags are much longer for investment (I), which, while it also can be influenced by fiscal policy (tax incentives), provides the main vehicle by which monetary policy affects aggregate demand. Planning for capacity expansion in a large corporation is a long, drawn-out process. Ideas must be submitted and approved. Plans must be drawn up, funding acquired, orders for machinery or contracts for new construction placed. And most of this occurs *before* any appreciable amount of money is spent. Economists have found that much of the response of investment to changes in interest rates or tax provisions is delayed for several years.

The fact that C responds more quickly than I has important implications for the choice among alternative stabilization policies. The reason is that the most common varieties of fiscal policy affect aggregate demand either directly (G is a component of C + I + G) or work through consumption with a relatively short lag, while monetary policy has its major effects on investment. Therefore:

Conventional types of fiscal policy actions, such as changes in G or in personal taxes, probably affect aggregate demand much more promptly than do monetary policy actions.

Notice that the statement says nothing about which instrument is more *powerful*. It simply asserts that the fiscal weapon, whether it is stronger or weaker, acts more *quickly*. This important fact has been used to build a case that fiscal policy should bear the major burden of economic stabilization. But before you jump to such a conclusion, you should realize that the sorts of lags we have been discussing are not the only ones affecting the timing of stabilization policy.

Apart from these lags in expenditure, which are beyond the control of policymakers, there are further lags that are due to the behavior of the policymakers themselves! We are referring here to the delays that occur while the policymakers are studying the state of the economy, contemplating what steps they should take, and putting their decisions into effect. And here most observers believe that monetary policy has an important edge; that is:

Policy lags are normally much shorter for monetary policy than for fiscal policy.

The reasons are apparent. The Federal Open Market Committee (FOMC) meets frequently, so monetary policy decisions are made almost every month. And once the Fed decides on a course of action, it normally can be executed almost instantly by buying or selling bonds on the open market.

Contrast this with fiscal policy. Federal budgeting procedures operate on an annual budget cycle. Except in rare circumstances, *major* fiscal policy initiatives that affect spending can occur only at the time of the annual budget. Tax laws can be changed at any time, but the wheels of Congress grind slowly and it may take many months before Congress acts on a presidential request to change taxes. In sum, one has to be very optimistic to suppose that important fiscal policy actions can be taken on short notice.

Where does the combined effect of expenditure lags and policy lags leave us? With nothing conclusive, we are afraid. As the late Arthur Okun put it, the debate over whether the nation should rely only on monetary policy or only on fiscal policy is a bit like arguing whether a safe car is one with good headlights or one with good brakes. It is unwise to drive at night unless you have both.

Keynesians Versus Monetarists: Control of the Money Supply Versus Control of Interest Rates

But the Keynesian–monetarist battles did not end there. As the debate over fiscal versus monetary policy fizzled, the two schools of thought regrouped along new, and more productive, battle lines.

One major controversy that is very much alive today is over how the Federal Reserve should conduct monetary policy. Keynesians argue that the Fed should use open-market operations and its other tools to control the rate of interest (r) while monetarists insist that the Fed should concentrate on controlling the money supply (M). To appreciate the nature of the debate, we must first understand why the Fed cannot do both. That is, why can it not control both M and r at the same time?

Figure 15–2 will help us see the answer. It shows an initial equilibrium in the money market at point E, where money demand curve $M_0 D_0$ crosses money supply curve MS. Here the interest rate is $r = 9$ percent and the money stock is $M = \$550$ billion. Let us assume that these are the Fed's targets for M and r; it wants to keep the money supply and interest rates just where they are.

If the demand curve for money holds still, this is possible. But suppose the demand for money is not so obliging. Suppose, instead, that the demand curve shifts outward to the position indicated by $M_1 D_1$ in Figure 15–2. As we learned in the last chapter (see, especially, Figure 14–4 on page 280) this might happen because output increases or because prices rise. Or it might happen simply because people decide to hold more money. Whatever the reason, the Fed can no longer achieve both of its previous targets.

If the Fed takes no action, the outward shift in the demand curve will push up both the quantity of money (M) and the rate of interest (r). Figure 15–2 shows this graphically. If the demand curve for money shifts outward from $M_0 D_0$ to $M_1 D_1$ and there is no change in monetary policy (so that supply

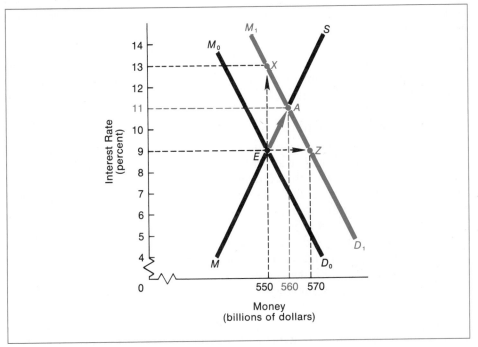

Figure 15–2

This diagram illustrates the dilemma facing the Fed when the demand schedule for money shifts. In this case, we suppose that it increases from $M_0 D_0$ to $M_1 D_1$. If the equilibrium at point E satisfied its goals both for the money supply ($550 billion) and for the rate of interest (9 percent), either one or both of these goals will have to be abandoned after the demand schedule shifts. Points X, A, and Z illustrate three of the many choices. At X, the Fed is keeping the money supply at $550 billion through contractionary policies, but at a cost of skyrocketing interest rates. At Z, the Fed is holding interest rates at 9 percent, but the required expansionary monetary policies raise the money supply to $570 billion. At A, the Fed is not adjusting its policy and is accepting an increase in both the money supply and the rate of interest.

schedule MS does not move), equilibrium moves from point E to point A. The money stock rises to $560 billion and the interest rate rises to 11 percent.

However, the supply of money is one of the major determinants of aggregate demand. Consequently, if the economy is already operating near full employment, the Fed might be unwilling to let M rise. In that case, it can use any of its contractionary weapons to prevent M from rising. But, if it does this, it will push r up even higher because, with no increase in the money supply, an even higher interest rate is necessary to keep quantity supplied and quantity demanded equal.

This is also shown in Figure 15–2. After the demand curve for money shifts, point E is unattainable. The Fed must choose from among the points on $M_1 D_1$, and point X is the point on this curve that keeps the money supply at $550 billion. If the supply curve is pushed inward so that it passes through point X, M will remain at $550 billion. However, the interest rate will skyrocket to 13 percent.

Alternatively, if the economy is operating at low levels of resource utilization, the Fed might decide that a rise in M is permissible, but that a rise in r is to be avoided. Why? Because, as we know, investment spending normally declines when interest rates rise. In this case, the Fed would be forced to engage in expansionary monetary policy to prevent the outward shift of the demand curve for money from pushing up r. The reason is that only by providing additional money can the Fed equate supply to the higher demand without a rise in interest rates. In terms of Figure 15–2, the interest rate can be held at 9 percent by shifting the supply curve outward to pass through point Z. But to do this, the Fed will have to push the money supply up to $570 billion. To summarize this discussion:

When the demand curve for money shifts outward, the Fed must tolerate a rise in interest rates, a rise in the money stock, or both. It simply does not have the weapons to control *both* the supply of money *and* the interest rate. If it tries to keep M steady, then r will rise sharply. Conversely, if it tries to stabilize r, then M will shoot up.

This explains why the Fed often finds it impossible to control both the money supply and the rate of interest. A shift in the demand schedule for money supply may make previously selected targets for M and r unattainable.

What Should the Fed Do?

Keynesians and monetarists have argued for years over what the Fed should do about this dilemma. Should it adhere rigidly to its target growth path for the money supply, regardless of the consequences for interest rates? Should it hold interest rates steady even if that causes wild gyrations in the money stock? Or is some middle ground more appropriate? Let us explore the issues before considering what has actually been done.

The main problem with rigid targets for the *supply* of money is that the *demand* for money does not cooperate by growing smoothly and predictably from month to month; instead it dances about quite a bit in the short run. This confronts the monetarist recommendation to control the money supply with two problems:

1. It is almost impossible to achieve. Since the volume of money in existence depends on *both* the demand *and* supply schedules, it would require exceptional dexterity on the part of the Fed to keep M on target in the face of significant fluctuations in demand for money.

2. For reasons that were just explained, rigid adherence to money-stock targets might lead to wide fluctuations in interest rates, which could create an unsettled atmosphere for business decisions.

By the same token, even more powerful objections can be raised against exclusive concentration on interest rate movements. Since increases in nominal GNP shift the demand schedule for money outward (as Figure 15–2 shows), a central bank determined to keep interest rates from rising would have to expand the money supply in response. Conversely, when GNP sagged, it would have to contract the money supply to keep rates from falling. Thus, interest rate *pegging* would make the money supply expand in boom times and contract in recessions—with potentially grave consequences for the stability of the economy. Ironically, this is precisely the sort of monetary behavior the Federal Reserve System was designed to prevent. Hence, if the Fed is to control interest rates, it had better formulate flexible targets, not fixed ones.

What Has the Fed Done?

In the early part of the postwar period, the predominant view held that the interest rate target was much the more important of the two. The rationale for this view was that gyrating interest rates would cause abrupt and unsettling changes in investment spending, and this in turn would make the whole economy fluctuate. In this view, stabilization of interest rates was the best way to stabilize GNP. If fluctuations in the money supply were required to keep interest rates on a steady course, that would be nothing to worry about. Consequently, the Fed looked mostly at interest rates.

In the 1960s, this prevailing view came under increasing attack by Professor Milton Friedman and other monetarists. They argued that the Fed's obsession with stabilization of interest rates actually *destabilized* the economy because it led to undue fluctuations in the money supply. The monetarist prescription was simple. The Fed should stop worrying about fluctuations in interest rates and make the money supply grow at a constant rate from month to month and year to year.

Monetarism made important inroads at the Fed during the inflationary 1970s. Early in the decade, the central bank began to keep much closer tabs on the money stock than it previously had. More important, a major change in the conduct of monetary policy was announced by then-Chairman Paul Volcker in October 1979. Henceforth, he asserted, the Fed would stick more closely to its target for money stock growth regardless of the implications for interest rates. Interest rates would go wherever the law of supply and demand took them.

According to our analysis, this change in policy should have led to wider fluctuations in interest rates. And it did. Unfortunately, the Fed ran into some bad luck. The ensuing three years were marked by unusually severe gyrations in the demand for money, so the ups and downs of interest rates were far more extreme than anyone had expected. Figure 15–3 gives an indication of just how volatile interest rates were between late 1979 and late 1982. Naturally, this erratic performance led to some heavy criticism of the Fed.

Then, in October 1982, Chairman Volcker announced that the Fed was temporarily abandoning its attempts to stick to a target growth path for the money supply. Although he did not say so, his announcement presumably meant that the Fed would once again pay more attention to interest rate targets. As you can see in Figure 15–3, interest rates have been much more stable — though certainly not constant — since the change in policy. Most observers think this is no coincidence.

Since late 1982, the Fed has distanced itself more and more from the monetarist position on control of the money supply. In early 1987, it actually stopped posting growth targets for M1. The central bank has essentially adopted the Keynesian position — though without saying so. In truth, it had little choice. The demand curve for money behaved so erratically and so

Figure 15–3
THE BEHAVIOR OF INTEREST RATES, 1979–1987
This chart traces interest rate movements from 1979 through 1987. Notice the extreme volatility of rates during the period from late 1979 to mid-1982 — the period in which the Fed was concentrating more on stabilizing the money supply. Since mid-1982, interest rates have been much less volatile.

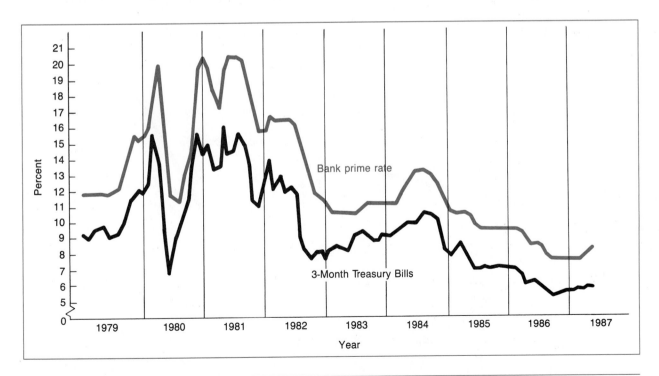

unpredictably between, say, 1981 and 1987 that stabilizing the money stock was probably impossible and certainly undesirable. Whether this situation will continue for the rest of the decade is anyone's guess.

Keynesians Versus Monetarists: The Aggregate Supply Curve

Another lively battleground in the Keynesian–monetarist debate today is over the shape of the economy's aggregate supply curve. As we have noted, either the Keynesian or the monetarist model must be supplemented by an aggregate supply curve if it is to tell us anything about output and prices. Most Keynesians tend to think of the aggregate supply curve as fairly flat in the short run, as in Figure 15–4(a), so that large increases in output can be achieved with little inflation. Monetarists, by contrast, envision the supply curve as steep, as in Figure 15–4(b), so that prices are very responsive to changes in output. The differences for public policy are substantial.

In the Keynesian view, expansionary fiscal or monetary policy that raises the aggregate demand curve can buy large gains in real GNP at little cost in terms of inflation. This is shown in Figure 15–5(a). Here, stimulation of demand raises the aggregate demand curve from $D_0 D_0$ to $D_1 D_1$ and moves the economy's equilibrium from point E to point A. There is a substantial rise in output ($400 billion) with only a pinch of inflation (1 percent).

Conversely, when the supply curve is flat, a restrictive stabilization policy is not a very effective way to cure inflation; instead, it serves mainly to reduce real output, as Figure 15–5(b) shows. Here, a leftward shift of the aggregate demand curve moves equilibrium from point E to point B, lowering real GNP by $400 billion but cutting the price level by merely 1 percent.

The monetarists see things differently. To them, the aggregate supply curve is so steep that expansionary fiscal or monetary policies are likely to cause a good deal of inflation without adding much to real GNP. [See

Figure 15–4
ALTERNATIVE VIEWS OF THE AGGREGATE SUPPLY CURVE
Keynesians tend to think of the economy's aggregate supply schedule as very flat, as in part (a), whereas monetarists tend to think of it as quite steep, as in part (b).

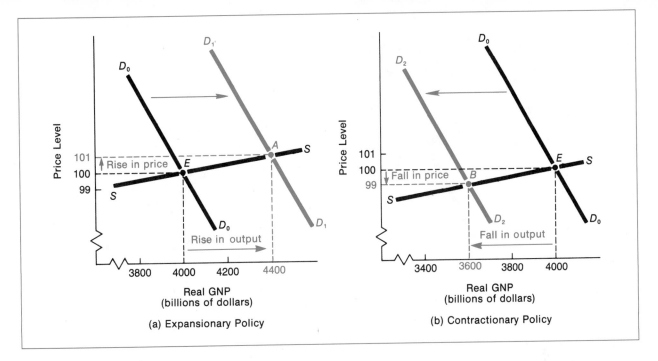

(a) Expansionary Policy

(b) Contractional Policy

Figure 15–6(a), where expansionary policies shift equilibrium from E to A.] Similarly, contractionary policies are effective ways of bringing down the price level without much sacrifice of output, as shown by the shift from E to B in Figure 15–6(b).

The resolution of this debate is of fundamental importance for the proper conduct of stabilization policy. If the Keynesian view is right, stabilization policy is much more effective at combating recession than inflation. If the monetarist view is correct, the reverse is true.

But why does the argument persist? Why cannot economists determine whether the aggregate supply curve is flat or steep, and stop arguing? The answer is that supply conditions in the real world are far more complicated than our simple diagrams suggest. Some industries may have flat supply curves while others have steep ones. For reasons explained in Chapter 11, supply curves shift over time. And, unlike many laboratory scientists, economists cannot perform the controlled experiments that would reveal the shape of the aggregate supply curve directly. Instead, they must use statistical inference to make educated guesses.

Although empirical research on aggregate supply is proceeding, our understanding of aggregate supply remains much less settled than our understanding of aggregate demand. Nevertheless, many economists believe that the dim outline of a consensus view has emerged. This view stresses that the steepness of the aggregate supply schedule depends on the degree of slack in the economy.

If industry has a great deal of spare capacity, then increases in demand will not call forth large price increases. Similarly, when many workers are unemployed, employment can rise without causing much acceleration in the rate at which wages are growing. In a word, the aggregate supply curve is quite flat. On the other hand, when businesses are producing near capacity and unemployment is near the frictional level, greater demand for goods will induce firms to raise prices; and greater demand for labor will push wages up faster. In brief, the aggregate supply schedule will be steep.

Figure 15–5
STABILIZATION POLICY WITH A FLAT AGGREGATE SUPPLY CURVE: THE KEYNESIAN CASE
These two diagrams show that stabilization policy is much more effective as an antirecession policy than as an anti-inflation policy when the aggregate supply curve is flat. In part (a), monetary or fiscal policies push the aggregate demand curve outward from $D_0 D_0$ to $D_1 D_1$, causing equilibrium to shift from point E to point A. It can be seen that output rises substantially (from $4000 billion to $4400 billion), while prices rise only slightly (from 100 to 101, or 1 percent). So the policy is quite successful. In part (b), contractionary policies are used to combat inflation by pushing the aggregate demand curve inward from $D_0 D_0$ to $D_2 D_2$. Prices do fall slightly (from 100 to 99) as equilibrium shifts from point E to point B, but real output falls much more dramatically (from $4000 billion to $3600 billion); so the policy has had little success. Keynesians tend to believe in this case.

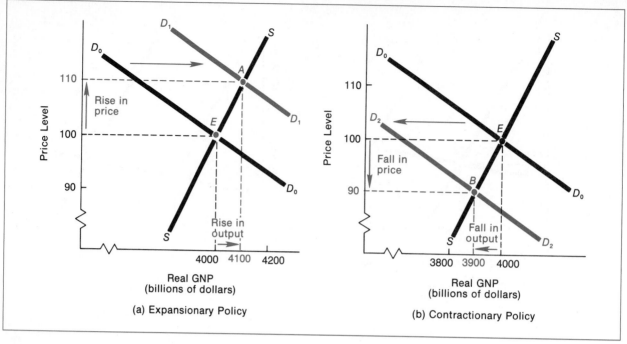

(a) Expansionary Policy

(b) Contractionary Policy

Figure 15–6

STABILIZATION POLICY WITH A STEEP AGGREGATE SUPPLY CURVE: THE MONETARIST CASE

These two diagrams show that stabilization policy is much more effective at fighting inflation than at fighting recession when the aggregate supply curve is steep. In part (a), expansionary policies that push aggregate demand outward from $D_0 D_0$ to $D_1 D_1$ raise output by only \$100 billion but push up prices by 10 percent as equilibrium moves from point E to point A. So demand management is not a good way to end a recession. In part (b), contractionary policies that pull aggregate demand inward to $D_2 D_2$ are successful in that they lower prices markedly (from 100 to 90, or about 10 percent) but reduce output only slightly (from \$4000 billion to \$3900 billion). Monetarists tend to believe in this case.

Figure 15–7 shows a version of the aggregate supply curve that embodies these ideas. It has the same general shape as most of the supply curves that we have used in this book. At low levels of GNP, like Y_1, it is nearly horizontal; then its slope starts to rise gradually until at very high levels of GNP, like Y_2, it becomes almost vertical. The implication is that any change in aggregate demand will have most of its effect on *output* when economic activity is slack (the Keynesian case) but on *prices* when the economy is operating near full employment (the monetarist case). In summary:

1. Keynesians believe that the aggregate supply curve is rather *flat* in many circumstances, especially when the economy is operating at low levels of resource utilization. They therefore stress the effects of demand management on output and belittle the effects on prices.

2. Monetarists believe that the aggregate supply curve is rather *steep* in many circumstances, especially when the economy has little slack. They therefore emphasize the effects of demand management on prices and belittle the effects on real output.

3. A middle-of-the-road view would hold that the Keynesian case is stronger when there is a great deal of unemployment, while the monetarist case is stronger when the economy is near full employment. Not all economists accept this middle-of-the-road view, but many do.

Keynesians Versus Monetarists: Should the Government Intervene?

We have yet to consider what may be the most fundamental and controversial issue of all: Is it likely that the government can conduct a successful stabilization policy? Or are its well-intentioned efforts likely to be harmful, so that it would be better to adhere to fixed rules?

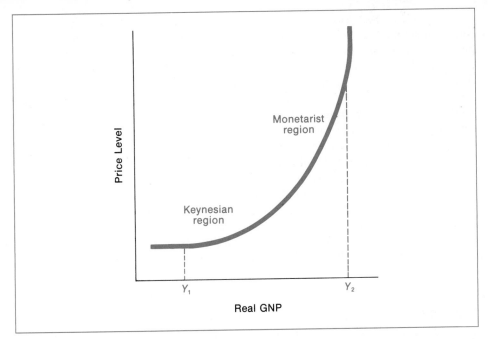

Figure 15–7
AN AGGREGATE SUPPLY CURVE WITH BOTH STEEP AND FLAT REGIONS
As this diagram suggests, either the Keynesians or the monetarists may be right under the appropriate circumstances. The Keynesian view of a flat supply curve is likely to be most accurate when there is much unemployment and unused capacity. The monetarist view of a steep supply curve is likely to be more accurate when there is full employment and high capacity utilization.

This controversy has raged for several decades now, with no end in sight. That Keynesians favor discretionary stabilization policy while monetarists favor noninterventionist rules is not surprising, given their political differences. As it happens, monetarists tend to be politically conservative while many Keynesians are liberal. So it is natural that Keynesians should be more intervention-minded and monetarists more inclined to keep the government's hands off the economy. But much more than political ideology propels the debate. We want to understand the economic issues.

Monetarists point to the lags and uncertainties that surround the operation of both fiscal and monetary policies—lags and uncertainties that we have stressed repeatedly in this and earlier chapters. Will the Fed's actions have the desired effects on the money supply? What will these actions do to interest rates? How will they affect spending, and how long will it take before the effects appear? Can fiscal policy actions be taken promptly? Will consumers view tax changes as temporary or permanent? How large is the expenditure multiplier? The list could go on and on.

Monetarists look at this formidable catalogue of difficulties, add a dash of skepticism about our ability to forecast the future state of the economy (see page 314), and conclude that stabilization policy is likely to do more harm than good. They advise both the fiscal and monetary authorities to pursue a passive policy rather than an active one—adhering to fixed rules that, while they will not iron out all the bumps in the economy's growth path, will at least keep it roughly on track in the long run.

Keynesians, though they admit that perfection is unattainable, are much *more optimistic* about the possibility of achieving a successful stabilization policy. And they are much *less optimistic* than the monetarists about how smoothly the economy would function in the absence of demand management. They therefore advocate discretionary increases in government spending (or decreases in taxes) and more rapid growth of the money supply when the economy has a recessionary gap. By this policy mix, they believe, government can keep the economy closer to its full-employment growth path.

Naturally, each side can point to evidence that buttresses its own view. Keynesians like to look back with pride at the tax cut of 1964 and the sustained period of economic growth that it helped usher in. They also point to the tax cut of 1975, which was enacted at just about the trough of a severe recession, the Federal Reserve's switch to easy money in 1982, and the accidentally Keynesian tax cuts of 1983 and 1984—all of which were helpful. Monetarists remind us of the government's refusal to curb what was obviously a situation of runaway demand during the 1966–1968 Vietnam buildup, its overexpansion of the economy in 1972, and the monetary overkill that helped bring on the sharp recessions of 1974–1975 and 1981–1982.

The historical record of fiscal and monetary policy is far from glorious. It shows that while there were many instances in which appropriate stabilization policy *could have been* helpful, the authorities instead either took inappropriate steps or did nothing at all. The question of whether the government should adopt passive rules or attempt an activist stabilization policy therefore merits a closer look. As we shall see, the lags in the effects of policy that we discussed earlier in this chapter play a pivotal role in the debate.

Lags and the Rules-Versus-Discretion Debate

The reason that lags lead to a fundamental difficulty for stabilization policy—a difficulty so formidable that it has led many economists to conclude that attempts to stabilize economic activity are likely to do more harm than good—can be explained best by reference to Figure 15–8. Here we chart the behavior of both actual and potential GNP over the course of a business cycle in a hypothetical economy in which no stabilization policy is attempted. At point A, the economy begins to slip into a recession and does not recover to full employment until point D. Then, between points D and E, it overshoots and is in an inflationary boom.

The case for stabilization policy runs like this. The recession is recognized to be a serious problem at point B, and appropriate actions are taken. These actions have their major effects around point C and therefore curb both the depth and the length of the recession.

Figure 15–8
A TYPICAL
BUSINESS CYCLE
This is a stylized representation of the relationship between actual and potential GNP during a typical business cycle. The imaginary economy slips into a recession at point A, bottoms out around point B, and is in a recovery period until point D. After point D, it enters an inflationary boom that lasts until point E.

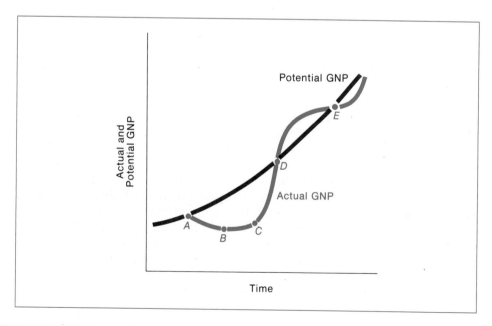

But suppose the lags are really much longer than this. Suppose, for example, that delays in taking action postpone policy initiatives until point C and that stimulative policies do not have their major effects until after point D. Then policy will be of little help during the recession and will actually do harm by overstimulating the economy during the ensuing boom. Thus:

In the presence of long lags, attempts at stabilizing the economy can actually succeed in destabilizing it.

Because of this, some economists, like Milton Friedman, have argued that we are better off letting the economy alone and relying on its natural self-corrective forces to cure recessions and inflations. Instead of embarking on periodic programs of monetary and fiscal stimulus or restraint, they advise policymakers to stick to fixed rules; that is, to rigid formulas that ignore current economic events.

Automatic Stabilizers

The rule most emphasized by monetarists is that the Fed keep the money supply growing at a constant rate. For fiscal policy, monetarists generally recommend that the government resist temptations to manage aggregate demand actively and rely instead on **automatic stabilizers**—features of the economy that reduce its sensitivity to shocks. Examples of automatic stabilizers are not hard to find in the federal budget. The personal income tax is the most obvious example.

The ability of the income tax to act as a shock absorber derives from the fact that it makes disposable income, and thus consumer spending, less sensitive to fluctuations in GNP. When GNP rises, disposable income (DI) rises also, but by less than the rise in GNP because part of the income is siphoned off by the U.S. Treasury. This helps limit the upward fluctuation in consumption spending. And when GNP falls, DI falls less sharply because part of the loss is absorbed by the Treasury rather than by consumers. So consumption does not drop as much as it otherwise might. Thus, as we noted in Chapter 12, income taxes lower the value of the multiplier. In truth, the unloved personal income tax is one of several modern institutions that help ensure us against a repeat performance of the Great Depression.

There are many other automatic stabilizers in our economy. For example, in Chapter 6 we studied the U.S. system of unemployment insurance. This serves as an automatic stabilizer in a similar way. When GNP begins to fall and people lose their jobs, unemployment benefits prevent the disposable incomes of the jobless from falling as much as their earnings. As a result, unemployed workers can maintain their spending, and consumption need not fluctuate as dramatically as employment.

And the list could continue. The basic principle is the same: Each of these automatic stabilizers, in one way or another, serves as a shock absorber, thereby lowering the multiplier. And each does so without the need for any decision-maker to take action. In a word, they work *automatically*.

An **automatic stabilizer** is any arrangement that automatically serves to support aggregate demand when it would otherwise sag and to hold down aggregate demand when it would otherwise surge ahead. In this way, an automatic stabilizer reduces the sensitivity of the economy to shifts in demand.

Stabilization Policy: Discretionary Measures or Fixed Rules?

Believers in fixed rules assert that we should forget about discretionary policy and rely solely on automatic stabilizers and the economy's natural, self-correcting mechanisms. Are they right? As usual, the answer depends on many factors.

How Fast Does the Economy's Self-Correcting Mechanism Work?

We stressed in Chapter 11 that the economy does have a self-correcting mechanism. If the economy can cure recessions and inflations quickly by itself, then the case for intervention is weak. For if such problems typically last only a short time, then lags in discretionary stabilization policy mean that the medicine will often have its major effects only after the disease is over. (In terms of Figure 15–8, this would be a case where point D comes very close to point A.)

While the more extreme advocates of rules argue that this is what indeed happens, most economists agree that the economy's self-correcting mechanism is slow and not terribly reliable, even when supplemented by the automatic stabilizers. On this count, then, a point is scored for the Keynesians and for discretionary policy.

How Long Are the Lags in Stabilization Policy?

As we explained, long lags before stabilization measures are adopted or take effect make it unlikely that policy can do much good, while short lags point in the other direction. Thus, advocates of fixed rules emphasize the length of lags while proponents of discretion discount them.

Who is really right depends on the circumstances. In the most optimistic scenario, fiscal policy actions are taken promptly, and the economy feels much of the stimulus from expansionary policy in less than a year after slipping into a recession. While far from an instant cure, such timely actions certainly would be felt soon enough to do some good. But, as we have seen, more pessimistic scenarios raise the possibility that policy may actually be destabilizing. History offers examples of both types of scenarios. No general conclusion can be drawn.

How Accurate Are Economic Forecasts?

One way to cut down the policy-making lag enormously is to have good economic forecasts. If we could see a recession coming a full year ahead of time (which we certainly *cannot* do), even a rather sluggish policy response would still be timely. (In terms of Figure 15–8, this would be a case where the recession is predicted well before point A.)

It therefore behooves us to take a look at the techniques that economists in universities, government agencies, and private businesses have developed over the years to assist them in predicting what the economy will do. There are a variety of techniques, none of them foolproof.

Techniques of Economic Forecasting

The Use of Econometric Models

An **econometric model** is a set of mathematical equations that embody the economist's model of the economy.

Among the most widely publicized forecasts are those generated by the use of **econometric models** of the economy. Put simply, an econometric model is merely a mathematical version of the models of macroeconomic activity that we have described in Parts 2–4. The difference is that the basic notions are cast in the form of mathematical equations rather than in diagrams. For example, our consumption function could have been expressed by the formula:

$$C = a + bDI,$$

where C is consumer spending and DI is disposable income, instead of by a graph.[2]

[2]This is nothing but the formula for a straight line with a slope of b and an intercept of a.

The builder of an econometric model takes equations like these and uses actual data to estimate the sizes of a and b. For example, statistical analysis may lead a forecaster to the conclusion that the correct magnitude of a in the previous formula is approximately 100 and that the most reasonable value of b is 0.8. Then the consumption function formula is:

$$C = 100 + 0.8\ DI.$$

This says that consumer spending is $100 (billion) plus 80 percent of disposable income. The economist can complete his model by adding a definition of disposable income as GNP minus tax receipts:

$$DI = Y - T,$$

and appending the fact that GNP is the sum of C, I, and G:

$$Y = C + I + G.$$

In this simple model, then, we have a total of three equations. If we hypothesize that government purchases, tax receipts, and investments are all unaffected by the relationships in the model, these three equations are just enough to determine the values of the three remaining variables: C, DI, and Y. These last three variables are called the model's *endogenous variables*, meaning that their values are determined *inside* the model. The remaining variables — G, T, and I — are called the model's *exogenous variables* because they must be provided from *outside* the model. With this nomenclature, it is easy to describe how the user of an econometric model forecasts the state of the economy:

An econometric forecaster uses a model to transform forecasts of the exogenous variables into corresponding forecasts of the endogenous variables.

Models actually used to forecast the behavior of the U.S. economy have hundreds of variables and equations. Because of their complexity, the only practical way to solve them for forecasts of all the endogenous variables is to use a high-speed computer. But making the forecasts accurate is another thing entirely because of the "garbage in, garbage out" problem: If you feed junk into a computer, that's exactly what comes out at the end. In the forecasting context, this "junk" can be either a bad set of predictions of the exogenous variables or an inaccurate set of equations. This is why model builders are constantly seeking to improve their equations. But they have yet to achieve anything like perfection. And, even if they did, their forecasts would still not be infallible because there is a certain amount of unavoidable randomness in macroeconomic behavior. After all, we are dealing with literally millions of individuals and business firms, and events essentially outside our control can sometimes exert a profound influence on our economy. (Example: Political turmoil in Iran in 1979 helped bring on the stagflation of 1979–1980.) So forecasts of the exogenous variables are bound to be wide of the mark at times.

Leading Indicators

A second forecasting method, pioneered at the National Bureau of Economic Research, exploits observed historical timing relationships through the use of certain **leading indicators** that have in the past given advance warning of economic events.

A **leading indicator** is a variable that, experience has shown, normally turns down before recessions start and turns up before expansions begin.

For example, the stock market is a leading indicator because stock market downturns normally begin several months before downturns in industrial production. Why does this happen? Does the decline in the stock market cause economic downturns by reducing consumer spending? Or are both the stock market and industrial production just reacting to some other influence, with the stock market's reaction coming sooner? Certainly these are fascinating questions. But the answers may not be crucial to a forecaster *if* the stock market continues to be as good a leading indicator for industrial production in the future as it has been in the past. In that event, we will be able to make use of the observed relationship between stock prices and industrial production for forecasting even if we do not entirely understand its origins.

As it turns out, however, excessive reliance on any single leading indicator produces an unimpressive forecasting record. An obvious solution is to look at many indicators. But once we start to do this, we will often receive conflicting signals. If one indicator is rising rapidly while another is falling, what are we to do?

One way to resolve this conflict is to form an average of several leading indicators. For example, every month the news media report the latest reading on the Commerce Department's composite index, which is a weighted average of 11 of their leading indicators. (See the boxed insert on page 313.) Figure 15–9 compares the behavior of this index with movements in real GNP. As you can see, the agreement is usually quite good. The leading indicators occasionally call for a recession that never comes (as in 1966), and occasionally they give clear early warning signals of a downturn (as in 1973 and 1979). But often movements of the leading indicators are followed so closely by movements in real gross national product that the advance warning they provide comes too late to be of much use to policymakers.

Figure 15–9
REAL GNP AND THE LEADING INDICATORS, 1950–1986
This diagram compares the path of the leading indicators (in blue) with that of real GNP (in black). The scales have been adjusted to make the two series comparable. It can be seen that the leading indicators sometimes give advance warning of a turning point in economic activity (for example, in 1979) but often give false signals of turning points that never occur (for example, 1966).
SOURCE: *Business Conditions Digest* and *Survey of Current Business*.

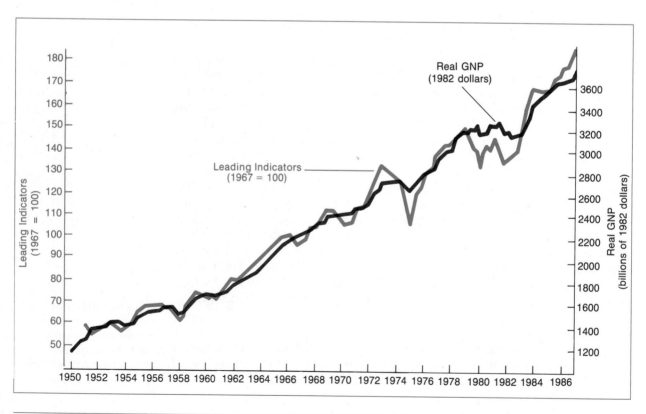

Survey Data

A third method of forecasting utilizes periodic surveys of the intentions of business and consumers. The Bureau of Economic Analysis of the Commerce Department and the Securities and Exchange Commission regularly ask firms how much money they plan to invest in factories and machinery over the next 3 to 12 months. These data are published in the financial press and are widely used by economists in industry, government, and academia. The Survey Research Center of the University of Michigan regularly conducts a survey of how consumers feel about both their personal finances and the general state of the economy. Some economists have found that this information on consumer sentiment helps improve forecasts of consumer spending.

Judgmental Forecasts

This term is used to describe the forecasts of those desperate (and probably prudent!) forecasters who refuse to rely on any one method, but look instead at every scrap of evidence they can get their hands on. They study the outputs of the econometric models; they watch the leading indicators; and they scrutinize the findings of surveys. At times, it seems, they even gaze at the stars. In any case, judgmental forecasters distill all this information in their heads and somehow arrive at a forecast of GNP and other key variables. How do they go about it? An outside observer can never really tell, since the very nature of judgmental forecasting precludes the existence of a formula that can be written down or described.

The Index of Leading Indicators

The Commerce Department's widely publicized index of leading indicators is a weighted average of 11 economic variables that have been shown to be useful in predicting business fluctuations. While the components of the index sometimes change, at the time of this writing they are:

1. Stock market prices.
2. The money supply (M2), expressed in 1982 dollars.
3. The change in business inventories.
4. The percentage change in sensitive commodity prices.
5. The average work week of production workers in manufacturing.
6. Initial claims for unemployment insurance. (This component enters negatively since rising unemployment is a sign of bad times.)
7. Building permits for private housing.
8. New orders for consumer goods and materials, in 1982 dollars.
9. Contracts and orders for investment goods, in 1982 dollars.
10. Change in business and consumer borrowing.
11. Vendor performance (an indicator of how easy or difficult it is for firms to get deliveries of inputs).

The Accuracy of Economic Forecasts

Which method wins the prize for the most accurate forecasts? First, no technique is clearly superior all the time. If it were, no one would do it any other way. Second, because econometric forecasters use surveys, lead–lag patterns, and judgment in forming their predictions of exogenous variables, and since judgmental forecasters watch the models closely, a clean comparison is impossible. In recent years, however, it seems that the most accurate forecasts have been derived by judgmental adjustment of forecasts from econometric models.

How accurate are economic forecasts? That depends both on the variable being forecast (consumption, for example, is easier than investment) and on the time period (for example, 1982–1983 were tough years for forecasters; 1984–1986 were much easier).

To give a rough idea of magnitudes, forecasts of the inflation rate for the year ahead typically err by plus or minus 1 to $1\frac{1}{2}$ percentage points. But in a rough year for forecasters, errors of 3 percentage points or so are common. Forecasts of real GNP for the coming year made during the 1970s and 1980s have also typically erred by between 1 and $1\frac{1}{2}$ percent. The biggest errors by far came in recession years like 1974–1975 and 1981–1982. Apart from these periods, errors of under 1 percent have been typical.[3]

Is this record good enough? That depends on what the forecasts are used for. It is certainly not good enough to support so-called fine tuning, that is, attempts to keep the economy always within a hair's breadth of full employment. But it probably is good enough if our interest in using discretionary stabilization policy is to close persistent and sizable gaps between actual and potential GNP.

Other Dimensions of the Rules-Versus-Discretion Debate

While lags and forecasting play major roles in the debate between advocates of rules and advocates of discretionary policy, these are not the only battlegrounds.

The Size of Government

One bogus argument that is nonetheless often heard is that an activist fiscal policy must inevitably lead to a growing public sector. Since proponents of fixed rules tend also to be opponents of big government, they view this as undesirable. Of course, others think that a large public sector is just what society needs. This argument, however, is completely beside the point because, as we pointed out in Chapter 12 (page 233): *One's opinion about the proper size of government should have nothing to do with one's view on stabilization policy.* For example, the Reagan administration promoted an extremely *activist* policy to spur the economy by *shrinking* the size of the public sector through reductions in taxes.

Uncertainties Caused by Government Policy

Advocates of rules are on stronger ground when they argue that frequent changes in tax laws, government spending programs, or monetary conditions make it difficult for firms and consumers to formulate and carry out rational plans. They argue that by adhering to fixed rules, which are known to businesses and consumers, the authorities can provide a more stable environment for the private sector.

---

[3]Victor Zarnowitz, "The Record and Improvability of Economic Forecasting," National Bureau of Economic Research, Working Paper No. 2099, December 1986.

While no one disputes that a more stable environment is better for private planning, supporters of discretionary policy point out the difference between stability in the government budget (or in Federal Reserve operations) and stability in the economy. The goal of stabilization policy is to help *prevent* gyrations in the pace of economic activity by *causing* timely gyrations in the government budget (or in monetary policy). Which atmosphere is better for business, they ask, one in which fiscal and monetary rules keep things peaceful on Capitol Hill and at the Federal Reserve System while recessions and inflations rack the economy, or one in which policy instruments are changed abruptly on occasion but the economy grows more steadily? They think that the answer is self-evident.

A Political Business Cycle?

A final argument used by advocates of rules is political rather than economic in nature. Fiscal policy, they note, is decided upon by elected politicians: the president and members of Congress. When elections are on the horizon (and for members of the House of Representatives they *always* are), these men and women are likely to be at least as concerned with keeping their offices as with doing what is right for the economy. This leaves fiscal policy subject to all sorts of "political manipulations," meaning that inappropriate actions may be taken to attain short-run political goals. In a system of purely automatic stabilization, its proponents argue, a rule of law would replace the rule of men, and this peril would be eliminated.

There is certainly a *possibility* that politicians could deliberately *cause* economic instability to help their own reelection. And some observers of these "political business cycles" have claimed that several American presidents have taken full advantage of the opportunity. Furthermore, even if there is no insidious intent, politicians may take the wrong actions for perfectly honorable reasons. Decisions in the political arena are never clear-cut, and it certainly is easy to find examples of grievous errors in the history of U.S. fiscal policy.

So, taken as a whole, the political argument against discretionary policy seems to have a great deal of merit. But what are we to do about it? It is foolhardy to believe that fiscal and monetary decisions could or should be made by a group of objective and nonpartisan technicians. Steering the economy is not like steering a rocket to the moon. Because policy actions that help on the employment front normally do harm on the inflation front, and vice versa, the "correct" policy action is almost always an inherently political matter. In a democracy, if we take such decisions out of the hands of elected officials, in whose hands shall we put them?

This harsh fact may seem worrisome in view of the possibilities for political chicanery, but it should not bother us any more (or any less!) than similar maneuvering in other areas of policy making. After all, the same thing applies to international relations, issues of national defense, formulation and enforcement of the law, and so on. Politicians make all these decisions for us, subject only to sporadic accountability at election times. Is there really any reason why economic decisions should be different?

Conclusion: What Should Be Done?

Where do all these considerations leave us? On balance, is it better to conduct discretionary policy as best we can, knowing full well that we will never do it perfectly? Or is it wiser to rely on fixed rules and the automatic stabilizers?

In weighing the pros and cons that we have discussed in this chapter, one's basic view of the economy is central. Some economists believe that the economy, if left unmanaged, would generate a series of ups and downs that are hard to predict, but that it would correct each of them by itself in a relatively short period of time. They conclude that, because of long lags and poor forecasts, our ability to anticipate whether the economy will be heading up or down by the time policy actions have their effects is quite limited. And so they are led to advocate fixed rules.

Other economists liken the economy to a giant glacier with a great deal of inertia. This means that if we observe an inflationary or recessionary gap today, it is likely still to be there a year or two from now because the self-correcting mechanism works so slowly. In such a world, accurate forecasting is not imperative, even if policy lags are long. If we base policy on a forecast of a $100 billion gap between actual and potential GNP a year from now, and the gap turns out to be only $50 billion, then we still will have done the right thing despite the horrible forecast. Holders of this view of the economy, then, are likely to advocate the use of discretionary policy.

While there is no consensus on this issue either among economists or among politicians, a prudent view might be that:

The case for active discretionary policy is strong when the economy has a serious deficiency or excess of aggregate demand. However, advocates of fixed rules are right that it is unwise to try to iron out every little wiggle in the growth path of GNP.

But the decision cannot be made solely on economic grounds. Political judgments enter as well. In the end:

The question of whether the government should take an active hand in managing the economy, which is one of the main bones of contention between Keynesians and monetarists today, is as much a matter of ideology as of economics. Liberals have always looked to government activism to solve social problems, while conservatives have consistently pointed out that many efforts of government fail despite the best intentions.

Table 15–1

MAJOR ISSUES IN THE KEYNESIAN–MONETARIST DEBATE

ISSUE	MONETARIST POSITION	KEYNESIAN POSITION	POSSIBLE COMPROMISE POSITION
View of velocity	stable	unstable	stable in some time periods; unstable in others
Best way to conduct monetary policy	control the money supply	control interest rates	watch both variables without rigidly controlling either
View of aggregate supply curve	steep	flat	flat in slack economy, steep near full employment
Should government try to stabilize the economy?	no	yes	only when gap between actual and potential GNP is large

Since no one can decide whether liberal or conservative political attitudes are the "correct" ones on purely objective criteria, the rules-versus-discretion debate is likely to go on for quite some time.

For your convenience, Table 15–1 summarizes the major issues in the Keynesian–monetarist debate and indicates a possible compromise position for each.

Summary

1. Monetarist and Keynesian analyses are two different ways of studying the determination of aggregate demand. Neither is a complete theory of the behavior of the economy until aggregate supply is brought into the picture.

2. Velocity (V) is the ratio of nominal GNP to the stock of money (M). It indicates how quickly money circulates, that is, how many times money changes hands in a year.

3. Among the determinants of velocity is the rate of interest (r). At higher interest rates, people find it less attractive to hold money because most money pays no interest. Thus, when r rises, money circulates faster, and V rises.

4. Monetarism is a type of analysis that focuses attention on velocity and the money supply (M). Though monetarists realize that V is not constant, they believe that it is predictable enough to make it a useful tool for policy analysis and forecasting.

5. Because it raises output and prices, and hence increases the demand for money, expansionary fiscal policy pushes interest rates higher. This is how a monetarist explains the effect of fiscal policy. Because higher r leads to higher velocity, it leads to a higher product $M \times V$ even if M is unchanged.

6. While Keynesian and monetarist theory both lead us to expect that fiscal *and* monetary policy can each affect aggregate demand, Keynesians tend to believe more in the effectiveness of fiscal policy while monetarists tend to believe more in the effectiveness of monetary policy.

7. Because fiscal policy actions affect aggregate demand either directly through G or indirectly through C, the expenditure lags between fiscal actions and their effects on aggregate demand are probably fairly short. By contrast, monetary policy operates mainly on investment, I, which responds slowly to changes in interest rates.

8. However, the policy-making lag normally is much longer for fiscal policy than for monetary policy. Hence, when the two lags are combined, it is not clear which type of policy acts more quickly.

9. Because it cannot control the demand curve for money, the Federal Reserve cannot control *both* M and r. If the demand for money changes, the Fed must decide whether it wants to hold M steady, hold r steady, or adopt some compromise position.

10. Monetarists emphasize the importance of stabilizing the growth path of the money supply while Keynesians put more emphasis on keeping interest rates on target.

11. In practice, the Fed has changed its views on this issue several times. For decades, it attached primary importance to interest rates. Between 1979 and 1982, it stressed its commitment to stable growth of the money supply. But since 1982 it has deemphasized money growth.

12. Keynesians believe that the aggregate supply curve is flat in the short run. This means that increases in aggregate demand will add much to the nation's real output and add little to the price level. Stabilization policy thus has much to recommend it as an antirecession device, but it has little power to combat inflation.

13. Monetarists believe that the aggregate supply curve is steep. This means that increases in aggregate demand increase real output rather little and succeed mostly in pushing up prices. Consequently, while stabilization policy can do much to fight inflation, it is not a very effective way to cure unemployment.

14. The Keynesian view probably is most applicable to an economy with much unemployment, while the monetarist view applies best to an economy producing near capacity levels.

15. When there are long lags in the operation of fiscal and monetary policy, it becomes possible that attempts to stabilize economic activity may actually succeed in destabilizing it.

16. The U.S. economy has a number of automatic stabilizers which make it less vulnerable to shocks than it would otherwise be. Among these are the personal income tax and unemployment benefits.

17. Economic forecasts are made by econometric models, by exploiting leading indicators, and by judgment. Each method seems to play a role in arriving at good forecasts; but no method is foolproof, and economic forecasts are not as accurate as many people would like them to be.

18. Many monetarists believe that our imperfect knowledge of the channels through which stabilization policy works, and the long lags involved, make it unlikely that discretionary stabilization

policy can succeed.

19. Keynesians recognize these difficulties but do not believe they are as serious as monetarists think. On the other hand, Keynesians place much less faith in the economy's ability to cure recessions and inflations on its own. They therefore think that discretionary policy is not only advisable, but essential.

20. Stabilizing the economy by fiscal policy does *not* imply a tendency toward "big government."

Concepts for Review

Quantity theory of money	Effect of fiscal policy on interest rates	Econometric models
Velocity	Lags in stabilization policy	Leading indicators
Equation of exchange	Shape of the aggregate supply curve	Judgmental forecasts
Effect of interest rate on velocity	Controlling M versus controlling r	Rules versus discretionary policy
Monetarism	Automatic stabilizers	

Questions for Discussion

1. How much money (including cash and checking account balances) do you typically have at any particular moment? Divide this into your total income over the past 12 months to obtain your own personal velocity. Are you typical of the nation as a whole?

2. In the next column you will find data on nominal gross national product and the money supply (M1 definition) for selected years. Compute velocity in each year. Can you see any trend?

YEAR	NOMINAL GNP (billions of dollars)	MONEY SUPPLY (M1) (billions of dollars) (end of year)
1966	772	174
1976	1783	310
1986	4235	731

3. Use the concept of opportunity cost to explain why velocity is higher at higher interest rates.

4. How does monetarism differ from the quantity theory of money? How does it differ from Keynesian analysis?

5. Distinguish between the expenditure lag and the policy lag in stabilization policy. Does monetary or fiscal policy have the shorter expenditure lag? What about the policy lag?

6. Explain why their contrasting views on the shape of the aggregate supply curve lead Keynesians to argue much more strongly for stabilization policies to fight unemployment while monetarists argue much more strongly for stabilization policies to fight inflation.

7. Use a supply and demand diagram similar to Figure 15–2 (page 301) to show the choices open to the Fed following an unexpected decline in the demand for money. If the Fed is following a monetarist policy rule, what will happen to the rate of interest?

8. Explain why lags make it possible for policy actions intended to stabilize the economy actually to destabilize it instead.

9. Name some automatic stabilizers and explain how and what they "stabilize."

10. Which of the following events would strengthen the argument for the use of discretionary policy, and which would strengthen the argument for rules?
   a. Structural changes make the economy's self-correcting mechanism faster and more reliable than before.
   b. New statistical methods are found that improve the accuracy of economic forecasts.
   c. A Republican president is elected when there is an overwhelmingly Democratic Congress. The Congress and the president differ sharply on what should be done about the national economy.

11. (More difficult) Use the following hypothetical econometric model of the U.S. economy to obtain a forecast of the GNP in 1991:

$$C = 100 + 0.8DI$$
$$DI = Y - T$$
$$Y = C + I + G.$$

T, I, and G are the exogenous variables, and their forecasted values for 1991 are $T = 1000$, $I = 700$, $G = 800$.

12. (More difficult) Answer the same question for an economy described by:

$$C = 18 + 0.9DI$$
$$DI = Y - T$$
$$T = 10 + \tfrac{1}{3}Y$$
$$Y = C + I + G$$

with forecasts $I = 200$, $G = 880$.

16

Budget Deficits and the National Debt: Fact and Fiction

Blessed are the young, for they shall inherit the national debt.

HERBERT HOOVER

There is a belief that runs deep in the American character that there is something inherently wrong with government budget deficits. Opinion polls consistently show that the public wants smaller deficits. Yet under President Reagan, surely the most conservative president in decades, the federal government has run the largest deficits in history.

How could such a thing have happened under a president who says he believes in balanced budgets? What kinds of problems do large deficits pose for the economy, both now and in the future? Should we strive to balance the budget? And if so, by what means? These are the questions to be addressed in this chapter.

We begin by explaining why the principles of stabilization policy that we have learned in Part 4 do not lead to the conclusion that the budget should always be balanced. (Neither, however, do they lead to the conclusion that it should always have a massive deficit!) Next we try to get the facts straight. We discuss the size of the national debt, and how it grew so large. Then we turn to the federal budget deficit and why some economists claim that it is badly mismeasured.

With the facts established, we examine the alleged ill effects of deficits. We shall see that many popular arguments against deficits are based on faulty reasoning. But not all are. In particular, we devote special attention to two potentially severe costs of deficit spending: It can be inflationary, and it can "crowd out" private investment spending.

The Partisan Political Debate over the Budget Deficit

Never has the budget deficit been more in the news than during the presidency of Ronald Reagan. Whatever else you think of President Reagan's controversial economic policies, it is clear that they have brought with them the biggest budget deficits in our history—a fact that has not been lost on his political foes. The endless debate between the president's supporters and opponents over the causes and consequences of large deficits, and how best to reduce them, has probably been the major public policy issue of the 1980s.

Critics of the president blame the large deficits directly on the tax cuts of 1981–1984, complain that the president has done little to stem the tide of red ink, argue that the deficit is a ticking time bomb that will ultimately cause grievous harm to the economy, and advocate higher taxes and lower defense spending to close the budget gap.

The president and his supporters have replied that the problem was inherited from the past, blamed Congress for refusing to trim civilian spending, and, at times, argued that a big deficit is the lesser evil if the alternatives are raising taxes or reducing military spending. They have frequently suggested that economic growth will eventually bring in enough tax revenue to balance the budget—provided that civilian spending is reduced enough.

The result of this partisan political struggle has been stalemate and continuing high deficits. The president has blocked tax increases and has bitterly, though unsuccessfully, opposed cutbacks in planned defense spending. Congress has slashed the president's requests for military spending, but turned down most of the large civilian budget cuts he has proposed. While the two sides argued over budget priorities, the deficit ballooned from $128 billion in fiscal year 1982 to $221 billion in fiscal 1986.

In this chapter, we will try to put politics aside and concentrate on the economic issues. You should keep in mind, however, that political, not economic, considerations have kept the deficit as large as it is for so long.

Should the Budget Be Balanced?

In December 1985, Congress passed a law—which it has since ignored—mandating a balanced budget by 1991. (See the boxed insert on page 340.) Is a zero deficit an appropriate target for fiscal policy?

The basic principles that we discussed in Chapter 12 certainly do not lead to the conclusion that the budget should always be balanced. Instead, they point to the desirability of budget *deficits* when private demand (C + I) is too weak and budget *surpluses* when private demand is too strong. The budget should be balanced, according to these principles, only when C + I + G under a balanced-budget policy approximately equals full-employment levels of output. This may sometimes occur, but it will not necessarily be the norm.

In brief, according to this approach, the focus of fiscal policy should be on *balancing aggregate supply and aggregate demand*, not on balancing the budget. The reason why a balanced budget may not achieve a balanced economy is clear from our earlier discussion of stabilization policy.

Consider the fiscal policy that would be followed if we lived under an effective balanced-budget law. If private spending sagged for some reason, the multiplier would pull GNP down. Since personal and corporate tax receipts fall sharply when GNP declines, the budget would start to swing into the red. That would require either lower spending or higher taxes—exactly the opposite of the appropriate policy response. Thus:

Attempts to balance the budget—as done, say, by President Hoover during the Great Depression—will prolong and deepen recessions.

Budget balancing can also lead to inappropriate fiscal policy when an economic boom begins. If rising tax receipts induce a budget-balancing government to spend more or cut taxes, fiscal policy will "boom the boom"—with disastrous inflationary consequences. Fortunately, believers in budget balancing usually are not alarmed by surpluses.

Actually, the issue is even more complicated than we have indicated so far. As we learned in Chapter 14, fiscal policy is not the only way the government affects aggregate demand. The government also influences aggregate demand through its monetary policy. For this reason:

The appropriate fiscal policy depends, among other things, on the stance of monetary policy. While a balanced budget may be appropriate under one monetary policy, a deficit or a surplus may be appropriate under another monetary policy.

An example will illustrate the point. Suppose Congress and the president believe that the aggregate supply and demand curves will intersect approximately at full employment if the budget is balanced. That would seem to call for a balanced-budget fiscal policy.

But suppose now that monetary policy turns contractionary, pulling the aggregate demand curve inward to the left as shown in Figure 16–1 and creating a recessionary gap. If the fiscal authorities wish to restore real GNP to its original level, they must shift the aggregate demand curve back out to its original position, $D_0 D_0$. To do this, they must either raise spending or cut taxes, thereby opening up a budget deficit. Thus the change in monetary policy changes the appropriate fiscal policy from a balanced budget to a deficit.

By the same token, a given target for aggregate demand implies that any change in fiscal policy will alter the appropriate monetary policy. For example, suppose Figure 16–1 indicates the effects of reducing the budget deficit by cutting government spending. If the authorities do not want real GNP to fall, monetary policy must become sufficiently more expansionary to restore the aggregate demand curve to $D_0 D_0$. As we shall see at the end of the chapter, it is precisely this outcome — a smaller budget deficit balanced by easier money — that many economists have sought in the 1980s.

So a balanced budget should not be expected to be the norm. Then how do we know whether any particular deficit is too large or too small? That is a good question, but a complicated one. Before attempting an answer, we should get some facts straight.

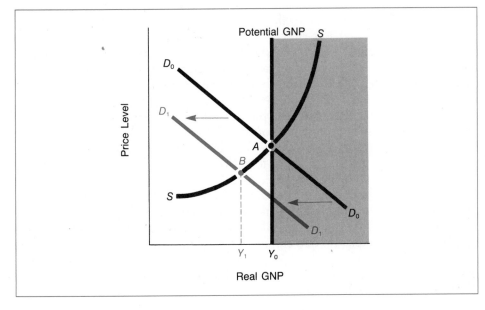

Figure 16–1
THE INTERACTION OF MONETARY AND FISCAL POLICY
Both monetary and fiscal policy affect the aggregate demand curve. If monetary policy turns contractionary, the aggregate demand curve shifts inward from $D_0 D_0$ to $D_1 D_1$ thereby lowering real GNP from Y_0 to Y_1. If Y_0 represented full employment with a balanced budget, then Y_1 represents a recessionary gap. Expansionary fiscal policy can push the aggregate demand curve back to $D_0 D_0$ but only by opening up a deficit in the government budget.

Deficits and Debt: Some Terminology

First some critical terminology. The title of this chapter contains two terms that seem similar but mean different things: *budget deficits* and the *national debt*. We must learn to distinguish between the two.

The **budget deficit** is the amount by which the government's expenditures exceed its receipts during some specified period of time, usually one year. For example, during fiscal year 1987, the government raised about $860 billion in taxes but spent almost $1020 billion, leaving a deficit of almost $160 billion.[1]

The **national debt,** also called the public debt, is the total value of the government's indebtedness at a moment in time. Thus, for example, the national debt at the end of fiscal year 1987 was over $2.3 trillion.

The two concepts — debt and deficits — are closely related because the government accumulates *debt* by running *deficits* or reduces its debt by running surpluses. The relationship between the debt and the deficit can be explained by a simple analogy. As you run water into a bathtub ("run a deficit"), the accumulated volume of water in the tub ("the debt") rises. Alternatively, if you let water out of the tub ("run a surplus"), the level of the water ("the debt") falls. Analogously, budget deficits raise the national debt while budget surpluses lower it.

Having made this distinction, let us look first at the size and nature of the accumulated public debt, and then at the annual budget deficit.

The **budget deficit** is the amount by which the government's expenditures exceed its receipts during a specified period of time, usually one year.

The **national debt** is the federal government's total indebtedness at a moment in time. It is the result of previous deficits.

Some Facts About the National Debt

How large a public debt do we have? How did we get it? Who owns it? Is it really growing rapidly?

To begin with the simplest question, the public debt is enormous. At the end of 1987 it amounted to over $2400 billion, almost $10,000 for every man, woman, and child in America. But nearly 30 percent of this outstanding debt was owned by agencies of the U.S. government — in other words, one branch of the government owed it to another. If we deduct this portion, the net national debt was only about $1750 billion, or around $7200 per person.

Furthermore, when we compare the debt with the gross national product — the volume of goods and services our economy produces in a year — it does not seem so large after all. With a GNP of over $4500 billion in late 1987, the net debt was just over one-third of the nation's yearly income. By contrast, many families who own homes owe *several years'* worth of income to the bank that granted them a mortgage. Many U.S. corporations also owe their bondholders much more than one-third of a year's sales.

But before these analogies make you feel too comfortable, we should point out that simple analogies between public and private debt are almost always misleading. A family with a large mortgage debt also owns a home with a value that presumably exceeds the mortgage. A solvent business firm has assets (factories, machinery, inventories, and so forth) that far exceed its outstanding bonds in value.

Is the same thing true of the U.S. government? Nobody knows for sure. How much is the White House worth? Or the national parks? And what about military bases, both here and abroad? Simply because these government assets are *not* sold on markets, no one can tell whether the federal government's assets

[1] *Reminder:* The fiscal year of the U.S. government ends on September 30. Thus, fiscal year 1987 ran from October 1, 1986, to September 30, 1987.

exceed its debt or not. One heroic attempt to measure the value of the government's assets concluded that they far exceeded the national debt in 1980, but fell slightly below the national debt by 1984.[2]

Figure 16–2 charts the irregular increase in the national debt from 1915 to 1987. You will notice that most of the debt was acquired either during wars, especially World War II, or during the last 15 years, which included two severe recessions. When economic activity falls, tax receipts of the federal government fall because of the heavy reliance on income taxes. As we shall see later, the

[2]Robert Eisner, *How Real Is the Federal Deficit?* (New York: Free Press, 1986), page 29.

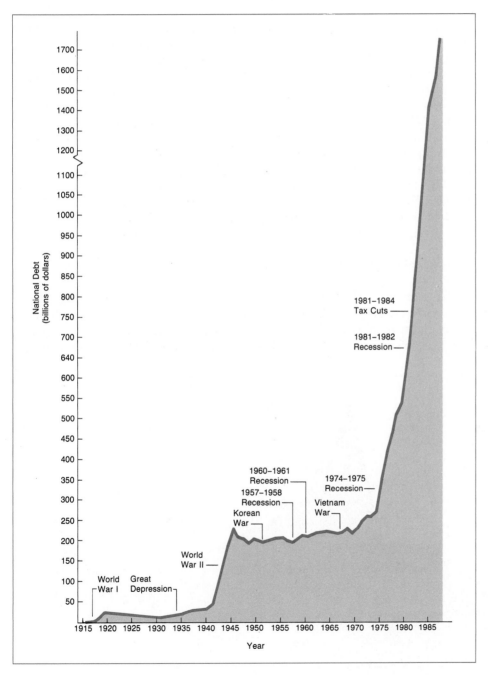

Figure 16–2
THE U.S. NATIONAL DEBT, 1915–1987
This graph charts the behavior of the public debt in the United States, after subtracting out the portion of the debt that is held by government agencies. It is clear that, until very recently, just about all the increases could be accounted for by wars and recessions. Few people realize that the public debt was about the same in 1972 as it was in 1945. But since 1972, it has grown rapidly.
SOURCE: Constructed by the authors from data in *Historical Statistics of the United States* and *Economic Report of the President*.

cause of the debt is quite germane to the question of whether or not the debt is a burden. So it is important to remember that:

Until about 1983, almost all of the U.S. national debt stemmed from financing wars and from losses of tax revenues that accompany recessions.

The growth of the debt looks enormous in Figure 16–2. But we must remember that everything grows in a growing economy. Private debt and business debt have grown rapidly since 1915; it would be surprising indeed if the public debt had not grown also. The fact is that federal debt grew less rapidly than private debt during most of the period since World War II—until about 1980.

In addition, the debt is measured in dollars and, in an inflationary environment, the amount of purchasing power that each dollar represents declines each year. A good way to put the numbers into perspective is to express each year's national debt as a fraction of that year's nominal GNP. This is done in Figure 16–3. Here, in contrast to Figure 16–2, we see an unmistakable downward trend from the dizzying heights of World War II until the recession of 1974–1975. In 1945, the national debt was the equivalent of 13 months' national income. By 1974 this figure had been whittled down to two months. If we use this as a crude indicator of the nation's ability to "pay off" its debt, then the burden of the debt was certainly far smaller in 1974 than it was in 1945.

This last graph also calls attention to a fact which is less comforting. During the 1980s, the national debt has been growing faster than GNP. By 1987, the debt was up to five months' GNP and growing. This is one reason why many economists are alarmed by continued large budget deficits.

Interpreting the Budget Deficit

We have observed that the federal government's annual budget deficits have been extremely large under President Reagan. As Figure 16–4 shows, the budget deficit for fiscal year 1981, which was affected in only minor ways by President Reagan's policies, was $79 billion. By fiscal year 1983, it had grown to a

Figure 16–3
RATIO OF PUBLIC DEBT TO GROSS NATIONAL PRODUCT
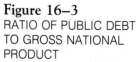
This graph takes the data from Figure 16–2 and divides each year's debt by the gross national product of that year. We can see that the debt grew relative to GNP during the two world wars, during the Great Depression, during the 1974–1975 recession, and since 1981. Other than that, the debt generally has fallen relative to GNP.

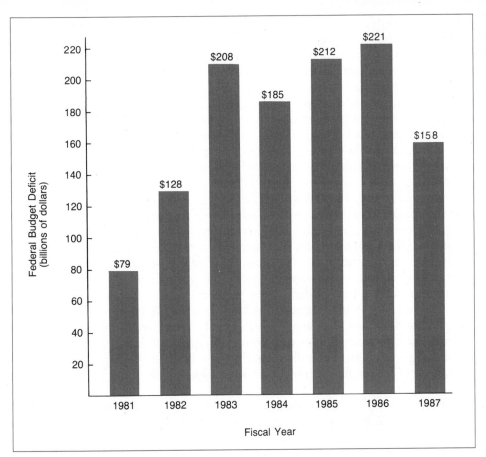

Figure 16–4
OFFICIAL BUDGET
DEFICITS SINCE 1981
(FISCAL YEARS)
The budget deficit almost
tripled between fiscal year
1981 and fiscal year 1983
and did not change much
between then and fiscal
1986. In fiscal year 1987, it
declined somewhat.

record $208 billion. But that record was broken in 1985 and again in 1986. The budget for fiscal year 1987, which ended just before this book went to press, still showed a deficit of $158 billion.

These are enormous, even mind-boggling, numbers. But what do they mean? In interpreting them, we begin with what many economists view as a serious measurement problem—the way interest payments are treated in the government's budget.

Inflation Accounting for Interest Payments*

At first blush, government accountants seem to treat interest payments in the sensible way: Every dollar of interest that the government pays on the national debt is counted as a dollar of spending—just like military purchases, social security payments, and the salaries of members of Congress. This seems the natural thing to do. But it ignores the fundamental distinction between real and nominal interest rates that we emphasized in Chapter 6. To review the analysis:

The **real interest rate** tells us the amount of purchasing power the borrower turns over to the lender for the privilege of borrowing. To this we must add an **inflation premium**, equal to the expected rate of inflation, to get the **nominal interest rate**. The inflation premium compensates the lender for the expected erosion of the purchasing power of her money and is best thought of as repayment of principal.[3]

---

*This section contains difficult material which may be skipped in shorter courses.
[3]If you need review, see pages 104–105.

The last sentence has important implications for the government budget—implications that few people understand.

From an economic point of view, the portion of the government's interest payments that merely compensates lenders for inflation should be counted as *repayment of principal*, not as *interest expense*, because it simply returns to lenders the purchasing power of their original loans. Only the *real* interest that the government pays should be treated as an expenditure item in the budget. Breaking up interest payments in this way is called **inflation accounting**. Since even sophisticated people have trouble understanding inflation accounting, it is worth taking the time to illustrate the idea with an analogy and a simple example.

Imagine that you lend a roommate, who is enrolled in a chemistry course, a bar of radium that you happen to own. Your roommate uses the radioactive bar in experiments for a year, and then returns it to you. Has your loan been repaid in full? Certainly not. Because of the natural process of radioactive decay, the bar you get back is smaller than the bar you originally loaned. To pay you back in full, your roommate must give you enough additional radium to replace the portion that eroded during the year.

The analogy to interest rates on loans is straightforward: Inflation erodes the purchasing power of money just as radioactive decay erodes radium. So, in figuring out how many dollars constitutes repayment of principal, we must take inflation into account. Let's illustrate this by a concrete example, comparing a loan made at zero inflation (no decay) with a loan made at 10 percent inflation (rapid decay).

First, suppose the government borrows $1000 for a year when the inflation rate is zero, paying 2 percent interest. At the end of the year it must pay back $1000 in principal and $20 in interest, for a total of $1020. Of this, only $20—the interest payment—is an expenditure item in the budget. The repayment of principal does not appear in the budget since it is not spending. The loan transaction is summarized simply in column 1 of Table 16–1.

Now let us see how inflation (radioactive decay of money) complicates the accountant's job. Suppose the same transaction takes place when the rate of inflation is 10 percent. If the real rate of interest is still 2 percent, the nominal rate of interest must be about 12 percent.

Inflation accounting means adjusting standard accounting procedures for the fact that inflation lowers the purchasing power of money.

Table 16–1
ACCOUNTING FOR A $1000 LOAN AT A 2 PERCENT REAL INTEREST RATE

ITEM	(1) AT ZERO INFLATION	(2) AT 10% INFLATION CONVENTIONAL ACCOUNTING	(3) AT 10% INFLATION INFLATION ACCOUNTING
Interest (included in budget)	$ 20	$ 122	$ 22
plus			
Principal (excluded from budget)	1,000	1,000	1,100
equals			
Total payment	$1,020	$1,122	$1,122
Addendum:			
Purchasing power of principal repayment	$1,000	$ 909	$1,000

More precisely, to compensate the lender for 10 percent inflation, and nothing more, the government must return $1.10 for each dollar originally borrowed. A real interest rate of 2 percent means that the government must return 2 percent more than this, or $1.02 \times \$1.10 = \$1.122$ per dollar borrowed. Thus, each dollar of lending earns 12.2 cents in interest, making the nominal interest rate 12.2 percent.

If the nominal interest rate is 12.2 percent, a government that borrows $1000 at the start of the year will have to repay $1,122 at year's end. Conventional accounting procedures will treat $1000 of this as repayment of principal (and hence not as an expenditure) and $122 as interest (which *is* an expenditure). This conventional accounting treatment is indicated in column 2 of Table 16–1.

But these numbers are misleading since $1000 at the end of the year is not adequate repayment of principal because inflation has eroded the real value of money. The correct inflation accounting treatment recognizes that it takes $1100 at the end of the year to buy what $1000 bought at the beginning of the year. So $1100 is treated as repayment of principal, leaving only $22 ($1122 − $1100) to be treated as interest. The correct inflation accounting treatment of the loan is shown in column 3 of Table 16–1.

To recapitulate, the proper economic treatment of a loan in an inflationary environment must recognize that more dollars (in our example, $1100) must be returned to the lender in order to give back the purchasing power of the original loan ($1000). Only the excess of the nominal interest payment ($122) over the compensation for inflation ($100) should be counted as interest.

This example holds the following lesson for interpreting budget deficit figures:

Inflation distorts the government budget under conventional accounting procedures by exaggerating interest expenses.

The example also suggests how this error can be corrected:

To correct the deficit for inflation, we must subtract the inflation premium from the interest paid on the national debt, thereby counting only *real* interest payments.

This treatment, by the way, corresponds exactly to the way inflation accounting is done by major corporations.

As Table 16–2 shows, making the inflation adjustment to interest payments would have reduced reported deficits by an average of about $45 billion in recent years, enough to turn apparently large deficits in 1980 and 1981 into small deficits. The table also shows that the years starting in fiscal 1982 stand out as exceptions to previous norms: The federal government began running large deficits *even after correction for inflation accounting.*

The High-Employment Budget

The second major issue in making sense of the budget deficit is not a problem of measurement, but rather one of interpretation.

As we learned in Chapter 12, the government's taxing and spending decisions profoundly affect the level of economic activity. For example, higher spending or lower taxes leads — via the multiplier process — to higher aggregate

Table 16–2
INFLATION ACCOUNTING AND THE DEFICIT

FISCAL YEAR	OFFICIAL DEFICIT (billions of dollars)	INFLATION ADJUSTMENT FOR INTEREST PAID (billions of dollars)	INFLATION ADJUSTED DEFICIT (−) OR SURPLUS (+) (billions of dollars)
1979	−40	+44	+4
1980	−74	+52	−22
1981	−79	+51	−28
1982	−128	+38	−90
1983	−208	+35	−173
1984	−185	+40	−145
1985	−212	+39	−173
1986	−221	+41	−180
1987	−158	+50	−108

SOURCE: Robert Eisner, *How Real Is the Federal Deficit?*, and authors' estimates.

demand and therefore to a higher GNP. This makes it natural to think that big deficits signify expansionary fiscal policy.

But that view may be incorrect because the state of the economy also affects the budget. In particular, *recessions tend to enlarge the budget deficit*. The reason is simple. Remember that the deficit is the difference between government expenditures and tax receipts, that is:

$$\text{Deficit} = G + \text{Transfers} - \text{Taxes}.$$

The government's most important sources of tax revenue — income taxes, corporate taxes, and payroll taxes — all shrink when GNP falls because firms and people pay less tax when they earn less. Similarly, some government spending, notably transfer payments like unemployment benefits, rises when GNP falls because more people are out of work. Since spending goes up and tax receipts go down as GNP falls:

The deficit rises in a recession and falls in a boom, even when there is no change in fiscal policy.

Because the deficit changes even when policy does not, the deficit is a poor measure of the government's fiscal policy. For this reason, many economists feel that we should pay less attention to the actual deficit or surplus and more attention to the deficit or surplus in what is called the **high-employment budget**. This is a hypothetical construct that replaces both the spending and taxes in the *actual* budget by estimates of how much the government *would be* spending and receiving, given current tax rates and expenditure rules, if the economy were operating near full employment.

Since it is based on the spending and taxing the government would be doing near full employment rather than on actual expenditures and receipts, the high-employment budget is not sensitive to the state of the economy. It will change only when policy changes. For this reason, most economists believe it is a better measure of the thrust of fiscal policy than the actual deficit. This new concept helps us understand the genesis of the large budget deficits of the 1980s: They were partly attributable to the consistently high unemployment rates that marked this period. Table 16–3 shows just how important the distinction between the actual deficit and the high-employment deficit has been in

The **high-employment budget** is the hypothetical budget we *would have* if the economy were operating near full employment.

Table 16–3

UNEMPLOYMENT AND THE DEFICIT

FISCAL YEAR	OFFICIAL DEFICIT (billions of dollars)	ADJUSTMENT TO HIGH EMPLOYMENT (billions of dollars)	HIGH-EMPLOYMENT DEFICIT (billions of dollars)
1980	−74	+23	−51
1981	−79	+31	−48
1982	−128	+77	−51
1983	−208	+102	−106
1984	−185	+55	−130
1985	−212	+41	−171
1986	−221	+36	−185
1987	−158	+36	−122

SOURCE: Congressional Budget Office.

recent years, particularly in the deep recession years 1982 and 1983. But since fiscal year 1983, even the high-employment budget has shown triple-digit deficits.

Other Measurement Issues

There are other complicated issues in measuring and interpreting the federal budget deficit. We conclude this section by mentioning just two of them.

1. *State and local budget surpluses.* Part of the reason for the federal deficit is that the federal government gives a good deal of money (over $100 billion in recent years) to state and local governments in the form of *grants-in-aid* each year. These funds have helped state and local governments run substantial surpluses—averaging between $30 and $50 billion annually in recent years. Thus, the *combined* deficits of governments at *all* levels has been considerably smaller than the *federal* deficit.

2. *Capital expenditures.* Some federal spending goes to purchase capital of various sorts—government buildings, military equipment, and so on. There is nothing unusual about borrowing to purchase assets. Private businesses and individuals do it all the time. For this reason, many people have suggested that the federal government compile a separate capital budget—which is precisely what most state and local governments do. The Office of Management and Budget is evaluating the merits of this idea.

Conclusion: What's New About the Recent Deficits?

Table 16–4 puts our two major adjustments—for inflation accounting and for unemployment—together and compares recent deficits (column 1) with corresponding figures on the high-employment, inflation-corrected deficit (column 4). The difference between the two columns is startling. The apparently substantial budget deficits of 1980–1982 were actually roughly balanced on the high-employment, inflation-corrected basis. Only since fiscal year 1983 has the high-employment, inflation-corrected budget been in deficit; and this concept of the deficit grew steadily from 1983 to 1986.

This, then, is the true swing in the federal budget position under President Reagan. Whereas the high-employment, inflation-corrected budget has historically shown an approximate balance, since fiscal 1983 it has shown a large deficit.

Table 16–4
ACTUAL AND ADJUSTED BUDGET DEFICITS

FISCAL YEAR	(1) OFFICIAL DEFICIT (billions of dollars)	(2) ADJUSTMENT FOR INFLATION (billions of dollars)	(3) ADJUSTMENT TO HIGH EMPLOYMENT (billions of dollars)	(4) ADJUSTED DEFICIT (−) OR SURPLUS (+) (billions of dollars)
1980	−74	+52	+23	+1
1981	−79	+51	+31	+3
1982	−128	+38	+77	−13
1983	−208	+35	+102	−71
1984	−185	+40	+55	−90
1985	−212	+39	+41	−132
1986	−221	+41	+36	−144
1987	−158	+50	+36	−72

SOURCE: Congressional Budget Office, Robert Eisner, and authors' calculations.

But what does all this mean? It certainly does *not* mean that in 1987, for example, only $72 billion in additional tax revenue (column 4) would have balanced the budget. What the numbers *do* mean is this. Of the $158 billion deficit in 1987 (column 1), about $50 billion was an artifact of poor accounting procedures and about $36 billion was attributable to the fact that the unemployment rate was still above full employment. This does not make the deficit disappear, but it does put it into some perspective.

Bogus Arguments About the Burden of the Debt

Having gained some perspective on the facts, let us now turn to some of the arguments advanced by those who claim that by running budget deficits we are placing an intolerable burden on future generations.

Argument 1: Our children and grandchildren will be burdened by heavy interest payments. To meet these payments there will have to be higher taxes.

Answer: It is certainly true that a higher debt will necessitate higher interest payments and, other things being equal, this will lead to higher taxes paid by our children and grandchildren. But think who will receive the higher interest payments as income: our children and grandchildren! Thus one group of future Americans will, essentially, be making interest payments to another group of future Americans. While some people will gain and others will lose, the future generation as a whole will come out even. We conclude that:

As long as the national debt is owned by domestic citizens, which the bulk of the U.S. debt is, future interest payments will merely shuffle money from one group of Americans to another. These transfers may or may not be desirable, but they hardly constitute a burden to the nation as a whole.

However, this argument *is* valid for the roughly 16 percent of our debt that is held by foreigners. Paying the interest on this portion of the debt will be a burden on future generations of Americans.

Argument 2: It will ruin the nation when we repay the enormous debt.

Answer: A first answer to this merely rephrases the answer to the previous argument: Only the part owned by foreigners involves any burden; the rest is paid by one group of Americans to another. But there is a much more fundamental point. *Unlike a private family, the nation need never pay off its debt.* Instead, each time the principal is due, the U.S. Treasury can simply "roll it over" by floating more debt. Indeed, this is precisely what the Treasury does.

Is this a bit of chicanery? How can the U.S. government get away with making loans that it never intends to pay back? The answer is found by recognizing the fallacy of comparing the U.S. government to a family or individual. People cannot be extended credit in perpetuity because they will not live that long. Sensible lenders will not extend long-term credit to very old people because their heirs cannot be forced to pay up. But the U.S. government will never "die"; at least, we hope not! So this problem does not arise. In this respect, the government is in much the same position as a large corporation. The American Telephone and Telegraph Company never worries about paying off its debt. It too rolls it over by floating new debt all the time.

Argument 3: Like any family or any business firm, a nation has a limited capacity to borrow. If it exceeds this limit, it is in danger of being unable to pay its creditors. It may go bankrupt with calamitous consequences for everyone.

Answer: This is another example of a false analogy. What is claimed about private debtors is certainly true. But the U.S. government need never fear defaulting on its debt. Why? First, because it has enormous power to raise revenues by taxation. If you had such power, you would never have to fear bankruptcy either.

But there is a still more fundamental point—one that distinguishes the U.S. debt from that of many foreign nations. *The American national debt is an obligation to pay U.S. dollars:* Each debt certificate obligates the Treasury to pay the holder so many U.S. dollars on a prescribed date. But the U.S. government is the source of these dollars; it prints them! *No nation need ever fear defaulting on debts that call for repayment in its own currency.* At the very worst, it can always print whatever money it needs to pay off its creditors.

It does not follow, however, that acquiring debt through budget deficits is therefore always a good idea. Sometimes it is clearly a bad idea. Printing money to pay the debt will expand aggregate demand and cause inflation, and this often will be undesirable. The point is not that budget deficits are either good or bad—we already know that they can be either under the appropriate circumstances. Rather, the point is that worrying about a possible default on the national debt is unnecessary and even foolish.

Having cleared the air of these fallacious arguments, we are now in a position to explore some real problems that may arise when the government spends more than it takes in through taxation.

Budget Deficits and Inflation

One indictment of deficit spending that certainly *does* have validity under most circumstances is the charge that it is inflationary. Why? Because when government policy pushes up aggregate demand, firms may find themselves unwilling or unable to produce the higher quantities that are being demanded at the going prices. Prices will therefore have to rise.

Figure 16–5

THE INFLATIONARY
EFFECTS OF DEFICIT
SPENDING

In this diagram, expansionary
fiscal policy pushes the
aggregate demand curve out
from $D_0 D_0$ to $D_1 D_1$, causing
equilibrium to move from E_0
(where there is
unemployment) to E_1 (where
there is full employment). But
because aggregate supply
curve SS slopes upward, the
price level is pushed up from
100 to 106; that is, there is a
6 percent inflation.

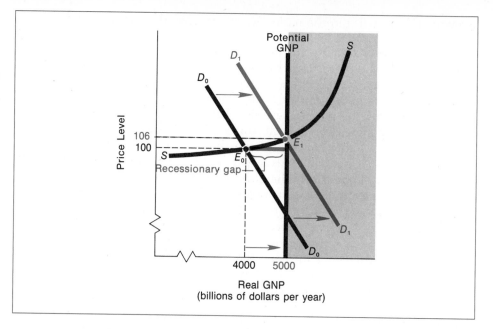

Figure 16–5 is an aggregate supply and demand diagram that shows this analysis graphically. Initially, equilibrium is at point E_0—where demand curve $D_0 D_0$ and supply curve SS intersect. Output is \$4000 billion, and the price index is at 100. The diagram indicates that the economy is operating below full employment; there is a recessionary gap. If the government does nothing to reduce the resulting unemployment, we know from Chapter 11 that this recessionary gap will linger for a long time. The economy will suffer through a prolonged period of unemployment.

Rather than permit such a long recession, we know that the government can raise its spending or cut its taxes enough to shift the aggregate demand schedule upward from $D_0 D_0$ to $D_1 D_1$. Such a policy can wipe out the recessionary gap and the associated unemployment—but not without an inflationary cost. The diagram shows that the new equilibrium price level is at 106, or 6 percent higher than before the government acted.

Thus the cries that budget deficits are "inflationary" have the ring of truth. How much truth, of course, depends on the slope of the aggregate supply curve. Deficit spending will not cause much inflation if the economy has lots of slack and the aggregate supply curve consequently is flat. But deficit spending will be highly inflationary in a fully-employed economy with a steep aggregate supply curve.

The Monetization Issue

Some people worry about the inflationary consequences of deficits for a rather different reason. They fear that the Federal Reserve may have to "monetize" part of the deficit, by which they mean that the Fed may feel compelled to purchase some of the newly issued government debt. Let us explain, first, why the Fed might make such purchases, and second, why these purchases are called **monetizing the deficit.**

The central bank is said
to **monetize the deficit**
when it purchases the
bonds that the
government issues.

Deficit spending, we have just noted, normally drives up both real GNP and the price level. As we have emphasized before, such an economic expansion shifts the demand curve for money outward to the right—as depicted in Figure 16–6. The figure shows that, if the Federal Reserve takes no actions to shift the money supply curve, interest rates will rise.

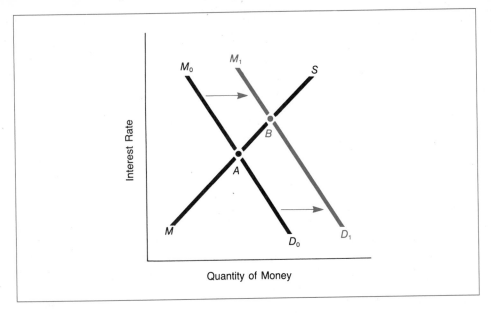

Figure 16–6
FISCAL EXPANSION AND
INTEREST RATES
If expansionary fiscal policy
pushes real GNP and the
price level higher, the
demand curve for money will
shift outward from $M_0 D_0$ to
$M_1 D_1$. Equilibrium in the
money market shifts from
point A to point B, so interest
rates rise.

Suppose now that the Fed does not want interest rates to rise. What can it do? To prevent the incipient rise in r, it must engage in *expansionary monetary policies* that shift the supply curve for money outward to the right—as indicated in Figure 16–7. And, as noted in Chapter 14, expansionary monetary policies normally take the form of open-market purchases of government bonds. For this reason, deficit spending sometimes induces the Federal Reserve to increase its purchases of government bonds, that is, to buy up some of the newly issued debt.

But why is this called *monetizing* the deficit? The reason is simple. As we learned in Chapter 14, open-market purchases of bonds by the Fed give banks more reserves, which leads, eventually, to an increase in the money supply. This is also shown in Figure 16–7: The outward shift of the money supply schedule from $M_0 S_0$ to $M_1 S_1$ leads to an increase in the money supply. By this

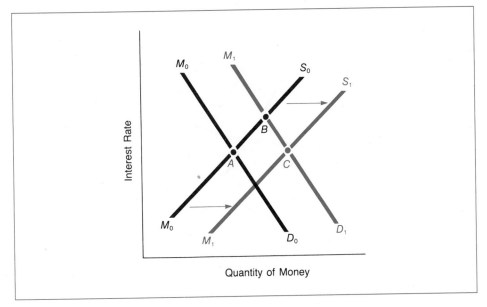

Figure 16–7
MONETIZATION AND
INTEREST RATES
If the Federal Reserve does
not want a fiscal expansion to
raise interest rates, it must
increase the money supply.
In this diagram, the fiscal
expansion shifts the demand
curve for money from $M_0 D_0$
to $M_1 D_1$, precisely as it did in
Figure 16–6. To keep the
rate of interest constant the
Fed will have to shift the
money supply curve outward
from $M_0 S_0$ to $M_1 S_1$. Points A
and C correspond to the
same rate of interest.

indirect route, then, larger budget deficits may lead to an expansion of the money supply. To summarize:

If the Federal Reserve takes no countervailing actions, an expansionary fiscal policy that raises the budget deficit will raise real GNP and prices, thereby shifting the demand curve for money outward and driving up interest rates. If the Fed does not want interest rates to rise, it can engage in expansionary open-market operations, that is, purchase more government debt. If the Fed does this, the money supply will increase. In this case, we say that part of the deficit is *monetized*.

Monetized deficits are more inflationary than nonmonetized deficits for the simple reason that expansionary monetary and fiscal policy *together* is more inflationary than expansionary fiscal policy *alone*. Figure 16–8 illustrates this conclusion. The aggregate supply curve and aggregate demand curves $D_0 D_0$ and $D_1 D_1$ are carried over without change from Figure 16–5. The shift from $D_0 D_0$ to $D_1 D_1$ represents the effect of expansionary fiscal policy (raising the budget deficit). If, in addition, the Fed monetizes part of the deficit, the aggregate demand curve will shift out still further—perhaps to the position indicated by $D_2 D_2$. Thus the price level will rise even more (compare points B and C).

Is this a real worry? Does the Fed actually monetize any substantial portion of the deficit? Sometimes it does, but normally it does not. For example, during the decade ending in 1986, the total federal debt held outside the government increased by about $1275 billion, but the Federal Reserve's holdings of government bonds increased by only about $85 billion. By this crude measure, less than 7 percent of the typical deficit was monetized.

Nonetheless, many economists and business leaders have been concerned about monetization in the 1980s. The reason is simple arithmetic. When budget deficits are extremely large, even a small percentage of monetization can lead to substantial increases in bank reserves and the money supply.

Figure 16–8
MONETIZED DEFICIT SPENDING
Expansionary fiscal policies that raise the budget deficit push the aggregate demand curve outward from $D_0 D_0$ to $D_1 D_1$. If the Fed monetizes some of the deficit, then expansionary monetary policy pushes the aggregate demand curve out even further—to $D_2 D_2$. Monetized deficits (point C) are therefore more inflationary than deficits that are not monetized (point B).

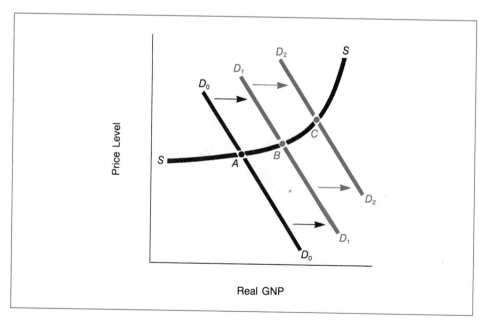

Deficits, Interest Rates, and Crowding Out

So far we have been looking for possible burdens of the national debt on the *demand* side of the economy. But the more serious burden probably comes on the *supply* side because large budget deficits discourage investment and therefore retard the growth of our nation's capital stock. The mechanism is easy to understand.

We have just seen that budget deficits tend to raise interest rates unless the Fed engages in substantial monetization. But the rate of interest (r) is a major determinant of investment spending (I). In particular, higher r leads to lower I. And if we spend less on I today, we will have a smaller capital stock tomorrow. This, according to most economists, is the true sense in which a large national debt may put a burden on future generations:

Because of the large national debt, we may bequeath less physical capital to future generations. If they inherit less plant and equipment, these generations will be burdened by a lower productive capacity—a lower potential GNP.

There is another way of looking at this problem—a way that explains why it is often called the **crowding-out effect**. Consider what happens in financial markets when the government engages in deficit spending. When it spends more than it takes in through tax revenues, the government must borrow the balance from private citizens. It does this by issuing bonds, and these bonds compete with corporate bonds and other financial instruments for the available supply of funds. When some private savers are persuaded to buy government bonds, there must be a decline in the funds remaining to invest in private bonds. Thus some private borrowers will get "crowded out" of the financial markets as the government claims an increasing share of the economy's total saving.

Crowding out occurs when deficit spending by the government forces private investment spending to contract.

Some critics of deficits who have taken this lesson to its illogical extreme argue that each $1 of deficit spending by government crowds out exactly $1 of private spending, so that expansionary fiscal policy has no net effect on total demand. In their view, when G rises, I falls by the same amount, so that $C + I + G$ is unchanged.

Under normal circumstances, this would not be expected to occur. Why? First, moderate budget deficits will push up interest rates only moderately. Second, the sensitivity of private spending to interest rates is not that great. Even at the higher interest rates that government deficits cause, most corporations will continue to borrow to finance their investments.

Furthermore, there is a counterforce that might be called the **crowding-in effect**. Deficit spending in time of economic slack presumably quickens the pace of economic activity; that, at least, is its purpose. As the economy expands, businesses find it both necessary and profitable to add to their capacity in order to meet the greater demands of consumers. Because of this *induced investment*, as we called it in earlier chapters, any increase in G tends to *increase* investment rather than *decrease* it as predicted by the crowding-out hypothesis.

Crowding in occurs when government spending, by raising real GNP, induces increases in private investment spending.

The strength of the crowding-in effect depends on how much additional real GNP is stimulated by government spending (that is, on the size of the multiplier) and on how sensitive investment spending is to the improved profit opportunities that accompany rapid growth. It is even conceivable that the crowding-in effect can dominate the crowding-out effect, so that I rises on balance when G rises.

But how can this be true in view of the crowding-out argument? Certainly, if government is borrowing more *and the total volume of private saving is fixed,* then private industry must be borrowing less. While this little bit of arithmetic is correct, the fallacy in the strict crowding-out argument comes in supposing that the economy's flow of saving is really fixed. If government deficits succeed in their goal of raising production, there will be more income and therefore more saving. In that way *both* government *and* industry can borrow more.

Which effect dominates, crowding out or crowding in? The crowding-out hypothesis stems from the increases in interest rates that deficit spending causes; this is certainly bad for investment. But the crowding-in hypothesis stems from the increases in production and profitability, which are good for investment. Under different sets of circumstances, one or the other force may prove to be stronger.

For example, a report issued by the Congressional Budget Office near the bottom of the deep recession of 1974–1975 argued that "on balance . . . it appears likely that more investments would be 'crowded in' by a stimulative fiscal policy than would be 'crowded out,' given the present state of the economy."[4] The report explained that, with so much slack in the economy, a surge in G would likely lead to a considerable increase in real output because the higher demand would not cause much inflation and, consequently, the multiplier would be large. In terms of our graphical apparatus, the aggregate supply curve would be rather flat when the economy is in the range indicated by Region I in Figure 16–9.

But the same report hastened to add, "The opposite conclusion might well be drawn if resources were more fully employed." This is because the economy would then be operating in the steep portion of Region III of the aggregate supply curve shown in Figure 16–9 so that demand stimulation would lead to only limited gains in real output.[5] If real GNP growth is minor, then so must be the

[4]Congressional Budget Office, *Inflation and Unemployment: A Report on the Economy* (Washington, D.C.: U.S. Government Printing Office, June 30, 1975), page 58.
[5]EXERCISE: Show that any given horizontal shift in the aggregate demand curve has a smaller effect on real GNP in Region III than it does in Region I.

Figure 16–9
A TYPICAL AGGREGATE SUPPLY CURVE
The aggregate supply curve depicted here has three regions. In Region I, output can increase with almost no change in prices because there is a great deal of unused labor and spare industrial capacity. Thus the supply curve is virtually horizontal. In Region III, resources are more or less fully employed, so even rather small increases in output necessitate substantial price increases; the supply curve is very steep. Region II is intermediate between these two extremes.

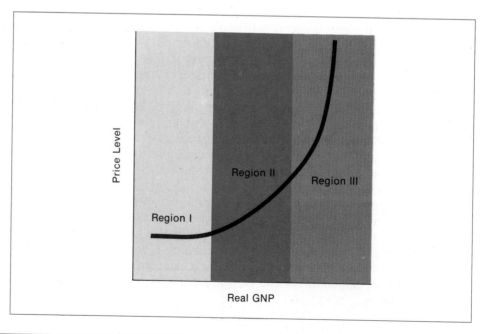

amount of induced investment. The crowding-in effect therefore would be weak. Instead, government spending would push up the price level, raise the demand for cash balances, and crowd out private borrowers.

Let us summarize what we have learned about the crowding-out controversy.

SUMMARY

1. The basic argument of the crowding-out hypothesis is sound: *Unless there is enough additional saving*, more government borrowing will force out some private borrowers who are discouraged by the high interest rates. This will reduce investment spending and cancel out some of the expansionary effects of higher government spending.

2. This force is rarely strong enough to cancel out the *entire* expansionary thrust of government spending, however. Some net stimulus to the economy remains.

3. If the deficit spending induces substantial growth in GNP, then there will be more saving. There might even be so much more that private industry could borrow *more* than before, despite the increase in government borrowing.

4. The crowding-out effect is likely to dominate when the economy is operating near full employment. The crowding-in effect is likely to dominate when there is a great deal of slack.

The True Burden of the National Debt

This analysis of crowding out versus crowding in, puts us in a position to understand why budget deficits might or might not impose a burden on future generations:

When government budget deficits take place in a high-employment economy, the crowding-out effect will probably dominate. So deficits will exact a burden by leaving a smaller capital stock to future generations. However, deficits in a slack economy may well lead to *more* investment rather than *less*. In this case, where the crowding-in effect dominates, the new debt is a blessing rather than a burden.

"Would you mind explaining again how high interest rates and the national deficit affect my allowance?"

Which case applies to the U.S. national debt? To answer this, let us go back to the historical facts and recall how we accumulated such a large debt. The first cause was the financing of wars, especially World War II. This debt was contracted in a fully-employed economy, and thus undoubtedly constituted a burden in the formal sense. It left future generations with less capital because some of our nation's resources were diverted from private investment into government production. The bombs, ships, and planes that it financed were used up in the war, not bequeathed as capital to future generations.

Yet what were the alternatives? We could have financed the entire war by taxation and thus placed the burden on consumption rather than on investment. But that would truly have been ruinous, and maybe even impossible, given the colossal wartime expenditures. Or we could have printed money. But that would have unleashed an inflation that nobody wanted. Or we could have just done much less government spending and perhaps not have won the war. So, in retrospect, the generations alive today and in the future may not feel unduly burdened by the decisions of the people in power in the 1940s. One need only imagine the sort of burden that would have been inherited had the United States not won the war.

The second major contributor to the national debt has been a series of recessions. But these are precisely the circumstances under which increasing the debt might prove to be a blessing rather than a burden. So, if we look for the classic type of deficit to which the valid burden-of-the-debt argument applies — deficits acquired in a fully-employed peacetime economy — we do not find many in the U.S. record until recently.

It is in this context that current budget deficits are a sharp departure from the past. Since 1986, the U.S. economy has been approaching the full employment zone. And it has been doing so in peacetime with deficits in the neighborhood of $200 billion per year. This is something that has never happened before, and it poses a real threat of severe crowding out and a serious potential burden on future generations.

The Burden of the National Debt

Let us now summarize our evaluation of the burden of the national debt and thereby clarify one of the **12 Ideas for Beyond the Final Exam** introduced in Chapter 1.

First, the arguments that a large national debt may lead the nation into bankruptcy, or unduly burden future generations who have to make onerous payments of interest and principal, are mostly bogus.

Second, the national debt *will* be a burden if it is contracted in a fully-employed peacetime economy, because in that case it will reduce the nation's capital stock.

Third, there are circumstances in which budget deficits are appropriate for stabilization reasons.

Fourth, until recently, the actual public debt of the U.S. government was mostly contracted as a result of wars and recessions — precisely the circumstances under which the valid burden-of-the-debt argument does not apply. However, the large deficits of recent years are worrisome from this point of view.

The Economic Effects of Budget Deficits: Causation Versus Correlation

Anyone who has followed the debate over budget deficits in the press is bound to have been confused by the contradictory claims and counter-claims. Do deficits lead to high interest rates? Some say yes, others say no. Are deficits inflationary? Some say yes, others say no. Are large deficits a roadblock to economic expansion? Some say yes, others say no. And somehow each participant in the debate finds data to support his or her view.

Who is right? Let us use what we have learned about the economic effects of budget deficits to make some sense of this confusion. We can do so by contrasting two imaginary case studies which, however, bear a certain resemblance to events in the United States in the early 1980s.

Case 1: A Tax Cut

Suppose the government opens up a budget deficit by reducing taxes. What should happen? According to the theory we have developed, aggregate demand should increase, and that should increase both real GNP (Y) and the price level

(P) — as in Figure 16–5 (page 332). The rise in Y and P should shift the demand curve for money outward, thereby raising the rate of interest (r) — as in Figure 16–6 (page 333) — and subsequently lowering investment. Thus, in response to the large deficit, the economy should experience rapid GNP growth, high inflation, and high interest rates. The general conclusion is:

If the government undertakes expansionary fiscal policies, like cutting taxes or raising spending, the deficit should rise and:

1. Real GNP should grow faster;
2. Interest rates should rise (which harms investment);
3. Inflation should rise.

This conclusion is recorded for future reference in the first column of Table 16–5.

Case 2: A Recession
Now suppose that the budget deficit increases for an entirely different reason. For example, suppose consumer spending declines sharply. What will happen? The decline in aggregate demand will lower both real GNP and prices. With both Y and P falling, the quantity of money demanded will decline. And the decrease in the demand for money will pull down interest rates, which will stimulate investment. Finally, as we have noted in this chapter, when GNP falls so do tax receipts; so the deficit will widen.[6] Thus, in this case, we expect larger deficits to be accompanied by weaker GNP growth, slower inflation, and lower interest rates. The general conclusion is:

If the economy experiences a recession for reasons having nothing to do with fiscal policy, the deficit should rise and:

1. Real GNP should fall;
2. Interest rates should fall;
3. Inflation should fall.

This conclusion is recorded in the second column of Table 16–5.

Table 16–5 shows how different the two cases are. The deficit rises in both cases. But in the first case Y, P, and r all rise, while in the second case they all fall.[7] In the real world, of course, deficits are sometimes caused by fiscal policy actions (as in Case 1) and sometimes caused by other factors (as in Case 2).

[6]EXERCISE: Test your understanding by working out the diagrams for this example.
[7]EXERCISE: To test your understanding, construct a version of Table 16–5 that applies to *falling* deficits caused by (a) a tax increase or (b) an autonomous increase in consumer spending. Be sure you can explain each entry in the table.

Table 16–5
DEFICITS AND THE ECONOMY: A SUMMARY

EXPECTED EFFECT ON:	CASE 1 FISCAL POLICY ACTIONS RAISE THE DEFICIT	CASE 2 A RECESSION RAISES THE DEFICIT
Real GNP growth	Up	Down
Interest rate	Up	Down
Inflation rate	Up	Down

Balancing The Budget
By Outlawing Deficits

The U.S. Congress has seriously considered enacting a balanced-budget amendment to the Constitution several times in the past decade. And a majority of the state legislatures has petitioned Congress to call a constitutional convention for precisely that purpose. If a few more states join the call, the first constitutional convention since 1787 may be convened. So some sort of constitutional prohibition of budget deficits, presumably with escape clauses, may one day become law.

Congress took a step in that direction in December 1985 when it passed the Balanced Budget Act, commonly known as the Gramm-Rudman-Hollings Act for its three senatorial sponsors. The act sets a strict numerical schedule for reducing the budget deficit from the $212 billion recorded in fiscal year 1985 to zero by fiscal year 1991. Despite the important effect of economic activity on the budget deficit that was discussed in this chapter (see especially pages 327–29), Congress made the deficit limit for each year a fixed number to apply whether the economy is booming or limping along. It did, however, provide for exceptional circumstances (such as a forecast of recession) under which the limits could be suspended.

The law set out a list of deadlines for Congress to follow in handling each year's budget. But its most stunning and important provision was a mechanical formula for cutting government spending by computer in the event that Congress failed to make the necessary deficit reductions by the specified date.

Early returns on the operation of the law have not been favorable. Congress set a $172 billion deficit limit for fiscal year 1986. But, since Gramm-Rudman was enacted after fiscal 1986 had started, the limit was not binding. In fact, the 1986 deficit turned out to be $221 billion—even higher than the 1985 deficit. An inauspicious beginning.

Then things got worse. In August 1986, as the House and Senate were nearing agreement over how to abide by Gramm-Rudman's fiscal 1987 deficit limit of $144 billion, the Supreme Court declared the automatic budget-cutting mechanism unconstitutional. The law had lost its teeth. Nonetheless, House Democrats and Senate Republicans miraculously agreed on a budget that claimed to produce a $144 billion deficit, and many observers gave Gramm-Rudman credit for disciplining Congress.

But the congratulations proved premature. First the president rejected Congress's budget proposal as too stingy on defense spending. Then the Congressional Budget Office reported that the budget failed to abide by the Gramm-Rudman deficit limit anyway. Discouraged, Congress simply ignored all the Gramm-Rudman deadlines. Then, after the fiscal year had begun, a jerry-built budget—replete with an embarrassing number of accounting gimmicks and other budgetary tricks—was rushed through both houses and signed into law by the president. In the end, the fiscal 1987 deficit came in at $158 billion despite surprisingly high revenues. Throughout the deliberations over the fiscal 1988 budget, both the administration and Congress more or less ignored the Gramm-Rudman deficit limit of $108 billion.

And that is why different people, looking at the same facts, can reach different conclusions about deficits.

The point is that "looking at the facts" is not enough. Simple correlations between the budget deficit and some other economic variable are not terribly informative. You must be able to distinguish between *cause* and *effect*. In

Case 1, changes in fiscal policy were the driving force; in a sense, a higher deficit *caused* Y, P, and r to rise. But in Case 2, there was no change in fiscal policy; a higher deficit was an *effect* of a recession.

Recent U.S. history has had elements of both cases. In the first years of the Reagan administration, we experienced a terrible recession that had very little to do with the president's fiscal policies (analogous to Case 2). Starting in 1983, however, the Reagan tax cuts began to have major effects on the deficit (as in Case 1). No wonder the charges and countercharges were so confused, and the evidence so confusing. (See Discussion Question 10 at the end of the chapter.)

Conclusion: The Partisan Debate over the Budget Deficit

Given what we have learned about the theory and facts of budget deficits, we are now in a position to address the issues debated by President Reagan and his critics.

1. *How did we get such a large deficit?* As we have seen in this chapter, triple-digit deficits began in 1982. At first, the most important cause was not Mr. Reagan's policies, but rather the steep recession. While the budget showed titanic deficits in 1982 and 1983, the high-employment deficits were roughly half as large (see Table 16–3 on page 329).

    But by 1984, with the economy improving and the tax cuts fully effective, the high-employment deficit was tremendous. Deliberate fiscal policy actions account for most of the 1984 deficit as well as subsequent deficits. Whether the blame should rest with the president or the Congress is a matter of politics, not economics.

2. *Is the deficit a problem?* Once again, the answer to the question was different in 1981–1983 from what it has been since. In 1981–1982, the economy went through a deep recession. And in 1983, the first year of the recovery, unemployment was still far above full employment. Under these circumstances, crowding out would not be expected to be a serious problem and actions to close the deficit would have threatened the recovery. According to the basic principles of fiscal policy, a large deficit was probably appropriate.

    But things are different now. Crowding out becomes a more serious issue as the economy nears full employment. So budget deficits should fall. But the actual deficit did not fall from 1983 to 1986 and the high-employment deficit rose dramatically. Since 1983 we have had large high-employment deficits in peacetime for the first time in our history; and worries about the burden of the national debt, once mostly myths, are becoming all too realistic.

3. *What should be done about the deficit?* It is a matter of simple arithmetic that you close a budget deficit by raising taxes and/or by reducing spending. Either of these routes is a contractionary fiscal policy and will retard the growth of real GNP and make it harder to return to full employment.

    Is there any way around this problem? There is, if fiscal and monetary policies can be coordinated better. If fiscal policy must turn contractionary to reduce the deficit, monetary policy can turn expansionary to counteract the effects on aggregate demand. In this way, we can hope to shrink the deficit without shrinking the economy in the process. Such a change in the policy "mix" would also bring down interest rates, since both tighter budgets and easier money tend to push interest rates down.

For these reasons, many economists — both liberal and conservative — have long advocated a shift in the policy mix toward tighter budgets and easier monetary policy. Some progress has been made in this direction. But, at this writing, most economists still feel that the federal deficit is too high.

Summary

1. Rigid adherence to budget balancing would make the economy less stable by reducing aggregate demand (via tax increases and reductions in government spending) when private spending is low, and raising aggregate demand when private spending is high.

2. Since both monetary and fiscal policy influence aggregate demand, the appropriate budget deficit or surplus depends on monetary policy. Similarly, the appropriate monetary policy depends on budget policy.

3. The national debt has grown dramatically since the mid-1970s. But until recently it was generally growing less rapidly than GNP.

4. Inflation makes the deficit look bigger than it really is because all nominal interest payments are counted as expenditures. Under inflation accounting, only real interest payments would count as expenditures, and the deficit would be seen to be much smaller.

5. Part of the reason for the large budget deficits of the 1980s is the fact that the economy has operated well below full employment. The high-employment deficit, which uses estimates of what the government's receipts and outlays would be at full employment, has been much smaller than the official deficit.

6. If we correct the official deficit for inflation and adjust it to high levels of employment, we find that deficits in the high-employment inflation-corrected budget began only in 1983. Before that there were balanced budgets or surpluses.

7. Arguments that the public debt will burden future generations, who will have to make huge payments of interest and principal, are based on false analogies. In fact, most of these payments are simply transfers from some Americans to other Americans. Besides, the Treasury can, and normally does, "roll over" its debt rather than pay it off.

8. The bogus argument that a large national debt can bankrupt a country like the United States ignores the fact that our national debt consists of obligations to pay U.S. dollars — a currency the government can raise by taxation or create by printing money.

9. Under normal circumstances, budget deficits are somewhat inflationary. They are even more inflationary if they are "monetized," that is, if the Federal Reserve buys some of the newly issued government debt in the open market.

10. Unless the deficit is substantially monetized, deficit spending forces interest rates higher and discourages private investment spending. This is called the crowding-out effect. If there is a great deal of crowding out, then deficits really do impose a burden on future generations by leaving them a smaller capital stock to work with.

11. But there is also a crowding-in effect from higher government spending (G). If expansionary fiscal policy succeeds in raising real output (Y), more investment will be induced by the higher Y.

12. Which effect is stronger, crowding out or crowding in, depends mainly on the state of the economy. When unemployment is high, crowding in probably dominates, so higher G does not cause lower investment. But when the economy is near full employment, the proponents of the crowding-out hypothesis are probably right: High government spending just displaces private investment.

13. Whether or not deficits are a burden therefore depends on how and why the government ran these deficits in the first place. If deficits are contracted to fight recessions, it is possible that more investment is crowded in by the increases in income that these deficits make possible than is crowded out by the increases in interest rates. Deficits contracted to carry on wars certainly impair the future capital stock, though they may not be considered a burden for noneconomic reasons. Since these two cases account for most of America's national debt, our debt cannot reasonably be considered a serious burden. This is one of the **12 Ideas for Beyond the Final Exam.**

14. If deficits arise from deliberate fiscal policy actions, then larger deficits should lead to more rapid growth of real output, higher prices, and higher interest rates.

15. But if deficits arise from a recession, we should find larger deficits accompanied by declining GNP, lower inflation, and lower interest rates.

Concepts for Review

Budget deficit

National debt

Real versus nominal interest rates

Inflation accounting

High-employment budget

Monetization of deficits

Crowding out

Crowding in

Burden of the national debt

Mix of monetary and fiscal policy

Questions for Discussion

1. Explain the difference between the budget deficit and the national debt. If we reduce the deficit, will the debt stop growing?

2. Explain how the U.S. government has managed to accumulate a debt of more than $2400 billion. To whom does it owe this debt? Can this debt be considered a burden on future generations?

3. Comment on the following: "Deficit spending paves the road to ruination. If we keep it up, the whole nation will go bankrupt. Even if things do not go this far, what right have we to burden our children and grandchildren with these debts while we live high on the hog?"

4. Calculate the budget deficit and the inflation-corrected deficit for an economy with the following data:

   Government expenditures other than interest = 90

   Tax receipts = 75

   Interest payments = 64

   Interest rate = 8 percent

   Inflation rate = 5 percent

   National debt at start of year = 800

   (*Note:* 8 percent interest on an $800 debt is $64.)

5. Explain why the high-employment budget might show a surplus while the actual budget is in deficit.

6. If the Federal Reserve begins to increase the money supply more slowly than before, what will happen to the government budget deficit? (*Hint:*

What will happen to tax receipts and interest expenses?) If the government wants to offset the effects of the Fed's actions on aggregate demand, what might it do? How will this affect the deficit?

7. Given the current state of the economy, do you think the Fed should monetize more of the deficit? (*Note:* There is no one correct answer to this question. It is a good question to discuss in class.)

8. Explain the difference between crowding out and crowding in. Given the current state of the economy, which effect would you expect to be dominant right now?

9. Suppose the Balanced Budget Act had been in effect in 1982, during the worst of the recession. What might have happened to the economy?

10. Evaluate each of the following statements. (*Note:* The facts in each case are correct; concentrate on the conclusion that is reached.)

    a. "In 1982, the deficit was larger than in 1981. But interest rates were lower. Therefore, larger deficits do not cause higher interest rates."

    b. "In 1978 we had a small deficit and strong GNP growth. In 1982, we had a huge deficit and a recession. Therefore, deficit spending does not stimulate the economy."

    c. "If we compare 1980–1981 with 1985–1986, we find much larger deficits but much lower inflation in the last two years than in the first two. Therefore, it is clear that deficit spending is not inflationary."

17

We must seek to reduce inflation at a lower cost in lost output and unemployment.

JIMMY CARTER
(JANUARY 1980)

The Trade-Off Between Inflation and Unemployment

The worldwide trend toward higher inflation was arrested during the first half of the 1980s. The rate of inflation in the United States declined from about 10 percent to under 4 percent. In Great Britain inflation fell from 20 percent to 4 percent; in Italy from 21 percent to 11 percent; in West Germany from $4\frac{1}{2}$ percent to about zero. As this was happening, the Western economies all suffered severe recessions. In the United States, for example, the unemployment rate topped 10 percent for the first time since the Great Depression.

Most economists believe that this conjunction of events was no coincidence. Rather, they insist, the period of high unemployment was the price we paid to reduce the rate of inflation. Although some optimists claim that it is possible to reduce inflation without suffering from unemployment, the world clearly paid a heavy price for the disinflation of the 1980s. Was this price inevitable, or could we have avoided it? That is the question for this chapter.

You may recall from Chapter 1 that the existence of an agonizing trade-off between inflation and unemployment is one of the **12 Ideas For Beyond the Final Exam.** The importance of this trade-off can hardly be overestimated. It is probably the one area of macroeconomics where confusion is most widespread. And because this confusion can have disastrous consequences for the conduct of stabilization policy, the trade-off merits the comprehensive examination that we give it in this chapter. Without a thorough understanding of the dimensions of this trade-off, it is impossible for a citizen to make an informed judgment about macroeconomic policy.

Demand-Side Inflation Versus Supply-Side Inflation: A Review

Let us begin our investigation of the trade-off by reviewing some of what we have learned about inflation in earlier chapters.

One major cause of inflation, though certainly not the only one, is *excessive growth of aggregate demand*. What happens if, for some reason, either consumers or investors or the government decides to increase spending? We know, first of all, that such an autonomous increase in spending will have a multiplier effect on aggregate demand; that is, each additional $1 of C or I or G will lead to more than $1 of additional demand. Second, we know that firms normally find it profitable to supply the additional output only at higher prices. Hence, such a stimulus to aggregate demand will normally pull up *both* real output *and* prices.

Figure 17–1, which is familiar from earlier chapters, reviews this conclusion. Initially, the economy is at point A, where aggregate demand curve D_0D_0 intersects aggregate supply curve SS. Then something happens to increase demand, and the aggregate demand curve shifts horizontally to D_1D_1. The new equilibrium is at point B, where both prices and output are higher than they were at A.

The slope of the aggregate supply curve measures the amount of inflation that accompanies any specified rise in output and therefore embodies the trade-off between unemployment and inflation. We concluded in the last chapter that this trade-off will be favorable when the economy is operating at low levels of capacity utilization and high levels of unemployment. Under such circumstances, firms can expand their operations substantially without running into higher costs. On the other hand, if the demand stimulus occurs in a fully employed economy, firms will find it difficult to raise output and so will respond mostly by raising prices. Thus, the tradeoff is unfavorable when unemployment is low.

But we have learned in this book (especially in Chapter 11) that inflation need not always emanate from the demand side. Restrictions in the growth of aggregate supply—caused, for example, by an increase in the price of foreign oil—can shift the economy's aggregate supply curve inward. This is illustrated in Figure 17–2, where the aggregate supply curve shifts from S_0S_0 to S_1S_1, and the economy's equilibrium consequently moves from point A to point B. Prices rise as output falls. We have *stagflation*.

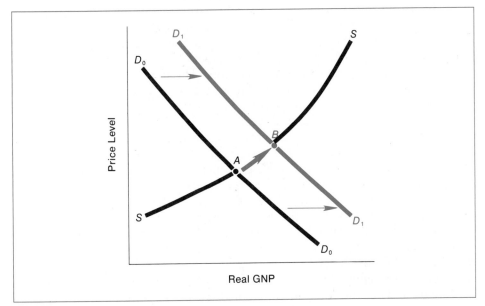

Figure 17–1
INFLATION FROM THE DEMAND SIDE
An increase in aggregate demand, whether it comes from consumers, investors, or the government, shifts the aggregate demand curve outward from D_0D_0 to D_1D_1. The economy's equilibrium moves from point A to point B. Since point B corresponds to a higher price level than does point A, there is inflation (that is, a rising price level) as the economy moves from A to B.

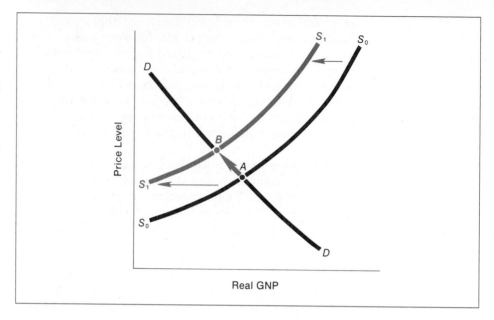

Figure 17–2

INFLATION FROM THE SUPPLY SIDE

A decrease in aggregate supply—which can be caused by such factors as an autonomous increase in wages, or by an increase in the price of foreign oil—can cause inflation. When the aggregate supply curve shifts to the left, from S_0S_0 to S_1S_1, the equilibrium point moves from A to B. Comparing B with A, we see that the price level is higher, which means there must have been *inflation* (rising prices) in the interim. Notice also that adverse supply shifts make real ouput decline while prices are rising; that is, they produce *stagflation*.

Thus, while inflation can be initiated from either the *demand* side or the *supply* side of the economy, there is a crucial difference. Demand-side inflation is normally accompanied by rising real GNP (see Figure 17–1), while supply-side inflation may well be accompanied by falling GNP (see Figure 17–2). This is an important distinction, as we shall see in this chapter.

Applying the Model to a Growing Economy

You may have noticed that our simple model of aggregate supply and aggregate demand determines an equilibrium *price level* and an equilibrium *level of real GNP*. But, in the real economy, we do not see an unchanged price level and an unchanged level of real GNP for long periods of time. Instead, the price level and the level of real GNP change every year.

This is illustrated in Figure 17–3, which is a scatter diagram of the U.S. price level and the level of GNP for every year from 1963 to 1986. The points are labeled to show the clear upward march of the economy through time— toward higher prices and higher levels of output.

It is certainly no mystery why this occurs. The normal state of affairs is for *both* the aggregate demand curve *and* the aggregate supply curve to shift to the right each year. Aggregate supply grows because there are more workers, more machinery, and more factories each year, and because technology is improving. Aggregate demand grows because a growing population means more demand for both consumer and investment goods, because the government increases its spending, and because the Federal Reserve increases the money supply. We can think of each point in Figure 17–3 as the intersection of an aggregate supply curve and an aggregate demand curve for that particular year. To help you visualize this, the curves for 1978 are sketched in the diagram.

Figure 17–4 illustrates how our theoretical model of aggregate supply and aggregate demand applies to a growing economy. The numbers are chosen so that curves D_0D_0 and S_0S_0 roughly represent the end of 1985, and the curves D_1D_1 and S_1S_1 roughly represent the end of 1986, except that nice round numbers are used. Thus the equilibrium late in 1985 was at point A, with real GNP

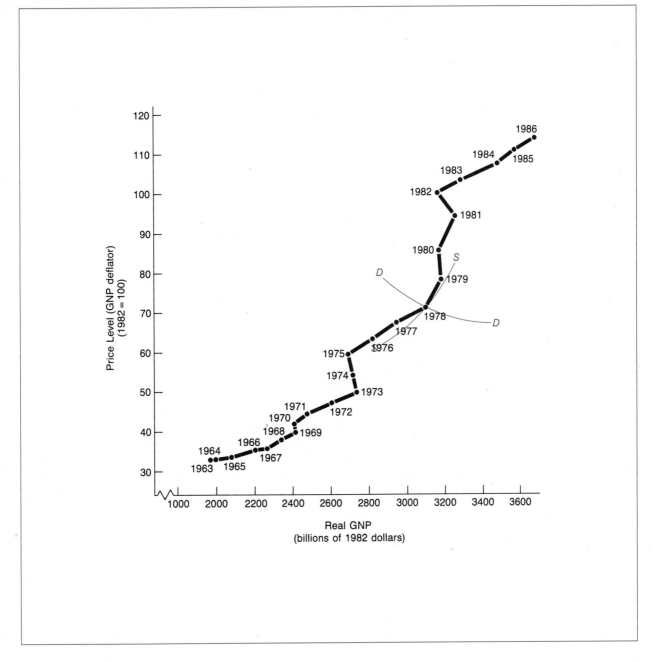

Figure 17–3
THE PRICE LEVEL AND REAL OUTPUT IN THE UNITED STATES, 1963–1986
This scatter diagram shows, for each year from 1963 to 1986, the price level (GNP deflator) and real GNP for the United States. Clearly the normal state of affairs is for both variables to rise from one year to the next.
SOURCE: U.S. Department of Commerce, Bureau of Economic Analysis

of $3600 billion (in 1982 dollars) and a price level of 113, while the equilibrium a year later was at point B, with real GNP at $3700 billion and the price level at 115, or 1.8 percent higher. The blue arrow in the diagram shows how equilibrium moved during 1986. It points upward and to the right, meaning that both prices and output increased.

Figure 17–4

AGGREGATE SUPPLY
AND DEMAND ANALYSIS
OF A GROWING
ECONOMY

This diagram illustrates how
the aggregate supply and
demand analysis of earlier
chapters can be applied to a
real-world economy, in which
both the supply curve and
the demand curve normally
shift outward from one year
to the next. In this example,
demand curve D_0D_0 and
supply curve S_0S_0 represent
the U.S. economy in late
1985. Equilibrium was at
point A, with a price level of
113 and real GNP of $3600
billion. Demand curve D_1D_1
and supply curve S_1S_1
represent the end of 1986.
During the year, the price
index rose by 2 points
(almost 2 percent) and output
increased by $100 billion
(almost 3 percent).

Demand-Side Inflation and the Phillips Curve

Let us now use our theoretical model to rerun history. Suppose that during 1986
the aggregate demand curve grew *faster* than it actually did. What difference
would this have made for the performance of the national economy? Figure
17–5 provides the answers. Here the demand curve D_0D_0 and both supply
curves are exactly as they were in the previous diagram, but the demand curve

Figure 17–5

THE EFFECTS OF
FASTER GROWTH OF
AGGREGATE DEMAND

In this hypothetical example,
we imagine that because
either private citizens spent
more or the government
pursued more expansionary
policies, aggregate demand
grew faster between late
1985 and late 1986 than it
did in Figure 17–4. The
consequence is that, in this
diagram, the price level rises
6 points (almost 6 percent)
during 1986 compared with
the 2 points (under 2
percent) in Figure 17–4.
Growth of real output is also
greater: $200 billion here
versus only $100 billion in the
previous figure.

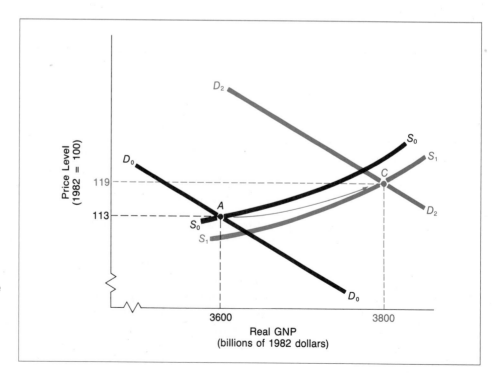

D_2D_2 is farther to the right than the demand curve D_1D_1 in Figure 17–4. Equilibrium is at point A late in 1985 and point C late in 1986. Comparing point C in Figure 17–5 with point B in Figure 17–4, we see that output would have increased more during 1986 ($200 billion versus $100 billion) and prices would also have increased more (to 119 instead of 115); that is, there would have been more *inflation*. This is generally what happens when the growth rate of aggregate demand speeds up.

For any given rate of growth of the aggregate supply curve, a faster rate of growth of the aggregate demand curve will lead to more inflation and faster growth of real output.

Figure 17–6 illustrates the opposite case. Here we imagine that the aggregate demand curve shifted out *less* than in Figure 17–4. That is, demand curve D_3D_3 in Figure 17–6 is to the left of demand curve D_1D_1 in Figure 17–4. The consequence, we see, is that the shift of the economy's equilibrium during 1986 (from point A to point E) would have entailed *less inflation* and *slower growth of real output* than actually took place. This again is generally the case.

For any given rate of growth of the aggregate supply curve, a slower rate of growth of the aggregate demand curve will lead to less inflation and slower growth of real output.

If we put these two findings together, we have a clear prediction from our theory:

If fluctuations in the economy's real growth rate from year to year are caused primarily by variations in the rate at which aggregate demand increases, then the data should show the most rapid inflation occurring when output expands most rapidly and the slowest inflation occurring when output expands most slowly.

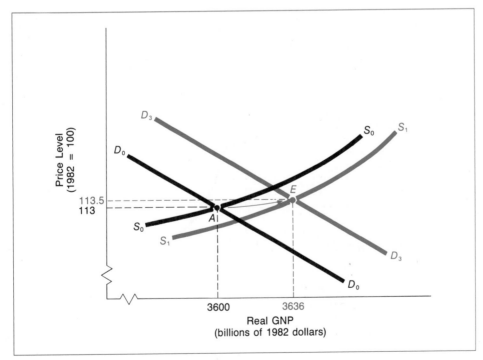

Figure 17–6
THE EFFECTS OF SLOWER GROWTH OF AGGREGATE DEMAND
Here, the aggregate demand curve is assumed to shift outward less than it did in Figure 17–4. Consequently, the movement from equilibrium point A to equilibrium point E during 1986 entails a smaller rise in the price level and a smaller increase in real output than actually occurred.

Does the theory fit the facts? We will put it to the test in a moment, but first let us translate it into a prediction about the relationship between inflation and unemployment. Faster growth of real output naturally means faster growth in the number of jobs and, hence, *lower unemployment*. Conversely, slower growth of real output means slower growth in the number of jobs and, hence, *higher unemployment*. So we conclude that, if business fluctuations emanate from the demand side, unemployment should be low when inflation is high and inflation should be low when unemployment is high.

Figure 17–7 illustrates this idea. The actual unemployment rate in the United States in late 1986 was about 6.5 percent, and the inflation rate during the year was about 1.8 percent. This is point *b* in Figure 17–7, which corresponds to equilibrium point B in Figure 17–4. The faster growth rate of demand depicted by point C in Figure 17–5 would have led to higher inflation and lower unemployment. For the sake of a concrete example, we suppose that unemployment would have been 5.5 percent and inflation would have been 5.3 percent; this is point *c* in Figure 17–7. Point E in Figure 17–6 summarized the results of slower growth of aggregate demand: Unemployment would have been higher and inflation lower. In Figure 17–7, this is represented by point *e*, with an unemployment rate of 7.5 percent and an inflation rate of about 1 percent. This figure shows graphically the principal empirical implication of our theoretical model:

If fluctuations in economic activity are primarily caused by variations in the rate at which the aggregate demand curve shifts outward from year to year, then the data should show an inverse relationship between unemployment and inflation, as in Figure 17–7.

Now we are ready to look at real data. Do we actually observe such an inverse relationship between inflation and unemployment? About 30 years ago,

Figure 17–7
ORIGINS OF THE PHILLIPS CURVE
The three previous diagrams indicated three different rates of growth of real GNP between late 1985 and late 1986 and three different inflation rates. Since each different real growth rate corresponds to a different rate of unemployment, we can put the information contained in the three preceding diagrams together in a scatter diagram to show the relationship between inflation and unemployment. Points *b, c,* and *e* in this figure correspond to points *B, C,* and *E* in Figures 17–4, 17–5, and 17–6, respectively. The inflation numbers are read directly from the previous three graphs. The unemployment numbers are fabricated to represent the fact that faster growth (Figure 17–5) is associated with lower unemployment (point *c*), while slower growth (Figure 17–6) is associated with higher unemployment (point *e*). Scatter diagrams like this one are called "Phillips curves," after their inventor, A. W. Phillips.

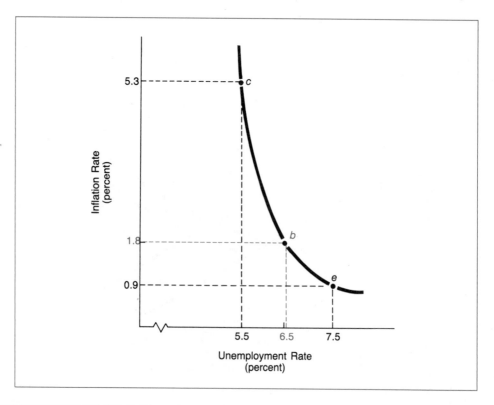

economist A. W. Phillips plotted data on unemployment and the rate of change of *wages* (not prices) for several extended periods of British history on a series of scatter diagrams, one of which is reproduced as Figure 17–8. He then sketched in a curve that seemed to "fit" the data. This type of curve, which is now called a **Phillips curve,** shows that wage inflation normally is high when unemployment is low and is low when unemployment is high. So far, so good.

Phillips curves have also been constructed for *price* inflation, and one of these for the postwar United States is shown in Figure 17–9. The curve appears to fit the data well, though not perfectly. As viewed through the eyes of our theory, these facts suggest that economic fluctuations in England between 1861 and 1913 and in the United States between 1954 and 1969 probably were accounted for primarily by changes in the growth of aggregate demand. The simple model of demand-side inflation really does seem to describe what happened.

During the 1960s and early 1970s, economists often thought of the Phillips curve as a "menu" of the choices available to policymakers. In this view, policymakers could opt for low unemployment and high inflation—as in 1969. Or

A **Phillips curve** is a graph depicting the rate of unemployment on the horizontal axis and either the rate of inflation or the rate of change of money wages on the vertical axis. Phillips curves are normally downward sloping, indicating that higher inflation rates are associated with lower unemployment rates.

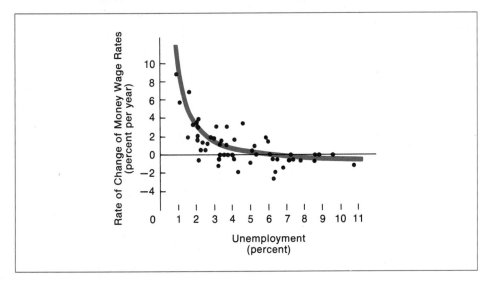

Figure 17–8
THE ORIGINAL PHILLIPS CURVE
This scatter diagram, reproduced from the original article by A. W. Phillips, shows the rate of change of money wages and the rate of unemployment in the United Kingdom between 1861 and 1913. Each year is represented by a point in the diagram.
SOURCE: A. W. Phillips, "The Relation Between Unemployment and the Rate of Change of Money Wages in the United Kingdom, 1861–1957." *Economica,* New Series, vol. 25, November 1958.

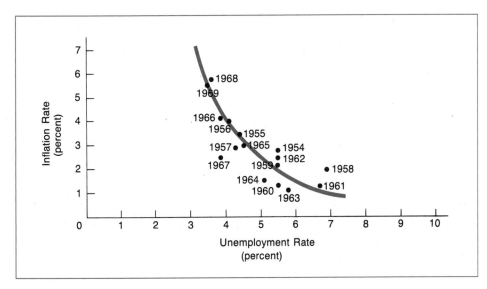

Figure 17–9
A PHILLIPS CURVE FOR THE UNITED STATES
This Phillips curve relates *price* inflation (rather than wage inflation) to the unemployment rate in the United States for the years 1954–1969. Though it misses badly in a few instances (for example, 1958), it generally "fits" the data well.

they might prefer higher unemployment coupled with lower inflation—as, for example, in 1961. The Phillips curve, it was thought, described the *quantitative* trade-off between inflation and unemployment. And, for a number of years, it worked rather well.

Then something happened. The economy in the 1970s behaved far worse than expected in terms of the Phillips curve shown in Figure 17–9. In particular, given the unemployment rates in each of those years, inflation was astonishingly high by historical standards. This is shown in Figure 17–10, which simply adds to Figure 17–9 the points for 1970–1986. Clearly something had gone wrong with the old view of the Phillips curve as a menu for policy choices. But what?

Supply-Side Inflation and the Collapse of the Phillips Curve

There are two major answers to this question, and the truth no doubt contains elements of each. We begin with the simpler explanation which claims that much of the inflation of the 1970s did not emanate from the demand side. Instead, the 1970s were full of adverse "supply shocks"—events like the crop failures of 1972–1973 and the oil price increases of 1973–1974 and 1979–1980—that pushed the economy's aggregate supply curve inward to the left. What kind of Phillips curve will be generated when economic fluctuations come from the supply side?

Figure 17–10

A PHILLIPS CURVE FOR THE UNITED STATES?

This scatter diagram adds the points for 1970–1986 to the scatter diagram shown in Figure 17–9. It is clear that inflation in each of those years was higher than the Phillips curve would have led us to predict.

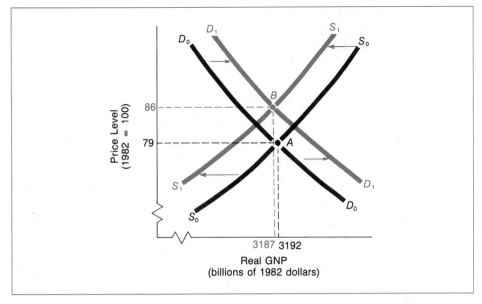

Figure 17–11
STAGFLATION FROM A SUPPLY SHOCK
Instead of shifting outward as it normally does, the aggregate supply curve shifted inward—from $S_0 S_0$ to $S_1 S_1$—between 1979 and 1980. Coupled with fairly slow growth of the aggregate demand curve—from $D_0 D_0$ in 1979 to $D_1 D_1$ in 1980—equilibrium moved from point A to point B. There was a slight decline of real output, and prices rose rapidly.

To find out, let us take the events of 1979 and 1980 as an example. In Figure 17–11, aggregate demand curve $D_0 D_0$ and aggregate supply curve $S_0 S_0$ represent the economic situation in 1979. Equilibrium was at point A, with a price level of 79 and real output of $3192 billion. By 1980, the aggregate demand curve had shifted out to the position indicated by $D_1 D_1$, and, under normal conditions, the aggregate supply curve would have shifted out as well. But 1979 was anything but normal. The Iranian revolution led to a shutdown of Iran's oilfields for months. The resulting worldwide scramble for oil led OPEC to double the price of its product during the year.

Thus, instead of shifting *outward* as it normally does from one year to the next, the aggregate supply curve shifted *inward* during 1979, to $S_1 S_1$. The equilibrium for 1980 (point B in the figure) therefore wound up almost vertically above the equilibrium point for 1979. Real output declined slightly and prices—led by energy costs—rose rapidly.

Now, in a growing population with more people looking for jobs each year, a stagnant economy that is not generating new jobs suffers a rise in the unemployment rate. This is precisely what happened in the United States; the unemployment rate averaged 5.8 percent in 1979 and 7.1 percent in 1980. Thus, inflation and unemployment increased at the same time: The Phillips curve basically shifted upward. A general conclusion is that:

If fluctuations in economic activity emanate from the supply side, higher rates of inflation will be associated with higher rates of unemployment, and lower rates of inflation will be associated with lower rates of unemployment.

The instances of major supply shocks during the 1970s stand out clearly in Figure 17–10. (Remember these are *real* data; they are not made up by some textbook writer.) Food prices boomed between 1972 and 1974 and again in 1978. Energy prices soared in 1973–1974 and again in 1979–1980. It is clear that the inflation and unemployment data generated by the U.S. economy between 1972 and 1974, and again between 1978 and 1980, are consistent with our theoretical model of supply-side inflation. Indeed, if you look at Figure 17–10 carefully, you can almost see the outlines of three separate Phillips curves: a low one for 1954–1969 (shown in the diagram), a high one for 1974–1983, and an intermediate one for 1970–1973 and 1984–1986. Many economists believe that the supply shocks of the 1970s account for these shifts of the Phillips curve.

What the Phillips Curve Is Not

But there is another view of what went wrong in the 1970s. This one holds that policymakers misinterpreted the Phillips curve and tried to pick unsustainable combinations of inflation and unemployment. Specifically, the Phillips curve is a *statistical relationship* between inflation and unemployment that we expect to emerge *if changes in the growth of aggregate demand are the predominant factor accounting for economic fluctuations*. But the curve was widely misinterpreted as depicting a number of *alternative equilibrium points* that the economy could achieve and from which policymakers could choose.

We can understand the flaw in this reasoning by quickly reviewing an earlier lesson. We know from Chapter 11 that the economy has a **self-correcting mechanism** that will cure both inflations and recessions *eventually* even if the government does nothing. Why is this relevant here? Because it tells us that many combinations of output and prices cannot be maintained indefinitely. Some will "self-destruct." Specifically, if the economy finds itself far away from the normal full-employment level of unemployment, forces will be set in motion that tend to erode the inflationary or recessionary gap.

For example, consider the case of a recessionary gap where aggregate supply curve S_0S_0 intersects aggregate demand curve DD at point A in Figure 17–12. With equilibrium output well below potential GNP, there is unused industrial capacity and unsold output. So firms will not raise prices much. At the same time, the availability of unemployed workers eager for jobs limits the rate at which labor can push up wage rates. But wages are the main component of business costs, so when wages decline (relative to what they would have been without a recession) so do costs. And lower costs stimulate greater production. This idea is depicted in Figure 17–12 as an outward shift of the aggregate supply curve—from S_0S_0 to S_1S_1.

Figure 17–12
THE ELIMINATION OF A RECESSIONARY GAP
When the aggregate supply curve is S_0S_0 and the aggregate demand curve is *DD*, the economy will reach an equilibrium with a recessionary gap (point *A*). The resulting deflation of wages will cause the aggregate supply curve to shift outward (downward) from S_0S_0 to S_1S_1 and eventually to S_2S_2. Here, with equilibrium at point *C*, the recessionary gap is gone and the economy is back at normal full employment.

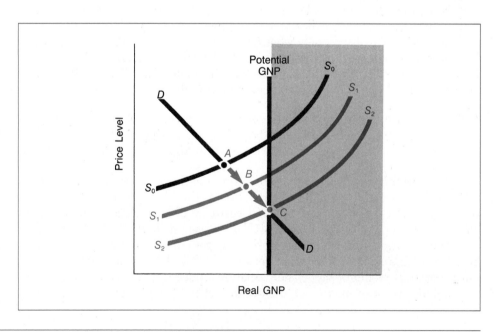

As can be seen in the figure, the outward shift of the aggregate supply curve brought on by the recession causes equilibrium output to rise as the economy moves from point A to point B. Thus the size of the recessionary gap begins to shrink. This process continues until the aggregate supply curve reaches the position indicated by S_2S_2 in Figure 17–12. Here wages have fallen enough to eliminate the recessionary gap, and the economy has reached a full-employment equilibrium at point C.[1]

We can relate this to our discussion of the origins of the Phillips curve with the help of Figure 17–13, which is a hypothetical Phillips curve.

Point a in Figure 17–13 corresponds to point A in Figure 17–12: it shows the initial recessionary gap with unemployment (at 8 percent) above full employment, which we assume to occur at 6 percent. But we have just seen that point A in Figure 17–12—and therefore also point a in Figure 17–13—is not sustainable. The economy tends to rid itself of the recessionary gap through the disinflation process we have just described. The adjustment path from A to C that we analyzed in Figure 17–12 would appear on our Phillips curve diagram as a movement toward less inflation and less unemployment—something like the blue arrow from point a to point c in Figure 17–13.

Similarly, points representing inflationary gaps—such as point d in Figure 17–13—are not sustainable. They are also gradually eliminated by the self-correcting mechanism that we studied in Chapter 11. Wages are forced up by the abnormally low unemployment, and this in turn pushes prices higher. Higher prices deter investment spending by forcing up interest rates and deter consumer spending by lowering the purchasing power of consumer wealth. The inflationary process continues until the amount people want to spend is brought into balance with the amount firms want to supply at normal full employment.

[1]This simple analysis assumes that the aggregate demand curve does not move during the adjustment period. If it is shifting to the right, the recessionary gap will disappear even faster, but inflation will not slow down as much.

EXERCISE: Construct the diagram for this case by adding a shift in the aggregate demand curve to Figure 17–12.

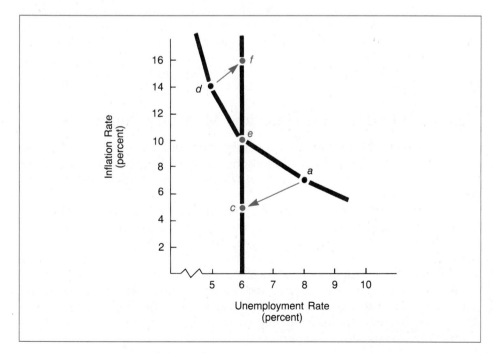

Figure 17–13
THE VERTICAL LONG-RUN PHILLIPS CURVE
In the long run, points like a, where unemployment is above the normal "full-employment" unemployment rate, are unsustainable. The economy's natural self-correcting mechanism (which was described in Figure 17–12) will erode the recessionary gap by reducing both inflation and unemployment. In the diagram, this will force the economy toward a point like c. The long-run choices, therefore, are among points like c and f, which constitute what is called the vertical (long-run) Phillips curve, not among points like d and a on the downward-sloping (short-run) Phillips curve.

During such an adjustment period, unemployment and inflation are both rising — as indicated by the blue path from point d to point f in Figure 17–13.

Putting these two conclusions together, we see that:

On a Phillips curve diagram, neither points corresponding to an inflationary gap (like d in Figure 17–13) nor points corresponding to a recessionary gap (like a in Figure 17–13) can be maintained indefinitely. Inflationary gaps lead to rising unemployment and rising inflation. Recessionary gaps lead to falling inflation and falling unemployment. All the points that are sustainable in the long run (such as c, e, and f in Figure 17–13) correspond to the same rate of unemployment, which is therefore called the **natural rate of unemployment.** The natural rate corresponds to what we have so far been calling the "full employment" unemployment rate.

The economy's self-correcting mechanism always tends to push the unemployment rate back toward a specific rate of unemployment that we call the **natural rate of unemployment.**

Thus the Phillips curve connecting points d, e, and a is not a menu of policy choices. While we can move from a point like e to a point like d by stimulating aggregate demand sufficiently, there is no way that we can stay at point d. Unemployment cannot be kept this low indefinitely. Instead, policymakers must choose from among points like c, e, and f, all of which are vertically above one another at the natural rate of unemployment. For rather obvious reasons, the line connecting these points has been dubbed the **vertical (long-run) Phillips curve.** It is this vertical Phillips curve (connecting points like e and f), that represents the true long-run menu of policy choices. We thus conclude that:

The **vertical (long run) Phillips curve** shows the menu of inflation/unemployment choices available to society in the long run. It is a vertical straight line at the natural rate of unemployment.

In the short-run, it is possible to "ride up the Phillips curve" toward lower levels of unemployment by stimulating aggregate demand. Conversely, by restricting the growth of demand, it is possible to "ride down the Phillips curve" toward lower rates of inflation (see, for example, point a in Figure 17–13). There is, thus, a *trade-off between unemployment and inflation*. Stimulating demand will improve the unemployment picture but worsen inflation; restricting demand will lower inflation but aggravate the unemployment problem.

However, there is no such trade-off in the long run. The economy's self-correcting mechanism ensures that unemployment eventually will return to the "natural rate," no matter what happens to aggregate demand. In the long run, faster growth of demand leads only to higher inflation, not to lower unemployment; and slower growth of demand leads only to lower inflation, not to higher unemployment.

Fighting Inflation with Fiscal and Monetary Policy

Now let us apply this analysis to a concrete policy problem, one that has troubled every president from Lyndon Johnson to Ronald Reagan. How should the government's ability to manage aggregate demand through fiscal and monetary policy be used to fight inflation?

We have already spent many chapters discussing how the government's monetary and fiscal policy tools — tax rates, government spending, open market operations, and so on — can be used to increase or decrease aggregate demand. We have also discussed some of the practical problems that arise in using each of these weapons and some of the issues involved in choosing among them. Rather than repeat all this, let us just suppose that the government somehow controls aggregate demand and wishes to use this ability to fight inflation. What has our discussion of the trade-off between inflation and unemployment taught us about this problem?

To create an example that comes close to that inherited by President Reagan in early 1981, let us imagine that a new president takes office when the inflation rate is 10 percent and the unemployment rate is 6 percent—point e in Figure 17–13.[2] Suppose the new president adopts a policy of restricting the growth of aggregate demand by contractionary fiscal and monetary policies, thereby opening up a recessionary gap. In a word—though no politician would ever use such blunt language—he decides to fight inflation by causing a recession.

At first, the economy "rides down" the short-run Phillips curve from point e to point a in Figure 17–13. The recession pushes unemployment up from 6 percent to 8 percent, but it reduces inflation from 10 percent to 7 percent. This scenario roughly describes what happened in the United States between early 1981 and late 1982, except that the recession was much more severe than in the example. Unemployment in the United States hit 10.7 percent.

But the anti-inflation dividends of recession do not end there. The economy's self-correcting mechanism begins to work and gradually erodes the recessionary gap. Inflation continues to decline as the economy recovers and unemployment falls. In the example, inflation falls from 7 percent to 5 percent as the economy recovers along the path from a to c in Figure 17–13. In the actual U.S. case, inflation continued to decline as recovery progressed, but the economy had still not returned to full employment when this book went to press in 1987.

When all the dust has settled, the economy in our hypothetical example has moved from point e to point c in Figure 17–13. Comparing these two points shows that, in the end, there is less inflation and no more unemployment. In what sense, then, do policymakers have to face up to a *trade-off* between inflation and unemployment? The answer is that:

The cost of reducing inflation by restrictive fiscal and monetary policies is a *temporary* rise in unemployment.

Figures 17–14 and 17–15 are intended to give the flavor of what the real menu of choices looks like to a policymaker who is considering embarking on such a program. Figure 17–14 contrasts the behavior of the inflation rate over time under a "status quo policy," which keeps the unemployment rate unchanged at 6 percent, with the behavior under a restrictive anti-inflationary policy, which deliberately slows the growth rate of aggregate demand and makes unemployment rise.

Inflation will continue at 10 percent per year if the government does not restrain the growth of demand and unemployment remains at 6 percent. This is the "status quo policy" path shown in black in Figure 17–14. It corresponds to the case where the economy stays indefinitely at point e in Figure 17–13.

On the other hand, if a restrictive policy is followed and the growth of aggregate demand is restrained, inflation will begin to fall, slowly at first but then with increasing speed. In the example, we suppose that the inflation rate falls little in the first year, more in the second year, and is essentially down to 5 percent after three years. This is the blue "restrictive policy" path in Figure 17–14. It corresponds to the path from e to a to c in Figure 17–13.

---

[2]The actual inflation rate was about 10 percent; but the unemployment rate was above 7 percent, so President Reagan had both inflation and unemployment to worry about. Our example will be easier to analyze, however, if we depart from reality by pretending that unemployment was not a problem initially.

Figure 17–14

THE PAYOFF TO
ANTI-INFLATION POLICY

If a recession is caused by
restrictive fiscal and
monetary policy, the inflation
rate will not respond much at
first. Gradually, however,
inflation will yield to the slack
caused by the restrictive
policy. In this example, the
inflation rate begins at 10
percent, falls only to 9
percent after one year, but is
down to 7$\frac{1}{2}$ percent after two
years, and 5 percent after
three years. The shaded area
indicates the gains that the
policy has reaped on the
inflation front.

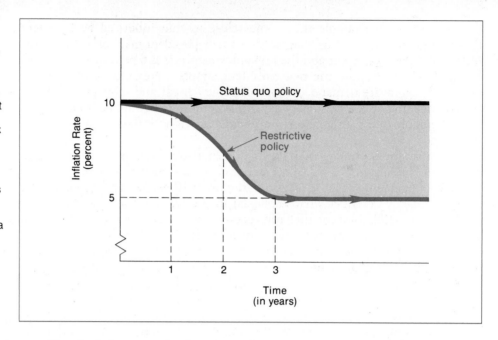

The shaded area in the figure summarizes the difference between these two
paths and therefore depicts the payoff to anti-inflation policy. But there are also
costs.

Figure 17–15

THE COST OF
ANTI-INFLATION POLICY

The inflation gains depicted
in the preceding figure do
not come to us without cost.
The restrictive policy
increases unemployment for
a period; that is, it induces a
recession. In this example
the unemployment rate takes
about a year to rise from 6
percent to 8 percent (the
recession period), and then
takes more than two years to
return to 6 percent (the
recovery period). The shaded
area indicates the extra
unemployment that must be
endured in order to get the
inflation rate down from 10
percent to 5 percent.

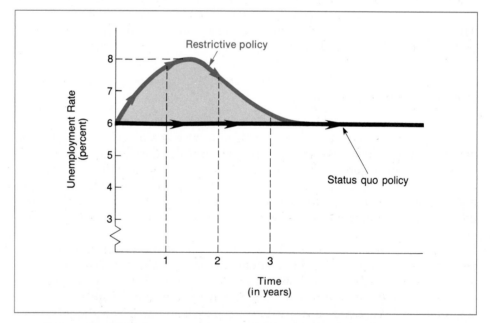

Figure 17–15 gives a rough impression of how the unemployment rate
might behave under the two alternative policies. The "status quo policy" keeps
the unemployment rate at 6 percent, which is the natural rate. The restrictive
policy results in a recession: Unemployment rises from 6 percent to 8 percent,
and then gradually falls back to the natural rate of 6 percent. The shaded area
in Figure 17–15 shows what it costs to get the inflation rate down: For over
three years unemployment is above the natural rate.

Notice the differences in timing between Figure 17–14 and Figure 17–15.
In the early stages of the disinflation program (say, the first year), progress

against inflation is meager even though the losses on the unemployment front are substantial. This reflects an underlying reality that we have mentioned before: Inflation gives way only grudgingly to economic slack. This, of course, makes anti-inflation policy politically distasteful. The costs of higher unemployment, though temporary, come right away; the benefits of lower inflation, though more durable, may not arrive until after the next election.

What Should Be Done?

Should the government pay the recessionary cost of fighting inflation? When the benefits depicted in Figure 17–14 are balanced against the costs shown in Figure 17–15, have we made a good bargain? While each of you will have to answer this question for yourself, our analysis highlights three critical issues on which your answer should rest.

The Costs of Inflation and Unemployment

We spent an entire chapter early in the book (Chapter 6) examining the social costs of inflation and unemployment. Most of the costs of the extra unemployment depicted in Figure 17–15, we concluded, are easy to translate into dollars and cents. Basically, we need only estimate the real GNP that is lost each year. However, the costs of inflation are harder to put a price tag on, and hence the benefits from reducing inflation are harder to measure. Thus there is considerable controversy over the costs and benefits of using recession to fight inflation.

Some economists and public figures believe that inflation is extremely costly, and so they look with favor on the trade-off that is embodied in Figures 17–14 and 17–15. Others have a lower estimate of the costs of inflation and find recession a terribly high price to pay. In particular, some observers believe that we paid an excessively high price to reduce inflation in the 1980s, while others applaud the policy and maintain that the price was worth paying.

The Position of the Economy

We have stated several times in this book that the shape of the economy's aggregate supply curve, and hence the shape of the short-run Phillips curve, depends on the degree of resource utilization. If resources are virtually fully employed, the aggregate supply curve (and thus the Phillips curve) will be steep, which means that the inflation gains will be substantial and the unemployment costs will be minimal. On the other hand, if there is a great deal of unemployed labor and unutilized industrial capacity, the aggregate supply curve (and hence the short-run Phillips curve) may be nearly horizontal. In that case, a great deal of unemployment will be needed to achieve even a slight reduction in inflation. The Phillips curves we have drawn in this chapter have this characteristic shape.

Because the Phillips curve is shaped this way, the trade-off for inflation-fighters looks more favorable when the economy is in a boom and less favorable when there is already a good deal of unemployment. This, of course, complicated the task faced by President Reagan, who took office at a time when inflation was high but unemployment was already above the natural rate.

The Efficiency of the Economy's Self-Correcting Mechanism

We have stressed that once government policy causes a recession, it is the economy's natural self-correcting mechanism that cures the recessionary gap.

The obvious question here is: How long do we have to wait? If the self-correcting mechanism—which works through reductions in the rate of wage inflation—is slow and halting, the costs of fighting inflation will be enormous. On the other hand, if wage inflation responds promptly, the recession necessary to bring down inflation may not be severe.

This is another issue that is surrounded by controversy. Most economists believe that the weight of the evidence points to extremely sluggish wage behavior. The rate of wage inflation appears to respond only slowly to economic slack. In terms of our Figure 17–13 (page 355), this means that the economy will traverse the path from *a* to *c* at an agonizingly slow pace, so that a long period of weak economic activity will be necessary if there is to be any appreciable effect on inflation.

But a significant minority opinion finds this assessment far too pessimistic. Economists in this group argue that the costs of reducing inflation are not nearly so severe and that the key to a successful anti-inflation policy is its effects on people's *expectations*. To understand this argument, we must first examine why expectations are relevant to the Phillips-curve trade-off.

Inflationary Expectations and the Phillips Curve

The explanation starts with more review. Recall from Chapter 11 that the main reason why the economy's aggregate supply curve slopes upward—that is, why output increases as the price level rises—is that businesses typically purchase labor and other inputs under long-term contracts that stipulate the cost of the input in *money* terms (for example, the money wage rate). If such contracts are in force when prices go up, then *real* wages fall as prices rise. From businesses' point of view, labor becomes cheaper in real terms, and firms are induced to expand employment and output. Buying cheaply and selling dearly is, after all, the route to higher profits. Long-term contracts that fix the money wage, then, explain why higher prices lead to more output; that is, why the aggregate supply curve slopes upward.

Table 17–1 illustrates how this works in a concrete example. We suppose that workers and firms agree today that the money wage to be paid a year from-now will be $10 per hour. The table then shows the real wage that corresponds to each alternative rate of inflation. Clearly, the higher the inflation rate, the higher the price level at the end of the year and the lower the real wage.

Lower real wages provide an incentive for the firm to increase output, as we have just noted. But lower real wages also impose losses of purchasing power

Table 17–1
MONEY AND REAL WAGES UNDER INFLATION

INFLATION RATE (percent)	PRICE LEVEL ONE YEAR FROM NOW	MONEY WAGE ONE YEAR FROM NOW (dollars per hour)	REAL WAGE ONE YEAR FROM NOW (dollars per hour)
0	100	10.00	10.00
2	102	10.00	9.80
4	104	10.00	9.62
6	106	10.00	9.43

NOTE: Each real wage figure is obtained by dividing the $10 nominal wage by the corresponding price level a year later and multiplying by 100. Thus, for example, when the inflation rate is 4 percent, the real wage at the end of the year is ($10/104) × 100 = $9.62.

on workers. Thus, there is a sense in which workers are being "cheated" by inflation if they sign a contract specifying a fixed money wage in an inflationary environment.

Many economists doubt that workers would sign such a contract if they can see inflation coming. Would it not be more reasonable, these economists ask, to insist on being compensated for inflation in advance? After all, firms should be willing to offer higher money wages when they expect inflation because they realize that higher money wages need not imply higher *real* wages.

Table 17–2 illustrates how the money wage specified in a contract can be adjusted for expected inflation. For example, if 4 percent inflation is expected, the contract could stipulate that the wage rate be increased to $10.40 (which is 4 percent more than $10) at the end of the year. That would keep the real wage at $10, the same as it would be under zero inflation. The remaining money wage figures in Table 17–2 are derived similarly.

If workers and firms actually adjust money wages in the way suggested in Table 17–2, then the expected real wage will not decline as the expected price level rises. In the example, the expected future real wage is always $10 per hour. Prices and wages will go up together if expectations prove correct, leaving the real wage unchanged. Workers will not lose from inflation, and firms will not gain. But, of course, that means that there will be no reason for firms to produce more as prices rise. In a word, the aggregate supply curve would become *vertical*. In general:

If workers can see inflation coming, and if they receive compensation for it in advance so that inflation does not erode *real* wages, then the economy's aggregate supply curve will not slope upward. It will be a vertical line at the level of output corresponding to potential GNP.

Such a curve is shown in part (a) of Figure 17–16. Since we derived the Phillips curve from the aggregate supply curve earlier in the chapter, it follows that even the *short-run* Phillips curve will become vertical under these circumstances [see part (b) of Figure 17–16].[3]

If this analysis is correct, it has profound implications for the costs and benefits of inflation fighting. This can be seen by referring back to Figure 17–13 on page 355, where we depicted the strategy of fighting inflation by causing a recession. We concluded there that in order to move from point e (representing 10 percent inflation) to point c (representing 5 percent inflation), the economy would have to take a long and unpleasant detour through point a; that is,

[3]See Discussion Question 10 at the end of the chapter.

Table 17–2
MONEY AND REAL WAGES UNDER EXPECTED INFLATION

EXPECTED INFLATION RATE (percent)	EXPECTED PRICE LEVEL ONE YEAR FROM NOW	MONEY WAGE ONE YEAR FROM NOW (dollars per hour)	EXPECTED REAL WAGE ONE YEAR FROM NOW (dollars per hour)
0	100	10.00	10.00
4	104	10.40	10.00
8	108	10.80	10.00
12	112	11.20	10.00

Figure 17–16

A VERTICAL AGGREGATE SUPPLY CURVE AND THE CORRESPONDING VERTICAL PHILLIPS CURVE

If workers foresee inflation, and if they also receive full compensation for it in advance, then inflation will no longer erode real wages. In that case, firms will have no incentive to raise production as prices rise, and the aggregate supply curve will be vertical as in part (a). Since we derived the short-run Phillips curve from the aggregate supply curve, the short-run Phillips curve will also become vertical [part (b)].

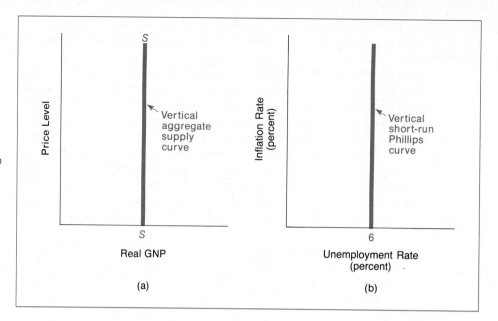

it would have to endure a recession. If, however, even the *short-run* Phillips curve were *vertical* rather than downward sloping, this detour would not be necessary. It would be possible for inflation to fall without unemployment rising. The economy could jump directly from point *e* to point *c*.

Is this analysis correct? Can we really slay the inflationary dragon so painlessly? As a piece of pure logic, the argument is impeccable. Yet things do not seem to work out this way. In practice, inflation fighting looks to be very costly. We must therefore ask ourselves whether the premises on which the analysis rests are realistic. There are several reasons why many economists think the expectations argument should not be applied uncritically to the modern economy.

Point 1. The argument is predicated on the notion that inflation can be accurately foreseen. But many contracts for labor and other raw materials cover such long periods of time that the expectations that were held when the contracts were written may be very different from current reality. If a restrictive policy reduces inflation below the rate firms and workers expected when they made their wage agreements, real wages wind up *higher* than intended, and hence firms want to reduce employment and produce less.

Point 2. Many people believe that inflationary expectations are sluggish, that they do not adapt quickly to changes in the economic environment. If, for example, the government embarks on an anti-inflation policy, workers will continue to expect high inflation for quite a while. Thus they will continue to insist on high rates of increase in money wages. Then, if inflation actually slows down, real wages will wind up rising faster than anyone expected. Firms will therefore find labor "too expensive" relative to current selling prices, and unemployment will result. With lags in the reaction of expectations, then, the short-run Phillips curve retains its downward slope, and inflation fighting is costly.

The Theory of Rational Expectations

These two points, and others we have not mentioned, have persuaded most economists that the expectations argument, while valid in part, should not be taken to extremes. Most economists nowadays accept the notion that the Phillips curve is downward sloping in the short run, and hence that a short-run trade-off does exist.

But a vocal minority of economists disagrees. This group, believers in the doctrine of **rational expectations,** insists that the only type of inflation that leads to *increases* in output is *unexpected* inflation, because only unexpected inflation reduces real wages. (To see this, compare Tables 17–1 and 17–2.) Similarly, they argue, the only type of reduction in inflation that leads to recession is an *unexpected* reduction.

To explain this point of view, we must first explain what *rational expectations* are. Once we do this, we will be in a position to understand why rational expectations have such radical implications for the Phillips curve.

What Are *Rational* Expectations?

In many economic contexts, people must formulate expectations about what the future will bring. For example, those who invest in the stock market need to forecast the future prices of the stocks they buy and sell. And we have just discussed why workers and businesses may want to forecast future prices before they agree on a money wage. *Rational expectations* is a controversial hypothesis about how such forecasts are made.

As used by economists, a forecast (an "expectation") of a future variable is considered rational if the forecaster makes *optimal* use of all information that is both *available* and *relevant*. Let us elaborate on the italicized words in this definition, using as an example a hypothetical stock market investor who has rational expectations.

First, believers in the doctrine of rational expectations recognize that *information is limited*. An investor who is interested in buying General Motors stock would like to know how much profit the company will make in the coming years. Armed with such information, she could predict the future price of GM stock more accurately. But that information is simply not available. Her forecast of the future price of GM stock is not "irrational" just because she does not know GM's future profits. On the other hand, if GM stock normally goes down on Fridays and up on Mondays, she should be aware of this fact.

Second, *not all information is important*. Some publicly available facts may be irrelevant to predicting the variables of interest. If so, a rational forecaster can afford to be ignorant of them. For example, anyone who cares to can find out how many babies were born last year in Peoria, Illinois. But this fact may not tell you much about the future performance of General Motors. So our investor need not have this information to be rational. However, if there is a clear Friday/Monday pattern in GM stock prices, she had better know what day of the week it is!

Finally, we have the word *optimal*. As used by economists, this means using proper statistical inference to process all the relevant information that is available before making a forecast. In a word, to have rational expectations, your forecasts do not have to be correct, but they cannot have systematic errors that could be avoided by applying better statistical methods. This requirement, while exacting, is not quite as outlandish as it may seem. A good billiards player makes expert use of the laws of physics, even though he may have no

Rational expectations are forecasts which, while not necessarily correct, are the best that can be made given the available data. Rational expectations, therefore, cannot err systematically. If expectations are rational, forecasting errors are pure random numbers.

understanding of the theory. Similarly, an experienced stock market investor may make good use of information even without formal training in statistics.

Rational Expectations and the Trade-Off

Let us now see how the doctrine of rational expectations has been applied to deny that there exists any trade-off between inflation and unemployment—even in the short run.

Though they recognize that inflation cannot always be predicted accurately, rational expectationists claim that workers will not make *systematic* errors in forecasting inflation. Note that Point 2 above suggests that inflationary expectations are typically *too low* when inflation is rising and *too high* when inflation is falling. Rational expectationists deny that this is possible. Workers, they argue, will always make the best possible forecast of inflation, using all the latest data and the best available economic models. Such forecasts will not err systematically in one direction or the other regardless of whether inflation is rising or falling. Consequently:

If expectations are rational, the difference between the *actual* rate of inflation and the *expected* rate of inflation (the forecasting error) will be a pure random number.

Now recall the basic expectationist argument summarized in the previous section: Employment is affected by inflation only to the extent that inflation *differs* from what was expected. But, under rational expectations, no *predictable* change in inflation can make the *expected* rate of inflation deviate from the *actual* rate of inflation. Hence, according to the rational expectationists, unemployment will always remain at the natural rate—except for random, and therefore totally unpredictable, gyrations due to forecasting errors.

The implications of rational expectations for the conduct of economic policy are revolutionary. For one thing:

If expectations are rational, the inflation rate can be reduced without the need for a period of high unemployment because the short-run Phillips curve is vertical.

According to the rational expectations view, the government's ability to manipulate aggregate demand gives it no ability to control real output and unemployment because the aggregate supply curve is vertical—even in the short run. [To see why, experiment by moving an aggregate demand curve when the aggregate supply curve is vertical, as in Figure 17–16(a).] Any *predictable* change in aggregate demand will lead to a change in the expected rate of inflation, and hence will leave real wages unaffected.

The government therefore can influence output only by making *unexpected* changes in aggregate demand. But this is not easy to do when expectations are rational because people understand what policymakers are up to. According to the rational expectationists, if the monetary and fiscal authorities typically react to high inflation by reducing aggregate demand, people will soon come to anticipate this reaction. And, as just mentioned, anticipated reductions in aggregate demand do not affect unemployment because they do not cause *unexpected* changes in inflation.

An Evaluation

Since rational expectationists believe that inflation can be reduced without losses of output, they tend to be hawks in the war against inflation. Though the doctrine has attracted many adherents, rational expectationists remain in the minority. There are several reasons for this.

For one, Point 1 above remains valid even if expectations are rational. When long-term contracts are made, people get locked into provisions which, while rational when they were made, may seem irrational from today's point of view. For example, consider a labor contract drawn up late in 1980 that specified money wages to be paid in 1981–1984. Given what people knew then, it may have been rational to expect the 1984 price level to be 30 percent higher than the 1981 price level. So the money wage may have been set to rise 33 percent over the three years. But, in fact, the price level rose only 15 percent. If the money wages specified in the contract were actually paid, the real wage wound up 15 percent higher than intended. But no one behaved irrationally.

Second, many observers of the labor market continue to believe that inflationary expectations are sluggish; that is, they are not *rational* expectations. Workers or managers may not be as well-informed as the rational expectations hypothesis assumes. Or they may not have a good understanding of how the economy works. Or they may not behave like the expert statisticians that the rational expectations hypothesis envisions.

Finally, the facts have not been kind to the rational expectations point of view. The theory suggests that unemployment should hover around the natural rate most of the time, with random gyrations in one direction or the other. Yet this does not seem to be the case. The theory also denies that predictable monetary and fiscal policy actions will have effects on real output. Yet most observers think they can identify episodes in the past where such actions had significant effects on real GNP and unemployment. And many direct tests of the rationality of expectations have cast doubt on the hypothesis. For example, survey data on peoples' expectations rarely meet the exacting requirements of rationality.

At this writing, there is a great deal of controversy over how best to apply the idea of rational expectations to macroeconomic issues. The issues are far from resolved. But the evidence to date leads most economists to reject the extreme rational expectationist position for short-run analysis. In the long run, however, the rational expectations view should be more or less correct since people will not hold systematically wrong expectations indefinitely. As Abraham Lincoln said, you cannot fool all of the people all of the time.

Fighting Recessions with Fiscal and Monetary Policy

At this point it may be useful to pause and take stock of what we have learned. A good way to test your understanding is to run the analysis in reverse. We have been considering the use of monetary and fiscal policies to combat *inflation*. Let us now suppose instead that the crucial macroeconomic problem is *unemployment*.

We again turn to the Phillips curve diagram, Figure 17–13 on page 355, for a concrete example. Suppose that the economy somehow finds itself at a point like *a*, in a recession. And suppose that the president and Congress want to get the economy back to full employment. What should they do?

We know from our previous analysis what will happen if the current rate of growth of aggregate demand is simply maintained. Since point *a* on the short-run Phillips curve represents a recessionary gap, the economy's self-correcting mechanism begins to work. High unemployment slows the rate of increase of money wages, which tends to push the aggregate supply curve outward — compared with where it would have been if full employment were maintained.

The slowdown in wages both puts a brake on inflation and stimulates employment. The economy slowly travels down the path indicated by the blue arrow in Figure 17–13, from point *a* to point *c*. But, as we have noted before, the road from *a* to *c* may be slow and bumpy.

Is there a better way out of our economic problems? Perhaps. As we know, expansionary measures such as tax cuts, increases in government spending, or open market purchases of government securities can speed up the rate at which the aggregate demand curve moves to the right. (Compare Figures 17–4 and 17–5 on page 348.) Such a policy would enable the economy to "ride up" the short-run Phillips curve toward point *e*.

Figure 17–17

THE PAYOFF TO ANTIRECESSION POLICY

By stimulating aggregate demand through monetary and fiscal policy, the government can reduce unemployment more rapidly. If it relies exclusively on the economy's ability to right itself, unemployment will follow the black "status quo policy" path. If, instead, the government takes an active hand in fighting the recession, unemployment will follow the blue "expansionary policy" path. The shaded area measures the reduction in unemployment that the expansionary policy achieves.

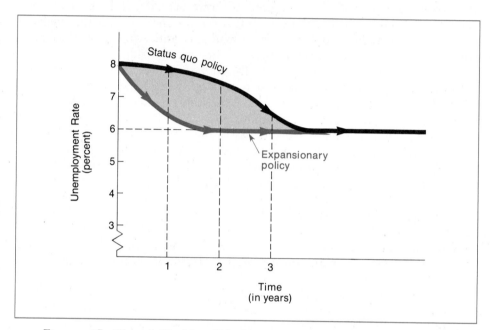

Figures 17–17 and 17–18 will help us compare this active antirecession policy with the more passive "status quo policy." Under the status quo policy of

Figure 17–18

THE COST OF ANTIRECESSION POLICY

The unemployment gains depicted in the previous figure are not obtained without cost. By stimulating the economy, the government policies cause a rise in the inflation rate—as shown by the blue "expansionary policy" path. If, instead, the government had simply waited for the economy's natural self-correcting mechanism to work, inflation would have fallen—see the black "status quo policy" path. The difference between these two paths (the shaded area) represents the inflationary cost of fighting the recession.

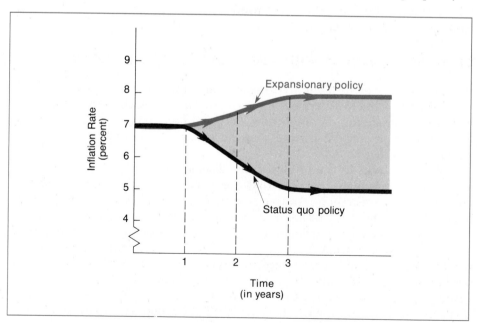

relying on the economy's self-correcting mechanism, the unemployment rate gradually falls from the 8 percent that corresponds to point *a* on the Phillips curve to the 6 percent that corresponds to point *c*. But progress is agonizingly slow. The "status quo policy" path shown in black in Figure 17–17 indicates that it takes more than three uncomfortable years to return to full employment.

By contrast, if expansionary monetary and fiscal policy actions are taken, the return to full employment is much quicker. According to the blue "expansionary policy" path in Figure 17–17, we get there in about one and one-half years. The shaded area in the figure measures the payoff to antirecession policy; it shows how much unemployment we save during the three-year period.

But, as we have by now come to expect, these gains are made at some cost. The black "status quo policy" path in Figure 17–18 shows the likely behavior of the inflation rate under the policy of waiting for the economy's self-corrective forces to work. Inflation falls gradually from the 7 percent rate that corresponds to point *a* on the Phillips curve to the 5 percent rate that corresponds to point *c*. But if expansionary policy is pursued, inflation will not creep downward; instead it will creep upward, as indicated by the blue "expansionary policy" path in Figure 17–18. The shaded area in this figure shows the cost of fighting recession with monetary and fiscal policy: We wind up with more inflation.

In considering whether or not to fight a recession, policymakers face a tradeoff between unemployment and inflation. If they take expansionary actions to reduce unemployment, they may end up with a higher inflation rate.

Are the inflationary costs depicted in Figure 17–18 worth the benefits of lower unemployment shown in Figure 17–17? This is not a question that can be answered with any assurance. The answer hinges on the same three issues we isolated in discussing anti-inflation policy:

1. *The social costs of inflation and unemployment.* Those who regard inflation as extremely costly will not want to pay the price of shortening the recession. Those who are more concerned with unemployment will find recession fighting a good idea.

2. *The position of the economy.* As we have noted, the Phillips curve is likely to be flatter at higher rates of unemployment. As you can see by studying Figure 17–13, if the Phillips curve is rather flat, the extra inflation caused by fighting a recession will be minimal. On the other hand, if the short-run Phillips curve is steep, the inflationary price tag will be high. Thus the case for fighting deep recessions is stronger than the case for fighting shallow ones.

3. *The efficiency of the economy's self-correcting mechanism,* which works as unemployment slows the rate of growth of wages. Naturally, if the economy's self-corrective forces work rapidly, there is little reason for the government to try to speed things up. On the other hand, if the mechanism is slow and unreliable or, worse yet, if it breaks down entirely, the case for government intervention is much stronger.

Why Economists (and Politicians) Disagree

These three factors help explain why economists sometimes differ so radically from one another in their recommendations as to the proper conduct of national economic policy. And they also help account for disagreements among politicians.

The question is: When a recession occurs, should the government take actions to bring it to a rapid end? You will say *yes* if you believe that (1) unemployment is more costly than inflation, (2) the short-run Phillips curve is rather flat, and (3) the economy's self-correcting mechanism is slow and unreliable. These views on the economy tend to be associated with economists of the Keynesian school, and with the (generally liberal) politicians who listen to them.

But you will say *no* if you believe that (1) inflation is more costly than unemployment, (2) the short-run Phillips curve is steep, and (3) the self-correcting mechanism works smoothly and quickly. These views are held by most monetarists and rational expectationists, so it is not surprising that the (generally conservative) politicians who follow their advice typically oppose strong measures to fight recessions.

The tables turn, however, when the question is whether or not to use policy to fight inflation. The Keynesian view of the world—that unemployment is costly, that the short-run Phillips curve is flat, and that the self-correcting mechanism is unreliable—leads to the conclusion that the costs of fighting inflation are high while the benefits are low. The monetarist and rational expectationist positions on these three issues are just the reverse, and so are the policy conclusions.

The Dilemma of Demand Management

So we have seen that the makers of monetary and fiscal policy face an agonizing trade-off. If they stimulate aggregate demand to reduce unemployment, they will aggravate inflation. If they restrict aggregate demand to fight inflation, they will cause higher unemployment.

But wait. Early in the chapter we learned that when inflation comes from the supply side, inflation and unemployment are *positively* associated: We suffer from more of both or enjoy less of each. Does this mean that monetary and fiscal policymakers can escape the trade-off between inflation and unemployment? Certainly not.

Adverse shifts in the aggregate supply curve can cause both inflation and unemployment to rise together, and thus can destroy the Phillips curve relationship. Nevertheless, anything that monetary and fiscal policy can do will make unemployment and inflation move in opposite directions because monetary and fiscal policy give the government control only over the *aggregate demand* curve, not over the *aggregate supply* curve.

Thus, no matter what the source of inflation, and no matter what happens to the Phillips curve, the makers of monetary and fiscal policy must still face up to the disagreeable trade-off between inflation and unemployment. This is a principle that many policymakers have failed to recognize, and one of the **12 Ideas** that we hope you will remember well **Beyond the Final Exam.**

Naturally, the unpleasant nature of this trade-off has led to a vigorous search for a way out of the dilemma. Both economists and public officials have sought a policy that might offer improvements on both fronts simultaneously, or that might ease the pain of either unemployment or inflation. The rest of this chapter considers some of these ideas.

Attempts to Improve the Trade-Off Directly

One class of policies aims to reduce the natural rate of unemployment. For example, vocational training and retraining programs, if successful, help unemployed workers with obsolete skills acquire abilities that are currently in demand. In doing so, they help alleviate upward pressures on wage rates in jobs where qualified workers are in short supply. For example, if an unemployed steelworker is taught to assemble computers, then progress is made against both inflation and unemployment, since one former steelworker leaves the ranks of the unemployed while one new worker helps alleviate the shortage of skilled labor in the computer industry. A similar role is played by the United States Employment Service and similar agencies at the state and local levels—which try to improve the match of workers to jobs by funneling information from prospective employers to prospective employees.

Although the idea sounds appealing and has attracted many adherents, successes achieved through training and placement programs have, in practice, been limited. Too often, people are trained for jobs that do not exist by the time they finish their training—if indeed they ever existed. Even when successful, these programs are expensive, which restricts the number of workers that can be accommodated.

Over the last decade, many government regulations over prices and provision of service have been reduced or made more flexible in such industries as airlines, trucking, railroads, telecommunications, and energy. Presidents Ford, Carter, and Reagan have all vigorously promoted deregulation, and each has cited the anti-inflationary impact as one of his reasons.[4] In addition, the Reagan administration halted the rise of the minimum wage and generally sought to reduce the amount of red tape imposed on businesses.

Prices have generally fallen in the deregulated industries. But most economists, while applauding deregulation on microeconomic grounds, doubt that it has had a large impact on the economy-wide inflation rate. The Reagan administration also sparked acrimonious debate by extending the deregulation drive into the areas of environmental protection and occupational health and safety.

Incomes Policy

Yet another way to improve the trade-off, one that has been tried intermittently in the United States, is incomes policy. As practiced in this country, incomes policy has run the gamut from verbal admonitions all the way to President Nixon's outright prohibition of wage and price increases in 1971. And in some foreign countries that rely upon incomes policy far more heavily than we do, a still more bewildering variety of alternative measures has emerged. Indeed, there may be only one common thread linking these disparate policies: No hard evidence exists that any of them has succeeded *permanently* in improving the trade-off between unemployment and inflation. Note that the emphasis here is on the word "permanently," for many attempts at incomes policy—including some in this country—have had temporary success.

> **Incomes policy** is a generic term used to describe a wide variety of measures aimed at curbing inflation *without* reducing aggregate demand.

Jawboning
The mildest form of incomes policy is commonly referred to as **jawboning.** The term is meant to conjure up in your mind an image of the president of the

> **Jawboning** refers to informal pressures on firms and unions to slow down the rates at which prices and wages are rising.

---

[4]For a full discussion of regulation and deregulation, see *Microeconomics* Chapter 15.

United States calling some corporate executive on the carpet for announcing a price increase deemed to be contrary to the national interest. Since corporate executives are likely to feel surrounded, perhaps even threatened, under these circumstances, jawboning has occasionally induced businesses to rescind previously-announced price increases.

Perhaps the most spectacular success was President Kennedy's confrontation with the steel industry in 1962. But President Johnson jawboned more than anyone else, and it was President Nixon who first established an official agency to monitor price increases and "blow the whistle" on those that were unwarranted. Since then, jawboning has become a partisan affair. President Ford rejected "open mouth policy," President Carter reinstated it, and President Reagan rejected it once again.

The main argument in favor of jawboning is that it is a relatively painless way to try to improve the trade-off between inflation and unemployment. Large corporations, it is argued, have the market power to raise prices even when price rises are not justified by cost increases. But, since these corporate giants are also public-relations conscious, proponents of jawboning argue, why not use the prestige of the federal government to dissuade them from exercising their market power?

Opponents of jawboning respond that market power can only explain *high* prices, not *rising* prices. Why, they ask, would a firm with market power wait until this month to raise prices when it could have done so last month? They answer that large corporations raise prices only when changes in demand or cost considerations make it profitable to do so, not because they have a residue of unused market power.

On balance, a fair assessment of jawboning would probably conclude that it does little good and little harm.

Wage–Price Guideposts

Wage–price guideposts are numerical standards for permissible wage and price increases.

The next step up from jawboning is the establishment of an official standard for "permissible" rates of increase in wages and prices. These so-called **wage–price guideposts** were initiated by the Kennedy administration in early 1962 but used most notably by the Johnson administration. Lacking an enforcement mechanism, they collapsed amid the inflationary pressures of 1967. Late in 1978, guideposts were resurrected by President Carter, who was by then convinced that jawboning was not enough. But inflation accelerated in 1979 and 1980 anyway, and President Reagan abandoned the guideposts immediately upon assuming office.

The logic behind guideposts is both simple and compelling. In an ideally functioning economy, if worker productivity rises by 2 percent a year, then wages can rise by 2 percent a year with no increase in costs or prices. Alternatively, wages can increase at a 4 percent annual rate while prices rise at 2 percent a year, and so on. In general, price inflation proceeds at a rate roughly 2 percentage points below wage inflation. A set of wage–price guideposts is obtained by picking a target rate of inflation, say 3 percent a year, and adding 2 percent to get a consistent target for wage increases—5 percent in this example. The government then announces that (a) wage increases that exceed this standard will be deemed "inflationary," (b) firms enjoying productivity increases faster than the national average are expected to raise their prices more slowly than 3 percent a year while, (c) firms obtaining sub-par productivity improvements are allowed to have higher-than-average price increases so that, (d) the overall price level can increase at a rate of 3 percent a year.

Such guideposts are logically sound. The problem comes in deciding what to do if some union or corporation violates them. Experience shows that voluntarism goes only so far when economic self-interest is threatened. If the government responds by jawboning—as frequently happened in the 1960s—we are back to the first type of incomes policy. Alternatively, we can give the guideposts the force of law, which brings us to the next variety of incomes policy.

Wage–Price Controls

Once the government is given the legal authority to *force* labor and industry to adhere to a set of guideposts, we have moved to a system of mandatory **wage–price controls.** While the United States used such a policy with great success during World War II and again during the Korean War, the Nixon administration's efforts to apply wage–price controls in peacetime is generally considered to have failed. This experience has soured many people on the idea of ever using them again.

Before considering some pros and cons of controls, let us be clear about what economists mean when they say that the 1971–1974 price controls "failed." They surely do *not* mean that inflation was not reduced by controls; most studies of the period have found that in fact it *was* reduced. Instead, they mean that the *lower* inflation rates that prevailed while controls were in effect were counterbalanced by *higher* inflation rates during the year or so after controls were lifted. Thus, instead of improving the tradeoff, the controls managed to increase the *variability* of inflation—making it lower in 1972–1973 and higher in 1974 than it would otherwise have been. In Chapter 6 we pointed out that the *variability* of inflation often exacts more serious social costs than the *average level*. In this sense, then, the controls program was counterproductive.

A major justification for controls, to which spokesmen for the Nixon administration appealed, is that inflation gathers a substantial momentum once workers, consumers, and business managers begin to expect that it will continue. **Inflationary expectations** encourage workers to demand higher wage increases. Firms, in turn, are willing to grant the workers' demands because they believe they will be able to pass the cost increases on to consumers in a general inflationary evironment. Thus, to a great extent, *inflation occurs because people expect it to occur*. Phrased in terms of our Phillips curve analysis, *inflationary expectations shift the Phillips curve upward*, so that any given rate of unemployment corresponds to a higher rate of inflation.

This analysis provides the best intellectual case for controls. A tough and thorough program of wage and price controls, it is argued, can break the vicious cycle of inflationary expectations. By announcing controls, the government serves notice on workers that they do not need anticipatory wage increases to preserve their purchasing power. And firms are warned that they may not be able to pass on higher costs to consumers. By breaking inflationary expectations, supporters argue, a controls program can shift the Phillips curve down and reduce the rate of inflation.

Under the right conditions, this argument may be correct. Several economists, for example, believe that controls helped both Argentina and Israel reduce galloping inflations in the 1980s. However, what if astute workers and business executives realize that no controls program can remain in force forever—at least not in a free-market economy like ours? They may then view the temporary dip in the inflation rate caused by controls as an aberration soon to be corrected, and therefore not as a major event that warrants changing their long-term expectations.

Wage–price controls are legal restrictions on the ability of industry and labor to raise wages and prices.

Why cannot wage–price controls be a permanent feature of the U.S. economy? We learned the answer to this back in Chapter 4. When price ceilings are effective, they force the price below the equilibrium price, so that quantity demanded exceeds quantity supplied. This is shown in Figure 17–19, where the equilibrium price of hamburgers is assumed to be $1. If controls do not allow the price of hamburgers to rise above 75 cents, quantity demanded will exceed quantity supplied by one million hamburgers.

With price no longer serving as the rationing device, some other method of rationing is necessary. One possibility is long lines of eager eaters waiting their turn for burgers. Scenes like this are typical in the Soviet Union, and they were witnessed in this country at gas stations during 1979, when gasoline was in short supply. Another is government ration coupons, giving the owner the right to buy a hamburger—a device used successfully for many goods during World War II. Neither of these measures is likely to be popular with the electorate in peacetime. And both are likely to spawn a black market, which erodes respect for law and order at the same time that it abrogates the effects of controls. As critics are fond of pointing out, controls give perfectly law-abiding citizens an incentive to break the law in an effort to circumvent the controls.

And the problems spawned by price controls go deeper than this. Among the principal factors determining the equilibrium price of hamburgers are the prices of raw agricultural commodities like beef. But prices of raw agricultural commodities cannot be controlled by the government because they depend on the weather and other acts of nature. If price controls hold the price of hamburgers at 75 cents while the price of beef skyrockets, it may become unprofitable to sell hamburgers. If so, firms will start leaving the hamburger industry.

With hamburgers unavailable, consumers will shift to other goods, thereby putting upward pressure on the prices of goods such as fish and soybeans. Thus, price controls on hamburgers will cause the hamburger industry to contract and necessitate additional price controls on fish and soybeans. And so it goes. Each extension of price controls to a new commodity requires additional controls to support it, in a never-ending chain. Thus, for price controls to be effective, they must be nearly universal—which is, of course, next to impossible except in times of acute national crisis.

Figure 17–19

THE EFFECTS OF PRICE CONTROLS

This diagram portrays the market for hamburgers under an effective price control system. Since the equilibrium price is $1 per hamburger, a regulation that holds the price at 75 cents makes the quantity of hamburgers demanded (2,500,000 per year) exceed the quantity supplied (1,500,000 per year). There is a shortage of one million hamburgers per year, and some sort of rationing scheme probably is necessary.

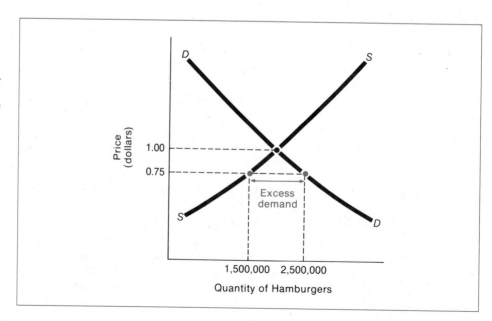

Wage–Price Freezes

An extreme case of mandatory controls is a **wage–price freeze**—a statute making it illegal to increase wages or prices above their levels on some specified date. President Nixon ushered in his controls program with a three-month freeze beginning in mid-August 1971. Such an action cannot last long, for it ossifies the market mechanism. It is meant to be a shock treatment—a dramatic action intended to break inflationary expectations. A wage–price freeze is generally a prelude to some milder form of incomes policy.

A wage–price freeze is an outright ban on wage or price increases.

Tax-Based Incomes Policy

A different approach to incomes policy—called **tax-based incomes policy** or TIP—seeks to use the tax system to fight inflation. The idea behind TIP is simple, though its practical implementation might be complex. TIP would give employers and employees a financial stake in fighting inflation by lowering taxes for firms or workers who abide by national guideposts for wage–price behavior, or by raising taxes for those who violate them.

Tax-based incomes policy uses the tax system to provide incentives favoring noninflationary behavior.

While there are many TIP plans, one particular example will bring out the flavor of them all. Suppose the government wants to limit wage increases to 5 percent a year. It could pass legislation granting a 2 percent payroll tax rebate to employees in firms in which average wages increase by no more than 5 percent. Then, for example, workers who settled for a $4\frac{1}{2}$ percent raise would actually wind up with *more* after-tax income than those who settled for a 6 percent raise. They would get $4\frac{1}{2}$ percent more from their employers, plus 2 percent more from the government in the form of lower taxes, for a total gain of $6\frac{1}{2}$ percent. This incentive, it is hoped, would lead labor and management to settle for slower growth in wages; and these slower wage increases, in turn, would lead to slower price increases.

Other TIP plans focus on corporation taxes rather than on payroll taxes, or utilize the "stick" rather than the "carrot" by penalizing violators of the wage–price guideposts rather than rewarding those who obey. But the basic goal is always the same: to make noninflationary behavior profitable for either firms or workers, or both.

Is TIP workable? Since it has never been tried, we have no idea how serious the many practical problems of implementation would be. For example, how would the government deal with a firm that simply promoted many workers into higher-paying job classifications rather than raising its wage scale?

The Share Economy

Recently, a new and imaginative approach to improving the trade-off has attracted the attention of politicians both here and abroad. Professor Martin Weitzman of M.I.T. has suggested that the introduction of **profit sharing,** a system in which workers are paid a base wage plus a share of company profits, would make the economy more resistant to unemployment.[5] His reasoning is as follows. If part of workers' pay comes from profit sharing rather than in straight wages, then labor costs automatically fall whenever business turns sour. With labor therefore "cheaper," firms will have less reason to lay workers off. In consequence, what Weitzman calls *a share economy* should normally have lower unemployment than an otherwise identical economy without profit sharing.

Profit sharing is a system of compensating labor in which workers receive both a fixed base wage and a share of the company's profits.

[5]Martin Weitzman, *The Share Economy* (Harvard University Press: 1984).

And because it would produce more goods, it should also normally have lower prices.

Weitzman's theoretical arguments are ingenious. And he bolsters his case by pointing to the low unemployment and low inflation of Japan—which has had extensive profit sharing for years. But organized labor has been cool to the idea of letting their earnings fluctuate with company profits. Furthermore, since we have no experience with widespread profit sharing, we can only guess at the practical problems that would arise in a share economy. Nonetheless, the potential benefits are large enough to justify the intensive scrutiny that profit sharing is now receiving.

Indexing

Indexing refers to provisions in a law or a contract whereby monetary payments are automatically adjusted whenever a specified price index changes. Wage rates, pensions, interest payments on bonds, income taxes, and many other things can be indexed in this way, and have been. Sometimes such contractual provisions are called *escalator clauses*.

Indexing—which refers to provisions in a law or contract whereby monetary payments are automatically adjusted whenever a specific price index changes—presents a very different approach to the inflation–unemployment dilemma. Whereas the other proposals discussed in this chapter are all designed *to lower the inflation rate*, the primary purpose of indexing is *to reduce the social costs of inflation*.

The mechanics of indexing are best explained by an example, and the most familiar example in the United States is an *escalator clause* in a wage agreement. An escalator clause provides for an automatic increase in money wages—without the need for new contract negotiations—any time the price level rises by more than a specified amount. Suppose that with the Consumer Price Index (CPI) sitting at 340, a union and a firm agree on a three-year contract setting wages at $8 per hour this year, $9 next year, and $10 in the third year. They might then add an escalator clause stating that wages will be increased above these stipulated amounts by 5 cents per hour for each point by which the CPI exceeds 370 in any future year of the contract. Then, if the CPI reaches 380 in the third year of the contract, workers will receive an additional 50 cents per hour (5 cents for each of the 10 points by which 380 exceeds 370), for a total wage of $10.50 per hour. In this way, workers are partly protected from inflation. Nowadays, less than half of all workers employed by large unionized firms in the United States are covered by some sort of escalator clause. And very few nonunion workers or employees of small firms enjoy such protection.

Interest payments on bonds or savings accounts can also be indexed, although this is not currently done in the United States.[6] The most extensive indexing to be found in the United States today is in government transfer payments. Social security benefits, for instance, are fully indexed so that retirees are not victimized by inflation. A variety of government income maintenance and social insurance programs also pay benefits that are tied directly to prices.

Indexing and the Social Costs of Inflation

Some economists believe that the United States should follow the example of several foreign countries and adopt a much more widespread system of indexing. Why? Because, they argue, it would take most of the sting out of inflation. To see how indexing would accomplish this, let us review some of the social costs of inflation that we enumerated in Chapter 6.

One important cost is the capricious redistribution of income caused by unexpected inflation. We saw that borrowers and lenders normally incorporate

---

[6]Some other countries, with much higher inflation than ours, do extensive indexing of interest rates. Brazil and Israel are notable examples.

an *inflation premium* equal to the *expected rate of inflation* into the nominal interest rate. Then, if inflation turns out to be higher than expected, the borrower has to pay to the lender only the agreed-upon nominal interest rate, including the premium for *expected* inflation; he does not have to compensate the lender for the (higher) *actual* inflation. Thus the borrower enjoys a windfall gain and the lender loses out. The opposite happens if inflation turns out to be lower than was expected. But if interest rates on loans were indexed, none of this would occur. Borrowers and lenders would agree on a fixed *real* rate of interest, and then the borrower would compensate the lender for whatever *actual inflation* occurred. No one would have to guess what the inflation rate would be.[7]

A second social cost we mentioned in Chapter 6 stems from the fact that our tax system levies taxes on nominal interest and nominal capital gains. As we learned, this flaw in the tax system leads to extremely high effective tax rates in an inflationary environment. But indexing could fix this problem easily. We need only rewrite the tax code so that only *real* interest payments and *real* capital gains are taxed.

A final problem noted in Chapter 6 is that uncertainty over future price levels makes it difficult to enter into long-term contracts — rental agreements, construction agreements, and so on. One way out of this problem is to write indexed contracts, which specify all future payments in real terms.

In the face of all these benefits, and others we have not mentioned here, why do many economists oppose indexing? Probably the major reason is the fear that indexing will lead to an acceleration of inflation. With the costs of inflation reduced so markedly, they argue, what will persuade governments to pay the price of fighting inflation? What will stop them from inflating more and more? They fear that the answer to these questions is, Nothing. Voters who stand to lose nothing from inflation are unlikely to pressure their legislators into stopping it. Opponents of indexing worry that a mild inflationary disease could turn into a ravaging epidemic in a highly indexed economy.

[7]For example, an indexed loan with a 2 percent real interest rate would require a 5 percent nominal interest payment if inflation were 3 percent, a 7 percent nominal interest payment if inflation were 5 percent, and so on.

Summary

1. Inflation can be caused either by rapid growth of aggregate demand or by sluggish growth of aggregate supply.
2. When fluctuations in economic activity emanate from the demand side, prices will rise rapidly when real output grows rapidly. Since rapid growth means more jobs, unemployment and inflation will be inversely related.
3. This inverse relationship between unemployment and inflation is called the Phillips curve. It explains U.S. data for the 1950s and 1960s rather well but fails miserably to account for the 1970s.
4. One reason for this failure is that the Phillips curve was misinterpreted as a menu of *long-run* policy choices for the economy. This view is incorrect because the economy's self-correcting mechanism guarantees that neither an inflationary gap nor a recessionary gap can last indefinitely.
5. Because of the self-correcting mechanism, the economy's true long-run choices lie along a *vertical* Phillips curve, which shows that the so-called *natural rate of unemployment* is the only unemployment rate that can persist indefinitely.
6. In the short-run, the economy can move up or down its short-run Phillips curve. *Temporary* reductions in unemployment can be achieved at the cost of higher inflation. Similarly, *temporary* increases in unemployment can be used to fight inflation.
7. Whether it is advisable to use unemployment to fight inflation depends on three principal factors: the relative social costs of inflation versus unemployment, the efficiency of the economy's self-correcting mechanism, and the current position of the economy.
8. If workers expect inflation to occur, and if they

demand (and receive) compensation for inflation, output will be independent of the price level. Both the aggregate supply curve and the short-run Phillips curve are vertical in this case.

9. However, errors in predicting inflation will still change real wages and hence will still change the quantity of output that firms wish to supply. Thus, *unpredicted* movements in the price level will lead to a normal, upward-sloping aggregate supply curve.

10. According to the doctrine of rational expectations, errors in predicting inflation are purely random. This means that, except for some random (and uncontrollable) gyrations, the aggregate supply curve is vertical even in the short run.

11. Many economists reject the rational expectations view of the world. Some deny that expectations are "rational" and believe instead that people tend, for example, to underpredict inflation when it is rising. Others point out that contracts signed years ago cannot possibly embody expectations that are "rational" in terms of what we know today.

12. When fluctuations in economic activity are caused by shifts of the aggregate supply curve, output will grow slowly (causing unemployment to rise) when inflation speeds up. Hence, the rates of unemployment and inflation will be positively related.

13. Many observers feel that the adverse supply shifts during the 1970s help explain why the Phillips curve collapsed.

14. Even if inflation is initiated by supply-side problems, so that inflation and unemployment occur together, the monetary and fiscal authorities still face this trade-off: Anything they do to improve unemployment is likely to worsen inflation, and anything they do to reduce inflation is likely to aggravate unemployment. The reason is that monetary and fiscal policy mainly influence the aggregate demand curve, not the aggregate supply curve. This is one of our **12 Ideas for Beyond the Final Exam.**

15. Policies that improve the functioning of the labor market—including retraining programs and employment services—can lower the natural rate of unemployment. To date, however, the U.S. government has had only modest success with these measures.

16. Some small amount of progress against inflation may also be made by eliminating government regulations that keep prices high. Indeed, some of this has already been done.

17. Many varieties of incomes policies have been used in this and other countries in an effort to improve the trade-off between inflation and unemployment. While some have led to notable temporary improvements, their lasting effects have been minimal.

18. The weakest varieties of incomes policies simply set up standards for permissible wage and price increases (wage–price guideposts) and apply verbal admonitions against violators (jawboning). Stronger variants may actually set legal limits on wage and price increases or even ban them outright (a wage–price freeze). But such policies seriously interfere with the workings of our market economy.

19. One argument in favor of short-term wage–price controls is that they can reduce inflationary expectations and thereby rob inflation of some of its momentum.

20. A new and different approach to incomes policy would use tax incentives to encourage more moderate wage and price increases. This so-called tax-based income policy has yet to be tried.

21. Some economists argue that we could improve both unemployment and inflation by including an important profit-sharing component in labor earnings.

22. Indexing is another way to approach the trade-off problem. Instead of trying to improve the trade-off, it concentrates on reducing the social costs of inflation—perhaps eliminating them, altogether. Opponents of indexing worry, however, that the economy's resistance to inflation may be lowered by indexing.

Concepts for Review

Demand-side inflation
Vertical (long-run) Phillips curve
Rational expectations
Supply-side inflation
Trade-off between unemployment and
  inflation in the short run and in the
  long run

Phillips curve
Stagflation caused by supply shocks
Self-correcting mechanism
Natural rate of unemployment
Inflationary expectations
Incomes policy
Wage–price freezes

Jawboning
Tax-based incomes policy (TIP)
Wage–price guideposts
Profit sharing
Indexing (escalator clauses)
Wage–price controls
Real versus nominal interest rates

Questions for Discussion

1. Some observers during the 1970s claimed that policymakers no longer face a trade-off between inflation and unemployment. Why did they think this? Were they correct?

2. "There is no sense in trying to shorten recessions through fiscal and monetary policy because the effects of these policies on the unemployment rate are sure to be temporary." Comment on both the truth of this statement and its relevance for policy formulation.

3. Why is the economy's self-correcting mechanism more efficient at eliminating inflationary gaps than it is at eliminating recessionary gaps?

4. Why is it said that decisions on fiscal and monetary policy are, at least in part, political decisions that cannot be made on "objective" economic criteria?

5. Does the economy have a recessionary gap or an inflationary gap today? What should be done about this? What facts would you want to know in preparing an answer to this question?

6. What is a "Phillips curve"? Why did it seem to work so much better in the 1954–1969 period than it did in the 1970s?

7. Explain the dilemma that policymakers face when there is an episode of supply inflation. What do you think should have been done in 1979? What would you recommend if there were a severe bout of supply inflation today?

8. Explain why expectations about inflation affect the wages that result from labor–management bargaining.

9. What is meant by "rational" expectations? Why does the doctrine of rational expectations have such stunning implications for economic policy? Would believers in rational expectations want to shorten a recession by expanding aggregate demand? Would they want to fight inflation by reducing aggregate demand?

10. Show that, if the economy's aggregate supply curve is vertical, fluctuations in the growth of aggregate demand produce only fluctuations in inflation with no effect on output. Relate this to your answer to the previous question.

11. Do you think it is proper for the president of the United States to "jawbone" some corporations into reducing their price increases?

12. Explain some of the differences between wage–price guideposts and wage–price controls.

13. Suppose that a program of wage–price controls is under consideration by the government. What are the possible benefits to the nation from such a program? What are the possible costs? How would you balance the benefits against the costs?

14. Explain the basic idea behind "TIP" (tax-based incomes policy). Try to devise a TIP plan of your own. Can you foresee some practical difficulties with your plan?

15. Ordinary savings accounts now pay approximately $5\frac{1}{2}$ percent *nominal* interest. Would you prefer to trade yours in for an indexed bank account that paid a zero *real* rate of interest? What if the real interest rate offered were 1 percent? What if it were −1 percent? What do your answers to these questions reveal about your personal attitudes toward inflation?

The United States in the World Economy

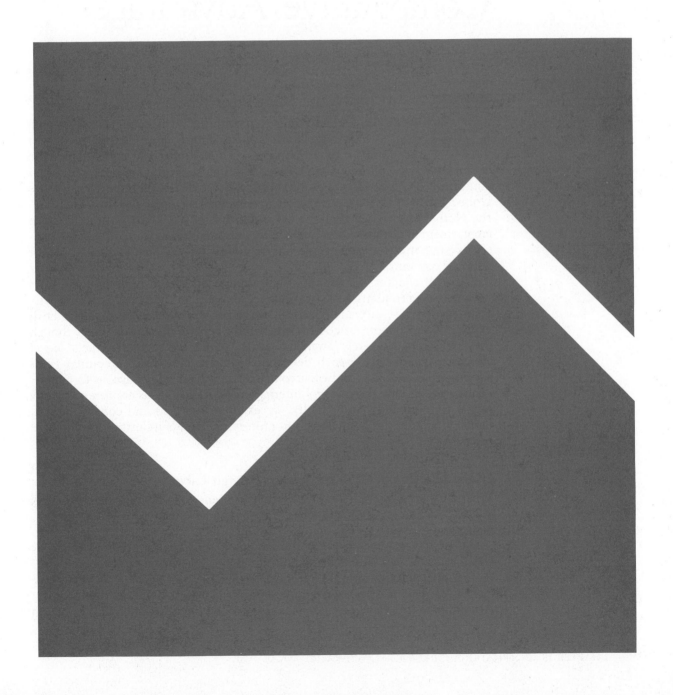

18

No nation was ever ruined by trade.

BENJAMIN FRANKLIN

International Trade and Comparative Advantage

While the United States can satisfy its own requirements for such goods as coal and sugar, it is almost *entirely* dependent on the rest of the world for other products, such as rubber and coffee. For these and many other vital inputs the United States must depend on trade with other countries. Though imports and exports are not nearly as important for the United States as they are for smaller nations such as Great Britain, Israel, and the Netherlands, they nonetheless make substantial contributions to both employment and standards of living here. Furthermore, as we shall see in Chapter 20, our international trade has profound effects on the health of our national economy.

In this chapter, we examine the purposes of foreign trade and the ways in which governments seek to influence or limit it. First, we examine why countries engage in trade. Second, we learn why the populations of both exporting and importing countries generally benefit from trade even though they are, in effect, merely "swapping goods." Third, we study the crucial *law of comparative advantage*, which determines what commodities a country finds advantageous to export and what commodities it finds advantageous to import. Fourth, we see how the prices of internationally traded goods are determined by supply and demand. And, finally, we examine the pros and cons of quotas, tariffs, and other devices designed to protect a country's industries from foreign competition.

Issue: The Competition of "Cheap Foreign Labor"

When analyzing international trade, common sense can be extremely valuable; indeed, there is no substitute for it. Yet sometimes conclusions based on common sense without factual confirmation and careful analysis can be misleading.

One important example is the argument that buying products made by cheap foreign labor is unfair and destructive to domestic interests. Some U.S. business people and union leaders argue that imports take bread out of the mouths of American workers and depress standards of living in this country. According to this view, cheap foreign goods cause job losses and put pressure on

U.S. businesses to lower wages. Moreover, imports allegedly encourage the continued exploitation of foreign workers by sweatshop proprietors abroad by making clear to them that low prices and, consequently, low wages are the only basis on which they can compete.

Yet, the facts are not consistent with this scenario. For one thing, wages in industrial countries that export to the United States rose spectacularly during the 1970s and 1980s. Table 18–1 shows that wages in seven leading industrial countries rose from an average of only 46 percent of American wages in 1970 to 82 percent by 1986. In fact, by 1986 labor costs in West Germany exceeded our own, and Sweden and the Netherlands were not far behind. Since 1986, this trend has continued, for the dollar is worth less now than it was then.[1] The fact is that American imports of Volkswagens from Germany, Volvos from Sweden, and Mazdas from Japan grew despite the fact that wages rose in those countries relative to those in the United States.

Although foreign labor became more expensive relative to U.S. labor during the 1960s and 1970s, America's position in the international marketplace deteriorated. In the 1950s, when European and Japanese wages were far below those in the United States, we had no trouble marketing our products abroad. In fact, the main problem then was to bring our imports up to the level at which they roughly balanced our bountiful exports. Then, as wages in Europe and Japan began to rise closer to those in the United States, America encountered serious trouble in its ability to sell goods abroad.

Clearly, then, cheap foreign labor need not serve as a crucial obstacle to U.S. sales abroad—as a "common sense" view of the matter suggests. In this chapter we will see what is wrong with that view.

Why Trade?

The main reason that countries trade with one another rather than try to run completely independent economies is that the earth's resources are not equally distributed across its surface. The United States has an abundant supply of coal, an energy source that is scarce in most of the rest of the world. Saudi Arabia has little land that is suitable for farming, but it sits atop a huge pool of oil. Because of the seemingly whimsical distribution of vital resources, every nation must trade with others to acquire what it lacks. In general, the more varied the

[1]Changes in international currency values are considered in the next chapter.

Table 18–1
LABOR COSTS IN INDUSTRIALIZED COUNTRIES

	1970	1986
	(percentage of U.S. labor costs)	
France	41	80
Great Britain	35	57
Italy	42	78
Japan	24	73
Netherlands	51	92
Sweden	70	93
West Germany	56	103

Data are compensation estimates per hour and relate to production workers in the manufacturing sector.
SOURCE: U.S. Bureau of Labor Statistics.

endowment of a particular country, the less it will have to depend on others to make up for its deficiencies.

Even if countries had all the resources they need, other differences in natural endowments — such as climate, terrain, and so on — would lead them to engage in trade. Americans *could*, with great difficulty, grow their own banana trees and coffee shrubs in hothouses; but these items are much more efficiently grown in such places as Honduras and Brazil, where the climate is appropriate. On the other hand, wheat grows in the United States with little difficulty, while mountainous Switzerland is not a good place to grow either bananas or wheat.

The skills of a country's labor force also play a role. If Argentina has a large group of efficient farmers and few workers with industrial experience while the opposite is true in Great Britain, it makes sense for Argentina to specialize in agriculture and let Great Britain concentrate on manufacturing.

This last point suggests one other important reason why countries trade — the advantages of **specialization.** If a small country were to try to produce every product, it would end up with many industries in which output was too small to utilize mass-production techniques, specialized training facilities, and other arrangements that give a cost advantage to large-scale operations. This is an acute problem for some countries, whose operation of their own international airlines or their own steel mills, for example, seems explainable only in political rather than economic terms. Inevitably, small nations that insist on operating in industries that are economical only when their scale of operation is large find that these enterprises can survive only with the aid of large government subsidies. To summarize:

Specialization means that a country devotes its energies and resources to only a small proportion of the world's productive activities.

International trade is essential for the prosperity of the trading nations because:

1. every country lacks some vital resources that it can get only by trading with others;

2. each country's climate, labor force, and other endowments make it a relatively efficient producer of some goods and an inefficient producer of other goods; and

3. specialization permits larger outputs and can therefore offer economies of large-scale production.

Mutual Gains from Trade

Centuries ago, it was believed that one nation could gain from an exchange only at the expense of another. Early writers on international trade pointed out that, since nothing is produced by the act of trading, the total collection of goods in the hands of the two parties at the end of an exchange is no greater than before the exchange took place. Therefore, they incorrectly argued, if one country gains from a swap, the other country must necessarily lose.

One of the consequences of this mistaken view was a policy prescription calling for each country to do its best to act to the disadvantage of its trading partners — in Adam Smith's terms, to "beggar its neighbors." The idea that one nation's gain must be another's loss means that a country can promote its own welfare only by harming others.

Yet, as Adam Smith and others after him emphasized, in any *voluntary exchange*, unless there is misunderstanding or misrepresentation of the facts, both parties *must* gain (or at least expect to gain) something from the transaction. Otherwise why would both parties agree to the exchange?

But how can mere exchange, in which no production takes place, leave *both* parties better off? The answer is that while trade does not increase the physical quantities of the goods available, it does allow each party to acquire items better suited to their needs and tastes. Suppose Scott has four sandwiches and nothing to drink, while William has four bottles of Coke and nothing to eat. A trade of two of Scott's sandwiches for two of William's Cokes does not increase the total supply of either food or beverages, but it clearly produces a net increase in the welfare of both boys.

Mutual Gains from Voluntary Exchange
Both parties must expect to gain from any *voluntary exchange*. Trade brings about mutual gains by redistributing products in such a way that both participants end up holding a combination of goods that is better adapted to their preferences than the goods they held before. This principle, which is one of our **12 Ideas for Beyond the Final Exam,** applies to nations just as it does to individuals.

International Versus Intranational Trade

The 50 states of the United States may be the most eloquent testimony to the gains from specialization and free trade. Florida specializes in growing oranges, Iowa in growing corn, Pennsylvania makes steel, and Michigan builds cars. All these states trade freely with one another and enjoy great material prosperity. Try to imagine how much lower living standards would be if your own state had to make all of these goods, plus the thousands of other things you consume each year.

The logic of international trade is essentially no different from that underlying trade among different states; the basic reasons for trade are equally applicable *within* a country or *among* countries. If we can learn about trade from strictly domestic exchanges, why study international trade as a special subject? There are at least three reasons.

Political Factors in International Trade
First, domestic trade takes place under a single national government, while foreign trade must involve at least two governments. At least in theory, the government of a nation is concerned with the welfare of all its citizens. But governments are usually much less deeply concerned with the welfare of citizens of other countries. For example, the Constitution of the United States prohibits overt tariffs and other impediments to domestic trade, barriers which seek to increase the gains from trade of some citizens at the expense of others. But the Constitution does not prohibit the United States from imposing tariffs on imports from abroad. A major issue in the economic analysis of international trade, and therefore of this chapter, is the use and misuse of impediments to free international trade.

The Many Currencies Involved in International Trade
Second, all trade within the borders of the United States is carried out in U.S. dollars. But trade across national borders must involve at least two currencies. Rates of exchange between different currencies can and do change. Thirty-five

years ago the pound was worth more than $4; now it is worth about $1.60. This variability in exchange rates brings with it a host of complications and policy problems that are discussed in the next chapter.

Impediments to Mobility of Labor and Capital

Third, it is usually much easier for labor and capital to move about within a country than to move from one country to another. If there are jobs in California but none in Michigan, workers can move freely to follow the job opportunities. Of course, there are personal costs—not only the dollar cost of moving, but also the psychological cost of giving up friends and familiar surroundings. But such relocations are not inhibited by immigration quotas, by laws restricting the employment of foreigners, or by the need to learn a new language, as are moves from one country to another.

There are also greater impediments to the transfer of capital from one country to another than to its movement within a country. The shipment of plant and equipment between countries can be expensive, and the international shipment of funds to be invested in foreign firms is likely to encounter many restrictions. For example, many countries have rules limiting the share of foreign ownership in a company. Foreign investment is also subject to special risks, such as the danger of outright expropriation if, say, after a political revolution the new government decides to take over all foreign properties without compensation. But even if nothing so extreme occurs, capital invested abroad faces risks from possible variations in exchange rates. An investment yielding a million pounds a year will be worth $2 million to American investors if the pound is worth $2 but only $1 million if the pound should fall to $1.

While labor, capital, and other factors of production do move from country to country when offered an opportunity to increase their earnings abroad, they are less likely to do so than to move from one region of a country to another to gain similar increases.

Comparative Advantage: The Fundamental Principle of Specialization

Some of the reasons why trade is beneficial to both parties are obvious. We now turn to an important source of mutual benefit which is far from obvious.

Coffee can be produced in Colombia using less labor and smaller quantities of other inputs than would be needed to grow it in the United States. And we know that the United States can produce large passenger aircraft at a lower resource cost than can Colombia. We say then that Colombia has an **absolute advantage** over the United States in coffee production, and the United States has an absolute advantage over Colombia in aircraft production.

A numerical example will illustrate the idea. According to Table 18–2, one year of labor time in the United States can produce either 50 pounds of

One country is said to have an **absolute advantage** over another in the production of a particular good if it can produce that good using smaller quantities of resources than can the other country.

Table 18–2
ALTERNATIVE OUTPUTS FROM ONE YEAR OF LABOR INPUT

	IN THE UNITED STATES	IN COLUMBIA
Coffee (pounds)	50	300
Airplanes	1/20	1/100

coffee or 1/20 of an airplane. By contrast, one year of labor time in Colombia can produce 300 pounds of coffee or 1/100 of an airplane. Thus, six years of labor input would be required to produce 300 pounds of coffee in the United States, whereas Colombia could do the job with only one year's worth of labor. On the other hand, it would take Colombia 100 years of labor to produce an airplane, a job the United States could do with only 20 years.

Obviously, if the United States wants coffee and Colombia wants airplanes, each can save resources by specializing in what it does best and trading with one another—each exporting the good in which it has an *absolute advantage*.

Suppose, however, that one country is more efficient than another in producing *every* item. Can they still gain by trading? The surprising answer is *definitely yes,* and a simple parable will help explain why.

The work of a highly paid business consultant frequently requires computer analysis. Suppose the consultant began her career as a computer operator, doing her own keypunching and programming, and is extremely good at it. She may sometimes grow impatient with the slow, sloppy work of some of the low-paid keypunchers who work for her and be tempted to do all the work herself. Good judgment, however, tells her that though she is better *both* at giving business advice *and* at keypunching than are her employees, it is foolish to devote any of her valuable time to the low-skilled keypunching job. That is because the opportunity cost of an hour devoted to keypunching is an hour less devoted to business consulting, which is a far more lucrative proposition.

This is an example of the principle of **comparative advantage** at work. The consultant specializes in business advice despite her absolute advantage in keypunching because she has a still greater absolute advantage as a business consultant. She suffers some direct loss by not doing her own keypunching. But that loss is more than compensated for by the earnings she makes selling her services to clients.

> One country is said to have a **comparative advantage** over another in the production of a particular good relative to other goods it can produce if it produces that good least inefficiently as compared with the other country.

This example brings out the fundamental principle that underlies the economic analysis of patterns of specialization and exchange among different nations and is one of our **12 Ideas for Beyond the Final Exam.** The principle, called the *law of comparative advantage,* was discovered by David Ricardo, one of the giants in the history of economic analysis.

The Law of Comparative Advantage

Even if one country is at an absolute disadvantage relative to another country in the production of *every* good, it is said to have a *comparative advantage* in making the good in whose production it is *least inefficient* in comparison with the other country.

Ricardo's basic finding was that two countries can still gain by trading even if one country is more efficient than another in the production of *every* commodity (that is, has an absolute advantage in every commodity).

In determining the most efficient patterns of production, what matters is *comparative* advantage, not *absolute* advantage. Thus one country will often gain by importing a certain good even if that good can be produced at home more efficiently than it can be produced abroad. Such imports will be profitable if the country is even more efficient at producing the goods that it exports in exchange.

The Arithmetic of Comparative Advantage

Let's see precisely how this works using numbers based on Ricardo's original example. Suppose labor is the only input used to produce wine and cloth in two countries, England and Portugal. Suppose further that Portugal has an absolute advantage in both goods, as indicated in Table 18–3. In this example, a week's worth of labor can produce either 12 yards of cloth or 6 barrels of wine in Portugal, but only 10 yards of cloth or 1 barrel of wine in England. So Portugal is the more efficient producer of both goods. Nonetheless, as our consultant-keypuncher example suggests, it pays for Portugal to specialize and trade with England.

We verify that this is so in two steps. First, we note that Portugal has a comparative advantage in wine while England has a comparative advantage in cloth. Then we show that both countries can gain if Portugal specializes in producing wine, England specializes in producing cloth, and the two countries trade with one another.

According to the numbers in Table 18–3, Portugal is 20 percent more efficient than England in producing cloth: It can produce 12 yards with a week's labor, whereas England can produce only 10. However, Portugal is six times as efficient as England in producing wine: It can produce 6 barrels per week rather than 1. Thus Portugal's competitive edge is far greater in wine than in cloth. That is precisely what we mean by saying that Portugal has a *comparative advantage* in wine. Looked at from the British perspective, these same numbers indicate that England is only slightly less efficient than Portugal in cloth production but drastically less efficient in wine production. So England's comparative advantage is in cloth. According to Ricardo's law of comparative advantage, then, the two countries can benefit if Portuguese wine is traded for English cloth. Let us check that this is true.

Suppose Portugal transfers a million weeks of labor out of the textile industry and into winemaking. According to the figures in Table 18–3, its cloth output falls by 12 million yards while its wine output rises by 6 million barrels. (See Table 18–4.) Suppose, at the same time, England transfers two million weeks of labor out of winemaking (thereby losing 2 million barrels of wine) and into clothmaking (thereby gaining 20 million yards of cloth). Table 18–4 shows us that these transfers of resources in the two countries increase the world's production of both outputs! Together, the two countries now have 4 million

Table 18–3
ALTERNATIVE OUTPUTS FROM ONE WEEK OF LABOR INPUT

	IN ENGLAND	IN PORTUGAL
Cloth (yards)	10	12
Wine (barrels)	1	6

Table 18–4
EXAMPLE OF THE GAINS FROM TRADE

	ENGLAND	PORTUGAL	TOTAL
Cloth (millions of yards)	+20	−12	+8
Wine (millions of barrels)	−2	+6	+4

additional barrels of wine and 8 million additional yards of cloth—surely a nice outcome.

But there seems to be some sleight of hand here. All that has taken place is an exchange. Yet, somehow Portugal and England gain both cloth and wine. How can such gains in physical output be possible? The explanation is that the trade process we have just described involves more than just a swap of a fixed

Biographical Note: David Ricardo (1772–1823)

David Ricardo was born four years before publication of Adam Smith's *Wealth of Nations*. Descended from a family of well-to-do stockbrokers of the Jewish faith who migrated to London from Amsterdam and were, in turn, descended from Portuguese Jews, he had about twenty brothers and sisters. At a school in Amsterdam, Ricardo's formal education ended at the age of 13, and so he was largely self-educated. He began his career by working in his father's brokerage firm. At age 21, Ricardo married a Quaker woman and decided to become a Unitarian, a sect then considered "little better than atheist." By Jewish custom, Ricardo's father broke with him, though apparently they remained friendly.

Ricardo then decided to go into the brokerage business on his own and was enormously successful. During the Napoleonic Wars he regularly scored business coups over leading British and foreign financiers, including the Rothschilds. After gaining a huge profit on government securities that he had bought just before the Battle of Waterloo, Ricardo decided to retire from business when he was just over 40 years old.

He purchased a country estate, Gatcomb (now owned by the royal family), where a brilliant group of intellectuals met regularly. Particularly remarkable for the period was the number of women included in the circle, among them Maria Edgeworth, the novelist (who wrote extravagant praise of Ricardo's mind), and Jane Marcet, an author of textbooks, one of which was probably the first text in economics. Ricardo's close friends included the economists T. R. Malthus and James Mill, father of John Stuart Mill, the noted philosopher-economist. Malthus remained a close friend of Ricardo even though they disagreed on many subjects and continued their arguments in personal correspondence and in their published works.

James Mill persuaded Ricardo to go into Parliament. As was then customary, Ricardo

purchased his seat by buying a piece of land that entitled its owner to a seat in Parliament. There he proved to be a noteworthy advocate of many causes that were against his personal interests.

James Mill also helped persuade Ricardo to write his masterpiece, *The Principles of Political Economy and Taxation,* which may have been the first book of pure economic theory. It was noteworthy that Ricardo, the most practical of practical men, had little patience with empirical economics and preferred instead to rest his analysis explicitly and exclusively on theory. His book made considerable contributions to the analysis of pricing, wage determination, and the effects of various types of taxes, among many other subjects. It also gave us the law of comparative advantage. In addition, the book described what has come to be called the Ricardian rent theory—even though Ricardo did not discover the analysis and explicitly denied having done so.

Ricardo died in 1823 at the age of 51. He seems to have been a wholly admirable person—honest, charming, witty, conscientious, brilliant—altogether too good to be true.

bundle of commodities. It is also a *change in the production arrangements*, with some of England's wine production taken over by the more efficient Portuguese wine producers, and with some of Portugal's cloth production taken over by English weavers who are *less* inefficient at producing cloth than English vintners are at producing wine.

When every country does what it can do best, all countries can benefit because more of every commodity can be produced without increasing the amounts of labor used.

If this result still seems a bit mysterious, the concept of opportunity cost will help remove the remaining mystery. If the two countries do not trade, Table 18–3 shows that England can acquire a barrel of wine on its own only by giving up 10 yards of cloth. Thus the opportunity cost of a barrel of wine in England is 10 yards of cloth. But in Portugal the opportunity cost of a barrel of wine is only 2 yards of cloth (see, again, Table 18–3). Thus, in terms of real resources foregone, it is cheaper—for *either* country—to acquire wine in Portugal. By a similar line of reasoning, the opportunity cost of cloth is higher in Portugal than in England, so it makes sense for both countries to acquire their cloth in England.[2]

The Graphics of Comparative Advantage

The gains from trade can also be displayed graphically, and doing so helps us to understand how these gains arise.

The lines *UK* and *PG* in Figure 18–1 are the production possibilities frontiers of the two countries, drawn on the assumption that each country has 6 million weeks of labor available.[3] For example, with 6 million weeks of labor, Table 18–3 tells us that England can produce 6 million barrels of wine and no cloth (point *K*), 60 million yards of cloth and no wine (point *U*), or any combination between (the line *UK*). Similar reasoning shows that *PG* is Portugal's production possibilities frontier.

[2]As an exercise, provide this line of reasoning.
[3]To review the concept of the production possibilities frontier, see Chapter 3.

Figure 18–1
ABSOLUTE AND COMPARATIVE ADVANTAGE SHOWN BY TWO COUNTRIES' PRODUCTION POSSIBILITIES FRONTIERS
Portugal's absolute advantage is shown by its ability to produce more of every commodity using the same quantity of labor as does England. Therefore, Portugal's production possibilities frontier, *PG*, is higher than England's, *UK*. But Portugal has a comparative advantage in wine production in which it is six times as productive as England. (It can produce 36 million barrels, point *P*, compared with England's 6 million, point *K*.) On the other hand, Portugal is only 20 percent more productive in cloth production (point *G*) than England (point *U*). Thus, England is less inefficient in producing cloth, where it consequently has a comparative advantage.

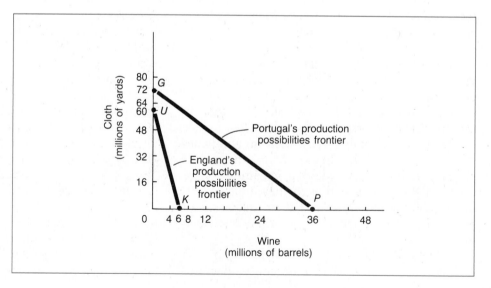

Note that Portugal's production possibilities frontier lies *above* England's throughout the diagram. That is because Portugal is the more efficient producer of *both* commodities. With the same amount of labor, it can obtain more wine and more cloth than England. Thus, the higher position of Portugal's frontier is the graph's way of showing Portugal's *absolute* advantage in both wine and cloth.

Portugal's comparative advantage in wine production and England's comparative advantage in cloth production are shown in a different way — by the relative *slopes* of the two production possibilities frontiers. Portugal's frontier is not only higher than England's, it is also flatter. What does this mean economically? One way of looking at the difference is to remember that while Portugal can produce six times as much wine as England (compare points P and K), it can produce only 20 percent more cloth than England (points G and U). England is, relatively speaking, much better at cloth production than at wine production. That is what is meant when we say it has a *comparative* advantage in the former.

We may express this difference more directly in terms of the slopes of the two lines. The slope of Portugal's production possibilities frontier is $OG/OP = 72/36 = 2$. This means that if Portugal reduces its wine production by one barrel, it will obtain two yards of cloth. Thus, the *opportunity cost* of a barrel of wine in Portugal is two yards of cloth, as we observed earlier.

In the case of England, the slope of the production possibilities frontier is $OU/OK = 60/6 = 10$. That is, if England reduces wine production by one barrel, it gets 10 additional yards of cloth. So in England the *opportunity cost* of a barrel of wine is 10 yards of cloth.

A country's absolute advantage in production over another country is shown by its having a higher production possibilities frontier. The difference in the comparative advantages of the two countries is shown by the difference in the slopes of their frontiers.

Because opportunity costs differ in the two countries, gains from trade are possible. How these gains are divided between the two countries depends on the prices for wine and cloth that emerge from world trade, which is the subject of the next section. But we already know enough to see that world trade must leave a barrel of wine costing less than 10 yards of cloth and more than 2 yards. Why? Because, if a barrel of wine cost more than 10 yards of cloth (its opportunity cost in England), England would be better off producing its own wine rather than trading with Portugal. Similarly, if a barrel of wine fetched less than two yards of cloth (its opportunity cost in Portugal), Portugal would prefer to produce its own cloth rather than trade with England.

We conclude, therefore, that if both countries are to trade, the rate of exchange between cloth and wine must be somewhere between 10 to 1 and 2 to 1. To illustrate the gains from trade in a concrete example, suppose the world price ratio settles at 4 to 1; that is, one barrel of wine costs 4 yards of cloth. How much, precisely, do England and Portugal gain from world trade?

Figure 18–2 is designed to help us see the answer. Production possibilities frontiers UK in part (a) and PG in part (b) are the same as in Figure 18–1. But England can do better than UK. Specifically, with a world price ratio of 4 to 1, England can buy a barrel of wine by giving up only 4 yards of cloth, rather than 10 (which is the opportunity cost of wine in England). Hence, if England produces only cloth [point U in Figure 18–2(a)] and buys its wine from Portugal, Britain's *consumption possibilities* will be as indicated by the blue line that begins

Figure 18–2

THE GAINS FROM TRADE
In this diagram, we suppose that trade opens up between England and Portugal and that the world price of wine is four times the world price of cloth. Now England's consumption possibilities are all the points on line *UN* (which starts at *U* and has a slope of 4), rather than just the points on its own production possibilities frontier, *UK*. Similarly, Portugal can choose any point on line *PR* (which begins at *P* and has a slope of 4), rather than just points on *PG*. Thus both nations gain from trade.

at point *U* and has a slope of 4—indicating that each additional barrel of wine costs England 4 yards of cloth. Since trade allows England to choose a point on *UN* rather than on *UK*, trade opens up consumption possibilities that were simply not available before.

The story is similar for Portugal. If the Portuguese produce only wine [point *P* in Figure 18–2(b)], they can acquire 4 yards of cloth from England for each barrel of wine they give up as they move along the blue line *PR* (whose slope is 4). This is better than they can do on their own, since a sacrifice of one barrel of wine yields only 2 yards of cloth in Portugal. Hence world trade enlarges Portugal's consumption possibilities from *PG* to *PR*.

Figure 18–2 shows graphically that gains from trade arise to the extent that world prices (4 to 1 in our example) differ from domestic opportunity costs (10 to 1 and 2 to 1 in our example). So it is a matter of some importance to understand how prices in international trade are established. Supply and demand is a natural place to start.

Supply–Demand Equilibrium and Pricing in Foreign Trade

When applied to international trade, the supply–demand model runs into several new complications. First, it involves at least two demand curves: that of the exporting country and that of the importing country. Second, it may also involve two supply curves, since the importing country may produce some part of its own consumption. Third, equilibrium does not take place at the intersection point of *either* pair of supply–demand curves. Why? Because if there is any trade, the exporting country's quantity supplied must be *greater* than its quantity demanded, while the quantity supplied by the importing country must be *less* than its quantity demanded.

These complications are illustrated in Figure 18–3, where we show the supply and demand curves of a country that exports wine, in part (a), and those

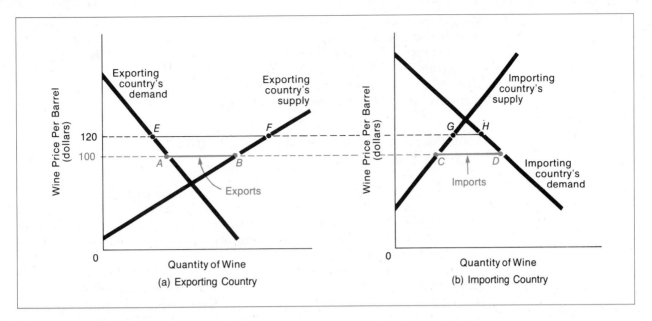

Figure 18–3
SUPPLY–DEMAND
EQUILIBRIUM IN THE
INTERNATIONAL WINE
TRADE
Equilibrium requires that
exports, *AB* (which is the
exporting nation's quantity
supplied, *B*, minus the
exporter's quantity
demanded, *A*), exactly
balance imports, *CD*, by the
importing country. At $100
per barrel of wine, there is
equilibrium. But at a higher
price, say $120, there is
disequilibrium because
export supply, *EF*, exceeds
import demand, *GH*.

of one that imports wine, in part (b). For simplicity, we assume that these countries do not deal in wine with anyone else.

Where will the two-country wine market reach equilibrium? The equilibrium price in a free market must satisfy two requirements:

1. The price of wine must be the same in both countries.
2. The quantity of wine exported must equal the quantity of wine imported.

In Figure 18–3, this happens at a price of $100 per barrel. At that price, the distance *AB* between what the exporting country produces (point *B*) and what it consumes (point *A*) equals the distance *CD* between the quantity demanded of the importing country (point *D*) and its quantity supplied (point *C*). At a price of $100 per barrel, the amount the exporting country has available to sell abroad is exactly equal to the amount the importer wants to buy, and so matters are in balance.

At any price above $100, producers in both countries will want to sell more and consumers in both countries will want to buy less. For example, if the price rises to $120 per barrel, the exporter's quantity supplied will rise from *B* to *F*, and the exporter's quantity demanded will fall from *A* to *E*, as shown in Figure 18–3(a). As a result, there will be a rise in the amount available for export, from *AB* to *EF*. For exactly the same reason, the price increase will cause higher production and lower sales in the importing country, leading to a shrinkage in the amount the importing country wants to import—from *CD* to *GH* in part (b). This means that the new price, $120 per barrel, cannot be sustained if the international market is free and competitive. With export supply *EF* far greater than import demand *GH*, there must be downward pressure on price and a move back toward the $100 equilibrium price. Similar reasoning shows that prices below $100 also cannot be sustained.

We can now see the straightforward role of supply–demand equilibrium in international trade:

In international trade, the equilibrium price must be at a level at which the amount the exporting country wants to export is exactly equal to the amount the importing country wants to import. Equilibrium will thus occur at a price at which the horizontal distance AB in Figure 18–3(a) (the excess of the exporter's quantity supplied over its quantity demanded) is equal to the horizontal distance CD in Figure 18–3(b) (the excess of the importer's quantity demanded over its quantity supplied). At this price, the *world's* quantity demanded is equal to the *world's* quantity supplied.

Comparative Advantage and Competition of "Cheap Foreign Labor"

The principle of comparative advantage takes us a good part of the way toward an explanation of the fallacy in the "cheap foreign labor" argument described earlier in the chapter. Given the assumed productive efficiency of Portuguese labor and the inefficiency of British labor, we would expect wages to be much higher in Portugal than in England.

In these circumstances, one can expect Portuguese workers to be apprehensive about an agreement to permit trade between the countries—"How can we hope to meet the unfair competition of those underpaid British workers?" And British laborers are also likely to be concerned—"How can we hope to meet the competition of those Portuguese, who are so efficient in producing everything?"

The principle of comparative advantage shows us that both fears are unjustified. As we have just seen, when trade is opened up between Portugal and England *workers in both countries will be able to earn higher real wages than before* because of the increased productivity that comes about through specialization.

Figure 18–2 (page 390) shows this fact directly. We have seen from our illustration that, with trade, England can end up with more wine and more cloth than it had before. So the living standards of its workers can rise even though they have been left vulnerable to the competition of the superefficient Portuguese. Portugal also can end up with more wine and with more cloth; so the living standards of its workers can rise even though they have been exposed to the competition of cheap British labor. These higher standards of living are, of course, a reflection of the higher real wages earned by workers in both countries.

The lesson to be learned here is elementary: Nothing helps raise standards of living more than does a greater abundance of goods.

Tariffs, Quotas, and Other Interferences with Trade

Despite the mutual gains obtained, international trade has historically been subjected to unrelenting pressure for government interference. In fact, until the rise of a free-trade movement in England at the end of the eighteenth and the beginning of the nineteenth centuries (with such economists as Adam Smith and David Ricardo as its vanguard), it was taken for granted that one of the essential tasks of government was to impose regulations that impede trade—presumably in the national interest.

There were many who argued then (and some who still argue today) that a nation's wealth consists of the amount of gold or other monies at its command. Consequently, the proper aim of government policy was to do everything it could to promote exports as a way to increase the amount foreigners would owe to it. Similarly the government was to discourage imports in order to decrease the amount the country owed to foreigners.

Obviously, there are limits to which this policy can be carried out. A country *must* import vital foodstuffs or critical raw materials that it cannot supply for itself; for if it does not, it must suffer a severe fall in living standards as well as a deterioration in its military strength. Morever, it is mathematically impossible for *every* country to sell more than it buys—one country's exports *must* be some other country's imports. If everyone competes in this game and cuts imports to the bone, then obviously exports must go the same way. The result will be that everyone is deprived of the mutual gains that trade can provide.

In more recent times, notably in the United States during the first three decades of the twentieth century, there was a return to an active policy designed to reduce competition from foreign imports. Since then, the United States has gradually assumed a leading role in attempts to promote freedom of trade, and barriers have gradually been reduced. However, recently a combination of high unemployment rates and a deterioration in America's competitive position in world trade has led to political pressures to move back in the other direction. The 1980s have seen new restrictions on U.S. trade in automobiles, lumber, semiconductors, and a variety of other products. Were it not for the free-trade proclivities of the Reagan administration, even more trade restrictions probably would have been enacted.

Three main devices have been used by modern governments seeking to control trade: tariffs, quotas, and export subsidies.

A **tariff** is simply a tax on imports. An importer of wine, for example, may be charged $10 for each barrel of wine he brings into the country. The United States is generally a low-tariff country. Although there are a few notable exceptions, most of our tariff rates are below 10 percent, and many items have no tariff at all. However, many other countries rely on heavy tariffs to protect their industries. Tariff rates of 100 percent or more are not unheard of.

A **quota** is a legal limit on the amount of a good that may be imported. For example, the government might allow no more than 5 million barrels of wine to be imported in a year. In some cases, governments ban the importation of certain goods outright—a quota of zero. (See the accompanying boxed insert for an example.) The United States imposes quotas on a smattering of goods, including steel, Japanese automobiles, textiles, sugar, and meat. But most imports are free of quotas.

An **export subsidy** is a payment by the government to an exporter. By reducing the exporter's costs, such subsidies permit exporters to lower their selling prices and compete more effectively in world trade. While export subsidies are minor in the United States, they are used extensively by some foreign governments to assist their industries—a practice that provokes bitter complaints from American manufacturers about "unfair competition."

A **tariff** is a tax on imports.

A **quota** specifies the maximum amount of a good that is permitted into the country from abroad per unit of time.

An **export subsidy** is a payment by the government to exporters to permit them to reduce the selling price of their goods so they can compete more effectively in foreign markets.

How Tariffs and Quotas Work

Both tariffs and quotas restrict supplies coming from abroad and drive up prices. The tariff works by raising prices and hence cutting the demand for imports, while the sequence associated with a quota goes the other way—restriction in supply forces prices up.

Let us use our international trade diagrams to see what a quota does. The supply and demand curves in Figure 18–4 are like those of Figure 18–3. Just as in Figure 18–3, equilibrium in a free international market occurs at a price of $100 per barrel (in both countries). At this price, the exporting country produces 10 million barrels [point B in part (a)] and consumes 5 million (point A),

Yes, Greeks Have No Bananas

ATHENS—Are there no bananas in Olympia? Yes.

Are there no bananas in Thebes? Yes. In Corinth? Yes. In Sparta, Marathon, Delphi? Yes, yes, yes.

Are there no bananas on Crete?

That depends on your definition of banana. Little green pods do grow on that Greek island, on scorched, drooping plants that look as though they want to be banana trees. They are called bananas, but they don't taste much like bananas—or, at least, that's what people say. A foreigner can't easily get a taste of a ripe Cretan banana. They are all sold secretly, on the black market. To buy a banana anywhere in Greece, you need a connection. All over the world, people take bananas for granted. A bunch of bananas off the boat from Panama isn't exactly what dreams are made of, right? Well, in this country, dreams *are* made of bananas. Alien bananas are contraband in Greece. For Greeks, a sweet, yellow, pulpy Panamanian banana is the forbidden fruit.

"Greece no banana," says the taxi driver at the Athens airport, ecstatically accepting an exotic beauty as a tip. A traveler has just slipped through customs with a bunch in a brown paper bag, defying a five-pound limit. The driver tenderly places his in the glove compartment. "I show it to my grandson," he says.

It has been 12 years now since the last banana boat sailed away from Piraeus. There are children in Greece today who don't even know what a banana is. Greece was a dictatorship in 1971, and dictatorships sometimes do strange things. The one in Greece outlawed the traffic in foreign bananas.

The head of internal security, Col. Stelios Pattakos, gave the order. He was born on Crete, a

bone-dry island, and was friendly toward some farmers there who had it in their heads to try growing a fruit native to equatorial jungles. The colonel got rid of the competition. Still, the Cretan crop was so puny it couldn't satisfy a 50th of the Greek passion for bananas. The price went up. The government imposed controls. And then the banana peddlers went underground.

When the dictatorship collapsed in 1974, Col. Pattakos was sentenced to life imprisonment for nonbanana-related offenses. Democracy returned—but bananas didn't. Bureaucrats do strange things, too.

A banana avalanche, they determined, would hurt the Greek apple business. Everybody would suddenly stop eating apples and start eating bananas. It didn't do any good to argue that comparing apples and bananas was like comparing apples and oranges. So Col. Pattakos got life, and the Greek people got life without bananas.

SOURCE: *The Wall Street Journal*, July 28, 1983, page 1.

---

so that exports are 5 million barrels—the distance *AB*. Similarly, the importing country consumes 8 million barrels [point *D* in part (b)] and produces only 3 million (point *C*), so that its imports are also 5 million barrels—the distance *CD*.

Now suppose the government of the importing nation imposes an import quota of (no more than) 3 million barrels. The free-trade equilibrium is no longer possible. Instead, the market must equilibrate at a point where both exports and imports are 3 million barrels. As Figure 18–4 indicates, this requires different prices in the two countries.

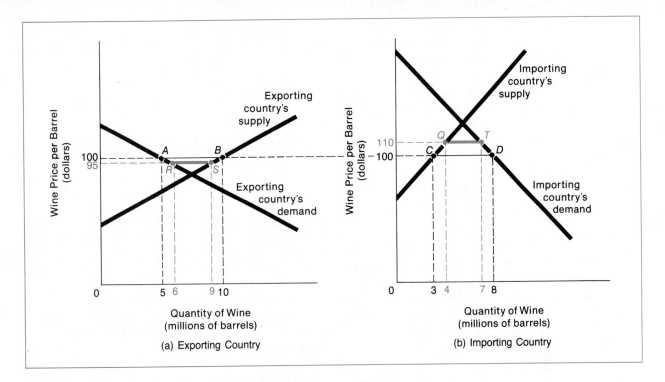

Wine Price per Barrel (dollars) *(a) Exporting Country axis)*

Quantity of Wine
(millions of barrels)

(a) Exporting Country

Wine Price per Barrel (dollars) *(b) Importing Country axis)*

Quantity of Wine
(millions of barrels)

(b) Importing Country

Imports in part (b) will be 3 million—the distance QT—only when the price of wine in the importing nation is $110 per barrel, because only at this price will quantity demanded exceed domestic quantity supplied by 3 million barrels. Similarly, exports in part (a) will be 3 million barrels—the distance RS—only when the price in the exporting country is $95 per barrel. At this price, quantity supplied exceeds domestic quantity demanded by 3 million barrels in the exporting country. Thus the quota *raises* the price in the importing country to $110 and *lowers* the price in the exporting country to $95. In general:

An import quota on a product normally will reduce the volume of that product traded, raise the price in the importing country, and reduce the price in the exporting country.

The same restriction of trade can be accomplished through a tariff. In the example we have just completed, a quota of 3 million barrels resulted in a price that was $15 higher in the importing country than in the exporting country ($110 − $95). Suppose that, instead of a quota, the importing nation posts a $15 per barrel tariff. International trade equilibrium then must satisfy the following two requirements:

1. The price that consumers in the importing country pay for wine must exceed the price that suppliers in the exporting country receive by $15 (the amount of the tariff).

2. The quantity of wine exported must equal the quantity of wine imported.

By consulting the graphs in Figure 18–4, you can see exactly where these two requirements are satisfied. If the exporter produces at S and consumes at R, while the importer produces at Q and consumes at T, then exports and imports

Figure 18–4
QUOTAS AND TARIFFS IN INTERNATIONAL TRADE
Under free trade, the equilibrium price of wine is $100 per barrel. The exporting country, in part (a), sends *AB,* or 5 million barrels, to the importing country (distance *CD*). If a quota of 3 million barrels is imposed by the importing country, these two distances must shrink to 3 million barrels. The solution is shown by distance *RS* for exports and distance *QT* for imports. Exports and imports are equal, as must be the case, but the quota forces prices to be unequal in the two countries. Wine sells for $110 per barrel in the importing country but only $95 per barrel in the exporting country. A tariff achieves the same result differently. It *requires* that the prices in the two countries be $15 apart. And this, as the graph shows, dictates that exports (= imports) will be equal at 3 million barrels.

are equal (at 3 million barrels), and the two domestic prices differ by exactly $15. (They are $110 and $95.) What we have just discovered is a general result of international trade theory:

Any restriction of imports that is accomplished by a quota normally can also be accomplished by a tariff.

In this case, the tariff corresponding to an import quota of 3 million barrels is $15 per barrel.

Tariffs versus Quotas

But while tariffs and quotas can accomplish the same reduction in international trade and lead to the same domestic prices in the two countries, there *are* some important differences between the two types of restrictions.

First, under a quota, profits from the price increases in the importing country usually go into the pockets of the foreign and domestic sellers of the product. Because supplies are limited by quotas, customers in the importing country must pay more for the product. So the suppliers, be they foreign or domestic, receive more for every unit they sell. For example, the U.S. quota on imports of Japanese automobiles that began in 1981 raised the "profits" of both American and Japanese automakers by billions of dollars per year.

On the other hand, when trade is restricted by a tariff, some of the profits go instead as tax revenues to the *government* of the importing country. In effect, the government increases its tax revenues partly at the expense of its citizens and partly at the expense of foreign exporters, who must accept a reduced price because of the resulting decrease in quantity demanded in the importing country. (Domestic producers again benefit, because they are exempt from the tariff.) In this respect, a tariff is certainly a better proposition than a quota from the viewpoint of the country that enacts it.

Another important distinction between the two measures is the difference in their implications for productive efficiency and prices in the long run. A tariff handicaps all foreign suppliers equally. It still awards sales to the firms and nations who are most efficient and can therefore supply the goods most cheaply.

A quota, on the other hand, necessarily awards its import licenses more or less capriciously—perhaps on a first-come, first-served basis or in proportion to past sales or even on political criteria. There is not the slightest reason to expect the most efficient and least costly suppliers to get the import permits. In the long run, the population of the importing country is likely to end up with significantly higher prices, poorer products, or both.

The U.S. quota on Japanese cars illustrates all of these effects. Japanese automakers responded to the limit on the number of cars by shipping bigger models equipped with more "optional" equipment. The "stripped down" Japanese car became a thing of the past. And the newer, smaller Japanese automakers—like Subaru and Mitsubishi—found it difficult to compete in the U.S. market because their quotas were so much smaller than those of Toyota, Datsun, and Honda.

If a country must inhibit imports, there are two important reasons for it to give preference to tariffs over quotas: (1) some of the resulting financial gains from tariffs go to the government of the importing country rather than to foreign and domestic producers; and (2) unlike quotas, tariffs offer no special benefits to inefficient exporters.

Why Inhibit Trade?

To state that tariffs are a better way to inhibit international trade than quotas leaves open a far more basic question: Why limit trade in the first place? There are two primary reasons for adopting measures that restrict trade: First, they may help the importing country get more advantageous prices for its goods, and second, they protect particular industries from foreign competition.

Shifting Prices in Your Favor

How can a tariff make prices more advantageous for the importing country if it raises consumer prices there? The answer is that it forces foreign exporters to sell more cheaply. Because their market is restricted by the tariff, they will be left with unsold goods unless they cut their prices. Suppose, as in Figure 18–4(b), that a $15 tariff on wine raises the price of wine in the importing country from $100 to $110 per barrel. This rise in price drives down imports from an amount represented by the length of the black line *CD* to the smaller amount represented by the blue line *QT*. And to the exporting country, this means an equal reduction in exports [see the change from *AB* to *RS* in Figure 18–4(a)].

As a result, the price at which the exporting country can sell its wine is driven down (from $100 to $95 in the example) while producers in the importing country—being exempt from the tariff—can charge $110 per barrel. In effect, such a tariff amounts to government intervention to rig prices in favor of domestic producers and to exploit foreign sellers by forcing them to sell more cheaply than they otherwise would.

However, this technique works only as long as foreigners accept tariff exploitation passively. And, as the accompanying boxed insert suggests, they rarely do. Instead, they retaliate, usually by imposing tariffs or quotas of their own on their imports from the country that first began the tariff game. This can easily lead to a trade war in which no one gains in terms of more favorable prices and everyone loses in terms of the resulting reductions in overall trade. Something like this happened to the world economy in the 1930s and helped prolong the worldwide depression. At present, it is threatening to happen again.

Tariffs or quotas can benefit particular domestic industries in a country that is able to impose them without fear of retaliation. But when every country uses them, everyone is likely to lose in the long run.

Protecting Particular Industries

The second, and probably more frequent, reason why countries restrict trade is to protect particular industries from foreign competition. If foreigners can produce steel or watches or shoes more cheaply, domestic businesses and unions in these industries are quick to demand protection; and their government is often reluctant to deny it to them. It is here that the cheap foreign labor argument is most likely to be invoked.

The fact is, however, that the firms that are unable to compete in the market are the ones whose relative inefficiency does not permit them to beat foreign exporters at their own game. In Ricardo's example of comparative advantage, one can well imagine the complaints from Portuguese clothmakers as the opening of trade led to increased importation of English cloth. At the same time, English grape growers would probably have expressed equal concern over the flood of imported wine from Portugal. Protective tariffs and quotas

An Eye for an Eye...and a Book for a Shingle?

Trade wars have a way of gathering momentum and moving in unpredictable directions, as the following excerpt shows.

As the authorities in the United States prepare to announce a decision on whether to impose a duty on imports of softwood lumber from Canada, the Canadian Government is threatening retaliation.

The lumber dispute is by far the biggest trade battle between Canada and the United States, the world's largest trading partners. A tariff of the magnitude requested by the American lumber industry would add more than $1 billion to the $3.5 billion price of softwood lumber imported from Canada each year.

"I think you can expect a strong response, but I'm not going to tell you what it is," Pat Carney, Canada's Minister for International Trade, said in an interview today.

She called the American lumber producers' request for a duty "total harassment."

After Washington imposed a tariff on Canadian cedar shingles last May, Ottawa imposed duties on a number of imports from the United States ranging from books to Christmas trees. But trade experts say it is unclear what retaliatory steps the Canadians could take now.

SOURCE: *The New York Times*, October 9, 1986.

---

are designed to undercut harsh competition coming from abroad. But it is precisely this competition that gives consumers the benefits of international specialization.

Usually, when an industry feels itself threatened by foreign competition, it is argued that some form of protection against imports is needed to prevent loss of jobs. We know from Part 4 that there are better ways to stimulate employment. But a program that limits foreign competition will do a better job of preserving employment in the particular protected industry. It will work, but often at a considerable cost to consumers in the form of higher prices and to the economy in the form of inefficient use of resources. Table 18–5 gives some

Table 18–5
ESTIMATED COSTS OF PROTECTIONISM

INDUSTRY	COST PER JOB SAVED
Automobiles	$105,000
Book manufacturing	100,000
Dairy products	220,000
Steel	750,000
Sugar	60,000
Textiles	42,000

SOURCE: Gary C. Hufbauer, Diane T. Berliner, and Kimberly Ann Elliott, *Trade Protection in the United States: 31 Case Studies* (Washington: Institute for International Economic Studies), 1986, Table 1.2.

recent estimates of the costs to American consumers of using tariffs and quotas to save jobs in selected industries. In every case, the costs far exceed the wages of the workers in the protected industries—ranging as high as a colossal $750,000 per job for the current quotas on steel products.

Nevertheless, union complaints over proposals to reduce a tariff or a quota are justified unless something is done to ease the cost to the individual workers of switching to those lines of production that trade has now made profitable.

The argument for free trade between countries cannot be considered compelling if there is no adequate program to assist the minority of citizens in each country who will be harmed whenever patterns of production change drastically, as would happen, for example, if tariff and quota barriers were suddenly brought down.

Owners of wineries in Britain and of textile mills in Portugal may see heavy investments suddenly rendered unprofitable. So would workers whose investments in acquiring special skills and training are no longer marketable. Nor are the costs to displaced workers only monetary. They may have to move to new locations as well as to new industries, uprooting their families, losing old friends and neighbors, and so on. That the *majority* of citizens undoubtedly will gain from free trade will be no consolation to those who are its victims.

To help alleviate this problem, the United States (and other countries) has set up programs to assist workers who lose jobs because of changing patterns of world trade. In the United States such **trade adjustment assistance** is provided to firms or workers who suffer idle facilities, unprofitability, and unemployment because of sharp increases in imports.

Firms may be eligible for technical assistance designed to improve their efficiency, financial assistance in the form of government loans or government guarantees of private loans, and permission to delay tax payments. Workers are eligible for retraining programs, lengthened periods of eligibility for unemployment compensation, and allowances to help pay for the cost of moving to other jobs. Each form of assistance is designed to ease the burden on the victims of free trade so that the rest of us can enjoy its considerable benefits.

Trade adjustment assistance in the U.S. began in 1962, and benefits to displaced workers had grown to be extremely generous by the 1970s. However, the Reagan administration—objecting that the program put too much emphasis on *assistance* and not enough on *adjustment*—cut benefits drastically in 1981. Now, very few workers qualify.

Trade adjustment assistance provides special unemployment benefits, loans, retraining programs, and other aid to workers and firms that are harmed by foreign competition.

Other Arguments for Protection

National Defense and Other Noneconomic Considerations

There are times when a tariff or some other measure to interfere with trade may be justified on noneconomic grounds. If a country considers itself vulnerable to military attack, it may be perfectly rational to keep alive industries whose outputs can be obtained more cheaply abroad but whose supplies might be cut off in an emergency. For example, airplane production by small countries makes sense only on these grounds.

The danger is that every industry, even those with the most peripheral relationship to defense, is likely to invoke this argument on its behalf. For instance, the U.S. watchmaking industry claimed protection for itself for many years on the grounds that its skilled craftsmen would be invaluable in wartime. Perhaps so, but a technicians' training program probably could have done the job more cheaply and even more effectively by teaching exactly the skills needed for military purposes.

Similarly, the U.S. has occasionally banned either exports to or imports from nations like Cuba, the Soviet Union, Libya, and Afghanistan on political grounds. Such actions often have important economic effects, creating either bonanzas or disasters for particular American industries. But they are justified by politics, not by economics. Noneconomic reasons also explain quotas on importation of whaling products and on the furs of other endangered species.

The Infant-Industry Argument

Another common argument for protectionism is the so-called infant-industry argument. Promising new industries, it is alleged, often need breathing room to flourish and grow. If we expose these infants to the rigors of international competition too soon, the argument goes, they may never develop to the point where they can survive on their own in the international marketplace.

The argument, while valid in certain instances, is less defensible than it at first appears. It makes sense only if the industry's prospective future gains are sufficient to repay the social losses incurred while it is being protected. But if the industry is likely to be so profitable in the future, why doesn't private capital rush in to take advantage of the prospective net profits? The annals of business are full of cases in which a new product or a new firm lost money at first but profited handsomely later. Only where funds are not available to a particular industry for some reason, despite its glowing profit prospects, does the infant-industry argument for protection stand up to scrutiny. And even then it may make more sense to provide a government loan than to provide trade protection.

It is hard to think of examples where the infant-industry argument applies. But even if such a case were found, one would have to be careful that the industry not remain in diapers forever. There are too many cases in which new industries were awarded protection when they were being established and, somehow, the time to withdraw that protection never arrived. One must beware of infant industries that never grow up.

Strategic Trade Policy

A new argument for (one hopes temporary) protectionism has become popular in recent years. Advocates of this argument agree that free trade for all is the best system. But they point out that we live in an imperfect world in which many nations refuse to play by the rules of the free-trade game. And they fear that a nation that pursues free trade in a protectionist world is likely to lose out. It therefore makes sense, they argue, to threaten to protect your markets unless other nations agree to open theirs. (See the article by columnist William Safire on page 401.)

This is a hard argument for economists to deal with. While it accepts the superiority of free trade, it argues that threatening protectionism is the best way to establish free trade. Such a strategy might work, but it clearly involves great risks. If threats that America will turn protectionist induce other countries to scrap existing protectionist policies, then the gamble will have succeeded. But, if the gamble fails, the world ends up with even more protection than it started with.

The analogy to arms negotiations with the Soviet Union is pretty obvious—and a little frightening. We threaten to install new missiles unless the Russians agree to dismantle some of theirs. If they do, the world is a safer place

Can Protectionism Save Free Trade?

In this 1983 column, William Safire shook off his longstanding attachment to free trade and argued eloquently for retaliation against protectionist nations.

WASHINGTON—Free trade is economic motherhood. Protectionism is economic evil incarnate...Never should government interfere in the efficiency of international competition.

Since childhood, these have been the tenets of my faith. If it meant that certain businesses in this country went belly-up, so be it...If it meant that Americans would be thrown out of work by overseas companies paying coolie wages, that was tough...

The thing to keep in mind, I was taught, was the Big Picture and the Long Run. America, the great exporter, had far more to gain than to lose from free trade; attempts to protect inefficient industries here would ultimately cost more American jobs.

While playing with my David Ricardo doll and learning nursery rhymes about comparative advantage, I was listening to another laissez-fairy tale: Government's role in the world of business should be limited to keeping business honest and competitive. In God we antitrusted. Let businesses operate in the free marketplace.

Now American businesses are no longer competing with foreign companies. They are competing with foreign governments who help their local businesses. That means the world arena no longer offers a free marketplace; instead, most other governments are pushing a policy that can be called *helpfulism*.

Helpfulism works like this: A government like Japan decides to get behind its baseball-bat industry. It pumps in capital, knocks off marginal operators, finds subtle ways to discourage imports of Louisville Sluggers, and selects target areas for export blitzes. Pretty soon, the favored Japanese companies are driving foreign competitors batty.

How do we compete with helpfulism? One way is to complain that it is unfair; that draws a horselaugh. Another way is to demand a "Reagan Round" of trade negotiations under GATT, the Gentlemen's Agreement To Talk, which is equally laughable. Yet another way is to join the helpfuls by subsidizing our exports and permitting our companies to try monopolistic tricks abroad not permitted at home. But all that makes us feel guilty, with good reason.

The other way to deal with helpfulism is through—here comes the dreadful word—*protection*. Or, if you prefer a euphemism, *retaliation*. Or if that is still too severe, *reciprocity*. Whatever its name, it is a way of saying to the cutthroat cartelists we sweetly call our trading partners: "You have bent the rules out of shape. Change your practices to conform to the agreed-upon rules, or we will export a taste of your own medicine."

A little balance, then, from the free trade theorists. The demand for what the Pentagon used to call "protective reaction" is not demagoguery, not shortsighted, not self-defeating.

On the contrary, the overseas pirates of protectionism and exemplars of helpfulism need to be taught the basic lesson in trade, which is: tit for tat.

SOURCE: William Safire, "Smoot-Hawley Lives," *The New York Times*, March 17, 1983. Copyright © 1983 by The New York Times Company. Reprinted by permission.

and everyone is better off. But, if they do not, the arms race accelerates and everyone is worse off. Is our threat to build new missiles therefore a wise or a foolish policy? There is no agreement on this question, and so we should not expect agreement on the advisability of using protectionist measures in a strategic way.

What Import Prices Benefit a Country?

Dumping means selling goods in a foreign market at lower prices than those charged in the home market.

One of the most curious features of the protectionist position is the fear of low prices charged by foreign sellers. Countries that subsidize exports are accused of **dumping** — of getting rid of their goods at unconscionably low prices. For example, Japan has frequently been accused of dumping various goods on the U.S. market — most recently, semiconductors.

Unfair Foreign Competition

Satire and ridicule are often more persuasive than logic and statistics. Exasperated by the spread of protectionism to so many industries under the prevailing Mercantilist philosophy, French economist Frédéric Bastiat decided to take the protectionist argument to its illogical conclusion. The fictitious petition of the French candlemakers to the Chamber of Deputies, written in 1845 and excerpted below, has become a classic in the battle for free trade.

We are subject to the intolerable competition of a foreign rival, who enjoys, it would seem, such superior facilities for the production of light, that he is enabled to *inundate* our *national market* at so exceedingly reduced a price, that, the moment he makes his appearance, he draws off all custom for us; and thus an important branch of French industry, with all its innumerable ramifications, is suddenly reduced to a state of complete stagnation. This rival is no other than the sun.

Our petition is, that it would please your honorable body to pass a law whereby shall be directed the shutting up of all windows, dormers, skylights, shutters, curtains, in a word, all openings, holes, chinks, and fissures through which the light of the sun is used to penetrate our dwellings, to the prejudice of the profitable manufactures which we flatter ourselves we have been enabled to bestow upon the country...

We foresee your objections, gentlemen; but there is not one that you can oppose to

us...which is not equally opposed to your own practice and the principle which guides your policy...

Labor and nature concur in different proportions, according to country and climate, in every article of production...If a Lisbon orange can be sold at half the price of a Parisian one, it is because a natural and gratuitous heat does for the one what the other only obtains from an artificial and consequently expensive one...

Does it not argue the greatest inconsistency to check as you do the importation of coal, iron, cheese, and goods of foreign manufacture, merely because and even in proportion as their price approaches *zero*, while at the same time you freely admit, and without limitation, the light of the sun, whose price is during the whole day at *zero*?

SOURCE: F. Bastiat, *Economic Sophisms* (New York: G. P. Putnam's Sons, 1922).

A moment's thought should indicate why this fear must be considered curious. As a nation of consumers, we should be indignant when foreigners charge us *high* prices, not *low* ones. That is the common-sense rule that guides every consumer, and the consumers of imported commodities should be no exception. Only from the topsy-turvy viewpoint of an industry seeking protection from competition are high prices seen as being in the public interest.

Ultimately, it must be in the best interest of a country to get its imports as cheaply as possible. It would be ideal for the United States if the rest of the world were willing to provide its exports to us free or virtually so. We could then live in luxury at the expense of the rest of the world.

But, of course, what benefits the United States as a whole does not necessarily benefit every single American. If quotas on, say, steel imports were dropped, American consumers and industries that purchase steel would gain from lower prices. But owners of steel companies and steelworkers would suffer serious losses in the form of lower profits, lower wages, and lost jobs—losses they will fight hard to prevent. For this reason, politics often leads to the adoption of protectionist measures that would likely be rejected on strictly economic criteria.

The notion that low import prices are bad for a country is a fitting companion to the idea—so often heard—that it is good for a country to export much more than it imports. True, this means that foreigners will end up owing us a good deal of money. But it also means that we will have given them large quantities of our products and have gotten relatively little in foreign products in return. That surely is not an ideal way for a country to reap gains from international trade.

Our gains from trade do not consist of accumulations of gold or of heavy debts owed us by foreigners. Rather, our gains are composed of goods and services that others provide minus goods and services we must provide in return.

Conclusion: A Last Look at the "Cheap Foreign Labor" Argument

The preceding discussion should indicate the fundamental fallacy in the argument that American workers have to fear cheap foreign labor. If workers in other countries are willing to supply their products to us with little compensation, this must ultimately *raise* the standard of living of the average American worker. As long as the government's monetary and fiscal policies succeed in maintaining high levels of employment at home, how can we possibly lose by getting the products of the world at bargain prices?

There are, however, some important qualifications. First, our employment policy may not be effective. If workers who are displaced by foreign competition cannot find jobs in other industries, then American workers will indeed suffer from international trade. But that is a shortcoming of the government's employment program, not of its international trade policies.

Second, we have noted that an abrupt stiffening of foreign competition resulting from a major innovation in another country, or from a discovery of a new and better source of raw materials, or from a sharp increase in export subsidies by a foreign country, *can* hurt U.S. workers by not giving them an adequate chance to adapt gradually to the new conditions. The more rapid the change, the more painful it will be. If it occurs fairly gradually, workers can retrain and move on to the industries that now require their services. If the change is even more gradual, no one may have to move. People who retire or leave the threatened industry for other reasons simply need not be replaced. But competition that inflicts its damage overnight is certain to impose real costs upon the affected workers, costs that are no less painful for being temporary.

But these are, after all, qualifications to an overwhelming argument. They call for intelligent monetary and fiscal policies and for transitional assistance to unemployed workers, not for abandonment of free trade.

In the long run, labor will be "cheap" only where it is not very productive. Wages will tend to be highest in countries in which high labor productivity keeps costs down and permits exporters to compete effectively despite high wages. It is thus misleading to say that the United States held its own in the international marketplace until recently *despite* the high wages of its workers. Rather it is much more illuminating to point out that the high wages of American workers were a result of high worker productivity, which gave the United States a heavy competitive edge.

We note that in this matter it is *absolute* advantage, not *comparative* advantage, that counts. The country that is most efficient in every output can pay its workers more in every industry.

Summary

1. Countries trade because differences in their natural resources and other inputs create discrepancies in the efficiency with which they can produce different goods, and because specialization may offer them greater economies of large-scale production.
2. Voluntary trade will generally be advantageous to both parties in an exchange. This is one of our **12 Ideas for Beyond the Final Exam.**
3. International trade is more complicated than trade within a nation because of political factors, different national currencies, and impediments to the movement of labor and capital across national borders.
4. Both countries will gain from trade with one another if each exports goods in which it has a comparative advantage. That is, even a country that is generally inefficient will benefit by exporting the goods in whose production it is *least inefficient*. This is another of the **12 Ideas for Beyond the Final Exam.**
5. When countries specialize and trade, each can enjoy consumption possibilities that exceed its production possibilities.
6. The prices of goods traded between countries are determined by supply and demand, but one must consider explicitly the demand curve and the supply curve of *each* country involved. Thus, in international trade, the equilibrium price must be where the excess of the exporter's quantity supplied over its domestic quantity demanded is equal to the excess of the importer's quantity demanded

over its quantity supplied.
7. The "cheap foreign labor" argument ignores the principle of comparative advantage, which shows that real wages can rise in both the importing and exporting countries as a result of specialization.
8. Tariffs and quotas are designed to protect a country's industries from foreign competition. Such protection may sometimes be advantageous to that country, but not if foreign countries adopt tariffs and quotas of their own as a means of retaliation.
9. While the same restriction of trade can be accomplished by either a tariff or a quota, tariffs offer at least two advantages to the country that imposes them: (1) some of the gains go to the government rather than to foreign producers; and (2) there is greater incentive for efficient production.
10. When a nation shifts from protection to free trade, some industries and their workers will lose out. Equity then demands that these people and firms be compensated in some way. The U.S. government offers various forms of trade adjustment assistance to do this, but these programs are small at present.
11. Several arguments for protectionism can, under the right circumstances, have validity. These include the national defense argument, the infant-industry argument, and the use of trade restrictions for strategic purposes. But each of these arguments is frequently abused.
12. Dumping may hurt domestic producers, but it always benefits domestic consumers.

Concepts for Review

Imports	Comparative advantage	Export subsidy
Exports	"Cheap foreign labor" argument	Trade adjustment assistance
Specialization	Tariff	Infant-industry argument
Mutual gains from trade	Quota	Dumping
Absolute advantage		

Questions for Discussion

1. You have a dozen eggs worth 80 cents and your neighbor has a pound of bacon worth about the same. You decide to swap six eggs for a half pound of bacon. In financial terms, neither of you gains anything. Explain why you are nevertheless both likely to be better off.
2. In the eighteenth century, some writers argued that one person in a trade could be made better off only by gaining at the expense of the other. Explain the fallacy in the argument.
3. Country A has lots of hydroelectric power, a cold climate, and a highly skilled labor force. What sorts of products do you think it is likely to produce? What are the characteristics of the countries with which you would expect it to trade?
4. Upon removal of a tariff on watches, a U.S. watch-making firm goes bankrupt. Discuss the pros and cons of the tariff removal in the short and long runs.
5. Country A's government believes that it is best always to export more (in money terms) than the value of its imports. As a consequence, it exports more to country B every year than it imports from country B. After 100 years of this arrangement, both countries are destroyed in an earthquake. What were the advantages and disadvantages of the surplus to country A? To country B?
6. The table below describes the number of red socks and white socks that can be produced with an hour of labor in two different cities:

	IN BOSTON	IN CHICAGO
Red socks (pairs)	3	2
White socks (pairs)	3	1

   a. If there is no trade, what is the price of white socks relative to red socks in Boston?
   b. If there is no trade, what is the price of white socks relative to red socks in Chicago?

   c. Suppose each city has 1000 hours of labor available per year. Draw the production possibilities frontier for each city.
   d. Which city has an absolute advantage in the production of which good(s)? Which city has a comparative advantage in the production of which good(s)?
   e. If the cities start trading with each other, which city will specialize and export which good?
   f. What can be said about the price at which trade will take place?
7. Suppose that the United States and Mexico are the only two countries in the world. In the United States, a worker can produce 6 bushels of wheat *or* 1 barrel of oil in a day. In Mexico, a worker can produce 2 bushels of wheat *or* 4 barrels of oil per day.
   a. What will be the price ratio between the two commodities (that is, the price of oil in terms of wheat) in each country if there is no trade?
   b. If free trade is allowed and there are no transportation costs, what commodity would the U.S. import? What about Mexico?
   c. In what range will the price ratio have to fall under free trade? Why?
   d. Picking one possible post-trade price ratio, show clearly how it is possible for both countries to benefit from free trade.
8. The table below presents the demand and supply curves for watches in Switzerland and the United States.
   a. Draw the demand and supply curves for the United States on one diagram and those for Switzerland on another one.
   b. If there is no trade between the United States and Switzerland, what are the equilibrium price and quantity in the watch market in the United States? In Switzerland?
   c. Now suppose trade is opened up between the two countries. What will be the equilibrium price in the world market for watches? What has happened to the price of watches in the United States? In Switzerland?

d. Which country will export watches? How many?
e. When trade opens, what happens to the quantity of watches produced, and therefore employment, in the watch industry in the United States? In Switzerland? Who benefits and who loses *initially* from free trade?

PRICE PER WATCH (dollars)	QUANTITY DEMANDED IN U.S. (thousands)	QUANTITY SUPPLIED IN U.S. (thousands)	QUANTITY DEMANDED IN SWITZERLAND (thousands)	QUANTITY SUPPLIED IN SWITZERLAND (thousands)
10	110	0	80	30
20	90	20	50	50
30	70	40	35	65
40	60	60	20	80
50	50	80	5	95
60	40	95	0	105
70	30	105	0	110
80	20	110	0	115

19

The International Monetary System: Order or Disorder?

In the last chapter, we discussed the reasons for international trade and the benefits that accrue to all nations when countries specialize in producing those goods in which they have a comparative advantage. But the movement of goods across national borders generally requires the movement of *money* in the opposite direction. For example, when the United States buys coffee from Brazil, we must send money to the Brazilians. When Japan purchases petroleum from Saudi Arabia, it must send money to the Saudis, and so on. This chapter takes a look at the system that has been set up to handle these international movements of money—the **international monetary system**.

We begin by investigating a system in which rates of exchange among national currencies are determined in free markets by the laws of supply and demand. Here the key concept to be studied is the *exchange rate*. We shall see that the main macroeconomic variables studied in Parts 2–4—output, the price level, and the rate of interest—each play a role in the determination of a country's exchange rate. This discussion sets the stage for Chapter 20, where we will learn how movements of the exchange rate, in turn, affect the national economy.

Next, we turn to the opposite polar form—an international monetary system in which exchange rates are fixed by government authority, rather than by the market. We do not now live in such a world. Yet studying it will help us understand the current international monetary system, which is a curious hybrid of fixed and floating exchange rates. Furthermore, by comparing how the two types of currency systems work, we can gain an understanding of the continuing controversy over whether the major trading nations should seek greater stability in exchange rates.

What Are Exchange Rates?

We noted in the previous chapter that international trade is more complicated than domestic trade. There are no national borders to be crossed when, say, California lettuce is shipped to Massachusetts. The consumer in Boston pays with *dollars*, just the currency that the farmer in Salinas wants. But if that same farmer ships his lettuce to Japan, consumers there will have only Japanese *yen* with which to pay, rather than the dollars the farmer in California wants. Thus if international trade is to take place, there must be a way to transform one currency (yen) into another (dollars). The rates at which such transformations are made are called **exchange rates**.

There is an exchange rate between every pair of currencies. For example, $1 is currently the equivalent of about 6 French francs. The exchange rate between the franc and the dollar, then, may be expressed as "6 francs to the dollar" (meaning that it costs 6 francs to buy a dollar) or about "17 cents to the franc" (meaning that it costs 17 cents to buy a franc).

Although exchange rates change all the time, Table 19–1 gives an indication of exchange rates prevailing in July 1980, February 1985, and September 1987, showing how many dollars or cents it cost at each of those times to buy each unit of foreign currency. You will note some dramatic changes in the international value of the dollar over time. In a nutshell, the dollar soared in the period from mid-1980 to early 1985 and has fallen against most major currencies since then. This chapter seeks to explain such currency realignments.

Under our present system, currency rates change frequently. When other currencies get more expensive in terms of dollars, we say that they have **appreciated** relative to the dollar. Alternatively, we can look at this same event as the dollar buying less foreign currency, meaning that the dollar has **depreciated** relative to another currency.

What is a depreciation to one country must be an appreciation to the other.

For example, if the dollar cost of a German mark rises from $33\frac{1}{3}$ cents to 50 cents, the cost of a U.S. dollar in terms of marks simultaneously falls from 3 marks to 2 marks. The Germans have had a currency *appreciation* while we have had a currency *depreciation*.

Notice also that, when many currencies are changing in value, the dollar may be appreciating with respect to one currency but depreciating with respect to another.

Table 19–1 shows that, between February 1985 and September 1987, the dollar *depreciated* sharply relative to the Japanese yen and most European

The **exchange rate** states the price, in terms of one currency, at which another currency can be bought.

A nation's currency is said to **appreciate** when exchange rates change so that a unit of its own currency can buy more units of foreign currency. The currency is said to **depreciate** when exchange rates change so that a unit of its currency can buy fewer units of foreign currency.

Table 19–1
EXCHANGE RATES WITH THE U.S. DOLLAR
(dollars per unit of foreign currency)

COUNTRY	CURRENCY UNIT	SYMBOL	JULY 1980	COST IN DOLLARS FEBRUARY 1985	SEPTEMBER 1987
Australia	dollar	$	$1.16	$0.74	$0.73
Canada	dollar	$	0.87	0.74	0.76
France	franc	FF	0.25	0.10	0.16
Germany	mark	DM	0.57	0.30	0.55
Italy	lira	L	0.0012	0.00049	0.00076
Japan	yen	¥	0.0045	0.0038	0.0069
Mexico	peso	$	0.044	0.0050	0.00065
Sweden	krona	Kr	0.24	0.11	0.16
Switzerland	franc	S. Fr.	0.62	0.36	0.66
United Kingdom	pound	£	2.37	1.10	1.64

SOURCE: International Financial Statistics and *The Wall Street Journal*.

currencies. For example, the British pound rose from $1.10 to $1.64. Yet during that same period the dollar *appreciated* dramatically relative to the Mexican peso; it bought about 200 pesos in 1985 but over 1500 in 1987.

While this is the terminology used to describe movements of exchange rates in free markets, another set of terms is used to describe decreases and increases in currency values when those values are set by government decree. When an officially set exchange rate is altered so that a unit of a nation's currency can buy *fewer* units of foreign currency, we say there has been a **devaluation** of that currency. When the exchange rate is altered so that the currency can buy *more* units of foreign currency, we say there has been a **revaluation**.

Exchange Rate Determination in a Free Market

Why is it that a German mark costs 56 cents and not 46 cents or 66 cents? In a world of **floating exchange rates**, with no government interferences, the answer would be fairly straightforward. Exchange rates would be determined by the forces of supply and demand, just like the prices of apples, or typewriters, or haircuts.

In a leap of abstraction, imagine that the United States and West Germany were the only countries on earth, so there was only one exchange rate to be determined. Figure 19–1 depicts the determination of this exchange rate at the point (denoted E in the figure) where demand curve DD crosses supply curve SS. At this price (56 cents per mark), the number of marks demanded is equal to the number of marks supplied.

In a free market, exchange rates are determined by the law of supply and demand. If the rate were below the equilibrium level, the quantity of marks demanded would exceed the quantity of marks supplied, and the price of a mark would be bid up. If the rate were above the equilibrium level, quantity supplied would exceed quantity demanded, and the price of a mark would fall. Only at the equilibrium exchange rate is there no tendency for the rate to change.

As usual, supply and demand determine price. What we must ask in this case is: Where do the supply and demand come from? Why does anyone demand a German mark? The answer comes in three parts:

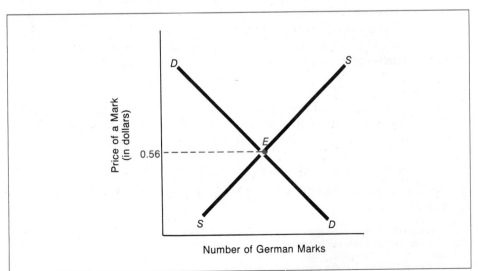

Figure 19–1
DETERMINATION OF EXCHANGE RATES IN A FREE MARKET
Like any price, an exchange rate will be determined by the intersection of the demand and supply curves in a free market. Point *E* depicts this point for the exchange rate between the U.S. dollar and the German mark, which settles at 56 cents per mark in this example.

1. *International trade in goods and services.* This was the subject of the last chapter. If, for example, Jane Doe, an American, wants to buy a German automobile, she will first have to buy marks with which to pay the dealer in Munich.[1] So Jane's demand for a German *car* leads to a demand for German *marks*. In general, *demand for a country's export goods and services leads to a demand for its currency.*[2]

2. *International trade in financial instruments like stocks and bonds.* For example, if American investors want to purchase German stocks, they will first have to acquire the marks that the sellers will insist upon. In this way, demand for German financial assets leads to demand for German marks. Thus, *demand for a country's financial assets leads to a demand for its currency.*

3. *Purchases of physical assets like factories and machinery overseas.* If IBM wants to buy out a small German computer manufacturer, the owners will no doubt want to receive marks. So IBM will first have to acquire German currency. In general, *direct foreign investment leads to a demand for a country's currency.*

Now, where does the supply come from? To answer this, we need only turn all of these transactions around. Germans wanting to buy U.S. goods and services, or to invest in U.S. financial markets, or to make direct investments in America will have to offer their marks for sale in the foreign-exchange market (which is similar to the stock market) to acquire the needed dollars. To summarize:

The *demand* for a country's currency is derived from the demands of foreigners for its export goods and services and for its assets, including financial assets, factories, and machinery. The *supply* of a country's foreign currency arises from its imports, and from foreign investment by its own citizens.

To appreciate the usefulness of even this simple supply and demand analysis, let us consider how the exchange rate between the dollar and the mark would change if there were an economic boom in the United States. One important effect of such a boom would be to stimulate American demand for German products, such as automobiles, cameras, and wines. In terms of the supply-demand diagram shown in Figure 19–2, the increased desires of Americans for German products would shift the demand curve for German marks out from $D_1 D_1$ (the black line in the figure) to $D_2 D_2$ (the blue line). Equilibrium would shift from point E to point A, and the exchange rate would rise from 56 cents per mark to 60 cents per mark. In a word, the increased demand for marks by U.S. citizens causes the mark to *appreciate* relative to the dollar.

EXERCISE

Test your understanding of the supply and demand analysis of exchange rates by showing why each of the following events would lead to a depreciation of the mark (appreciation of the dollar) in a free market:

1. A recession in the United States cuts American purchases of German goods.

2. German investors are attracted by prospects for profit in the American stock market.

---

[1]Actually she will not do this because banks generally handle foreign exchange transactions for consumers. An American bank probably will buy the marks for her. But the effect is exactly the same as if Jane had done it herself.

[2]See Discussion Question 2 at the end of the chapter (page 429).

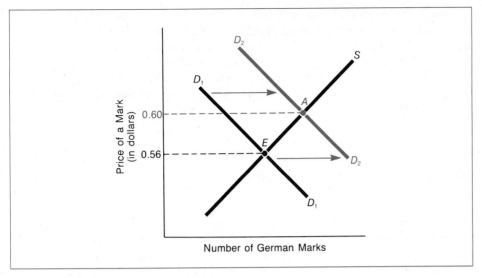

Figure 19–2
THE EFFECT OF AN ECONOMIC BOOM ON THE EXCHANGE RATE
If the U.S. economy suddenly booms, Americans will spend more on imports from Germany. Thus the demand curve for German marks will rise from $D_1 D_1$ to $D_2 D_2$ as Americans seek to acquire the marks they need. The diagram shows that this will cause the mark to appreciate, from 56 cents to 60 cents, as equilibrium shifts from point E to point A. Looked at from the U.S. perspective, the dollar will depreciate.

3. Interest rates on government bonds rise in the United States but are stable in Germany (*Hint:* Which country's citizens will be attracted by high interest rates in the other country?)

To say that supply and demand determine exchange rates in a free market is at once to say everything and to say nothing. If we are to acquire some understanding of the reasons why some currencies appreciate while others depreciate, we must look into the factors that move the supply and demand curves. Economists believe that the principal determinants of exchange rate movements are rather different in the long, medium, and short runs. So we turn in the next three sections to the analysis of exchange rate movements over these three "runs," beginning with the long run.

The Purchasing-Power Parity Theory: The Long Run

As long as there is free trade across national borders, exchange rates should eventually adjust so that the same product costs the same number of dollars (or the same amount of any other currency) in every country, except for differences attributable to transportation costs and the like. This simple statement forms the basis of the major theory of exchange rate determination in the long run.

The **purchasing-power parity theory of exchange rate determination** holds that the exchange rate between any two national currencies adjusts to reflect differences in the price levels in the two countries.

An example will bring out the basic truth in this theory and also suggest some of its limitations. Suppose that Swedish and American steel are identical and that these two nations are the only producers of steel for the world market. Suppose further that steel is the only tradable good that either country produces.

Question: If American steel costs $160 per ton and Swedish steel costs 1000 kronor per ton, what must be the exchange rate between the dollar and the krona?

Answer: Since 1000 kronor or $160 each buys a ton of steel, they must be of equal value. Hence, each krona must be worth 16 cents. Why? A higher price of a krona, like 20 cents, would mean that steel would cost $200 per ton (1000 kronor at 20 cents each) in Sweden but only $160 per ton in the United States. Then all foreign customers would shop for their steel in the United States. Similarly, any exchange rate below 16 cents per krona would send all the steel business to Sweden.

EXERCISE
Show why an exchange rate of 12 cents per krona is too low.

The purchasing-power parity theory is used to make long-run predictions about the effects of inflation on exchange rates. To continue our example, suppose that over a five-year period, prices in the United States rise by 25 percent while prices in Sweden rise by 100 percent. The purchasing-power parity theory predicts that the krona will depreciate relative to the dollar. It also predicts the amount of the depreciation. After the inflation, American steel costs $200 per ton (one-fourth more than $160), while Swedish steel costs 2000 kronor per ton (100 percent more than 1000 kronor). For these two prices to be equivalent, 2000 kronor must be worth $200, or one krona must be worth 10 cents. The krona, therefore, must have fallen from 16 cents to 10 cents.

According to the purchasing-power parity theory, differences in domestic inflation rates are a major cause of adjustments in exchange rates. If one country has a faster rate of inflation than another, then its exchange rate should be depreciating.

For many years, the theory seemed to work tolerably well. While precise numerical predictions based on purchasing power parity calculations were not very accurate (see the accompanying box), nations with higher inflation did at least experience depreciating currencies. But in the 1980s, even this broke down. For example, while the U.S. inflation rate was higher than both West Germany's and Japan's between 1980 and 1985, the dollar nonetheless rose relative to both the mark and the yen. Clearly, the theory is missing something. There are a number of complications which the purchasing-power theory ignores.

First, changes in any of the interferences with free trade, such as tariffs and quotas, can upset simple calculations based on purchasing-power parity. For example, if Swedish prices rise faster than American prices but, at the same time, foreign countries erect tariff barriers to keep American (but not Swedish) steel out, then the krona might not have to depreciate.

Second, some goods and services cannot be traded across national frontiers. Land and buildings are only the most obvious examples; most services can be traded only to a limited extent (as when tourists from one country have their hair cut in another). Inflation rates for goods and services that are *not tradable* have little bearing on exchange rates.

Third, few of the goods that different nations produce and trade are as uniform as the Swedish and American steel in our example. A Volvo and a Buick, for example, are not identical products. So the price of a Volvo *in U.S. dollars*

Purchasing-Power Parity and the Big Mac

In 1983, *The New York Times* used a well-known international commodity to assess the purchasing-power parity theory. As this article shows, the theory did not work very well.

The French have been most vociferous in complaining that the dollar's value has been too high. But if the cost of lunch at McDonald's is any guide, it is the franc, more than the dollar, that should be devalued.

Theoretically, at least, if all exchange rates were where they should be, prices of the same goods should be identical in every country. Using McDonald's as an example, exchange rates, indeed, are out of line and the dollar is overvalued against all the major currencies, except the franc.

Last Wednesday in New York, it cost $3.39 to buy a Big Mac, a small order of fries and a small Coke. This was substantially higher than the cost of a comparable McDonald's lunch in five major foreign cities.

In Paris, however, the dollar-equivalent price was $3.82, based on the franc's June 28 value of 13.08 cents. The biggest bargain was in Amsterdam, where the price of a McDonald's lunch was only $2.40. In Switzerland, the cost of a comparable meal was $3.23; in Tokyo, $2.62; in Germany, $2.57; and in London, $2.40.

If the seven currencies were to be made equal on the "MacIndex," using the New York price as a yardstick, the Swiss franc would have to be revalued upward by 4.7 percent against the dollar; the Japanese yen 22.7 percent; the German mark 24 percent; the British pound 25.7 percent and the Dutch guilder 29.2 percent. The French franc would have to be devalued 11.3 percent.

SOURCE: *The New York Times*, July 3, 1983.

AUTHORS' NOTE: Actually, the theory did not do all that badly. Over the next several months, the French franc depreciated 10.9 percent relative to the dollar.

---

can rise faster than the price of a Buick without driving Volvos out of the market entirely. On balance:

Most economists believe that other factors are much more important than relative price levels for exchange rate determination in the short run. But in the long run, purchasing-power parity plays an important role.

Economic Activity and Exchange Rates: The Medium Run

Since consumer spending increases when income expands and decreases when income contracts, the same is likely to happen to spending on imported goods. For this reason:

A country's imports will rise quickly when its economy is booming and slowly when its economy is stagnating.

We have already illustrated this point with Figure 19–2. There we saw that a boom in the United States would shift the demand curve for marks outward and therefore lead to an appreciation of the mark (depreciation of the dollar) as American imports from Germany surge. However, if Germany were booming at the same time, German citizens would be buying more American exports, which would shift the supply curve of marks outward. On balance, the value of the dollar might or might not fall. What matters is whether exports are growing faster than imports. The general lesson is that:

Holding other things equal, a country that grows faster than the rest of the world normally finds its currency depreciating because its imports grow faster than its exports, so that its demand curve for foreign currency shifts outward more rapidly than its supply curve.

A recent policy controversy involving the United States, West Germany, and Japan is a case in point. As the dollar fell in 1986 and 1987, the U.S. government tried to persuade the Germans and Japanese to give their economies a boost as a way of spurring U.S. exports and propping up the dollar.

Interest Rates and Exchange Rates: The Short Run

While economic activity is important for exchange rate determination in the medium run, "other things" often are not equal in the short run. Specifically, one factor that often seems to call the tune in determining exchange rate movements in the short run is *interest rate differentials*. There is an enormous fund of so-called hot money — owned by banks, multinational corporations, and wealthy individuals of all nations, and amounting to perhaps a trillion dollars — that travels around the globe in search of the highest interest rates.

Thus suppose that British government bonds are paying an 8 percent rate of interest when yields on equally safe American government securities rise to 10 percent. British investors will be attracted by the high interest rates in the United States and will offer pounds for sale in order to buy dollars, planning to use those dollars to buy American securities. At the same time, American investors will find investing in the United States more attractive than ever, so fewer pounds will be demanded by Americans.

When the demand schedule falls and the supply curve rises, the effect on price is predictable: The pound will depreciate, as Figure 19–3 shows. In the figure, the supply curve of pounds shifts outward from $S_1 S_1$ to $S_2 S_2$ when British

Figure 19–3

THE EFFECT OF A RISE IN U.S. INTEREST RATES
When the U.S. raises its interest rates, more English investors will want to buy American bonds, and so the supply curve of pounds will shift outward from $S_1 S_1$ to $S_2 S_2$. At the same time, fewer Americans will seek to buy British bonds, so the demand curve for pounds will shift inward from $D_1 D_1$ to $D_2 D_2$. The combined effect of these two shifts is to move the market equilibrium from point E_1 to point E_2. The British pound depreciates, and the dollar appreciates.

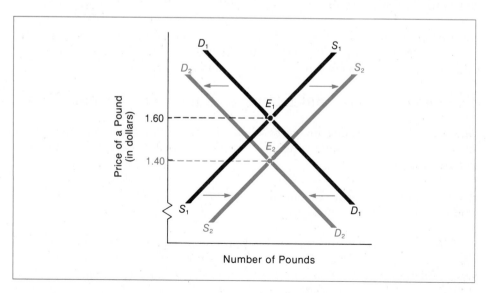

investors seek to sell pounds in order to purchase U.S. securities. At the same time, American investors wish to buy fewer pounds because they no longer wish to invest in British securities. Thus the demand curve shifts inward from $D_1 D_1$ to $D_2 D_2$. The result, in our example, is a depreciation of the pound from $1.60 to $1.40. In general:

Holding other things equal, countries with high interest rates are able to attract more capital than are countries with low interest rates. Thus a rise in interest rates often will lead to an appreciation of the currency, and a drop in interest rates will lead to a depreciation.

This factor, most experts in international finance believe, is the major determinant of exchange rates in the short run. It certainly played a predominant role in the stunning movements of the U.S. dollar during the 1980s. Beginning in 1980, American interest rates rose well above comparable interest rates abroad. In consequence, foreign capital was attracted here, American capital stayed at home, and the dollar soared. Then, in the mid-1980s, the gap between U.S. and foreign interest rates narrowed and the dollar fell.

Market Determination of Exchange Rates: Summary

We can summarize this discussion of exchange rate determination in free markets as follows:

1. Currency values generally will be *appreciating* in countries whose inflation rates are lower than the rest of the world because buyers in foreign countries will demand their goods, and thus drive up the currency.
2. Exchange rates would also be expected to rise in countries whose levels of economic activity are lower than average, because these countries will be importing rather little.
3. We expect to find appreciating currencies in countries whose interest rates are high because these countries will attract capital from all over the world.

Reversing each of these, we expect that currencies will be *depreciating* in countries with relatively high inflation rates, or high levels of economic activity, or low interest rates.

Fixed Exchange Rates and the Definition of the Balance of Payments

Some exchange rates today are truly floating, determined by the forces of supply and demand without government interference. But many are not. For this reason, we turn our attention next to the opposite of floating exchange rates, a system of **fixed exchange rates**, or rates that are set by government. Naturally, under such a system the exchange rate, being fixed, is not closely watched. Instead, international financial specialists focus on a country's **balance of payments** — a term we must now define.

Fixed exchange rates are rates set by government decisions and maintained by government actions.

To understand what the balance of payments is, look at Figure 19–4, which depicts a situation that might represent, say, Great Britain before its major devaluation in 1967 — an *overvalued* currency. While the supply and demand curves for British pounds indicate an equilibrium exchange rate of $2.40 to the pound (point E), the British government is keeping the rate at

Figure 19–4

A BALANCE OF PAYMENTS DEFICIT

At a fixed exchange rate of $2.80 per pound, which is well above the equilibrium level of $2.40 per pound, England's currency is overvalued in this example. As a consequence, more pounds will be supplied (point B) than are demanded (point A). The difference—distance AB, or £2 billion per year—represents Britain's balance of payments deficit.

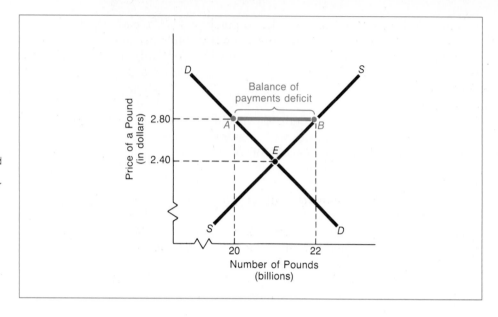

$2.80. Notice that at $2.80 more people are supplying pounds than are demanding them. In the example, suppliers are selling £22 billion per year, but demanders are purchasing only £20 billion.

This gap between the £22 billion that some people sell and the £20 billion that other people buy is what we mean by Britain's **balance of payments deficit**—£2 billion per year in this case. It is shown by the horizontal distance between points A and B in Figure 19–4.

How can market forces be flouted in this way? Since sales and purchases on any market must be equal, as a simple piece of arithmetic, the excess of quantity supplied over quantity demanded of British currency (£2 billion per year in this example) must be bought by the Bank of England, Britain's central bank. In buying these pounds, it must give up some of the gold and foreign currencies that it keeps as *reserves*. Thus the Bank of England would be losing £2 billion in reserves per year as the cost of keeping the pound at $2.80.

Naturally, this cannot go on forever; the reserves eventually will run out. And this is the fatal flaw in the system of fixed exchange rates. Once speculators become convinced that the exchange rate can be held only a short while longer, they will sell pounds in massive amounts rather than hold on to a currency whose value they soon expect to fall sharply. The supply curve of pounds will shift outward drastically, as shown in Figure 19–5, causing a sharp rise in the balance of payments deficit (from £2 billion to £4 billion in the example). This is called a "run" on the currency. Lacking sufficient reserves, the central bank will have to permit the exchange rate to fall to its equilibrium level, and this might amount to an even larger devaluation than would have been required before the speculative run on the pound began.

For an example of the reverse case, a severely *undervalued* currency, let us consider Germany in 1973. Figure 19–6 depicts demand and supply curves for marks that intersect at an equilibrium price of 40 cents per mark (point E in the diagram). Yet, in the example, we suppose that the German authorities are holding the rate at 35 cents. At this rate, the quantity of marks demanded (50 billion) greatly exceeds the quantity supplied (40 billion). The difference is Germany's **balance of payments surplus**, and is shown by the horizontal distance AB.

The **balance of payments deficit** is the amount by which the quantity supplied of a country's currency (per year) exceeds the quantity demanded. Balance of payments deficits arise whenever the exchange rate is pegged at an artificially high level.

The **balance of payments surplus** is the amount by which the quantity demanded of a country's currency (per year) exceeds the quantity supplied. Balance of payments surpluses arise whenever the exchange rate is pegged at an artificially low level.

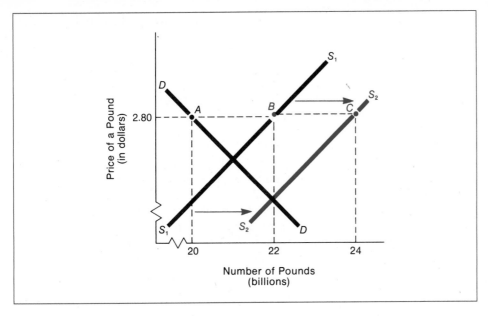

Figure 19–5
A SPECULATIVE RUN ON
THE POUND
When speculators become
convinced that a devaluation
of the pound is in the offing,
they will rush to sell pounds.
Their actions shift the supply
curve outward from $S_1 S_1$ to
$S_2 S_2$ and, in the process,
widen England's balance of
payments deficit from AB to
AC.

Germany can keep the rate at 35 cents only by providing the marks that foreigners want to buy: 10 billion marks per year in this example. In return, it receives U.S. dollars, British pounds, French francs, gold, and so on. All of this serves to increase Germany's reserves of foreign currencies. But notice the important difference between this case and Britain's overvalued pound.

The accumulation of reserves rarely will *force* a central bank to revalue in the way that depletion of reserves can force a devaluation.

This was another weakness of the system of fixed exchange rates that prevailed between 1944 and 1971. In principle, imbalances in exchange rates could be cured either by a devaluation by the country with a balance of payments deficit or by an upward revaluation by the country with a balance of

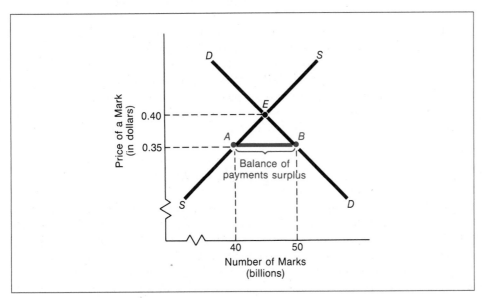

Figure 19–6
A BALANCE OF
PAYMENTS SURPLUS
In this example, Germany's
currency is undervalued at
35 cents per mark since the
equilibrium exchange rate is
40 cents per mark.
Consequently, more marks
are being demanded (point
B) than are being supplied
(point A). The gap between
quantity demanded and
quantity supplied—distance
AB, or 10 billion marks per
year—measures Germany's
balance of payments surplus.

payments surplus. In practice, though, it was almost always the deficit countries that were forced to act.

Why did the surplus countries refuse to revalue? One reason was a stubborn refusal to recognize some basic economic realities. They viewed the disequilibrium as the problem of the deficit countries and believed that the deficit countries, therefore, should take the corrective steps. This, of course, is nonsense. Some currencies are overvalued *because* some other currencies are undervalued. In fact, the two statements mean exactly the same thing.

The other reason why exporters in Germany, Japan, and other surplus countries resisted upward revaluations is that such actions would make their products more expensive to foreigners and thus cut into their sales. And these exporters had the political clout to make their views stick. Meanwhile, since the values of the mark and the yen on world markets were artificially held down, German and Japanese consumers were put in the unenviable position of having to pay more for imported goods than they need have paid. Rather than buy these excessively expensive foreign goods, they watched domestically produced goods go overseas in return for pieces of paper (dollars, francs, pounds, and so on).

Defining the Balance of Payments in Practice

From the preceding discussion it may seem that measuring a nation's balance of payments position is a simple task: We simply count up the private demand for and supply of its currency and subtract quantity supplied from quantity demanded. Conceptually, this is all there is to it. But in practice, the difficulties are great because we never have statistics on the number of dollars demanded and supplied. There is no way to observe these directly.

If we look at actual market transactions, we will see that the number of U.S. dollars actually *purchased* and the number of U.S. dollars actually *sold* are identical. Unless someone has made a bookkeeping error, this must always be so. How, then, can we recognize a balance of payments surplus or deficit? Easy, you say. Just look at the transactions of the central bank, whose purchases or sales must make up the difference between private demand and private supply. If the Federal Reserve is buying dollars, its purchases measure our balance of payments deficit. If it is selling, its sales represent our balance of payments surplus.

Thus the suggestion is to measure the balance of payments by *excluding official transactions among governments*. This is roughly how the balance of payments surplus or deficit is defined today, though, for a variety of complicated reasons, the U.S. government decided long ago to stop publishing any official statistic called "the balance of payments deficit." Instead, all foreign transactions are listed, and readers are invited to define the balance of payments in any way they wish. Let us now see just what data are published in these official accounts.

The U.S. Balance of Payments Accounts

Using 1986 as an example, Table 19–2 shows the official U.S. balance of payments accounts. There is nothing that purports to measure America's overall balance of payments surplus or deficit. The top section of the table summarizes America's trade in currently produced goods and services—the so-called *current account*. The positive or negative sign attached to each entry indicates whether the transaction represented a *gain* (+) or a *loss* (−) of foreign currency.

Table 19–2
U.S. BALANCE OF PAYMENTS ACCOUNTS, 1986 (billions of dollars)

Current Account

(1) Balance of trade		−$144.3
(2) Merchandise exports	+224.4	
(3) Merchandise imports	−368.7	
(4) Net military transactions		−3.7
(5) Travel and transportation (net)		−9.9
(6) Net income from investments and other services		+32.2
(7) Balance on goods and services (Lines 1 plus 5 plus 6)		−125.7
(8) Unilateral transfers		−15.7
(9) Private	−1.7	
(10) U.S. government (nonmilitary)	−14.0	
(11) Balance on current account (Lines 7 plus 8)		−141.4

Capital Account

(12) Net private capital flows		+84.3
(13) Change in U.S. assets abroad	−94.4	
(14) Change in foreign assets in the U.S.	+178.7	
(15) Net governmental capital flows		+33.1
(16) Change in U.S. government assets	−1.6	
(17) Change in foreign official assets in the U.S.	+34.7	
(18) Balance on capital account (Lines 12 plus 15)		+117.4

Addendum

(19) Sum of lines (11) and (18)		−24.0
(20) Statistical discrepancy		−24.0

SOURCE: *Survey of Current Business*, June 1987. Organization of table changed by authors.

Looking first at the top of the table, we see that in merchandise transactions, Americans imported about $144 billion more than they exported, leading to a whopping deficit in what is called the *balance of trade* (see lines 1–3). Because it is available on a monthly basis, this is the number reported most frequently by the news media. The incredibly large trade deficit shown in line 1, probably the largest ever run by any nation, caused great consternation and political controversy. For example, it was a major factor behind the drive for more trade protection that we discussed in Chapter 18.

The entry in line 4 indicates the net effect of a large number of dollars spent by U.S. military installations abroad (transactions that cost us foreign currency) and a large amount of foreign currency earned by selling armaments. On balance, these cost the United States about $3.7 billion in foreign currency. Line 5 shows that in 1986 American tourists and shippers spent about $10 billion more on foreign services than foreign tourists and shippers spent here. Line 6 displays our major source of foreign currency earnings in the services category: We earned about $32 billion more on our investments overseas (and on some other miscellaneous services) than foreign investors earned here.

Line 7 gives the net result of all trading in goods and services—*the balance on goods and services*. The entry in line 7 means that the United States spent over $125 billion more than it received during 1986. Lines 8–10 indicate the so-called unilateral transfers, including both private gifts to foreigners and official foreign aid. Together these cost us over $15 billion in foreign currency. When these unilateral transfers are subtracted from the deficit on goods and services, we find (in line 11) a huge deficit of $141.4 billion in America's *current account*. Many economists take the balance on current account to be the most basic measure of a nation's international transactions.

But this hardly represents our "balance of payments," as it leaves out all purchases and sales of assets. This group of transactions is shown in the *capital account* (lines 12–18). Line 12 shows that, on balance, foreign individuals and businesses bought about $84 billion more in assets here than private American investors bought from foreigners. The net entry is *plus* $84.3 billion because $94.4 billion dollars flowed *out of* the United States to buy foreign assets (line 13), while $178.7 billion in foreign money flowed *into* the United States to buy American assets (line 14).

This large surplus in private capital flows, coupled with a much larger deficit in the current account, left the United States with a gigantic balance of payments deficit in 1986. How are such deficits financed? Normally, by government capital flows in the opposite direction (such as when foreign governments buy U.S. government bonds). Line 15 tells us that such was the case in 1986. Foreign governments bought $34.7 billion worth of U.S. assets (line 17), while our government bought only $1.6 billion in foreign assets (line 16), leaving a large surplus in governmental capital flows of $33.1 billion (line 15).

You may notice that the accounts do not balance. When we add up the current account (line 11) plus the overall (private plus government) capital account (line 18), we get a $24.0 billion deficit (line 19). But, of course, this is impossible. Since it is a simple matter of arithmetic that the two accounts together must balance (dollars purchased = dollars sold), the difference is considered a *statistical discrepancy* (line 20). While part of this huge discrepancy simply comes from errors in data collection and computation, the lion's share reflects the U.S. government's inability to monitor all the flows of money, goods, and services across its borders. When we fail to record the cargo of a truck hauling U.S. goods to Canada, we overstate our current account deficit. When we fail to record foreign capital movements into the United States, we understate our capital account surplus. Such errors and omissions have left a big statistical discrepancy in the U.S. balance of payments accounts for years.

A Bit of History: The Gold Standard

It is hard to find examples of strictly fixed exchange rates in the historical record. About the only time exchange rates were truly fixed was under the old **gold standard**, at least when it was practiced in its ideal form.[3] Under the gold standard, fixed exchange rates were maintained by an automatic equilibrating mechanism that went something like this: All currencies were defined in terms of gold; indeed, some were actually made of gold. When a nation had a deficit in its balance of payments, this meant, essentially, that more gold was flowing *out* than was flowing *in*. Since the domestic money supply was based on gold, losing gold to foreigners meant that the quantity of money *automatically* fell. This raised interest rates and attracted foreign capital. At the same time, the restrictive "monetary policy" pulled down national output and prices, thus discouraging imports and encouraging exports. The balance of payments problem quickly rectified itself. This meant, however, that:

Under the gold standard, no nation had control of its domestic monetary policy, and therefore no country could control its domestic economy very well.

[3]As a matter of fact, while the gold standard lasted (on and off) for hundreds of years, it was rarely practiced in its ideal form. Except for a brief period of fixed exchange rates in the late nineteenth and early twentieth centuries, there were periodic adjustments of exchange rates even under the gold standard.

At least in principle, the effects on surplus countries were perfectly symmetrical under the gold standard. A balance of payments surplus led, via gold inflows, to an increase in the domestic money supply, whether the surplus country liked the idea or not. This raised prices and output, thereby increasing imports and decreasing exports. And it also lowered interest rates, thereby encouraging outflows of capital. Because of these automatic adjustments, nations rarely reached the point at which devaluations or revaluations were necessary. Exchange rates were fixed as long as countries abided by the rules of the gold standard game.

In addition to the loss of control over domestic monetary conditions, the gold standard posed one other serious difficulty.

A fundamental problem with the gold standard was that the world's commerce was at the mercy of gold discoveries.

Discoveries of gold meant higher prices in the long run and higher real economic activity in the short run, through the standard monetary-policy mechanisms that we studied in Part 4. And when the supply of gold did not keep pace with growth of the world economy, prices had to fall in the long run and employment had to fall in the short run.

The Bretton Woods System and the International Monetary Fund

The gold standard, which had faltered many times before, finally collapsed for good amid the financial chaos of the Great Depression of the 1930s and the Second World War. Without it, the world struggled through an almost complete breakdown in international trade.

Then, as World War II drew to a close, with much of Europe in ruins and with the United States holding the lion's share of the free world's reserves, officials of the industrial nations met at Bretton Woods, New Hampshire, in 1944 to try to establish a stable monetary environment that would facilitate world trade. Since the dollar was the only "strong" currency at that time, it was natural for them to turn to the dollar as the basis of the new international economic order.

That is just what they did. The Bretton Woods agreements reestablished a system of fixed exchange rates based not on the old gold standard but on the free convertibility of the U.S. dollar into gold. The United States agreed to buy or sell gold to maintain the $35 per ounce price that had been established by President Franklin Roosevelt in 1933. The other signatory nations, which had almost no gold in any case, agreed to buy and sell dollars to maintain their exchange rates at agreed-upon levels. Thus all currencies were indirectly on a modified "gold standard." A holder of French francs, for example, could exchange these for dollars at (roughly) 5 francs per dollar and then exchange these into gold at $35 per ounce. In this way, the value of the franc was fixed at 175 francs per ounce of gold (5 francs per dollar times 35 dollars per ounce). The new system was dubbed the **gold-exchange system**, and it was often referred to as the **Bretton Woods system**.

The **International Monetary Fund (IMF)** was set up to police and manage this new system. Using funds that had been contributed by member countries, the IMF was empowered to make loans to countries that were running low on reserves. A change in exchange rates was to be permitted only in the case of a "fundamental disequilibrium" in a nation's balance of payments—for it was believed that only relatively fixed exchange rates could provide the stable climate needed to restore world trade.

Of course, the Bretton Woods conferees did not define clearly what a "fundamental disequilibrium" was, nor could they have. As the system evolved, it came to mean a chronic *deficit* in the balance of payments of sizable proportions. Such nations would then *devalue* their currencies relative to the dollar. So the system was not really one of fixed exchange rates but rather one where rates were "fixed until further notice."

Several flaws in the Bretton Woods system have already been mentioned in our discussion of the pure system of fixed exchange rates. First, since devaluations were permitted only after a long run of balance of payments deficits, these devaluations (a) could be clearly foreseen and (b) normally had to be large. Speculators then saw opportunities for profit and would "attack" weak currencies with a wave of selling.

This problem led many economists to question whether the system of fixed exchange rates was really providing the stable climate for world trade that had been intended. Was a system where rates were constant for long periods and then altered by large amounts really more conducive to international trade than one where overvalued currencies would gradually depreciate, as they would under a system of floating rates?

The second problem arose from the custom that deficit nations were expected to devalue when forced to, while surplus nations (mainly Germany and Japan) could resist upward revaluations. Since the U.S. dollar defined the monetary value of gold (at $35 per ounce), America was the one nation in the world that had no way to devalue its currency relative to gold, no matter how "fundamental" the disequilibrium became. The only way exchange rates between the dollar and foreign currencies could change was if the surplus nations revalued their currencies upward relative to the dollar. They did not do this frequently enough, so the United States, with its chronically overvalued currency, ran persistent balance of payments deficits in the 1960s.

Adjustment Mechanisms Under the Bretton Woods System

Under the Bretton Woods system, devaluation was viewed as a last resort, to be used only after other methods of adjusting to payments imbalances had failed. What were these other methods?

We have already encountered most of them in our discussion of exchange rate determination in free markets (see pages 409–15). Any factor that increases the demand for, say, British pounds or that reduces the supply will push the value of the pound upward if it is free to adjust. If, however, the exchange rate is pegged, it is the balance of payments deficit rather than the exchange rate that will adjust when supply of or demand for a nation's money changes. Specifically, the British balance of payments deficit will shrink if either the demand for pounds increases or the supply decreases.

The two panels of Figure 19–7 illustrate this adjustment. In each case, Great Britain has a payments deficit, since the official exchange rate ($2.80) exceeds the equilibrium rate ($2.40). The deficit starts at AB in each diagram. Then either the demand curve moves outward as in part (a), or the supply curve moves inward as in part (b). With the exchange rate held at $2.80, the balance of payments deficit shrinks—to CB in part (a) or to AC in part (b).

Referring back to our earlier discussions of the factors that underlie the demand and supply curves, then, we see that one way a deficit nation can

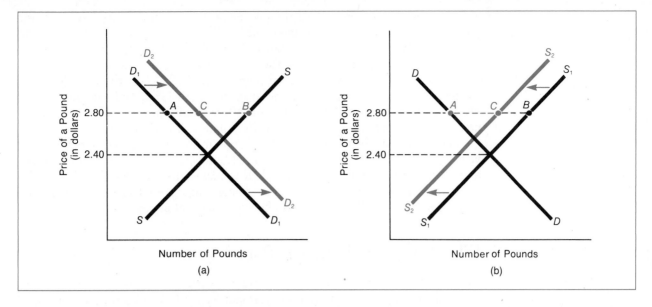

Number of Pounds
(a)

Number of Pounds
(b)

improve its balance of payments is to *reduce its aggregate demand,* thus discouraging imports and cutting down its demand for foreign currency. Another is to *slow its rate of inflation,* thus encouraging exports and discouraging imports. Finally, it can *raise its interest rates* in order to attract more foreign capital.

In a word, deficit nations were expected to follow restrictive monetary and fiscal policies *voluntarily* just as they would *automatically* have done under the old gold standard. However, just as under the gold standard, this medicine was often unpalatable, so deficit nations frequently resorted to a bewildering variety of **exchange controls** — laws and regulations that made it very difficult for its nationals to sell their own currency to get foreign exchange. Many countries still have such controls.

Surplus nations could, of course, have taken the opposite measures: pursuing expansive monetary and fiscal policies to increase economic growth and lower interest rates. Such actions, by increasing the supply of the country's currency and reducing the demand for it, would have reduced the balance of payments surplus. But often the countries did not relish the inflation that accompanies expansionary policies; and so, once again, they left the burden of adjustment to the deficit nations. The general point about fixed exchange rates is that:

Under a system of fixed exchange rates, the government of a country loses some control over its domestic economy. There may be times when balance of payments considerations force it to contract its economy in order to cut down its demand for foreign currency, even though domestic needs are calling for expansion. Conversely, there may be times when the domestic economy needs to be reined in, but balance of payments considerations suggest expansion.

The Bretton Woods system worked fairly well for a number of years, but it finally broke down over its inability to devalue the U.S. dollar. In August 1971, the rapid depletion of America's reserves and the accumulation of foreign debts resulting from America's chronic balance of payments deficits forced President Richard M. Nixon to end fixed exchange rates. He unilaterally abolished the gold exchange system by announcing that the United States would no longer peg the value of the dollar by buying and selling gold. After some futile

Figure 19–7
ADJUSTING TO BALANCE OF PAYMENTS DEFICITS
The two parts of this diagram illustrate alternative ways to cut England's balance of payments deficit while maintaining the exchange rate at $2.80 per pound. Part (a) might represent a reduction in British inflation, which would increase world demand for her export products. Or it could represent a rise in British interest rates, which would attract foreign capital. Part (b) might represent a reduction in British incomes, which would diminish English appetites for foreign goods. In either case, whether demand rises or supply falls, the balance of payments deficit is reduced: from *AB* to *CB* in part (a) and from *AB* to *AC* in part (b).

Exchange controls are laws restricting the exchange of one nation's currency for another's.

attempts by the major trading nations to reestablish fixed rates in 1971 and 1972, the Bretton Woods system ended in 1973.

Most observers today agree that the gold-exchange system could not have survived the incredible events of the 1970s in any case. The worldwide inflationary boom of 1972, the poor food harvests in 1972–1974, the huge increases in the price of oil in 1973–1974 and again in 1979–1980, and the great worldwide recessions of 1974–1976 and the 1980s created a world in which the major countries were experiencing dramatically different inflation rates.

For example, between 1975 and 1985, inflation averaged 4 percent per year in Germany, 7 percent in the United States, 11 percent in Great Britain, and 15 percent in Italy. As the purchasing-power theory reminds us, large differences in inflation rates call for *major* changes in currency values. The Bretton Woods system was ill-suited to handle such major changes.

Why Try to Fix Exchange Rates?

"Then it's agreed. Until the dollar firms up, we let the clamshell float."
Drawing by Ed Fisher © 1971, The New Yorker Magazine, Inc.

In view of these and other severe problems with the Bretton Woods system, why did the international financial community work so hard to maintain fixed rates for so many years? The answer is that floating exchange rates, determined in free markets by supply and demand, also pose problems.

Chief among these is the possibility that freely floating rates might prove to be highly variable rates, which add an unwanted element of risk to foreign trade. For example, if the exchange rate is 16 cents to the French franc, then a 2000-franc Parisian dress will cost $320. But should the franc appreciate to 20 cents, this same dress would cost $400. An American department store thinking of buying this dress may need to place its order far in advance and will want to know the cost *in dollars*. It may be worried about the possibility that the value of the franc will rise, so that the dress will cost more than $320. And such worries might inhibit trade.

There are two answers to this concern. First, we could hope that freely floating rates would prove not to be very volatile. Prices of many domestic consumer goods, for example, are determined by supply and demand in free markets and yet do not fluctuate unduly.

Second, speculators might relieve business firms of exchange rate risks—for a fee, of course. Consider the deparment store example. If French francs cost 16 cents today, the department store manager can assure herself of paying exactly $320 for the dress several months from now by arranging for a speculator to deliver francs to her at 16 cents on the day she needs them. If the franc appreciates in the interim, it is the speculator, not the department store, that will take the financial beating. (And, of course, if the franc depreciates, the speculator will pocket the profits.) Thus speculators play an important role in a system of floating exchange rates.

The widespread fears that speculative activity in free markets will lead to wild gyrations in prices, while occasionally valid, are more often unfounded. The reason is simple. International currency speculators, if they are to make profits, must buy a currency when its value is low (thus helping to support the currency by pushing up its demand curve) and sell it when its value is high (thus holding down the price by adding to the supply curve).

This means that, if they are successful, speculators will be coming into the market as *buyers* just when demand is weak (or when supply is strong), and coming in as *sellers* just when demand is strong (or supply is scant). In doing so, they will help limit price fluctuations. Looked at the other way around, speculators can destabilize prices only if they are systematically willing to lose money.[4]

Notice the stark contrast to the system of fixed exchange rates in which speculation often led to wild "runs" on currencies that were on the verge of devaluation. Speculative activity, which may well be destabilizing under fixed rates, is likely to be stabilizing under floating rates.

We do not mean to imply here that there are no difficulties at all under floating exchange rates. At the very least, speculators will demand a fee for their services—a fee that adds to the costs of trading across national borders. In addition, it may be impossible to eliminate all exchange-rate risks through speculation. Currently, for example, contracts on foreign currencies offered in speculative markets cover at most a few months. Thus no business can protect itself from exchange-rate changes over periods measured in years.

The experience under floating rates since 1973 has delivered clear verdicts on these two issues. First, exchange rates have in fact proven to be extremely volatile—much more volatile than advocates of floating rates anticipated. This volatility has led, in recent years, to more and more talk about moving back toward fixed exchange rates. Second, however, international trade has flourished despite all this volatility.

The Current Mixed System

Our current international financial system—where some currencies are still pegged in the old Bretton Woods manner, others are floating freely, and many more are floating subject to government interferences—has evolved gradually since President Nixon severed the dollar's link to gold. Though it continues to change and adapt, at least three features are evident.

The first is the decline in the notion that exchange rates should be fixed for relatively long periods of time. The demand by many countries in the early 1970s that the world quickly return to fixed exchange rates had largely subsided by the mid-1970s. Even where rates are still pegged to the dollar, devaluations and revaluations are now much more frequent—and smaller—than they were in the 1944–1971 period. Most free-world currency rates change slightly on a day-to-day basis, and market forces generally determine the basic trends, up or down. Even advocates of greater fixity in exchange rates generally propose that governments keep rates within certain *ranges*, rather than literally fix them as under Bretton Woods.

Second, however, some central banks do not hesitate to intervene to moderate exchange movements whenever they feel that such actions are appropriate. Typically, these interventions are aimed at ironing out transitory fluctuations. But there are times in which central banks oppose basic trends in exchange rates. Deficit nations buy their own currencies to prevent them from depreciating. Surplus nations sell their own currencies to prevent them from appreciating. While we certainly no longer have many fixed exchange rates, many of the major currencies are floating less than freely. The terms **"dirty float"** or **"managed float"** have been coined to describe this mongrel system.

The third unmistakable feature of the present international monetary system is the virtual elimination of any role for gold. The trend away from gold actually began before President Nixon's dramatic announcement in 1971, and

---

[4] See Discussion Question 11 at the end of the chapter.

by now it is only a minor exaggeration to say that gold plays no role in the world's financial system. Nowadays there is a *free market* in gold, which enables those who wish to invest in gold—dentists, jewelers, industrial users, speculators, and ordinary citizens who think of gold as a good store of value—to buy or sell as they wish. The price of gold, determined each day by the law of supply and demand, has proved to be quite volatile. Fortunes have been made and lost by investors in gold.

Figure 19–8
THE UPS AND DOWNS OF THE DOLLAR, 1970–1987
This graph charts the behavior of the international value of the dollar relative to a basket of ten major foreign currencies since 1970. (The index is based on March 1973 = 100.) The net change in the value of the dollar since 1972 has not been large, but the ups and downs have been pronounced. The stunning climb of the dollar from its 1980 low to its 1985 high stands out on the graph, as do the sharp declines in 1971–1973, 1977–1978, and 1985–1986.
SOURCE: Federal Reserve System.

Recent Developments in International Financial Markets

The Dancing Dollar

We mentioned earlier that floating exchange rates have not been stable exchange rates. No currency illustrates this better than the U.S. dollar. (See Figure 19–8.)

After several years of considerable stability, the international value of the dollar plummeted from late 1977 until late 1978. Compared to a weighted average of currencies of other nations, the dollar depreciated by 17 percent—enough to grab headlines in the United States. Where would it all end, Americans wondered? Then a rescue mission arrested the fall, and the dollar stabilized for almost two years.

Starting in mid-1980, however, the dollar began rising like a rocket. For example, in 1980 a U.S. dollar bought less than 2 German marks, about 4 French francs, and about 830 Italian lira. By the time it peaked in February 1985, the dollar could buy more than 3 German marks, about 10 French francs, and over 2000 Italian lira. The mighty dollar was a blessing to Americans who

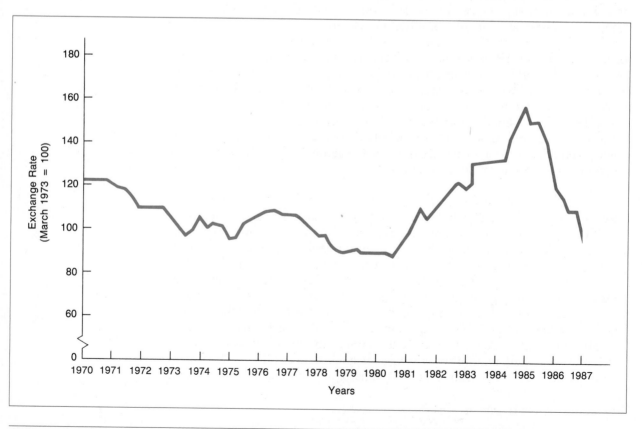

traveled abroad or who bought foreign goods because foreign prices, when translated to dollars by the exchange rate, looked cheap to Americans.[5]

But the arithmetic worked the other way for U.S. firms seeking to sell their goods abroad; foreign buyers found everything American very expensive.[6] It was no surprise, therefore, that as the dollar climbed our exports fell, our imports rose, and our current account registered all-time record deficits. An expensive currency, Americans came to learn, is a mixed blessing.

Since early 1985, the value of the dollar has generally been falling against most major currencies and is now back down to 1981 levels. The cheaper dollar is curbing American appetites for imports and alleviating some of the problems of our export industries. However, rising prices for imported goods and foreign vacations have been a source of consternation to many American consumers. An uncertainty over the future of the dollar may have contributed to the stock market crash of October 1987.

The European Monetary System

As noted earlier, floating exchange rates are no magical cure-all. One particular problem beset the members of the European Economic Community (EEC). These Common Market countries seek a unified market like the United States and have a long-range goal of establishing a single currency for all member countries. Floating rates would make this goal impossible. So in 1973 some of the member countries entered into an agreement whereby exchange rates among their currencies would remain relatively *fixed* while Common Market currencies as a group would rise or fall *relative to the rest of the world*.

Within a short time, however, both Britain and Italy found themselves unable to maintain parity with the strong currencies of Germany and the Netherlands. Britain was the first to let the pound float, but soon Italy and France also had to devalue relative to the mark. In 1979 the arrangement was strengthened and formalized into the **European Monetary System (EMS),** which currently has eight member nations. The EMS makes periodic adjustments to exchange rates which get out of line with the others, and it is widely regarded as the first step, albeit a small one, toward a unified European currency. In practice, the German mark is the dominant currency in the EMS, playing a role within Europe analogous to that played by the dollar under the Bretton Woods system.

The LDC Debt Problem[7]

The enormous debts of many less developed countries (LDCs), and the difficulties they are having in meeting their burdensome interest payments, have frequently grabbed the headlines during the 1980s. Many experts feel that the still-unresolved LDC debt problem poses the most serious threat to the stability of the international monetary system.

The seeds of the problem were sown in the 1970s. When real interest rates were low, many of these countries, particularly in Latin America, borrowed heavily to finance their development. In some cases, the money was put to good use. But, in others, unwise policies frittered away the funds. Then, in the 1980s, well-managed and poorly managed countries alike were hit by three common shocks. First, the worldwide recession of the 1980s made it harder for them to earn foreign currency by exporting goods to the industrial countries;

[5]EXAMPLE: How much does a 200-franc hotel room in Paris cost in dollars when the franc is worth 20 cents? 16 cents? 10 cents?
[6]EXAMPLE: How much does a $55 American camera cost a German consumer when the mark is worth 55 cents? 44 cents? 33.33 cents?
[7]For more on this problem, see Chapter 21, especially page 474.

their markets simply contracted. Second, real interest rates rose dramatically, making the burden of paying interest on the debt much harder to bear. Third, the value of the dollar rose, making their international debts—which were denominated in dollars—more onerous.

Beginning with Mexico's problems in 1982, the 1980s have been marked by a series of near-crises in the international financial system as countries like Argentina, Brazil, Peru, the Phillipines, and others have postponed or scaled back payments and renegotiated their debt obligations. Citizens of many of these countries have suffered severe declines in their standards of living as the LDCs scramble to meet their interest and principal payments. Some banks have absorbed sizable losses. But, so far, a series of special arrangements negotiated by governments and banks has managed to keep the system afloat and avoid a panic.

However, no one is declaring the problem solved. Many business people, politicians, and economists doubt that the LDCs will ever be able to repay their debts in full and advocate some sort of partial forgiveness of interest or principal, perhaps on a selective basis. To date, American banks have opposed such plans. But there is continued concern that widespread defaults on loans by LDCs could threaten the solvency of some major U.S. banks.

Summary

1. Exchange rates state the value of one currency in terms of another and thus influence the patterns of world trade in important ways.
2. If governments do not interfere, exchange rates will be determined in free markets by the usual laws of supply and demand. Such a system is called floating exchange rates.
3. Demand for a nation's currency is derived from foreigners' desires to purchase that country's goods and services or to invest in its assets. Any change that increases the demand for a nation's currency will cause its exchange rate to appreciate under floating rates.
4. Supply of a nation's currency is derived from the desire of that country's citizens to purchase foreign goods and services or to invest in foreign assets. Any change that increases the supply of a nation's currency will cause its exchange rate to depreciate under floating rates.
5. In the long run, purchasing-power parity plays a major role in exchange rate movements. The purchasing-power parity theory states that relative price levels in any two countries determine the exchange rate between their currencies. Therefore, countries with relatively low inflation rates normally will have appreciating currencies.
6. Over shorter periods, the pace of economic activity and the level of interest rates exert a greater influence on the exchange rate. In particular, interest rate movements are typically the dominant factor in the short run.
7. Exchange rates can be fixed at nonequilibrium levels by governments that are willing and able to mop up any excess of quantity supplied over quantity demanded, or provide any excess of quantity demanded over quantity supplied. In the first case, the country is suffering from a balance of payments deficit because of its overvalued currency. In the second, an undervalued currency has given it a balance of payments surplus.
8. In the early part of this century, the world was on a particular system of fixed exchange rates called the gold standard, in which the value of every nation's currency was fixed in terms of gold. But this created problems because nations could not control their own money supplies and because the world could not control its total supply of gold.
9. After World War II, the gold standard was replaced by the gold-exchange (or Bretton Woods) system where rates were again fixed, or rather, fixed until further notice. In this system, the U.S. dollar was the basis of international currency values.
10. The gold-exchange system served the world well and helped restore world trade, but it got into trouble when the dollar became chronically overvalued since the system provided no way to remedy this situation.
11. After 1971, the world gradually moved toward a system of relatively free exchange rates, though there are plenty of exceptions. We now have a thoroughly mixed system of "dirty" or "managed" floating which continues to evolve and adapt.
12. Floating rates are not without their problems. For

example, importers and exporters justifiably worry about fluctuations in exchange rates. Though these problems seem manageable, some people think that a return to fixed exchange rates is desirable.

13. Under floating exchange rates, investors who speculate on international currency values provide a valuable service by assuming the risks of those who do not wish to speculate. Normally, speculators stabilize rather than destabilize exchange rates, because that is how they make profits.

14. The U.S. dollar rose dramatically in value from 1980 to 1985, making our imports cheaper and our exports more expensive. Since 1985, however, the dollar has been tumbling.

Concepts for Review

International monetary system	Floating exchange rates	Gold standard
Exchange rate	Purchasing-power parity theory	Gold-exchange system
Appreciation	Fixed exchange rates	(Bretton Woods system)
Depreciation	Balance of payments deficit	International Monetary Fund (IMF)
Devaluation	and surplus	Exchange controls
Revaluation	Current account	"Dirty" or "managed" floating
Supply of and demand for	Capital account	The European Monetary System (EMS)
foreign exchange	Balance of trade	The LDC debt problem

Questions for Discussion

1. What items do you own or routinely consume that are produced abroad? What countries do these come from? How have your purchases affected the exchange rates between the dollar and these currencies?

2. If the dollar depreciates relative to the Japanese yen, will the Sony stereo you have longed for become more or less expensive? What effect do you imagine this will have on American demands for Sonys? Does the American demand curve for yen, therefore, slope upward or downward? Explain.

3. During the 1980s, inflation in West Germany has generally been below that in the United States. What, then, does the purchasing-power parity theory predict should have happened to the exchange rate between the mark and the dollar? (Look at Table 19–1 to see what actually has happened.)

4. Use supply and demand diagrams to analyze the effect on the exchange rate between the dollar and the British pound if:
   a. Britain's flow of North Sea oil increases.
   b. British dockworkers refuse to unload ships that arrive with cargo from America but continue to load ships that sail from Britain.
   c. The Federal Reserve raises interest rates in America.
   d. The U.S. government, to help settle the problems of the Middle East, gives huge amounts of foreign aid to Israel and her Arab neighbors.
   e. Both Britain and the United States slip into recession, but the British recession is far more severe.
   f. Polls suggest that Britain's conservative government will be replaced by radicals, who vow to nationalize all foreign-owned assets.

5. How are the problems of a country faced with a balance of payments deficit similar to those posed by a government regulation that holds the price of peanuts above the equilibrium level? (*Hint:* Think of each in terms of a supply-demand diagram.)

6. Look at the U.S. balance of payments accounts table in the text (Table 19–2 on page 419). Figure out where each of the following actions you could have taken in 1986 would have been recorded in these accounts:
   a. You spent the summer traveling in Europe.
   b. Your uncle in Canada sent you $25 as a birthday present.
   c. You bought a new Volvo.
   d. You sold your stock on the Japanese stock market.
   e. You drove over the Canadian border carrying American records in your trunk and sold them to a friend in Canada. (*Hint:* Would your sale have been recorded anywhere?)

7. For each of the transactions listed in Question 6, indicate how it would affect:
   a. the U.S. balance of payments, if exchange rates were fixed;
   b. the international value of the dollar, if exchange rates were floating.

8. Under the old gold standard, what do you think happened to world prices when there was a huge gold strike in California in 1849? What do you think happened when the world went without any

important new gold strikes for 20 years or so?

9. Explain why the members of the Bretton Woods conference in 1944 wanted to establish a system of fixed exchange rates. What was the flaw that led to the ultimate breakdown of the system in 1971?

10. Suppose you want to reserve a hotel room in Paris for the coming summer but are worried that the value of the franc may rise between now and then, making the rooms too expensive for your budget. Explain how a speculator could relieve you of this worry. (Don't actually try it. Speculators deal only in very large sums!)

11. On page 425, it is pointed out that successful speculators buy a currency when demand is weak and sell it when demand is strong. Use supply and demand diagrams for two different periods (one with weak demand, the other with strong demand) to show why this will limit price fluctuations.

12. Use the following statistics to produce a balance of payments table for the United States, identifying separately the current and capital accounts. (Assume no statistical discrepancy.)

U.S. income on foreign investment	20
U.S. government grants to foreigners	40
Merchandise exports	400
U.S. tourist expenditures abroad	30
U.S. private direct investment abroad	200
Merchandise imports	600

a. Does the balance of payments show a surplus or a deficit?

b. What would happen to the exchange rate under flexible exchange rates?

20

Macroeconomics in a World Economy

No man is an island, entire of itself.

JOHN DONNE

America is no longer an isolated economy immune to foreign influences, if indeed it ever was one. More than ever before, the nations of the world are locked together in an uneasy economic union. Fluctuations in foreign GNP growth, foreign inflation, and foreign interest rates profoundly affect the U.S. economy. Economic events that originate within our borders reverberate around the globe. Before we complete our study of macroeconomics, we must become acquainted with these international linkages, for otherwise it is truly impossible to understand many of the most important economic developments of the 1980s.

One simple fact will drive home the point. Between 1981 and 1986, the sum of $C + I + G$ in the United States, measured in constant 1982 dollars, advanced by about $660 billion, or 3.8 percent per year. Yet during this same five-year period, real GNP grew only about $465 billion, or 2.7 percent per year. (See Figure 20–1.) The large gap between these two numbers suggests that a model that equates Y to $C + I + G$ must be missing something important. It is, and this chapter is designed to remedy the omissions.

The analysis is explained in a step by step manner. We begin by studying how international trade in goods and services affects macroeconomic activity in different countries, paying no attention to changes in exchange rates or to international movements of capital. Then we bring in exchange rate adjustments, which change the price of one country's goods in terms of the currency of another. In Chapter 19, we learned how changes in major macroeconomic variables like GNP, prices, and interest rates affect exchange rates. In this chapter, we complete the circle by looking at international linkages in the opposite direction—studying how changes in the exchange rate affect the domestic economy. Finally, we bring international capital flows into the picture and learn how monetary and fiscal policy work in an international economy.

Policy Issue: The U.S. Trade Deficit

Everybody knows that the United States has been importing much more than it has been exporting in recent years. In 1986, for example, our real imports of Japanese automobiles, Korean textiles, French wine, and other products

Figure 20–1

GROWTH IN DOMESTIC
DEMAND AND GNP,
1981–1986
Between 1981 and 1986, real
GNP in the United States
expanded by about $465
billion, or almost $200 billion
less than the growth of the
sum of C + I + G. The
difference between Y and
C + I + G is net exports,
X − IM, which fell by almost
$200 billion over this period.
SOURCE: U.S. Bureau of
Economic Analysis.

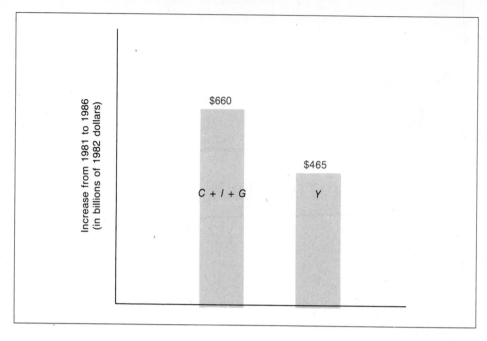

amounted to $523 billion while our real exports of wheat, computers, banking services, and the like were just $377 billion. In absolute magnitude, this trade deficit was the largest ever run by any nation in the history of the world. Naturally, it attracted a great deal of attention not only from economists, but also from politicians, the business community, and the news media. Indeed, America's gaping trade deficit rivals the federal budget deficit as the major economic news story of the 1980s. And both have been blamed by some for the October 1987 stock market crash.

Yet few people realize that American foreign trade was roughly in balance as recently as 1982–1983. And fewer still understand how we came to acquire such a mammoth trade deficit in so short a time. This lack of knowledge, however, has not inhibited these same people from prescribing—and in some cases seeking to legislate—"cures" for our trade problems. By the end of this chapter, you will have acquired an understanding of the origins of America's trade deficit and will be able to make up your own mind about how it can best be cured.

International Trade and National Incomes

If you turn back to the circular flow diagram of Chapter 8 (see page 140), you will see that there is an additional source of spending aside from the usual C + I + G. That final component of aggregate demand is *net exports*, which we symbolize by X − IM, where X is **exports** and IM is **imports.** The condition for equilibrium on the demand side of the economy remains what it was: Total spending must equal total production. But in an **open economy,** the total output available for purchase consists of domestic production plus imports (which are foreign goods that we purchase):

An **open economy** is one that trades with other nations in goods and services, and perhaps also in financial assets.

$$\text{Total available output} = Y + IM.$$

And total expenditure consists of domestic demand plus exports (foreign demand for our products):

$$\text{Total expenditure} = C + I + G + X.$$

So, in the presence of international trade, output and expenditure are in balance when:

$$Y + IM = C + I + G + X,$$

or, rearranging slightly:

$$Y = C + I + G + X - IM.$$

In a strictly arithmetic sense, this revised equilibrium condition for an open economy explains how Y could have expanded by $200 billion less than $C + I + G$ in the United States between 1981 and 1986: Real net exports, $X - IM$, fell by about $200 billion. But this is a rather shallow explanation. To gain a deeper understanding, we must study the determinants of exports and imports.

While both exports and imports depend on many factors, the predominant one is national income. Some of the additional consumption and investment goods that American consumers and firms buy as their spending rises are foreign goods. So:

Our imports rise as our GNP rises and fall as our GNP falls.

Similarly, our *exports* are the *imports* of other countries, so it is natural to assume that our exports depend on *their* GNPs, not on our own. Thus:

Our exports are relatively insensitive to our own GNP, but are quite sensitive to the GNPs of other countries.

These two observations enable us to bring international trade into our model of income determination and the multiplier. Table 20–1 displays the mechanics in a concrete example adapted from Chapter 12. The first two columns are an abbreviated version of Table 12–3 on page 226; they show the sum of $C + I + G$ —now labelled "Domestic Expenditure" at alternative levels of GNP.

Columns 3 and 4 record specific numerical versions of the assumed behavior of exports and imports. Exports are fixed at $400 billion regardless of (our)

Table 20–1
INCOME DETERMINATION WITH INTERNATIONAL TRADE

(1) GROSS NATIONAL PRODUCT (Y) (billions)	(2) DOMESTIC EXPENDITURE (C + I + G) (billions)	(3) EXPORTS (X) (billions)	(4) IMPORTS (IM) (billions)	(5) NET EXPORTS (X − IM) (billions)	(6) TOTAL EXPENDITURE (C + I + G + X − IM) (billions)
$2500	$3100	$400	$250	$150	$3250
3000	3400	400	300	100	3500
3500	3700	400	350	50	3750
4000	4000	400	400	0	4000
4500	4300	400	450	−50	4250
5000	4600	400	500	−100	4500
5500	4900	400	550	−150	4750

GNP, and imports are assumed to rise by $50 billion for every $500 billion rise in GNP. Column 5 simply subtracts imports from exports to get net exports, $X - IM$, and column 6 adds net exports to domestic expenditure to get total expenditure, $C + I + G + X - IM$.

The equilibrium, you can see, occurs at $Y = \$4000$ billion. At any lower level of GNP, Y is less than $C + I + G + X - IM$, so output will rise. At any higher level of GNP, Y is greater than $C + I + G + X - IM$, so output will fall.

Figures 20–2 and 20–3 derive the same conclusion graphically. The upper panel of Figure 20–2 shows that exports are fixed at $400 billion regardless of GNP while imports increase as GNP rises, just as in Table 20–1. The difference between exports and imports, or net exports, is positive until GNP reaches $4000 billion and negative once GNP surpasses that amount. The bottom panel of Figure 20–2 shows the subtraction explicitly and makes it clear that:

Net exports decline as GNP rises.

Figure 20–3 carries this analysis over to the 45° line diagram. We begin with a familiar $C + I + G$ line, in black; this simply duplicates the $C + I + G$ line from Figure 12–4 (page 226). Equilibrium in an open economy occurs where $Y = C + I + G + X - IM$, so we must now add net exports to domestic expenditure. Figure 20–3 does this by first repeating the $X - IM$ line from Figure 20–2 at the bottom of the graph and then adding the two black lines vertically to produce the blue line labelled $C + I + G + X - IM$. The $C + I$

Figure 20–2

THE DEPENDENCE OF NET EXPORTS ON GNP

This graph displays the data on exports, imports, and net exports found in Table 20–1. Exports, X, are independent of GNP while imports, IM, rise as GNP rises (top panel). As a result, net exports, $X - IM$, decline as GNP rises (bottom panel).

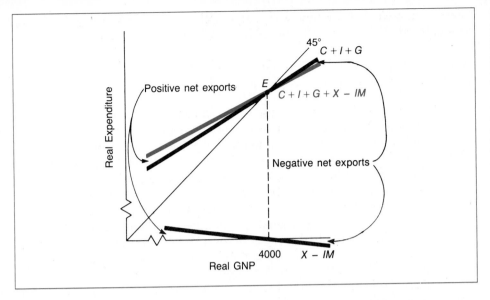

Figure 20–3
EQUILIBRIUM GNP WITH
FOREIGN TRADE
In the presence of foreign
trade, equilibrium GNP
occurs where the $C + I + G$
$+ X - IM$ line crosses the
45° line, for here $Y = C + I +$
$G + X - IM$. In the graph,
equilibrium is at point E,
where GNP is $4000 billion.
This matches the equilibrium
we found in Chapter 12
(Figure 12–4 on page xxx)
without international trade
because our example
assumes that net exports are
zero when $Y = 4000. In the
diagram, net exports are
shown by the vertical
distance — positive or
negative — between the
$C + I + G + X - IM$ line
and the $C + I + G$ line. The
$C + I + G + X - IM$ line is
flatter than the $C + I + G$ line
because net exports decline
as GNP rises.

A **closed economy** is one
that does not trade with
other nations in either
goods or assets.

$+ G + X - IM$ line crosses the 45° line at point E, which is the equilibrium level of GNP with international trade.

If you turn back to page 226 in Chapter 12, you will see that $Y = 4000 is also the equilibrium we found in a **closed economy** with no international trade. (Figure 20–3 shows this quite clearly, since the $C + I + G$ and $C + I + G +$ $X - IM$ lines both cross the 45° line at $Y = 4000.) Does international trade therefore not affect domestic income?

Hardly. Notice in the table or in the figure that we have constructed our example so that exports exactly balance imports ($X - IM = 0$) when GNP is $4000 billion. This is just an artifact of our example. It is because of this artifact that net exports have no effect on equilibrium GNP.

When net exports are zero, foreign trade has no net effect on domestic GNP.

The Multiplier in the Presence of Foreign Trade

But this is not the normal state of affairs. Let us consider what happens if exports rise to $650 billion while imports remain as in Table 20–1. Table 20–2

Table 20–2
EQUILIBRIUM GNP AFTER A RISE IN EXPORTS

GROSS NATIONAL PRODUCT (Y) (billions)	DOMESTIC EXPENDITURE (C + I + G) (billions)	EXPORTS (X) (billions)	IMPORTS (IM) (billions)	NET EXPORTS (X − IM) (billions)	TOTAL EXPENDITURE (C + I + G + X − IM) (billions)
$2500	$3100	$650	$250	$400	$3500
3000	3400	650	300	350	3750
3500	3700	650	350	300	4000
4000	4000	650	400	250	4250
4500	4300	650	450	200	4500
5000	4600	650	500	150	4750
5500	4900	650	550	100	5000

shows us that equilibrium now occurs at a GNP of $Y = \$4500$ billion. So international trade has raised domestic GNP. In general:

When net exports are positive, international trade raises equilibrium GNP. When net exports are negative, international trade lowers equilibrium GNP.

The reason is hardly mysterious. When foreigners buy U.S. products, they put income into the hands of Americans, just as domestic investment does. As this income is spent and respent, a multiplier process is set in motion, raising GNP. Specifically, in this example an increase of $250 billion in exports (from $400 billion to $650 billion) leads to an increase of $500 billion in GNP (from $4000 billion to $4500 billion). So the multiplier is 2 (= $500/$250).[1] This same conclusion is shown graphically in Figure 20–4, where the line $C + I + G + X_0 - IM$ represents the original expenditure schedule and the line $C + I + G + X_1 - IM$ represents the expenditure schedule after the rise in exports. Equilibrium shifts from point E to point A, and GNP rises by $500 billion.

Notice that the multiplier in this example is 2, whereas in the absence of international trade (in Chapter 12) it was $2\frac{1}{2}$. There is nothing special that makes the multiplier for exports different from any other multiplier. The same multiplier of 2 would apply to an autonomous change in *any* component of total expenditure.[2] What we have discovered is that:

International trade lowers the value of the multiplier.

Figure 20–3 shows us graphically why this is true. Because net exports decline as GNP rises, the total expenditure line is *flatter* in the presence of international trade ($C + I + G + X - IM$) than in its absence ($C + I + G$). As we know from earlier chapters, the *size* of the multiplier depends on the *slope* of the expenditure schedule—steeper expenditure schedules lead to larger

[1]EXERCISE: Construct a version of Table 20–1 to show what would happen if imports rose by $250 billion at every level of GNP while exports remained at $400 billion. You should be able to show that the new equilibrium would be $Y = \$3500$ billion.
[2]EXERCISE: Construct a version of Table 20–1 that shows the effects of a rise in domestic expenditure by $250 billion at every level of GNP. Show that the new equilibrium occurs at $Y = \$4500$.

Figure 20–4
THE MULTIPLIER WITH FOREIGN TRADE
This diagram shows a $250 billion increase in exports as a vertical shift of the total expenditure schedule from $C + I + G + X_0 - IM$, to $C + I + G + X_1 - IM$. As a result, equilibrium shifts from point E to point A, and GNP rises from $4000 billion to $4500 billion. The multiplier is therefore 2 (= $500/$250).

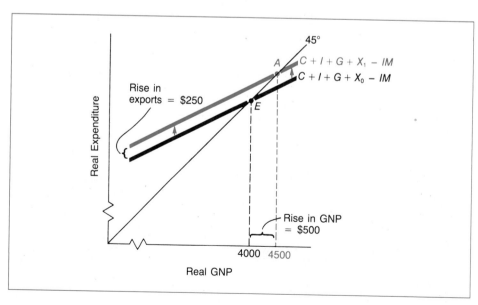

mulipliers. Since international trade flattens the expenditure schedule, it lowers the multiplier.[3]

Thus international trade gives us yet another reason why the oversimplified multiplier formula first given in Chapter 10 (page 189) overstates the true value of the multiplier. We now have accumulated four such reasons:

REASONS WHY THE OVERSIMPLIFIED MULTIPLIER FORMULA IS WRONG

1. It ignores price-level changes, which reduce the size of the multiplier.

2. It ignores the income tax, which reduces the size of the multiplier.

3. It ignores the rising interest rates that accompany any autonomous increase in spending, which reduce the size of the multiplier.

4. It ignores international trade, which also reduces the size of the multiplier.

Although we have much more to learn about how the U.S. economy is linked to the economies of other countries, this simple analysis of the multiplier in the presence of foreign trade already teaches us an important lesson: *Booms and recessions tend to be transmitted across national borders*.

Why is that? Figure 20–4 shows how a rise in our exports will, via the multiplier, raise GNP in the United States. But we have said nothing so far about what might cause our exports to rise. One possibility is that a boom abroad raises aggregate demand and GNP in foreign countries. With rising incomes, foreigners will buy more American goods—which means that United States exports will rise. By this mechanism, rapid economic growth abroad contributes to rapid economic growth here.

Of course, the same mechanism also operates in the downward direction. Suppose some of the foreign countries that trade with us slip into recession. As their GNPs decline, so do their imports. But this means that the U.S. will experience a decline in exports which, through the multiplier, will pull down GNP in the U.S. Hence a recession abroad can contribute to recessionary conditions in the United States.

Naturally, what foreign countries do to us, we also do to them. Thus rapid economic growth in the U.S. tends to produce boom conditions in the countries from which we buy, and recessions here tend quickly to spill beyond our borders. In summary:

The GNPs of the major economies are linked by trade. A boom in one country tends to raise its imports and hence push up exports and GNP in other countries. Similarly, a recession in one country tends to pull GNP down in other countries.

[3]For those who like formulas, we can amend the multiplier formula given in the appendix to Chapter 12 (page 246) to allow for international trade. That formula was:

$$\text{Multiplier} = \frac{1}{1 - b(1 - t)}$$

where b is the marginal propensity to consume and t is the tax rate. If we define the marginal propensity to import as the rise in imports per dollar of GNP (the marginal propensity to import is 0.1 in our example) and symbolize it by the letter m, the formula for the multiplier with foreign trade is:

$$\text{Multiplier} = \frac{1}{1 - b(1 - t) + m}.$$

This formula clearly shows that a higher value of m leads to a lower multiplier.

Relative Prices, Exports, and Imports

While GNP levels at home and abroad are important influences on a country's net exports, they are not the only relevant factor. International prices matter, too. To make things concrete, let us focus on trade between the United States and Japan and assume—just for this short section—that the yen/dollar exchange rate is *fixed*.

Suppose now that the prices of American export goods rise while Japanese prices are constant. This makes U.S. products more expensive *relative to Japanese goods* than was true previously. If American consumers react to the new relative price structure by buying more Japanese goods, our *imports rise*. If Japanese consumers react to the same relative price changes by buying fewer American products, our *exports fall*. Both reactions reduce America's net exports. And since $X - IM$ is a component of $C + I + G + X - IM$, the result is less aggregate demand and GNP in the United States.

Figure 20–5 shows this conclusion graphically. In the figure, the black lines labelled $X_0 - IM_0$ and $C + I + G + X_0 - IM_0$ are carried over without change from Figure 20–3. A rise in American prices, we have just concluded, shifts the $X - IM$ schedule (and hence the $C + I + G + X - IM$ schedule) downward as shown in the diagram. Equilibrium therefore shifts from E_0 to E_1, leading to lower GNP in the United States.

Naturally, the effects of a decline in American prices are precisely the opposite of those depicted in Figure 20–5. Net exports are stimulated, the $C + I + G + X - IM$ line shifts up, and GNP rises. Thus:

For given foreign prices, a rise in the prices of a country's exports will lead to a reduction in that country's net exports, and hence to a decline in its real GNP. Analogously, a fall in the prices of a country's exports will raise that country's net exports and GNP.

Notice that this analysis leads us to conclude that a *higher* domestic price level leads, other things equal, to a *lower* equilibrium GNP on the demand side.

Figure 20–5
RELATIVE INTERNATIONAL PRICES AND EQUILIBRIUM GNP
If American prices rise or foreign prices fall, U.S. exports decline and U.S. imports rise. Hence, America's net export schedule declines from the black $X_0 - IM_0$ line to the blue $X_1 - IM_1$ line. In the upper part of the diagram, the total expenditure curve shifts downward correspondingly. As a result, equilibrium GNP falls.

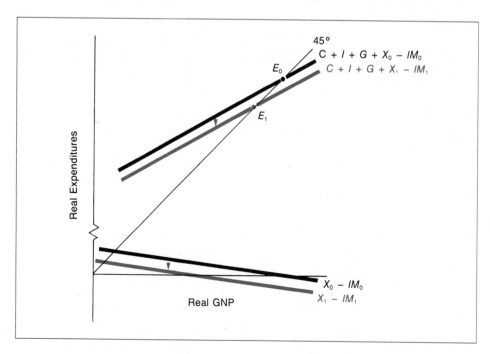

(See Figure 20–5.) That is simply a long-winded way of saying that the economy's *aggregate demand curve slopes downward*, something we have previously concluded on other grounds. Hence:

International trade provides yet another reason for a downward-sloping aggregate demand curve. As the price level rises, domestic goods become more expensive relative to foreign goods, which reduces net exports and lowers equilibrium real GNP on the demand side of the economy.

Since trade patterns are governed by the prices of U.S. goods *relative to* Japanese goods, precisely the same logic applies to changes in Japanese prices. Suppose Japanese prices fall. Americans will import more and export less. So X − IM will decline, dragging down GNP in the United States. Figure 20–5 applies to this case without change. By similar reasoning, rising Japanese prices increase U.S. net exports and stimulate our economy. Thus:

Price increases abroad raise a country's net exports and hence its GNP. Price decreases abroad have the opposite effects.

The Effects of Changes in Exchange Rates

From here it is a simple matter to figure out how changes in *exchange rates* affect a country's net exports, for currency appreciations or depreciations are like changes in international relative prices.

Recall that the basic role of an exchange rate is to convert one country's prices into the currency of another. Table 20–3 uses two examples of U.S.–Japanese trade to remind us of this role. Suppose the dollar depreciates from 150 yen to only 120 yen. Then, from the viewpoint of American consumers, a television set that costs ¥60,000 in Japan goes up in price from $400 to $500. To Americans, it is just as if TV prices in Japan had risen by 25 percent. Naturally, Americans react by purchasing fewer Japanese products. So American imports go down.

Now consider the implications for Japanese consumers interested in buying American microcomputers that cost $2000. When the dollar falls from 150 yen to 120 yen, they see the price of this computer falling from ¥300,000 to ¥240,000. To them, it is just as if American producers had offered a 20 percent markdown. Under such circumstances, we expect U.S. sales to the Japanese to rise. So U.S. exports should increase. Putting these two findings together, we conclude that:

A currency depreciation should raise net exports and therefore increase aggregate demand. Conversely, a currency appreciation should reduce net exports and therefore decrease aggregate demand. (Figure 20–5 can be thought of as applying to an *appreciation* of the currency.)

Table 20–3
EXCHANGE RATES AND HOME-CURRENCY PRICES

EXCHANGE RATE	60,000 YEN JAPANESE TV SET		$2000 U.S. HOME COMPUTER	
	PRICE IN JAPAN	PRICE IN U.S.	PRICE IN U.S.	PRICE IN JAPAN
$1 = 150 yen	¥60,000	$400	$2,000	¥300,000
$1 = 120 yen	¥60,000	$500	$2,000	¥240,000

For later reference, this conclusion is depicted on an aggregate supply and demand diagram in Figure 20–6. If the currency depreciates, net exports rise and the aggregate demand curve shifts outward from D_0D_0 to D_1D_1. Both prices and output rise as the economy's equilibrium moves from E_0 to E_1. If the currency appreciates, everything operates in reverse: net exports fall, the aggregate demand curve shifts inward to D_2D_2, and both prices and output decline.

Now we are in a position to understand one of the main reasons why the U.S. trade deficit grew so large in the 1980s. Recall from Chapter 19 that the international value of the dollar soared from mid-1980 until early 1985. (You may wish to refer back to Figure 19–8 on page 426.) According to the analysis we have just completed, such a stunning appreciation of the dollar should have encouraged U.S. imports, damaged U.S. exports, and been a drag on aggregate demand. That is precisely what happened. In real 1982 dollars, American imports soared by 52 percent between 1981 and 1986 while American exports declined by 4 percent. The result is that a $49 billion net export surplus turned into a $146 billion deficit. In consequence, strong growth in $C + I + G$ translated into only mediocre growth in GNP.

Lags in International Trade and the J Curve

The exchange value of the dollar peaked in early 1985 and began to decline. Yet our trade deficit continued to climb in 1985 and through most of 1986. Something seems wrong here. Since the dollar was falling, our analysis predicts that America's net export position should have improved. Instead, it continued to deteriorate.

Actually, there is nothing wrong with our analysis. It is simply incomplete, for we have failed to note that international trade patterns take time to respond to changes in exchange rates. These lags in international trade give rise to a phenomenon known as the **J curve**. (See Figure 20–7.) The J curve indicates that, following a devaluation or depreciation, a country's trade deficit actually deteriorates for a while (from A to B in Figure 20–7) before improving (beyond point B). Thus a considerable period of time may elapse before any

The **J curve** shows the typical pattern of response of net exports to a change in currency values. Following a depreciation or a devaluation, net exports usually decline at first and then rise.

Figure 20–6
THE EFFECTS OF EXCHANGE RATE CHANGES ON AGGREGATE DEMAND
A depreciation of the exchange rate raises net exports and hence shifts the aggregate demand curve outward to the right, from D_0D_0 to D_1D_1 in the diagram. An appreciation of the currency shifts the aggregate demand curve inward to the left, to D_2D_2. Thus depreciations are expansionary and appreciations are contractionary.

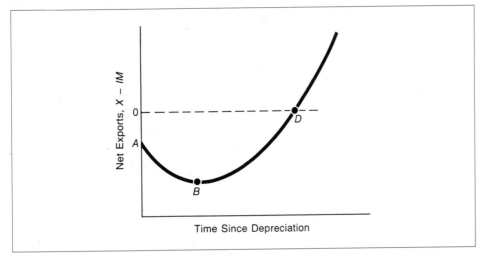

Figure 20–7
THE J CURVE
The response of a country's net exports to a decline in the value of its currency tends to follow a J-shaped pattern. In the period immediately following the depreciation or devaluation, everyone imports and exports about the same volume of goods as they did before. But imports cost more in terms of home currency, so net exports decline. This is the descending portion of the J curve, from point A to point B. After a while, however, imports decline and exports rise, so net exports improve. This is the rising portion of the curve, beyond point B.

improvement in net exports is apparent. In the U.S. case, net exports first began to turn around late in 1986.

To explain the origins of the J curve, let us continue the example of an appreciating yen (depreciating dollar). On the day after the yen rises in value, the dollar prices of, say, Sony television sets in American stores and warehouses will be the same as they were on the previous day. Similarly, the yen prices of IBM PCs in Japan will be the same. Hence there is no reason for Americans to buy fewer Japanese TVs nor for Japanese to buy more American computers. Gradually, however, the profit motive will force Sony to raise its U.S. dollar prices and induce IBM to cut its Japanese yen prices. Only then do international trade patterns start to adjust. But that, too, takes time. American wholesalers and retailers with long-term contracts with Japanese TV manufacturers will only gradually redirect their orders to American suppliers. Similarly, Japanese merchants accustomed to dealing with local computer manufacturers will only gradually begin to place orders with American firms.

These gradual adjustments of international trade patterns lead to a J curve in the following manner. In the short run, Americans will be buying almost as many Japanese TV sets after the dollar depreciates as they did before. But we will be paying more — in U.S. dollars — for each set. Hence our imports from Japan, *when measured in U.S. dollars*, actually rise while our exports are unchanged. So our trade deficit deteriorates at first. Only after the passage of some time will the volume of U.S. imports decline enough to improve America's trade position with Japan.[4]

Some illustrative numbers will clarify the arithmetic behind the J curve. Suppose that, when the dollar was worth 150 yen, the United States was importing 1 million TV sets at $400 each and exporting 150,000 computers at $2000 each. Then the dollar value of our imports was $400 million and the dollar value of our exports was $300 million, leading to a trade deficit with Japan of $100 million.

Now the dollar depreciates to 120 yen and the dollar price of Japanese TVs rises to $500 (see Table 20–3). At first, purchases are unchanged; so our import bill for the 1 million Japanese TVs increases to $500 million. With exports

---

[4]Actually, improvement occurs only if consumers in the two countries are sufficiently responsive to price changes. The precise condition is best left to more advanced courses in international economics.

remaining at $300 million, our trade deficit balloons to $200 million. We are on the downward portion of the J, between A and B in Figure 20–7.

After some time, however, Americans curtail their purchase of Japanese TVs and the Japanese buy more American computers. For the sake of concreteness, suppose that we now import 800,000 TVs and export 200,000 computers. At a price of $500 each, our TV imports cost $400 million. At a price of $2000 each, our computer exports earn us $400 million. Thus our trade with Japan is now balanced. In terms of Figure 20–7, we have reached point D.

Applying the J-curve analysis to the recent U.S. experience is no easy matter because the dollar did not decline all at once, but rather in stages beginning in early 1985. Each depreciation set in motion its own little J curve, forming a complex pattern. However, there is no doubt that the J-curve phenomenon goes a long way toward explaining why U.S. net exports responded so sluggishly to the falling dollar.

Aggregate Supply in an Open Economy

So we have concluded that, after a lag described by the J curve, a currency depreciation increases aggregate demand while a currency appreciation decreases it. To complete our model of macroeconomics in an open economy, we must now turn to the implications of international trade for *aggregate supply*.

Part of the story is familiar. As we know from previous chapters, the U.S., like all economies, purchases some of its productive inputs from abroad. Oil is only the most prominent example. We also rely on foreign suppliers for various metals (like titanium), many raw agricultural products (like coffee beans), and thousands of other items that are used by American industry. If these imported inputs rise in price, American firms will charge higher prices at any given level of output. Graphically, this means that *the aggregate supply curve will shift upward*.

There are also direct inflationary effects of rising foreign prices. First, prices of imported goods are included in American price indexes like the Consumer Price Index (CPI). So when prices of Japanese cars, French wine, and Swiss watches increase, the CPI goes up even if no American price rises. Second, higher import prices provide less foreign competition for American producers of cars, wine, and watches, who may react by raising their own prices. All of this can be summarized by saying:

When foreign prices rise, the U.S. aggregate supply curve is likely to shift inward, pushing up U.S. prices. When foreign prices fall, the U.S. aggregate supply curve shifts outward, pushing U.S. prices down.

Similarly, rising or falling prices in the U.S. contribute to inflation or deflation in other countries.

This analysis makes it easy to think through the consequences of a change in the *exchange rate*. Suppose the dollar depreciates. Then foreign goods cost more in terms of dollars, just as if foreign prices had risen. The consequence, we now know, is that the aggregate supply curve shifts *inward*. Similarly, an appreciation of the dollar makes foreign goods less expensive to Americans and shifts the aggregate supply curve *outward*. Thus (refer to Figure 20–8):

A currency depreciation shifts the aggregate supply curve inward and drives up the domestic price level. A currency appreciation has the opposite effects.

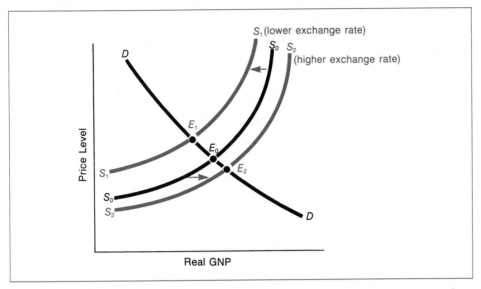

Figure 20–8
THE EFFECTS OF
EXCHANGE RATE
CHANGES ON
AGGREGATE SUPPLY
A depreciation of the
currency pushes the
aggregate supply curve
inward, from S_0S_0 to S_1S_1 in
the diagram, and is therefore
inflationary. A currency
appreciation has a
deflationary effect because it
pushes the aggregate supply
curve outward, from S_0S_0 to
S_2S_2.

The Macroeconomic Effects of Exchange Rates

We can now put aggregate demand and aggregate supply together and study the macroeconomic effects of changes in exchange rates.

First suppose that the international value of the dollar falls. Referring back to Figures 20–6 and 20–8, we see that this will shift the aggregate demand curve *outward* and the aggregate supply curve *inward*. The result, as Figure 20–9 shows, is that the U.S. price level certainly rises. Whether real GNP rises or falls depends on whether the supply or demand shift is the dominant influence. The evidence strongly suggests that aggregate *demand* shifts are usually more important, so we expect GNP to rise.

A currency depreciation is inflationary and probably also expansionary.

What is the intuitive explanation for this result? When the dollar falls, foreign goods become more expensive to Americans. That is directly inflationary.

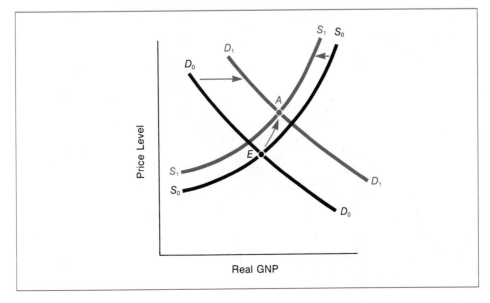

Figure 20–9
THE EFFECTS OF A
CURRENCY
DEPRECIATION
If the currency depreciates,
aggregate demand increases
because net exports are
stimulated and aggregate
supply decreases because
foreign goods become more
expensive. Prices rise as
equilibrium moves from point
E to point A. If the demand
shift is the more important
influence, output increases,
too.

At the same time, aggregate demand in the U.S. is stimulated by rising net exports. As long as the expansion of demand outweighs the adverse shift of the aggregate supply curve brought on by the depreciation, real GNP should rise.

Now let's reverse things. Suppose the dollar *appreciates*. In this case, net exports *fall* so the aggregate demand curve shifts *inward*. At the same time, foreign goods become cheaper, so the aggregate supply curve shifts *outward*. (See Figure 20–10.) Once again, we can be sure of the movement of the price level: It falls. Output will also fall if the demand shift is more important than the supply shift, as is likely. Hence:

A currency appreciation is certainly disinflationary and is probably contractionary.

In the rest of the chapter, we shall assume that the effect of the exchange rate on aggregate *demand* dominates its effect on aggregate *supply*, because that is what the evidence suggests.

Interest Rates and International Capital Flows

There is one important piece left in our international economic puzzle. We have analyzed international trade in goods and services rather fully, but have ignored international movements of capital.

For some nations, this omission is of little concern because they are rarely involved in international capital flows. But things are quite different for the United States, whose dollar is the world's major international currency. The vast majority of international capital flows involve either the buying or the selling of assets whose values are stated in dollars. Fortunately, given what we have just learned about the effects of exchange rates, it is not difficult to add international capital flows to our analysis.

Recall from Chapter 19 that interest-rate differentials and capital flows are typically the most important determinants of exchange rate movements in the short run. Specifically, suppose interest rates in the United States rise while foreign interest rates remain unchanged. We learned in Chapter 19 that this will attract capital to the United States and cause the dollar to appreciate. This

Figure 20–10
THE EFFECTS OF A CURRENCY APPRECIATION

If the currency appreciates, aggregate demand declines because net exports fall and aggregate supply increases because foreign goods become cheaper. Prices fall as equilibrium moves from point *E* to point *B*. If the demand shift is the more important influence, output also falls.

Real GNP

chapter has taught us that an appreciating dollar, in turn, will reduce net exports, prices, and output in the U.S. — as indicated in Figure 20–10. Thus:

A rise in interest rates tends to contract the economy by appreciating the currency and reducing net exports.

Notice that this conclusion has a familiar ring. In Chapter 14, while studying how monetary policy works, we observed that higher interest rates deter investment spending and hence reduce the I component of $C + I + G + X - IM$. Now, in studying an open economy with international capital flows, we see that higher interest rates also reduce the $X - IM$ component. Thus *international capital flows strengthen the negative effects of interest rates on aggregate demand.*

If interest rates in the United States fall, or if those abroad rise, everything we have just said is turned in the opposite direction. There is no need to repeat the analysis. The conclusion is:[5]

A fall in interest rates tends to expand the economy by depreciating the exchange rate and raising net exports.

Fiscal Policy in an Open Economy

Now we are ready to use our model to study how fiscal and monetary policy work when the exchange rate is floating and capital is internationally mobile. In addition to teaching us how international economic relations modify the effects of stabilization policies, this discussion will serve as a review of what we have learned up to this point in the chapter, for no new theoretical apparatus is necessary. We begin with fiscal policy.

Suppose the government cuts taxes or raises spending. Aggregate demand increases, which pushes up both real GNP and the price level in the usual manner. This is shown as the shift from $D_0 D_0$ to $D_1 D_1$ in Figure 20–11. In a closed economy, that is the end of the story. But in an open economy with international capital flows, the fact that a fiscal expansion pushes up interest rates assumes great importance.

[5]EXERCISE: Provide the reasoning behind this conclusion.

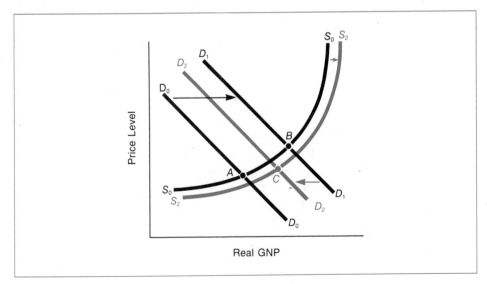

Figure 20–11

A FISCAL EXPANSION IN AN OPEN ECONOMY

A fiscal expansion pushes the aggregate demand outward, from $D_0 D_0$ to $D_1 D_1$ in the diagram. But it also raises interest rates which attracts international capital and appreciates the currency. The currency appreciation, in turn, reduces aggregate demand and raises aggregate supply — as shown by the blue curves $S_2 S_2$ and $D_2 D_2$. The result is that equilibrium occurs at point C rather than at point B. Output and prices both rise less than they would in a closed economy.

What happens in international financial markets as a result of higher U.S. interest rates? American securities become more attractive to foreign investors who then go to the foreign exchange market to buy dollars for use in purchasing American securities. That drives up the value of the dollar. The rising dollar, in turn, makes American goods more expensive abroad and foreign goods cheaper here. So exports fall and imports rise. The $X - IM$ component of aggregate demand therefore falls.

The fiscal expansion thus winds up increasing both America's *capital* account *surplus* and *current* account *deficit*. In fact, the two must rise by equal amounts because, under floating exchange rates, it is always true that:[6]

$$\text{current account surplus} + \text{capital account surplus} = 0.$$

Since a fiscal expansion leads to a trade deficit, many economists believe that the U.S. trade deficit of the 1980s was a side-effect of the Reagan tax cuts. We will come back to that issue shortly.

But first note that the induced rise in the dollar will shift the aggregate supply curve *outward* and the aggregate demand curve *inward*, as we saw in Figure 20–10 (page 444). Figure 20–11 adds these two shifts (in blue) to the effect of the original fiscal expansion (in black). The final equilibrium in an open economy is point C, whereas in a closed economy it would be point B. By comparing points B and C we can see how international linkages change the picture of fiscal policy that we painted in Part 4.

There are two main differences. First, a rising exchange rate offsets part of the inflationary effect of a fiscal expansion by making imports cheaper. Second, a rising exchange rate reduces the expansionary effect on real GNP by reducing $X - IM$. Here we have a new kind of "crowding out," different from the one we studied in Chapter 16. In the earlier chapter, we learned that an increase in G, by raising interest rates, will crowd out some private investment spending. Here a rise in G crowds out *net exports*. But the effect is the same: The fiscal multiplier is reduced. Thus, we conclude that:

International capital flows reduce the power of fiscal policy.

Table 20–4 shows that this new international variety of crowding out has been much more important than the traditional type of crowding out in the 1980s. Between 1981 and 1986, the share of investment in GNP actually *increased* (from 16.8 percent to 17.6 percent) despite the rise in the share of government purchases (from 19.4 percent to 20.3 percent). Only the share of net exports, $X - IM$, fell—from 1.5 percent to −3.9 percent.

[6]If you need review, turn back to Chapter 19, pages 415–20.

Table 20–4
PERCENTAGE SHARES OF REAL GNP IN THE UNITED STATES: 1981 AND 1986

YEAR	C	I	G	X − IM
1981	62.3%	16.8%	19.4%	1.5%
1986	66.0%	17.6%	20.3%	−3.9%
Change	+3.7	+0.8	+0.9	−5.4

Monetary Policy in an Open Economy

Now let us consider how monetary policy works in an open economy with floating exchange rates and international capital mobility.

As we know from earlier chapters, expansionary monetary policy raises aggregate demand, which pushes up both Y and P. This is shown in Figure 20–12 by the shift from D_0D_0 to D_1D_1, and it looks exactly the same as a fiscal expansion. However, we know that a monetary expansion pushes interest rates *down*, whereas a fiscal expansion pushes them *up*. Hence the ramifications in international capital markets are reversed. Funds start to flow *out of* the United States in search of better rates of return abroad. The exchange rate *falls*. The depreciating dollar discourages imports and encourages exports; so $X - IM$ *rises*.

America therefore winds up with capital flowing out (a deficit on capital account) and an increase in its trade surplus—or a reduction in its trade deficit. This time, as you will notice from Figure 20–12:

International capital flows increase the power of monetary policy.

International Aspects of Reaganomics

This completes our theoretical analysis of the macroeconomics of open economies. Now let us put the theory through its paces by applying it to the changes in U.S. macroeconomic policy since 1981. In the process, we will see that Reaganomics had important international implications that we did not mention in Part 4.

In broadest outline, the Reagan administration engineered a dramatic change in the policy mix toward tighter money and much easier fiscal policy. The Federal Reserve's tight monetary policy was already in progress when President Reagan was elected; the new administration simply encouraged the Fed to

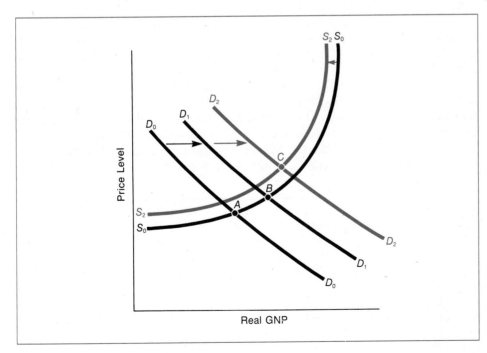

Figure 20–12
A MONETARY EXPANSION IN AN OPEN ECONOMY
A monetary expansion pushes the aggregate demand outward, from D_0D_0 to D_1D_1, just like a fiscal expansion. But it lowers, rather than raises, interest rates which leads to international capital outflows and a currency depreciation. The depreciation increases net exports and therefore raises aggregate demand—which shifts outward from D_1D_1 to D_2D_2. But it also raises foreign prices and reduces aggregate supply—as indicated by the shift from S_0S_0 to S_2S_2. The result is that output and prices both rise more in an open economy (point C) than they would in a closed economy (point B).

persevere. The expansionary fiscal policy was mainly the result of the tax cuts of 1981–1984, which led to very large and persistent federal budget deficits.

Table 20–5 indicates what the theory predicts should have happened under such circumstances. Look first at column 1. We have just concluded that a fiscal expansion should raise real interest rates, make the dollar appreciate, raise real GNP (though perhaps weakly because the rising dollar should reduce net exports), and be less inflationary than normal because of the rising dollar. This information is recorded by entering + signs for increases and − signs for decreases.

Our analysis of a monetary *expansion* can be turned on its head to predict the likely effects of a monetary *contraction*. Column 2 notes that the theory says that the tight money component of Reaganomics should have raised real interest rates, made the dollar appreciate, reduced real GNP (probably strongly because the rising dollar should reduce net exports), and been more disinflationary than usual because of the rising dollar.

Column 3 puts the two pieces together. We conclude that the Reaganomics policy mix of fiscal expansion and monetary contraction should have raised interest rates strongly, pushed the value of the dollar up dramatically, devastated our foreign trade, and had uncertain effects on output and inflation — the balance depends on whether fiscal expansion overwhelmed monetary contraction or vice-versa.

How well do these predictions square with the facts? Let us take them one at a time. We know from Chapter 19 that the international value of the dollar soared — rising about 80 percent from its low in mid-1980 to its high in early 1985. We have also observed in this chapter that American foreign trade was clobbered. Real net exports fell from about +$49 billion in 1981 to about −$146 billion in 1986 — a swing of $195 billion in just five years. These two facts accord extremely well with the theory.

What about interest rates? Figure 20–13 shows an estimate of the real interest rate on long-term U.S. government bonds from 1978 to 1987. (The historic norm for this rate is between 2 and 3 percent.) The real rate of interest rose dramatically between the time of the 1980 election campaign and the time the Reagan economic program was enacted into law (by September 1981). It then fell during the 1982 recession, but rose again to very high levels in mid-1984. Again, this is just as our theory predicts.

What about real GNP? As we know, the U.S. economy suffered through a terrible recession in 1981–1982. However, it then rebounded and grew strongly for about a year and a half. Thus output growth sagged at first and then spurted. To appraise the effects of Reaganomics on real output, we must look over a longer period. If we take the full five-year period from 1981 to 1986, the average annual growth rate of real GNP was 2.7 percent. Since this almost precisely

Table 20–5
EXPECTED EFFECTS OF POLICY

VARIABLE	(1) FISCAL EXPANSION	(2) MONETARY CONTRACTION	(3) REAGANOMICS
Real interest rate	+	+	+
Exchange rate	+	+	+
Real GNP	+ (small)	− (large)	?
Net exports	−	−	−
Inflation	+ (small)	− (large)	?

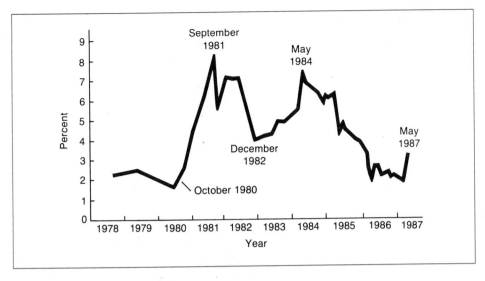

Figure 20–13
REAL INTEREST RATES
IN THE UNITED STATES,
1978–1987
This figure charts the
behavior of the real interest
rate on ten-year U.S.
government bonds on the
basis of a survey of
inflationary expectations. It
rises steeply in 1980–1981.
SOURCE: Richard B. Hoey,
Drexel Burnham Lambert.

matches the average growth rate achieved during the preceding 15 years, the conclusion seems to be that the monetary contraction cancelled out the demand-increasing effects of the fiscal expansion, leaving no net effect on the growth rate of aggregate demand.

If this is so, that would leave only the supply shifts caused by the appreciating dollar. Figures 20–11 and 20–12 show that fiscal expansions and monetary contractions both *increase* aggregate supply by appreciating the currency. (Remember, Figure 20–12 applies to a monetary *expansion*.) The rising dollar certainly helped slow inflation in the early 1980s. In addition, the fact that the deep recession came early in President Reagan's term of office meant that the economy had a recessionary gap throughout the 1981–1986 period. Finally, as we saw in earlier chapters, energy prices were falling rapidly. Each of these factors played a role in the rapid disinflation.

The Link Between the Budget Deficit and the Trade Deficit

There is another useful way to look at the connection between fiscal policy and the trade deficit. But to understand it we need to do some simple arithmetic.

We begin by recalling two definitions: that GNP equals disposable income (DI) plus taxes (T):

$$Y = DI + T,$$

and that disposable income can either be consumed or saved:

$$DI = C + S.$$

These two definitions jointly imply that:

$$Y = C + S + T,$$

which simply says that national income can be spent, saved, or taxed away.

Now remember the equilibrium condition for GNP in an open economy:

$$Y = C + I + G + X - IM.$$

Equating these two expressions for Y gives:

$$C + I + G + X - IM = C + S + T.$$

Subtracting C from both sides and grouping terms in a natural way leads to this conclusion:

$$G - T = (S - I) - (X - IM).$$

In words, the government budget deficit must be equal to the surplus of savings over investment plus the trade deficit.

This fundamental equation suggests that there is a potentially tight connection between the budget deficit and the trade deficit. Let us examine how this link worked out in the case of Reaganomics.

Since the Reagan tax cuts led to a large budget deficit, the United States could have avoided a large trade deficit only by saving much more or investing much less. The latter is not a very appetizing option and, in any case, generous business tax cuts in 1981 shielded investment spending from the ravages of high real interest rates. (As we saw in Table 20–4, investment *rose* as a share of GNP.) That leaves saving. Supply-siders did indeed promise that the tax cuts would raise savings by extraordinary amounts. Had these promises been redeemed, the budget deficit need not have caused a trade deficit. But they were not. With S not rising and I not falling, our equation leaves only one possibility: A rise in $G - T$ must be reflected in a fall in $X - IM$. The government budget deficit thus led to a massive trade deficit.

This story seems overly mechanical. It may also appear to differ from the one we told earlier; after all, the last paragraph never mentioned interest rates or exchange rates. One last piece of arithmetic, however, will both show that the two stories are equivalent and bring out the intuition behind our fundamental equation.

As we noted in Chapter 19 and earlier in this chapter, the current account and capital account surpluses must sum to zero under floating rates. Thus:

$$(X - IM) + \text{Capital inflows} = 0.$$

Using this to replace $X - IM$ in the previous equation gives:

$$G - T = (S - I) + \text{Capital inflows}.$$

This last equation is simply common sense: If American savers will not save enough to meet the borrowing requirements of both the U.S. government and American investors, then the balance must be borrowed from foreigners.

And it is no mystery how this happens. To attract foreign capital, we must offer interest rates higher than those available abroad. As capital flows into the United States, the exchange rate is driven up. And the high exchange rate leads to a trade deficit. Thus the adjustments of interest rates and exchange rates that we discussed earlier are precisely the way the economy matches the budget deficit with a trade deficit.

On Curing the Trade Deficit

We now have a thorough understanding of how the United States acquired its massive twin deficits and became the world's most indebted nation. Next comes the hard question that we raised at the beginning of the chapter: What can be done about it; how can we cure our foreign trade problem and end our addiction to foreign borrowing?

The answer, of course, is highly controversial. Both economists and politicians disagree over the appropriate course of action. The best we can do here is outline some alternatives.

1. **Reduce the Government Budget Deficit:** The equation:

$$G - T = (S - I) - (X - IM)$$

points to a reduction in the budget deficit as one good way to reduce the trade deficit. Lower G or higher T would lead to lower real interest rates in the United States, a depreciating dollar and, after a lag summarized by the J curve, a shrinking trade deficit.

In fact, American policymakers have been trying to follow this route for some years now, the dollar has come down considerably, and our trade deficit has begun to shrink. However, partisan political bickering over how best to reduce the budget deficit has made progress on this front agonizingly slow and painful.

2. **Expansionary Monetary Policy:** When the government curtails its spending or raises taxes to reduce its budget deficit, aggregate demand falls. If we do not want deficit reduction to contract the U.S. economy, we must compensate for it by monetary stimulus. Like contractionary fiscal policy, expansionary monetary policy also lowers interest rates and depreciates the dollar.

Once again, American policymakers have been pursuing this policy for years. Interest rates here have generally been falling since mid-1984 and the money supply has been growing rapidly. In 1987, however, the Fed became concerned about the possible inflationary consequences of rapid money growth (and of the falling dollar) and grew more cautious.

Notice that these two remedies, in combination, amount to undoing the Reaganomics policy mix of tight money and loose budgets. Between 1980 and 1984, the United States experienced a monetary contraction followed by a fiscal expansion. What we need now to cure the trade deficit, according to many economists, is precisely the reverse: a monetary expansion coupled with a fiscal contraction.

3. **Rapid Economic Growth Abroad:** If foreign economies grew faster, residents of these countries would buy more American goods. That would raise American exports and GNP and reduce our trade deficit. Since about 1985, the U.S. has been urging our major trading partners—especially West Germany and Japan—to stimulate their economies, though with little success.

4. **Raise Domestic Savings or Reduce Domestic Investment:** Our fundamental equation calls attention to two other routes to a smaller trade deficit: higher savings or lower investment.

U.S. personal saving rates are now near all-time lows. If Americans would save more, we could finance more of our government budget deficit at home and therefore would need to borrow less abroad. This, too, would lead to a cheaper dollar and a smaller trade deficit. The only trouble is that no one has yet found a reliable way to induce Americans to save more. We seem to be a nation of consumers.

If the other cures for our trade deficit fail to work in time, the trade deficit may cure itself in a particularly unpleasant way: by dramatically

Saving Patterns and Trade Deficits: The Arithmetic Of U.S.–Japanese Economic Relations

The huge U.S. trade deficit with Japan is a significant source of friction between the two countries and has led to frequent calls for protectionist measures in this country. Our fundamental equation,

$$G - T = (S - I) - (X - IM),$$

teaches us that part of the problem traces to different saving habits in the two countries.

The Japanese people are among the biggest savers in the world. So $S - I$ is a large positive number in Japan. Like the U.S. government, the Japanese government has a budget deficit. However, Japan's $G - T$ is far smaller than its $S - I$. It therefore follows that, in order to balance the international books, Japan must generate a trade surplus.

The contrast between the United States and Japan in this regard is marked. While the American people and government together are big net *borrowers*, the Japanese people and government together are big net *savers*. In an integrated world financial system, it is therefore natural that the Japanese should be lending to us. In short, Japan should have capital *outflows* and we should have capital *inflows* — which is just what has been happening in recent years. Remembering that:

$$\text{current account} + \text{capital account} = 0,$$
$$\text{surplus} \qquad \text{surplus}$$

the implication is that Japan should have a current account *surplus*, and we should have a current account *deficit*.

Once again this is only natural. In fact, the United States has had a trade deficit with Japan for a long time — even when our overall trade position and Japan's were nearly balanced. Being an island nation almost devoid of natural resources, Japan must run huge trade deficits in primary products. Much of this trade is with developing countries. To offset this trade deficit in primary products, Japan needs a surplus in trade in manufactured goods. And who is likely to be the leading customer for these goods? The biggest consumers on earth, of course — the Americans.

So it is natural for the United States to run a bilateral deficit in trading goods with Japan. However, that does not imply that an annual deficit of $60 billion or more is appropriate, nor that the Japanese are blameless.

For one thing, Japan has long been among the most protectionist of all the advanced industrial nations. Much of this protectionism has been subtle, coming not through high tariffs but through bureaucratic regulations that make importing difficult. But Japan also has its share of high tariffs and quotas. So one possible solution to the U.S.–Japan trade problem is to persuade Japan to open its markets more. But no one really thinks that, even in a completely free market, we could sell in Japan nearly as much as they sell here.

Macroeconomic policy might be a more effective tool. Look once again at the fundamental equation:

$$G - T = (S - I) - (X - M).$$

If Japan stimulated its economy by more expansionary fiscal policy, $G - T$ would rise and $X - M$ would fall. If, at the same time, the U.S. reduced its budget deficit, $G - T$ would fall here and $X - M$ would rise. In all likelihood, our bilateral trade deficit with Japan would narrow.

reducing U.S. domestic investment. Let us see how this might work. As our trade deficits and foreign borrowing persist, foreigners wind up holding more and more U.S. dollar assets. At some point, their willingness to acquire yet more dollar assets will begin to wear thin and they will start charging us much higher interest rates. Of course, higher interest rates lead to lower investment in the United States. Some economists fear a worst-case scenario in which foreigners cease lending to the United States, interest rates here shoot up, and we experience a severe recession. A recession, of course, would reduce our trade deficit substantially by curbing our appetite for imports. But it is a painful cure.

5. **Protectionism:** We have saved the worst approach for last. One seemingly obvious way to cure our trade deficit is to limit imports by imposing stiff tariffs, strict quotas, and other protectionist devices. We discussed protectionism, and the reasons why almost all economists oppose it, in Chapter 18. Despite the economic arguments against it, protectionism has an undeniable political allure. It seems, superficially, to "save American jobs." And it conveniently shifts the blame for our trade problems onto foreigners.

In addition to robbing s and other countries of the benefits of comparative advantage studied in Chapter 18, there are reasons why protectionism might not even succeed in reducing our trade deficit. One is that other nations may retaliate. We erect trade barriers to reduce our imports, thereby reducing *IM*. But if foreign countries erect corresponding barriers to our exports, *X* declines. On balance, our *net* exports, $X - IM$, may or may not improve. But world trade will surely suffer. This is a game that may have no winners, only losers.

Even if other nations do not retaliate, tariffs and quotas may not improve our trade deficit much. Why? If they succeed in reducing American spending on imports, tariffs and quotas thereby reduce the supply of dollars on the world market and push the value of the dollar up. A rising dollar, of course, hurts U.S. exports and encourages more imports. The fundamental equation,

$$G - T = (S - I) - (X - M),$$

reminds us that protectionism can raise $X - IM$ only if it reduces the budget deficit, raises saving, or reduces investment.[7]

Conclusion: We Are Not Alone

We do indeed live in a world economy. The major trading nations of the world are linked by exports and imports, by capital flows, and by exchange rates. What happens to national income, prices, and interest rates in one country affects other nations.

Thus policymakers in Europe, Asia, and South America take a keen interest in developments in the U.S. economy. If the U.S. economy expands, these other countries have better markets for their exports. If we pursue policies that make the dollar depreciate, they find their currencies appreciating. If interest rates rise in the United States, they see capital flowing out of their countries into ours. As the "big guy on the block," America bears a special responsibility for the health of the world economy.

[7]Here tariffs, which raise revenue for the government, have a clear advantage over quotas, which do not.

Coordinating Economic Policies: The Group of Seven

Six somberly suited men and one, the Italian, who invariably arrives in open sports coats, convene every three months or so in the opulent gilded chambers of the Louvre Palace, in the clubby rooms of No. 11 Downing Street or beneath the swooping brass chandeliers of the American Treasury's third-floor conference room. All ministers of finance, they...come armed with briefing books, kept at their fingertips, and with the weight of their economies on their backs...

Collectively, they are known as the Group of Seven, for the industrial democracies—the United States, Japan, West Germany, France, Britain, Canada and Italy—that join in the annual economic summit conferences. Formed only a year ago, the group has an impressive mandate: to devise a way the countries can work together to manage the world economy. That is easier said than done.

In a simpler era...when the world's economies were less interdependent...a similar group of men wrote the treaty of Bretton Woods, which tied the finances of the Western world to gold and kept them in some kind of balance. That era is now past; most financial experts agree that the same volatile forces that pushed that system to its limits by the early 1970's, leading President Richard M. Nixon to abandon the gold standard, make it impossible to return to such simple mechanisms as rigidly fixed relationships among currencies.

But finding a workable replacement...pushes economic theory to its limits...[and] assumes a hefty dose of political clout among its participants, if they are to put into effect at home the promises they make to each other. "One of the most difficult jobs in the world," said Treasury Secre-

tary James A. Baker 3d, "is coordinating economic policy. Of necessity, a country's domestic agenda has to come first unless you're going to cede sovereignty, and we're not going to do that."

...What the Western finance ministers have established so far is a "framework," they call it, for holding their economies on course...Already, the countries have put into effect one feature of the broader concept of policy coordination. They have been setting ranges for currency exchange rates, a partial step back to the system of fixed exchange rates that prevailed from 1944 until the early 1970's...

The idea is that when a currency departs from the range, the countries will act in some way...For all the ministers' progress, the most important component of an attempt to coordinate economic policies—a willingness to alter countries' fiscal policies of taxation and spending—has yet to be demonstrated. So far, they have been willing only to alter monetary policies—mainly interest rates—in response to unwanted changes in exchange rates.

SOURCE: Excerpted from Peter Kilborn, "Can the Big Seven Learn to Waltz?" *The New York Times* (business section), May 31, 1987.

But we are not the *only* guys on the block. What happens in Germany, Japan, and elsewhere affects the U.S. economy, too. The depression in Latin America and the near-depression in Europe during the 1980s damaged our export markets and contributed to our trade deficit. As mentioned in the previous section, the U.S. government has been urging the Japanese and the Germans to pursue more expansionary policies to help the world economy get back on its feet.

That the major economies of the world are linked suggests the need for greater policy coordination among nations. But since the national interests of particular countries often differ, countries are understandably reluctant to surrender any of their sovereignty. Hence international policy coordination remains an elusive goal. (See the boxed insert on page 454.) Economically speaking, we all live in one world. Politically, however, we live in a world of separate nation-states.

Summary

1. The nations of the world are linked together economically because national income, prices, and interest rates in one country affect those in another.
2. Equilibrium in an open economy requires that $Y = C + I + G + X - IM$. Thus international trade raises GNP if net exports $(X - IM)$ are positive and reduces GNP if net exports are negative.
3. Because imports rise as GNP rises while exports are insensitive to (domestic) GNP, net exports decline as GNP rises.
4. International trade reduces the value of the multiplier.
5. Rapid (or sluggish) economic growth in one country contributes to rapid (or sluggish) growth in other countries.
6. Net exports depend on a country's prices relative to prices in other countries. This provides another reason why the aggregate demand curve slopes downward.
7. If the currency depreciates, net exports rise and aggregate demand increases, thereby raising both real GNP and the price level. A depreciating currency also reduces aggregate supply by making imported goods more expensive.
8. If the currency appreciates, net exports fall and aggregate demand, real GNP, and the price level all decrease. But an appreciating currency also increases aggregate supply by making imports cheaper.
9. Because there are lags in international trade, net exports follow a J-shaped pattern after a currency depreciation; that is, the trade deficit gets worse before it gets better.
10. International capital flows respond strongly to interest rate differentials among countries. Hence higher domestic interest rates lead to currency appreciations and lower interest rates lead to depreciations.
11. For this reason, international capital flows make monetary policy more powerful and fiscal policy less powerful.
12. Since Reaganomics combined tight money with highly expansionary fiscal policy, it raised interest rates, pushed the dollar up, and caused a large trade deficit in the United States.
13. Budget deficits and trade deficits are linked by the fundamental equation $G - T = (S - I) - (X - IM)$. This also implies that $G - T = S - I +$ capital inflows.
14. It follows from this equation that the U.S. trade deficit must be cured by some combination of lower budget deficits, higher savings, and lower investment.
15. A change in the policy mix toward easier monetary policy and smaller budget deficits is one way to reduce the U.S. trade deficit without contracting the U.S. economy.
16. Protectionist policies might not cure the U.S. trade deficit because (a) they will cause the dollar to appreciate and (b) they may provoke foreign retaliation.
17. International coordination of economic policies is important. But it is also elusive in a world of sovereign nations.

Concepts for Review

Exports	Equilibrium GNP with foreign trade	J curve
Imports	Exchange rate	International capital flows
Net exports	Appreciation	Budget deficits and trade deficits
Closed economy	Depreciation	$G - T = (S - I) - (X - IM)$
Open economy	Trade deficit	

Questions for Discussion

1. Suppose exports and imports of a country are given by:

GNP	EXPORTS	IMPORTS
$500	$300	$ 50
750	300	100
1000	300	150
1250	300	200
1500	300	250
1750	300	300

   Calculate net exports at each level of GNP.

2. If domestic expenditure in the economy described in Question 1 is as shown below, construct a 45°-line diagram and locate the equilibrium level of GNP.

GNP	DOMESTIC EXPENDITURES
$ 500	$ 450
750	650
1000	850
1250	1050
1500	1250
1750	1500

3. Now raise exports to $400 and find the equilibrium again. How large is the multiplier?

4. For years, the U.S. government has been trying to get West Germany to expand its economy faster. Explain how more rapid growth in Germany would affect the U.S. economy.

5. If inflation is higher in the United States than in Taiwan, and the exchange rate between the two countries is fixed, what is likely to happen to the balance of trade between the two countries?

6. Explain why a currency depreciation leads to an improvement in a country's trade balance. If there is a "J curve," what happens in the short run? Why?

7. Explain why American fiscal policy is less powerful and American monetary policy is more powerful than indicated in the closed-economy model of Part 4.

8. Use an aggregate supply-and-demand diagram to analyze the effects of a currency appreciation.

9. Explain why $G - T = (S - I) - (X - IM)$.

10. Given what you now know, evaluate Reaganomics.

11. What, in your view, is the best way for America to reduce its trade deficit?

12. (More difficult) Suppose consumption and investment are described by:

$$C = 120 + .8DI \quad (DI = \text{disposable income})$$

$$I = 1100 + .1Y - 100r \quad (Y = GNP)$$

Here r, the interest rate, is measured in percentage points (for example, a 9 percent interest rate is $r = 9$). Exports and imports are as follows:

$$X = 250$$

$$IM = 110 + .2Y$$

Government purchases are $G = 500$ and taxes depend on income as follows:

$$T = -50 + .25Y.$$

The price level is fixed and the demand for money is:

$$M^D = 50 + .2Y - 20r.$$

a. The central bank (called the "Fed") uses its monetary policy to peg the interest rate at $r = 9$. Find equilibrium GNP, the budget deficit or surplus, and the trade deficit or surplus.

b. Suppose the currency depreciates and, as a result, exports and imports change to:

$$X = 400$$

$$IM = -40 + .2Y.$$

   Now find equilibrium GNP, the budget deficit or surplus, and the trade deficit or surplus.

PART 6

Alternative Economic Systems

21

Growth in Developed and Developing Countries

The development of capitalist production... compels [the capitalist] to keep constantly extending his capital... by means of progressive accumulation.... Fanatically bent on making value expand itself, he... forces the development of the productive powers of society, and creates those material conditions, which alone can form the real basis of a higher form of society.

KARL MARX

In this chapter we discuss the factors that determine the rate at which an economy grows and examine the desirability of rapid growth. We begin by considering how growth can be measured and go on to examine the effects of population growth on prospects for rising per capita incomes. Next, we examine the views of those who have argued that in wealthier countries economic growth is a mixed blessing that may do more harm than good. Then, in the second part of the chapter, we turn to the special problems of the less developed countries (LDCs) and look at the measures that have been proposed to increase their rates of growth. We show that although in the 1970s standards of living in some of the LDCs began to rise significantly, their rapid population growth and their vulnerability to such external shocks as periods of drought, a rise in oil prices, an accumulation of debts, and other similar perils more recently held back the economic growth of many of the LDCs. Indeed, as we saw in Chapter 7, real per capita incomes in some LDCs have been falling further and further behind that of the industrial countries. Next, we examine the problems that impede growth in the LDCs, including scarcity of capital, lack of education, and unemployment. While doing this we consider what the LDCs can do to help themselves and what the rest of the world can do to help them.

Growth in General

How to Measure Growth:
Total Output or Output per Capita?

Adam Smith, like many of his successors, took it for granted that expansion of productive capacity is inherently desirable. But he also took it for granted, apparently without examining the matter very closely, that growth in the size of population is to be wished for. His reason was that a larger population provides a larger work force, and a larger work force makes a larger national output possible. Few economists since Smith's time have argued in this way. Nowadays we usually measure a nation's prosperity not in terms of its total output but in terms of its output *per person*. India has a GNP more than twice as large as Sweden's. But with a population more than 90 times as large as Sweden's, India remains a poor country while Sweden is highly prosperous. The point is that:

If the objective of growth is the material welfare *of the individuals* who make up a country, then the proper measure of the success of a program of economic development is how much it adds to output per person. The relevant index is not total output. It is total output *divided by total population* that is, **output per capita.**

From this point of view, the appropriate objective of growth is not, as the old cliché puts it, "the greatest good for the *greatest number*" — it is the greatest good *per person* in the economy. Per capita figures tell this story well. To make the appropriate comparison of well-being in Sweden and India, we note that per capita GNP in Sweden is more than $12,000 a year, whereas in India, even after a generous adjustment to correct for lower prices in that country, the figure is about $900 a year.

Only where the objective of the government is grandeur or military strength may the number of inhabitants alone seem an appropriate part of its goal. A small country like Finland, for instance, cannot hope to overwhelm a giant neighbor like the Soviet Union, even if Finland has a much higher per capita GNP than the Soviet Union.[1] But where the goal of the government is not national power but the elimination of poverty, illiteracy, and inadequate medical care, sheer increase in population becomes a questionable pursuit.

On Growth in Population: Is Less Really More?

In 1798, the Reverend Thomas R. Malthus (who was to become England's first professor of political economy) published *An Essay on the Principle of Population*. This book was to have a profound effect on people's attitudes toward population growth. Malthus argued that sexual drives and other influences induce people to reproduce themselves as rapidly as their means permit. Unfortunately, he said, when the number of humans increases, the production of food and other consumption goods generally cannot keep up.

The problem is the noted *law of diminishing returns* to additional labor used with a fixed supply of land, a relationship we encountered before (in *Microeconomics* Chapter 7). This states that if we use more and more labor to cultivate a fixed stock of land, we will eventually reach a point at which each additional laborer will contribute less additional output than the previous laborer. Ultimately, as the labor force increases, output per worker will decline.

Malthus and his followers concluded that the tendency of humankind to reproduce itself must constantly exert pressure on the economy to keep living standards from rising. Wages will gravitate toward some minimal subsistence level — the lowest income on which people are willing to marry and raise a

---

[1]Even where military power is the primary objective, a large but impoverished population may not be a very effective means to that end. China has long had an enormous population, but in the modern era its military presence is certainly quite recent.

family. If wages are above subsistence, the population can and will grow. Thus, a wage that is above subsistence will set forces into motion that will drive wages down toward subsistence because of diminishing returns.

Sometimes, according to Malthus, the population will grow beyond the capability of the economy to support it. Then the number of people will be brought back into line by means that are far more unpleasant than a decrease in wages — by starvation and disease or by wars that produce the required number of casualties.

Later in the nineteenth century and during the first half of the twentieth century, the gloomy Malthusian vision seemed to lose credibility. New technology and improved agricultural practices generally enabled the output of food and other agricultural products to increase faster than the population (at least in the wealthier industrialized nations). In addition, it turned out that as living standards rose, people became less anxious to reproduce, and so the expansion of population slowed substantially. Figure 21-1 illustrates this trend in Germany over a period considerably longer than a century. All in all, it began to look as though population growth constituted no significant threat — it was something with which human technological skills and ingenuity could cope.

More recently, however, there has been renewed concern over population. With improvements in medicine — notably, improved hygiene in hospitals, the use of such public health measures as swamp drainage, and the discovery of antibiotics — death rates have plunged in the developing countries, especially for infants. At the same time, birth control programs in most of these countries have, at least until quite recently, not been very successful. As a result, the populations of developing countries have continued to expand dramatically, eating up a good proportion of any output increases obtained through their governments' economic development programs.

It has been widely concluded that significant improvement in living standards in the developing areas is impossible without a substantial reduction in their population growth. But the "neo-Malthusians" go further than this, arguing that a rapid approach to birthrates so low that populations cease expanding — that is, to *zero population growth* — is virtually a matter of life and death even for the most prosperous nations. It is illuminating to consider the logic of their argument.

Figure 21–1
GERMAN BIRTHRATES, 1850–1985
This chart shows that birthrates in Germany have generally been declining since 1850.
SOURCE: Statistisches Bundesamt, *Statistisches Jahrbuch* (Weisbaden, Germany).

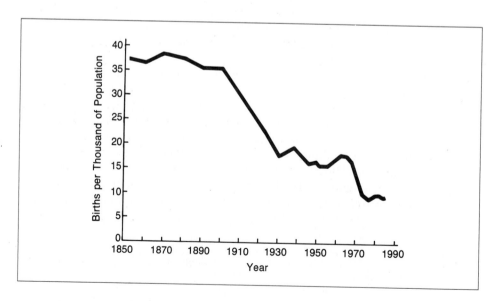

The Crowded Planet:
Exponential Population Growth

Malthus used an argument that has caught many imaginations ever since:

Population, when unchecked, increases in a geometrical ratio. Subsistence increases only in an arithmetical ratio. A slight acquaintance with numbers will shew the immensity of the first power in comparison of the second.[2]

In modern discussions, such a "geometric" growth pattern is referred to as **exponential growth,** or "compounded growth" or "snowballing." Exponential growth is growth at a constant *percentage rate*. For example, at a 10 percent growth rate, a population of 100 persons will increase by 10 persons a year; but a population of a million persons will increase by 100,000 persons a year. Thus, although the *rate* of growth is the same for large and small populations, the *numbers* are dramatically different. The bigger the population, the more it will add annually. And each year's growth implies still faster growth in the following year. It is like a snowball rolling downhill, accumulating more snow the bigger it gets, thus expanding faster and faster all the time.

If the population doubles (grows 100 percent) in 35 years, it will quadruple (grow another 100 percent) in 70 years, increase 8-fold in 105 years, 16-fold in 140 years, and so on indefinitely. The doubling sequence 2, 4, 8, 16, 32, 64, and so on, is the basic pattern of exponential growth. Figure 21–2 shows how astronomical such a growth sequence is. Projecting the world's population 175 years into the future on the assumption that population will grow exponentially at about its current rate, it shows that by the year 2160 the population will have reached about 92 billion—almost 20 times as many people as there are today.

Exponential growth is growth at a constant percentage rate.

[2]Malthus, *An Essay on the Principle of Population*, (London, 1798), page 20.

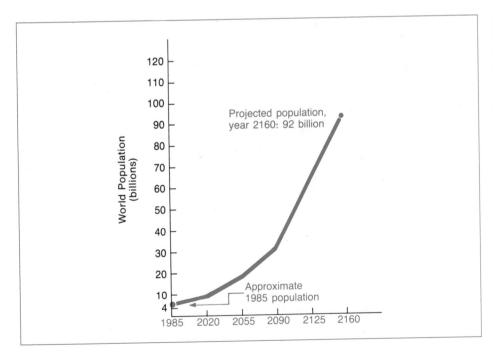

Figure 21–2
PROJECTED GROWTH OF THE WORLD'S POPULATION IN 175 YEARS AT CURRENT RATE OF GROWTH
This figure shows the sensational acceleration of population growth *if* population expands exponentially.

It turns out that in describing the consequences of exponential growth, Malthus was conservative. He did not begin to spell out the wonders and the horrors that his premise implied. Consider some calculations by one leading authority on population (who derived his conclusions simply by carrying through the arithmetic of exponential growth rates):

- *If population were to grow at today's rates for another 600–700 years, every square foot of the surface of the earth would contain a human being;*

- *If it were to expand at the same rate for 1200 years, the combined weight of the human population would exceed that of the earth itself;*

- *If that growth rate were to go on for 6000 years (a very short period of time in terms of biological history), the globe would constitute a sphere whose diameter was growing with the speed of light.*[3]

And none of this is conjecture. It is *sure* to come about *if* the present (exponential) rate of growth of the earth's population continues unabated.

Of course, none of this can really happen. Our finite earth just does not have room for that sort of expansion. The fate of humanity is not determined by the rules of arithmetic—it depends on the course of nature and on the behavior of the human race. It is true that if the number of humans continues to swell until it presses upon the earth's capacity, the process will ultimately be brought to a halt in a Malthusian apocalypse. Disease, famine, and war must finally put a stop to the expansion process.

But there is a better alternative. People can choose to stop raising large families. There is no inevitability about the family of six or ten children. As we have just noted, there has in fact been a decline in the rate of expansion in the wealthier societies—so much so that in the United States in the last few years the rate of reproduction has reached what can ultimately give us zero population growth (see Figure 21–3). Even in the developing nations, as we will see later in this chapter, the birthrate has recently been declining.

A more balanced view of the matter recognizes the serious difficulties that rapid population growth can lead to, and suggests that its encouragement will

[3]Ansley J. Coale, "Man and His Environment," *Science,* vol. 179 (October 9, 1970), pages 132–36. Copyright 1970 by the American Association for the Advancement of Science.

Figure 21–3
ANNUAL PERCENTAGE GROWTH RATE OF THE U.S. POPULATION
Note how rapidly the rate has fallen in recent years. It has just about returned to the low level of the Great Depression. (The years after 1986 are a projection.)
SOURCE: U.S. Bureau of the Census, *Current Population Reports,* Series P-25.

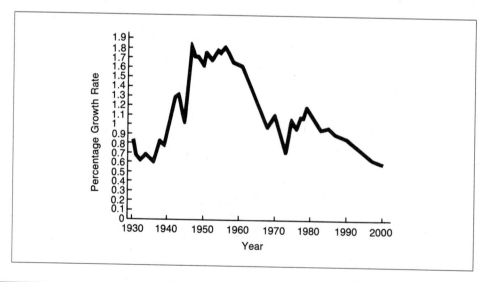

not serve the interests of society. Yet, it does *not* imply that a great catastrophe is at hand or that the appropriate reaction is panic.

Requirements for Increased Growth

What can be done to increase the growth rate of an economy? Unfortunately, no one has a handy list of sure-fire recipes.

Growth can be attributed to a number of factors that no one knows how to explain: (1) *inventiveness,* which produces the new technology and other innovations that have contributed so much to economic expansion; (2) *entrepreneurship,* the leadership that recognizes no obstacles and undertakes the daring industrial ventures needed to move the economy ahead; and (3) *the work ethic* that leads a work force to high levels of productivity. No one really knows what features of economic organization and social psychology actually lead a community to adopt these goals, as Great Britain is said to have done at the beginning of the nineteenth century, as the United States is reputed to have done in the first half of the twentieth century, and as Japan is apparently doing today. We do know, however, that:

Growth requires two things that people can influence directly:

1. A large expenditure on *capital equipment:* factories, machinery, transportation, and telecommunications equipment.
2. The devotion of considerable effort to research and development from which innovations are derived.

Both these types of expenditures help to increase the economy's ability to *supply* goods, which brings us back to the analysis of Parts 2–4. There we stressed that the level (and, consequently, the growth) of national income is determined by the interaction of *aggregate supply and aggregate demand.* It is the need for capital equipment in any growth process that provides a vital link between aggregate demand and aggregate supply, for an economy acquires a larger capital stock by investing. Recall that aggregate demand is the sum of consumption, investment, government spending, and net exports $Y = C + I + G + X - IM$. But I is the only part of Y that creates more capital for the future. Such investment can be carried out either by the private sector of the economy or by government. In free market economies government investment is, of course, a much smaller share of the total than it is in centrally directed economies.

The *composition* of aggregate demand is a major determinant of the rate of economic growth. If a larger fraction of total spending goes toward investment rather than toward consumption, government purchases, or net exports, the capital stock will grow faster and the aggregate supply schedule will shift more quickly to the right.

Accumulating Capital by Sacrificing Consumption: The Case of Soviet Russia

The importance of the *composition* of demand stands out sharply if we turn away from the United States and consider a *centrally planned* economy, such as the Soviet Union.

When the Soviet Union undertook to expand its industrial output very rapidly, it was clear from the earliest stage of planning that a tremendous amount of capital equipment would be required to carry out the expansion. Not only did the Russians have to build modern factories and acquire sophisticated machinery, they also needed a **social infrastructure**—a transportation network to bring raw materials to the factories and take finished products to the markets, an efficient telecommunications system, and schools in which to train the population sufficiently to be an effective labor force. All this and much more was needed, and all of it required labor, raw material, and fuel for its construction.

Obviously, such a use of resources has its *opportunity cost*. Fuel and steel that are employed to build a train become unavailable for the production of refrigerators and washing machines. The real price of accumulating plant, equipment, and infrastructure is paid in the form of consumer goods that must be given up in order to build that capital equipment. In other words:

Through saving, the public gives up some consumption, which is the price it must pay for the accumulation of plant, equipment, and infrastructure. Without this sacrifice, growth generally cannot occur.

This is the hard lesson that the inhabitants of the Soviet Union have been living with for over half a century. Ever since the Russian Revolution in 1917, the Soviet leadership has been determined to promote rapid economic growth and has imposed on the general public whatever sacrifices of current consumption were deemed necessary for the purpose. Only in the most recent decades has an increase in the supply of consumer goods been assigned any priority. Yet, even now, investment in the U.S.S.R. is still about one-third of GNP, while in the United States the figure is less than half that amount. As a result, Soviet living standards have been rising very slowly, particularly because the demands of the military forces have joined those of the growth planners in competing for the resources that might otherwise go into consumption.

The reason for this harsh trade-off is clear enough. If the economy is producing at its full potential, then real output Y cannot be increased further. Since $Y = C + I + G + X - IM$, a decision to devote more resources to the production of heavy machinery (which is in I) or armaments (which are in G) is simultaneously a decision to forgo some consumption or to import more. Where resources are already fully employed, it is simply not possible to have both more guns *and* more butter.

The Payoff to Growth: Higher Consumption in the Future

We may seem to be painting a rather grim picture of growth, and indeed, the process has often been harsh in the U.S.S.R. and in other nations that have enforced a high rate of economic growth. But it is also true that if the growth process is successful, the sacrifice of consumption that it requires is only a temporary loss. Consumers give up goods and services now in order to make possible the construction of productive capacity that will permit them to consume even more goods and services at a later date. After all, from the consumers' point of view, that is what growth is all about. It is not an end in itself, but a means to an end—a standard of living higher than they could have attained without the process of economic expansion.

At least in a consumer-oriented economy, the decision to save in order to promote economic growth is simply an *exchange between present and future consumption*. Consumers sacrifice consumption now in order to be able to increase consumption in the future by more than they gave up in the past.

Of course, the payoff may never come if something goes wrong. An earthquake may destroy factories and roads, or a government with military ambitions may divert the increased productive capacity into the manufacture of armaments. So there is a risk in the decision to give up consumption now for increased consumption later. The growth process is a gamble—it means trading in a relatively sure thing (present consumption) for a risky future return (increased future consumption).

But betting on the future is not necessarily foolhardy. Economies would remain stagnant if people were unwilling to take chances. And some of the risk of investment plans can be reduced if decision makers understand fully the terms of the trade-off.

Growth Without Sacrificing Consumption: Something for Nothing?

Of course, some growth can be achieved without much sacrifice of present consumption. For at least one of the main engines of growth can be powered with relatively small increases in the nation's stock of factories, equipment, and infrastructure. Research and development can teach society new and more efficient ways of using the nation's productive resources. Thus, *innovation* — the process of putting inventions into operation—can permit an economy to get more output from the same inputs rather than by *expansion* of capital stock.

Everyone knows that this has in fact occurred. From the invention of the steam engine to that of the modern computer, our economy has benefited from a stream of inventions—some sensational, some more routine—which together have increased enormously the productivity of the nation's resources. Estimates of the relative contributions of innovation and accumulation to the growth process differ. A number of analysts attribute considerably more than half of the economic growth of the United States to research and invention. But whatever the correct figure, it is certainly large.

Another way of describing this conclusion is to say that while a substantial proportion of growth is **embodied** in increased quantities of plant, equipment, and infrastructure, a very large proportion of the economy's growth is **disembodied.** That is, it is attributable to better ideas—to improved methods of finding and using the same quantities of resources.

Embodied growth has two serious costs that disembodied growth avoids. First, embodied growth necessarily speeds up the use of society's depletable resources: its iron ore, its petroleum supplies, and its stocks of other minerals and fuels. Second, the resources that are used up in a process of embodied growth must ultimately end up on society's garbage heap. The physical laws of conservation of matter and energy tell us that no raw material can ever disappear. It can be transformed into smoke or solid waste, but unless it is recycled *entirely* (something that is both beyond the capability of our technology and impractical for other reasons), the greater the quantity of resources used in the productive process, the greater the quantity of wastes that must ultimately result.

Economist Kenneth Boulding has likened our planet to a spaceship hurtling through the solar system but constrained by terrestrial littering laws to keep its garbage on board. In spaceship Earth, we can transform waste materials into other forms—as by melting old bottles for reuse or converting them into energy, or by burning combustible garbage for heat—but we cannot simply toss them overboard.

So far, we have enjoyed substantial success in our efforts to achieve growth in output without commensurate increases in our use of resources. One statistical analysis, for example, attributes only about half of the growth in the United States to increased use of physical inputs. The remainder must be ascribed to improvements in technology as well as to increased education and skill of the labor force.[4]

One final remark on disembodied growth is in order. Economists are fond of pointing out that there is no such thing as a free lunch. Except in rare instances, improvements in technology are not "manna from heaven." They result, instead, from the work of scientists and technicians in government and industrial laboratories, from the labor of inventors in their basements or garages, and from the effort of management specialists studying the organization of factories and assembly lines. This means that labor (along with other resources) is diverted from other activities into the production of knowledge. *In a fully employed economy, the opportunity costs of investing in the discovery of new knowledge are the consumption of and physical investment in goods that would otherwise have been produced.* So even here, we cannot get something for nothing.

Is More Growth Really Better?

A number of writers have raised questions about the desirability of faster economic growth as an end in itself, at least in the wealthier industrialized countries. Yet faster growth does mean more wealth, and to most people the desirability of wealth is beyond question. "I've been rich and I've been poor—and I can tell you, rich is better," a noted stage personality is said to have told an interviewer, and most people seem to have the same attitude about the economy as a whole. To those who hold this belief, a healthy economy is one that is capable of turning out vast quantities of shoes, food, cars, and TV sets. An economy whose capacity to provide all these things is not expanding is said to have succumbed to the disease of *stagnation*.

Economists from Adam Smith to Karl Marx saw great virtue in economic growth. Marx argued that capitalism, at least in its earlier historical stages, was a vital form of economic organization by which society got out of the rut in which the medieval stage of history had trapped it. As we saw in the opening quotation of this chapter, Marx believed that "the development of the productive powers of society . . . alone can form the real basis of a higher form of society. . . ." Marx went on to tell us that only where such great productive powers have been unleashed can one have "a society in which the full and free development of every individual forms the ruling principle."[5] In other words, only a wealthy economy can afford to give all individuals the opportunity for full personal satisfaction through the use of their special abilities in their jobs and through increased leisure activities.

Yet the desirability of further economic growth for a society that is already wealthy has been questioned on grounds that undoubtedly have a good deal of

---

[4]Edward F. Denison, *Accounting for United States Economic Growth 1929–1969* (Washington, D.C.: The Brookings Institution, 1974). More recently, however, there has been a decline in the rate of growth in output relative to input quantities used. See E. F. Denison, *Accounting for Slower Economic Growth* (Washington, D.C.: The Brookings Institution, 1979), page 62. This slowdown was discussed in Chapter 7.
[5]Marx, *Capital*, vol. I (Chicago: Charles H. Kerr Publishing Co., 1906), page 649.

validity. It is pointed out that the sheer increase in quantity of products has imposed an enormous cost on society in the form of pollution, crowding, proliferation of wastes that need disposal, and some claim it has had very unfortunate psychological and social effects. It is said that industry has transformed the satisfying and creative tasks of the artisan into the mechanical and dehumanizing routine of the assembly line. It has dotted our roadsides with junkyards, filled our air with smoke, and poisoned our food with dangerous chemicals. The question is whether the outpouring of frozen foods, talking dolls, CB radios, and headache remedies is worth its high cost to society. As one well-known economist put it:

The continued pursuit of economic growth by Western societies is more likely on balance to reduce rather than increase social welfare. . . . Technological innovations may offer to add to men's material opportunities. But by increasing the risks of their obsolescence it adds also to their anxiety. Swifter means of communications have the paradoxical effect of isolating people; increased mobility has led to more hours commuting; increased automobilization to increased separation; more television to less communication. In consequence, people know less of their neighbors than ever before in history.[6]

Virtually every economist agrees that these concerns are valid, though many question whether economic growth is their major cause. Nevertheless, they all emphasize that pollution of air and water, noise and congestion, and the mechanization of the work process are very real and very serious problems. There is every reason for society to undertake programs that grapple with these problems. *Microeconomics* Chapter 18, which dealt with problems of the environment, examined these issues more closely and described some policies to deal with them.

Despite the costs of growth in terms of human and environmental damage, there is strong evidence that if the economy's total output were kept at its present level, the community would pay a high price over and above the loss of additional goods and services.

First, it is not easy to carry out a decision to prevent further economic growth. Mandatory controls are abhorrent to most Americans. We cannot *order* people to stop inventing means to expand productivity. Nor does it make any sense to order every firm and industry to freeze its output level, since changing tastes and needs require some industries to expand their outputs at the same time that others are contracting. But who is to decide which should grow and which should contract, and how shall such decisions be made? *The achievement of zero economic growth may very well require government intervention on a scale that becomes expensive and even repressive.*

Second, without continued growth it will be no easy matter to finance effective programs of environmental protection. To improve the purity of our air and water and to clean up urban neighborhoods, tens of billions of dollars must be made available every year. Continued growth would enable the required resources to be provided without any reduction in the availability of consumer goods. But without such growth, we may actually be forced to cut back on our programs to protect the environment. Society could thus end up with less goods and a worse environment.

Finally, zero economic growth may seriously hamper efforts to eliminate poverty both within our economy and throughout the world. Much of the

[6]E. J. Mishan, *The Costs of Economic Growth* (New York: Frederick A. Praeger Publishers, 1967), pages 171, 175.

earth's population today lives in a state of extreme want. And though wealthier nations have been reluctant to provide more than token amounts of help to the **less developed countries (LDCs),** less wealth means there would be even less to share. So perhaps the only hope for improved living standards in the impoverished countries of Africa, Asia, and Latin America lies in continued increases in output.

Problems of the Less Developed Countries

Living in the LDCs

Three quarters of the world's population lives in areas whose average per capita GNP is about $1,500 or less per year, evaluated (as well as it is possible to do) in terms of today's prices in the United States. Table 21–1 shows that there are countries in which annual per capita GNP is under $300. Even after adjustment for differences in measurement of GNP in the United States and the poorer countries, this probably comes to an annual GNP figure under $1000.

To us, residents of an economy that offers an average GNP nearly 15 times as high as this, such a figure is not only likely to seem incredible, it is all but incomprehensible. Few of us can *really* imagine what life would be like if our family income were reduced to, say, $2000 per year. It is even hard to envision survival on such amounts. It must be emphasized that these figures do *not* represent the living standards of a small group of outcasts from their own societies. Rather, they are *typical* of perhaps a majority of those who live in Asia, Africa, and Latin America.

What can life be like in such circumstances? No brief description can really bridge the gulf between our range of experience and theirs. Yet it can offer us a glimpse into a way of life that few of us will want to share.

Inhabitants of many of the less developed countries live with their large families in one-room shanties or apartments, their water supplies are scanty, polluted, and often miles from home, their only source of energy is that of man and beast, and their sparse harvests are wrung from miserable soil in good years,

Table 21–1
PER CAPITA GNP IN DEVELOPED AND LESS DEVELOPED COUNTRIES, 1983

	(measured in U.S. dollars)
Developed Countries	
United States	$14,080
West Germany	11,400
Sweden	12,440
Less Developed Countries	
Bolivia	$480
China	300
Egypt	690
Ethiopia	120
Haiti	290
India	260

SOURCE: Population Reference Bureau, 1986.

with starvation threatened perhaps every five years when the rains do not come and the crops fail.[7] With no surplus in production, no food can be put into reserves, and the old, the infirm, and the very young are likely to perish.

The life of a man in an LDC is hard enough, with its low nutritional level, its lack of equipment to help him in his work, and its frequency of debilitating diseases. But his life is luxurious compared with that of his wife. She is usually married by the age of 14, bears 8 or 10 children, and by 35 is often a toothless old crone. If (as is true of some 80 percent of the population) she inhabits a rural area, she may have to trudge miles every day to fetch water for the family. She sews all the family's clothes by hand and cooks its meals. There is not enough money for preground flour, so part of the woman's daily work is to pound the grain by hand for food for the family—perhaps an additional two hours of hard labor. She also tends the gardens that produce food for the family, although, except in Moslem countries where women are sequestered, she is also expected to put in a full day in the fields during the six months of the agricultural season.

Another duty of the woman in an LDC is to bring produce, wood, or whatever she has to trade to market a couple of times a week, and she must often walk as many as 10 miles each way with bundles as heavy as she can carry on her back or on her head. She has no respite in the raising of her children, since they are likely not to have a school to attend when they are well or a hospital to go to when they are sick. It is no wonder that she ages so much faster than a woman in our society.

Table 21–2 gives the percentage of infant deaths for each 1000 live births and the average life expectancy of a newborn child in some countries ranging from the most underdeveloped to the most affluent. The contrasts are dramatic. In Bolivia, 119 babies die of every 1000 that are born, while the comparable figure in Sweden is only six. In many countries people survive only until their

[7]It has been estimated that in some famine years in the 1970s, half a million people died as a result in Bangladesh; 200,000 in Ethiopia; 100,000–250,000 in the Sahelian zone of Africa; and more than 800,000 in just three of the states of India (*The New York Times*, October 27, 1976).

Table 21–2
INFANT MORTALITY AND LIFE EXPECTANCY IN DEVELOPED AND LESS DEVELOPED COUNTRIES, 1981–85

	INFANT MORTALITY (deaths per 1000 live births)	LIFE EXPECTANCY AT BIRTH (years)
Developed Countries		
United States	10.5	75
West Germany	9.6	74
Sweden	6.4	77
Less Developed Countries		
Bolivia	119	51
China	50	64
Egypt	100	58
Ethiopia	168	41
Haiti	108	53
India	110	53

SOURCE: Population Reference Bureau, 1986.

40s or 50s, while in Scandinavia they live to be 77. There is little question about the quality of life in less developed lands.

Most of the inhabitants of many LDCs are shockingly poor. Malnutrition and disease are widespread. The sheer process of living and surviving taxes the people to the utmost and makes them old before their time.

Recent Trends

Do recent trends offer hope of improvement? Here there is both good news and bad. The good news is perhaps the most remarkable. In the decade of the 1970s, real GNP in the LDCs grew, on average, more than 5 percent a year. (See Table 21–3 for examples.) Even more important, income per capita grew at an annual rate greater than $2\frac{1}{2}$ percent. The world recession of the early 1980s hit some LDCs very hard and enmeshed them in a serious debt burden (see page 472). Nevertheless, for some of the LDCs the long-term outlook continues to be promising. This means that:

Despite population increases, some LDCs have succeeded in breaking out of the stagnation trap. If growth continues as it has recently, an average family in the successful developing areas can look forward to a doubling of its living standards in less than 30 years. Or put another way, standards of living will be increasing faster than they did in the United States in the nineteenth century!

Clearly, the experience of the 1970s offered hope for a major reduction in absolute poverty in at least some LDCs.

While there was good news in the 1970s, the beginning of the 1980s was not so favorable. Aside from their debt problems, which will be discussed a bit later, there are several developments that can be considered either as merely unfortunate or as thoroughly ominous for the LDCs.

First, while the percentage rates of growth of per capita incomes in the LDCs have been impressive, the industrialized countries, with their initially

Table 21–3
AVERAGE ANNUAL GROWTH RATES OF REAL GROSS DOMESTIC PRODUCT IN DEVELOPED AND LESS DEVELOPED COUNTRIES, APPROXIMATELY 1970–1983

	1970–1975 (percent)	1975–1980 (percent)	1980–83 (percent)
Developed Countries			
United States	2.8	3.7	0.7
Italy	3.1	3.6	−0.5
Sweden	2.8	1.3	1.0
Less Developed Countries			
Colombia	6.0	5.6	1.3
Haiti	3.8	5.3	−2.3
Pakistan	4.5	6.7	5.5
Zimbabwe	6.8	1.5	5.0
Zambia	2.9	−0.6	0.1
Sri Lanka	3.3	5.6	5.2
Uganda	0.1	−4.0	6.6

SOURCE: United Nations, *Statistical Yearbook*, 1983–84.

high incomes, have not exactly been standing still. Indeed, largely because their population growth has been slower, the percentage growth rate in per capita incomes has been higher in the developed countries. But even if the *percentage* increases in their per capita incomes had been very similar, *absolute* incomes would have continued to rise more quickly in the richer lands. Where per capita income is $100 a year, a $2\frac{1}{2}$ percent growth rate translates into a $2.50 annual improvement; however, where per capita income is $5000 a year, the same $2\frac{1}{2}$ percent rate of growth adds $125 a year to the income of the average person. As a result:

The purchasing power of the average family in an LDC is falling further behind that of a typical family in a wealthy economy.

Second, many critics, notably those on the left, emphasize that the $2\frac{1}{2}$ percent growth rate has been accompanied by a worsening distribution of income in some of the LDCs. The rise in population has worsened the living standards of people on marginal lands with inadequate rain (about 40 percent of Indian farmers and a large proportion of Africans). Partly as a result, there have been entire economies among the less developed countries that have been falling behind the rest of the world. Add the massive explosion of urban unemployment, and one gets several hundred million people who are no better off and possibly worse off.

Third, a continuing problem within the LDCs is the relatively high growth rate of their populations.

While net population growth has fallen almost to zero in the United States and some countries of Western Europe, the population explosion continues in some of the LDCs, particularly in Africa.

Table 21–4 tells the story. For the sample of LDCs shown, the annual growth rate of population continues perhaps ten times as high as it is in the industrialized countries. Clearly, the more closely the growth in population

Table 21–4
BIRTHRATE MINUS DEATH RATE IN DEVELOPED AND LESS DEVELOPED COUNTRIES, 1981–85 (ESTIMATED)

	(births minus deaths as percent of population)
Developed Countries	
United States	0.7
West Germany	−0.2
Sweden	0.0
Less Developed Countries	
Bolivia	2.8
China	1.0
Egypt	3.2
Ethiopia	2.1
Haiti	2.3
India	2.3

SOURCE: Population Reference Bureau, 1986.

approximates the growth in national income, the more slowly standards of living will rise, since there will be that many more persons among whom the additional product must be divided.

Fourth, the relatively high growth rate in per capita incomes has not been uniform throughout the LDCs. In some countries, such as Sri Lanka, Ghana, Chad, and Cuba, growth rates have been extremely low. In some cases, as in Uganda and Nigeria, real per capita incomes actually seem to have fallen. Yet in others, notably the Ivory Coast, Singapore, South Korea, and Taiwan, growth has been so spectacular that some of them are no longer considered LDCs, despite oil shocks, increasing restrictions against their exports, and lack of mineral resources.

Finally, the LDCs have shown themselves highly vulnerable to such events as the oil crisis in 1979 and the high real interest rates of the 1980s. Much as the fall in Iranian exports and rise in oil prices affected the industrialized economies, it undoubtedly damaged the LDCs even more, leading to enormous deficits and foreign debts for the countries least able to afford them. (See the boxed insert on pages 474–75.) In other words, the new growth trends in the LDCs may be quite fragile, and their continuation cannot simply be taken for granted.

It is ironic that the leveling-off of oil prices at the beginning of the 1980s not only left many oil-importing LDCs with their crippling debts, but caused similar problems for some of the oil exporters. As a result, Mexico and Venezuela joined Brazil in the group of countries whose economies are severely constrained by huge indebtedness to the rest of the world.

Impediments to Development in the LDCs

No one has produced a definitive list of causes of the poverty of the LDCs, just as no one can pretend to have produced a foolproof prescription for its cure. Yet there is general agreement on the main conditions contributing to the economic problems of LDCs. These include lack of physical capital, rapid growth of populations, lack of education, unemployment, and social and political impediments to business activity. Let us consider each of these.

Scarcity of Physical Capital

The LDCs are obviously handicapped by their lack of modern factories and machinery. In addition, they lack infrastructure — good roads, railroads, port facilities, and so on. But capital is not easy to acquire. If it is to be provided by the populations of the LDCs themselves, they must save the required resources — that is, as we saw earlier in this chapter, they must give up consumption in order to free the resources needed to build plants, equipment, and roads. That is fairly easy in a rich community, where substantial saving still leaves the public well off in terms of current consumption. But in an LDC, where malnutrition is a constant threat, the bulk of the inhabitants cannot save except at enormous sacrifice to their families. Moreover, in many of the LDCs, tradition imputes little virtue to investment in business, so that even the wealthy are not terribly anxious to put their savings into productive equipment. Thus:

Because of poverty, which makes saving difficult, if not impossible, and because of traditions that do not encourage investment, the LDCs' growth rates of domestically financed capital are lower than those in the developed countries.

One way to help matters is to obtain the funds for investment from abroad. There is a long tradition of foreign investment in developing countries. For example, throughout the first half of the nineteenth century the United States almost constantly drew capital from abroad, though the amounts involved were only a small proportion of U.S. GNP. In recent decades a considerable share of the resources going to the LDCs from abroad has come from foreign governments as part of their aid programs. While some of the resources provided in this way have been used wastefully, informed observers generally agree that the waste incurred under these programs has not been spectacularly great, and they conclude that these capital transfers from the rich countries to the poor have at least worked in the right direction.

Capital can also be transferred to an LDC when a private firm chooses to invest money in such a country to build a factory or to explore for oil in order to increase its own profits. This too seems to have been helpful to the LDCs. In earlier days, it sometimes gave an unacceptable degree of political influence to the foreign firms, particularly when the LDC was a colony of an industrial country. In recent years this difficulty may have become rarer. Nowadays, it is more often the outside firm that is afraid of the government of the LDC rather than vice versa, with foreign proprietors frequently fearful of rigid control by the government of the LDC in which it invests. Sometimes it even fears outright expropriation—that the government will simply take over its property in the LDC with, or even without, compensation because of the hostile attitudes that residents of many LDCs hold toward large foreign companies.

It is difficult for a resident of an industrialized country like the United States to realize how much hatred and resentment is felt in less developed countries toward the "northern imperialist powers." This resentment is focused in particular on **multinational corporations**—companies like IBM, Royal Dutch Shell, Volkswagen, and Unilever—which have their headquarters in an industrialized country and their operations in a variety of less developed countries. Multinationals may first process their own raw materials in one country, ship them to another to make them into parts, and assemble them in still a third. Some of these corporations, among them the oil companies, specialize in the extraction and/or marketing of raw materials, while others, like IBM and Volkswagen, specialize in manufacturing. Many LDCs regard these and other giant foreign corporations as instruments of imperialist exploitation, not as firms which happen to carry on their activities wherever the dictates of efficiency require, contributing benefits to each of the countries in which they operate.

It is true that foreign firms hope to make more money out of an LDC than they put into it, but that is only natural, since otherwise their investment would not have been expected to be profitable, and the funds would therefore not have been invested in the first place. But there are usually *mutual* gains from trade. Investment will be useful to the LDCs if in the process of earning these profits foreign firms build factories, infrastructure, and provide jobs that leave the community wealthier than it would otherwise have been. The evidence is that this is in fact what foreign private investment has typically accomplished in recent decades.

A problem with foreign business investment that is more serious is the danger that foreign firms will fail to train native personnel in the skills necessary to run the factories built by those companies. Often the firm brings with them their own managers, engineers, and technicians, and the work force from the LDCs is kept in menial jobs in which on-the-job training is minimal. In

The Continuing Debt Crisis of the Developing Countries

Although there had been previous isolated cracks in the international debt terrain, it was not until 1982 that the problem erupted in dramatic proportions. In August of that year, Mexico announced that it was unable to meet its debt obligations to foreign creditors, although it was taking steps to rectify the situation. In response, the U.S. government mounted a rescue operation, involving the creditor banks, the International Monetary Fund (IMF), and other creditor governments. The package included a strict program of adjustment for the Mexican economy and a rescheduling of much of the debt. Nervous banks began to cut back lending to other countries that appeared to be heavily indebted, with Brazil the most obvious target. As long as the banks had been willing to continue lending, the debtor countries had had the foreign exchange necessary to continue servicing their accumulated debt, i.e., making scheduled payments of interest and amortization of principal. As the banks cut back, the debtors found debt-service obligations increasingly difficult to meet. One by one, Brazil, Argentina, and many other debtor countries found it necessary to seek debt relief from their creditors, while implementing programs of economic adjustment monitored by the IMF.

The following is from a U.S. government report:

The debt problem threatens to undermine growth in much of Latin America, particularly Mexico, Brazil, Argentina, and Venezuela, and African countries such as Nigeria. It was caused by overborrowing and overspending during the 1970s when prosperity and growth seemed easy to

recent years the LDCs have begun to deal with this problem by restricting immigration of foreign personnel, giving them work permits only for limited periods and requiring at least some minimum employment of native personnel in key positions.

Another danger posed by foreign investment is that it may prevent future financial independence. Profits are a major source of the funds used for investment. If foreign investment takes over the LDCs' most profitable industries, then newly formed capital—new plants and equipment—will also be owned predominantly by foreigners.

Population Growth

Population growth is often described as the primary villain in the LDCs. We have already noted that their populations grow far more rapidly than those in the wealthier countries. And though the growth rate has recently been declining in many of the less developed countries, overall, the population of the LDCs is expanding at a rate that will double in less than 30 years, requiring a doubling of housing, schools, hospitals, and so on—a heavy real cost for an LDC.

The growth in population has been stimulated by improvements in medical care, which have reduced death rates spectacularly. Today, in some areas, sustain; by the high oil prices of the 1970s, which hurt the oil-importing LDCs; by the fall in oil prices in the early 1980s, which hurt the oil-exporting LDCs; and by high interest rates, which hurt them all.

The debt crisis is forcing widespread adoption of austerity policies — reducing already low consumption levels so that less has to be imported and more goods are left over for export. It prevents any ambitious investment programs for the same reason, thus impeding future growth. It is indeed a major problem for the LDCs and, incidentally, for the large banks in the industrialized countries to whom the money is owed and who fear the loss of their loans.

SOURCE: From the *Economic Report of the President*, February 1984, page 71.

According to *The Wall Street Journal*:

The international debt crisis that erupted in 1982 is flaring up again, and it holds new risks for U.S. banks and debtor countries alike. . . .

Brazil a week and a half ago . . . announced it was suspending payments on about $67 billion of foreign debt and freezing about $15 billion of short-term credits and money-market deposits lent by foreign banks.

Like other Third World nations, from Ecuador and Argentina to the Philippines, Brazil hopes to win a "restructuring" of its debt and possibly get new financing as well. That for example, was what Mexico was able to negotiate last fall, in a deal expected to be concluded later this month. . . .

In the Mexican and other past negotiations, [the] Federal Reserve Board Chairman . . . has succeeded in holding the international debt structure together by getting the creditor banks to agree to new terms and new financings.

But this time [the Chairman] may be losing some of his tight control of the situation. Deep schisms have developed among creditors. New York's Citicorp has differed with other big money-center banks, insisting that the terms in restructurings be as strict as possible.* More and more regional banks are refusing to lend money to sickly debtors . . .

For their part, some of the debtors, realizing their economies can't readily support current levels of debt, have become bolder. Peru has gone so far as to essentially default on its $14 billion of debt by limiting interest payments to a fraction of its scant export earnings. . . .

*Author's Note: Citicorp has since declared a substantial portion of these debts to be uncollectable, as have other banks.

SOURCE: Charles F. McCoy and Peter Truell, *The Wall Street Journal*, March 3, 1987, page 1.

---

death rates (ratio of deaths to population) are only one-quarter or one-fifth as high as birthrates. While formerly it was not unusual for half a nation's children to die before the age of 20, today in many countries this is true of only some 4 percent of those populations. This dramatic decline can be attributed primarily to inexpensive public health measures — reduction in intestinal diseases through purer water supplies, reduction in the incidence of malaria by the draining of swamps, insecticide spraying of the breeding grounds of infectious mosquitoes, eradication of smallpox by vaccination, and so forth. The more expensive treatment of illness, using modern medical techniques and miracle drugs, seems to have contributed far less.

But not all LDCs suffer from serious population problems. India, Indonesia, and Egypt are frequently cited examples of population pressures. On the other hand, many African countries and parts of Latin America still have populations so small that they are denied economies of larger scale communication and transportation. The economy of a sparsely settled country whose electric power and telecommunication lines must traverse great unpopulated areas is under a costly handicap.

Governments in a number of LDCs have been struggling to find workable ways to cut population growth. Programs set up to distribute contraceptives and propaganda against large families have achieved modest success; but in some countries with particularly severe population problems the governments have been dissatisfied with the results of these voluntary efforts. In India, a program making use of compulsory sterilization aroused the anger of the public and finally led to the downfall of the government.

Ironically enough, it was communist China which, along with Singapore, decided to employ strong financial incentives for the purpose. In China, government support is provided for a first child. For a second, the support is withdrawn and some financial penalties imposed; and for a third child, the penalties are really prohibitive for most people. Observers come away impressed with its initial impact in the cities. Everywhere in Chinese urban areas one meets people who say they are determined to have only one child. However, reports indicate that in rural areas the program has been considerably less effective.

Educational and Technical Training

Everyone knows that educational levels in the LDCs are much lower than they are in the wealthier countries. There are fewer graduates of elementary schools, far fewer graduates of high schools, and enormously fewer college graduates. The percentage of the population that is literate is much lower than in industrialized nations. The issue is how much of a handicap this constitutes for economic growth.

If, by "education," we refer to general learning rather than technical (trade) schooling, the evidence is that it makes considerably less difference for economic growth than is often believed. For example, the number of jobs that clearly require secondary (high school) education rarely seems to exceed 10 percent of the labor force. Various studies that have investigated whether there is a statistical relationship between the economic growth of an economy and its typical educational level have failed to turn up any significant correlation between the two. Other suggestive evidence can easily be cited. For example, in 1840 when Great Britain ruled the markets of the world, only 59 percent of the British adult population was literate, while in the United States, Scandinavia, and Germany, then all relatively undeveloped countries, the figure was about 80 percent.

All of this is not meant to imply that education is worthless. On the contrary, it obviously offers many benefits in and of itself, which need not be discussed here. But it does suggest that if a government invests in education *purely as a means to stimulate economic growth,* only a very limited outlay is justifiable on these grounds.

Matters are quite different when we turn to technical training. There is clearly a high payoff to the training of electricians, machinists, draftsmen, construction workers, and the like. While the number of persons involved need not be very high in proportion to the population, the role played by such specialists is crucial. However, the LDCs would find it a very heavy drain upon their scarce foreign currency to send young people abroad to learn these skills in the numbers called for by the needs of the economy. One of the main inhibitions to adequate training in these areas is that in many countries such skills are held in low esteem and considered inferior to training in the liberal arts. Consequently, technical education is often handicapped by low budgets, low teacher salaries—which discourage good people from entering the field—and the prejudice of potential students against such fields.

Training in improved farming methods also has a great deal to contribute. In many of the LDCs, agricultural methods produce yields far lower than the best of the known techniques can offer. As one leading observer, Nobel Prizewinner Sir W. Arthur Lewis, has remarked:

If this gap could be closed, the economies of these countries would be unrecognizable. Indeed . . . no impact can be made on mass living standards without revolutionizing agricultural performance.[8]

There seem to be no easy ways to provide the necessary education to the farmers who cannot spare the time to attend schools, and training their children also involves a number of critical obstacles. Religious beliefs often lead parents to object to schooling of their children, particularly of girls; in areas where literacy is low (where the problem is generally most serious), truly literate and knowledgeable teachers are almost impossible to find in any substantial numbers; and children who do complete schooling have a tendency to leave the farms and move to the cities.

Programs to provide help to the peasants on their own farms have had only limited success. Indeed, lack of training is only part of the problem. Many other things are needed to make modern farming methods possible — farms larger than the five acres that are typical in a number of countries are required to permit the use of modern machinery where it is appropriate. Roads and storage facilities must be built. Credit must be made available to farmers. Financial arrangements must be changed so the farmer need no longer give up half his crop to landlords and tax collectors whom he can surely regard as little more than parasites and who undermine his incentives for improved productivity.

Unemployment

One of the most noteworthy features of the growth of the LDCs has been an increase in unemployment as population shifted out of agriculture into the cities. Increased schooling has stimulated the migration out of the rural areas, as has unionization, which has often produced a huge gap between urban and rural wages. Government investment policies have also favored construction of schools, hospitals, and other facilities in the cities, and as a result, large numbers of migrants have entered the cities to swell the ranks of the unemployed. The unemployment rate among young urban workers has been particularly high; indeed, rates as high as 50 percent are not unheard of.

These figures are compounded by the phenomenon of **disguised unemployment.** For example, ten persons may do a job for which only six are needed. The statistics would show no unemployment among the ten workers, even though four of them really contribute nothing to output. Some observers believe that this is such a widespread problem in rural areas that even a substantial reverse migration of the urban unemployed back to the farms would add very little to production, at least in some of the LDCs.

An important consequence of all this is that in many LDCs unemployment may not be accompanied by any substantial reduction in output, in contrast to the situation in industrialized economies. But this does not mean that unemployment in the LDCs is not a serious problem. What it does mean is that it may sometimes be desirable for those economies to avoid the use of labor-saving equipment, partly because it will result in better use of an abundant resource and partly because it will contribute to the solution of a serious social problem. Thus, increased jobs are desirable perhaps primarily because they sop up unemployed labor. This is in contrast to the usual situation in the developed countries in which increased employment is desirable perhaps primarily because it increases income and output.

[8]W. A. Lewis, *Development Economics, An Outline* (Morristown, N.J.: General Learning Press, 1974), page 25.

Social Impediments to Entrepreneurship

As we saw earlier in this chapter, one of the magic ingredients of economic growth is **entrepreneurship.** It is clear that the LDCs need entrepreneurs if their economies are to grow rapidly. But in many of these economies, there are serious inhibitions to entrepreneurship. Traditional social values often accord relatively low status to business activity. Indeed, those traditional values even prevent businesses from seeking ways to attract and please their customers and their work force. In addition, high positions in business in many LDCs are often determined by family connections and inheritance, not by ability.

In the LDCs, growth will be inhibited until customs can be modified to increase the social status of economic activity, to make it respectable for private business people and managers of public enterprises to do their best to attract business and increase productivity, and to assign responsibility on the basis of ability rather than family connections.

Government Inhibition of Business Activity

In addition to social impediments to business, the political situation in the LDCs often is detrimental to business success. Business is not helped by unstable governments or by the uncertainty that accompanies such an environment, especially if there is a high likelihood of revolution. Foreign investment will be discouraged where there is fear of expropriation or of unstable currencies that may fall in value and wipe out hard-earned profits. And native business people may live in fear of nationalization or even imprisonment—possibilities that are not likely to encourage investment.

In addition, in the normal course of events, governments in the LDCs are often inclined to interfere with business activity in a variety of ways that seem relatively innocuous—but whose effects can be deadly. Price controls are often imposed at levels that make the controlled activity totally unprofitable and cause it to wither. Licenses and other direct controls are frequently administered by incompetent bureaucrats, who tie up business activity in red tape. As a matter of prestige of the currency, exchange rates are often set so high that exports from the LDC cannot compete on the world market. The governments sometimes expropriate and seek to operate foreign firms before they have trained native personnel to run them. In short:

Poorly conceived economic policies can impede business activity and hence economic growth in the LDCs. But, then, it must be admitted that the LDCs have no monopoly on foolish economic policies!

Help from Industrialized Economies

We have just seen that the two primary needs of the LDCs are technical skills and capital resources. Happily, these are precisely the things that the more prosperous nations are in a position to offer. We have the trained teachers, classrooms, laboratories, and equipment necessary to provide an education of the highest quality to students from the LDCs. However, there is a danger here that has received a great deal of attention, the so-called **brain drain.** This refers to the temptation for students from LDCs to try to stay in the countries where they have studied and enjoy the higher living standard, rather than to return home where their abilities are needed so badly.

There are several ways to deal with this. For example, one can require students to return to their homelands for at least some given number of years after completion of the educational program, or offer higher wages for trained persons in the LDCs to make returning more attractive. Yet the problem is there, and the large number of doctors, teachers, and other skilled personnel from LDCs who are seeking jobs in the developed countries suggests that it is not negligible.

A second major contribution that the wealthier countries can make to the LDCs is to offer them trained technicians and technical advice from their own populations. Such counseling and personnel can be very helpful as a temporary measure, but in the long run they can prove detrimental if provision for the training of local personnel for the ultimate replacement of the foreign technicians and advisers is not built into the program.

Third, the world can help the LDCs through research. One of the hardest problems for the developing world is what to do in the rural areas that suffer from inadequate rainfall, where several hundred million people live in both Asia and Africa. These people are badly in need of new dry-farming techniques. Until some are discovered, their poverty will increase as their numbers grow. An international research organization devoted to food production in problem areas in the LDCs would have much to contribute.

Fourth, the developed countries can help by encouraging freedom of trade and investment. This will help those LDCs whose exports are now being held back by barriers to trade. Exports of sugar, meat, cotton, and other agricultural products are inhibited by industrialized countries' tariffs and other restrictions. LDCs would also benefit substantially from a lifting of tariffs and quotas upon the export of processed or manufactured goods. Such restrictive measures make it difficult for LDCs to export anything but raw materials and impedes their industrialization and modernization. All in all, increased freedom of trade is a matter of highest priority for the LDCs.[9]

A last, and very important, type of assistance from the developed to the less developed countries takes the form of money or physical resources provided either as loans made on favorable terms or as outright grants (gifts).

Loans and Grants by the United States and Others

Since World War II a number of countries have provided capital to the LDCs. An international organization, the International Bank for Reconstruction and Development (the **World Bank**), was created largely for this purpose. It has 144 member countries, each providing an amount of capital related to its wealth; for instance, the United States has contributed approximately one-third of the total. The Bank makes loans that finance its bonds and has acted as guarantor of repayment to encourage some private lending. Since its inception the Bank has approved loans totalling $131.5 billion to 104 countries, mostly for infrastructure, dams, communications, and transportation. In addition, it provided technical assistance and planning advice.

United States' loans and grants have exceeded the total given by all other countries and international agencies, with U.S. interest and repayment terms generally far more generous than those of other governments. However, the

---

[9]Not everyone agrees with this conclusion. There are those who have argued that participation of LDCs in international trade is bad for them because it weakens their capacity to develop as self-reliant, mature economies. It is held that new manufacturing industries in the LDCs will not take off without protection from foreign competition; that development of raw material exports creates a politically powerful vested interest that inhibits manufacturing; and that foreign participation in trade and production of exports inhibits domestic investment and the development of local entrepreneurship.

In this view, LDCs are therefore held back by international trade and they would do better to integrate regionally and develop their own home markets without foreigners, who also bring unsuitable habits, tastes, and technology, and impart a crippling inferiority complex to the natives.

bulk of the assistance provided by the United States has gone to a small number of countries, such as India, Pakistan, South Korea, and Turkey.

During the 1960s, our expenditures on aid ran to more than $3 billion per year. In the past decade, expenditures on foreign aid have become less popular politically, and the amounts provided consequently have gone down sharply and steadily from about half a percent of U.S. GNP in 1965 to under 0.3 percent of GNP in 1984–85.

France, Great Britain, West Germany, and other industrialized noncommunist countries now provide about $29 billion per year, which is about 0.4 percent of their GNP. The Soviet Union has also become a major source of assistance to the LDCs, now providing, along with its associated countries, about $3.4 billion, or 0.23 percent of their GNP. While the Soviet funds have obviously been distributed in a way intended to maximize its political advantage, it can hardly be claimed that the U.S. foreign aid program has been entirely free of political considerations.

Many economists have advocated greater generosity in our assistance to LDCs. It is argued that an effective aid program that really helps the growth of LDCs will also serve our own interests. By making those countries more stable economically and politically, we can contribute to our own economic tranquility. By increasing the LDCs' power to buy and sell, we contribute to the prosperity of the entire world.

Can LDCs Break Away from Poverty?

It is easy to jump to the conclusion that the economic problems of the LDCs are staggering and that the prospects of their ever catching up with the industrialized countries are negligible. Yet a number of LDCs and former LDCs have made enormous progress. The African countries Kenya, Cameroon, and the Ivory Coast increased their GNPs during the 1970s at a rate of about 5 to 6 percent a year, which is considerably faster than their population growth. In the Americas, Costa Rica's performance has been comparable. Even more striking is the expansion of output in a number of places in the Far East—particularly Hong Kong, Taiwan, South Korea, and Singapore, where prosperity is unprecedented and economic activity is expanding at an astonishing rate. Here per capita GNPs have been growing at a rate of 6.5 percent a year and more.

But the most impressive case is that of Japan. Many of your professors will remember clearly when U.S. business feared the flood of goods produced by cheap Japanese labor, and when the label "made in Japan" suggested inexpensive and shoddy merchandise. From one of the world's impoverished countries, Japan has risen to one of the world's richest. Its goods are now feared by American manufacturers not because they are produced and sold so cheaply, but because their quality is so high. Japanese cars and sophisticated electronic equipment find a ready market in the United States. And as a result, per capita income in Japan has surpassed that in Great Britain. A less developed country need not lag behind forever.

Summary

1. If growth is evaluated in terms of its effect upon the well-being of individuals, a country's economic growth should be measured in terms of *per capita* income, not in terms of GNP or some other index of total output of the economy.

2. A rapidly rising population poses a threat to growth of per capita incomes.

3. On our finite planet, exponential growth (growth at a constant percentage rate) is, in general, impossible except for relatively brief periods.

4. Increases in growth depend heavily on entrepreneurship, accumulation of capital equipment, and research and development.

5. Saving is necessary for the accumulation of resources with which to produce factories, machinery, and other capital equipment. Thus, saving is a critical requisite for growth, particularly in less developed countries.

6. Many observers argue that even if continued growth does not lead to catastrophically rapid depletion of resources (as some have predicted), its desirability is nevertheless questionable because it produces pollution, overcrowding, and many other undesirable consequences.

7. Those who favor growth argue that without it there is no chance of ridding the world of poverty.

8. Standards of living in many LDCs are extremely low; per capita incomes that are equivalent to $1500 a year are not uncommon. Life expectancy is low and daily living is very difficult, particularly for women.

9. GNP and per capita incomes in the LDCs grew considerably in the 1970s, though in many cases they slowed in the 1980s.

10. Nevertheless, the gap between family incomes in the less developed and the industrialized countries has continued to widen.

11. In many LDCs, population continues to grow much faster than that in the industrialized countries.

12. Growth in the LDCs is impeded by shortages of capital caused by poverty, traditions that do not encourage investment, rapid population growth, poor education, unemployment, lack of entrepreneurship, and government impediments to business.

13. Industrialized countries can help the LDCs by providing capital through loans and grants, by offering training and education to people from those lands, and by encouraging freedom of trade with the LDCs.

14. In the post-World War II period many countries, including the United States and the Soviet Union, have provided large amounts of money to the LDCs in the form of loans and grants.

15. Several international organizations, most notably the World Bank, have been organized to provide economic assistance to the LDCs.

Concepts for Review

Output per capita
Exponential growth
Social infrastructure
Exchange between present and
  future consumption

Embodied growth
Disembodied growth
Less developed countries (LDCs)
Growth rate in GNP vs. per capita income
Multinational corporations

Disguised unemployment
Entrepreneurship
Brain drain
World Bank

Questions for Discussion

1. Which do you think has the higher total GNP, Pakistan or Luxembourg? Which has the higher per capita GNP? In which do you think people are better off economically?

2. Suppose population grows at a constant exponential rate and doubles every 10 years. How many times will it have grown in 30 years? How many years does it require to expand to 16 times its initial level?

3. Can you think of any innovations that permit growth without proportionate increases in use of inputs?

4. Name as many undesirable consequences of growth as you can think of.

5. Are the undesirable consequences of growth more likely to be considered serious in a less developed country or in an industrialized country? Why?

6. To many families living in less developed countries, an income equivalent to $2000 per year is considered a high standard of living. Can you make up a budget for a U.S. family of four earning $2000 a year?

7. Explain how it is possible for the per capita income of an LDC to grow at a faster rate than that in the United States and yet for the difference between the incomes of average families in both countries to increase. Can you give a numerical example showing how this happens?

8. Discuss the advantages and disadvantages to an LDC of a U.S. manufacturing company investing in that country.
9. If you were economic adviser to the president of an LDC, what might you suggest that he or she do to encourage increases in saving and investment?
10. No one knows what encourages or discourages the supply of entrepreneurs. Do you have any ideas about policies that may be capable of stimulating entrepreneurship?
11. Name some countries in which entrepreneurship seems to be abundant these days and some countries in which it seems to be scarce. What is your impression about what is happening to the supply of entrepreneurs in the United States?
12. Discuss what you have read in the newspapers and heard from other sources about the Japanese "growth miracle." What does it portend for the future of the Japanese economy? For that of the United States?

Appendix

Selected U.S. Macroeconomic Data 1929–1986 and, Quarterly, 1978–1987

SELECTED U.S. MACROECONOMIC DATA 1929–1986

Year	Gross National Product	Personal Consumption Expenditure	Gross Private Domestic Investment	Government Purchases	Net Exports	Gross National Product	Personal Consumption Expenditure	Gross Private Domestic Investment	Government Purchases	Net Exports	Potential GNP*	Real GNP per capita
	(in billions of dollars)					(in billions of 1982 dollars)						(in 1982 dollars)
1929	103.9	77.3	16.7	8.9	1.1	709.6	471.4	139.2	94.2	4.7	709.6	5822
1933	56.0	45.8	1.6	8.3	.4	498.5	378.7	22.7	98.5	−1.4	779.5	3966
1939	91.3	67.0	9.5	13.6	1.2	716.6	480.5	86.0	144.1	6.1	893.5	5469
1945	213.4	119.6	11.3	83.0	−.5	1354.8	592.7	76.5	704.5	−18.9	1024.3	9682
1950	288.3	192.1	55.1	38.8	2.2	1203.7	733.2	234.9	230.8	4.7	1186.7	7935
1955	405.9	257.9	69.7	75.3	3.0	1494.9	873.8	259.8	361.3	0	1465.7	9045
1956	428.2	270.6	72.7	79.7	5.3	1525.6	899.8	257.8	363.7	4.3	1510.1	9069
1957	451.0	285.3	71.1	87.3	7.3	1551.1	919.7	243.4	381.8	7.0	1556.0	9056
1958	456.8	294.6	63.6	95.4	3.3	1539.2	932.9	221.4	395.3	−10.3	1606.6	8839
1959	495.8	316.3	80.2	97.9	1.5	1629.1	979.4	270.3	397.7	−18.2	1658.3	9200
1960	515.3	330.7	78.2	100.6	5.9	1665.3	1005.1	260.5	403.7	−4.0	1712.2	9213
1961	533.8	341.1	77.1	108.4	7.2	1708.7	1025.2	259.1	427.1	−2.7	1768.0	9299
1962	574.6	361.9	87.6	118.2	6.9	1799.4	1069.0	288.6	449.4	−7.5	1825.6	9644
1963	606.9	381.7	93.1	123.8	8.2	1873.3	1108.4	307.1	459.8	−1.9	1885.4	9896
1964	649.8	409.3	99.6	130.0	10.9	1973.3	1170.6	325.9	470.8	5.9	1952.5	10281
1965	705.1	440.7	116.2	138.6	9.7	2087.6	1236.4	367.0	487.0	−2.7	2023.2	10741
1966	772.0	477.3	128.6	158.6	7.5	2208.3	1298.9	390.5	532.6	−13.7	2096.5	11233
1967	816.4	503.6	125.7	179.7	7.4	2271.4	1337.7	374.4	576.2	−16.9	2172.5	11428
1968	892.7	552.5	137.0	197.7	5.5	2365.6	1405.9	391.8	597.6	−29.7	2251.2	11784
1969	963.9	597.9	153.2	207.3	5.6	2423.3	1456.7	410.3	591.2	−34.9	2332.8	11953
1970	1015.5	640.0	148.8	218.2	8.5	2416.2	1492.0	381.5	572.6	−30.0	2416.5	11781
1971	1102.7	691.6	172.5	232.4	6.3	2484.8	1538.8	419.3	566.5	−39.8	2500.0	11964
1972	1212.8	757.6	202.0	250.0	3.2	2608.5	1621.9	465.4	570.7	−49.4	2586.0	12426
1973	1359.3	837.2	238.8	266.5	16.8	2744.1	1689.6	520.8	565.3	−31.5	2675.0	12948
1974	1472.8	916.5	240.8	299.1	16.3	2729.3	1674.0	481.3	573.2	.8	2764.4	12760
1975	1598.4	1012.8	219.6	335.0	31.1	2695.0	1711.9	383.3	580.9	18.9	2846.5	12478
1976	1782.8	1129.3	277.7	356.9	18.8	2826.7	1803.9	453.5	580.3	−11.0	2930.1	12961
1977	1990.5	1257.2	344.1	387.3	1.9	2958.6	1883.8	521.3	589.1	−35.5	3016.2	13431
1978	2249.7	1403.5	416.8	425.2	4.1	3115.2	1961.0	576.9	604.1	−26.8	3104.7	13993
1979	2508.2	1566.8	454.8	467.8	18.8	3192.4	2004.4	575.2	609.1	3.6	3195.3	14182
1980	2732.0	1732.6	437.0	530.3	32.1	3187.1	2000.4	509.3	620.5	57.0	3281.3	13994
1981	3052.6	1915.1	515.5	588.1	33.9	3248.8	2024.2	545.5	629.7	49.4	3367.7	14114
1982	3166.0	2050.7	447.3	641.7	26.3	3166.0	2050.7	447.3	641.7	26.3	3456.4	13614
1983	3405.7	2234.5	502.3	675.0	−6.1	3279.1	2146.0	504.1	649.0	−19.9	3547.5	13964
1984	3772.2	2430.5	664.8	735.9	−58.9	3501.4	2249.3	658.4	677.7	−84.0	3640.9	14771
1985	4010.3	2629.4	641.6	818.6	−79.2	3607.5	2352.6	636.1	726.9	−108.2	3736.8	15074
1986	4235.0	2799.8	671.0	869.7	−105.5	3713.3	2450.5	654.0	754.5	−145.8	3835.0	15368

*From Robert J. Gordon, *Macroeconomics*, fourth edition (Boston: Little, Brown, 1987), Table B-1. Reprinted by permission. Updated by authors.
SOURCES: U.S. Department of Commerce, Bureau of Labor Statistics, Federal Reserve System, and Professor R. J. Gordon.

Year	Price Level GNP Deflator (1982=100)	Consumer Price Index (1967=100)	Real Average Hourly Earnings (1977=100)	Population (millions)	Labor Force*	Civilian Unemployment Rate (percent)	Money Supply M1 (in December) (billions of dollars)	M2	Interest Rates Treasury Bills (percent)	Corporate Bonds†	Exchange Value of U.S. Dollar a (March 1973=100)	Federal Budget Surplus(+) or Deficit(−) (billions of dollars)
1929	14.6	51.3	—	121.9	49.2	3.2	—	—	—	4.73	—	+1.2
1933	11.2	38.8	—	125.7	51.6	24.9	—	—	0.52	4.49	—	−1.3
1939	12.7	41.6	—	131.0	55.2	17.2	—	—	0.02	3.01	—	−2.2
1945	15.7	53.9	—	139.9	53.9	1.9	—	—	0.38	2.62	—	−42.1
1950	23.9	72.1	64.0	151.7	62.2	5.3	—	—	1.22	2.62	—	+9.2
1955	27.2	80.2	73.3	165.3	65.0	4.4	—	—	1.75	3.06	—	+4.4
1956	28.1	81.4	75.9	168.2	66.5	4.1	—	—	2.66	3.36	—	+6.1
1957	29.1	84.3	76.9	171.3	66.9	4.3	—	—	3.27	3.89	—	+2.3
1958	29.7	86.6	78.0	174.1	67.6	6.8	—	—	1.84	3.79	—	−10.3
1959	30.4	87.3	80.0	177.1	68.4	5.5	141.0	297.8	3.41	4.38	—	−1.1
1960	30.9	88.7	81.4	180.8	69.6	5.5	141.8	312.3	2.93	4.41	—	+3.0
1961	31.2	89.6	83.0	183.7	70.5	6.7	146.5	335.5	2.38	4.35	—	−3.9
1962	31.9	90.6	85.0	186.6	70.6	5.5	149.2	362.7	2.78	4.33	—	−4.2
1963	32.4	91.7	86.3	189.3	71.8	5.7	154.7	393.2	3.16	4.26	—	+0.3
1964	32.9	92.9	87.5	191.9	73.1	5.2	161.9	424.8	3.55	4.40	—	−3.3
1965	33.8	94.5	89.0	194.3	74.4	4.5	169.5	459.4	3.95	4.49	—	+0.5
1966	35.0	97.2	90.3	196.6	75.7	3.8	173.7	480.0	4.88	5.13	—	−1.8
1967	35.9	100.0	92.2	198.7	77.3	3.8	185.1	524.3	4.32	5.51	120.0	−13.2
1968	37.7	104.2	94.0	200.7	78.7	3.6	199.4	566.3	5.34	6.18	122.1	−6.0
1969	39.8	109.8	95.0	202.7	80.7	3.5	205.8	589.5	6.68	7.03	122.4	+8.4
1970	42.0	116.3	95.7	205.1	82.8	4.9	216.6	628.2	6.46	8.04	121.1	−12.4
1971	44.4	121.3	98.3	207.7	84.4	5.9	230.8	712.7	4.35	7.39	117.8	−22.0
1972	46.5	125.3	101.2	209.9	87.0	5.6	252.0	805.1	4.07	7.21	109.1	−16.8
1973	49.5	133.1	101.1	211.9	89.4	4.9	265.9	861.0	7.04	7.44	99.1	−5.6
1974	54.0	147.7	98.3	213.9	92.0	5.6	277.5	908.5	7.89	8.57	101.4	−11.6
1975	59.3	161.2	97.6	216.0	93.8	8.5	291.1	1023.2	5.84	8.83	98.5	−69.4
1976	63.1	170.5	99.0	218.1	96.2	7.7	310.4	1163.7	4.99	8.43	105.6	−53.5
1977	67.3	181.5	100.0	220.3	99.0	7.1	335.3	1286.8	5.27	8.02	103.3	−46.0
1978	72.2	195.4	100.5	222.6	102.2	6.1	363.0	1389.2	7.22	8.73	92.4	−29.3
1979	78.6	217.4	97.4	225.1	105.0	5.8	391.1	1500.3	10.04	9.63	88.1	−16.1
1980	85.7	246.8	93.5	227.8	107.0	7.1	416.6	1633.1	11.51	11.94	87.4	−61.3
1981	94.0	272.4	92.6	230.2	109.0	7.6	443.2	1795.5	14.03	14.17	102.9	−63.8
1982	100.0	289.1	93.4	232.5	110.2	9.7	481.3	1953.8	10.69	13.79	116.6	−145.9
1983	103.9	298.4	94.9	234.8	111.6	9.6	526.9	2184.6	8.63	12.04	125.3	−176.0
1984	107.7	311.1	94.6	237.1	113.5	7.5	557.5	2369.1	9.58	12.71	138.3	−169.6
1985	111.2	322.2	94.1	239.3	115.5	7.2	627.0	2569.6	7.48	11.37	143.2	−196.0
1986	114.1	328.4	95.0	241.6	117.8	7.0	730.5	2798.4	5.98	9.02	112.0	−204.7

* Counts persons 14 years and older 1929–1946, 16 years and older 1947–present.
† Moody's Aaa rating.
a Multilateral trade-weighted average. Federal Reserve series.

SELECTED U.S. MACROECONOMIC DATA, QUARTERLY 1978–1987

Year	Gross National Product	Personal Consumption Expenditure	Gross Private Domestic Investment	Government Purchases	Net Exports	Gross National Product	Personal Consumption Expenditure	Gross Private Domestic Investment	Government Purchases	Net Exports	Potential GNP*
	(in billions of dollars)					(in billions of 1982 dollars)					
1978:1	2111.4	1332.6	379.7	405.6	−6.6	3020.5	1923.0	544.0	592.5	−39.0	3071.1
1978:2	2230.3	1391.1	420.2	417.6	1.3	3115.9	1960.8	584.6	601.3	−30.7	3093.4
1978:3	2289.5	1424.6	424.7	433.4	6.8	3142.6	1970.3	583.3	611.5	−22.4	3115.9
1978:4	2367.6	1465.7	442.7	444.2	15.0	3181.6	1989.7	595.8	611.1	−15.1	3138.5
1979:1	2420.5	1501.8	446.9	449.2	22.7	3181.7	1997.5	582.2	606.7	−4.8	3161.3
1979:2	2474.5	1537.6	463.2	458.6	15.2	3178.7	1994.1	590.1	606.9	−12.4	3184.3
1979:3	2546.1	1590.0	461.5	472.8	21.8	3207.4	2007.9	575.7	611.3	12.5	3207.4
1979:4	2591.5	1637.5	447.8	490.7	15.4	3201.3	2018.0	552.9	611.7	18.7	3228.3
1980:1	2673.0	1682.2	461.0	509.1	20.7	3233.4	2015.4	556.7	617.8	43.5	3249.4
1980:2	2672.2	1688.9	425.0	528.2	30.1	3157.0	1974.1	499.2	625.1	58.6	3270.6
1980:3	2734.0	1749.3	405.4	532.6	46.8	3159.1	1996.3	467.7	621.1	74.1	3291.9
1980:4	2848.6	1810.0	456.4	551.4	30.8	3199.2	2015.6	513.5	617.9	52.2	3313.4
1981:1	2978.8	1862.9	506.9	570.1	38.9	3261.1	2022.9	552.3	626.3	59.7	3335.0
1981:2	3017.7	1896.4	515.3	577.0	29.0	3250.2	2022.4	551.2	626.4	50.2	3356.7
1981:3	3099.6	1940.9	535.9	591.9	30.9	3264.6	2031.5	560.7	630.2	42.1	3378.6
1981:4	3114.4	1960.2	504.0	613.3	36.9	3219.0	2020.0	517.9	635.9	45.3	3400.6
1982:1	3112.6	1996.3	459.5	622.1	34.7	3170.4	2031.2	464.2	634.6	40.4	3422.8
1982:2	3159.5	2023.8	467.8	625.7	42.1	3179.9	2041.0	467.5	629.7	41.7	3445.1
1982:3	3179.4	2065.6	452.2	647.1	14.5	3154.5	2051.8	448.6	642.5	11.7	3467.6
1982:4	3212.5	2117.0	409.6	671.8	14.1	3159.3	2078.7	408.8	660.1	11.7	3490.2
1983:1	3265.8	2146.6	428.3	668.1	22.8	3186.6	2094.2	427.1	649.2	16.1	3513.0
1983:2	3367.4	2213.0	481.3	675.2	−2.1	3258.3	2135.1	486.9	650.9	−14.6	3535.9
1983:3	3443.9	2262.8	519.7	680.7	−19.3	3306.4	2163.0	524.8	653.6	−35.0	3558.9
1983:4	3545.8	2315.8	579.8	676.1	−25.8	3365.1	2191.9	577.2	642.2	−46.2	3582.1
1984:1	3674.9	2361.1	663.0	696.5	−45.7	3451.7	2212.1	655.2	653.0	−68.6	3605.5
1984:2	3754.2	2417.0	664.2	735.8	−62.8	3498.0	2246.7	658.4	680.2	−87.3	3629.0
1984:3	3807.9	2450.3	670.3	746.6	−59.3	3520.6	2257.3	664.2	684.5	−85.5	3652.7
1984:4	3851.8	2493.4	661.8	764.5	−67.9	3535.2	2281.1	655.7	693.2	−94.8	3676.5
1985:1	3921.1	2549.9	638.6	784.1	−51.5	3568.7	2314.1	632.1	703.4	−81.0	3700.5
1985:2	3973.6	2602.0	648.4	800.5	−77.3	3587.1	2337.0	645.7	712.1	−107.7	3724.6
1985:3	4042.0	2665.4	628.6	832.8	−84.7	3623.0	2376.1	623.2	738.6	−114.9	3748.9
1985:4	4104.4	2700.1	650.8	857.0	−103.5	3650.9	2383.2	643.3	753.7	−129.3	3773.3
1986:1	4174.4	2737.9	683.4	846.9	−93.8	3698.8	2409.7	674.4	737.6	−123.0	3797.9
1986:2	4211.6	2765.8	679.4	867.2	−100.8	3704.7	2434.3	665.6	751.6	−146.8	3822.7
1986:3	4265.9	2837.1	660.8	878.5	−110.5	3718.0	2477.5	645.0	757.2	−161.6	3847.7
1986:4	4288.1	2858.6	660.2	886.3	−116.9	3731.5	2480.5	631.0	771.8	−151.8	3872.8
1987:1	4377.7	2893.8	699.9	896.2	−112.2	3772.2	2475.9	671.8	759.6	−135.2	3898.1
1987:2	4447.7	2947.3	700.9	918.2	−118.6	3793.7	2489.0	670.5	767.5	−133.3	3923.5

*From Robert J. Gordon, *Macroeconomics*, fourth edition (Boston: Little, Brown, 1987), Table B-1. Reprinted by permission. Updated by authors.
SOURCES: U.S. Department of Commerce, Bureau of Labor Statistics, Federal Reserve System, and Professor R. J. Gordon.

Year	Price Level GNP Deflator (1982=100)	Consumer Price Index (1967=100)	Real Average Hourly Earnings (1977=100)	Population (millions)	Labor Force*	Civilian Unemployment Rate (percent)	Money Supply M1 (quarterly average) (billions of dollars)	M2	Interest Rates Treasury Bills (percent)	Corporate Bonds†	Exchange Value of U.S. Dollar[a] (March 1973=100)	Federal Budget Surplus(+) or Deficit(−) (billions of dollars)
1978:1	69.9	188.8	100.8	221.6	100.9	6.3	339.7	1301.9	6.41	8.45	95.9	−47.5
1978:2	71.6	193.1	100.7	222.2	101.9	6.0	347.3	1324.9	6.48	8.67	95.2	−25.3
1978:3	72.9	197.6	100.3	222.8	102.6	6.0	354.4	1351.3	7.31	8.75	90.6	−24.2
1978:4	74.4	202.2	99.9	223.5	103.5	5.9	360.7	1380.4	8.68	9.03	87.8	−20.4
1979:1	76.1	207.2	99.4	224.1	104.4	5.9	365.1	1403.0	9.36	9.29	88.1	−9.8
1979:2	77.8	214.0	97.8	224.6	104.3	5.7	371.9	1432.8	9.37	9.39	89.8	−6.0
1979:3	79.4	220.8	96.7	225.3	105.2	5.9	384.7	1471.8	9.63	9.29	87.0	−20.0
1979:4	81.0	227.8	95.7	226.0	105.9	6.0	389.1	1493.7	11.80	10.54	87.4	−28.7
1980:1	82.7	236.8	94.2	226.6	106.6	6.3	393.3	1517.9	13.46	12.14	87.4	−37.8
1980:2	84.6	244.8	93.2	227.3	106.8	7.3	387.5	1531.9	10.05	11.20	87.8	−64.5
1980:3	86.5	249.2	93.6	228.0	107.1	7.7	406.5	1589.8	9.23	11.58	85.4	−75.0
1980:4	89.0	256.3	93.2	228.6	107.4	7.4	417.5	1627.3	13.71	12.83	89.0	−68.0
1981:1	91.3	263.3	92.9	229.1	108.3	7.4	419.3	1652.9	14.37	13.16	94.5	−47.4
1981:2	92.8	268.9	92.8	229.6	108.9	7.3	426.2	1692.2	14.83	13.98	103.1	−49.2
1981:3	94.9	276.3	92.2	230.2	108.5	7.4	433.3	1733.1	15.09	14.92	110.0	−62.5
1981:4	96.7	280.8	92.4	231.0	109.0	8.2	438.7	1777.8	12.02	14.62	105.4	−96.0
1982:1	98.2	283.4	93.2	231.4	109.4	8.8	446.7	1816.8	12.89	15.01	110.0	−109.2
1982:2	99.4	287.2	93.4	232.1	110.2	9.4	448.6	1846.8	12.36	14.51	114.0	−112.9
1982:3	100.8	292.3	93.2	232.7	110.5	10.0	458.2	1893.0	9.70	13.75	119.8	−158.8
1982:4	101.7	293.4	93.8	233.4	110.8	10.6	476.6	1938.9	7.93	11.88	122.2	−202.6
1983:1	102.5	293.6	95.1	233.8	110.7	10.4	488.9	2037.1	8.08	11.84	119.4	−186.2
1983:2	103.3	296.8	94.8	234.3	111.3	10.1	502.7	2090.3	8.42	11.57	123.0	−171.4
1983:3	104.2	299.8	94.6	235.0	112.1	9.4	516.6	2130.8	9.19	12.34	128.7	−177.3
1983:4	105.4	303.1	94.7	235.7	112.0	8.5	525.0	2173.8	8.79	12.41	130.2	−169.2
1984:1	106.5	306.8	94.9	236.2	112.5	7.9	533.2	2213.7	9.13	12.28	131.6	−154.6
1984:2	107.3	309.6	95.2	236.7	113.5	7.4	541.7	2252.7	9.84	13.21	132.8	−163.5
1984:3	108.2	313.1	94.5	237.3	113.8	7.4	547.5	2288.0	10.34	12.99	141.7	−172.8
1984:4	109.0	315.4	94.3	237.9	114.3	7.3	553.3	2344.7	8.97	12.35	147.2	−187.5
1985:1	109.9	317.4	94.3	238.5	115.0	7.3	568.3	2415.2	8.18	12.26	156.5	−162.9
1985:2	110.8	321.2	94.1	239.0	115.2	7.3	583.1	2451.4	7.46	11.63	149.1	−210.3
1985:3	111.6	323.6	94.1	239.6	115.5	7.2	603.8	2509.7	7.11	11.03	139.2	−195.8
1985:4	112.4	326.5	94.0	240.2	116.2	7.0	620.2	2551.3	7.17	10.58	128.2	−215.0
1986:1	112.9	327.3	94.3	240.8	117.0	7.1	633.9	2585.3	6.90	9.57	119.5	−196.1
1986:2	113.7	326.5	95.3	241.3	117.6	7.1	658.4	2646.2	6.14	9.00	114.2	−230.2
1986:3	114.7	328.9	95.1	241.9	118.2	6.9	685.6	2716.2	5.52	8.83	108.3	−203.7
1986:4	114.9	330.8	95.3	242.5	118.6	6.8	714.8	2778.7	5.35	8.68	107.0	−188.7
1987:1	116.1	334.5	94.6	243.0	119.2	6.7	738.2	2822.8	5.54	8.37	99.9	−170.5
1987:2	117.2	338.3	94.0	243.5	119.6	6.2	750.0	2839.5	5.66	9.17	97.0	−141.9

* Counts persons 14 years and older 1929–1946, 16 years and older 1947–present.
† Moody's Aaa rating.
[a] Multilateral trade-weighted average. Federal Reserve series.

Glossary

Page numbers for *Macroeconomics* are shown in regular type, those for *Microeconomics* in boldface type.

Numbers in parentheses indicate pages in the text where the terms are discussed.

Ability-to-pay principle The idea that persons with greater ability to pay taxes should pay higher taxes. (**342**)

Absolute advantage Of one country over another in the production of a particular good is said to occur if it can produce that good using smaller quantities of resources than can the other country. (384)

Abstraction Ignoring many details in order to focus on the most important factors in a problem. (10) (**10**)

Affirmative action Active efforts to locate and hire members of minority groups. (**457**)

Aggregate demand The total amount that all consumers, business firms, and government agencies are willing to spend on final goods and services. (139)

Aggregate demand curve Graphic presentation of the quantity of national product that is demanded at each possible value of the price level. (77, 174)

Aggregate saving The difference between disposable income and consumer expenditure. (155)

Aggregate supply The total amount that all business firms are willing to produce. (198)

Aggregate supply curve A graph that shows, for each possible price level, the quantity of goods and services that all the nation's businesses are willing to produce, holding all other determinants of aggregate quantity supplied constant. (77, 198)

Aggregation Combining many individual markets into one overall market. Economic aggregates are the focus of macroeconomics. (75)

Aid to Families with Dependent Children (AFDC) Major transfer program that pays cash benefits to poor families with dependent children. (**453**)

Allocation of resources The decision on how to divide up the economy's scarce input resources among the different outputs produced in the economy and among the different firms or other organizations that produce those outputs. (**37**)

Antitrust policy Programs designed to control the growth of monopoly and to prevent powerful firms from engaging in practices considered "undesirable," as defined by certain federal laws and court decisions. (**315**)

Appreciation Of a nation's currency is said to occur when exchange rates change so that a unit of its own currency can buy more units of foreign currency. (408)

Arbitration Process in which an outsider is authorized to dictate the terms of a settlement of a labor-management dispute if a voluntary agreement cannot be reached. (**430**)

Asset An item that an individual or a firm owns. (258)

Automatic stabilizer An arrangement that automatically supports aggregate demand when it would otherwise sag and holds down aggregate demand when it would otherwise surge ahead; thus reduces the sensitivity of the economy to shifts in demand. (309)

Autonomous increase in consumption An increase in consumer spending without any increase in incomes. Represented graphically as a shift of the entire consumption function. (190)

Average cost curve Shows, for each output, the cost per unit, that is, total cost divided by output. (**121**)

Average physical product (APP) Total physical product (TPP) divided by the total quantity of input used. (**117**)

Average revenue (AR) Total revenue (TR) divided by quantity. (**152**)

Balance sheet An account statement listing the values of all assets on the left-hand side and of all liabilities and net worth on the right-hand side. (258)

Barter A system of exchange in which people directly trade one good for another, without using money as an intermediate step. (250)

Benefits principle of taxation The idea that people who derive benefits from a service should pay the taxes that finance it. (**342**)

Bilateral monopoly Market situation in which there is both a monopoly on the selling side and a monopoly on the buying side. (**428**)

Bond A corporation's promise to pay the holder a fixed sum of money at the specified *maturity* date and some other fixed amount of money (the coupon or interest payment) every year up to the date of maturity. (**276**)

Brain drain Occurs when the educated natives of a less developed country emigrate to wealthier nations. (478)

Budget deficit Amount by which the government's expenditures exceed its receipts during a specified period of time, usually one year. (322)

Budget line Represents graphically all the possible combinations of two commodities that a household can purchase, given the prices of the commodities and some fixed amount of money at its disposal. (**85**)

Burden of a tax The amount of money an individual would have to be given to make him just as well off with the tax as he was without it. (**343**)

Capital Inventory (stock) of plant, equipment, and other productive resources held by a business firm, an individual, or some other organization. (**390**)

Capitalism Method of economic organization in which private individuals own the means of production, either directly or indirectly through corporations. (**479**)

Capital gain An increase in the market value of a piece of property that occurs between the time it is bought and the time it is sold. (235)

Capital good An item that is used to produce other goods and services in the future, rather than being consumed today. (42) (**42**)

Capital loss A decrease in the market value of a piece of property that occurs between the time it is bought and the time it is sold. (235)

Cartel Group of sellers of a product who have joined together to control its production, sale, and price in the hope of obtaining the advantages of monopoly. (**235**)

Central bank A bank for banks. The central bank of the United States is the Federal Reserve System. (269)

Closed economy An economy that does not trade with other nations in either goods or services. (435)

Closed shop An arrangement that permits only union members to be hired. (**424**)

Collective bargaining Negotiations between union representatives of an industry's labor force and the employers of those workers. (**428**)

Commodity money An object used as a medium of exchange but which also has substantial value in alternative (nonmonetary) uses. (251)

Common stock A piece of paper that gives the stockholder a share in ownership of the company. (276)

Comparable worth A pay standard that assigns equal wages to jobs judged "comparable." (444)

Comparative advantage Of one country over another in the production of a particular good relative to other goods it can produce is said to occur if it produces that good least inefficiently compared with the other country. (385)

Complements Refers to two goods if an increase in the price of one reduces the quality demanded of the other, all other things remaining constant. (107)

Concentration of industry The share of the industry's total output (in money terms) supplied by some given number (usually four) of its largest firms. (322)

Concentration ratio Percentage of an industry's output produced by its *four* largest firms. It is intended to measure the degree to which the industry is dominated by large firms, that is, how closely it approximates a monopoly. (323)

Consumer expenditure (consumption) Symbolized by the letter C; the total amount spent by consumers on newly produced goods and services (excluding purchases of new homes, which are considered investment goods). (139)

Consumer Price Index The most popular index number for the price level. Its weights are based on the spending patterns of a typical urban household. (113)

Consumer sovereignty Consumer preferences determine what goods shall be produced, and in what amounts. (479)

Consumption function Relationship between total consumer expenditure and total disposable income in the economy, holding all other determinants of consumer spending constant. (147)

Consumption good An item which is available for immediate use by households and which satisfies wants of members of households without contributing directly to future production by the economy. (42) (42)

Corporation A firm with the legal status of a fictional individual. It is owned by stockholders and run by elected officers and a board of directors, whose chairman often influences the firm's affairs. (272)

Correlation A relationship between two variables such that they tend to go up or down together. Correlation need not imply causation. (14) (14)

Cost disease of personal services Tendency of the cost of services such as auto repair and legal counsel to rise faster than the economy's overall inflation rate because it is difficult to increase productivity (output per person hours) in these services. (256)

Craft union Represents a particular type of skilled worker regardless of the industry. (424)

Cross elasticity of demand For product X to a change in the price of another product, Y, is the ratio of the percentage change in quantity demanded of product X to the percentage change in the price of product Y that brings about the change in quantity demanded. (107)

Cross-subsidization Selling one product at a loss, which is balanced by higher profits on another product. (296)

Crowding in Occurs when government spending, by raising real GNP, induces increases in private investment spending. (335)

Crowding out Occurs when deficit spending by the government forces private investment spending to contract. (335)

Cyclical unemployment The portion of unemployment that is attributable to a decline in the economy's total production. Cyclical unemployment rises during recessions and falls as prosperity is restored. (96)

Deficit, balance of payments Amount by which the quantity supplied of a country's currency (per year) exceeds the quantity demanded. Such deficits arise when the exchange rate is artificially high. (416)

Deflating (by a price index) Dividing some nominal magnitude by a price index in order to express that magnitude in dollars of constant purchasing power. (114)

Deflation A sustained decrease in the general price level. (81)

Demand, law of States that a lower price generally increases the amount of a commodity that people in a market are willing to buy. Thus, for most goods, demand curves have a negative slope. (95)

Demand curve A graph showing how the quantity demanded of a certain product during a specified period of time changes as the price of the product changes, holding all other determinants of quantity demanded constant. (53) (53)

Demand schedule A table showing how the quantity demanded of a

certain product during a given period of time changes as the price of the product changes, holding all other determinants of quantity demanded constant. (53) (53)

Deposit creation Process by which the banking system turns a dollar of reserves into several dollars of deposits. (259)

Deposit insurance A system that guarantees that most depositors will not lose money even if their bank goes bankrupt. Most deposits are insured against loss by the Federal Deposit Insurance Corporation (FDIC) or the Federal Savings and Loan Insurance Corporation (FSLIC). (257)

Depreciation (of capital goods) The value of the portion of the nation's capital equipment that is used up within the year. It indicates how much output is needed just to keep the economy's capital stock intact. (160)

Depreciation (of a currency) Is said to occur when exchange rates change so that a unit of its own currency can buy fewer units of foreign currency. (408)

Depreciation allowances Tax deductions that businesses may claim when they spend money on investment goods. (167)

Devaluation Reduction in the official value of a currency. (409)

Direct taxes Taxes levied directly on the people. (334)

Discount rate The interest rate the Fed charges on loans it makes to banks. (276)

Discounting Process of determining the present worth of a quantity of money receivable or payable at some future date. (407)

Discouraged worker An unemployed person who gives up looking for work and is therefore no longer counted as part of the labor force. (94)

Discrimination, economic Occurs when equivalent factors of production receive different payments for equal contributions to output. (447)

Discrimination, statistical Occurs when the productivity of a particular worker is estimated to be low just because that worker belongs to a particular group. (449)

Disguised unemployment Occurs when tasks are carried out by a number of persons larger than the number that can complete them most efficiently. (477)

Disposable income A measure of income derived by subtracting personal income taxes from personal income. (140)

Diversification Including a number and variety of stocks, bonds, and other such items in an individual's portfolio of investments. (279)

Division of labor Breaking up a task into smaller, more specialized tasks so that each worker can become more skilled in the particular job. Division of labor creates efficiency and increases productivity. (44) (44)

Dual labor market theory Asserts that workers generally work in one of two types of jobs—those which offer opportunities for acquisition of skills and promotions, and "dead end jobs" which offer little scope for improvement. (419)

Dumping Selling goods in a foreign market at lower prices than those charged in the home market. (402)

Econometric model A set of mathematical equations that embody the economist's model of the economy. (310)

Economic growth A condition in which an economy is able to produce more goods and services for each consumer. (42) (42)

Economic model A simplified, small-scale version of some aspect of the economy. Economic models are often expressed in equations, graphs, or words. (14) (14)

Economic power A buyer or seller is said to have economic power if, by his own actions, he can influence the market price. (507)

Economic profit Net earnings minus the firm's opportunity cost of capital. (187)

Economic profit, total Of a firm or an industry, is the total revenue it derives from the sale of its products minus the total cost of its inputs, including the opportunity cost of any inputs supplied by the proprietors. (151)

Economic rent Said to be earned whenever a factor of production receives a reward that exceeds the minimum amount necessary to keep the factor in its present employment. (399)

Economies of scale Savings acquired through increases in quantities produced. (135, 295)

Economies of scope Savings acquired through simultaneous production of many different products. (296)

Efficiency The absence of waste, achieved primarily by gains in productivity resulting from specialization, division of labor, and a system of exchange. (43) (43)

Efficient allocation of resources One that takes advantage of every opportunity to make some individuals better off in their own estimation while not worsening the lot of anyone else. (193)

Elasticity of demand, price Ratio of the *percentage* change in quantity demanded to the *percentage* change in price that brings about the change in quantity demanded. (99)

Employment Act of 1946 Act in which Congress declared the achievement of full employment to be a goal of national policy. (96)

Entrepreneurship The act of starting new firms, introducing new products and technological innovations, and, in general, taking the risks necessary in seeking out business opportunities. (386)

Equation of exchange States that the money value of GNP transactions must be equal to the product of the average stock of money times velocity (M x V = P x Y). (291)

Equilibrium A situation in which there are no inherent forces that produce change. Changes away from an equilibrium position occur only as a result of "outside events" that disturb the status quo. (57, 169) (57)

Equilibrium level of GNP (on the demand side) Level of GNP which makes aggregate demand equal to production. (169)

Equilibrium price Price at which quantity demanded and quantity supplied are equal. This common quantity is called the equilibrium quantity. (175)

Excess burden of a tax The amount by which the burden of the tax exceeds the tax that is paid. (344)

Excess capacity theorem Asserts that monopolistic competitive firms will tend to produce outputs lower than those that minimize average costs, that is, that they will tend to produce less than their capacity. (232)

Excess reserves Reserves held in excess of the legal minimum. (259)

Exchange A mechanism by which workers can trade the various products resulting from specialization and the division of labor. (45) (45)

Exchange controls Laws restricting the exchange of one nation's currency for that of another. (423)

Exchange rate States the price, in terms of one currency, at which another currency can be bought. (408)

Exchange rates, fixed Rates set by government decisions and maintained by government actions. (415)

Exchange rates, floating Rates determined in free markets by the law of supply and demand. (409)

Excise tax Sales tax on a specific commodity. (97)

Expected rate of inflation Forecasted rate of price change. Also, the

difference between the nominal interest rate and the real interest rate. (105)

Expediture schedule Illustration of the relationship between national income (GNP) and total spending. (170)

Exponential growth Growth at a constant percentage rate. (461)

Export subsidy Payment by the government to exporters to permit them to reduce the selling price of their goods so they can compete more effectively in foreign markets. (394)

Externality, beneficial Result of an activity that causes incidental benefits to others with no corresponding compensation provided to or paid by those who generate the externality. (250)

Externality, detrimental Result of an activity that causes damages to others with no corresponding compensation provided to or paid by those who generate the externality. (250)

Federal Open Market Committee (FOMC) Chief policymaking committee of the Federal Reserve System. (271)

Federal Reserve System The central bank of the United States. (269)

Fiat money Money decreed as such by the government. It has little value as a commodity, but it maintains its value as a medium of exchange because people believe the issuer will back it and limit its production. (252)

Final goods and services Those that are purchased by their ultimate users. (79)

Fiscal federalism The system of grants from one level of government to the next. (341)

Fiscal policy The government's plan for spending and taxation, designed to direct aggregate demand in a desired direction. (221)

Fixed cost Cost of the indivisible inputs which the firm needs to produce any output at all. The total cost of these inputs does not change when output changes. (122)

Food Stamps Transfer program under which poor families receive coupons which they can exchange for food. (454)

A 45° line A ray through the origin with a slope of + 1. It marks off points where the variables measured on each axis have equal values, assuming that both variables are measured in the same units. (23) (23)

Fractional reserve banking A system under which bankers keep in their vaults as reserves only a fraction of the funds they hold on deposit. (256)

Frictional unemployment Unemployment resulting from the normal workings of the labor market. Includes people who are temporarily between jobs because they are moving or changing occupations, or for similar reasons. (95)

Game theory Analyzes the behavior of competing firms mathematically, treating this as analogous to the strategies of rival players in a competitive game. (238)

Gold-exchange system (Bretton Woods system) International monetary system that prevailed from 1944 to 1971. Under this system, the United States fixed the value of the dollar in terms of gold, and other countries fixed the values of their currencies in terms of the dollar. (421)

Gold standard System in which exchange rates are set in terms of gold and pegged by buying or selling gold as necessary. (420)

Government purchases Symbolized by the Letter G, all the goods and services purchased by all levels of government. Transfer payments, such as social security and unemployment benefits, are not included. (139)

Gross national product (GNP) The sum of the money values of all final goods and services produced by the economy during a specified period, usually one year. (78, 158)

Gross national product, nominal Calculated by valuing all outputs at current prices. (79)

Gross national product, real The sum of the real values of all final goods and services produced by the economy during a specified period, using the prices that prevailed in some agreed-upon year (currently 1982). (79)

Gross national product deflator Price index obtained by dividing nominal GNP by real GNP. (114)

Growth, disembodied Refers to increases in an economy's output which can occur without being accompanied by (embodied in) additional capital stock. (465)

Growth, embodied Refers to increases in an economy's output which are made possible by increased or improved plant, equipment, or other forms of capital. (465)

High-employment budget Hypothetical budget the United States *would have* if the economy were operating near full employment. (328)

Historical materialism Marx's theory that we cannot understand an economy without recognizing its place in history. Also, while historical events are influenced primarily (though not exclusively) by economic conditions, the form of this influence is often indirect and subtle, filtering through current social customs, political organizations, and similar structures. (464)

Horizontal equity The notion that equally situated persons should be taxed equally. (341)

Human capital theory Interprets education as an investment in a human being's earning power, just as an improvement in a factory is an investment in the factory's earning capacity. (417)

Incidence of a tax An allocation of the burden of the tax to specific individuals or groups. (344)

Income effect A portion of the change in quantity of a good demanded when its price changes. A rise in price cuts the consumer's purchasing power (real income), which leads to a change in the quantity demanded of that commodity. That change is the income effect. (81)

Income-expenditure diagram (45° line diagram) A plotting of total real expenditures (on the vertical axis) against real income (on the horizontal axis). The 45° line marks off points where income and expenditure are equal. (173)

Incomes policy Variety of measures to curb inflation *without* reducing aggregate demand. (369)

Increasing costs, principle of As the production of a good expands, the opportunity cost of producing another such unit generally increases. (39) (39)

Indexing Provisions in a law or contract whereby monetary payments are automatically adjusted whenever a specified price index changes; sometimes called *escalator clauses*. (374)

Index number A number indicating the percentage change in some variable (such as the price level) between the base period and some other period. Typically, the value of the index number in the base period is arbitrarily set to 100. (112)

Indicative planning Government guidance rather than direct control of economic activity. (487)

Indifference curve Line connecting all combinations of commodities that are equally desirable to the consumer. (87)

Indirect taxes Taxes levied on specific economic activities. (334)

Induced increase in consumption An increase in consumer spending that stems from an increase in consumer incomes. Represented graphically as a movement along a fixed consumption function. (190)

Induced investment Investment which rises when GNP rises and falls when GNP falls. (171)

Industrial union Represents all types of workers in a single industry. (424)

Inferior good A commodity whose quantity demanded falls when the purchaser's real income rises, all other things remaining equal. (81)

Inflation A sustained increase in the general price level. (77)

Inflation, creeping An inflation that proceeds for a long time at a moderate and fairly steady pace. (109)

Inflation, galloping An inflation that proceeds at an exceptionally high rate, perhaps for only a relatively brief period. This type of inflation is generally characterized by accelerating inflation rates, so that the inflation rate is higher this month than last month. (109)

Inflation accounting Adjusting standard accounting procedures for the fact that inflation lowers the purchasing power of money. (326)

Inflationary gap The amount by which equilibrium real GNP exceeds the full-employment level of GNP. (176)

Innovation The act of putting a new idea into practical use. (404)

Input Any item which a firm uses in its production process. (117)

Interest Payment for the use of funds employed in the production of capital; measured as a percent per year of the value of the funds tied up in the capital. (391)

Intermediate good One that is bought for resale or for use in producing another good. (79)

International Monetary Fund (IMF) International organization set up originally to police and manage the gold-exchange system. (421)

Invention The act of generating a new idea. (404)

Investment Flow of resources into the production of new capital. (390)

Investment, gross private domestic Sum of business investment expenditures on plant and equipment, residential construction expenditures, and inventory change. (158)

Investment schedule Table or curve showing how investment spending depends on GNP. (171)

Investment spending Symbolized by the letter *I*, the sum of the expenditures of business firms on new plant and equipment, plus the expenditures of households on new homes. Financial investments and resales of existing physical assets are not included. (139)

J curve A curve that shows the typical pattern of response of net exports to a change in currency values. (440)

Jawboning Informal pressures on firms and unions to slow down the rates at which prices and wages are rising. (369)

Labor force The number of people seeking jobs. (94)

Labor productivity A measure of total output divided by the amount of labor used to produce it. It is a measure of output per unit of labor employed. (120)

Laissez faire A program of minimal interference with the workings of the market system. (198)

Leading indicator A variable that, experience has shown, normally turns down before recessions start and turns up before expansions begin. (311)

Less developed countries (LDCs) Countries whose share of output composed of agricultural products, mining, and the like is relatively high, which engage in relatively little industrial high-technology activity, and whose per capita incomes are generally comparatively low. (468)

Liability An item that an individual or a firm owes; collectively, liabilities are known as *debts*. (258)

Liability, limited Legal obligation of a firm's owners to pay back company debts only with the money they have already invested in the firm. (272)

Liability, unlimited Legal obligation of a firm's owners to repay company debts with whatever resources they own. (270)

Libertarianism School of thought that emphasizes the importance of individual freedom. (503)

Limited partnership A firm, generally small, which though organized as a partnership, gives some of the partners the legal protection of limited liability. (274)

Liquidity, of an asset The ease with which it can be converted into cash. (255)

Long run Period of time long enough for all the firm's commitments to come to an end. (127)

Loophole, tax Special provision in the tax code that reduces taxation below normal rates (perhaps to zero) if certain conditions are met. (386)

Lorenz curve Graph depicting the distribution of income. (444)

M1 The narrowly defined money supply, which is the sum of all coins and paper money in circulation, plus certain checkable deposit balances at banks and savings institutions. (254)

M2 The broadly defined money supply, which is the sum of all coins and paper money in circulation, plus all types of checking account balances, most forms of savings account balances, shares in money market mutual funds, and a few other minor items. (255)

Macroeconomics The study of the behavior of economies. (75)

Marginal cost, long-run *Addition* to the supplier's total cost resulting from the supply of the output *including whatever additional plant and equipment* is needed in the long run to provide that output. Inclusion of this marginal capital cost (of the necessary additions to plant and equipment) is the crucial distinction between *long-run* and *short-run* marginal cost. (300)

Marginal cost curve Shows, for each output, the increase in the firm's total cost required if it increases its output by an additional unit. (121)

Marginal land Land that is just on the borderline of being used. (397)

Marginal physical product (MPP) Increase in total output that results from a one-unit increase in the input, holding the amounts of all other inputs constant. (118, 387)

Marginal profit The addition to total profit resulting from one more unit of output. (154)

Marginal propensity to consume (MPC) Ratio of the change in consumption to the change in disposable income that produces the change in consumption. On a graph, it appears as the slope of the consumption function. (148)

Marginal propensity to save (MPS) Graphically, the slope of the saving function, which indicates how much more consumers will save if disposable income rises by $1 billion. (156)

Marginal returns, law of diminishing To an input, X, asserts that if the quantities of all other inputs are held constant, the employment of additional quantities of X by a firm or an industry will eventually yield smaller and smaller (marginal) increases in output. (120)

Marginal revenue (MR) The addition to total revenue resulting from the addition of one unit to total output. (183)

Marginal revenue product (MRP) Additional revenue earned from increased sales of an input when an additional unit of the input is used. (130, 387)

Marginal social cost (MSC) The sum of *marginal private cost (MPC)*, which is the share of marginal cost caused by an activity that is paid for by the persons who carry out the activity, and *incidental cost*, which is the share borne by others. (251)

Marginal utility, law of diminishing Asserts that additional units of a commodity are worth less and less to a consumer in money terms. As the individual's consumption increases, the marginal utility of each additional unit declines. (76)

Market The set of all sale and purchase transactions that affect the price of some commodity. (173)

Market demand curve Shows how the total quantity demanded of some product during a specified period of time changes as the price of the product changes, other things being constant. (94)

Market power The ability of a firm to raise its price significantly above the competitive price level and to maintain this high price profitably for a considerable period. (328)

Market system A form of organization of the economy in which decisions on resource allocation are left to the independent decisions of individual producers and consumers acting in their own best interests without central direction. (46) (46)

Maximin criterion Selecting the strategy that yields the maximum payoff, on the assumption that your opponent does as much damage to you as he can. (241)

Mediation Process in which an outsider is brought into a labor management negotiation in the hope that this person can lead the two sides to a voluntary agreement through persuasion. (430)

Merger The combining of two previously independent firms under a single owner or group of owners. A **horizontal merger** involves two firms producing similar products. A **vertical merger** involves two firms one of which supplies an ingredient of the other's product. A **conglomerate merger** is the union of two unrelated firms. (321)

Microeconomics The study of the behavior of individual decision-making units, such as farmers or consumers. (74)

Minimum-wage law Requires all employees (with some specified exceptions) to be paid at least some fixed given dollar amount per hour. Congress has increased this minimum wage several times in the past. (411)

Monetarism Mode of analysis that uses the equation of exchange to organize macroeconomic data. (295)

Monetary policy Actions that the Federal Reserve System takes to change the equilibrium of the money market; that is, to alter the money supply, move interest rates, or both. (281)

Monetizing the deficit The effect of the central bank's purchasing the bonds the government issues. (332)

Money Medium of exchange; that is, the standard object used in exchanging goods and services. (251)

Money fixed asset Asset with a face value fixed in terms of dollars, such as money, government bonds, and corporate bonds. (150)

Monopolistic competition Competition among firms each of which has products that are somewhat different from those of its rivals. (228)

Monopoly, pure Industry in which there is only one supplier of a product for which there are no close substitutes, and in which it is difficult or impossible for another firm to coexist. (214)

Monopsony Market situation in which there is only one buyer. (428)

Moral hazard Tendency of insurance to encourage risk taking. (263)

Moral suasion Informal requests and warnings designed to persuade banks to limit their borrowings from the Fed. (277)

Multinational corporations Corporations whose production activities occur in a number of different countries. (473)

The multiplier The ratio of the change in equilibrium GNP (Y) divided by the original change in spending that causes the change in GNP. (184)

National debt Federal government's total indebtedness, which has resulted from previous deficits. (322)

National income The sum of the incomes of all individuals in the economy earned in the forms of wages, interest, rents, and profits. It excludes transfer payments and is calculated before any deductions are taken for income taxes. (140)

National income accounting Bookkeeping and measurement system for national economic data. (157)

Nationalization Government ownership and operation of a business firm. (311)

National product The total production of a nation's economy. (75)

Natural monopoly Industry in which advantages of large-scale production make it possible for a single firm to produce the entire output of the market at lower average cost than a

number of firms each producing a smaller quantity. (215)

Natural rate of unemployment The unemployment rate when the economy is at "full employment." (356)

Near moneys Liquid assets that are close substitutes for money. (255)

Negative income tax Transfer program under which families with income below a certain threshold (the "breakeven level") would receive cash benefits from the government; these benefits would decline as income rose. (**454**)

Net exports Exports minus imports. (139)

Net national product (NNP) Gross national product minus depreciation. (160)

Net worth The value of all assets minus the value of all liabilities. (258)

Oligopoly Market dominated by a few sellers, at least several of which are large enough relative to the total market to be able to influence the market price. (233)

Open-market operations The Fed's purchase or sale of government securities through transactions in the open market. (272)

Open economy An economy that trades with other nations in goods and services. (432)

Opportunity cost The foregone value of the next best alternative that is not chosen. (36) (**36**)

Origin The lower left-hand corner of a graph where the two axes meet. In two-variable diagrams, both variables equal zero at the origin. (19) (**19**)

Output The good or service that a firm produces. (**117**)

Paradox of thrift The fact that an effort by a nation to save more may simply reduce national income and fail to raise total savings. (192)

Partnership A firm whose ownership is shared by a fixed number of proprietors. (271)

Patent A temporary grant of monopoly rights over an innovation. (327)

Perfectly contestable market One in which entry and exit are costless and unimpeded. (245)

Personal income A measure of income derived by subtracting corporate profits, retained earnings, and payroll taxes from national income, then adding in transfer payments. Personal income measures the income that actually accrues to individuals. (163)

Phillips curve Graph depicting the rate

of unemployment on the horizontal axis and either the rate of inflation or the rate of change of money wages on the vertical axis; normally downward sloping, indicating that higher inflation rates are associated with lower unemployment rates. (351)

Phillips curve, vertical (long run) Shows the menu of inflation/unemployment choices available to society in the long run; a vertical straight line at the natural rate of unemployment. (356)

Potential gross national product The real GNP the economy would produce if its labor and other resources were fully employed. (99)

Poverty line Amount of income below which a family is considered "poor." (**440**)

Price ceiling Legal maximum price that can be charged. (64) (**64**)

Price discrimination Charging different prices to different buyers of the same product. (319)

Price floor Legal minimum price that can be charged. (66) (**66**)

Price leadership One firm sets the price for the industry and the others follow. (236)

Price war A situation in which each competing firm is determined to sell at a price that is lower than the price of its rivals, usually regardless of whether that price covers the pertinent cost. (237)

Private good Commodity or service whose benefits are depleted by an additional user and for which people are excluded from its benefits. (**255**)

Production function The *maximum* amount of product that can be obtained from any specified *combination* of inputs, given the current state of knowledge. (131)

Production indifference curve (sometimes called an *isoquant*), a curve in a graph showing quantities of *inputs* on its axes. Each indifference curve indicates *all* combinations of input quantities capable of producing *a given* quantity of output. (141)

Production possibilities frontier A graphical presentation of the different combinations of various goods that a producer can turn out, given the available resources and existing technology. (38) (**38**)

Productivity The amount of output produced by a unit of input. (201)

Profit sharing A system of compensating labor in which workers receive both a fixed base wage and a share of the company's profits. (373)

Progressive tax One in which the average tax rate paid by an individual rises as his income rises. (334)

Property tax Tax on assessed value of real property. (340)

Proportional tax One in which the average tax rate is the same at all income levels. (334)

Proprietorship Business firm owned by a single person. (270)

Public good Commodity or service whose benefits are *not depleted* by an additional user and for which it is generally difficult or *impossible to exclude* people from its benefits, even if they are unwilling to pay for it. (255)

Purchasing power The purchasing power of a given sum of money is the volume of goods and services it will buy. (100)

Purchasing-power parity theory (of exchange rates) Theory that the exchange rate between any two national currencies adjusts to reflect differences in the price levels of the two nations. (411)

Quantity demanded The number of units consumers want to buy. (52) (52)

Quantity supplied The number of units sellers want to sell. (54) (54)

Quantity theory of money A simple theory of aggregate demand based on the idea that velocity is constant, so that norminal GNP is proportional to the money stock. (291)

Quota Specifies the maximum amount of a good that is permitted into the country from abroad per unit of time. (394)

Random walk The time path of a variable, such as the price of a stock, when its magnitude in one period equals its value in the preceding period plus a completely random number. (288)

Rate of interest, nominal The percentage by which the money the borrower pays back exceeds the money that he borrowed, making no adjustment for any fall in the purchasing power of this money that results from inflation. (105)

Rate of interest, real The percentage increase in purchasing power that the borrower pays to the lender for the privilege of borrowing. It indicates the increased ability to purchase goods and services that the lender earns. (105)

Rational decision A decision that best serves the objective of the decision maker, whatever the objective may be. The term "rational" connotes neither approval nor disapproval of the objective. (36) (36)

Rational expectations Forecasts which,

while not necessarily correct, are the best that can be made given the available data. If expectations are rational, forecasting errors are pure random numbers. (363)

Ray through the origin (or ray) A straight line emanating from the origin, or zero point on a graph. (23) (23)

Recession A period during which the total output of the economy declines. (78)

Recessionary gap The amount by which the equilibrium level of real GNP falls short of potential GNP. (176)

Regressive tax One in which the average tax rate falls as income rises. (334)

Relative price The price of an item in terms of some other item rather than in terms of dollars. (102)

Regulation of industry A process established by law which restricts or controls some specified decisions made by the affected firms. (252)

Rent seeking Unproductive activity in the pursuit of profit. (282)

Required reserves The minimum amount of reserves (in cash or the equivalent) required by law. Required reserves are usually proportional to the volume of deposits. (258)

Resources The instruments provided by nature or by people that are used to create the goods and services people want. (35) (35)

Research and Development (R and D) The activity of business firms in which systematic efforts are undertaken to invent new or improved products or productive techniques and to make them ready to market or for use in production processes. (127)

Retained earnings (plowback) The portion of a corporation's profits that management decides to keep and reinvest in the firm's operations rather than pay out directly to stockholders in the form of dividends. (275)

Revaluation Increase in the official value of a currency. (409)

Run on a bank An event that occurs when many depositors withdraw cash from their accounts almost simultaneously. (249)

Sales maximizing firm One whose objective is to sell as much of its outputs as possible (measured in terms of the revenue they bring in) rather than to maximize the company's product. (237)

Saving function The schedule relating total consumer saving to disposable income in the economy, holding

other determinants of saving constant. (156)

Saving schedule Table or curve showing how saving depends on GNP. (173)

Scatter diagram Graph showing the relationship between two variables. Each year is represented by a point in the diagram. The coordinates of each year's point show the value of the two variables in that year. (145)

Self-correcting mechanism The economy's way of curing inflationary or recessionary gaps automatically via inflation or deflation. (327)

Seniority rules Rules which give special job-related advantages to workers who have held their jobs longest. (425)

Service industry One that does not turn out physical products. (128)

Shortage An excess of quantity demanded over quantity supplied. When a shortage exists, buyers cannot purchase the quantities they want. (57) (57)

Short run A shorter period of time than the long run so that some, but not all, of the firm's commitments will have ended. (511)

Slope of a budget line Amount of one commodity the market requires an individual to give up in order to obtain one additional unit of another commodity without any change in the amount of money spent. (89)

Slope of a curved line At any particular point, the slope of the straight line that is tangent to the curved line at that point. (21) (21)

Slope of an indifference curve Referred to as the marginal rate of substitution between the commodities involved, represents the maximum amount of one commodity the consumer is willing to give up in exchange for one more unit of another commodity. (89)

Slope of a straight line The ratio of the vertical change to the corresponding horizontal change as we move to the right along the line. The ratio of the "rise" over the "run." (20) (20)

Socialism Method of economic organization in which the state owns the means of production. (479)

Specialization The process whereby a worker becomes more skilled at a particular job. Specialization enables division of labor and the consequent increase in productivity. (382)

Speculation Investment in risky assets in the hope of obtaining a profit from unexpected changes in the prices of these assets. (285)

Stabilization policy The name given to government programs designed to prevent or shorten recessions and to counteract inflation (that is, to stabilize prices). (88)

Stagflation Inflation that occurs while the economy is growing slowly ("stagnating") or having a recession. (86)

Store of value An item used to store wealth from one point in time to another. (251)

Structural unemployment Refers to workers who have lost their jobs because they have been displaced by automation, because their skills are no longer in demand, or for similar reasons. (95)

Subchapter S corporation A small corporation which is permitted to escape part of the burden of double taxation. (274)

Substitutes Refers to two goods if an increase in the price of one raises the quantity demanded of the other, all other things remaining constant. (107)

Substitution effect Change in quantity demanded of a good resulting from a change in its relative price, exclusive of whatever change in quantity demanded may be attributable to the associated change in real income. (81)

Sunk cost A cost to which a firm is precommitted for some limited period, either because the firm has signed a contract to make the payments or because the firm has already paid for some durable item and cannot get its money back except by using that item to produce output for some period of time. (127)

Supply curve A graph showing how the quantity supplied of some product during a specified period of time changes as the price of that product changes, holding all other determinants of quantity supplied constant. (55) (55)

Supply-demand diagram Diagram showing both a supply curve and a demand curve. (56) (56)

Supply schedule A table showing how the quantity supplied of some product during a specified period of time changes as the price of that product changes, holding all other determinants of quantity supplied constant. (55) (55)

Surplus An excess of quantity supplied over quantity demanded. When there is a surplus, sellers cannot sell the quantities they want to supply. (57) (57)

Surplus, balance of payment Amount by which the quantity demanded of a country's currency (per year) exceeds the quantity supplied. Such

surpluses arise when the exchange rate is artificially low. (416)

Tariff Tax on imports. (394)

Tax-based incomes policy An incomes policy that uses the tax system to provide incentives favoring noninflationary behavior. (373)

Tax deduction A sum of money that may be subtracted before the taxpayer computes his or her taxable income. (336)

Tax rate, average Ratio of taxes to income. (334)

Tax rate, marginal Fraction of each *additional* dollar of income that is paid in taxes. (718) (334)

Tax shifting Occurs when the economic reactions to a tax cause prices and outputs in the economy to change, thereby shifting part of the burden of the tax onto others. (345)

Technostructure Professionals who, according to Galbraith, run most of the important economic institutions, including corporations, government bureaus, and large unions. (508)

Theory A deliberate simplification of relationships whose purpose is to explain how those relationships work. (13) (13)

Time series graph A type of two-variable diagram that depicts the change in a variable over time. The horizontal axis always represents time. (25) (25)

Total cost curve Shows, for each possible quantity of output, the total amount which the firm must spend for its inputs to produce that amount of output plus any opportunity cost incurred in the process. (121)

Total physical product (TPP) curve A curve that shows what happens to the quantity of a firm's output as one changes the quantity of one of the firm's inputs while holding the quantities of all other inputs unchanged. (117)

Trade adjustment assistance Provides special unemployment benefits, loans, retraining programs, and other aid to workers and firms that are harmed by foreign competition. (399)

Transfer payments Sums of money that certain individuals receive as outright grants from the government rather than as payments for services rendered to employers. (141)

Unemployment insurance Government program under which some, but not all, employed workers receive transfer payments. (97)

Unemployment rate The number of unemployed people, expressed as a percentage of the labor force. (94)

Union shop An arrangement under which nonunion workers may be hired but then must join the union within a specified period of time. (424)

Unit of account The standard unit for quoting prices. (251)

Usury law Establishes a maximum permissible interest rate for a particular type of loan. Loans at rates above the usury ceiling are illegal. (106)

Utility, marginal Of a commodity to a consumer (measured in money terms) is the maximum amount of money he or she is willing to pay for *one more unit* of it. (78)

Utility, total Of a quantity of goods to a consumer (measured in money terms) is the maximum amount of money he or she is willing to give in exchange for it. (79)

Value added The value added by a company is its revenue from selling a product minus the amount paid for goods and services purchased from other firms. (161)

Variable An object, such as price, whose magnitude is measured by a number. (18) (18)

Variable cost Any cost that is not a fixed cost. (122)

Velocity Number of times per year that an "average dollar" is spent on goods and services; the ratio of nominal GNP to the number of dollars in the money stock. (291)

Vertical equity The notion that differently situated persons should be taxed differently in a way that society deems fair. (342)

Wage-price controls Legal restrictions on the ability of industry and labor to raise wages and prices. (371)

Wage-price freeze An outright ban on wage or price increases. (373)

Wage-price guideposts Numerical standards for permissible wage and price increases. (370)

Wage rate, real The wage rate adjusted for inflation. It indicates the volume of goods and services that money wages will buy. (100)

Welfare state A variety of government programs aimed at assisting the poor and protecting individuals from the rigors of the marketplace. (486)

Workers' management System under which employees of an enterprise make most of the decisions normally reserved for management. (489)

Index

Page numbers for *Macroeconomics* are shown in regular type. Those for *Microeconomics* are shown in boldface.

A

Ability-to-pay principle, **342**
Absolute advantage, 384
Abstraction
  defined, 10 **10**
  determination of national income and, 11–12, **11–12**
  distribution of income and, 11 **11**
Accelerated depreciation, 235
Accounting, national income, 157–58
Accounting profits, **188**
Addyston Pipe case, 320
Adelman, M. A., 324
Advertising, **108–109, 114**
  oligopoly and, **228**
AFDC-UF programs, **454**
Affirmative action, **458–59**
Agents, defined, **263**
Aggregate demand, 165
  algebraic treatment of, 244–47
  defined, 139
  inflation and, 207, 345–46
  interest rates and, 282–83
  in the Keynesian model, 283–85
  monetarist versus Keynesian prediction of, 295–96
  unemployment and, 89
Aggregate demand curve, 77, 173–75
  downward slope of, 287
  inflationary gaps and, 206–207
  international trade and, 439
  multiplier and, 193–94
Aggregate saving, 155–56
Aggregate supply, 165, 202–204
  in an open economy, 442
Aggregate supply curve, 77, 198–202
  capital and, 201–202
  defined, 198
  Keynesian–monetarist debate over, 304–306
  shape of, 202
  shifts of, 200–202
Aggregation, 75–76
Aid to Families with Dependent Children (AFDC), **453–54**
Airline industry, equilibrium in, 60–61, **60–61**
Air pollution, **357**
Alienation, **472–73, 515**
American Capitalism (Galbraith), **507**
American Federation of Labor (AFL), **422**
American Stock Exchange, **282**
American Telephone and Telegraph (AT&T), 295, 299
  breakup of, **316**
American Tobacco Company, 320
AMTRAK, 307
Analytical cost curve, **138**
Antitrust laws, **317–20**
Antitrust policy, **315–17**
  issues in, **328–29**

Antitrust suits, **315**
Appreciation, of currency, 408
Arbitration, defined, **430**
Asset, defined, 258
Assymetric information, **263**
Automatic stabilizers, 309
Autonomous increase in consumption, 190
Average cost curve (ACC), **121**
  long-run, **137**
  shape of, **125–26**
  in the short and long runs, **127–28**
Average curves, **168**
Average fixed costs (AFC), **124**
Average physical product (APP), **117**
Average revenue (AR), **152**
Average tax rate, **334**
Average variable cost (AVC), **180**

B

Balance of payments, 415–18
  in practice, 418
Balance of payments deficit, 416
Balance of payments surplus, 416
Balance of trade, 419
Balance sheet, 258
Banking
  bank regulation, 257–58
  bookkeeping of, 258–59
  deposit creation, 259–61, 265–66
  deposit destruction, 264–65
  deregulation of, 248–49
  fractional reserve, 256–57
  lending to banks, 276–77
  money supply mechanism, 278–79
  multiple money creation, 261–64
  origins of, 255–57
  principles of bank management, 257
  see also Federal Reserve System
Banks, investment, **282**
Barriers to entry, **215**
Barter system, 250
Bastiat, Frederic, 402
Beneficial externality, **250, 332**
Benefits principle of taxation, **342–43**
Bilateral monopoly, **428**
Black market, 64–65, **64–65**
Board of Governors (Federal Reserve System), 270–71
Bonds, 273–74, **276–77**
  buying, **278–79**
  interest rates and, **277–78**
  risk and, **278**
Boulding, Kenneth, 465–66
Brain drain, defined, **478**
Break-even analysis, **179–81**
Bretton Woods system, 421–22
  adjustment mechanisms under, 422–24
Bretton Woods treaty, **454**
Bubble concept, **370–71**
Budget deficit, 4, **4**

crowding-out and crowding-in effects, 335–37
  debate over, 341–42
  defined, 322
  economic effects of, 338–41
  inflation and, 331–34
  interest rates and, 335
  interpreting the, 324–30
  outlawing, to balance the budget, 340
  Reaganomics and, 319–20, 329–30, 341–42
  trade deficit and, 449–50
  versus national debt, 322
  see also National debt
Budget line, **85–86**
  for firms, **144–45**
  production indifference curve and, **144–45**
  properties of, **86–87**
  slope of, **88–90**
Budget surpluses, state and local, 329
Burden of a tax, **343**
Bureau of Economic Analysis, 313
Bureau of Labor Statistics (BLS), 94, 113
Business confidence, 166
Business cycles, 81, 82
Business firm
  budget line for, **144–45**
  cost curves of, **134–35**
  discrimination and, **448–49**
  economies of scale and, **135–37**
  maximizing profits of, **150–51**
  price-quantity decisions of, **148–50**
  short-run profit of, **177–78**
  short-term losses of, **178–79**
  shut-down of, **179**
  total profit and, **151–53**
  types of, **269–76**
  see also Marginal analysis
Business firms (one-variable input case)
  physical products of, **117–18**
Business losses, short-term, **178–79**

C

Capacity utilization, investment and, 166–67
Capital
  aggregate supply curve and, 201–202
  defined, **390**
Capital account, 419
Capital flows, international, 444–45
Capital gain, defined, 235
Capital goods, 42, **42**
Capitalism
  defined, **479**
  Marx's view of, **475**
  versus socialism, **483–84**
Capitalism and Freedom (Friedman), **506**
Capital loss, defined, 235
Cartel, **235–36**

Carter, Jimmy, 369, 370, **196**, **295**
Celler-Kefauver Antimerger Act, **318**, **319**
Central bank, 269
Centrally planned economy, 463–64
Central planning, **201–202**
Chamberlin, Edward, **228**
"Chicago School," **503**
China
  in the 1970s and 1980s, **499–500**
  under Mao Tse-tung, **497–99**
Choice
  for a single firm, 37–39, **37–39**
  for the entire society, 39–41, **39–41**
  for households, **41**, 41
  necessity and, 34–35, **34–35**
  scarcity and, **35**, 35
Circular flow diagram, 140, 141–42,
  167–68
Civil Rights Act of 1964, **457**
Clayton Act, **318**, **319**
Closed economy, **435**
Closed shop, **424**
Collective bargaining, **428–31**
  in the public sector, **431–32**
Commodities. *See* Public goods
Commodity money, 251–52, 253
Common Market, **427**
Common stocks, **276**
Communism
  in China, **497–500**
  nature of communist society, **466–67**
Communist Manifesto (Marx), **464**, **465**,
  475
Comparable worth, **458**
Comparative advantage, 398
  arithmetic of, 386–88
  competition of foreign labor and, 392
  graphics of, 388–90
  law of, 4–5, 384–85, **4–5**
Competition
  monopolistic, **173**
  perfect, **173**, **174**
  self-destructive, **297**
Competitive firm
  demand curve of, **175**
  short-run equilibrium of, **175–77**
  short-run supply curve of, **181**
Competitive industry
  equilibrium in the long run, **183–86**
  equilibrium in the short run, **182–83**
  long-run supply curve for, **186–87**
  regulation of, **292–94**
  short-run supply curve of, **181–82**
Complements, 108, **110–11**
Computer industry, equilibrium in, 63, **63**
Concentration, market power and, **328–29**
Concentration of industry, **322–23**
  statistics on, **323–25**
Concentration ratio, **323–24**
Conglomerate merger, **321**
Congress of Industrial Organizations
  (CIO), **424**
Conservatism, 46–47, **46–47**
Constant returns to scale, **136**
Consumer choice
  rule of, **90**
  theory of, 83
  see also Budget line
Consumer expenditure, elasticity and, **105**
  see also Consumption

Consumer Price Index (CPI), 113–14, **442**
Consumer protection, regulation and, **298**
Consumers
  incomes of, 58–59, **58–59**
  manipulation of, **513–14**
  preferences of, 60, **60**
  in the Soviet Union, **493**
Consumer sovereignty, **479**
Consumer spending
  changes in tax laws and, 153–54
  determinants of, 150–52
  income and, 144–47
  multiplier effect of, 190–91
Consumption (C)
  autonomous increase in, 190
  defined, 139
  elasticity and, **105**
  induced increase in, 190
Consumption function, 147–48
  movements along versus shifts in,
  149–50
Consumption good, 42, **42**
Consumption possibilities, 389–90
Contour maps, 24, **24**
Contracts, long-term, 108
Corporate income tax, 235, **335**, **338**
Corporations, 269, **272–74**
  double taxation of, 272, **273–74**
  financing, **274–76**
  multinational, **473**
  subchapter S, **274**
  see also Stocks; Bonds
Correlation, defined, 14, **14**
Cost, as defined by economists, 16, **16**
Cost curve
  of business firms, **134–35**
  historical versus analytical, **138–40**
Cost curves, **121–22**
  of business firms, **134–35**
  under monopoly, **223**
Cost minimization, 129, **140–41**
  for firms, **145**
Costs, long-run versus short-run, **126–27**
Craft union, **424**
Creeping inflation, 109–11
Crisis theory (Marx), **473–75**
Cross elasticity of demand, **107–108**
  DuPont case and, 110
Cross-subsidization, **296–97**
Cross-subsidy, **299**
Crowding-in effect, 335
Crowding-out effect, 335, 446
Cultural Revolution (China), **499**
Currency
  appreciation of, 408
  appreciations and depreciations of, 439,
  442, 443–44
  depreciation of, 408
  devaluation and revaluation of, 409
  exchange rates for, 407–408
  gold standard, 420–21
  supply and demand for, 410
Current account, 418, 419–20
Cyclical unemployment, 96

D

Das Kapital (Marx), **465**, **469**, **475**
Decreasing returns to scale, **136**

Deflating by a price index, defined, 114
Deflation, 81, 208–10
Deindustrialization, 132
Demand
  cross elasticity of, **107–108**
  investment and, 166–67
  law of, **95–96**
  quantity demanded and, 52–53, **52–53**
Demand curve, 19, 53, **19**, **53**
  advertising and prices of complements
  and substitutes and, **108–109**
  of competitive firms, 175
  downward slope of aggregate, 287
  horizontal, **179**, **180**
  kinked, **241–43**
  law of diminishing marginal utility and,
  78–79
  under monopoly, **222–23**
  perfectly elastic, **103**
  perfectly inelastic, **102–103**
  price changes and, **91–92**
  role of the shape of, **98–99**
  shifts in, 58–60, **58–60**
  time dimension of, **109–11**
Demand for money, 279
Demand inflation, 207
Demand management, 142–44, 368
Demand relationships, statistical analysis of,
  112–14
Demand schedule, 53, **53**
Demand-side equilibrium, 169–79
  employment and, **175–77**
  income determination and, 171–73
Demand-side inflation, Phillips curve and,
  348–52
Department of Agriculture, **294**
Department of Justice, mergers and, **321**
Depletability, **255**
Deposit creation, 259
Deposit destruction, 264–65
Deposit insurance, 257
Depreciation
  accelerated, 235
  of currency, 408
  defined, 160
Depreciation allowances, 167, 235
Deregulation, 369, 293, 306
  consequences of, **310–11**
  effects of, **308–10**
  see also Government regulation
Derived demand, **389**
Detrimental externality, **250**
Devaluation, defined, 409
Diagrams
  circular-flow, 140, 141–42
  income-expenditure, 173
  supply–demand, 56, **56**
  two-variable, 18–20, **18–20**
Diamond-water paradox, 75
  marginal and total utility and, 80
Diminishing marginal returns, 119–20
Diminishing returns, 130–31
Direct taxes, **334**
"Dirty float," **425**
Discounting, 392
  present value and, **407–408**
Discount rate, 276
Discouraged workers, 94
Discretionary stabilization policy, 307, 310,
  316

Discrimination. *See* Economic discrimination
Disembodied growth, 469
Disguised unemployment, 477
Disposable income (DI), 140, 144, 163
Distribution of goods, efficient, **209–211**
Diversification, defined, **279**
Division of labor, 34, 44, **34, 44**
Dollars, U.S., 426–27
Domestic savings, trade deficit and, 451–53
Double taxation, 272, 273, **273–74**
Dual labor market theory, 419
Dumping, defined, 402
DuPont antitrust case, **110**

E

E. C. Knight case, **320**
Earnings. *See* Wages
Ecological costs, 81
Economic Consequences of the Peace (Keynes), 178
Economic costs, 6–7, **6–7**
Economic discrimination, **447–48**
    policies to combat, **457–59**
    theory of, **448–50**
Economic efficiency, **188–89**
Economic forecasting
    accuracy of, 310, 314
    judgmental, 313
    techniques of, 310–13
Economic growth
    defined, 42, **42**
    desirability of, 466–68
    embodied versus disembodied, 465–66
    measuring, 458–59
    price of, 464–65
    requirements for, 463
    of the United States, 81
    in the United States and Japan, 42–43, **42–43**
Economic models, 14, 310–11, **14**
Economic policy, politics of, **265**
Economic power, 507
Economic profit, **402–403**
    opportunity cost and, **187–88**
    public opinion on, **403**
    taxation of, **404–405**
Economic rent, 399
Economics
    as a discipline, 9, **9**
    basic concepts of, 2–9, **2–9**
    disagreements concerning, 15, **15**
    need for abstraction in, 9–11, **9–11**
    radical, **511–17**
    radical views of mainstream, **572–74**
    role of economic theory, 13, **13**
    supply-side, 8, 87, 197–98, 234–37, 241, **8**
Economics of Welfare, The (Pigou), 355
Economic systems, **477**
    choosing among, **478**
    distinctions among, **478–79**
    free markets versus planning, **479–82**
Economic theory, 13–14, **13–14**
Economies of scale, 116
    analytical cost curve and, **139–40**
    of business firms, 135–37
    natural monopolies and, **295–96**

Economies of scope, **296**
Economists
    Keynes on, 9, **9**
    radical, **502**
    views on national economic policy, 367–68
    vocabulary of, 16–17, **16–17**
Economy
    centrally planned, 463–64
    closed, 435
    coordination tasks of, **198–201**
    growth of aggregate supply and demand in, 346–47
    Keynesian versus monetarist views of, 296–97
    planned, **482–83**
    self-correcting mechanism of, 210–11, 310, 354, 359–60, 367
    specialization, division of labor, and exchange in, 44–45, **44–45**
    see also Open economy
"Edifice" complex, **358–59**
Education
    earnings and, **417–18**
    in less developed countries, 126, 476–77
    spending on, **331**
Efficiency, 34, 43–44, **34, 43–44**
    economic decisions and, **197–98**
    equality and, **451–53**
    perfect competition and, **203–206**
    in pollution control, **365–66**
    price system and, **194–95**
    in public enterprise, 312
    regulation and, **304–306**
    in taxation, **343–44**
Elasticity, **99**
    as a general concept, **106–107**
    shape of demand curves and, **102–104**
    total expenditure and, **104–106**
Elasticity formula, **101–102**
Elasticity of demand, **99–102**
    determinants of, **106**
Embodied growth, 465
Emissions offset program, 370
Emissions permits, 369
Emissions taxes, **364–65**
Employment
    demand-side equilibrium and, **175–77**
    full, 96
    see also Unemployment
Employment Act of 1946, 96
Energy, **371**
    aggregate supply curve and, 201
    prices of, 128–29
    see also Natural resources
Engels, Friedrich, **465**, **469–70**
England. *See* Great Britain
Entrepreneurs, **403**
Entrepreneurship, **386**
    in less developed countries, 477–78
Environmental protection, **355–59**
    approaches to, **362–64**
    emissions taxes versus direct controls, **364–67**
    enforcement of, **364–65**
    environmental damage as an externality, **360–61**
    financial devices for, **367–69**
    supply–demand analysis of

environmental problems, **361–62**
Environmental Protection Agency (EPA), **294**, 363
    bubble concept, **370**
    emissions offset program, 370
Equal Employment Opportunities Commission (EEOC), **457**
Equality of incomes, efficiency and, **451–53**
Equation of exchange, 291, 295
Equilibrium, **168–70**
    of aggregate demand and supply, 202–204
    of the competitive firm, **175–77**, **183–86**
    defined, 57, 169, **57**
    demand-side, 169–70
    in the money market, 280–81
    under monopolistic competition, **230–31**
    of supply and demand, 56–58, **56–58**
Equilibrium GNP, 168–69, 202–204
    on the demand side, 169–79
Equilibrium income, 168
    tax policy and, 225–27
Equilibrium level of GNP, international trade and, 434–35
Equilibrium output, determination of, 172
Equilibrium price, 57, **57**
Equilibrium price level, 202–204
Equilibrium quantity, 57, **57**
Escalator clause, 374
Essay on the Principle of Population, An (Malthus), 459
Estate taxes, **456–57**
European Economic Community (EEC), 427
European Monetary System (EMS), 427
Excess burden of a tax, **344**, **346–47**
Excess capacity theorem of monopolistic competition, **232–33**
Excess reserves, 259
Exchange, 34, **34**
Exchange controls, 423
Exchange rate determination, purchasing-power parity theory of, 411–13
Exchange rates, **407–408**
    in a free market, 409–11
    economic activity and, 413–14
    effects of changes in, 439–40
    fixed, 415
    floating, 409
    interest rates and, 414–15
    macroeconomic effects of, 443–44
    market determination of, 415
    reasons for fixing, 424–25
Exchange value, **468**
Excise taxes, 480–81, **338**, **339**
    incidence of, **347**
Excludability, **255**
Expansionary fiscal policy, 449
Expansionary monetary policy, **279**, 281, 284, 285, 286, 451
    budget deficit and, 333
Expansion path, **145**
Expected rate of inflation, 105
Expenditure schedule, 170–71
Exponential growth, defined, 461
Exports, relative prices and, 438–39
    see also International trade
Export subsidy, 394

Externalities, 6, **6**, 250–51, 355, 480
  beneficial, 250, 332
  detrimental, **250**
  environmental damage and, 360–61
  Friedman on, **505**
  government policy and, 254–55
  inefficiency and, 251–53
  universality of, 253

F

Factors of production, **386**
Featherbedding, defined, **427**
Federal Communications Commission
  (FCC), **294**
Federal Deposit Insurance Corporation
  (FDIC), 257
Federal Energy Regulatory Commission
  (FERC), **294–95**
Federal Open Market Committee (FOMC),
  271
Federal Power Commission (FPC), **294**
Federal Reserve System
  independence of, 271
  lending to banks, 276–77
  monetary policy and, 300–304
  origins and structure of, 269–71
  proposals for tightening monetary
    control, 277–78
  reserve requirements, 274–76
Federal Savings and Loan Insurance
  Corporation (FSLIC), 257
Federal taxes, 335–38
Federal Trade Commission (FTC), mergers
  and, 321
Federal Trade Commission Act, **318**, 319
Fiat money, 252
Final goods and services, 79, 158–59
Financial markets, international, 426–28
Firefighters Local vs. Stotts, 458
Firefighters vs. City of Cleveland, 458
Firms. *See* Business firm; Competitive firm
Fiscal federalism, **341**
Fiscal policy
  algebraic treatment of, 244–47
  balancing the budget and, 320–21
  defined, 221
  effect on interest rates, 296–97
  expansive, 230–31
  inflation and, 356–60
  Keynesian analysis and, 298–300
  in an open economy, 445–46
  for recession, 365–67
  restrictive, 231–32
  tax reform and, 220–21
Five-year plans, **492–94**
Fixed cost, **122–25**
  profit-maximizing price and, **158–60**
Fixed exchange rates, 415, 423
  1944–1971, 417–18
Fixed prices, 199
Floating exchange rates, 409
Flypaper theory of tax incidence, **344–45**
Food and Drug Administration (FDA), **294**
Food stamps, 454
Ford, Gerald, 143, 369, **196**, 295
Forecasting. *See* Economic forecasting
Foreign economies, growth of, 451
Foreign labor, 380–81, 392, 403–404
45-degree line, 23–24, 172–73, **23–24**

45-degree line diagram, 173
Fractional reserve banking, 256–57
France, economy of, **487–89**
Free market
  distribution of products in, **200–201**
  exchange rates in, 409–11
  output selection in, **198–99**
  pricing of natural resources and, 373–75
  production planning in, **199–200**
  resource depletion and, 379–81
"Free-rider" problem, **255–56**
Frictional unemployment, 95
Friedman, Milton, 302, 309
  libertarian economics of, **503–505**
Fuel, depletion of, **372**
Full-bodied paper money, 252
Full employment, 96
Full employment level of GNP, 175–77
Fullilove vs. Klutznick, 458
Fully distributed costs, **300**, 301
Funds
  demand curve for, **392–93**
  supply of, **393–94**

G

G.E.-Westinghouse case, **320**
Galbraith, John Kenneth, 232, **502**, **507**
  on American economy, **509**
  on conventional economic theory,
    507–509
  critique of, **510–11**
Galloping inflation, 109–111
Game theory, **238–41**
  entry deterrence and, **240**
GDP per capita, 122
GDP per labor hour, 122
*General Theory of Employment, Interest, and
  Money, The* (Keynes), 84–85, 157, 175,
    178
Germany, productivity in, 130, 132, 134
GNP. *See* Gross National Product (GNP)
GNP deflator, 114–15
GNP in constant dollars, 79
GNP per capita, 120
Gold exchange system, 421
Gold standard, 420–21
Gompers, Samuel, **422**
Goods, prices of related, 491–92
Gorbachev, Mikhail, **482**, 491
Gosplan (USSR), **491**, 492
Government
  capital expenditures and, 329
  policy on externalities, **254–55**
Government purchases of goods and
  services (G), 139, 221–23
Government regulation, **292–94**
  higher prices and, 298–99
  history of, **294–95**
  justifications for, **295–98**
  proposals for change in, **306–308**
  of public utilities, 107–108
  of railroads, 303
  during Reagan administration, 309
  U.S. productivity slowdown and, 128
Government spending, 331–32
Gramm-Rudman-Hollings Act (1985),
  4, 340, **4**
Graphs, 18–32, **18–32**
  45-degree line, 172–73

  contour maps, 24, **24**
  dangers of omitting the origin, 29–30,
    29–30
  definition and measurement of slope,
    20–23, **20–23**
  demand curve, 53–54, **53–54**
  distorting trends by choice of time
    period, 26–28, **26–28**
  interpretation of growth trends, 25–26,
    25–26
  of marginal and average curves, **168**
  rays through the origin and 45-degree
    lines, 23–24, **23–24**
  steepness and choice of units, 30–32,
    30–32
  supply and demand curves, 50, **50**
  supply curve, 54, **54**
  supply–demand diagram, 56, **56**
  two-variable diagrams, 18–20, **18–20**
Great Britain, productivity in, 130, 132,
  133–34
Great Depression, 83–85, 146
  productivity growth during, 130
Great Leap Forward (China), **498**
Greenspan, Alan, 270, **339**
Gross Domestic Product (GDP), 121
  per capita, 122
  per labor hour, 122
Gross National Product (GNP)
  defined, 78
  exceptions to, 158
  full-employment level of, 175–77
  limitations of the, 80–81
  under monetarism, 295
  net exports and, 434
  nominal, 79
  potential, 99
  public debt and, 322, 324
  real, 79, 98, 99
  research and development and, 127–28
  savings and investment approach to
    determining, 181–82
  as the sum of all factor payments,
    159–61
  as the sum of final goods and services,
    158–59
  as the sum of values added, 161–62
Gross private domestic investment, 158
Group of Seven, 454
Growth trends
  distorting by choice of time period,
    26–28, **26–28**
  interpretation of, 25–26, **25–26**
Gurley, John, 512

H

Harrington, Michael, **439**
Head tax, **334**
Hegel, Georg Wilhelm Friedrich, **465**
Hicks, J. R., 165, 166
High-employment budget, 327–29
Historical costs, 138
Historical materialism, **464**
Hooks, Benjamin, **301**
Hoover, Herbert, 84
Horizontal axis, 19, **19**
Horizontal demand curve, 175, 176
Horizontal equity, **341**
Horizontal merger, **321**

Hotelling, Harold, **373**
Human capital, investment in, **417–18**
Human capital theory, **417–18**

I

Iacocca, Lee, **399–400**
Imports
    of Canadian lumber, 397
    of Japanese autos, 396
    prices of, 402–403
    relative prices and, 438–39
    see also International trade
Incidence of a tax, **344**
Income
    consumer spending and, 144–47
    as defined by economists, 16, **16**
    determination of national, 11–12, **11–12**
    disposable, 140, 144, 163
    distribution of, 11, **11**
    effect on quantity demanded, **80–81**
    effects of supply-side policies on
        distribution of, 239
    inequality of, **441–44**
    inferior goods and, **91**
    national, 432–35
    personal, 163
    reasons for unequal, **446–47**
    spending and production and, 140–42
    versus money, 281–82
    versus wealth, 150
Income determination, 171–73
    algebra of, 182–83
Income distribution, **480–81**
    abstraction and, 11, **11**
    effect of price on, **206–208**
    Lorenz curve, **444–45**
    politics and economics of inequality,
        438–39
Income effect, **81–82**
    supply of labor and, **412**
Income-expenditure diagram, 173
Income redistribution, **332**
Incomes policy, 369
Income tax. *See* Personal income tax
Income taxes
    consumption schedule and, 224–25
    under supply-side economics, 236
Increasing costs, principle of, 39, **39**
Increasing marginal returns, **119**
Increasing returns to scale, **135**
Indexing, 374–75
Index numbers, 112–13
Index of leading indicators, 313
Indicative planning, **487**
Indifference curve
    defined, **87**
    properties of, **88**
    slope of, **88–90**
Indifference curve analysis, **85–92**
    see also Budget line
Indirect taxes, **334**
Induced increase in consumption, 190
Induced investment, 171, 181
Industrial Revolution, 45, **45**
Industrial union, **424**
Industry. *See* Competitive industry
Inequality of incomes, **441–44**
    optimal amount of, **450–51**
Infant mortality, 469

Inferior goods, **81–82**
    income changes and, **91**
Inflation
    aggregate demand and, 207, 345–46
    budget deficits and, 331–36
    costs of, 108–109, 359
    creeping versus galloping, 109–111
    defined, 77–78
    demand-side versus supply-side, 344–46
    effect on interest rates, 294
    expected rate of, 105
    fiscal and monetary policy for, 356–60
    indexing and, 374–75
    interest rates and, 104–105, 106–107
    multiplier and, 213–15
    myth versus reality, 100–103
    profit rates and, 108
    public utilities and, 107–108
    as a redistribution of income and wealth,
        103–104
    social costs of, 367
    statistics on, 112–15
    supply-side policies and, 239
    taxation and, 105–106
    U.S. history of, 81–87
    unemployment and, 3, 16, **3**, **16**
    usury laws and, 106–107
Inflation accounting, 325–27
Inflationary expectations, 360–62, 371
Inflationary gaps, 176, 202, 204–207,
    355, 356
Inflation premium, 325
Inflation rate, 151
Information
    imperfect, **262**
    symmetric versus assymetric, **263**
Inheritance taxes, **456–57**
Innovation, defined, **404**
Input
    defined, **117**
    derived demand curve for an, **388–89**
    optimal quantity of an, **129–31**
Input combination, 128–41, 144–45
    substitutability and, **128–29**
Input–output analysis, **201–202**
Input–output equations, **203**
Input prices, changes in, **145–47**
Input proportions, **131–34**
Inputs, 37, **37**
    allocation of, **211–12**
    prices of, 63, **63**
Input substitution, **136**
Interest, defined, **391**
Interest payments, inflation accounting for,
    325–27
Interest rate differentials, 414
Interest rates, 3, **3**
    affect on velocity, 294
    aggregate demand and, 282–83
    attempts to control, 51, **51**
    bond prices and, **277–78**
    on bonds, 273–74
    budget deficits and, 335
    control of by the Federal Reserve System,
        300–304
    as determinants of velocity, 294
    effect of fiscal policy on, 296–97
    exchange rates and, 414–15
    international capital flows and, 444–45
    investment and, 166

market determination of, **392–95**
    real versus nominal, 104–105, 108,
        325–26
    regulation of, 106–107
    usury laws and, **389–90**
Intermediate goods, 79, 160
International Bank for Reconstruction and
    Development, 479
International capital flows, 444–45
International financial markets, recent
    developments in, 426–28
International Ladies Garment Workers'
    Union, **423**
International Monetary Fund (IMF),
    421–22
International monetary system, 407
International trade
    aggregate demand curve and, 439
    foreign labor and, 380–81
    gains from, 382–83
    in goods and services, 410
    government interference in, 392–94
    lags in, 440–42
    multiplier and, 435–37
    national defense and, 399–400
    national incomes and, 432–35
    reasons for, 381–82
    restricting, 397–99
    in stocks and bonds, 410
    supply–demand equilibrium and pricing
        in, 390–92
    versus intranational trade, 383–84
Interstate Commerce Commission (ICC),
    294, 303–304
Invention, defined, **404**
Investment
    defined, 159, 390
    in land, 396–99
    risk bearing in, **403–404**
    selecting a portfolio, 279–80
    stocks and bonds, 278–79
    tax credit for, 167
Investment bank, **282**
Investment spending (I), 165, 166
    defined, 139
    demand and, 166–67
    tax provisions and, 167
Investment tax credit, 167
Invisible hand, **205–206**
    in distribution of goods and production
        planning, **209–12**
Irreversible decisions, **261**
Isoquant. *See* Production indifference curve

J

Japan
    economic relations with the United
        States, 452
    productivity in, **119**
    trade with, 441–42
Jawboning, 369–70
J curve, 440–42
Johnson, Lyndon B., 143, 370
    War on Poverty, **440**
Judgmental forecasting, 313

K

Kahn, Alfred, **265**

Kennedy, John F., 143, 370
  unemployment and, 96
Keynes, John Maynard, 9, 157, 166, 167,
  175, 179
  biographical notes, 178
  on managing economies, 84–85
  on personal investment, 289
Keynesian analysis
  aggregate supply curve and, 304–306
  fiscal policy and, 298–300
  versus monetarism, 296–97
Keynesian model
  aggregate demand in, 283–85
  money and the price level in, 285–87
Keynesian theory, 13, 13
  Phillips machine and, 14, 14
Kinked demand curve, 241–43
Knights of Labor, 421–22
Krushchev, Nikita, 478, 480
Kuznets, Simon, 157–58

L

Labor
  as a factor of production, 410
  aggregate supply curve and, 201–202
  demand for, 414
  division of, 34, 44, 34, 44
  dual labor market theory, 419
  foreign, 380–81, 392, 403–404
  historical trends in supply of, 413–14
  marginal labor costs, 435
  supply of, 412–13
Labor force, 94
  changes in, 128
Labor productivity, 120–23
Laissez-faire, 198, 199, 200
Land, investment in, 396–99
Law of comparative advantage, 4–5,
  384–85, 4–5
Law of demand, 95–96
Law of diminishing marginal returns, 120
Law of diminishing marginal utility,
  76–77
  demand curves and, 78–79
Law of diminishing returns to scale,
  137–38
Law of supply and demand, interferences
  with, 197
Law on Worker Management of Enterprise
  (Yugoslavia), 489
Leading indicators, 311–12
  index of, 313
Leisure, 80–81
Lenin, V. I., 490
Less developed countries (LDCs), 126
  debt crisis in, 474
  debt problem of, 427–28
  growth in, 458
  help from industrialized economies,
  478–80
  impediments to development, 472–78
  physical capital in, 472–75
  population in, 475–76
  problems of, 468–70
  recent growth trends, 470–72
Lewis, John L., 424
Lewis, W. Arthur, 476
Liability, 258
Libertarianism, 502, 503

public policy and, 505
Life expectancy, 469
Limited liability, 272
Limited partnership, 274
Line
  45-degree, 23–24, 23–24
  slope of a straight, 20, 20
  slopes of curved, 21, 21
Liquidity, 255
Local 28 vs. Equal Employment Opportunity
  Commission, 458
Lock-out, 429
Longfield, Mountifort, 196
Long-run average cost curve, 137
Long-run costs, 126–27
Loopholes. See Tax loopholes
Lorenz curve, 444–45
Losses
  capital, 235
  short-term business, 178–79

M

Macroeconomics, 3, 3
  aggregation and, 75–76
  effects of exchange rates in, 443–44
  stabilization in, 87–89
  supply and demand in, 76–78
  versus microeconomics, 74–75, 76
Malthus, Thomas R., 459–60, 461
"Managed float," 425
Mao Tse-tung, 497–99
Maps, contour, 24, 24
Marginal analysis, 7, 459, 7
  changes in income and, 80–81
  examples of, 160–63
  maximization of total profit and, 155–57
  relationship among total, average, and
  marginal data, 166–68
  role of, 163–65
Marginal cost (MC), 7, 7
  price floors and, 300, 301
  profit maximization and, 157–58
Marginal cost (MC) curve, 121
Marginal cost pricing, 301–302
Marginal curves, 168
Marginal labor costs, 435
Marginal land, 397
Marginal physical product (MPP), 118, 387
Marginal physical product curve, 119
Marginal private cost (MPC), 251
Marginal productivity, 387–88
Marginal productivity theory, criticisms of,
  405–406
Marginal profit, 156
Marginal propensity to consume (MPC),
  147–48
Marginal propensity to save (MPS),
  156–57
Marginal rate of substitution, 89
Marginal returns, 119–120
Marginal revenue (MR), 153
  for monopolies, 218
  profit maximization and, 157–58
Marginal revenue product (MRP), 130,
  387
  price and, 133
Marginal social cost (MSC), 251
Marginal tax rate, 242, 334
Marginal utility (MU), 76

law of diminishing, 76–77
  scarcity and, 80
Market
  defined, 173
  environmental protection and, 369–71
  perfectly contestable, 244, 245
  role of, 46, 46
  see also Free market
Market demand curve, 95
Market failure, 262–64
  government failure and, 264
Market mechanism, 46–48, 46, 48,
  247–48
  equality and, 459
Market power, 328
Market structure, varieties of, 173–74
Market system, 46, 46, 172
  strengths and weaknesses of, 479–82
Marshall, John, 484
Marx, Karl, 466, 463–64, 466–67
  on alienation, 472–73
  biographical notes, 465
  crisis theory of, 473–75
  economic terms of, 467–68
  on surplus value, 469–70
  value theory of, 468–69
Marxian analysis, 464–66
  of pricing and profit, 470–71
  purpose of price–value analysis, 471–72
Marxism, on concentration of industry, 322
Material balance, defined, 494
Material incentives, 497
Maximin criterion, 241
Mediation, defined, 430
Medicaid, 454
Medium of exchange, 251
Mercantilist philosophy, 402
Merger policy, 321–22
Mergers, 310, 321
Microeconomics, 3, 3
  versus macroeconomics, 74–75, 76
Minimum wage laws, 411, 420–21
  under monopsony, 436–37
Monetarism, 294–96
  aggregate supply curve and, 304–306
  control of money supply and, 300–304
  Keynesian analysis and, 296–97
  monetary policy and, 298–300
Monetary policy, 281
  contractionary, 279, 281
  expansionary, 279, 281, 284, 285, 286,
  333, 451
  Federal Reserve System and, 300–304
  inflation and, 356–60
  in an open economy, 447
  for recessions, 365–67
  restrictive, 357
  versus fiscal policy, 298–300
Monetizing the deficit, 332–34
Money
  barter versus monetary exchange,
  249–50
  commodities that serve as, 251–52
  contractionary monetary policy, 279, 281
  controlling the supply of, 272–79
  defined, 251
  as defined by economists, 16, 16
  demand for, 279
  equilibrium in the money market,
  280–81

expansionary monetary policy, 279, 281, 284
measuring the quantity of, 253–55
monetary control, 266–67
origins of paper money, 256
quantity theory of, 290–92
supply mechanism of, 278–79
utility and, 459
versus income, 281–82
see also Banking; Federal Reserve System
Money cost, 36–37, **36–37**
Money fixed asset, 150
Money GNP, 79
Money market deposit accounts, 254
Money market mutual funds, 255
Money multiplier formula, 263–64
Money supply
M1, 254
M2, 255
Money wage rate, 200–201
Monopolistic competition, 173, 227, 228–29
excess capacity theorem of, **232–33**
price and output under, **230–31**
public welfare and, **243–45**
Monopoly, 292–93
advantages and disadvantages of, **326–27**
bilateral, **428**
causes of, **214–15**
compared with perfect competition, 220–22
natural, **215–16**
pollution charges and, 213–14, 224–25
price and marginal revenue for, **218**
pure, 173, **214**
supply decisions for, **216–17**
Monopoly power, **403**
Monopoly profits, **219–20**
Monopsony, **428**
minimum wage laws under, **436–37**
unions under, **435–36**
Moral hazard, **263**
Moral suasion, 277
Morgan, J. P., **317**, 318
Morgenstern, Oskar, **238**
Multinational corporations, 473
Multiplier
aggregate demand curve and, 193–94
algebra of the, 195–96
automatic stabilizers and, 309
calculation of, 215
consumer spending and, 190–91
defined, 184–85
foreign trade and, 435–37
formula for, 188–90, 297
function of, 186–88
inflation and, 213–15
mechanics of, 229–30
money multiplier formula, 263–64
multiplier process in reverse, 191–92
for tax policy, 227–28
Multiplier analysis, 184–96
Multiplier formula, 437
Multiplier spending chain, 187
Municipal bonds, **336**

N

Nader, Ralph, 14, **14**

National debt
burden of the, 330–31, 337–38
defined, 322
facts about, 322–24
see also Budget deficit
National defense, 399–400, **331**
National income, 140, 141, 168
alternative measures of, 162–63
National income accounting, 157–58
Nationalization, 293, **311–13**
National Labor Relations Act, **422**
National Labor Relations Board, **422–23**
National product, 168
Natural monopoly, **215–16, 223, 295**
Friedman on, **504**
Natural rate of unemployment, 356
Natural resources, **371–72**
depletion of, **379–81**
fuel crisis, 372
pricing of, **373–79**
reserves of, **382–83**
Near moneys, 255
Necessity, choice and, 34–35, **34–35**
Negative income tax (NIT), **454–55**
work incentives and, **455–56**
Negative marginal returns, **119**
Negotiable order of withdrawal (NOW) accounts, 254
Neo-Malthusians, 460
Net exports, 139, 432
GNP and, 434, 435–36
Net national product (NNP), 160–61
Net worth, 258
Neumann, John von, **238**
New Economic Policy (Lenin), **490**
"New Economics" (Keynes), 85
New Frontier (Kennedy), 96
New Industrial State, The (Galbraith), **507**
New York Stock Exchange, **281**
Nixon, Richard M., 85–86, 369, 373, 423, 425, 454, 378–79
Nominal GNP, 79
Nominal interest rate, 105, 108, 325–26
Normal good, **81**

O

Oil, prices of, **196, 380**
Okun, Arthur, 300, **453**
Oligopolistic interdependence, **235**
Oligopoly, 173, 227
advertising and, **228**
defined, **233**
difficulty in analyzing, **234**
game theory approach to analyzing, 238–41
kinked demand curve model, **241–43**
models of, **235–37**
public welfare and, **243–45**
One-year plans, **494**
Open economy, 432
aggregate supply in, 442
fiscal policy in, 445–46
monetary policy in, 447
Open market operations, 272, 273–74, 300
Opportunity cost, 7, 34, **7, 34**
defined, 16, **16**
of holding money, 279–80
money cost and, 36–37, **36–37**
principle of, 36, **36**

resource allocation and, **248**
Opportunity cost of capital, **187–88**
Optimal purchase rule, 461–62, **77–78**
Optimal use of inputs, rule for, **130**
Organization for Economic Cooperation and Development (OECD), **445**
Organization of Petroleum Exporting Countries (OPEC), 86, 212–13, 353, **196, 380, 381**
as a cartel, **235–36**
Origin
dangers of omitting, 29–30, **29–30**
defined, 19, 23, **19, 23**
Other America, The (Harrington), **439**
Output
defined, **117**
equality and, 8, **8**
under monopoly, **220–21**
quantity of, **149–50**
total cost and, **120–21**
Output decisions, **148–49**
Output per capita, 120, 459
Outputs, 37, **37**
prices of, 63, **63**
Output selection, **198–99**
rule for efficient, **204**

P

Paradox of thrift, 192
Partnerships, **271–72**
limited, **274**
Patents, 215, **327–28**
Payoff matrix, **239**
Payroll tax, 335, **337–38**
incidence of, **348–49**
Social Security system and, **338–39**
Peirce, C. S., 13, **13**
Perfect competition, 173
compared with monopoly, **220–22**
defined, **174**
economic efficiency and, **188–89**
efficiency and, **203–206**
Perfectly contestable markets, **244, 245**
Perfectly elastic demand curve, **103**
Perfectly inelastic demand curve, **102–103**
Personal income, 163
Personal income tax, **335–37**
equality and, **456**
negative, **454–55**
state and local, 341
Phillips, A. W., 14, **14**
Phillips curve, 14, **14**
defined, 351
demand-side inflation and, 348–52
inflationary expectations and, 360–62
misinterpretations of, 354–56
supply-side inflation and, 352–54
vertical (long-run), 356
Physical capital, in less developed countries, **472–75**
Pigou, A. C., **261**, 355
Planned economy, **482–83**
see also Soviet Union
Plowback, **275–76**
Political business cycles, 315
Pollution. *See* Environmental protection
Pollution charges
monopoly and, 213–14, **224–25**
see also Emissions taxes

Population, in less developed countries, 475–76
Population growth, **459–60**
    exponential, **461–63**
Portfolio of investments, **279–80**
Potential GNP, 99
Poverty, **439–41**
    in less developed countries, 472–73
    policies to combat, **453–54**
Poverty line, **440**
Present value, **407–408**
Price
    aggregate supply curve and, 201
    availability of goods and, 60, **60**
    deregulation and, 308
    effect on real income, 81
    income distribution and fairness and, 206–208
    for monopolies, 218
    profit-maximizing, **158–60**
    quantity demanded and, 80
    quantity of output and, 149–50
    sticky, 241
Price ceiling, 64–65, **64–65**
Price changes, demand curve and, **91–92**
Price controls
    for natural resources, 378
    problems associated with, 67–68, **67–68**
    during the Revolutionary War, 51–52, **51–52**
Price decisions, **148–49**
Price discrimination, 319, 329
(Price) elasticity of demand, **99–102**
Price floor, 66–67, **66–67**
    marginal versus full-cost, **299–300**
Price index, 114
Price leadership, **236–37**
Price level
    1963–1986, 346–47
    consumer spending and, 150–51
Price mechanism, assessment of, 208
Price supports, 66–67, **66–67**
Price system, **192**
    Adam Smith on, 50, **50**
    distribution of products and, 200
    under perfect competition, **204–205**
    pricing to promote efficiency, **194–95**
    public interest and, **195–97**
Price taker, defined, **175**
Price war, 237
Pricing
    in foreign trade, 390–92
    under perfect competition, 175
Principals, defined, **263**
Principles of Political Economy and Taxation, The (Ricardo), 387
Private good, **255**
Production
    factors of, **386**
    input quantities and cost and, 120
    means of, 37, **37**
Production function, **131–34**
Production indifference curve, **142–46**
    budget line and, **144–45**
    characteristics of, **143–44**
Production planning, **199–200**
    efficient, **211–12**
Production possibilities frontier, 38, 39, **38, 39, 193, 248–49**
Productivity, 5, **5**

costs of lagging, 131
    defined, 201
    unemployment and, **131–34**
    wages and, 134
Productivity growth
    convergence of, 123–25
    equalization of, 125–26, 131
    in other industrialized nations, 123–25
    slowdown in the United States, 126–31
    in the United States, 120–23
Products, distribution of, **200–201**
Profit, **150–53**
    accounting, **188**
    business, 150–51, 177–78, **402–403**
    deregulation and, **308**
    for monopolies, 219–20
    regulation of, **304–306**
    zero economic, 151, **187–88**
Profit maximization, **154–55**
Profit-maximizing price, **158–60**
Profit sharing, 373
Progressive tax, **334**
Property taxes, **340–41**
Proportional tax, **334**
Proprietorships, **270–71**
Protectionism, **397–402**, 453
Public goods, **255–56**, 332
Public utilities, regulation of, 107–108
Purchasing power, 100, 102
Purchasing-power parity theory of exchange rate determination, 411–13
    assessment of, 413
Pure monopoly, 173, **214**

Q

Quantity demanded, 52, **52**
Quantity supplied, 54, **54**
Quantity theory of money, **290–92**
    under monetarism, **294–96**
Quota, 394, 412
    function of, **394–96**
    versus tariff, 396

R

Radical economics, **511–17**
    view of the American economy, **516**
Radical economists, **502**
Radicalism, 46–48, **46–48**
Railroads, regulation of, **303**
Ramsey, Frank, **302**
Ramsey pricing rule, **302–303**
Random walks, **286–89**
Rate averaging, **296–97**
Rational choice, 6–7, **6–7**
Rational decisions, 36, **36**
Rational expectations
    defined, 363
    inflation and unemployment and, 364–65
Rays through the origin, 23, **23**
Reagan, Ronald, 34, 35, 369, 370, 295
    on budget deficits, 4, **4**
    personal income tax and, **335**
    tax cuts and, 143
    tax reform and, **352**
Reagan administration
    supply-side economics and, 197–98
    tax policy and, 220–21

Reaganomics, 3, 8, 86–87, **3, 8**
    the budget and, 240
    budget and trade deficits and, 450
    budget deficits and, 319–20, 341–42
    international aspects of, 447–49
Real GNP, **98–99**
    1963–1986, 346–47
Real interest rate, 105, 108, 325
Real wage rate, 100
Recession, 78, 138
    fiscal and monetary policy for, 365–67
Recessionary gap, 176, 202, 204, 205, 208–210, 355, 356
Recycling, **358**
Regents of the University of California vs. Bakke, **458**
Regressive tax, **334**
Regulation. *See* Government regulation
Regulatory agencies, **294–95**
Regulatory lag, **306**
    institutionalized, **307–308**
Relative price, 102
Rent
    controls on, 65–66, **65, 66, 401–402**
    determination of, **395–96**
    economic, **399**
    of land, **396–99**
    theory of, **399–401**
Rent seeking, **262**
Required reserves, 258
Resale price maintenance, **316**
Research and development (R and D), 127–28
    tax credits for, 236
Resource allocation, 37, **37**
    efficient, **192–94, 248–50**
    monopoly and, **221–22**
    for the present versus the future, **259–62**
    production and scarcity and, 37, **37**
Resource depletion, prices and, **381–82**
Resources
    defined, 35, **35**
    waste of, 44, **44**
    scarce, **215**
    see also Natural resources
Retained earnings, **275–76**
Returns to scale, **135–38**
Revaluation, defined, 409
Ricardo, David, 385, 386, 398, **468**
    biographical notes, 387
Risk, bonds and, **278**
Robinson, Joan, **228**
Robinson-Patman Act, 318, 319
Rockefeller, John D., Sr., 294, 317
Roosevelt, Franklin D., 421
Roosevelt, Theodore, 318
Rule of reason, **320–21**
Run on a bank, 249

S

Safire, William, 401
Sales maximization, **237–38**
Sales taxes, 339
"Satisficing," **151**
Saving and investment, 177, 179
    GNP and, 181–82
Saving function, **155–56**
Saving schedule, 181
Say, J. B., **473**

Say's Law, 473–74
Scarce resources, monopoly and, 215
Scarcity
    for a single firm, 37–39, **37–39**
    choice and, 35, **35**
    coordinating economic decisions and,
        197–98
    for the entire society, 39–41, **39–41**
    for households, 41, **41**
    marginal utility and, **80**
Scatter diagram, 145–46
Schumpeter, Joseph, 223
Securities and Exchange Commission
    (SEC), 295
Self-correcting mechanism, 210–11, 354,
    359–60, 367
Self-destructive competition, 297
Seniority rules, 425
Service industries, 128
Service sector, costs of, 8, **8**, **256–59**
Sherman Antitrust Act, 317, 318
    courts and, **320–21**
Shortage, 57, **57**
Short-run costs, **126–27**
Simon, Herbert, 151
Single tax, 398
Slope, 18, **18**
    of a budget line, **89**
    of curved lines, 21, **21**
    definition and measurement of, 20–23,
        20–23
    how to measure, 21, 22, **21, 22**
    of an indifference curve, **89, 143**
    of the production possibilities frontier,
        39, 40–41, **39, 40–41**
Smith, Adam, 44–45, 47, 382, **44–45, 47,**
    80, 293
    on perfect competition, **174**
    on price system, 50, **50**
    on utility, 458–59
Social infrastructure, 464
Socialism
    defined, **479**
    planning and freedom and, **484–85**
    versus capitalism, **483–84**
Social Security benefits, 103
Social Security system, payroll tax and,
    338–39
Solow, Robert, **510–11**
Soviet Union
    consumerism in, **493**
    economy of, 463–64
    five-year and one-year plans, **492–95**
    historical background, **490–91**
    markets and prices in, **492**
    performance and planning in, **495–97**
    structure of the economy, **491–92**
Specialization, 44–45, **44–45**
    comparative advantage and, 384–85
    defined, 382
Speculation, **285–86**
Spending
    production and income and, 140–42
    see also Consumer spending
Spending policy, versus tax policy, 232–33
Stabilization policy, 88, 215
    automatic stabilizers, 309
    discretionary measures versus fixed rules
        for, 309–10, 314–17
    effect of lags on, 308–309

Keynesian versus monetarist views of,
    306–308
    lags in, 299–300, 310
Stagflation, 86, 345
    1966–1970, 207–208
    defined, 207
    from supply shifts, 212–13
Stalin, Joseph, **482, 490–91**
Stand-alone cost (SAC), **304**
Standard of living, 120
Standard Oil Company, **294, 317, 320**
Standard Oil Trust, 317
State, radical and mainstream views of,
    515–16
Statistical discrimination, **449–50**
Statistics
    on inflation, 112–15
    on unemployment, 94–95
Status quo policy, 357, 358, 366–67
Sticky price, 241
Stock exchanges, **281–82**
    corporate capital needs and, **282–83**
Stockman, David, 238, 240
Stock market
    speculation in, **285–86**
    takeover battles in, **283–85**
Stocks, **276–77**
    buying, **278–79**
    predicting prices of, **287**
    risk and, **278**
    stock prices as random walks, **286–89**
Store of value, 251
Straight line, slope of a, 20, **20**
Straight-line demand curve, **103**
Strikes, **429–31**
Structural unemployment, 95
Student Price Index (SPI), 113–14
Subchapter S corporation, **274**
Subsidies
    for reduced emissions, **367–69**
    for suppliers of resources, **378**
Substitutability, **128–29**
Substitutes, 107, **108–109**
Substitution effect, **81–82**
    supply of labor and, **412**
Sunk costs, 179
Supply, quantity supplied and, 54, **54**
Supply and demand, 37, **37**
    in a free market, 58, **58**
    equilibrium of, 56–58, **56–58**
    exchange rates and, 409
    laws of, 5–6, 50, 52, **5–6, 50, 52**
    in macroeconomics, 76–78
Supply and demand curves, 50, **50**
Supply curve, 55, **55**
    backward-bending, **413**
    of the competitive firm, **181**
    of the competitive industry, **181–82**
    effect of taxes on, **97–98**
    long-run industry, **186–87**
    shifts in, 61–63, **61–63**
Supply–demand analysis
    of environmental problems, **361–62**
    of exchange rates, 409–410
Supply–demand diagram, 56, **56**
    for housing, 65, **65**
Supply–demand equilibrium, in foreign
    trade, 390–92
Supply schedule, 55, **55**
Supply shocks, 352–53

Supply-side economics, 8, 87, **8**
    assessment of, 241
    Reagan administration and, 197–98
    tax cuts and, 234–37
Supply-side inflation, Phillips curve and,
    352–54
Supply-side tax cuts, **234–37**
    objections to, 237–39
Supreme Court, affirmative action and, **458**
Surplus, 57, **57**
Surplus value, **469–70**
Sweden, welfare state of, **485–87**

T

Taft-Hartley Act of 1947, **424**
Takeover, defined, **283**
Tangent to the curve, 21, **21**
Tariff, 394, 412
    function of, 394–96
    versus quota, 396
Tawney, R. H., **477**
Taxation
    benefits principle of, **342–43**
    double, 272, **273–74**
    efficiency in, **343–44**
    equity in, **341–43, 350–51**
    improving efficiency and, **349–50**
Tax-based incomes policy (TIP), 373
Tax credit for investments, 167
Tax deductions, **336–37**
Taxes
    1964 tax reduction, 143
    1968 tax reduction, 143, 152–53
    1975 tax reduction, 143, 152–53
    1981–1984 tax cuts, 143–44
    burden and excess burden of, **343–44**
    consumer behavior and, 153–54
    direct versus indirect, **334**
    effect on supply curve, **97–98**
    on emissions, 364
    excise, 96–97, 338, 339, 347
    federal, **335–38**
    indirect, 334
    inflation and, 105–106
    on inheritances and estates, **456–57**
    progressive, proportional, and regressive,
        334
    state and local, 341
    supply-side tax cuts, 234–37, 237–39
    in the United States, **332–34**
Tax exemption, **336**
Tax incidence, **344–45**
Tax loopholes, 336, 351
Tax policy
    equilibrium income and, 225–27
    multipliers for, 227–28
    versus spending policy, 232–33
Tax provisions, investments and, 167
Tax rate, average, 334
Tax reform, 352
    1984 and 1986, 106
    fiscal policy and, 220–21
Tax Reform Act of 1986, 336, 351
Tax revenues, under supply-side policies,
    239
Tax shifting, **345**
Technology, aggregate supply curve and,
    201
Technostructure, **508**

Telecommunications industry, cost curve of, **139–40**
Theory, defined, 13, **13**
Third market, **282**
Third World countries. *See* Less developed countries (LDCs)
Thrift, paradox of, 192
Time series graph, 25–26, **25–26**
Tobin, James, **513**
Total cost (TC), **120–21**, **151**
Total cost (TC) curve, **121**
  shape of, **125–26**
Total fixed costs (TFC), **124**
Total physical product (TPP), **117**
Total revenue (TR), **151**
Total utility, **75**
Tract on Monetary Reform (Keynes), 178
Trade
  balance of, 419
  U.S. trade deficit, 431–32
  see also International trade
Trade adjustment assistance, 399
Trade deficit
  budget deficit and, 449–50
  curing, 450–53
  saving patterns and, 452
  in the United States, 431–32
Trade wars, 397
Transfer payments, 139, 159, 228–29
  defined, 141
Transportation Reform Alliance, **309**
Treasury bills, 272
Triumph of Politics: Why the Reagan Revolution Failed (Stockman), 240
Two-dimensional graph, 19, **19**
Tying contracts, **319**

U

Underconsumption models, **474**
Underground economy, 80
Unemployment, 93–100, **410–11**
  aggregate demand and, 89
  budget deficit and, 329
  costs of, 359
  cyclical, 96
  disguised, 477
  economic costs of, 97–100
  full employment, defined, 96
  inflation and, 3, 16, **3**, **16**
  in less developed countries, 477
  natural rate of, 356

productivity and, 131–34
recessionary gaps and, 208–210
restrictive fiscal and monetary policies and, 357–60
social costs of, 367
statistics on, 94–95
structural, 95
types of, 95–96
Unemployment insurance, 97
Unemployment rate, 94
Unions, **421**
  1980–1984, **429**
  deregulation and, **310**
  as a labor monopoly, **424–28**
  history of, **421–24**
  under monopsony, **435–36**
Union shop, **424**
United States
  average physical product of, **119**
  balance of payments accounts in, 418–20
  disposable income since 1929, 144
  economic relations with Japan, 452
  living conditions in the nineteenth century, 117–20
  productivity growth in, 120–23
  slowdown in productivity growth, 126–31
  trade deficit in the 1980s, 440
  trade deficit of, 431–32
United States, economic history of, 81–87
  1870–1940, 82
  1973–1980, 86
  Great Depression, 83–85
  Reagan years, 86–87
  World War II–1973, 85–86
United Steel Workers vs. Weber, **458**
Unit-elastic demand curve, **103**
Unit of account, 251
Universal service, **296**
Unlimited liability, **270**
Unsafe at Any Speed (Nader), 14, **14**
USSR. *See* Soviet Union
Usury laws, 106–107, **389–90**
Utility
  defined, 459
  marginal and total, 459–60

V

Value added, 161
Value-added tax, **334**

Vanderbilt, W. H., **318**
Variable, defined, 18, **18**
Variable cost, **122–25**
Velocity
  defined, 291
  determinants of, 293–94
Vertical (long-run) Phillips curve, 356
Vertical axis, 19, **19**
Vertical equity, **342**
Vertical merger, **321**
Vietnam War, 143
Volcker, Paul, 303
Voluntary exchange, 4, 45, **4**, **45**
  gains from, 383

W

Wage–price controls, 371–72
Wage–price freeze, 373
Wage–price guideposts, 370–71
Wages
  ability and, **416–17**
  determination of, **414**
  differences in, **415–16**
  education and, **418–19**
  productivity and, 134
  unions and, **427–28**
Wages foregone, 37, **37**
Wagner Act, **422**
"War on Poverty" (Johnson), **440**
Wealth, versus income, 150
Wealth of Nations, The (Smith), 44–45, 47, **44–45**, **47**, 293
Weitzman, Martin, 373–74
Welfare, **453–54**
Welfare state, **485–87**
Workers' management, **489**
Work incentives, **455–56**
World Bank, 479
World War II
  productivity growth during, 130
  rationing during, **379**

Y

Y-intercept, 23
Yugoslavia, economy of, **489–90**

Z

Zero economic profit, **151**, **187–88**